CHILTON'S
REPAIR & TUNE-UP GUIDE

DATSUN
Z and ZX
1970-82

240-Z • 260-Z • 280-Z • 280-ZX
All models including Turbocharged engines.

Managing Editor KERRY A. FREEMAN, S.A.E.
Senior Editor RICHARD J. RIVELE, S.A.E.

President GARY A. INGERSOLL
Executive Vice President JAMES A. MIADES
Vice President and General Manager JOHN P. KUSHNERICK

CHILTON BOOK COMPANY
Radnor, Pennsylvania
19089

SAFETY NOTICE

Proper service and repair procedures are vital to the safe, reliable operation of all motor vehicles, as well as the personal safety of those performing repairs. This book outlines procedures for servicing and repairing vehicles using safe, effective methods. The procedures contain many NOTES, CAUTIONS and WARNINGS which should be followed along with standard safety procedures to eliminate the possibility of personal injury or improper service which could damage the vehicle or compromise its safety.

It is important to note that repair procedures and techniques, tools and parts for servicing motor vehicles, as well as the skill and experience of the individual performing the work vary widely. It is not possible to anticipate all of the conceivable ways or conditions under which vehicles may be serviced, or to provide cautions as to all of the possible hazards that may result. Standard and accepted safety precautions and equipment should be used when handling toxic or flammable fluids, and safety goggles or other protection should be used during cutting, grinding, chiseling, prying, or any other process that can cause material removal or projectiles.

Some procedures require the use of tools specially designed for a specific purpose. Before substituting another tool or procedure, you must be completely satisfied that neither your personal safety, nor the performance of the vehicle will be endangered.

Although information in this guide is based on industry sources and is as complete as possible at the time of publication, the possibility exists that the manufacturer made later changes which could not be included here. While striving for total accuracy, Chilton Book Company cannot assume responsibility for any errors, changes, or omissions that may occur in the compilation of this data.

PART NUMBERS

Part numbers listed in this reference are not recommendations by Chilton for any product by brand name. They are references that can be used with interchange manuals and aftermarket supplier catalogs to locate each brand supplier's discrete part number.

ACKNOWLEDGMENTS

The Chilton Book Company expresses its appreciation to the Nissan Motor Corporation for their generous assistance in the preparation of this book.

Copyright © 1982 by Chilton Book Company
All Rights Reserved
Published in Radnor, Pa., by Chilton Book Company
and simultaneously in Canada,
by VNR Publishers, 1410 Birchmount Road,
Scarborough, Ontario M1P 2E7

Manufactured in the United States of America
  234567890   109876543

Chilton's Repair & Tune-Up Guide: Datsun Z and ZX 1970–82
ISBN 0-8019-7172-1 pbk.
Library of Congress Catalog Card No. 81-70231

CONTENTS

1 General Information and Maintenance
- 1 How to Use this Book
- 2 Tools and Equipment
- 8 Routine Maintenance and Lubrication

2 Tune-Up
- 38 Tune-Up Procedures
- 40 Tune-Up Specifications

3 Engine and Engine Rebuilding
- 60 Engine Electrical System
- 73 Engine Service and Specifications
- 94 Engine Rebuilding

4 Emission Controls and Fuel System
- 113 Emission Control System and Service
- 132 Fuel System Service

5 Chassis Electrical
- 146 Accessory Service
- 156 Instrument Panel Service
- 158 Lights, Fuses and Flashers

6 Clutch and Transmission
- 162 Manual Transmission
- 164 Clutch
- 168 Automatic Transmission

7 Drive Train
- 171 Driveshaft and U-Joints
- 174 Rear Axle

8 Suspension and Steering
- 176 Front Suspension
- 182 Rear Suspension
- 186 Steering

9 Brakes
- 194 Front Brakes
- 200 Rear Brakes
- 206 Brake Specifications

10 Body
- 212 Repairing Scratches and Small Dents
- 216 Repairing Rust
- 222 Body Care

11 Troubleshooting
- 225 Problem Diagnosis

- 259 Appendix
- 263 Index

140 Chilton's Fuel Economy and Tune-Up Tips

Quick Reference Specifications For Your Vehicle

Fill in this chart with the most commonly used specifications for your vehicle. Specifications can be found in Chapters 1 through 3 or on the tune-up decal under the hood of the vehicle.

 ## Tune-Up

Firing Order_____

Spark Plugs:

   Type_____

   Gap (in.)_____

Point Gap (in.)_____

Dwell Angle (°)_____

Ignition Timing (°)_____

   Vacuum (Connected/Disconnected)_____

Valve Clearance (in.)

   Intake_____ Exhaust_____

Capacities

Engine Oil (qts)

   With Filter Change_____

   Without Filter Change_____

Cooling System (qts)_____

Manual Transmission (pts)_____

   Type_____

Automatic Transmission (pts)_____

   Type_____

Front Differential (pts)_____

   Type_____

Rear Differential (pts)_____

   Type_____

Transfer Case (pts)_____

   Type_____

FREQUENTLY REPLACED PARTS

Use these spaces to record the part numbers of frequently replaced parts.

PCV VALVE   **OIL FILTER**   **AIR FILTER**

Manufacturer_____   Manufacturer_____   Manufacturer_____

Part No._____   Part No._____   Part No._____

General Information and Maintenance

HOW TO USE THIS BOOK

This book is organized so that the most often used portions appear at the front, the least used portions at the rear. The first chapter covers all the information that may be required at a moment's notice—information like the locations of the various serial numbers, and proper towing instructions. Chapter 1 will probably be the most often used part of the book because of the need to carefully follow the maintenance schedule which it includes to ensure good performance and long component life. Chapter 2 covers tune-up and will be used regularly to keep the engine running at peak performance and to restore operation in case of failure of any of the more delicate components. Chapters 3 through 9 cover repairs (rather than maintenance) for various portions of the car, with each chapter covering either one system or two related systems. Chapter 10 covers body repair and Chapter 11 is designed to diagnose automotive problems. The appendix then lists general information which may be used in rebuilding the engine or performing some other operation on any car.

In using the Table of Contents, refer to the bold listings for the beginning of the chapter. See the smaller listings or the index for information on a particular component or specifications.

In general, there are three things a proficient mechanic has which must be allowed for when a nonprofessional does work on his car. These are:

1. A sound knowledge of the construction of the parts he is working with, their order of assembly, etc.
2. A knowledge of potentially hazardous situations.
3. Manual dexterity, which includes the ability to put the right amount of torque on a part to ensure that it will not be damaged or warped.

This book provides step-by-step instructions and illustrations wherever possible. Use them carefully and wisely—do not just jump headlong into disassembly. Where you are not sure about being able to readily reassemble something, make a careful drawing of it before beginning to take it apart. Assembly always looks simple when everything is still assembled.

Cautions and notes will be provided where appropriate to help keep you from injuring yourself or damaging the car. Therefore, you should read through the entire procedure before beginning work, and make sure that

2 GENERAL INFORMATION AND MAINTENANCE

you are aware of the warnings. Since no number of warnings could cover every possible situation, you should work slowly and try to envision what is going to happen in each operation ahead of time.

When it comes to tightening things, there is generally a slim area between too loose to properly seal or resist vibration and so tight as to risk damage or warping. When dealing with major engine parts, or with any aluminum component, it pays to procure a torque wrench and go by the recommended figures.

When reference is made in this book to the "right side" or "left side" of the car, it should be understood that these positions are to be viewed from the front seat. Thus, the left side of the car is always the driver's side, even when one is facing the car, as when working on the engine.

We have attempted to eliminate the use of special tools wherever possible, substituting more readily available hand tools. However, in some cases, the special tools are necessary. These can be purchased from your Datsun dealer, or from an automotive parts store.

Always be conscious of the need for safety in your work. Never crawl under the car unless it is firmly supported by jackstands or ramps. Never smoke near or allow flame to get near the battery or fuel system. Keep your clothing, hands and hair clear of the fan and pulleys when working near the engine, if it is running. Most importantly, try to be patient, even in the midst of an argument with a particularly stubborn bolt; reaching for the largest hammer in the garage is usually a cause for later regret and more extensive repair. As you gain confidence and experience, working on your car will become a source of pride and satisfaction.

TOOLS AND EQUIPMENT

The service procedures in this book presuppose a familiarity with hand tools and their proper use. However, it is possible that you may have a limited amount of experience with the sort of equipment needed to work on an automobile. This section is designed to help you assemble a basic set of tools that will handle most of the jobs you may undertake.

In addition to the normal assortment of screwdrivers and pliers, automotive service work requires an investment in wrenches, sockets and the handles needed to drive them, and various measuring tools such as torque wrenches and feeler gauges.

You will find that virtually every nut and bolt on your Z-car is metric. Therefore, despite a few close size similarities, standard inch-size tools will not fit and must not be

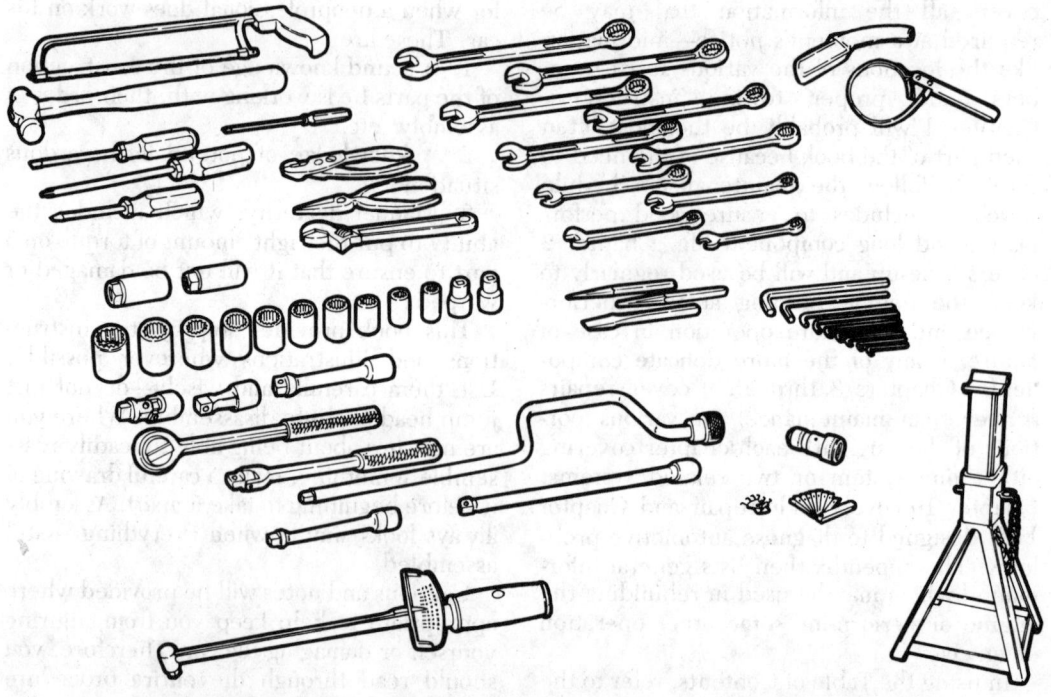

A basic collection of hand tools is necessary for automotive service

GENERAL INFORMATION AND MAINTENANCE

used. You will need a set of metric wrenches as your most basic tool kit, ranging from about 6 mm to 17 mm in size. High quality forged wrenches are available in three styles: open end, box end, and combination open/box end. The combination tools are generally the most desirable as a starter set; the wrenches shown in the accompanying illustration are of the combination type.

The other set of tools inevitably required is a ratchet handle and socket set. This set should have the same size range as your wrench set. The ratchet, extension, and flex drives for the sockets are available in many sizes; it is advisable to choose a ⅜ inch drive set initially. One break in the inch/metric sizing war is that metric-sized sockets sold in the U.S. have inch-sized drive (¼, ⅜, ½, etc.). Thus, if you already have an inch-sized socket set, you need only buy new metric sockets in the sizes needed. Sockets are available in six and twelve point versions; six point types are stronger and are a good choice for a first set. The choice of a drive handle for the sockets should be made with some care. If this is your first set, take the plunge and invest in a flex-head ratchet; it will get into many places otherwise accessible only through a long chain of universal joints, extensions, and adapters. An alternative is a flex handle, which lacks the ratcheting feature but has a head which pivots 180°; such a tool is shown below the ratchet handle in the illustration. In addition to the range of sockets mentioned, a rubber-lined spark plug socket should be purchased. The correct size for the plugs in your Datsun's engine is $^{13}/_{16}$ inch.

The most important thing to consider when purchasing hand tools is quality. Don't be misled by the low cost of "bargain" tools. Forged wrenches, tempered screwdriver blades, and fine tooth ratchets are much better investments than their less expensive counterparts. The skinned knuckles and frustration inflicted by poor quality tools make any job an unhappy chore. Another consideration is that quality tools come with an unbeatable replacement guarantee—if the tools breaks, you get a new one, no questions asked.

Most jobs can be accomplished using the tools on the accompanying lists. There will be an occasional need for a special tool, such as snap ring pliers; that need will be mentioned in the text. It would not be wise to buy a large assortment of tools on the premise that someday they will be needed. Instead, the tools should be acquired one at a time, each for a specific job, both to avoid unnecessary expense and to be certain that you have the right tool.

The tools needed for basic maintenance jobs, in addition to the wrenches and sockets mentioned, include:
1. Jackstands, for support;
2. Oil filter wrench;
3. Oil filler spout or funnel;
4. Grease gun;
5. Battery post and clamp cleaner;
6. Container for draining oil;
7. Many rags for the inevitable spills.

In addition to these items there are several others which are not absolutely necessary, but handy to have around. These include a transmission funnel and filler tube, a drop (trouble) light on a long cord, an adjustable (crescent) wrench, and slip joint pliers.

A more advanced list of tools, suitable for tune-up work, can be drawn up easily. While the tools are slightly more sophisticated, they need not be outrageously expensive. The key to these purchases is to make them with an eye towards adaptability and wide range. A basic list of tune-up tools could include:
1. Tachometer/dwell meter;
2. Spark plug gauge and gapping tool;
3. Feeler gauges for valve adjustment;
4. Timing light.

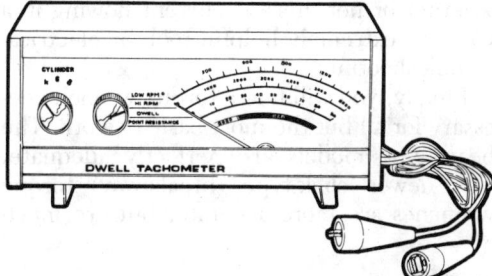

A dwell/tachometer is useful for tune-up work; you won't need a dwell meter if your car has electronic ignition

Note that if your Z-car has electronic ignition, you will have no need for a dwell meter, and of course a tachometer is provided on the instrument panel of the car. You will need both wire-type and flat-type feeler gauges, the former for the spark plugs and the latter for the valves. The choice of a timing light should be made carefully. A light which works on the DC current supplied by the car battery is the best choice; it should have a

4 GENERAL INFORMATION AND MAINTENANCE

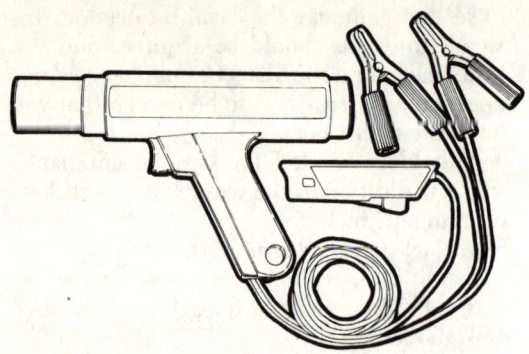

An inductive pickup simplifies timing light connection to the spark plug wire

xenon tube for brightness. Since most of the Z-cars have electronic ignition, and since nearly all cars will have it in the future, the light should have an inductive pickup which clamps around the number one spark plug cable (the timing light illustrated has one of these pickups).

In addition to these basic tools, there are several other tools and gauges which you may find useful. These include:

1. A compression gauge. The screw-in type is slower to use, but eliminates the possibility of a faulty reading due to escaping pressure;
2. A manifold vacuum gauge;
3. A test light;
4. A combination volt/ohmmeter;
5. An induction meter, used to determine whether or not there is current flowing in a wire, an extremely helpful tool for electrical troubleshooting.

Finally, you will find a torque wrench necessary for all but the most basic of work. The beam-type models are perfectly adequate. The newer click-type (breakaway) torque wrenches are more accurate, but are much more expensive, and must be periodically recalibrated.

Special Tools

Special tools are available from:
- Kent-Moore Corporation
  29784 Little Mack
  Roseville, Michigan 48066
  In Canada:
- Kent-Moore of Canada, Ltd.
  2395 Cawthra
  Mississauga, Ontario
  Canada L5A 3P2

SERVICING YOUR CAR SAFELY

It is virtually impossible to anticipate all of the hazards involved with automotive maintenance and service, but care and common sense will prevent most accidents.

The rules of safety for mechanics range from "don't smoke around gasoline," to "use the proper tool for the job." The trick to avoiding injuries is to develop safe work habits and take every possible precaution.

Dos

- Do keep a fire extinguisher and first aid kit within easy reach.
- Do wear safety glasses or goggles when cutting, drilling, grinding or prying. If you wear glasses for the sake of vision, they should be made of hardened glass that can serve also as safety glasses, or wear safety goggles over your regular glasses.
- Do shield your eyes whenever you work around the battery. Batteries contain sulphuric acid. In case of contact with the eyes or skin, flush the area with water or a mixture of water and baking soda and get medical attention immediately.

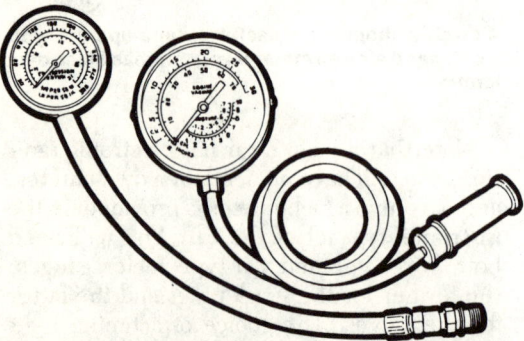

A compression gauge and a combination vacuum/fuel pressure gauge are handy for troubleshooting and tune-up work

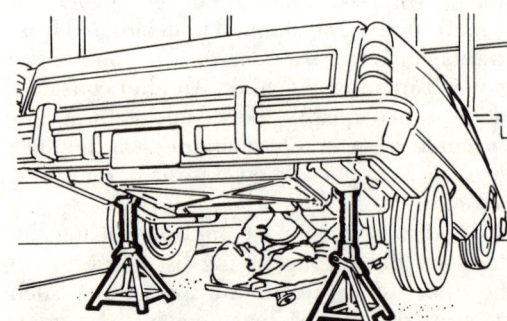

Always support the car on jackstands when working under it

GENERAL INFORMATION AND MAINTENANCE

- Do use safety stands for any undercar service. Jacks are for raising vehicles; safety stands are for making sure the vehicle stays raised until you want it to come down. Whenever the car is raised, block the wheels remaining on the ground and set the parking brake.
- Do use adequate ventilation when working with any chemicals or hazardous materials. Like carbon monoxide, the asbestos dust resulting from brake lining wear can be poisonous in sufficient quantities.
- Do disconnect the negative battery cable when working on the electrical system. The secondary ignition system can contain up to 40,000 volts.
- Do follow manufacturer's directions whenever working with potentially hazardous materials. Both brake fluid and antifreeze are poisonous if taken internally.
- Do properly maintain your tools. Loose hammerheads, mushroomed punches and chisels, frayed or poorly grounded electrical cords, excessively worn screwdrivers, spread open end wrenches, cracked sockets, slipping ratchets, or faulty droplight sockets can cause accidents.
- Do use the proper size and type of tool for the job being done.
- Do when possible, pull on a wrench handle rather than push on it, and adjust your stance to prevent a fall.
- Do be sure that adjustable wrenches are tightly closed on the nut or bolt and pulled so that the face is on the side of the fixed jaw.
- Do select a wrench or socket that fits the nut or bolt. The wrench or socket should sit straight, not cocked.
- Do strike squarely with a hammer; avoid glancing blows.
- Do set the parking brake and block the drive wheels if the work requires the engine running.

Don'ts

- Don't run an engine in a garage or anywhere else without proper ventilation—EVER! Carbon monoxide is poisonous; it takes a long time to leave the human body and you can build up a deadly supply of it in your system by simply breathing in a little every day. You may not realize you are slowly poisoning yourself. Always use power vents, windows, fans or open the garage doors.
- Don't work around moving parts while wearing a necktie or other loose clothing. Short sleeves are much safer than long, loose sleeves; hard-toed shoes with neoprene soles protect your toes and give a better grip on slippery surfaces. Jewelry such as watches, fancy belt buckles, beads or body adornment of any kind is not safe working around a car. Long hair should be hidden under a hat or cap.
- Don't use pockets for toolboxes. A fall or bump can drive a screwdriver deep into your body. Even a wiping cloth hanging from the back pocket can wrap around a spinning shaft or fan.
- Don't smoke when working around gasoline, cleaning solvent.or other flammable material.
- Don't smoke when working around the battery. When the battery is being charged, it gives off explosive hydrogen gas.
- Don't use gasoline to wash your hands; there are excellent soaps available. Gasoline may contain lead, and lead can enter the body through a cut, accumulating in the body until you are very ill. Gasoline also removes all the natural oils from the skin so that bone dry hands will suck up oil and grease.
- Don't service the air conditioning system unless you are equipped with the necessary tools and training. The refrigerant, R-12, is extremely cold when compressed, and when released into the air will instantly freeze any surface it contacts, including your eyes. Although the refrigerant is normally non-toxic, R-12 becomes a deadly poisonous gas in the presence of an open flame. One good whiff of the vapors from burning refrigerant can be fatal.

HISTORY

It was not long after the introduction of the Datsun 240-Z in 1969 that the term "Z-car" became a part of the language. For many, the Z-car represented a perfect compromise between the large size of American "personal" cars and the primitiveness of the traditional sports car. The 240-Z was within the financial reach of many who could not afford a traditional grand touring car, and yet it sported the overhead cam, fully independent suspension, and exciting appearance and performance which they had dreamed of.

Datsun called the 260-Z an "encore" to the 240-Z. While it was not a radical departure from the 240-Z, it represented a surprising

6 GENERAL INFORMATION AND MAINTENANCE

change in direction. While most cars simply continued to sport more and more modest performance, the 260-Z's slight increase in displacement and fully redesigned emission control system meant full performance with a minimal penalty in fuel economy, hitting the Z-car owner or potential owner right where he wanted to be hit.

The 260-Z 2+2 allowed the Z-car to become an exciting alternative to the conventional family sedan, while formerly it sometimes had to be dismissed because the entire family could not be accommodated. The 280-Z was introduced in 1975 and was equipped with a larger 2800 cc, fuel injected engine. A 5-speed transmission was made optional in 1977. A 280-Z 2+2 model continued the choice in passenger accommodations.

When the 240-Z was introduced, it had virtually no direct competition, but instead created an entirely new class of car. Over the years, however, more and more cars were introduced by other manufacturers in successful attempts to cash in on the Z-car's market. Increasing competition forced Nissan executives to re-evaluate the Z-car's market position. Additionally, inevitable price increases slowly but irreversibly moved the Z-car away from its original market segment, toward a new class of more affluent buyers. Nissan determined that this new breed of buyer valued attributes traditionally considered part of a luxury car's appeal, not a sports car's.

Accordingly, in 1979, an entirely new Z-car was introduced, the 280-ZX. Conceding the "sports car" market to the Mazda RX-7, Volkswagen Scirocco, Triumph TR-7 and similar cars, the ZX offered luxury in place of sports car performance. Although similar in appearance to the Z, the ZX shared few components other than the engine and transmission. The crisp lines of the Z-car (originally designed by either Albrecht Goertz, according to Goertz, or by Nissan committee, according to Nissan) gave way to a bulkier, more rounded committee form, which shared basic styling elements with the Z but nothing else. The suspension was completely revised for a more luxurious ride, at some expense of handling; the rear suspension was directly lifted from the Datsun 810, and the front suspension was hybridized from various existing designs. Inside the car, elements of both luxury and gimmickry competed for attention. Functional and pleasing touches, such as automatic checkout of fluid levels and light operation, or low distortion stereo, nestled next to dual-meter gasoline gauges.

Overall, the 280-ZX hit the mark at which Nissan aimed. Although its price had risen to a level unimaginable ten years before, it offered the new type of ZX buyer the exact blend of comfort, luxury, and performance unavailable in other cars.

SERIAL NUMBER IDENTIFICATION

Vehicle
1970–78

On all cars, the identification number is located on the top of the instrument panel so that it can be seen from outside the vehicle. This number also appears on the car identification plate, which is located on the right front strut housing on 1970–72 models, and on the right panel of the hood ledge on later models.

The model identification code of the serial number may be interpreted as follows:

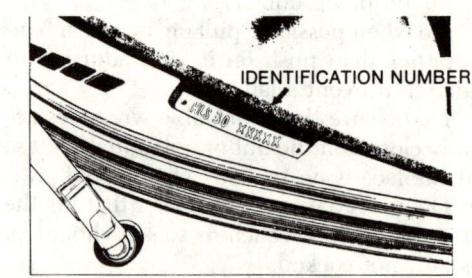

Vehicle serial number location

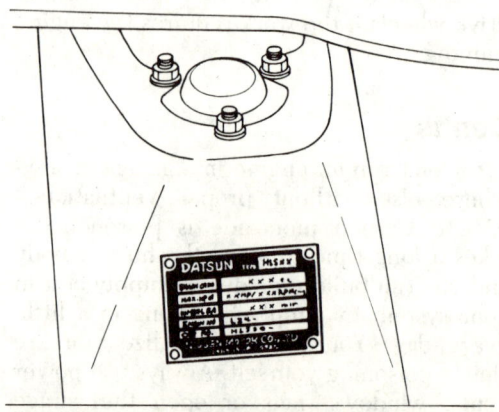

1970–72 car identification plate location

GENERAL INFORMATION AND MAINTENANCE

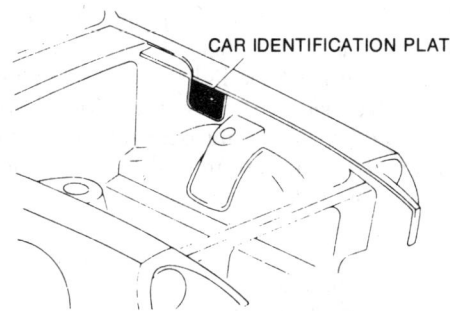

1973–78 car identification plate location

1. The first letter will be either an "H" (for L24 or L28 engine) or "R" (for L26 engine). 2 + 2 models will start with a "G."
2. Following this, an "L" will appear if the vehicle is left-hand drive.
3. Then the designation "S30" will appear for all models.
4. If the vehicle has an automatic transmission, an "A" will then appear. "F" designates a 5-speed.
5. The letter "U" will then appear for all vehicles designed for U.S. and Canadian markets.
6. An "N" will then appear for Canadian vehicles. California vehicles are designated by a "V."
7. If the vehicle is air conditioned, a "C" will appear at the end of the suffix.
8. On pre-1973 vehicles, a dash will follow the S30 designation. The L24 engine is the 2400 cc engine used in the 240-Z, the L26 engine refers to the 2600 cc engine in the 260-Z and the L28 for the 2800 cc engine.

Thus, a 260-Z designed for Canadian use only and equipped with automatic transmission and air conditioning would have the code:
"RLS30AUNC"

1979 and Later

The Vehicle Identification Number (VIN) is stamped on a plate located on the left front of the instrument panel. It is visible through the windshield. The serial number also appears on the firewall, just behind the engine's valve cover. The car identification plate, which contains the car type identification, engine and car serial numbers, and other information, is located on the cowl in the engine compartment, just behind the battery.

The car type identification can be interpreted as follows:

1. The first letter (fifth prefix) will be a K or a blank. K indicates a T-bar roof.
2. The second letter (fourth prefix) is an H, for the L28 engine.
3. The third letter (third prefix) is an L, for left-hand drive.
4. The fourth letter (second prefix) is a G or a blank. G indicates a 2 + 2 model.
5. The fifth letter (first prefix) is an S. This is the prefix for all 280-ZX models.
6. The designation for all 280-ZX models is 130.
7. The sixth letter (first suffix) is a J, for Grand Luxury model.
8. The seventh letter (second suffix) is an A, for automatic transmission, an F, for a five-speed transmission, or a blank for a four-speed transmission.
9. The eighth letter (third suffix) is a V for a California model, a U for a U.S.A.—non-California model, a UD for a U.S.A.—non-California model with a catalytic converter (1979 only) or an N for a Canadian model.
NOTE: *On models equipped with a turbocharger (1981 and later) the eighth letter (third suffix) is a T.*
10. The ninth letter (fourth suffix) is a B, for power steering.
11. The tenth letter (fifth suffix) is a C, for air conditioning, or a C1 for air conditioning with automatic temperature control.

Engine

The engine serial number is located on the right rear of the block at the cylinder head contact surface. The prefix will be "L24," "L26," or "L28," depending on the engine displacement, and the three-digit (1973 and earlier), four-digit (1974), or six-digit (1975 and later) serial number will appear next to it.

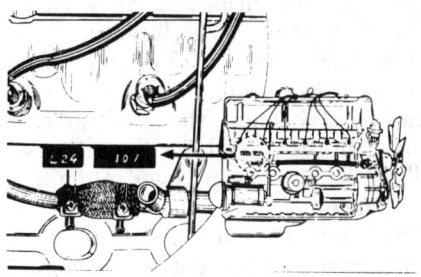

Engine serial number location

8 GENERAL INFORMATION AND MAINTENANCE

Transmission

The transmission serial number is stamped on the front upper face of the transmission case on manual transmissions, or on the right side of the transmission case on automatic transmissions.

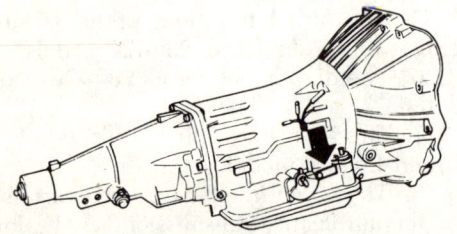

Automatic transmission serial number location

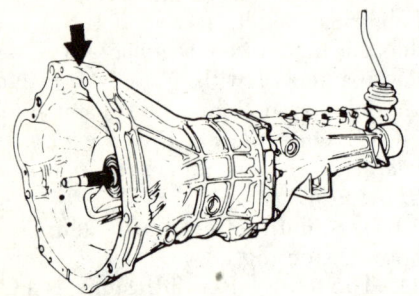

Manual transmission serial number location

Body Color

A body color number plate is attached to the top face of the radiator core support on 1973 and later vehicles.

ROUTINE MAINTENANCE

Air Cleaner

An air cleaner is used to keep air-borne dirt and dust out of the air flowing through the engine. Proper maintenance is vital, as a clogged element will undesirably richen the fuel mixture, restrict airflow and power, and allow excessive contamination of the oil with abrasives. To remove the air cleaner, simply remove the two or three thumbscrews and pull off the air cleaner cover. Then, pull out the element.

The element must be replaced every 24,000 miles (30,000 miles, 1979 and later), or more often if the car is driven in dusty areas. The condition of the element should be checked at every tune-up. Replace the element if it is so heavily coated with dust that you cannot see light through it. The element has been specially treated to eliminate the need for cleaning between replacement intervals, so no attempt should be made to clean it with compressed air.

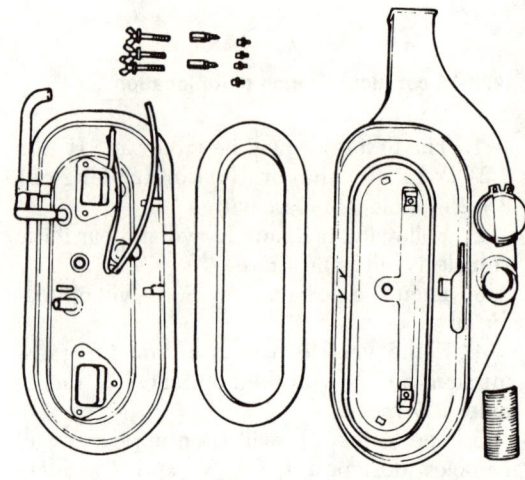

Disassembled view of the 1970–74 air cleaner case

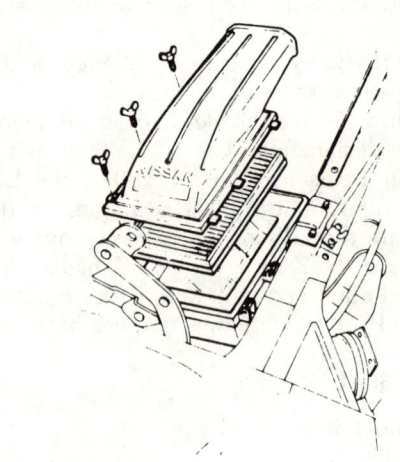

1975–78 air cleaner

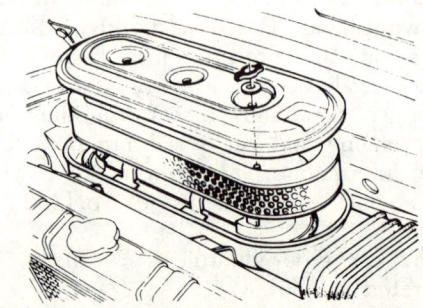

1979 and later air cleaner

GENERAL INFORMATION AND MAINTENANCE

Air Induction Filter

1980 Only

Most 1980 ZX models sold in the U.S. have an air induction system for the purpose of emission controls. Cars sold in California and Canada do not have the air induction system. The system relies on exhaust pulses to siphon fresh air into the exhaust manifold to continue combustion of any unburned intake charge. More details on this system, which resembles an ordinary air injection system except for the air pump, can be found in Chapter 4.

Every 24 months or 30,000 miles, the air induction valve filter must be replaced.

1. Disconnect the negative cable from the battery.
2. Remove the ignition coil to facilitate access to the air induction filter.

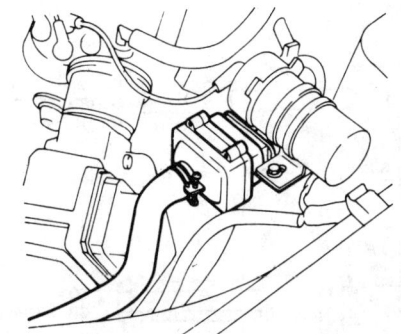

Air induction filter location

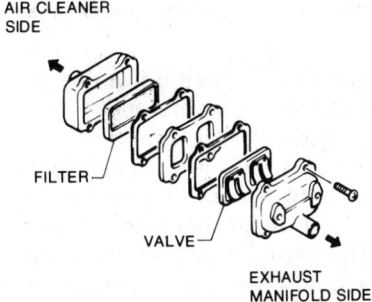

Exploded view of the air induction filter

3. Unscrew the clamps and disconnect the hoses from the valve assembly. Remove the valve assembly, noting its installed position before removal.
4. Remove the four retaining screws and disassemble the air induction valve. Remove the old filter and discard.
5. Install the new filter and assemble the valve.
6. Install the valve and connect the hoses. Be certain the valve is facing in the correct direction, so that the exhaust gases do not flow backward. Replace the ignition coil and connect the negative battery cable.

PCV System

Every 12,000 miles or 1 year, whichever comes first, perform the following checks on the function of the PCV system:

1. Check the ventilation hoses for leaks or clogging, and clean or replace as necessary.
2. Remove the ventilator hose from the PCV valve with the engine idling and place a finger over the valve inlet. If a strong vacuum is felt and a hissing noise is evident, the valve is functional. Otherwise, replace it.

On models through 1974, the PCV valve must be replaced every 12 months or 12,000 miles, whichever comes first. To replace the valve, unscrew it from its fitting on the intake manifold with the proper size wrench and screw the replacement valve into the manifold. Replace any brittle or cracked hoses at the same time.

On 1975–79 models, the valve must be replaced every 24 months or 24,000 miles. To replace the valve, simply disconnect it from its hose fittings and install a new valve into the hoses. Replace any brittle or cracked hoses at the same time.

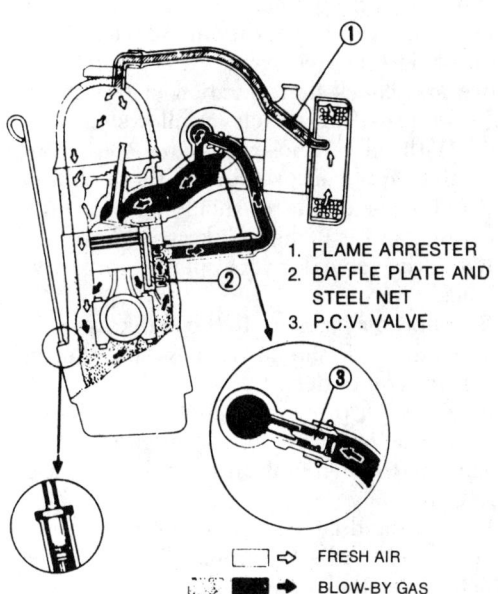

1970–74 PCV system

10 GENERAL INFORMATION AND MAINTENANCE

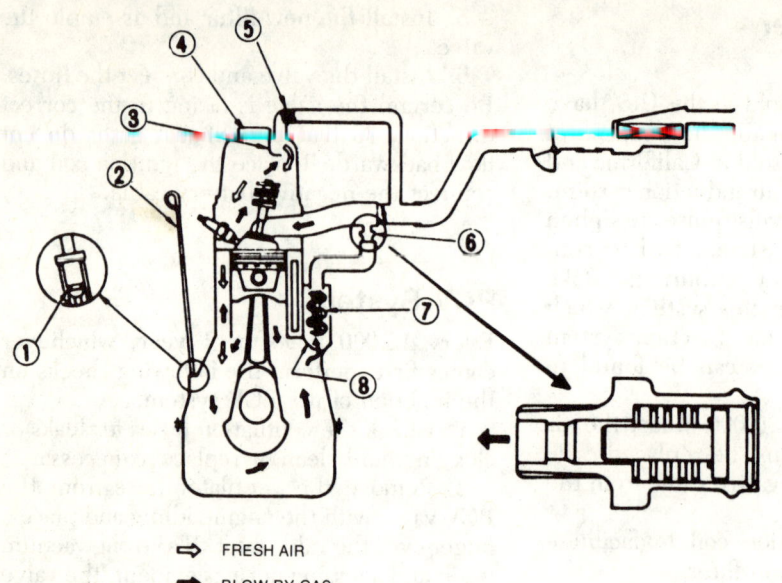

1. O-ring
2. Oil level gauge
3. Baffle plate
4. Oil cap
5. Flame arrester
6. Throttle chamber
7. P.C.V. valve
8. Steel net
9. Baffle plate

⇒ FRESH AIR
➡ BLOW-BY GAS

1975 and later PCV system

On 1980 and later ZX models, no regularly scheduled replacement of the valve is called for. The valve must be replaced whenever it is clogged, as determined by the test given in Step 2. The valve is of the same type as the 1975–79 PCV valve.

Evaporative Emissions System

Check the evaporation control system every 12,000 miles. Check the fuel and vapor lines and hoses for proper connections and correct routing, as well as condition. Replace damaged or deteriorated parts as necessary. Remove and check the operation of the check valve on pre-1974 models as follows:

1. With all the hoses disconnected from the valve, apply air pressure to the fuel tank side of the valve. The air should flow through the valve and exit the crankcase side of the valve. If the valve does not operate correctly, replace it.
2. Apply air pressure to the crankcase side of the valve. Air should not pass to either of the other two outlets.
3. When air pressure is applied to the carburetor side of the valve, the air should pass to exit out the fuel tank and/or the crankcase side of the valve.

On 1974 and later models, the flow guide is replaced with a carbon-filled canister which stores fuel vapors until the engine is

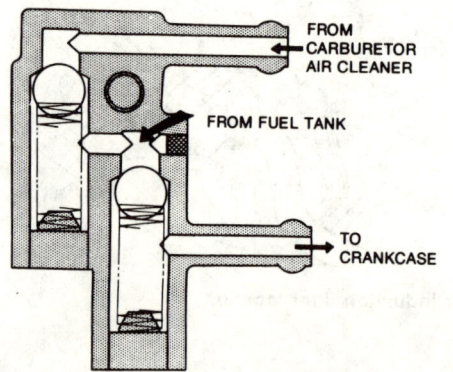

Diagram of the evaporative emission check valve

started; vapors are then drawn into the combustion chambers and burned.

To check the operation of the carbon canister purge control valve, disconnect the rubber hose between the canister control valve and the T-fitting at the T-fitting. Apply vacuum to the hose leading to the control valve. The vacuum should be maintained indefinitely. If the control valve leaks, remove the top cover of the valve and check for a dislocated or cracked diaphragm. If the diaphragm is damaged, a repair kit containing a new diaphragm, retainer, and spring is available and should be installed.

The carbon canister has an air filter in the bottom of the canister. The filter element should be checked and replaced as indicated in the "Maintenance Intervals" chart. Re-

GENERAL INFORMATION AND MAINTENANCE 11

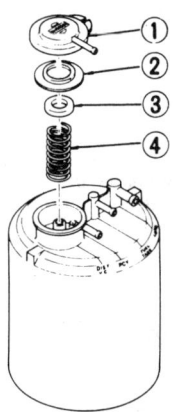

1. Cover
2. Diaphragm
3. Retainer
4. Diaphragm spring

Components of the carbon canister purge control valve

place the filter by removing the canister, pulling the filter out of the bottom of the canister, and installing a new filter.

NOTE: *Sealant has been applied to the base of the canister and the canister tray on 1979 and later ZXs. To remove, pull the tray from the canister, while twisting the canister at the same time. Apply sealer to the canister tray before replacement. Note that the filter replacement is not a regularly scheduled emissions service on 1980 models. On these cars, the filter must be replaced only when it is clogged.*

More details on the Evaporative Emissions System can be found in Chapter 4.

Belts

At engine tune-up (every 12,000 miles), check the condition of the drive belts and check and adjust belt tension as below:

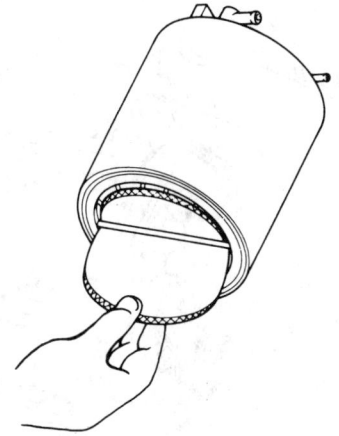

Replacing the carbon canister filter

1. Inspect belts for signs of glazing or cracking. A glazed belt will be perfectly smooth from slippage, while a good belt will have a slight texture of fabric visible. Cracks will usually start at the inner edge of the belt and run outward. Replace the belt at the first sign of cracking or if glazing is severe.

2. Belt tension does not refer to play or droop. By placing your thumb midway between two pulleys, it should be possible to depress each belt about .4 in. (10 mm) with about 20 lbs (10 Kg) pressure. The air pump belt runs looser than this. You should be able to depress it about .6 in. (7 mm). If the belt can be depressed more than this, or cannot be depressed this much, adjust the tension. Inadequate tension will result in slippage and wear, while excessive tension will damage bearings and cause belts to fray and crack.

To adjust the tension on all components except the factory-installed air conditioning compressor and the 1979–81 power steering pump, loosen the pivot and mounting bolts of the component which the belt is driving. Use a soft wooden hammer handle, a broomstick, or the like to pry the component toward or away from the engine until the proper tension is achieved.

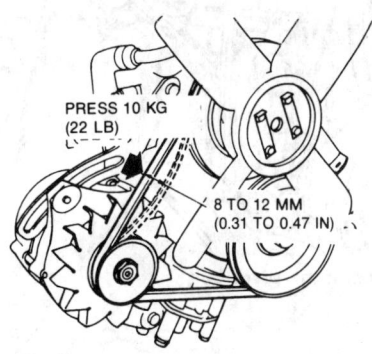

Belt tension

CAUTION: *Do not use a screwdriver or other metal device, such as a prybar, as a lever.*

Tighten the component mounting bolts securely. If a new belt has been installed, recheck the tension after about 200 miles of driving.

Belt tension adjustment for the factory-installed air conditioning compressor and power steering pump is made at the idler pulley bracket. Loosen the locknut, then turn the adjusting bolt to move the idler

12 GENERAL INFORMATION AND MAINTENANCE

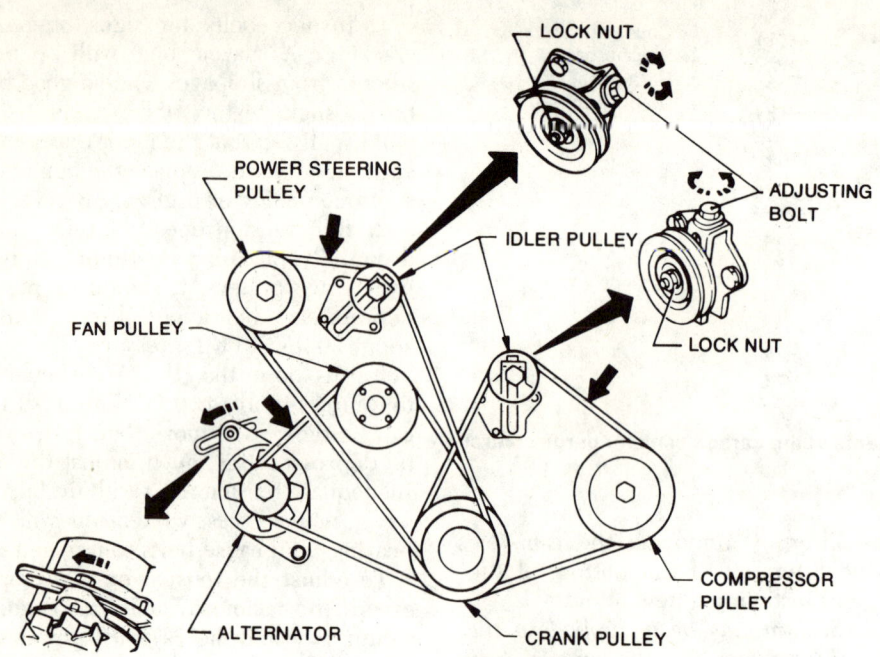

Adjustment points for belt tension

1. Loosen the pivot bolt

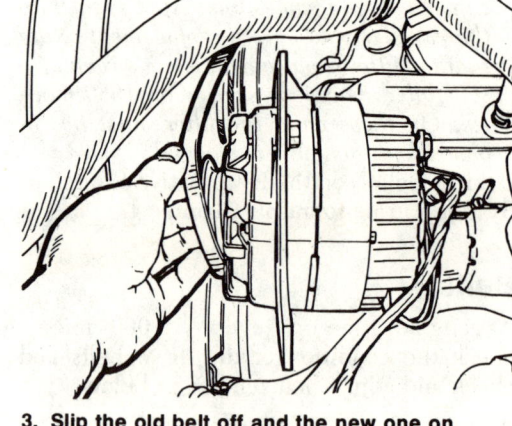

3. Slip the old belt off and the new one on

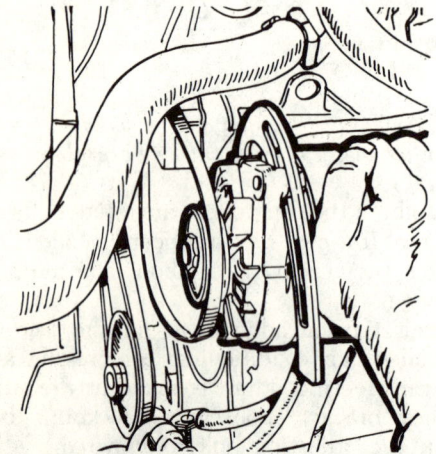

2. Push the component inwards

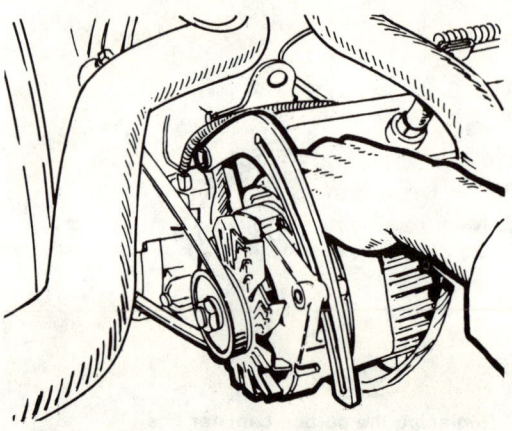

4. Pull outwards to tension the belt

GENERAL INFORMATION AND MAINTENANCE

How to Spot Worn V-Belts

V-Belts are vital to efficient engine operation—they drive the fan, water pump and other accessories. They require little maintenance (occasional tightening) but they will not last forever. Slipping or failure of the V-belt will lead to overheating. If your V-belt looks like any of these, it should be replaced.

Cracking or weathering

This belt has deep cracks, which cause it to flex. Too much flexing leads to heat build-up and premature failure. These cracks can be caused by using the belt on a pulley that is too small. Notched belts are available for small diameter pulleys.

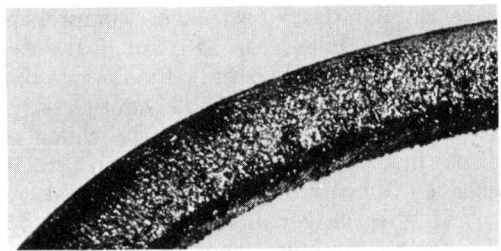

Softening (grease and oil)

Oil and grease on a belt can cause the belt's rubber compounds to soften and separate from the reinforcing cords that hold the belt together. The belt will first slip, then finally fail altogether.

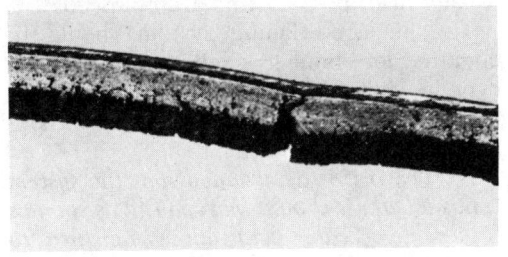

Glazing

Glazing is caused by a belt that is slipping. A slipping belt can cause a run-down battery, erratic power steering, overheating or poor accessory performance. The more the belt slips, the more glazing will be built up on the surface of the belt. The more the belt is glazed, the more it will slip. If the glazing is light, tighten the belt.

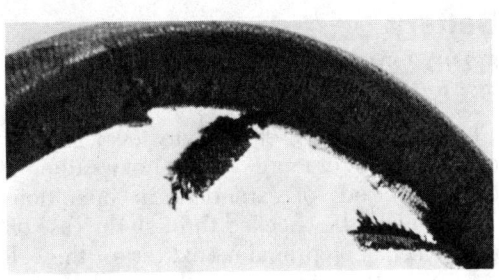

Worn cover

The cover of this belt is worn off and is peeling away. The reinforcing cords will begin to wear and the belt will shortly break. When the belt cover wears in spots or has a rough jagged appearance, check the pulley grooves for roughness.

Separation

This belt is on the verge of breaking and leaving you stranded. The layers of the belt are separating and the reinforcing cords are exposed. It's just a matter of time before it breaks completely.

GENERAL INFORMATION AND MAINTENANCE

pulley up or down until the belt tension is correct. Tighten the locknut securely and recheck the adjustment.

Air Conditioning System Check

Datsun factory units have a sight glass for checking the refrigerant charge. This is on top of the receiver-dehydrator.

CAUTION: *Do not attempt to charge or discharge the refrigerant system unless you are thoroughly familiar with its operation and the hazards involved. The compressed refrigerant used in the air conditioning system expands and evaporates (boils) into the atmosphere at a temperature of $-29.8°$ C $(-21.7°$ F) or less. This will freeze any surface that it contacts, including your eyes. In addition, the refrigerant decomposes into a poisonous gas in the presence of flame.*

NOTE: *If your car is equipped with an aftermarket air conditioner, the following system check may not apply. You should contact the manufacturer of the unit for instructions on system checks.*

Air conditioner receiver-dehydrator sight glass

This test works best if the outside air temperature is warm (above 70° F).

1. Place the automatic transmission in Park or the manual transmission in Neutral. Set the parking brake.
2. Run the engine at a fast idle (about 1,500 rpm) either with the help of a friend, or by temporarily readjusting the idle speed screw.
3. Set the controls for maximum cold with the blower on high.
4. Locate the sight glass on top of the receiver-dehydrator. If a steady stream of bubbles are present in the sight glass, the system is low on charge. Very likely there is a leak in the system.
5. If no bubbles are present, the system is either fully charged or empty. Feel the high and low pressure lines at the compressor. If no appreciable temperature difference is felt, the system is empty, or nearly so.
6. If one hose (high pressure) is warm and the other (low pressure) is cold, the system may be OK. However, you are probably making these tests because there is something wrong with the system, so proceed to the next step.
7. Either disconnect the compressor clutch wire, or have an assistant in the car turn the fan control on and off to operate the compressor clutch. Watch the sight glass.
8. If bubbles appear when the clutch is disengaged and disappear when it is engaged, the system is properly charged.
9. If the refrigerant takes more than 45 seconds to bubble when the clutch is disengaged, the system is overcharged. This usually cases poor cooling at low speeds.

The air conditioning system should be operated for about five minutes each week, even in winter. This will circulate lubricating oil within the system to prevent the various seals from drying out.

NOTE: *If it is determined that the system has a leak, it should be repaired as soon as possible. Leaks may allow moisture to enter, causing an expensive rust problem.*

Battery

FLUID LEVEL (EXCEPT "MAINTENANCE FREE" BATTERIES)

Check the battery electrolyte level at least once a month, or more often in hot weather or during periods of extended car operation. The level can be checked through the case on translucent polypropylene batteries; the cell caps must be removed on other models. The electrolyte level in each cell should be kept filled to the split ring inside, or the line marked on the outside of the case.

If the level is low, add only distilled water, or colorless, odorless drinking water, through the opening until the level is correct. Each cell is completely separate from

GENERAL INFORMATION AND MAINTENANCE 15

Fill the battery to the bottom of the split ring

the others, so each must be checked and filled individually.

If water is added in freezing weather, the car should be driven several miles to allow the water to mix with the electrolyte. Otherwise, the battery could freeze.

SPECIFIC GRAVITY (EXCEPT "MAINTENANCE FREE" BATTERIES)

At least once a year, check the specific gravity of the battery. It should be between 1.20 and 1.26 at room temperature.

The specific gravity can be checked with the use of an hydrometer, an inexpensive instrument available from many sources, including auto parts stores. The hydrometer has a squeeze bulb at one end and a nozzle at the other. Battery electrolyte is sucked into the hydrometer until the float is lifted from its seat. The specific gravity is then read by noting the position of the float. Generally, if after charging, the specific gravity between any two cells varies more than 50 points (.050), the battery is bad and should be replaced.

It is not possible to check the specific gravity in this manner on sealed ("maintenance free") batteries. Instead, the indicator built into the top of the case must be relied on to display any signs of battery deterioration. If the indicator is dark, the battery can be assumed to be OK. If the indicator is light, the specific gravity is low, and the battery should be charged or replaced.

CABLES AND CLAMPS

Once a year, the battery terminals and the cable clamps should be cleaned. Loosen the clamps and remove the cables, negative cable first. On batteries with posts on top, the use of a puller specially made for the purpose is recommended. These are inexpensive, and available in auto parts stores. Side terminal battery cables are secured with a bolt.

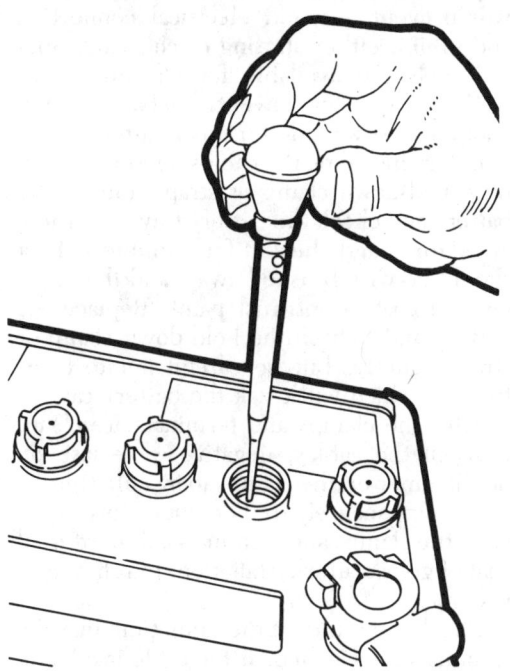

Specific gravity can be checked with an hydrometer

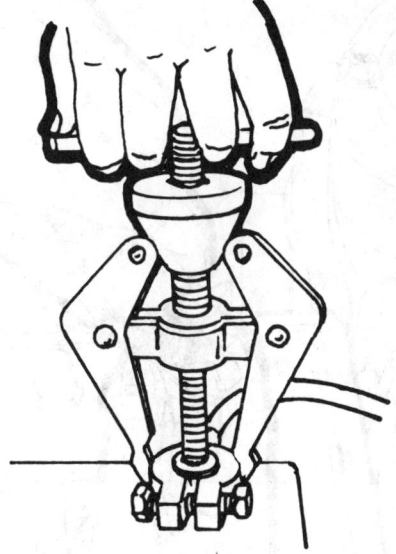

Pullers make clamp removal easier

Clean the cable clamps and the battery terminal with a wire brush, until all corrosion, grease, etc. is removed and the metal is shiny. It is especially important to clean the

16 GENERAL INFORMATION AND MAINTENANCE

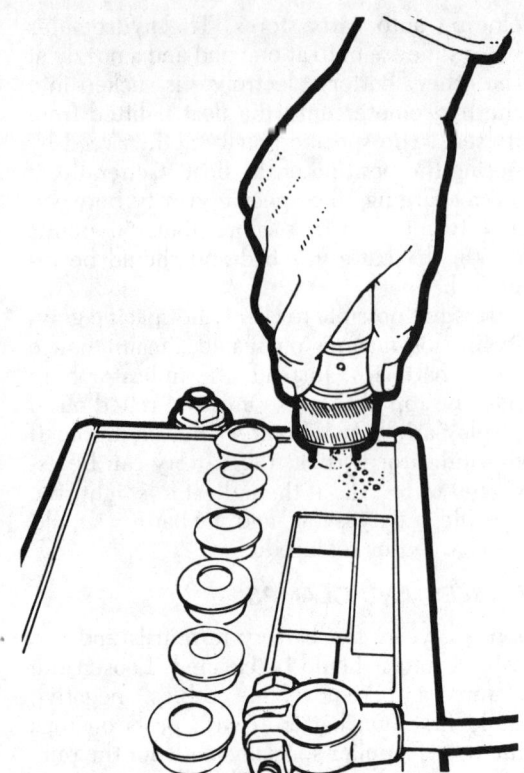

Clean the posts with a wire brush, or a terminal cleaner made for the purpose (shown)

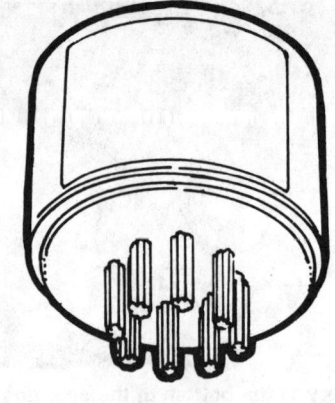

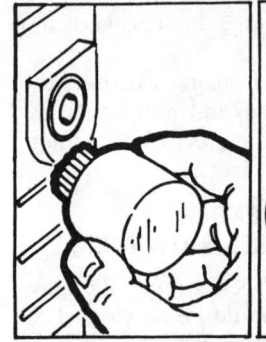 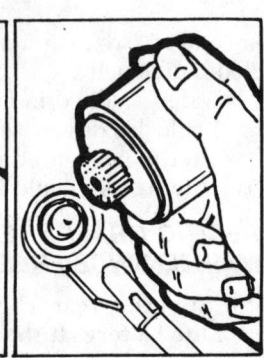

Special tools are also available for cleaning the posts and clamps on side terminal batteries

Clean the inside of the clamps with a wire brush, or the special tool

inside of the clamp thoroughly, since a small deposit of foreign material or oxidation there will prevent a sound electrical connection and inhibit either starting or charging. Special tools are available for cleaning these parts, one type for conventional batteries and another type for side terminal batteries.

Before installing the cables, loosen the battery hold-down clamp or strap, remove the battery and check the battery tray. Clear it of any debris, and check it for soundness. Rust should be wire brushed away, and the metal given a coat of anti-rust paint. Replace the battery and tighten the hold-down clamp or strap securely, but be careful not to overtighten, which will crack the battery case.

After the clamps and terminals are clean, reinstall the cables, negative cable last; do not hammer on the clamps to install. Tighten the clamps securely, but do not distort them. Give the clamps and terminals a thin external coat of grease after installation, to retard corrosion.

Check the cables at the same time that the terminals are cleaned. If the cable insulation is cracked or broken, or if the ends are frayed, the cable should be replaced with a new cable of the same length and gauge.

GENERAL INFORMATION AND MAINTENANCE

NOTE: *Keep flame or sparks away from the battery; it gives off explosive hydrogen gas. Battery electrolyte contains sulphuric acid. If you should splash any on your skin or in your eyes, flush the affected area with plenty of clear water; if it lands in your eyes, get medical help immediately.*

REPLACEMENT

When it becomes necessary to replace the battery, select a battery with a rating equal to or greater than the battery originally installed. Deterioration, embrittlement and just plain aging of the battery cables, starter motor, and associated wires makes the battery's job harder in successive years. The slow increase in electrical resistance over time makes it prudent to install a new battery with a greater capacity than the old. Details on battery removal and installation are covered in Chapter 3.

Cooling System

Dealing with the cooling system can be a dangerous matter unless the proper precautions are observed. It is best to check the coolant level in the radiator when the engine is cold. This is done by removing the radiator cap and seeing that the coolant is within two inches of the bottom of the filler neck. On 1976 and later models the cooling system has, as one of its components, an expansion tank. If coolant is visible above the "Min" mark on the tank, the level is satisfactory. Always be certain that the filler caps on both the radiator and the reservoir are tightly closed.

In the event that the coolant level must be checked when the engine is warm on engines

On models without a coolant overflow tank, the coolant level should be about one inch below the filler neck (engine cold)

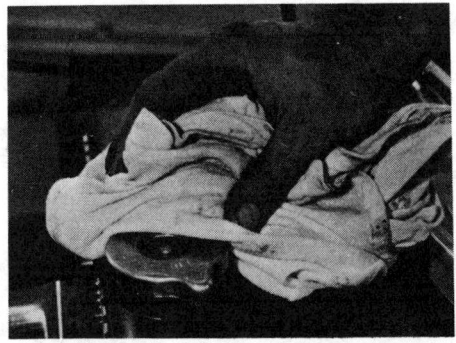

If the engine is hot, cover the radiator cap with a rag

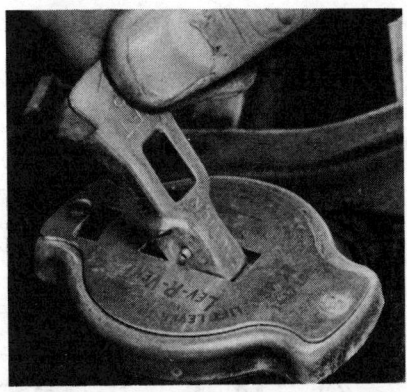

Some radiator caps have pressure release levers

without the expansion tank, place a thick rag over the radiator cap and slowly turn the cap counterclockwise until it reaches the first detent. Allow all the hot steam to escape. This will allow the pressure in the system to drop gradually, preventing an explosion of hot coolant. When the hissing noise stops, remove the cap the rest of the way.

If the coolant level is low, add equal amounts of ethylene glycol-based antifreeze and clean water. On models without an expansion tank, add coolant through the radiator filler neck. Fill the expansion tank to the "Max" level on cars with that system.

CAUTION: *Never add cold coolant to a hot engine unless the engine is running, to avoid cracking the engine block.*

If the coolant level is chronically low or rusty, refer to the Troubleshooting section at the end of Chapter 2 for diagnosis of the problem.

The radiator hoses and clamps and the radiator cap should be checked at the same time as the coolant level. Hoses which are brittle, cracked, or swollen should be replaced. Clamps should be checked for tightness (screwdriver tight only—do not

18 GENERAL INFORMATION AND MAINTENANCE

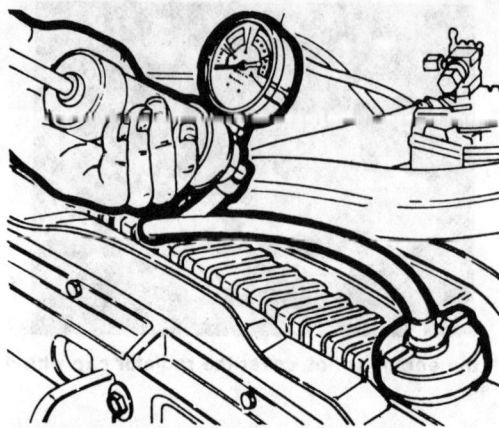

Pressurize the cooling system with the special tool shown to check for leaks

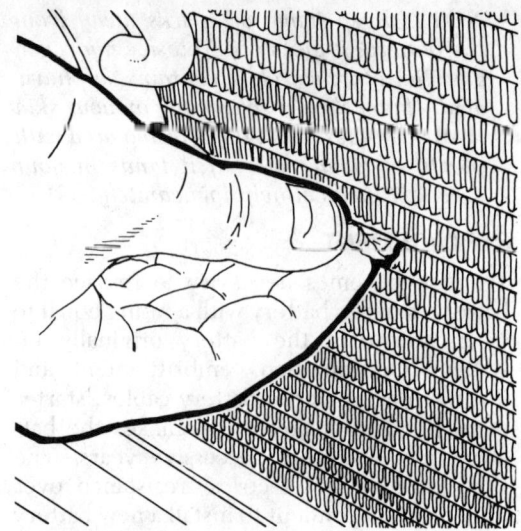

Clean the radiator fins of any debris which impedes air flow

COOLANT CHANGES

Once every 24 months or 24,000 miles, the cooling system should be drained, thoroughly flushed, and refilled. This should be done with the engine cold.

1. Remove the radiator cap.
2. There are two drain plugs in the cooling system; one at the bottom of the radiator and one at the rear of the driver's side of the engine. Both should be loosened to allow the coolant to drain.

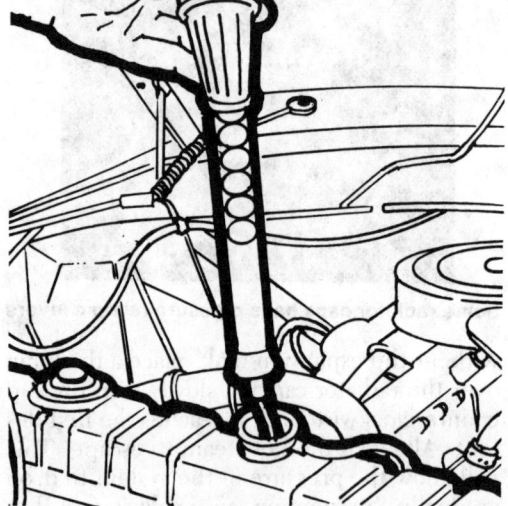

Coolant protection quality can be checked with an inexpensive float-type tester

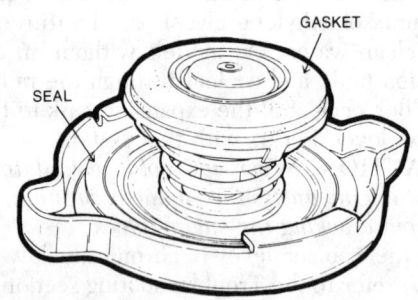

Check the radiator cap seal and gasket condition

allow the clamp to cut into the hose or crush the fitting). The radiator cap gasket should be checked for any obvious tears, cracks or swelling, or any signs of incorrect seating in the radiator neck.

Open the radiator cap and radiator drain petcock to change the coolant

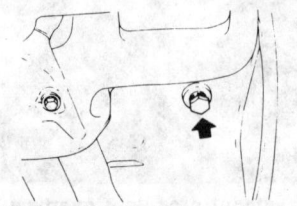

The engine block coolant drain plug is located at the left rear of the engine

GENERAL INFORMATION AND MAINTENANCE

How to Spot Bad Hoses

Both the upper and lower radiator hoses are called upon to perform difficult jobs in an inhospitable environment. They are subject to nearly 18 psi at under hood temperatures often over 280°F., and must circulate nearly 7500 gallons of coolant an hour—3 good reasons to have good hoses.

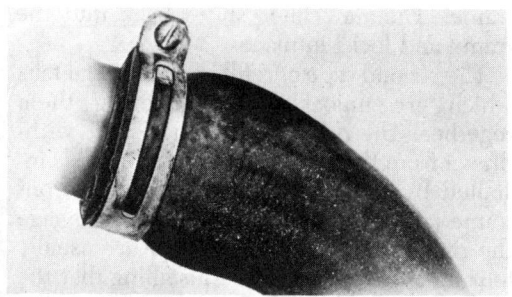

Swollen hose

A good test for any hose is to feel it for soft or spongy spots. Frequently these will appear as swollen areas of the hose. The most likely cause is oil soaking. This hose could burst at any time, when hot or under pressure.

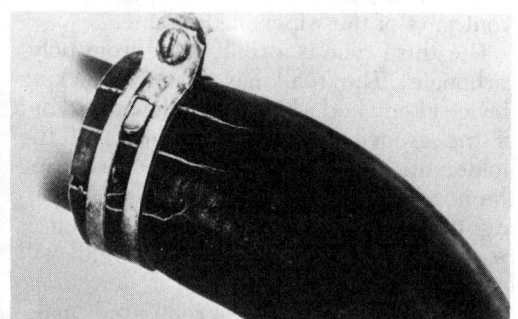

Cracked hose

Cracked hoses can usually be seen but feel the hoses to be sure they have not hardened; a prime cause of cracking. This hose has cracked down to the reinforcing cords and could split at any of the cracks.

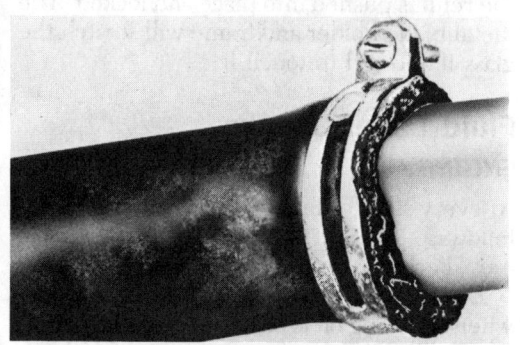

Frayed hose end (due to weak clamp)

Weakened clamps frequently are the cause of hose and cooling system failure. The connection between the pipe and hose has deteriorated enough to allow coolant to escape when the engine is hot.

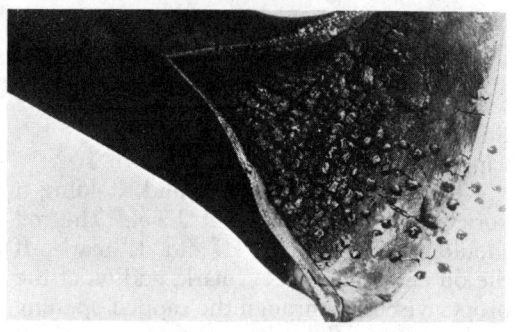

Debris in cooling system

Debris, rust and scale in the cooling system can cause the inside of a hose to weaken. This can usually be felt on the outside of the hose as soft or thinner areas.

GENERAL INFORMATION AND MAINTENANCE

3. Turn on the heater inside the car to its hottest position. This ensures that the heater core is flushed out completely. Flush out the system thoroughly by refilling it with clean water through the radiator opening as it escapes from the two drain cocks. Continue until the water running out is clear. Be sure to clean out the coolant recovery tank as well if your car has one.

4. If the system is badly contaminated with rust or scale, you can use a commercial flushing solution to clear it out. Follow the manufacturer's instructions. Some causes of rust are air in the system, caused by a leaky radiator cap or an insufficiently filled or leaking system; failure to change the coolant regularly; use of excessively hard or soft water; and failure to use a proper mix of antifreeze and water.

5. When the system is clear, allow all the water to drain, then close the drain plugs. Fill the system through the radiator with a 50/50 mix of ethylene glycol type antifreeze and water.

6. Start the engine and top off the radiator with the antifreeze and water mixture. If your car has a coolant recovery tank, fill it half full with the coolant mix.

7. Replace the radiator and coolant tank caps, and check for leaks. When the engine has reached normal operating temperature, shut it off, allow it to cool, then top off the radiator or coolant tank as necessary.

Windshield Wipers

For maximum effectiveness and longest element life, the windshield and wiper blades should be kept clean. Dirt, tree sap, road tar and so on will cause streaking, smearing and blade deterioration if left on the glass. It is advisable to wash the windshield carefully with a commercial glass cleaner at least once a month. Wipe off the rubber blades with the wet rag afterwards. Do not attempt to move the wipers by hand; damage to the motor and drive mechanism will result.

If the blades are found to be cracked, broken or torn, they should be replaced immediately. Replacement intervals will vary with usage, although ozone deterioration usually limits blade life to about one year. If the wiper pattern is smeared or streaked, or if the blade chatters across the glass, the elements should be replaced. It is easiest and most sensible to replace the elements in pairs.

There are basically three different types of refills, which differ in their method of replacement. One type has two release buttons, approximately one-third of the way up from the ends of the blade frame. Pushing the buttons down releases a lock and allows the rubber filler to be removed from the frame. The new filler slides back into the frame and locks in place.

The second type of refill has two metal tabs which are unlocked by squeezing them together. The rubber filler can then be withdrawn from the frame jaws. A new refill is installed by inserting the refill into the front frame jaws and sliding it rearward to engage the remaining frame jaws. There are usually four jaws; be certain when installing that the refill is engaged in all of them. At the end of its travel, the tabs will lock into place on the front jaws of the wiper blade frame.

The third type is a refill made from polycarbonate. The refill has a simple locking device at one end which flexes downward out of the groove into which the jaws of the holder fit, allowing easy release. By sliding the new refill through all the jaws and pushing through the slight resistance when it reaches the end of its travel, the refill will lock into position.

Regardless of the type of refill used, make sure that all of the frame jaws are engaged as the refill is pushed into place and locked. The metal blade holder and frame will scratch the glass if allowed to touch it.

Fluid Level Checks

ENGINE OIL

At every stop for fuel, check the engine oil as follows:

1. Park the car on the level.
2. The engine may be either hot or cold when checking oil level. However, if it is hot, wait a few minutes after the engine has been shut off to allow the oil to drain back into the crankcase. If the engine is cold, do not start it before checking the oil level.
3. Open the hood and locate the dipstick, which is on the right side (passenger's side) of the engine. Pull the dipstick from its tube, wipe it clean, and reinsert it.
4. Pull the dipstick again and, holding it horizontally, read the oil level. The oil should be between the "H" and "L" marks. If the oil is below the "L" mark, add oil of the proper viscosity through the capped opening in the front of the valve cover. See the "Oil

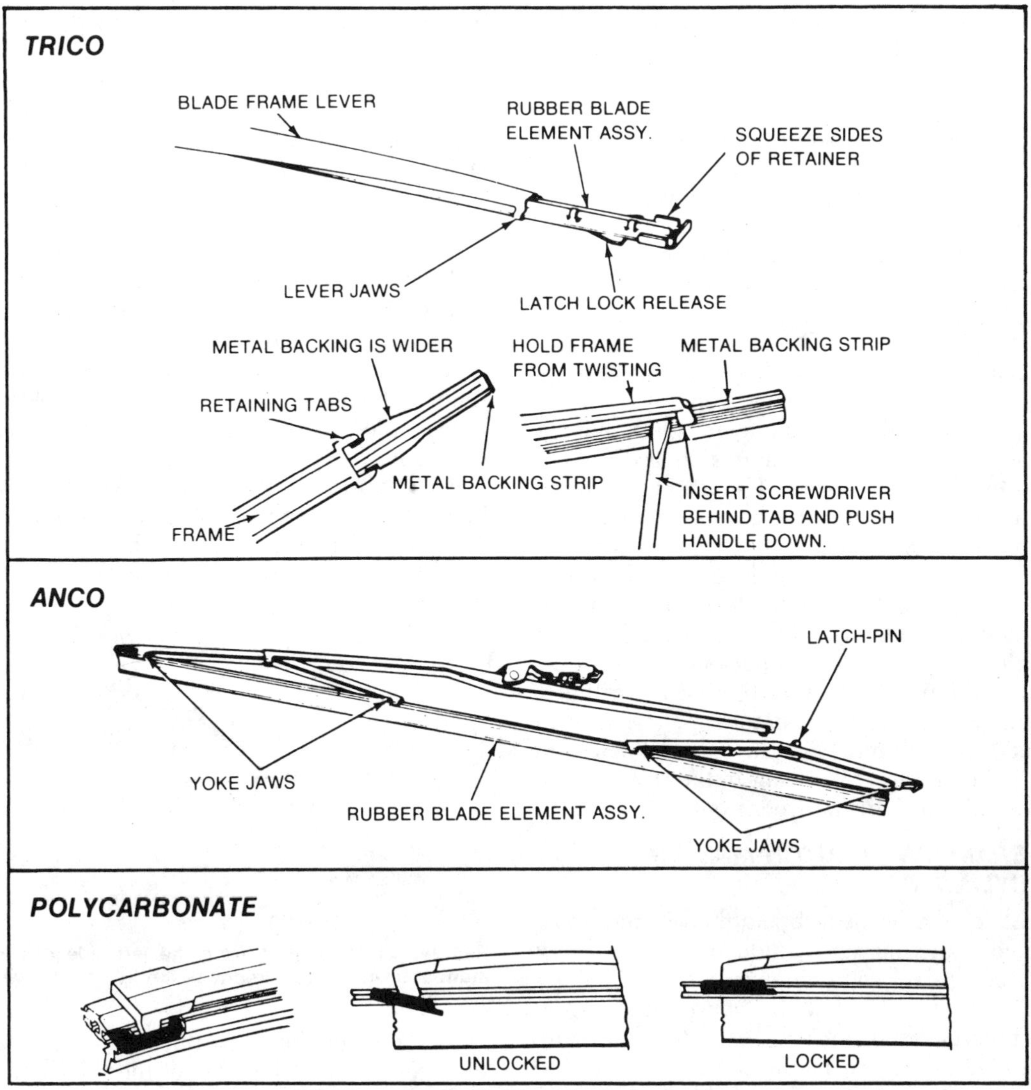

GENERAL INFORMATION AND MAINTENANCE

TRICO

- BLADE FRAME LEVER
- RUBBER BLADE ELEMENT ASSY.
- SQUEEZE SIDES OF RETAINER
- LEVER JAWS
- LATCH LOCK RELEASE
- METAL BACKING IS WIDER
- HOLD FRAME FROM TWISTING
- METAL BACKING STRIP
- RETAINING TABS
- METAL BACKING STRIP
- FRAME
- INSERT SCREWDRIVER BEHIND TAB AND PUSH HANDLE DOWN.

ANCO

- LATCH-PIN
- YOKE JAWS
- RUBBER BLADE ELEMENT ASSY.
- YOKE JAWS

POLYCARBONATE

UNLOCKED   LOCKED

The three types of wiper element retention

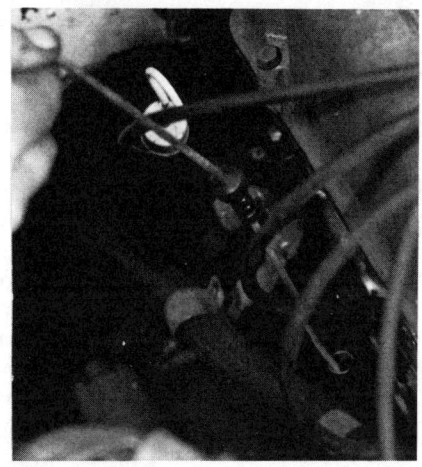

Oil level is checked with the dipstick, on the right side of the engine

Add oil through the capped opening in the valve cover

and Fuel Recommendations" section in this chapter for the proper viscosity and rating of oil to use.

5. Replace the dipstick, and check the level again after adding any oil. Be careful not to overfill the crankcase. Approximately one quart of oil will raise the level from "L" to "H". Excess oil will generally be consumed at an accelerated rate even if no damage to the engine seals occurs.

RADIATOR COOLANT

Datsun recommends checking the radiator coolant every time you stop for gas. On 1970–75 models if the engine is hot, allow it to cool for several minutes to reduce the pressure in the system. Using a rag, turn the radiator cap ¼ turn to the stop and allow all pressure to escape. Then, remove the cap. On 1976 and later models equipped with an expansion tank, check the level visually in the tank. It should be above the low mark. Never fill the tank over the upper mark.

Fill the radiator until the level is within 1 in. (25 mm) of the radiator cap. It is best to add a 50-50 mix of antifreeze and water to avoid diluting the coolant in the system. Use permanent type antifreeze only.

BRAKE AND CLUTCH MASTER CYLINDERS

Check the levels of brake fluid in the brake and clutch master cylinder reservoirs every 3,000 miles. The fluid should be maintained to a level not below the bottom line on the reservoirs and not above the top line. Any sudden decrease in the level in any of the reservoirs indicates a probable leak in that particular system and should be checked out immediately.

When making additions of fluid, use only fresh, uncontaminated brake fluid meeting or exceeding DOT 3 standards. Be careful not to spill any brake fluid on painted surfaces, because it eats paint. Do not allow the fluid container or master cylinder reservoirs to remain open any longer than necessary; brake fluid absorbs moisture from the air, reducing its effectiveness and causing brake and clutch line corrosion.

TRANSMISSION

Manual

Check the lubricant level at the interval specified in the maintenance chart.

1. With the car parked on a level surface, remove the filler plug from the left side of the transmission case. The filler plug has a square head.
2. If lubricant begins to trickle out the hole, there is enough. Otherwise, carefully insert a finger (watch out for sharp threads) and check to see if the oil is up to the edge of the hole.

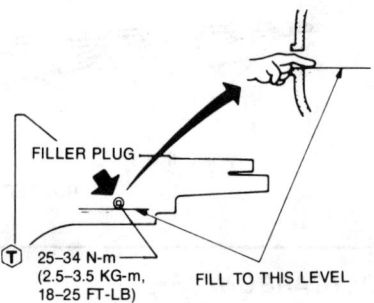

Remove the filler plug from the left side of the manual transmission to check the lubricant level

3. If not, add lubricant through the hole to raise the level to the edge of the filler hole. Most gear lubricants come in a plastic squeeze bottle with a nozzle, making additions easy. You can also use a squeeze bulb. Add API GL-4 gear oil of the proper viscosity (see the viscosity chart under "Oil and Fuel Recommendations").
4. Replace the plug and check for leaks.

Automatic

Check the level of the automatic transmission fluid every 2,000 miles. There is a dipstick at the right rear of the engine under the hood. The dipstick has "H" and "L" markings, which are accurate for level indications only when the transmission is hot (normal operating temperature). The transmission is considered hot after 15 miles of highway driving.

1. Park the car on a level surface with the engine idling. Apply the parking brake.
2. Shift the transmission to Park.

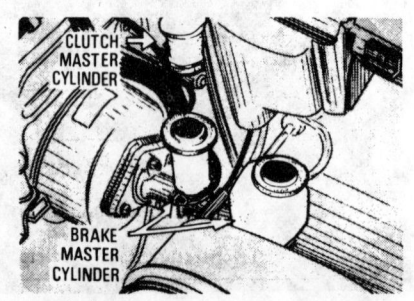

Check the fluid levels in the brake and clutch master cylinders

GENERAL INFORMATION AND MAINTENANCE

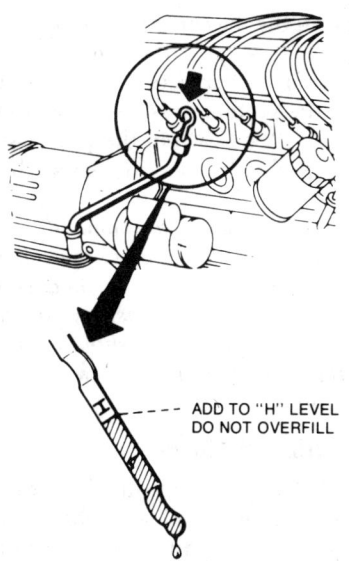

The automatic transmission fluid level is checked with the dipstick

3. Remove the dipstick, wipe it clean, then reinsert it firmly. Be certain that it has been pushed fully home. Remove the dipstick and check the fluid level while holding the dipstick horizontally. The level should be at or near the "H" mark.

4. If the fluid level is below the "L" mark, add DEXRON® type automatic transmission fluid through the dipstick tube. This is more easily accomplished with the aid of a funnel and hose. Check the level often between additions, being careful not to overfill the transmission. Overfilling will cause slippage, seal damage, and overheating. Approximately one quart of fluid will raise the level from "L" to "H".

NOTE: *The fluid on the dipstick should be a bright red color. If it is discolored (brown or black), or smells burnt, serious transmission troubles, probably due to overheating, should be suspected. The transmission should be inspected by a qualified mechanic to locate the cause of the burnt fluid.*

REAR AXLE

Check the differential fluid level at the interval specified in the maintenance chart. Park the car on a level surface. Remove the filler plug in the rear center of the differential housing. The lubricant should be up to the level of the hole. You can check this with your finger (watch out for sharp threads). If the fluid is below the level of the hole, add API GL-5 gear oil of the proper viscosity (see

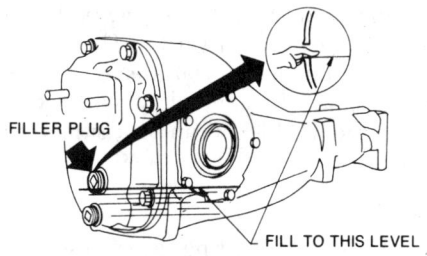

The differential fluid level is checked through the filler hole

"Oil and Fuel Recommendations") through the hole to bring the lubricant up to the proper level. Gear oil usually comes in a plastic squeeze bottle with a nozzle, but you can use a squeeze bulb or a kitchen baster to squirt the stuff in.

BATTERY

Check the battery electrolyte level at least once a month. Fluid level checks are covered earlier in this chapter, under routine maintenance for the battery.

CARBURETOR DAMPER OIL

On 1970–74 models, every 3,000 miles, check the level of the carburetor damper oil by removing the oil cap nut. If the oil level is below the lower line, add SAE 20 to restore the proper level. Do not use SAE 30!

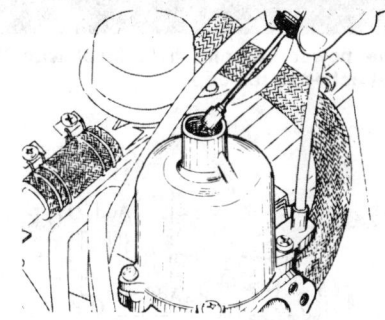

Check the carburetor damper oil level on the cap nut dipstick

STEERING GEAR
Manual

The manual rack and pinion steering gear should be inspected for leaks or seepage every 30,000 miles. The factory recommends inspection of the lubricant level at the same time. However, there is no filler plug on the gear housing. Consequently, level checks require removal of the backlash adjusting

GENERAL INFORMATION AND MAINTENANCE

screw and locknut, and resetting of the backlash adjustment afterwards. These procedures should be left to your dealer or a qualified mechanic. In general, if no leakage is evident, the fluid level can be assumed to be satisfactory.

Power

The ZF power steering gear reservoir is equipped with a level dipstick, attached to the filler cap. The dipstick has a scale on each side, one for cold and the other for hot.

1. The level is checked with the engine off and wheels pointed straight ahead.
2. Remove the fluid reservoir cap and check the level on the dipstick. Use the "HOT" or "COLD" scale as appropriate.

Check the power steering fluid level with the dipstick attached to the cap

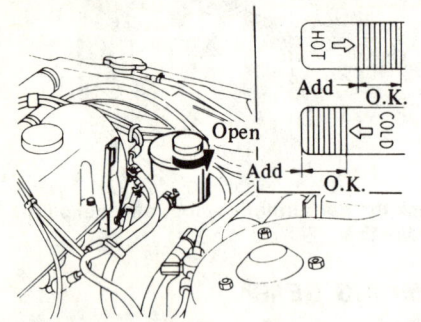

The power steering dipstick has hot and cold level markings

3. If the level is incorrect, add DEXRON® automatic transmission fluid until the proper level is reached. Be careful not to overfill the reservoir; overfilling will cause foaming and fluid loss.

Check all the various lines, hoses, and connections for leakage. Hose, line, and connection leaks can be corrected by replacement of the part; the system must be bled afterwards (see Chapter 8). Leaks in the power steering gear itself should be corrected by your dealer.

NOTE: *The fluid recommendation and level check procedure given here is for the factory-installed unit on ZX models only. If your 1970–78 Z-car has an aftermarket power steering unit, you should consult the manufacturer for fluid checks and recommendations.*

WINDSHIELD WASHER

Check the fluid level in the windshield washer tank at every oil level check. (The ZX rear wiper/washer unit shares the tank with the front washer system.) The fluid can be mixed in a 50% solution with water, if desired, as long as temperatures remain above freezing. Below freezing, the fluid should be used full strength. Never add engine coolant antifreeze to the washer fluid, because it will damage the car's paint.

HEADLIGHT WASHER

The headlight washer tank is located in the left front of the engine compartment. Use the same washing fluid as that used in the windshield washer tank. As with the windshield washer, the fluid should be used full strength in freezing weather.

Tires

Tires should be checked weekly for proper air pressure. A chart, located either in the glove compartment or on the driver's or passenger's door, gives the recommended inflation pressures. Maximum fuel economy and tire life will result if the pressure is maintained at the highest figure given on the chart. Pressures should be checked before driving since pressure can increase as much as six pounds per square inch (psi) due to heat buildup. It is a good idea to have your own accurate pressure gauge, because not all gauges on service station air pumps can be trusted. When checking pressures, do not neglect the spare tire. Note that some spare tires require pressures considerably higher than those used in the other tires.

While you are about the task of checking air pressure, inspect the tire treads for cuts, bruises and other damage. Check the air

GENERAL INFORMATION AND MAINTENANCE

Tread wear indicators will appear when the tire is worn out

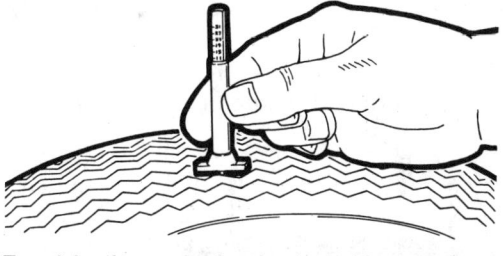

Tread depth can also be checked with an inexpensive gauge

A penny works as well as anything for checking tire tread depth

valves to be sure that they are tight. Replace any missing valve caps.

Check the tires for uneven wear that might indicate the need for front end alignment or tire rotation. Tires should be replaced when a tread wear indicator appears as a solid band across the tread.

When buying new tires, give some thought to the following points, especially if you are considering a switch to larger tires or a different profile series:

1. All four tires must be of the same construction type. This rule cannot be violated. Radial, bias, and bias-belted tires must not be mixed.

2. The wheels should be the correct width for the tire. Tire dealers have charts of tire and rim compatibility. A mismatch will cause sloppy handling and rapid tire wear. The tread width should match the rim width (inside bead to inside bead) within an inch. For

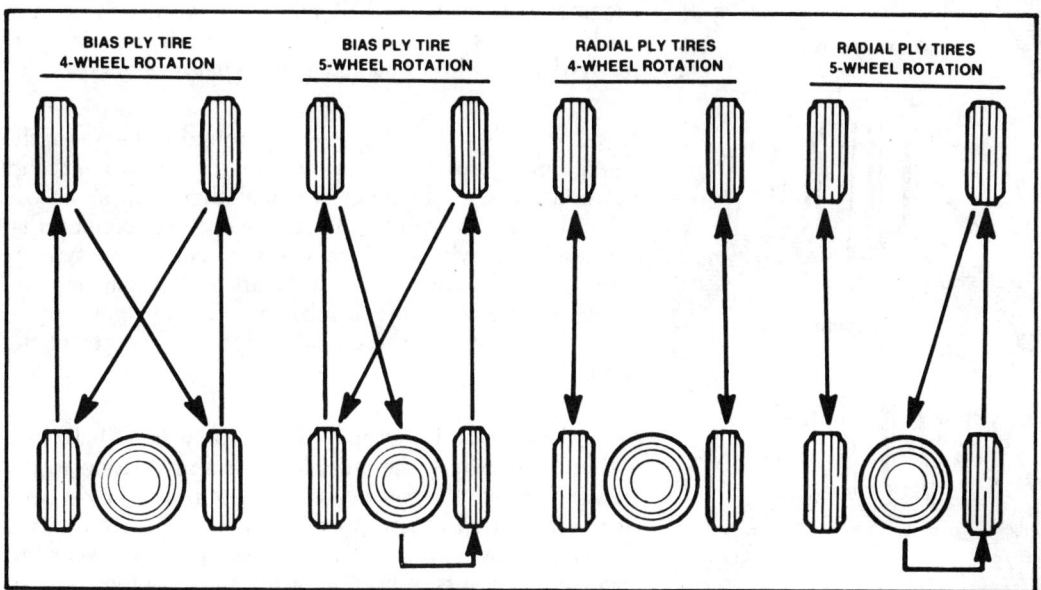

Tire rotation diagrams; note that radials should not be cross-switched

GENERAL INFORMATION AND MAINTENANCE

How to Read Tire Wear

The way your tires wear is a good indicator of other parts of your car. Abnormal wear patterns are often caused by the need for simple tire maintenance, or for front end alignment.

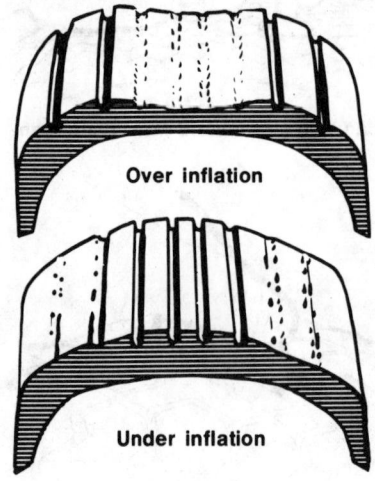
Over inflation

Excessive wear at the center of the tread indicates that the air pressure in the tire is consistently too high. The tire is riding on the center of the tread and wearing it prematurely. Occasionally, this wear pattern can result from outrageously wide tires on narrow rims. The cure for this is to replace either the tires or the wheels.

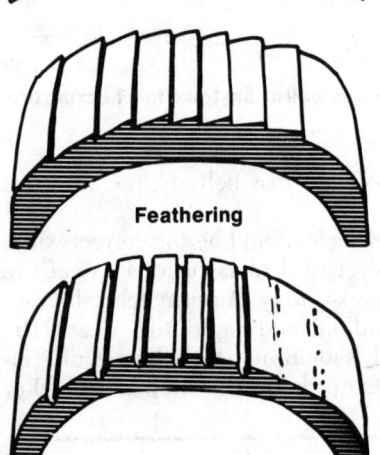
Under inflation

This type of wear usually results from consistent under-inflation. When a tire is under inflated, there is too much contact with the road by the outer treads, which wear prematurely. When this type of wear occurs, and the tire pressure is known to be consistently correct, a bent or worn steering component or the need for wheel alignment could be indicated.

Feathering

Feathering is a condition when the edge of each tread rib develops a slightly rounded edge on one side and a sharp edge on the other. By running your hand over the tire, you can usually feel the sharper edges before you'll be able to see them. The most common causes of feathering are incorrect toe-in setting or deteriorated bushings in the front suspension.

One side wear

When an inner or outer rib wears faster than the rest of the tire, the need for wheel alignment is indicated. There is excessive camber in the front suspension, causing the wheel to lean too much putting excessive load on one side of the tire. Misalignment could also be due to sagging springs, worn ball joints, or worn control arm bushings. Be sure the vehicle is loaded the way it's normally driven when you have the wheels aligned.

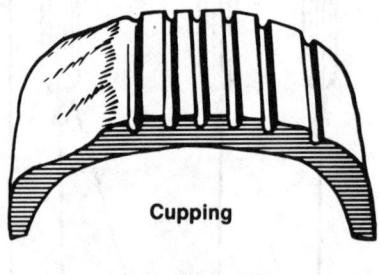
Cupping

Cups or scalloped dips appearing around the edge of the tread almost always indicate worn (sometimes bent) suspension parts. Adjustment of wheel alignment alone will seldom cure the problem. Any worn component that connects the wheel to the car can cause this type of wear. Occasionally, wheels that are out of balance will wear like this, but wheel imbalance usually shows up as bald spots between the outside edges and center of the tread.

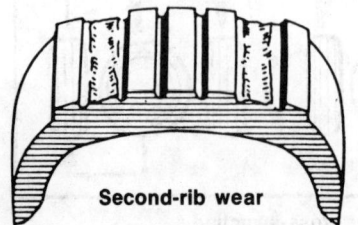
Second-rib wear

Second-rib wear is normally found only in radial tires, and appears where the steel belts end in relation to the tread. Normally, it can be kept to a minimum by paying careful attention to tire pressure and frequently rotating the tires. This is frequently considered normal wear but excessive amounts indicate that the tires are too wide for the wheels.

GENERAL INFORMATION AND MAINTENANCE

radial tires, the rim width should be 80% or less of the tire (not tread) width.

3. The height (mounted diameter) of the new tires can change speedometer accuracy, engine speed at a given road speed, fuel mileage, acceleration, and ground clearance. Tire manufacturers furnish full measurement specifications.

4. The spare tire should be usable, at least for short distance and low speed operation, with the new tires.

5. There shouldn't be any body interference when loaded, on bumps, or in turns.

TIRE ROTATION

Tire rotation is recommended every 6000 miles or so, to obtain maximum tire wear. The pattern you use depends on whether or not your car has a usable spare. Radial tires should not be cross-switched (from one side of the car to the other); they last longer if their direction of rotation is not changed. Snow tires sometimes have directional arrows molded into the side of the carcass; the arrow shows the direction of rotation. They will wear very rapidly if the rotation is reversed. Studded tires will lose their studs if their rotational direction is reversed.

NOTE: *Mark the wheel position or direction of rotation on radial tires or studded snow tires before removing them.*

Tire Inflation Chart

Recommended cold tire inflation pressure–psi

Model	Under 100 mph	Over 100 mph
All	28	32

STORAGE

Store the tires at the proper inflation pressure if they are mounted on wheels. Keep them in a cool dry place, laid on their sides. If the tires are stored in the garage or basement, do not let them stand on a concrete floor; set them on strips of wood.

Fuel Filter

The fuel filter should be replaced every 2 years or 25,000 miles. The filter should be replaced only when the engine is cold. Always place some absorbent cloths under the filter before disconnecting any lines, because some gas will spill from the bottom of the filter during removal.

Capacities

Year	Model	Displacement cu in. (cc)	Engine Crankcase Qts (liters) With Filter	Engine Crankcase Qts (liters) Without Filter	Transmission Pts (liters) Manual	Transmission Pts (liters) Automatic	Drive Axle Pts (liters)	Gasoline Tank Gals (liters)	Cooling System Qts (liters)
1970–73	240-Z	146 (2393)	5 (4.7)	4.25 (4)	3⅛ (1.5)	11¾ (5.5)	2⅛ (1)	15⅞ (60)	10½ (9.9)
1974	260-Z	156.5 (2565)	5 (4.7)	4.25 (4)	3⅛ (1.5)	11¾ (5.5)	2⅛ (1)	15⅞ (60)	10 (9.4)
1975	280-Z	168 (2753)	5 (4.7)	4.25 (4)	3.13 (1.5)	11.75 (5.5)	2.75 (1.3)	17.25 (65)	10 (9.4)
1976	280-Z	168 (2753)	5 (4.7)	4.25 (4)	3.13 (1.5)	11.75 (5.5)	2.75 (1.3)	17.25 (65)	11 (10.4)
1977–78	280-Z	168 (2753)	5 (4.7)	4.25 (4)	3.63 (1.7) ①	11.75 (5.5)	2.75 (1.3) ②	17.25 (65)	11 (10.4)
1979–82	280-ZX	168 (2753)	4.75 (4.5) ③	4.25 (4.0) ④	3.63 (1.7) ①	11.75 (5.5)	2.75 (1.3) ②	21.12 (80)	11.12 (10.5)

① For 4-speed; 5-speed capacity is 4.25 pts (2 liters)
② For rear axle used with manual transmissions; with automatic capacity is 2.13 pts (1 liter)
③ Turbocharged engines—5.5 qts.
④ Turbocharged engines—5.0 qts.

28 GENERAL INFORMATION AND MAINTENANCE

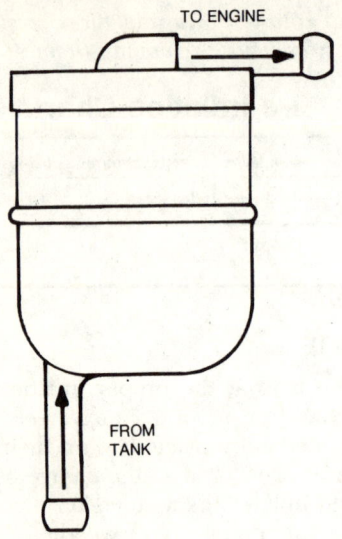

1970–73 fuel filter

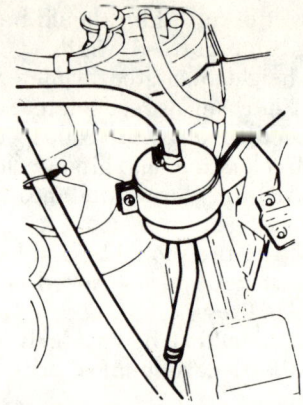

1975 and later fuel filter

REPLACEMENT

1970–73

The fuel filter is a clear plastic unit mounted in a clamp in the engine compartment.

1. Unsnap the filter from its clamp.
2. Disconnect the fuel lines from both ends of the filter.
3. Discard the old filter.
4. Install the fuel lines onto the replacement filter and tighten the clamps.
5. Replace the filter in the clamp.
6. Start the engine and check for leaks.

1974

This filter is similar to the one used on earlier models, but it is located near the rear axle along with electric fuel pump. Raise the rear of the car and safely support it. Use the method given for earlier models to replace the filter.

1975–79

The fuel filter is retained by a bracket to the inner fender directly behind the evaporative canister. Before the filter can be replaced, the high pressure in the fuel system must be released.

1. Disconnect the ground cable from the battery.
2. Disconnect the cold start valve electrical connector. The cold start valve is located in the intake runner.
3. Use two jumper wires from the battery to connect to the terminals on the cold start valve.

CAUTION: *Be careful not to short these against each other.*

Hold the jumpers to the valve terminal for about two or three seconds. This will relieve the pressure in the fuel system.

4. Remove the fuel lines from the fuel filter by loosening the clamps.
5. Remove the bolt from the filter retaining bracket and remove the filter.
6. Install the replacement filter in the reverse order of removal. Use new hose clamps.

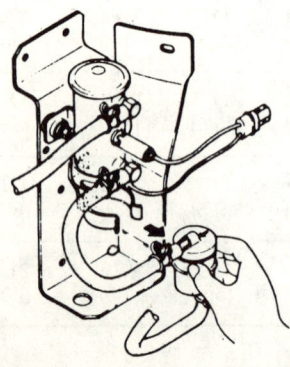

1974 fuel filter

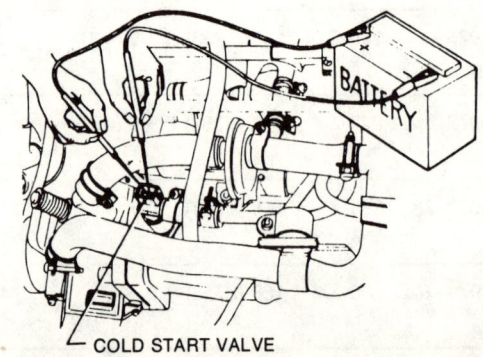

Energizing the cold start valve to release fuel system pressure on 1975–79 models

GENERAL INFORMATION AND MAINTENANCE

7. Connect the cold start valve and the battery ground cable.
8. Start the engine and check for leaks.

1980 and Later

The fuel filter is of the same type as that used on the other fuel injected models, but the method for discharging the fuel injection system is different.
1. Start the engine.
2. Remove the fuel pump relay (#1 in the diagram) from the relay connector while the engine is running. The relay is located on the right front fender in the engine compartment, just aft of the windshield washer reservoir.
3. After the engine stalls, crank the engine two or three more times.
4. Turn the ignition switch off. Install the fuel pump relay.
5. Release the clamps securing the fuel hoses to the filter. Be careful not to spill fuel on the engine. Disconnect the hoses from the filter.

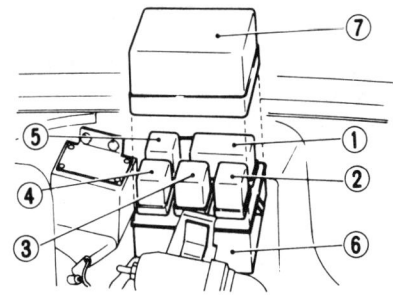

1. Fuel pump relay #2
2. Lighting relay
3. Bulb check relay
4. Air conditioning relay
5. Inhibitor relay
6. Relay box
7. Relay cover

Location of the fuel pump relay # 2—1980 and later

6. Remove the bolt securing the filter to the bracket; remove the filter.
7. Install the new filter. Connect the fuel hoses and secure them with new clamps.
8. Start the engine and check for leaks.

Maintenance Intervals Chart

Intervals are for numbers of months or thousands of miles, whichever comes first.
NOTE: *Heavy-duty operation (trailer towing, prolonged idling, severe stop and start driving, winter operation on salted roads) should be accompanied by a 50% increase in maintenance. Cut the interval in half for these conditions. Operation in extremely dusty conditions may require immediate changes of engine oil and all filters.*

Maintenance	1970–71	1972–73	1974	1975–78	1979	1980–82
Air cleaner (Replace)	24	24	24	24	24	24
PCV valve						
Check	12	12	12	12	12	12
Replace	12	12	12	24	24	①
Carbon canister filter						
(Replace)	—	—	24	24	24	①
Belt tension (Adjust)	6	6	12	12	12	12
Engine oil (Change)	3	3	4	6	6	6
Engine oil filter						
(Change)	6	6	8	6	6	6
Fuel filter (Replace)	24	24	24	24	24	24
Manual transmission						
Check	3	3	4	6	6	12
Change	30	30	36	24	24	48

GENERAL INFORMATION AND MAINTENANCE

Maintenance Intervals Chart (cont.)

Maintenance	1970–71	1972–73	1974	1975–78	1979	1980–82
Automatic transmission						
Check	—	3	4	6	6	12
Change	—	30	36	—	—	—
Differential						
Check	3	3	4	6	6	12
Change	30	30	36	24	48	48
Front wheel bearings (Clean and repack)	24	24	24	24	24	24
Engine coolant (Change)	24	24	24	24	24	24
Steering gear (Check)	6	6	12	12	12	12
Chassis lubrication Linkage and suspension ball joints	24	24	24	24	24	24
Axle shaft lubrication	30	30	36	24	24	24
Rotate tires	6	6	8	12	12	12
Valve lash ② (Check and adjust)	6	6	12	12	12	12
Brake and clutch fluid						
Check	3	3	4	6	6	12
Change ③	12	12	12	12	12	12
Air induction filter (Replace)	—	—	—	—	—	24
Oxygen sensor ⑤	—	—	—	—	—	30

① As necessary   ③ See Chapters 6 and 9   ⑤ See Chapter 4
② See Chapter 2   ④ 1980 only

LUBRICATION
Oil and Fuel Recommendations

OIL

The SAE (Society of Automotive Engineers) grade number indicates the viscosity of the engine oil, and thus its ability to lubricate at a given temperature. The lower the SAE grade number, the lighter the oil; the lower the viscosity, the easier it is to crank the engine in cold weather.

Oil viscosities should be chosen from those oils recommended for the lowest anticipated temperatures during the oil change interval.

Multi-viscosity oils (10W-30, 20W-50, etc.) offer the important advantage of being adaptable to temperature extremes. They allow easy starting at low temperatures, yet give good protection at high speeds and engine temperatures. This is a decided advantage in changeable climates or in long distance touring.

The API (American Petroleum Institute) designation indicates the classification of engine oil for use under given operating conditions. Only oils designated for use "Service SF" should be used. Oils of the SF type perform a variety of functions inside the engine in addition to the basic function as a lubricant. Through a balanced system of metallic detergents and polymeric dispersants, the oil prevents the formation of high and low temperature deposits, and also keeps sludge and

GENERAL INFORMATION AND MAINTENANCE

dirt particles in suspension. Acids, particularly sulfuric acid, as well as other byproducts of combustion, are neutralized. Both the SAE grade number and the API designation can be found on the top of the oil can.

NOTE: *Non-detergent or straight mineral oils must never be used.*

FUEL

The Z-car engine is designed to operate on regular leaded fuel, 1970–71, or regular, low-lead, or unleaded fuel, 1972–79, with the exception of 1975 and later cars sold in California, which have a catalytic converter. Converter-equipped cars must use unleaded fuel. This also applies to all 1980 and later ZX models, since all have a converter. The use of leaded fuel will plug the catalyst rendering it inoperative, and will increase the exhaust back pressure to the point where engine output will be severely reduced. In all cases, the minimum octane rating of the fuel used must be at least 91 RON. All unleaded fuels sold in the U.S. are required to meet this minimum octane rating.

Use of a fuel too low in octane (a measurement of anti-knock quality) will result in spark knock. Since many factors affect operating efficiency, such as altitude, terrain, and air temperature and humidity, knocking may result even though the recommended fuel is being used. If persistent knocking occurs, it may be necessary to switch to a slightly higher grade of gasoline. Continuous or heavy knocking may result in engine damage.

NOTE: *Your engine's fuel requirement can change with time, mainly due to carbon buildup, which changes the compression ratio. If your engine pings, knocks, or runs on, switch to a higher grade of fuel, if possible, and check the ignition timing. If your engine requires unleaded fuel, sometimes changing brands will cure the problem. If it is necessary to retard timing from specifications, don't change it more than a few degrees. Retarded timing will reduce power output and fuel mileage, and will increase engine temperature.*

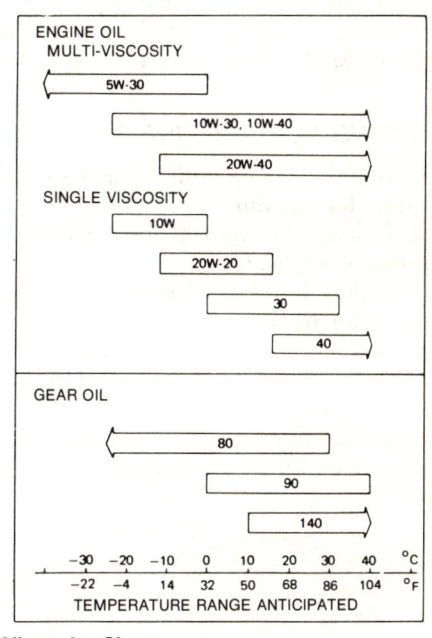

Recommended Lubricants

Lubricant	Classification
Engine Oil	API SE or SF
Manual Transmission	API GL-4
Automatic Transmission	DEXRON® or DEXRON II®
Differential	API GL-5
Wheel Bearings	NLGI #2
Chassis Grease	NLGI #2
Driveshaft	NLGI #2
Brake Fluid	DOT 3
Clutch Fluid	DOT 3
Steering Gear: manual	API GL-4
power	DEXRON® or DEXRON II®
Antifreeze	Ethylene Glycol

Oil Viscosity Chart

Oil Changes

The mileage figures given in the "Maintenance Intervals" chart are the Datsun recommended intervals for oil and filter changes assuming average driving. If your Datsun is being used under dusty, polluted, or off-road conditions, change the oil and filter sooner than specified. The same thing goes for cars driven in stop-and-go traffic or only for short distances.

32 GENERAL INFORMATION AND MAINTENANCE

Always drain the oil after the engine has been running long enough to bring it to operating temperature. Hot oil will flow easier and more contaminants will be removed along with the oil than if it were drained cold. You will need a large capacity drain pin, which you can purchase at any store which sells automotive parts. Another necessity is containers for the used oil. You will find that plastic bottles, such as those used for bleach or fabric softener, make excellent storage jugs. One ecologically desirable solution to the used oil disposal problem is to find a cooperative gas station owner who will allow you to dump your used oil into his tank.

Datsun recommends changing both the oil and filter during the first oil change and the filter every other oil change thereafter. For the small price of an oil filter, it's cheap insurance to replace the filter at every oil change. One of the larger filter manufacturers points out in its advertisements that not changing the filter leaves one quart of dirty oil in the engine. This claim is true and should be kept in mind when changing your oil.

CHANGING YOUR ENGINE OIL

1. Run the engine until it reaches normal operating temperature.
2. Jack up the front of the car and support it on safety stands.
3. Slide a drain pan of at least 6 quarts capacity under the oil pan.
4. Loosen the drain plug. Turn the plug out by hand. By keeping an inward pressure on the plug as you unscrew it, oil won't escape past the threads and you can remove it without being burned by hot oil.

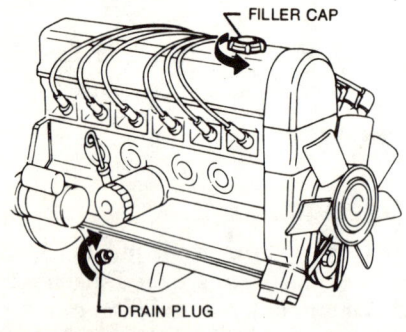

Oil drain plug location

5. Allow the oil to drain completely and then install the drain plug. Don't overtighten the plug, or you'll be buying a new pan or a trick replacement plug for stripped threads.

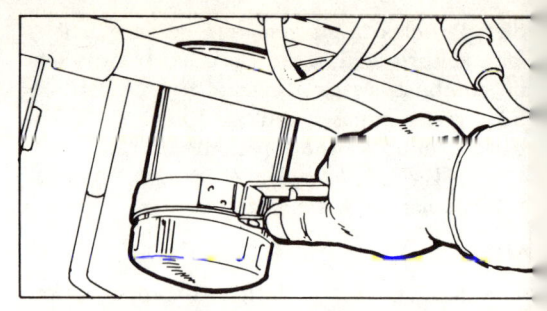

Remove the oil filter with a strap wrench

6. Using a strap wrench, remove the oil filter. Keep in mind that it's holding about one quart of dirty, hot oil.
7. Empty the old filter into the drain pan and dispose of the filter.
8. Using a clean rag, wipe off the filter adapter on the engine block. Be sure that the rag doesn't leave any lint which could clog an oil passage.
9. Coat the rubber gasket on the filter with fresh oil. Spin it onto the engine *by hand;* when the gasket touches the adapter surface give it another ½–¾ turn. No more, or you'll squash the gasket and it will leak.

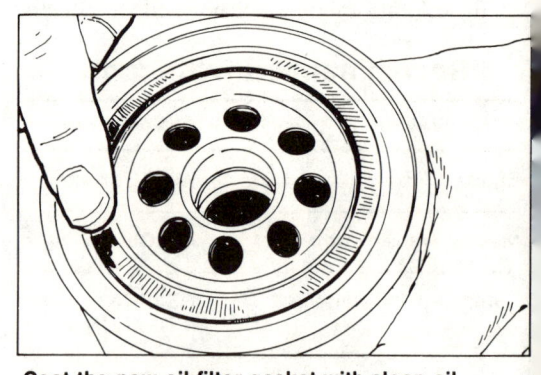

Coat the new oil filter gasket with clean oil

Install the new filter by hand

10. Refill the engine with the correct amount of fresh oil. See the "Capacities" chart.
11. Check the oil level on the dipstick. It

GENERAL INFORMATION AND MAINTENANCE

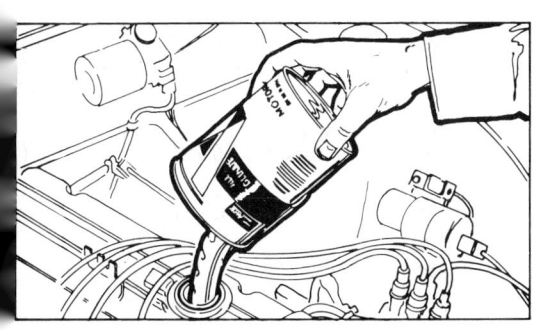

Add oil through the valve cover

is normal for the level to be a bit above the full mark. Start the engine and allow it to idle for a few minutes.

CAUTION: *Do not run the engine above idle speed until it has built up oil pressure, indicated when the oil light goes out.*

12. Shut off the engine, allow the oil to drain for a minute, and check the oil level. Check around the filter and drain plug for any leaks, and correct as necessary.

Transmission

MANUAL

Change the manual transmission oil according to the schedule in the "Maintenance Intervals" chart. You may also want to change it if you have bought your car used, or if it has been driven in water deep enough to reach the transmission case.

1. The oil should be hot before it is drained. If the car is driven until the engine is at normal operating temperature, the oil should be hot enough.
2. Remove the filler plug from the left side of the transmission to provide a vent.
3. The drain plug is located on the bottom of the transmission case. Place a pan under the drain plug and remove it.

CAUTION: *The oil will be HOT. Push up against the threads as you unscrew the plug to prevent leakage.*

4. Allow the oil to drain completely. Clean off the plug and replace, tightening it until it is just snug.
5. Fill the transmission with gear oil through the filler plug hole. Use API service GL-4 gear oil of the proper viscosity (see the "Viscosity Chart" in this chapter for recommendations). This oil usually comes in a squeeze bottle with a long nozzle. If yours isn't, you can use a rubber squeeze bulb of the type used for kitchen basting to squirt the

stuff in. Refer to the "Capacities" chart for the amount of oil needed.

6. The oil level should come right up to the edge of the filler hole. You can stick your finger in to verify this. Watch out for sharp threads.
7. Replace the filler plug. Dispose of the old oil in the same manner as old engine oil. Take a drive in the car, stop, and check for leaks.

AUTOMATIC

The fluid should be changed according to the schedule in the "Maintenance Intervals" chart. If the car is normally used in severe service, such as start-and-stop driving, trailer towing, or the like, the interval should be halved. The fluid must be hot before it is drained; a 20 minute drive should accomplish this.

1. There is no drain plug; the fluid pan must be removed. Partially remove the pan screws until the pan can be pulled down at one corner. Place a container under the transmission, lower a rear corner of the pan, and allow the fluid to drain.

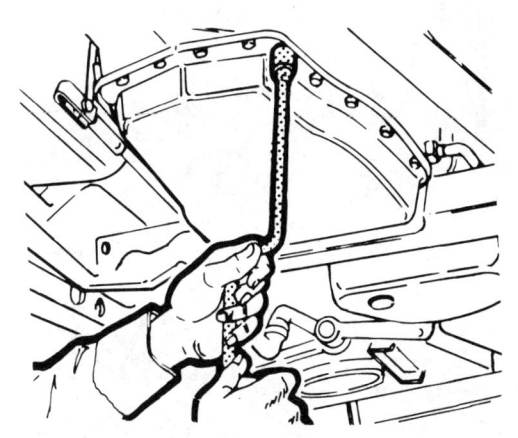

Remove the pan to drain the automatic transmission

2. After draining, remove the pan screws completely, and remove the pan and gasket.
3. Clean the pan thoroughly and allow it to air dry. If you wipe it out with a rag you risk leaving bits of lint in the pan which will clog the tiny hydraulic passages in the transmission.
4. Install the pan using a new gasket. If you decide to use sealer on the gasket apply it only in a very thin bead running to the outside of the pan screw holes. Tighten the pan screws evenly in rotation from the center outwards, to 3–5 ft lbs.

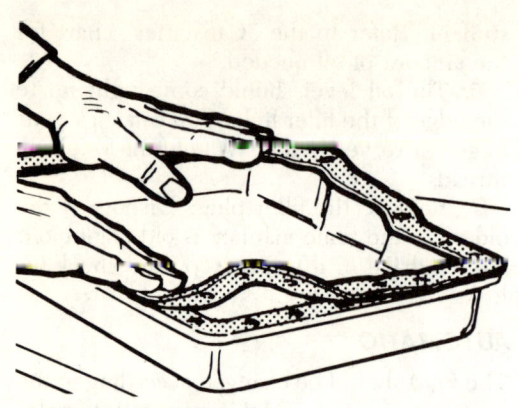

Install a new gasket

5. It is a good idea to measure the amount of fluid drained to determine how much fresh fluid to add. This is because some parts of the transmission, such as the torque converter, will not drain completely, and using the dry refill amount specified in the "Capacities" chart may lead to overfilling. Fluid is added through the dipstick tube. Make sure that the funnel, hose, or whatever you are using is completely clean and dry before pouring transmission fluid through it. Use DEXRON® or DEXRON II® automatic transmission fluid.

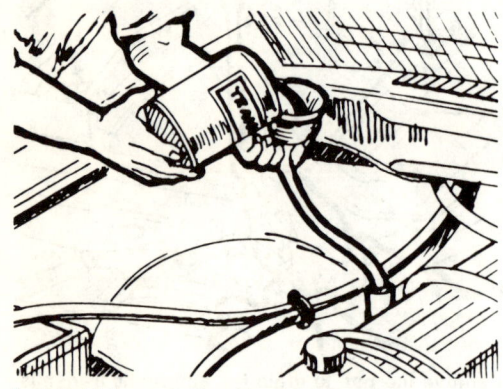

Add fluid through the dipstick tube

6. Replace the dipstick after filling. Start the engine and allow it to idle. Do NOT race the engine.

7. After the engine has idled for a few minutes, shift the transmission slowly through the gears, then return the lever to Park. With the engine idling, check the fluid level on the dipstick. It should be between the "H" and "L" marks. If below "L", add sufficient fluid to raise the level to between the marks.

8. Drive the car until the transmission is at operating temperature. The fluid should be at the "H" mark. If not, add sufficient fluid until this is the case. Be careful not to overfill; overfilling causes slippage, overheating, and seal damage.

NOTE: *If the drained fluid is discolored (brown or black), thick, or smells burnt, serious transmission problems due to overheating should be suspected. Your car's transmission should be inspected by a transmission specialist to determine the cause.*

Rear Axle

The axle lubricant should be changed according to the schedule in the "Maintenance Intervals" chart; you may also want to change it if you have bought your car used, or if it has been driven in water deep enough to reach the axle.

1. Park the car on a level surface. Place a pan of at least two quarts capacity underneath the drain plug. The drain plug is located on the center rear of the differential carrier, just below the filler plug. See the illustration earlier in this chapter, under "Fluid Level Checks" for a drawing of the location of these plugs. Remove the drain plug.

2. Allow the lubricant to drain completely.

3. Install the drain plug. Tighten it so that it will not leak, but do not overtighten. If you have a torque wrench, recommended torque is 29–43 ft lbs.

4. Refill the differential housing with API GL-5 gear oil of the proper viscosity. The correct level is to the edge of the filler hole.

5. Install the filler plug. Tighten to 29–43 ft lbs.

Chassis Greasing

Lubricate the accelerator linkage every 6,000 miles. Lubricate the foot pedal bushings every 12,000 miles.

Every 30,000 miles or 30 months, whichever comes first:

1. Lubricate the steering and suspension ball joints and the rear axle shaft joints as follows: Remove the grease plug and install a grease fitting. Install the grease gun connector and *slowly* feed grease into the joint to avoid forcing it out of the joint except at the grease bleeder. Lubricate the joint with multipurpose grease until new grease emerges at the bleeder point.

2. Apply multipurpose grease to the ball

GENERAL INFORMATION AND MAINTENANCE

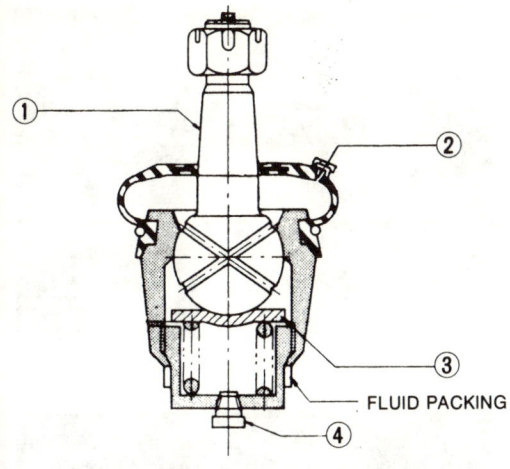

1. Ball stud
2. Grease bleeder
3. Spring seat
4. Plug

Cross-section of a suspension ball joint

splines of the driveshafts and repack the universal joints on the driveshaft and axle shafts. This will require major disassembly operations—see Chapter 7.

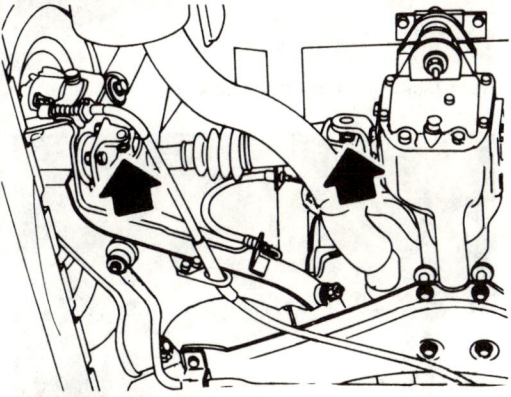

Axle shaft greasing locations

Body Lubrication

Lubricate all locks and hinges with multipurpose grease every 6,000.

Wheel Bearings

Clean and repack wheel bearings every 30,000 miles. See Chapter 9.

TOWING

Manual Transmission

Tow forward using the hook shown in the illustration. *Do not attempt to tow the vehicle by the front suspension.* Tow the vehicle so as to avoid a sudden impact on the hook.

Towing with manual transmission

Automatic Transmission

If the distance to be traveled is six miles or less, the vehicle may be towed with the front wheels off the ground. The speed must not exceed 20 mph under these conditions.

If the transmission is not operating properly, greater distance is involved, or higher speeds are required, tow the vehicle with the rear wheels off the ground and the steering wheel secured in a straight-ahead position. The ignition key should be left in the lock in the "Off" position. If the car is towed on the front wheels with the ignition key removed (steering column locked), damage to the steering column or lock will result.

JUMP STARTING

When jump starting a car, be sure to observe the proper polarity of the battery connections.

CAUTION: *Always hook up the positive (+) terminal of the booster battery to the positive terminal of the discharged battery and the negative terminal (−) to a good ground.*

If the battery terminals are unmarked, the correct polarity of each battery may be determined by examining the battery cables. The negative (ground) cable will run to the chassis and the positive (hot) cable will run to the starter motor. A 12 volt fully charged battery should be used for jump starting.

To jump start the car, proceed in the following manner:

1. Put the transmission in Park (P) or Neutral (N) and set the parking brake. Make sure that all electrical loads are turned off (lights, wipers, etc.).

2. Remove the vent caps from both batteries. Cover the opened vents of both batteries

36   GENERAL INFORMATION AND MAINTENANCE

with a clean cloth. These two steps help reduce the hazard of an explosion.

3. Connect the positive (+) terminals of both batteries first. Be sure that the cars are not touching or the ground circuit may be completed accidentally.

4. Connect the negative (−) terminal of the booster battery to a suitable ground (engine lifting bracket, alternator bracket, etc.) on the engine of the car with the dead battery. Do not connect the negative jumper cable to the ground post of the dead battery.

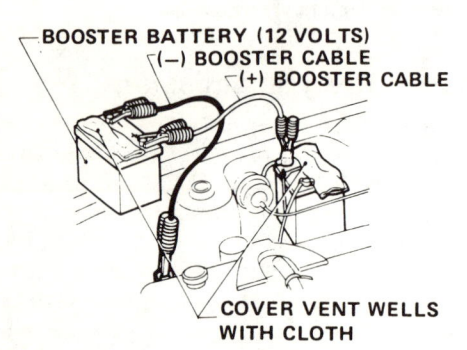

Proper jumper cable connections. Connect the negative cable of the booster battery last, and connect it to a metal part of the engine, not to the other battery

5. Start the car's engine in the usual manner.

6. Remove the jumper cables in *exactly* the reverse order used to hook them up.

JACKING AND HOISTING

The vehicle is supplied with a scissors jack for emergency road repairs. The scissors jack may be used to raise the car via the notches on either side at the front and rear of the doors. *Do not attempt to use the jack in any other places.* Always block the diagonally opposite wheel when using a jack. When using

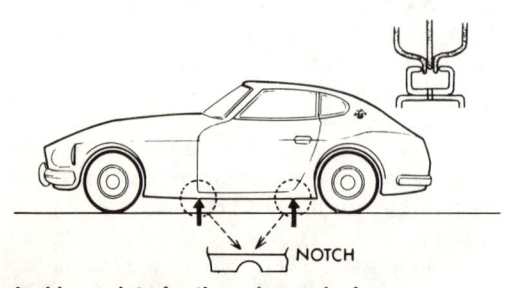

Jacking points for the scissors jack

Front jacking point—floor jack

Rear jacking point—floor jack

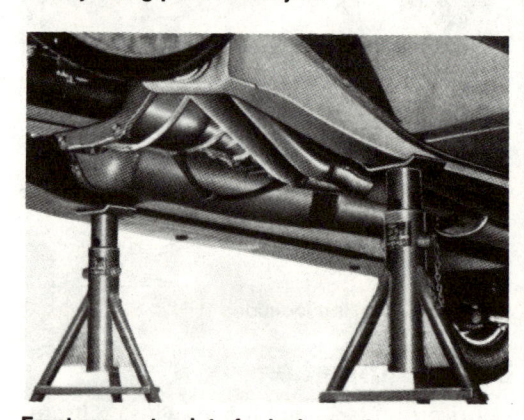

Front support points for jack stands

Rear support points for jack stands

GENERAL INFORMATION AND MAINTENANCE

a garage jack, support the car at the center of the front suspension member or at the differential carrier. *Do not attempt to jack the car at the front suspension transverse link.* Block both wheels at the opposite end of the car.

When using stands, use the side members at the front and the differential front mounting crossmember at the back for placement points.

Whenever you plan to work under the car, you must support it on jackstands or ramps. Never use cinder blocks or stacks of wood to support the car, even if you're only going to be under it for a few minutes. Never crawl under the car when it is supported only by the tire-changing jack.

Small hydraulic, screw, or scissors jacks are satisfactory for raising the car. Drive-on trestles or ramps are also a handy and safe way to both raise and support the car. These can be bought or constructed from wood or steel.

If the Datsun is to be raised with a hoist such as the type used in service stations, the pads of the hoist should be positioned on the frame rails of the car, or at the points indicated for jackstand support in the illustrations. Never support the car on any suspension member or underbody panel.

Tune-Up 2

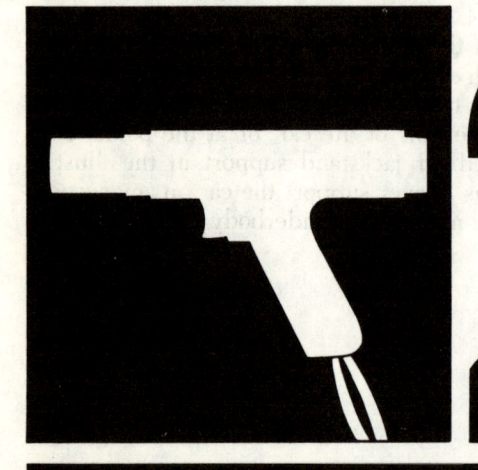

TUNE-UP PROCEDURES

In order to extract the full measure of performance and economy from your engine it is essential that it be properly tuned at regular intervals. A regular tune-up will keep your Datsun's engine running smoothly and will prevent the annoying minor breakdowns and poor performance associated with an untuned engine.

NOTE: *All Datsun Z-cars use a conventional breaker points ignition system through 1973. Models through 1973 with automatic transmission use a dual points system for emission control purposes. Models through 1973 with manual transmission have single breaker points. All 1974 and later models use a fully transistorized ignition system. 1974 automatic transmission models, and all 1975–76 49 States and Canada models have dual pick-ups. 1975–76 California models have only one pick-up. All 1977 and later models have single pick-up electronic ignition.*

A complete tune-up should be performed every 12,000 miles or twelve months, whichever comes first. This interval should be halved if the car is operated under severe conditions, such as trailer towing, prolonged idling, continual stop and start driving, or if starting or running problems are noticed. It is assumed that the routine maintenance described in Chapter 1 has been kept up, as this will have a decided effect on the results of a tune-up. All of the applicable steps of a tune-up should be followed in order, as the result is a cumulative one.

If the specifications on the tune-up sticker in the engine compartment of your Datsun disagree with the "Tune-Up Specifications" chart in this chapter, the figures on the sticker must be used. The sticker often reflects changes made during the production run.

Spark Plugs

Spark plugs ignite the air and fuel mixture in the cylinder as the piston reaches the top of the compression stroke. The controlled explosion that results forces the piston down, turning the crankshaft and the rest of the drive train.

The average life of a spark plug is 12,000 miles. This is, however, dependent on a number of factors: the mechanical condition of the engine; the type of fuel; the driving conditions; and the driver.

When you remove the spark plugs, check their condition. They are a good indicator of the condition of the engine. It is a good idea to remove the spark plugs every 6,000 miles

TUNE-UP

to keep an eye on the mechanical state of the engine.

A small deposit of light tan or gray material (or rust red with unleaded fuel) on a spark plug that has been used for any period of time is to be considered normal. Any other color, or abnormal amounts of deposit, indicates that there is something amiss in the engine.

The gap between the center electrode and the side or ground electrode can be expected to increase not more than 0.001 in. every 1,000 miles under normal conditions.

When a spark plug is functioning normally or, more accurately, when the plug is installed in an engine that is functioning properly, the plugs can be taken out, cleaned, regapped, and reinstalled in the engine without doing the engine any harm.

When, and if, a plug fouls and begins to misfire, you will have to investigate, correct the cause of the fouling, and either clean or replace the plug.

There are several reasons why a spark plug will foul and you can learn which is at fault by just looking at the plug. A few of the most common reasons for plug fouling, and a description of the fouled plug's appearance, are listed in the color section, which also offers solutions to the problems.

Spark plugs suitable for use in your Datsun's engine are offered in a number of different heat ranges. The amount of heat which the plug absorbs is determined by the length of the lower insulator. The longer the insulator, the hotter the plug will operate; the shorter the insulator, the cooler it will operate. A spark plug that absorbs (or retains) little heat and remains too cool will accumulate deposits of lead, oil, and carbon, because it is not hot enough to burn them off. This leads to fouling and consequent misfiring. A spark plug that absorbs too much heat will have no deposits, but the electrodes will burn away quickly and, in some cases, preignition may result. Preignition occurs when the spark plug tips get so hot that they ignite the fuel/air mixture before the actual spark fires. This premature ignition will usually cause a pinging sound under conditions of low speed and heavy load. In severe cases, the heat may become high enough to start the fuel/air mixture burning throughout the combustion chamber rather than just to the front of the plug. In this case, the resultant explosion will be strong enough to damage pistons, rings, and valves.

In most cases the factory recommended heat range is correct; it is chosen to perform well under a wide range of operating conditions. However, if most of your driving is long distance, high speed travel, you may want to install a spark plug one step colder than standard. If most of your driving is of the short trip variety, when the engine may not always reach operating temperature, a hotter plug may help burn off the deposits normally accumulated under those conditions.

REMOVAL

1. Number the wires so that you won't cross them when you replace them.
2. Remove the wire from the end of the spark plug by grasping the wire by the rubber boot. If the boot sticks to the plug, remove it by twisting and pulling at the same time. Do not pull the wire itself or you will damage the core.

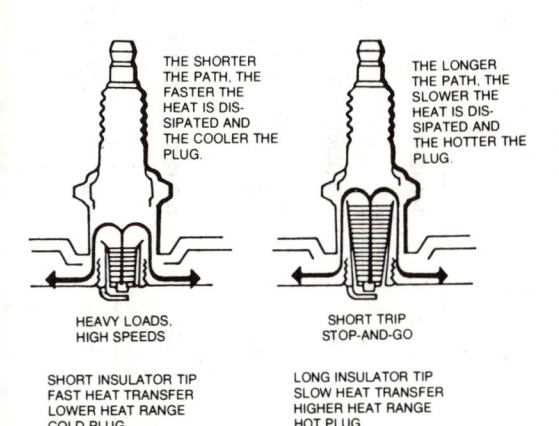

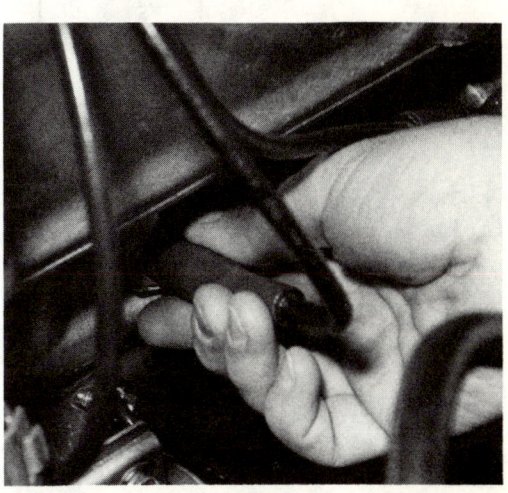

Spark plug heat range

Pull on the spark plug boot, not on the wire

TUNE-UP

Tune-Up Specifications

Year	Engine Displacement cu in. (cc)	Spark Plugs Type	Gap (in.) (mm)	Distributor Point Dwell (deg)	Point Gap (in.) (mm)	Ignition Timing (deg) MT	Ignition Timing (deg) AT	Compression Pressure (psi) (kg/cm^2)	Idle Speed (rpm) MT	Idle Speed (rpm) AT	Hot Valve Clearance In	Hot Valve Clearance Ex
1970–71	146 (2393)	BP6E	.031–.035 (.8–.9)	35–41	.016–.019 (.4–.5)	5B	—	171–185 (12–13)	750	—	.010 (.25)	.012 (.30)
1972	146 (2393)	BP6ES	.031–.035 (.8–.9)	35–41	.016–.019 (.4–.5)	5B	TDC ②	171–185 (12–13)	750	600	.010 (.25)	.012 (.30)
1973	146 (2393)	BP6ES	.031–.035 (.8–.9)	35–41	.018–.021 (.45–.55)	7B	5B ③	171–185 (12–13)	750	600	.010 (.25)	.012 (.30)
1974	156 (2565)	BP6ES	.031–.035 (.8–.9)	—	.012–.016 ① (.3–.4)	8B	8B ③	171–185 (12–13)	750	600	.010 (.25)	.012 (.30)
1975	168 (2753)	BP6ES	.028–.031 (.7–.8)	—	.008–.016 ① (.2–.4)	7B ④ ⑤	7B ④ ⑤	164–178 (11.5–12.5)	800	700	.010 (.25)	.012 (.30)
1976	168 (2753)	BP6ES	.028–.031 (.7–.8)	—	.008–.016 ① (.2–.4)	7B ④ ⑤	7B ④ ⑤	164–178 (11.5–12.5)	800	700	.010 (.25)	.012 (.30)
1977	168 (2753)	BP6ES-11 ⑥	.039–.043 ⑦ (1.0–1.1)	—	.008–.016 ① (.2–.4)	10B	10B	164–178 (11.5–12.5)	800	700	.010 (.25)	.012 (.30)

TUNE-UP

Year									
1978	168 (2753)	BP6ES-11 ⑥	.039–.043 ⑦ (1.0–1.1)	—	.008–.016 ① (.2–.4)	10B	10B	164–178 (11.5–12.5)	800	700	.010 (.25)	.012 (.30)
1979	168 (2753)	B6ES-11 ⑧	.039–.043 (1.0–1.1)	—	.012–.020 ① (.3–.5)	10B	10B	171 (12)	800 ⑨	700	.010 (.25)	.012 (.30)
1980	168 (2753)	BP6ES-11 ⑩	.039–.043 (1.0–1.1)	—	.012.020 ① (.3–.5)	10B	10B	171 (12)	700	700	.010 (.25)	.012 (.30)
1981	168 (2753)	BPR6ES-11	.039–.043 (1.0–1.1)	—	.012–.020 ① (.3–.5)	8B ⑪	8B ⑪	171 (12)	700	700	.010 (.25)	.012 (.30)
1981 (turbo)	168 (2753)	BPR6ES-11	.039–.043 (1.0–1.1)	—	—	20B	20B	141 (10)	650	650	.010 (.25)	.012 (.30)

See Underhood Specifications Sticker

Part numbers in this chart are not recommendations by Chilton for any product by brand name.
— Not Applicable
① Refers to air gap—electronic ignition
② 10B @ 600 below 30°F
③ 15B @ 600 advance
④ 10B on California models
⑤ 13B with engine cold on dual reluctor models
⑥ BR6ES—Canada
⑦ .028–.031 (.7–.8)—Canada
⑧ BR6ES-11—Canada
⑨ 700—Non-California models with catalytic converter
⑩ BPR6ES-11—Canada
⑪ Canada—10B

TUNE-UP

3. Use a 13/16 in. spark plug socket to loosen all of the plugs about two turns.

NOTE: *The cylinder head is cast from aluminum. Remove the spark plugs when the engine is cold, if possible, to prevent damage to the threads.*

If removal of the plugs is difficult, apply a few drops of penetrating oil or silicone spray to the area around the base of the plug, and allow it a few minutes to work.

4. If compressed air is available, apply it to the area around the spark plug holes. Otherwise, use a rag or a brush to clean the area. Be careful not to allow any foreign material to drop into the spark plug holes.

5. Remove the plugs by unscrewing them the rest of the way from the engine.

INSPECTION

Check the plugs for deposits and wear. If they are not going to be replaced, clean the plugs thoroughly. Remember that any kind of deposit will decrease the efficiency of the plug. Plugs can be cleaned on a spark plug cleaning machine, which can sometimes be found in service stations, or you can do an acceptable job of cleaning with a stiff brush. If the plugs are cleaned, the electrodes must be filed flat. Use an ignition points file, not an emery board or the like, which will leave deposits. The electrodes must be filed perfectly flat with sharp edges; rounded edges reduce the spark plug voltage by as much as 50%.

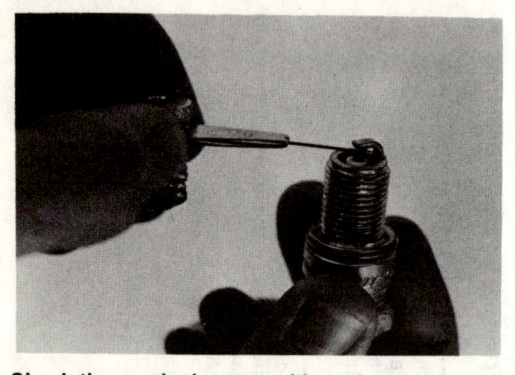

Check the spark plug gap with a wire gauge

Check spark plug gap before installation. The ground electrode must be parallel to the center electrode and the specified size wire gauge should pass through the gap with a slight drag. Always check the gap on new plugs, too; they are not always correctly set at the factory. Do not use a flat feeler gauge when measuring the gap, because the reading will be inaccurate. Wire gapping tools

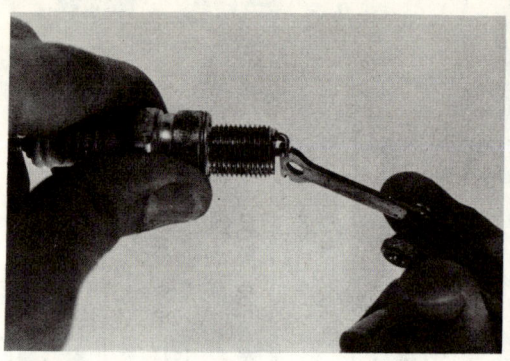

Bend the side electrode to adjust the gap

usually have a bending tool attached. Use that to adjust the side electrode until the proper distance is obtained. Absolutely never bend the center electrode. Also, be careful not to bend the side electrode too far or too often; it may weaken and break off within the engine, requiring removal of the cylinder head to retrieve it.

INSTALLATION

1. Lubricate the threads of the spark plugs with a drop of oil. Install the plugs and tighten them hand-tight. Take care not to cross-thread them.

2. Tighten the spark plugs with the socket. Do not apply the same amount of force you would use for a bolt; just snug them in. If a torque wrench is available, tighten to 11–15 ft lbs.

3. Install the wires on their respective plugs. Make sure the wires are firmly connected. You will be able to feel them click into place.

CHECKING AND REPLACING SPARK PLUG CABLES

At every tune-up, visually inspect the spark plug cables for burns, cuts, or breaks in the insulation. Check the boots and the nipples on the distributor cap and coil. Replace any damaged wiring.

Every 36,000 miles or so, the resistance of the wires should be checked with an ohmmeter. Wires with excessive resistance will cause misfiring, and may make the engine difficult to start in damp weather. Generally, the useful life of the cables is 36,000–50,000 miles.

To check resistance, remove the distributor cap, leaving the wires attached. Connect one lead of an ohmmeter to an electrode within the cap; connect the other lead to the corresponding spark plug terminal (remove it from the plug for this test). Replace any wire which shows a resistance over 50,000 ohms. Generally speaking, however, resistance should not be over 30,000 ohms, and 50,000 ohms must be considered the outer limit of acceptability. Test the high tension lead from the coil by connecting the ohmmeter between the center contact in the distributor cap and either of the primary terminals of the coil. If resistance is more than 25,000 ohms, remove the cable from the coil and check the resistance of the cable alone. Anything over 15,000 ohms is cause for replacement. It should be remembered that resistance is also a function of length; the longer the cable, the greater the resistance. Thus, if the cables on your car are longer than the factory originals, resistance will be higher, quite possibly outside these limits.

When installing new cables, replace them one at a time to avoid mixups. Start by replacing the longest one first. Install the boot firmly over the spark plug. Route the wire over the same path as the original. Insert the nipple firmly into the tower on the cap or the coil.

Breaker Points and Condenser

The points function as a circuit breaker for the primary circuit of the ignition system. The ignition coil must boost the 12 volts of electrical pressure supplied by the battery to as much as 25,000 volts in order to fire the plugs. To do this, the coil depends on the points and the condenser to make a clean break in the primary circuit.

The coil has both primary and secondary circuits. When the ignition is turned on, the battery supplies voltage through the coil and onto the points. The points are connected to ground, completing the primary circuit. As the current passes through the coil, a magnetic field is created in the iron center core of the coil. When the cam in the distributor turns, the points open, breaking the primary circuit. The magnetic field in the primary circuit of the coil then collapses and cuts through the secondary circuit windings around the iron core. Because of the physical principle called "electromagnetic induction," the battery voltage is increased to a level sufficient to fire the spark plugs.

When the points open, the electrical charge in the primary circuit tries to jump the gap created between the two open contacts of the points. If this electrical charge were not transferred elsewhere, the metal contacts of the points would start to change rapidly.

The function of the condenser is to absorb excessive voltage from the points when they open and thus prevent the points from becoming pitted or burned.

INSPECTION OF THE POINTS

1. Disconnect the high-tension wire from the top of the distributor and the coil.
2. The distributor cap is retained by two spring clips. Insert a screwdriver under their ends and release them. Lift off the cap with the spark plug wires attached. Inspect the inside of the cap. Wipe it clean with a rag and check for burned contacts, cracks and carbon tracks. A carbon track shows as a dark line running from one terminal to another. It cannot be successfully removed, so replace the cap if it has one of these. Generally, a cap and rotor will last 36,000 miles.
3. Remove the rotor from the distributor shaft by pulling it straight up. Examine the condition of the rotor. If it is cracked or the metal tip is excessively worn or burned, it should be replaced. Clean the metal tip with a clean cloth, but don't file it.
4. Pry open the contacts of the points with a screwdriver and check the condition of the contacts. If they are excessively worn, burned or pitted, they should be replaced.
5. If the points are in good condition, adjust them and replace the rotor and the distributor cap. If the points need to be replaced, follow the replacement procedure given next.

REPLACEMENT OF THE BREAKER POINTS AND CONDENSER

1. Remove the cap and rotor as outlined in steps 1–3 of the preceding section.
2. On single points distributors, loosen the two screws securing the points. Use a magnetic screwdriver to avoid losing a screw down the distributor. Loosen the screw in the side of the distributor and slip the points wire out. Remove the point set.

On dual points distributors you will first have to decide if the tools available to you will enable you to remove the two condensers on the outside of the distributor body. If you have a flexible screwdriver, or one bent at a 90° angle, you should be able to get at them. Otherwise, it may be best to remove the distributor from the engine for points and condenser replacement.

TUNE-UP

To remove the distributor, first note and mark the position of the distributor on the small timing scale on the front of the distributor. Then mark the position of the rotor in relation to the distributor body. Do this by simply replacing the rotor on the distributor shaft and marking the spot on the distributor body where the rotor is pointing. Remove the small bolt at the rear of the distributor, and lift the distributor out of the block. DO NOT CRANK THE ENGINE WITH THE DISTRIBUTOR REMOVED.

3. On dual points distributors, loosen the two mounting screws which secure the points. Do not loosen the factory pre-set phase adjusting screw (#3 in the photograph). Loosen the screws retaining the points wires and remove each points set. The bottom of the points set is slotted; thus, it is not necessary to completely remove the points mounting screws.

On dual point distributors, #1 and #2 are the mounting screws. Do not loosen #3, the phase adjusting screw

4. On single points distributors, the condenser is mounted on the side of the distributor. Disconnect the wire and remove the condenser.

On dual points distributors, the two condensers are mounted on the outside of the distributor body. Note that the two are different. When new condensers are installed, they must be replaced in the same relationship as the originals. This is important, because they have different electrical capacities. Remove the condenser mounting screws, loosen the condenser lead screws, and remove the condensers.

5. Before installing the new points and condenser(s), place a matchhead-sized dab of grease on the distributor shaft cam and smear it evenly around the cam. Do not use oil, because it will lead to rapid point burning.

6. Install the new points set(s) and condenser(s). Be sure you are putting the dual points condensers in their proper locations. The different mounting ears on each make them pretty much idiot-proof. Tighten the condenser mounting screws, but leave the points screws slightly loose.

7. Check that the faces of the points meet squarely. If not, the fixed mount can be bent slightly with gentle force and a set of needle-nose pliers. Do not bend the movable contact.

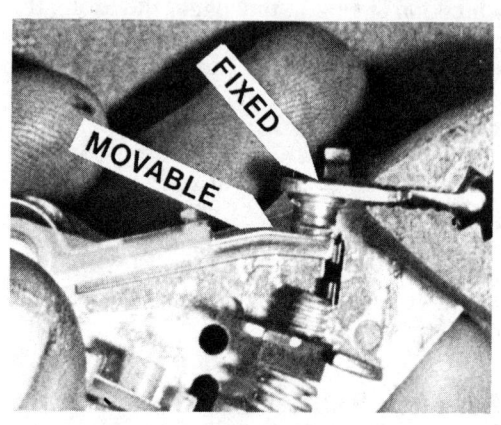

Bend the fixed point until the faces are square

8. The point gap must be adjusted next. The gap is adjusted with the rubbing block of the points resting on one of the six high spots of the distributor cam. To get it there, the engine can be rotated by bumping the starter with the ignition key, or the crankshaft can be turned with a wrench on the crankshaft pulley bolt; this is easier to do with the spark plugs removed.

If the distributor is removed (dual points) the distributor shaft can be rotated until the points blocks are resting on the high spots of the cam. It won't matter if you move the distributor shaft; it can only go back into the engine one way. Just note the position from which it is moved, and move it back there prior to replacing the distributor in the engine.

9. Insert a 0.018 in. thick flat feeler gauge between the points. A slight drag should be felt. If no drag can be felt, or if the gauge cannot be inserted at all, insert a screwdriver into the eccentric adjusting screw, or into the notch provided for adjustment, and use it to open or close the gap between the points until it is correct.

TUNE-UP 45

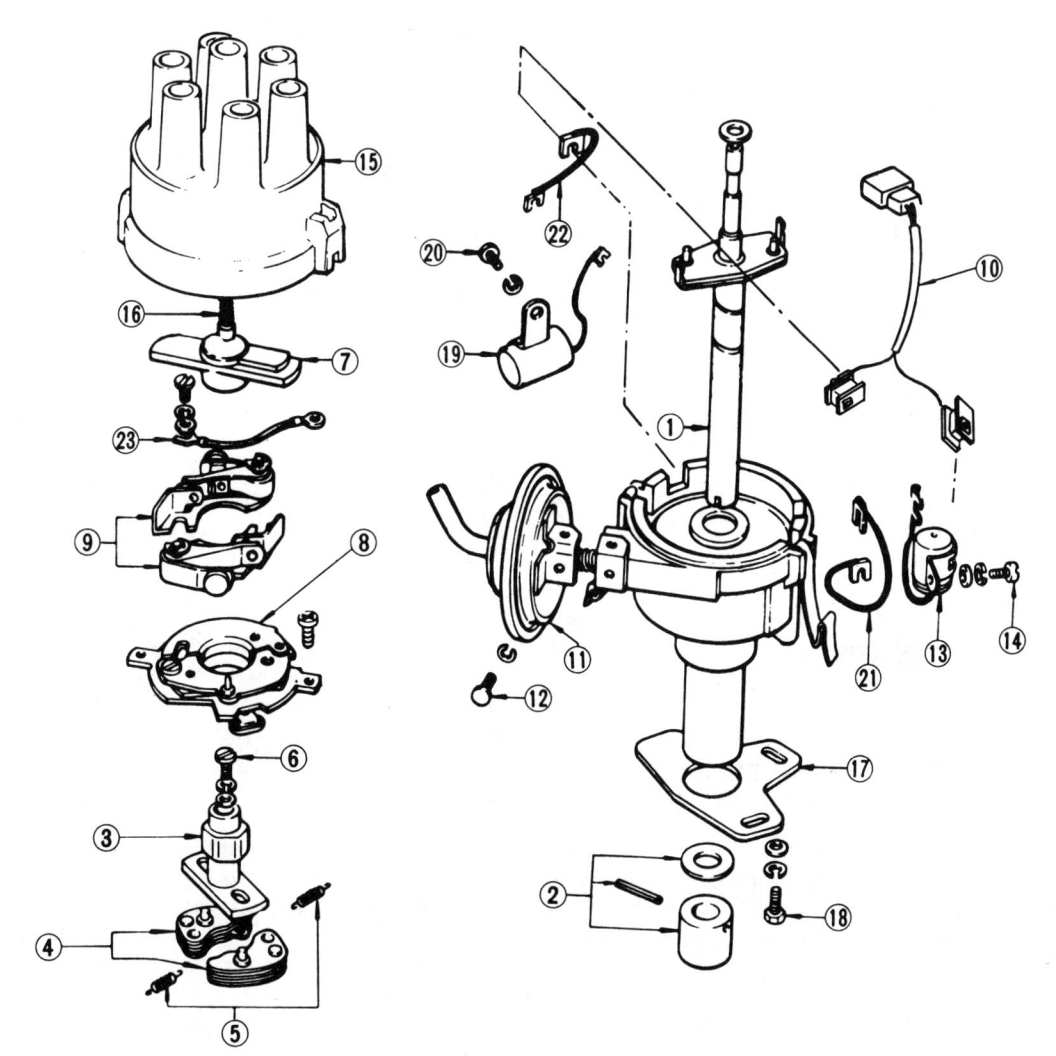

1. Shaft assembly
2. Collar set assembly
3. Cam assembly
4. Governor weight assembly
5. Governor spring set
7. Screw
7. Rotor head assembly
8. Breaker assembly
9. Contact set
10. Connector assembly
11. Vacuum control assembly
12. Screw
13. Condenser assembly (for Advanced point)
14. Screw
15. Distributor cap assembly
16. Carbon point assembly
17. Fixing plate
18. Bolt
19. Condenser assembly (for Retarded point)
20. Screw
21. Lead wire assembly (for Advanced point)
22. Lead wire assembly (for Retarded point)
23. Ground wire assembly

Exploded view of the dual point distributor

10. When the gap is set, tighten the points screws, and then recheck the gap. Sometimes it takes three or four tries to get it correct, so don't feel frustrated if they seem to move around on you a little. It is not easy to feel the correct gap, either. Use gauges 0.002 in. larger and smaller than 0.018 as a test. If the points are spread slightly by a 0.020 in. gauge, and not touched at all by a 0.016 in. gauge, the setting should be right.

11. After all the adjustments are complete, pull a clean piece of tissue or a white business card between the points to clear any bits of grit.

12. On dual points distributors, if the distributor was removed, reset the shaft and rotor to their original positions, and install the distributor. Note that the slot for the oil pump drive is tapered and will only fit one way. Be sure the marks you made earlier line up, and tighten the distributor hold down bolt.

46 TUNE-UP

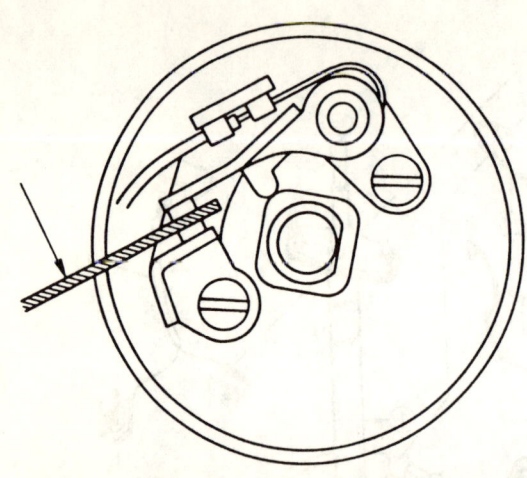

The arrow indicates the feeler gauge used to check point gap

13. Replace the rotor and distributor cap, and snap on the clips. If you have a dwell meter (recommended) you should next set the dwell. Otherwise, go on to the ignition timing.

ADJUSTMENT OF THE BREAKER POINTS WITH A DWELL METER

Single Point Distributor

The dwell angle is the number of degrees of distributor cam rotation through which the points remain closed (conducting electricity). Increasing the point gap decreases dwell, while decreasing the gap increases dwell.

The dwell angle may be checked with the distributor cap and rotor installed and the engine running, or with the cap and rotor removed and the engine cranking at starter speed. The meter gives a constant reading with the engine running. With the engine cranking, the meter will fluctuate between zero degrees dwell and the maximum figure for that setting. Never attempt to adjust the points when the ignition is on, or you may receive a shock.

1. Connect a meter as per the manufacturer's instructions (usually one lead to the distributor's terminal of the coil and the other lead to a ground). Zero the meter, if necessary.
2. Check the dwell by either the cranking method, or with the engine running. If the setting is incorrect, the points must be adjusted.

CAUTION: *Keep your hands, hair and clothing clear of the engine fan and pulleys. Be sure the wires from the dwell meter are routed out of the way. If the engine is running, block the front wheels, put the transmission in Neutral, and set the parking brake.*

3. To change the dwell angle, turn the ignition off, loosen the points hold down screw and adjust the point gap; increase the gap to decrease dwell, and vice versa. Tighten the hold down screw and check the dwell angle with the engine cranking. If it seems to be correct, replace the cap and rotor and check dwell with the engine running. Readjust as necessary.
4. Run the engine speed up to about 2,500 rpm, and then let the speed drop abruptly; the dwell reading should not change. If it does, a worn distributor shaft, bushing or cam, or a worn breaker plate is indicated. The parts must be inspected and replaced, if necessary.
5. After adjusting dwell angle, go on to the Ignition Timing section following. Ignition timing must be checked after adjusting the point gap, as a 1° increase in dwell results in an ignition timing retard of 2°, and vice versa.

Dual Point Distributor

Adjust the point gap of a dual point distributor with a dwell meter as follows:

1. Disconnect the wiring harness of the distributor from the engine wiring harness.
2. Using a jumper wire (a length of wire with an alligator clip at each end), connect the black wire of the engine side of the harness to the black wire of the distributor side of the harness (advance points).
3. Start the engine and observe the reading on the dwell meter. Shut the engine off and adjust the points accordingly as pre-

Use the terminals provided (arrows) for jumper wire connection

viously outlined for single point distributors.

4. Disconnect the jumper wire from the black wire of the distributor side of the wiring harness and connect it to the yellow wire (retard points).

5. Adjust the point gap as necessary in the manner previously discussed.

6. After the dwell of both sets of points is correct, remove the jumper wire and connect the engine-to-distributor wiring harness securely.

Electronic Ignition—Non Turbocharged Engines

All 1974 and later cars are equipped with electronic ignition as standard equipment. 1974 models with automatic transmission, and 1975–76 49 States and Canada models have two pick-ups in the distributor. All 1975–76 California models, and all 1977 and later models have only one pick-up.

The 1974 system has a different electronic module than later systems, which precludes troubleshooting of the system by the home mechanic. However, pick-up air gap adjustments and ignition timing adjustments can be performed in the same manner as for 1975–78 models. The 1978 system differs somewhat from the 1975–77 system; the 1979 and later electronic ignition is markedly different, although the operating principle is the same.

The electronic ignition differs from its conventional counterpart only in the distributor component area. The secondary side of the ignition system is the same as a conventional breaker points system.

Located in the distributor, in addition to the normal ignition rotor, is a six spoke rotor (reluctor) which rests on the distributor shaft where the breaker points cam is found on earlier systems. A pick-up coil, consisting of a magnet, coil, and wiring, rests on the "breaker plate" next to the reluctor. The system also uses a transistor ignition unit, located on the right side of the firewall in the passenger compartment, through 1978. 1979 and later models have an integrated circuit (IC) ignition unit, which is mounted on the side of the distributor. In addition, 1979–80 models use a ring-type pick-up coil, which surrounds the reluctor, rather than the arm-type coil used through 1978.

When a reluctor spoke is not aligned with the pick-up coil, it generates large lines of flux between itself, the magnet, and the pick-up coil. This large flux variation results in a high generated voltage in the pick-up coil, preventing current from flowing to the pick-up coil. When a reluctor spoke lines up with the pick-up coil, the flux variation is low—thus, zero voltage is generated, allowing current to flow to the pick-up coil. Ignition primary current is then cut off by the electronic unit, allowing the field in the ignition coil to collapse, inducing high secondary voltage in the conventional manner. The high voltage then flows through the distributor to the spark plug, as usual.

Because no points or condenser are used, and because dwell is determined by the electronic unit, no adjustments are necessary. Ignition timing is checked in the usual way, but unless the distributor is disturbed it is not likely to ever change very much.

Service consists of inspection of the distributor cap, rotor, and ignition wires, replacing when necessary. These parts can be expected to last for at least 40,000 miles. In addition, the reluctor air gap should be checked periodically.

1. The distributor cap is held on by two clips. Release them with a screwdriver and lift the cap straight up and off, with the wires attached. Inspect the cap for cracks, carbon tracks, or a worn center contact. Replace it if necessary, transferring the wires one at a time from the old cap to the new.

2. Pull the ignition rotor (not the spoked reluctor) straight up to remove. Replace it if its contacts are worn, burned, or pitted. Do not file the contacts. To replace, press it firmly onto the shaft. It only goes on one way, so be sure it is fully seated.

3. Before replacing the ignition rotor, check the reluctor air gap. Use a non-magnetic feeler gauge. Rotate the engine until a reluctor spoke is aligned with the pick-up coil (either bump the engine around with the starter, or turn it with a wrench on the crankshaft pulley bolt). The gap should measure 0.012–0.016 in. (0.3–0.4 mm) in 1974, 0.008–0.016 in. (0.2–0.4 mm) from 1975 to 1978, or 0.012–0.020 in. (0.3–0.5 mm) in 1979 and later. Adjustment, if necessary, is made by loosening the pick-up coil mounting screws and shifting its position on the "breaker plate" either closer to or farther from the reluctor, through 1978. On 1979 and later models, center the pick-up coil (toothed stator ring) around the reluctor. Tighten the screws and recheck the gap.

4. Inspect the ignition wires for cracks or brittleness. Replace them one at a time to

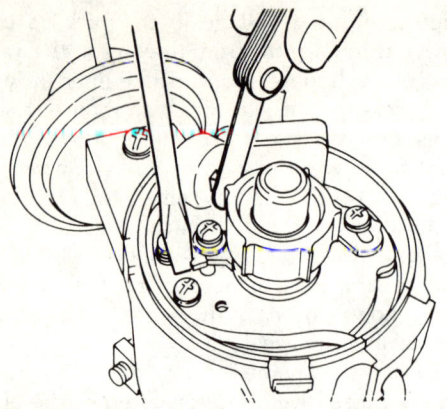

TUNE-UP

Measure the air gap with a non-magnetic feeler gauge

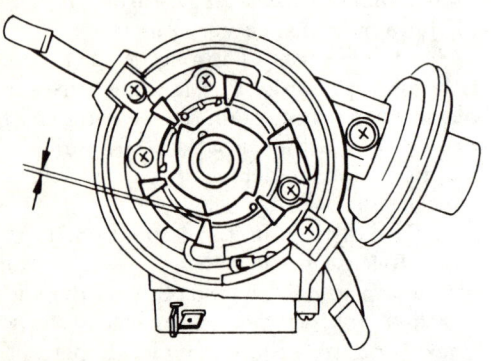

1979 and later air gap

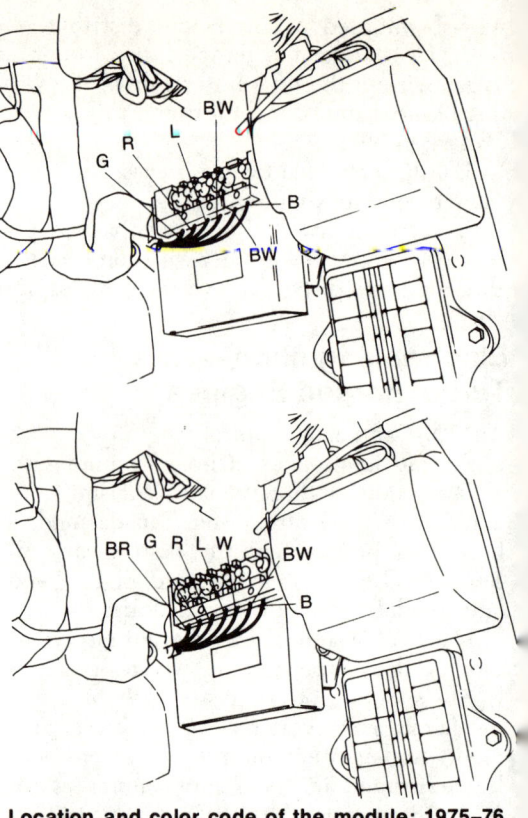

Location and color code of the module: 1975–76 California and all 1977, top; 1975–76 49 States and Canada, bottom

prevent crosswiring, carefully pressing the replacement wires into place. The cores of wires used with electronic ignition are more susceptible to breakage than those of standard wires, so treat them gently.

TROUBLESHOOTING

1974

The 1974 electronic ignition cannot be tested using conventional equipment. It must be checked by a dealer with a Datsun-made transistor ignition unit tester. The only alternative available to the home mechanic is a substitution test of the control unit. If a unit known to be good operates correctly in the car, the old unit is presumably faulty. This method is far from satisfactory; it ignores all of the associated systems, and can result in a protracted and needless waste of money and time. It is strongly recommended that problems with the 1974 ignition system be referred to your dealer.

1975–78

The components used in these systems are basically similar. However, differences exist, which affect the troubleshooting process.

There are two different systems used in 1975 and 1976. One is for Z-cars sold in California, which have one pick-up in the distributor. The wiring harness to the module is composed of six wires: one black (B), two black with white stripe (BW), one blue (L), one red (R), and one green (G). The 49 States and Canada models have seven wires in the harness: black (B), black with white stripe (BW), white (W), blue (L), red (R), green (G), and brown (Br). The 1977 system is the same as the 1975–76 California system.

The main differences between the 1975–77 and the 1978 systems are: (1) the

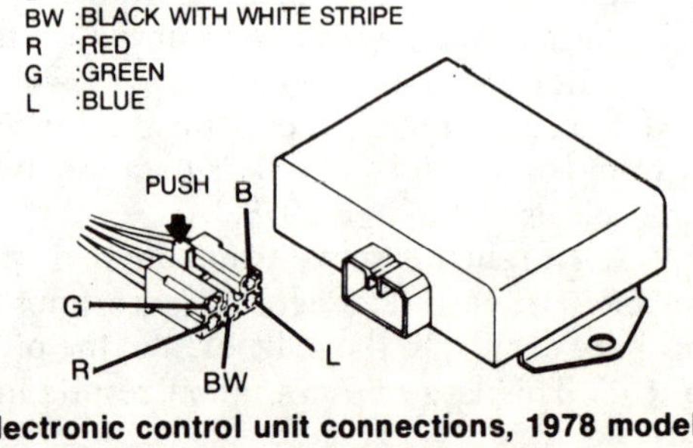

COLOR CODE

B : BLACK
BW : BLACK WITH WHITE STRIPE
R : RED
G : GREEN
L : BLUE

Electronic control unit connections, 1978 models

TUNE-UP 49

1975-77 system uses an external ballast resistor located next to the ignition coil, and (2) the earlier system uses a wiring harness with individual eyelet connectors to the electronic unit, while the later system uses a multiple plug connector.

You will need an accurate voltmeter and ohmmeter for these tests, which must be performed in the order given.

1. Check all connections for corrosion, looseness, breaks, etc., and correct if necessary. Clean and gap the spark plugs.

2a. Disconnect the harness (connector or plug) from the electronic unit. Turn the ignition switch On. Set the voltmeter to the DC 50v range. Connect the positive (+) voltmeter lead to the black/white wire terminal, and the negative (−) lead to the black wire terminal. On 1975-76 California models, and all 1977 models, you will have to perform this test twice, first at one black/white wire and then the other. Battery voltage should be obtained. If not, check the black/white and black wires for continuity; check the battery terminals for corrosion; check the battery state of charge.

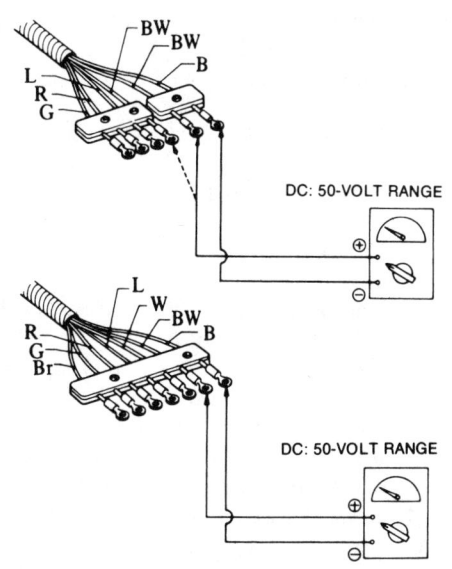

Check the power supply at the harness: 1975-76 California and all 1977, top; 1975-76 49 States and Canada, bottom

2b. Connect the voltmeter positive lead to the blue wire and the negative lead to the black wire. Battery voltage should be obtained. If not, check the blue wire for continuity; check the ignition coil terminals for corrosion or looseness; check the coil for continuity. On 1975-77 models, also check the external ballast resistor connections.

3. Disconnect the distributor harness wires from the ignition coil ballast resistor on 1975-77 models, leaving the ballast resistor-to-coil wires attached. On 1978 models, disconnect the ignition coil wires. Connect the leads of an ohmmeter to the ballast resistor outside terminals (at each end) through 1977: resistance should be 1.6-2.0 ohms (1.6-1.8 ohms in 1975). In 1978, connect the ohmmeter to the coil primary terminals: resistance should be zero ohms. If more than 1.8 ohms in 1975, 2.0 ohms, 1976-77, or 1.8 ohms, 1978, replace the coil.

4. Disconnect the harness from the electronic control unit. Connect an ohmmeter to the red and green wire terminals. Resistance should be 720 ohms. If far more or far less, replace the distributor pick-up coil (retarded side pick-up coil on 1975-76 49 States and Canada models).

5. This step is only for 1975-76 49 States and Canada models with two pick-up coils in the distributor. Skip this step if your car has only one pick-up coil.

Disconnect the brown wire from the control unit. Connect an ohmmeter between the brown and green wire terminals. Resistance should be approximately 720 ohms. If far more or far less, replace the advance side pick-up coil in the distributor.

6. Turn off the ignition. Disconnect the fuel injection wiring harness from the cold start valve. Connect a voltmeter to the red and green terminals of the electronic control harness. When the starter is cranked, the needle of the voltmeter should deflect slightly. If not, replace the distributor pick-up coil. This would be the retarded side coil or models with two pick-up coils. Repeat the test between the brown and green terminals to check the advance side pick-up coil (1975-76 49 States and Canada models only).

7. Reconnect the ignition coil and the electronic control unit harness. Disconnect the fuel injection wiring harness from the injectors and the cold start valve. Unplug the high tension lead (coil to distributor) from the distributor and hold it 1/8-1/4 in. from the cylinder head with a pair of insulated pliers and a heavy glove. When the engine is cranked, a spark should be observed. If not, check the lead and replace if necessary. If still no spark, replace the electronic control unit.

CAUTION: *Do not make this test near the fuel injection wiring harness. Damage to the fuel injection control unit will result if sparks travel to the harness.*

8. Reconnect all wires.

50 TUNE-UP

1975–77: connect the voltmeter positive lead to the blue control unit wire terminal and the negative lead to the black wire terminal. The harness should be attached to the control unit.

1978: connect the voltmeter positive lead to the negative terminal of the ignition coil and the negative lead to a good ground.

As soon as the ignition switch is turned On, the meter should indicate battery voltage. If not, replace the electronic control unit.

1979 and Later

1. Turn the ignition switch OFF. Disconnect the fusible link connector for the fuel injection wiring harness. Be sure the ignition is off before doing this. Disconnect the cold start valve wiring harness connector. Disconnect the high tension lead (coil to distributor) at the distributor and hold it ⅛–¼ in. away from the cylinder head with a pair of insulated pliers and a heavy glove. When the engine is cranked, a spark should be observed. If not, check the lead and replace as necessary. If there is still no spark, go on with the following system checks.

2. Make a check of the power supply circuit. Turn the ignition OFF. Disconnect the connector from the top of the IC unit. Turn the ignition ON. Measure the voltage at each terminal of the connector in turn by touching the probe of the positive lead of the voltmeter to one of the terminals, and touching the probe of the negative lead of the voltmeter to a ground, such as the engine. In each case, battery voltage should be indicated. If not, check all wiring, the ignition switch, and all connectors for breaks, corrosion, discontinuity, etc., and repair as necessary.

3. Check the primary windings of the ignition coil. Turn the ignition OFF. Disconnect the harness connector from the negative coil terminal. Use an ohmmeter to measure the resistance between the positive and negative coil terminals. If resistance is 0.84–1.02 ohms, the coil is OK. Replace if far from this range.

If the power supply, circuits, wiring, and coil are in good shape, check the IC unit and pick-up coil, as follows:

4. Turn the ignition OFF. Remove the distributor cap and ignition rotor. Use an ohmmeter to measure the resistance between the two terminals of the pick-up coil, where they attach to the IC unit. Measure the resistance by reversing the polarity of the probes. If approximately 400 ohms are indicated, the pick-up coil is OK, but the IC unit is bad and must be replaced. If other than 400 ohms are measured, go to the next Step.

5. Be certain the two pin connector to the IC unit is secure. Turn the ignition ON. Measure the voltage at the ignition coil negative terminal. Turn the ignition OFF.

CAUTION: *Remove the tester probe from the coil negative terminal before switching the ignition OFF, to prevent burning out the tester.*

If zero voltage is indicated, the IC unit is bad and must be replaced. If battery voltage is indicated, proceed.

6. Remove the IC unit from the distributor:

   a. Disconnect the battery ground (negative) cable.

   b. Remove the distributor cap and ignition rotor.

   c. Disconnect the harness connector at the top of the IC unit.

   d. Remove the two screws securing the IC unit to the distributor.

   e. Disconnect the two pick-up coil wires from the IC unit.

CAUTION: *Pull the connectors free with a pair of needlenose pliers. Do not pull on the wires to detach the connectors.*

   f. Remove the IC unit.

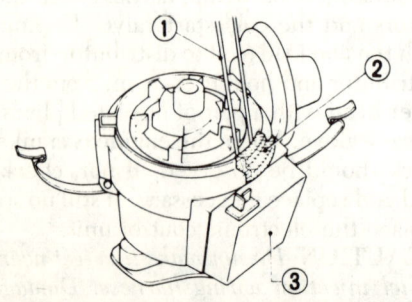

1 Tester probes   2 Grommet   3 IC ignition unit
Ohmmeter connection to the pick-up coil terminals, 1979 and later

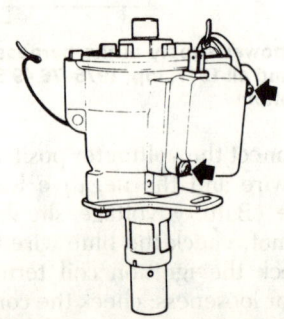

The arrows indicate the IC unit retaining screws, 1979 and later

TUNE-UP

7. Measure the resistance between the terminals of the pick-up coil. It should be approximately 400 ohms. If so, the pick-up coil is OK, and the IC unit is bad. If not approximately 400 ohms, the pick-up coil is bad and must be replaced.

PICK-UP COIL AND RELUCTOR REPLACEMENT

1974–78

The reluctor cannot be removed on some early 1974 models—it is an integral part of the distributor shaft. Non-removable reluctors can be distinguished by the absence of a "roll pin" (retaining pin) which locks the reluctor in place on the shaft.

To replace the pick-up coil on all 1974–78 models:

1. Remove the distributor cap by releasing the two spring clips. Remove the ignition rotor by pulling it straight up and off the shaft.
2. Disconnect the distributor wiring harness at the terminal block.
3. Remove the two pick-up coil mounting screws. Remove the screws retaining the wiring harness to the distributor.

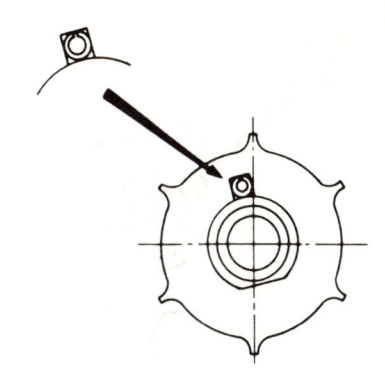

Roll pin installation, 1974–78

slit facing away from the distributor shaft. Do not re-use the old roll pin.

1979 and Later

1. Remove the distributor cap (release the two spring clips) and the ignition rotor (pull straight up and off the shaft).
2. Use a pair of needlenose pliers to disconnect the pick-up coil spade connectors from the ignition unit. Do not pull on the pick-up coil wires themselves.

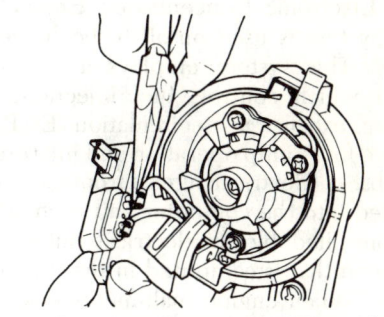

Pick-up coil connecter removal, 1979 and later

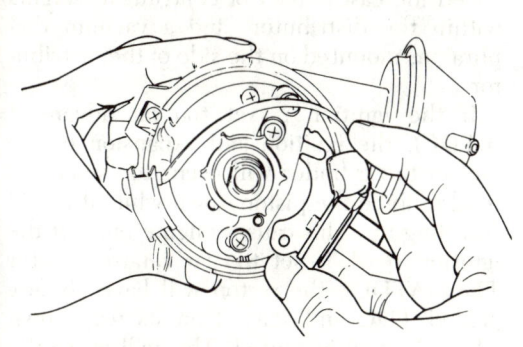

Removing the 1974–78 pick-up coil

4. Remove the pick-up coil.

To replace the pick-up coil, reverse the removal procedure, but leave the mounting screws slightly loose to facilitate air gap adjustment.

To replace the reluctor on models with a roll pin:

1. Remove the distributor cap, ignition rotor and the pick-up coil.
2. Use two screwdrivers or pry bars to pry the reluctor from the distributor shaft. Be extremely careful not to damage the reluctor teeth. Remove the roll pin.
3. To replace, press the reluctor firmly onto the shaft. Install a new roll pin with the

3. Remove the toothed stator and the ring magnet underneath it by removing the three mounting screws.
4. Remove the reluctor by prying it from the distributor shaft with two screwdrivers or pry bars. Be careful not to damage any of the reluctor teeth. Remove the roll pin.
5. Remove the screw retaining the pick-up coil wiring harness to the distributor. Remove the pick-up coil.
6. Install the pick-up coil into place in the distributor body. Replace the wiring harness retainer.
7. Press the reluctor firmly into place on the shaft. Install a new roll pin with the slit in the pin parallel to the flat on the shaft.
8. Install the magnet and stator, and center the stator around the reluctor. Air gap is 0.3–0.4 mm (0.012–0.020 in.).

52 TUNE-UP

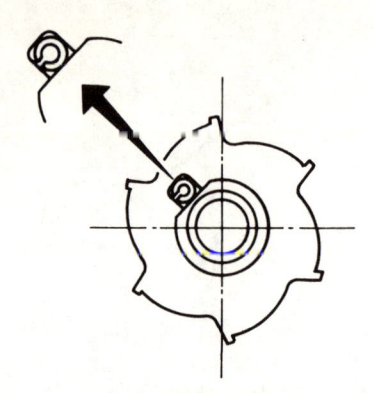

Roll pin installation, 1979 and later

9. Press the pick-up coil spade connectors onto the ignition unit terminals with your fingers. The proper connections can be determined from the color code marked on the grommet. Replace the ignition rotor and the distributor cap.

Electronic Ignition— Turbocharged Engines

The Electronic Concentrated Engine Control System is used on all turbocharged engines. This system employs a micro-computer which controls fuel injection, spark timing, exhaust gas recirculation (EGR), idle speed, fuel pump operation and mixture ratio feedback. Electrical signals from each sensor are fed into the computer and each actuator is controlled by an electrical pulse with a duration that is computed in the micro-computer. When engine malfunctions occur the use of an E.C.C.S. analyzer is necessary to accurately diagnose the problem.

The E.C.C.S. analyzer monitors several input and output signals that are emitted in response to various engine operating conditions and when the engine stops. Input signals are compared to computerized signal values stored in the C.E.C.U. (Central Electronic Control Unit) while output signals are monitored to ensure they are properly attuned before they are emitted from the C.E.C.U. unit to actuators. In other words, this analyzer analyzes all electrical signals that are transmitted to and emitted from the C.E.C.U. unit.

Since this analyzer would be very expensive to purchase, any suspected malfunction of the engine that cannot be corrected by an obvious visual inspection, should be left to a qualified repair shop that contains this equipment.

Ignition Timing

Ignition timing is the measurement, in degrees of crankshaft rotation, of the point at which the spark plugs fire in each of the cylinders. It is measured in degrees before or after Top Dead Center (TDC) of the compression stroke.

Because it takes a fraction of a second for the spark plug to ignite the mixture in the cylinder, the spark plug must fire a little before the piston reaches TDC. Otherwise, the mixture will not be completely ignited as the piston passes TDC and the full power of the explosion will not be used by the engine.

The timing measurement is given in degrees of crankshaft rotation before the piston reaches TDC (BTDC). If the setting for the ignition timing is 5° BTDC, the spark plug must fire 5° before each piston reaches TDC. This only holds true, however, when the engine is at idle speed.

As the engine speed increases, the pistons go faster. The spark plugs have to ignite the fuel even sooner if it is to be completely ignited when the piston reaches TDC. To do this, the distributor has two means to advance the timing of the spark as the engine speed increases: a set of centrifugal weights within the distributor, and a vacuum diaphragm, mounted on the side of the distributor.

If the ignition is set too far advanced (BTDC), the ignition and expansion of the fuel in the cylinder will occur too soon and tend to force the piston down while it is still traveling up. This causes engine ping. If the ignition spark is set too far retarded, after TDC (ATDC), the piston will have already passed TDC and started on its way down when the fuel is ignited. This will cause the piston to be forced down for only a portion of its travel. This will result in poor engine performance and lack of power.

Timing marks consist of a notch on the rim of the crankshaft pulley and a scale of degrees attached to the front of the engine. The notch corresponds to the position of the piston in the number 1 cylinder. A stroboscopic (dynamic) timing light is used, which is hooked into the circuit of the No. 1 cylinder spark plug. Every time the spark plug fires, the timing light flashes. By aiming the timing light at the timing marks, the exact position of the piston within the cylinder can be read, since the stroboscopic flash makes the mark on the pulley appear to be standing still.

TUNE-UP 53

Proper timing is indicated when the notch is aligned with the correct number on the scale.

There are three basic types of timing light available. The first is a simple neon bulb with two wire connections (one for the spark plug and one for the plug wire, connecting the light in series). This type of light is quite dim, and must be held closely to the marks to be seen, but it is inexpensive. The second type of light operates from the car battery. Two alligator clips connect to the battery terminals, while a third wire connects to the spark plug with an adapter. This type of light is more expensive, but the xenon bulb provides a nice bright flash which can even be seen in sunlight. The third type replaces the battery source with 110 volt house current. Some timing lights have other functions built into them, such as dwell meters, tachometers, or remote starting switches. These are convenient, in that they reduce the tangle of wires under the hood, but may duplicate the functions of tools you already have.

If your Datsun has electronic ignition, you should use a timing light with an inductive pickup. This pickup simply clamps onto the No. 1 plug wire, eliminating the adapter. It is not susceptible to crossfiring or false triggering, which may occur with a conventional light, due to the greater voltages produced by electronic ignition.

IGNITION TIMING ADJUSTMENT

All Except Turbocharged Engine

Refer to Chapter 4, "Emission Controls and Fuel System," for the procedure to check and adjust the phase timing of the dual points or dual pick-ups in 1973–76 models.

1. Set the dwell of the breaker points to the proper specification.
2. Locate the timing marks on the crankshaft pulley and the front of the engine.

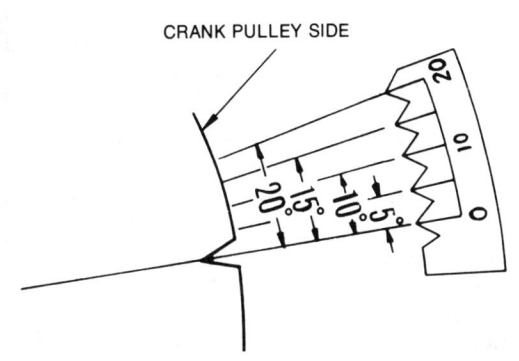

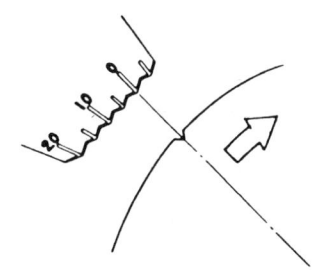

1974 and later timing scale

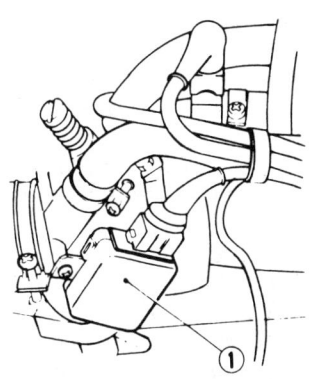

1980 and later throttle valve switch (1)

3. Clean off the timing marks, so that you can see them.
4. Use chalk or white paint to color the mark on the crankshaft pulley and the mark on the scale which will indicate the correct timing when aligned with the notch on the crankshaft pulley.
5. Attach a tachometer to the engine.
6. Attach a timing light to the engine, according to the manufacturer's instructions. If the timing light has three wires, one, usually green or blue, is attached to the No. 1 spark plug with an adapter. The other wires are connected to the battery. The red wire goes to the positive side of the battery and the black wire is connected to the negative terminal of the battery.

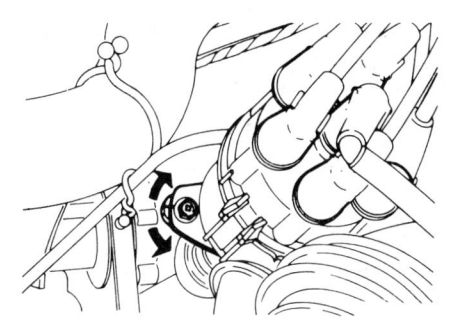

The crankshaft pulley and timing scale, 1973 240-Z

Loosen the distributor lockbolt and turn the distributor slightly to advance (upper arrow) or retard (lower arrow) the timing

TUNE-UP

7. Leave the vacuum hose connected to the distributor advance vacuum diaphragm on all models through 1979.

On 1980 models: disconnect the throttle valve switch harness connector. Disconnect and plug the canister purge hose from the intake manifold. Plug the opening in the intake manifold. On 1980 49 States models, also disconnect the hose from the air induction pipe and cap the pipe, and disconnect and plug the vacuum advance hose at the distributor. Note that the disconnect and plug instructions for the air induction pipe and the distributor vacuum advance do not apply to 1980 models sold in California or Canada.

8. Check that all of the wires clear the fan, pulleys, and belts, and then start the engine. Allow the engine to reach normal operating temperature.

CAUTION: *Block the front wheels and set the parking brake. Shift the manual transmission to Neutral or the automatic transmission to Drive. Do not stand in front of the car when making adjustments!*

9. Adjust the idle to the correct setting. See the "Idle Speed and Mixture" section later in this chapter.

10. Aim the timing light at the timing marks. If the marks which you put on the pulley and the engine are aligned when the light flashes, the timing is correct. Turn off the engine and remove the tachometer and the timing light. If the marks are not in alignment, proceed with the following steps.

11. Turn off the engine.

12. Loosen the distributor lockbolt just enough so that the distributor can be turned with a little effort.

13. Start the engine. Keep the wires of the timing light clear of the fan.

14. With the timing light aimed at the pulley and the marks on the engine, turn the distributor in the direction of rotor rotation to retard the spark, and in the opposite direction of rotor rotation to advance the spark. Align the marks on the pulley and the engine with the flashes of the timing light.

15. Tighten the distributor lockbolt and recheck the timing.

Turbocharged Engines

The ignition timing is controlled by the central electronic control unit adjusting to the engine operating conditions: that is, as the best ignition timing in each driving condition has been memorized in the unit, the ignition timing is determined by the electric signal calculated in the unit.

The signals used for the determination of ignition timing are cylinder head temperature, engine rpm, engine load, engine crank angle, detonation sensor and so forth.

Then, the signal from the central electronic control unit is transmitted to the power transistor of the ignition coil, and controls the ignition timing. If there is engine knocking, a detonation sensor monitors its condition and the signal is transmitted to the central electronic control unit. After receiving it, the control unit controls the ignition timing to avoid the knocking condition.

Ignition timing is automatically controlled by the control unit, and it is usually unnecessary to adjust it. However, the ignition timing can go wrong if the crank angle sensor mounting position gets out of alignment. When this happens, the crank angle sensor must be adjusted.

This adjustment should be left to a qualified technician since it should be preceded by a system test using an E.C.C.S. analyzer. (See the explanation given under Electronic Ignition—Turbocharged Engines)

Valve Lash

Valve adjustment determines how far the valves enter the cylinder and how long they stay open and closed.

If the valve clearance is too large, part of the lift of the camshaft will be used in removing the excessive clearance. Consequently, the valve will not be opening for as long as it should. This condition has two effects: the valve train components will emit a tapping sound as they take up the excessive clearance and the engine will perform poorly because the valves don't open fully and allow the proper amount of gases to flow into and out of the engine.

If the valve clearance is too small, the intake valves and the exhaust valves will open too far and they will not fully seat on the cylinder head when they close. When a valve seats itself on the cylinder head, it does two things: it seals the combustion chamber so that none of the gases in the cylinder escape and it cools itself by transferring some of the heat it absorbs from the combustion in the cylinder to the cylinder head and to the engine's cooling system. If the valve clearance is too small, the engine will run poorly

TUNE-UP

because of the gases escaping from the combustion chamber. The valves will also become overheated and will warp, since they cannot transfer heat unless they are touching the valve seat in the cylinder head.

NOTE: *While all valve adjustments must be made as accurately as possible, it is better to have the valve adjustment slightly loose than slightly tight, as a burned valve may result from overly tight adjustments.*

ADJUSTMENT

1. The valves are adjusted with the engine at normal operating temperature. Oil temperature, and the resultant parts expansion, is much more important than water temperature. Run the engine for at least fifteen minutes to ensure that all the parts have reached their full expansion. After the engine is warmed up, shut it off.

2. Purchase either a new gasket or some silicone gasket seal before removing the camshaft cover. Note the location of any wires and hoses which may interfere with cam cover removal, disconnect them and move them aside. Then remove the bolts which hold the cam cover in place and remove the cam cover.

3. Place a wrench on the crankshaft pulley bolt and turn the engine over until the valves for No. 1 cylinder are closed. When both cam lobes are pointing up, the valves are closed. If you have not done this before, it is a good idea to turn the engine over slowly several times and watch the valve action until you have a clear idea of just when the valve is closed.

Valve arrangement as seen from the left side of the engine (E = exhaust; I = intake)

4. Adjust the clearance of only half of the valves. Adjust only 1,3,7,8,9, and 11 valves.

5. Using a feeler gauge, measure the clearance between the cam lobe and the valve rocker. The valve clearance should be (hot) intake—(3, 8, 11) 0.010 in. (0.25 mm), exhaust—(1, 7, 9) 0.012 (0.30 mm)

6. If the clearance is not the specified value, loosen the pivot lock nut and turn the valve rocker pivot to provide proper clearance. The feeler gauge should move with a very slight drag when rechecked.

7. Turn the crankshaft again so that the

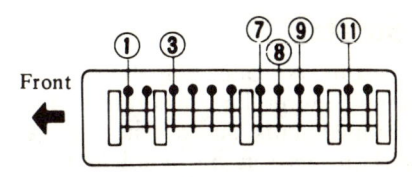

Adjust valves—1, 3, 7, 8, 9, and 11

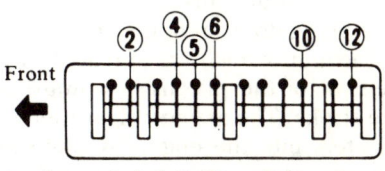

Adjust valves—2, 4, 5, 6, 10 and 12

high point of the No. 1 cam lobe points down. Adjust the clearance of the other half of the valves 2,4,5,6,10 and 12, using the same procedure as in step 6. The valve clearance should be (hot) intake—(2,5,10) 0.010 in. (0.25 mm), exhaust—(4,6,12) 0.012 in. (0.30 mm).

8. Install the cam cover gasket, the cam cover, and any wires and hoses which were removed.

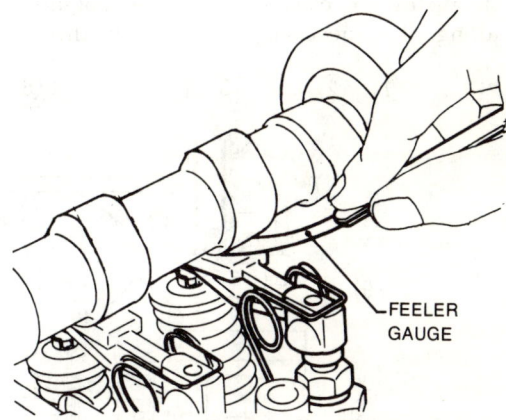

Check the clearance with a flat feeler gauge

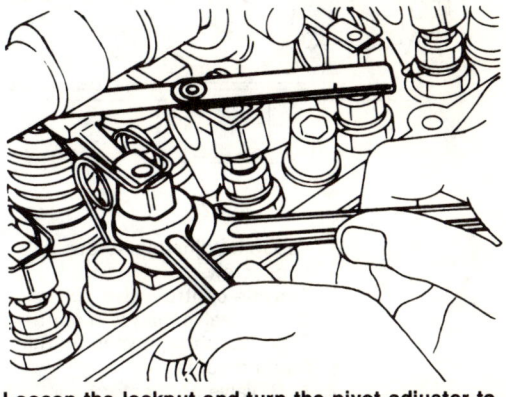

Loosen the locknut and turn the pivot adjuster to change the clearance

Carburetor

This section contains only tune-up adjustment procedures for carburetors. Descriptions, adjustments, and overhaul procedures for carburetors can be found in the "Fuel System" section.

When the engine in your Datsun is running, the air-fuel mixture from the carburetor is being drawn into the engine by a partial vacuum which is created by the movement of the pistons downward on the intake stroke. The amount of air-fuel mixture that enters into the engine is controlled by the throttle plates in the bottom of the carburetor. When the engine is not running the throttle plates are closed, completely blocking off the bottom of the carburetor from the inside of the engine. The throttle plates are connected by the throttle linkage to the accelerator pedal in the passenger compartment of the Datsun. When you depress the pedal, you open the throttle plates in the carburetor to admit more air-fuel mixture to the engine.

When the engine is not running, the throttle plates are closed. When the engine is idling, it is necessary to have the throttle plates open slightly. To prevent having to hold your foot on the pedal when the engine is idling, an idle speed adjusting screw is added to the carburetor linkage.

The idle adjusting screw contacts a lever (throttle lever) on the outside of the carburetor. When the screw is turned, it either opens or closes the throttle plates of the carburetor, raising or lowering the idle speed of the engine. This screw is called the curb idle adjusting screw.

A special mixture circuit is incorporated into the carburetor to enable the engine to run smoothly at idle. This circuit is controlled by the mixture screw, which determines the amount of fuel admitted at idle.

IDLE SPEED AND MIXTURE ADJUSTMENT

1970–72

1. Run the engine until it is at operating temperature. Remove the air cleaner.

2. Adjust the idle speed to 750 rpm. Apply an air flow meter for one or two seconds to one of the carburetor air horns, holding it vertically. Then, check the flow of the other

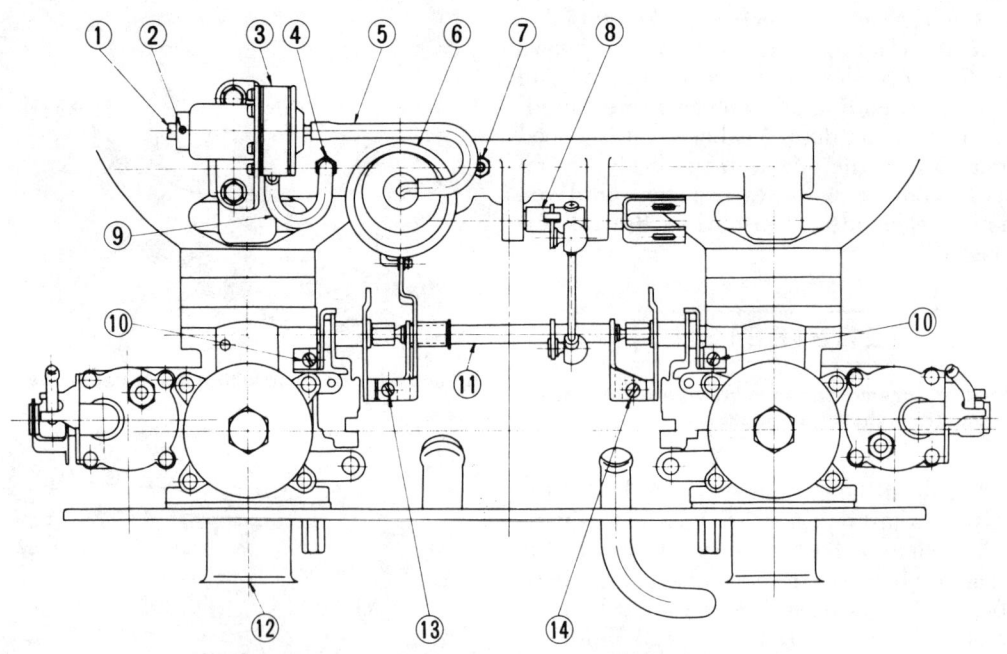

1. Vacuum adjusting screw
2. Lockscrew
3. Throttle control valve
4. Control valve manifold connection
5. Servo diaphragm vacuum tube
6. Servo diaphragm
7. A. B. valve connector
8. Auxiliary throttle shaft
9. Control valve vacuum tube
10. Throttle adjusting screw
11. Throttle shaft
12. Airhorn
13. Opener adjusting screw
14. Balance screw

Location of the throttle linkage and carburetor components on 1972 and earlier models

TUNE-UP

Idle mixture adjusting nut—1972 and earlier models

caburetor. Adjust the throttle adjusting screws so that the airflow is equal and the rpm is 750.

3. Disconnect the control vacuum tube from the connector on the manifold and connect the servo diaphragm vacuum tube in its place, in order to apply full vacuum to the diaphragm.

4. Adjust the opener adjusting screw to give an rpm of 1,200.

5. Using the flow meter as described above, adjust the balance screw so that the airflow is equal for the carburetors.

6. Disconnect and then reconnect the servo diaphragm vacuum tube where it is connected to the manifold. Check the rpm and flow rates and, if necessary, readjust as in Steps 4 and 5.

7. Return the vacuum hoses to their original positions, disconnect the diaphragm tube from the manifold and reconnect it to the control valve, and then reconnect the control valve hose to the manifold connection.

8. *If a CO meter is available*, adjust CO as follows:

   a. Disconnect the air pump belt so that the pump will be inoperative.

   b. Gently tighten the mixture adjusting nuts located under the carburetors until they hit their stops.

   c. Turn both nuts equally outward until CO is 5–7%.

   d. Reconnect the air pump belt.

1973–74

1. Run the engine until it is at operating temperature. Remove the air cleaner.

2. Loosen the throttle adjusting screw all the way. Except on 1974 automatics, loosen the throttle opener adjusting screw all the way.

3. Adjust the idle speed to 750 rpm using the idle speed adjusting screw. On automatic transmission models, securely apply the parking brake and then put the transmission in gear. Then, adjust the idle speed adjusting screw to bring the idle to 600 rpm. Return the selector to "N" position.

4. With 260-Z automatic transmission models, proceed to Step 7 as these cars do not employ a throttle opener control valve.

5. Disconnect the hose which runs between the vacuum control valve and the servo diaphragm. Do the same with the hose running between the control valve and the intake manifold.

6. Connect a longer hose of the same diameter between the servo diaphragm and the open connector on the manifold.

7. On all but 1974 260-Z automatics, adjust the throttle opener adjusting screw for 1,400 rpm. On automatic 260-Zs, do the same with the fast idle adjusting screw.

8. Apply a flow meter briefly to the front carburetor intake. Turn the adjusting screw on the flow meter and align the upper end of the float with the scale. Then, tighten the screw.

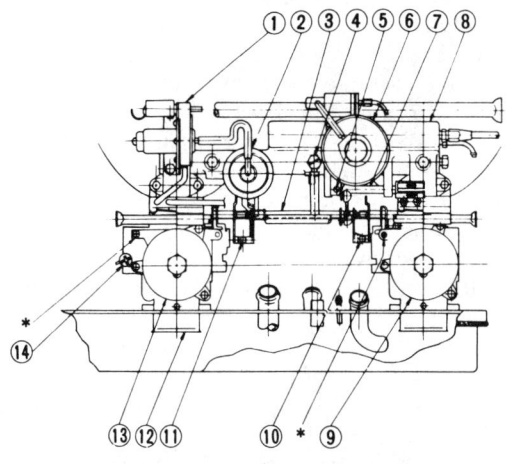

1. Throttle opener control valve
2. Servo diaphragm
3. Throttle shaft
4. Idle speed adjusting screw
5. Fast idle screw
6. E.G.R. valve
7. Auxiliary throttle shaft
8. Balance tube
9. Rear carburetor
10. Balance adjusting screw
11. Throttle opener adjusting screw
12. Airhorn
13. Front carburetor
14. Idle mixture adjusting screw

Throttle linkage and carburetor components on 1973–74 models

TUNE-UP

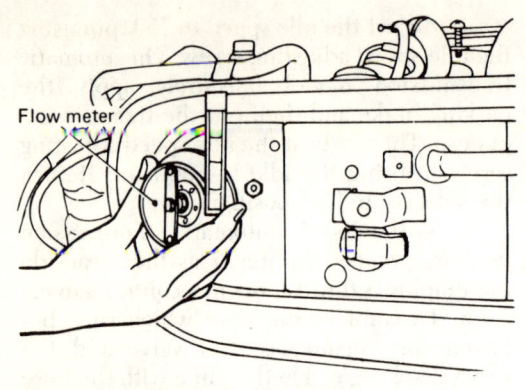

Measuring airflow with flow meter

9. Apply the meter to the rear carburetor air intake and adjust the balance adjusting screw until the float in the meter is aligned with the scale.

10. Reinstall the air cleaner, connecting the vacuum motor to the temperature sensor with the vacuum hose.

11. Readjust the engine speed to 1,400 rpm as in Step 7.

12. Raise the engine speed briefly to 3,000 rpm. Then, raise it to 1,700 rpm with the throttle opener or fast idle screw (depending on the model as specified above). Finally, gradually lower the speed down to 1,400 rpm.

13. Disconnect the air pump check valve hose and plug the check valve.

14. With a CO meter, adjust the CO to 1.0–1.6% with manual transmission; 0.6–1.2% with automatics (in Neutral). This adjustment is made at the idle mixture adjusting screw.

15. On all cars but 260-Z automatics, disconnect the servo diaphragm vacuum for two to three seconds and then reconnect it. Make sure that the rpm returns to 1,400. If not, readjust it at the throttle opener adjusting screw.

16. On all but 1974 260-Zs, remove the long vacuum hose and reconnect the hoses so that one runs from the manifold to the throttle opener control valve and the other runs from the end of the control valve to the servo. On late model automatics, turn the fast idle screw out until there is a clearance of 0.078 in. (2 mm) between the lever and the tip of the screw.

17. Race the engine several times to verify that the idle speed is correct. Readjust it if necessary.

18. Unplug the check valve and reconnect the hose.

19. Measure the CO percentage and make sure that it is below 2.7%.

Fuel Injection

1975 and later models have electronic fuel injection as standard equipment. The only regular tune-up maintenance required with this system is an idle speed check, and, on 1975–79 manual transmission models, a dashpot adjustment. Idle mixture is not adjustable through 1976. Mixture can be adjusted on 1977 and later models, but it requires the use of a CO meter. It is unlikely you will ever have need to adjust the mixture, and because of the expense of a CO meter, it is suggested that any mixture adjustments be referred to your dealer or a qualified mechanic with access to the proper equipment.

IDLE SPEED

1. Warm the engine to normal operating temperature, either by driving the car or allowing it to idle. When warm, continue to run the engine with the hood open for about five minutes at 2000 rpm. If the car has air conditioning, it should be off.

2. Race the engine two or three times under no load. Allow the engine to return to idle.

3. Set the parking brake and block the front wheels. Shift manual transmissions to Neutral and automatic transmissions to Drive.

4. Adjust the idle speed to specifications by turning the idle speed screw, which is

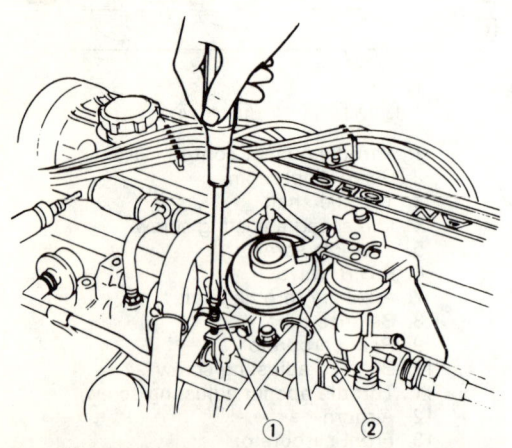

1. Fast idle screw   2. E.G.R. valve

Location of the fast idle screw on 1974 automatic transmission models

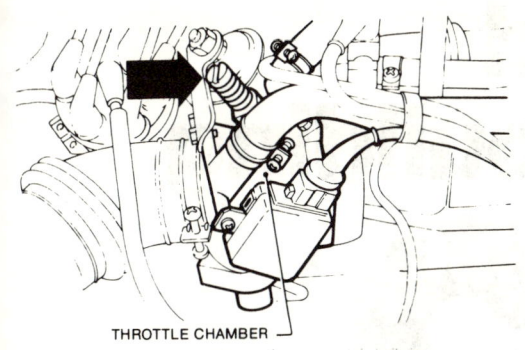

TUNE-UP 59

1975 and later idle speed screw

located in the throttle chamber, next to the distributor.

DASHPOT ADJUSTMENT
1975-79 With Manual Transmission

1. Start the engine and run it at 2000 rpm under no load. The air conditioning should be off, if the car has it.

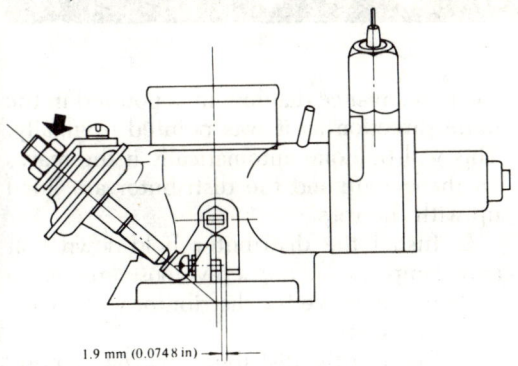

2. The clearance between the idle set-screw (preset at the factory) and the throttle lever should be eactly 1.9 mm (0.075 in.).

3. The dashpot plunger, when fully extended, should be in contact with the throttle lever.

4. If adjustment is necessary, loosen the dashpot mounting nut and turn the dashpot assembly until the clearance is correct. Tighten the nut and recheck the clearance.

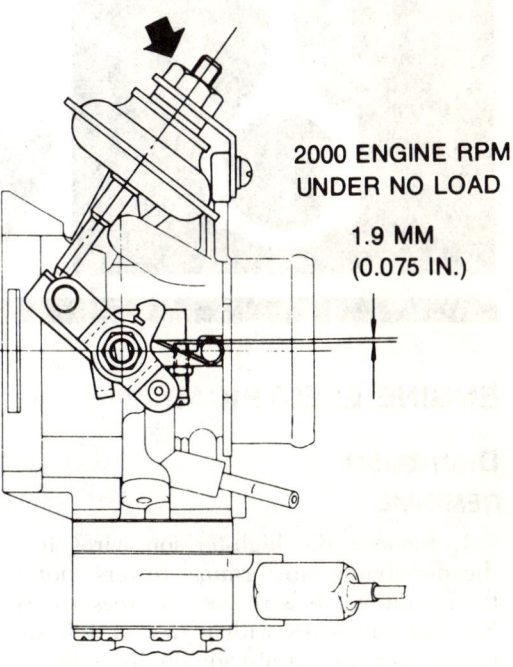

Dashpot measurement through 1978—adjust at the locknut (arrow)

1979 dashpot measurement—adjustment is made at the locknut (arrow)

Engine and Engine Rebuilding

ENGINE ELECTRICAL

Distributor

REMOVAL

1. Remove the high-tension wires from the distributor cap terminal towers, noting their positions to assure correct reassembly. Number the wires with pieces of adhesive tape if they are not already numbered.
2. Disconnect the distributor wiring harness.
3. Disconnect the vacuum line(s).
4. Unlatch the two distributor cap retaining clips and remove the distributor cap.
5. Note the position of the rotor in relation to the base. Scribe a mark on the base of the distributor and on the engine block to facilitate reinstallation. Align the marks with the direction the metal tip of the rotor is pointing.
6. Remove the bolt which holds the distributor to the engine.
7. Lift the distributor assembly from the engine.

INSTALLATION

1. Insert the distributor shaft and assembly into the engine. Line up the mark on the distributor and the one on the engine with the metal tip of the rotor. Make sure that the vacuum advance diaphragm is pointed in the same direction as it was pointed originally. This will be done automatically if the marks on the engine and the distributor are lined up with the rotor.
2. Install the distributor hold-down bolt and clamp. Leave the screw loose enough so that you can move the distributor with heavy hand pressure.
3. Connect the distributor wiring harness. Install the distributor cap on the distributor housing. Secure the distributor cap with the spring clips.
4. Install the spark plug wires. Make sure that the wires are pressed all the way into the top of the distributor cap and firmly onto the spark plug.
5. Adjust the point dwell and set the ignition timing.

NOTE: *If the crankshaft has been turned or the engine disturbed in any manner (i.e., disassembled and rebuilt) while the distributor was removed, or if the marks were not drawn, it will be necessary to initially time the engine. Follow the procedure given below.*

1. It is necessary to place the No. 1 cylinder in the firing position to correctly install the distributor. To locate this position, the ignition timing marks on the crankshaft front pulley are used.

ENGINE AND ENGINE REBUILDING 61

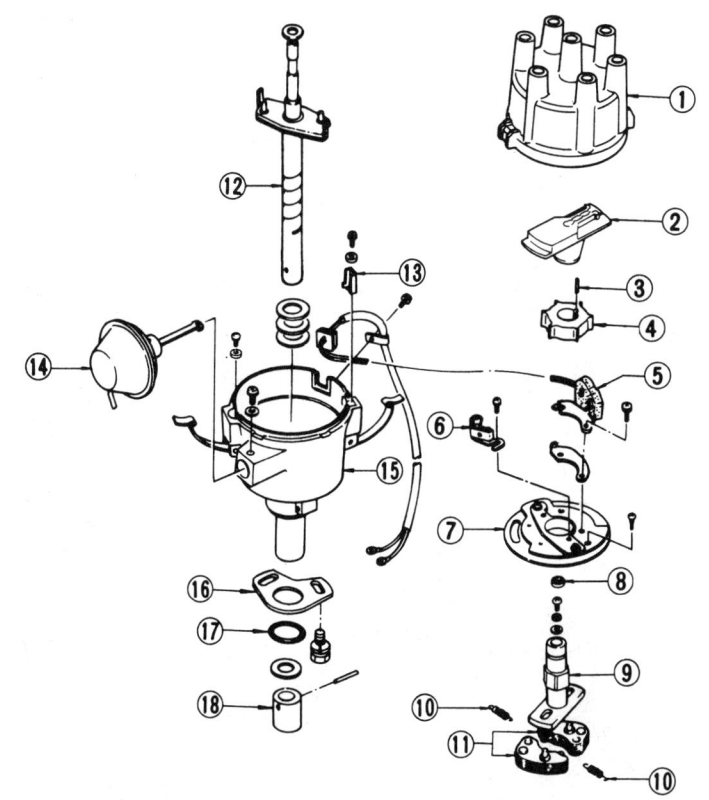

1. Cap assembly
2. Rotor head assembly
3. Roll pin
4. Reluctor
5. Pick-up coil
6. Contactor
7. Breaker plate assembly
8. Packing
9. Rotor shaft
10. Governor spring
11. Governor weight
12. Shaft assembly
13. Cap setter
14. Vacuum controller
15. Housing
16. Fixing plate
17. O-ring
18. Collar

Exploded view of the single pick-up electronic ignition distributor, through 1978

2. Remove the No. 1 cylinder spark plug. Turn the crankshaft until the piston in the No. 1 cylinder is moving up on the compression stroke. This can be determined by placing your thumb over the spark plug hole and feeling the air being forced out of the cylinder. Stop turning the crankshaft when the timing marks that are used to time the engine are aligned.

3. Oil the distributor housing lightly where the distributor bears on the cylinder block.

4. Install the distributor so that the rotor, which is mounted on the shaft, points toward the No. 1 spark plug terminal tower position when the cap is installed. Of course you won't be able to see the direction in which the rotor is pointing if the cap is on the distributor. Set the cap on the top of the distributor and make a mark on the side of the distributor housing just below the No. 1 spark plug terminal. Make sure that the rotor points toward that mark when you install the distributor.

5. When the distributor shaft has reached the bottom of the hole, move the rotor back and forth slightly until the driving lug on the end of the oil pump shaft enters the slots cut in the end of the distributor shaft, and the distributor assembly slides down into place.

6. When the distributor is correctly installed, the breaker points should be in such a position that they are just ready to break contact with each other; or, on engines with electronic ignition, the reluctor teeth should be aligned with the pick-up coil. This can be accomplished by rotating the distributor body after it has been installed in the engine. Once again, line up the marks that you made before the distributor was removed.

7. Install the distributor hold-down bolt.

8. Install the spark plug into the No. 1 cylinder and continue from Step 3 of the installation procedure, engine undisturbed.

62 ENGINE AND ENGINE REBUILDING

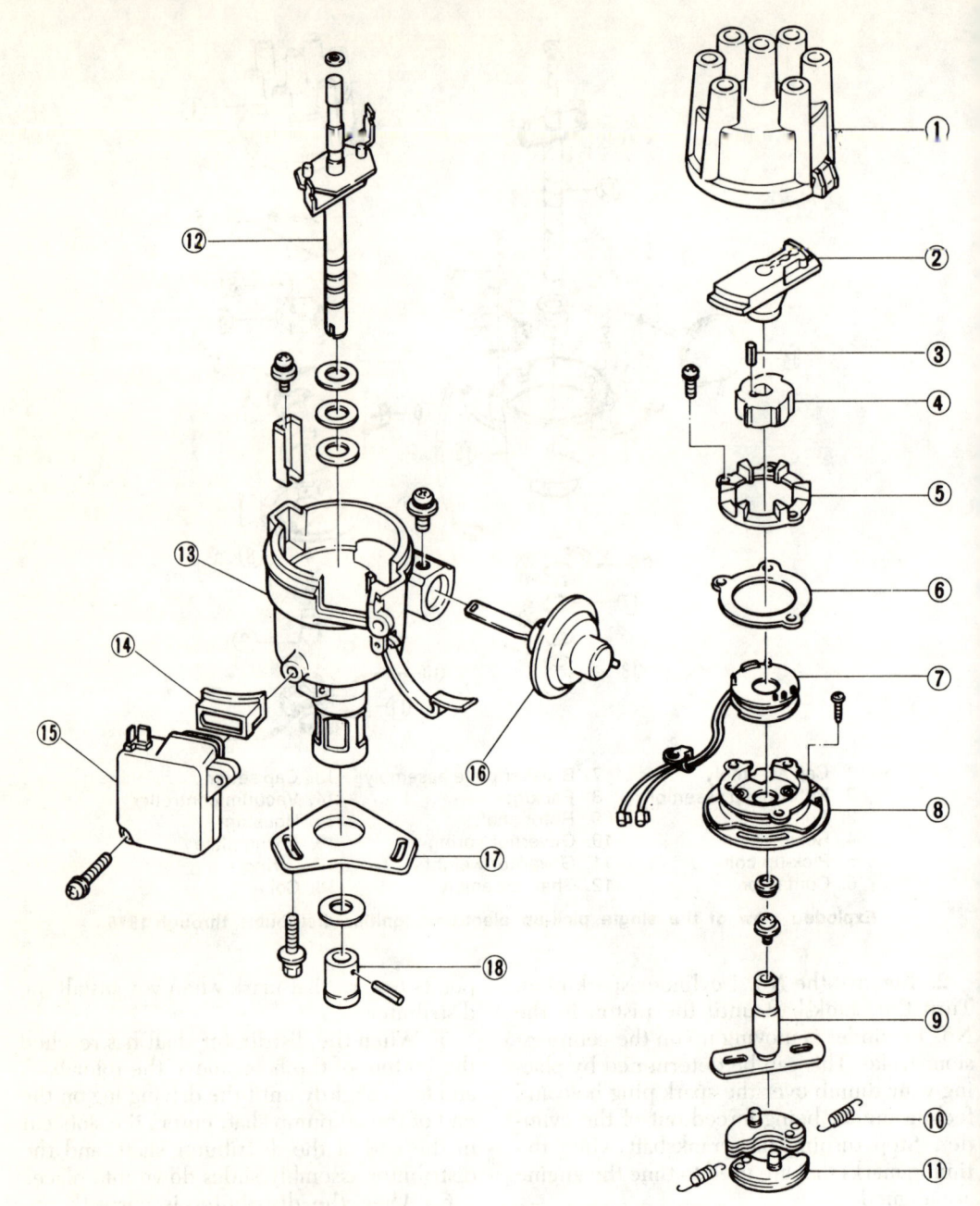

1. Cap assembly
2. Rotor head assembly
3. Roll pin
4. Reluctor
5. Stator
6. Magnet assembly
7. Pick-up coil assembly
8. Breaker plate assembly
9. Rotor shaft assembly
10. Governor spring
11. Governor weight
12. Shaft assembly
13. Housing
14. Grommet
15. IC ignition unit
16. Vacuum controller
17. Fixing plate
18. Collar

Exploded view of the 1979 and later distributor, except engines with turbocharger

ENGINE AND ENGINE REBUILDING 63

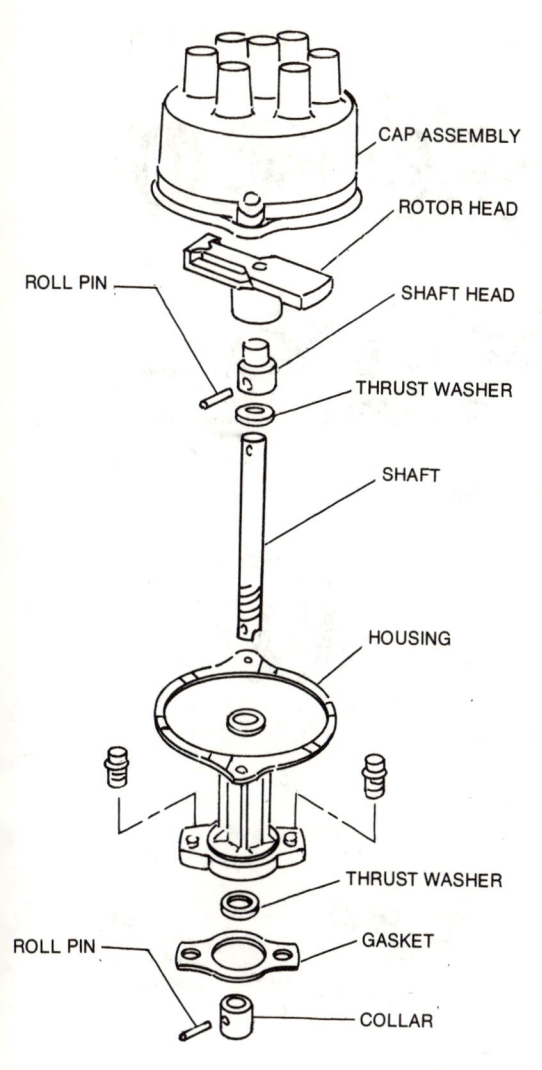

Exploded view of the distributor, turbocharged engines

Firing Order
Always number the spark plug wires before removal to prevent crosswiring.

Firing order

Alternator
Datsun Z-cars use 12 volt alternators, with amperage ratings varying according to year and model. Through 1977, an electromechanical, adjustable voltage regulator is used. 1978 and later models have a transistorized, non-adjustable regulator integral with the alternator.

ALTERNATOR PRECAUTIONS
To prevent damage to the alternator and regulator, the following precautionary measures must be taken when working with the electrical system.

1. Never reverse battery connections. Always check the battery polarity visually. This is to be done before any connections are made to ensure that all of the connections correspond to the battery ground polarity of the car.
2. Booster batteries must be connected properly. Make sure the positive cable of the booster battery is connected to the positive terminal of the battery which is getting the boost.
3. Disconnect the battery cables before using a fast charger; the charger has a tendency to force current through the diodes in the opposite direction for which they were designed.
4. Never use a fast charger as a booster for starting the car.
5. Never disconnect the voltage regulator while the engine is running, unless as noted for testing purposes.
6. Do not ground the alternator output terminal.
7. Do not operate the alternator on an open circuit with the field energized.
8. Do not attempt to polarize the alternator.
9. Disconnect the battery cables and remove the alternator before using an electric arc welder on the car.
10. Protect the alternator from excessive moisture. If the engine is to be steam cleaned, cover or remove the alternator.

REMOVAL AND INSTALLATION
1. Disconnect the negative (−) battery terminal. *Failure to do this will damage the electrical system.*
2. Disconnect the plug connecting alternator to the wiring harness. Disconnect and label the two lead wires.
3. Remove the alternator adjusting bolt, move the alternator toward the crankshaft

64 ENGINE AND ENGINE REBUILDING

1. Pulley assembly
2. Through bolt
3. Front cover
4. Front bearing
5. Rotor
6. Rear bearing
7. Stator
8. Diode set plate assembly
9. Lead wire assembly
10. Brush assembly
11. Rear cover

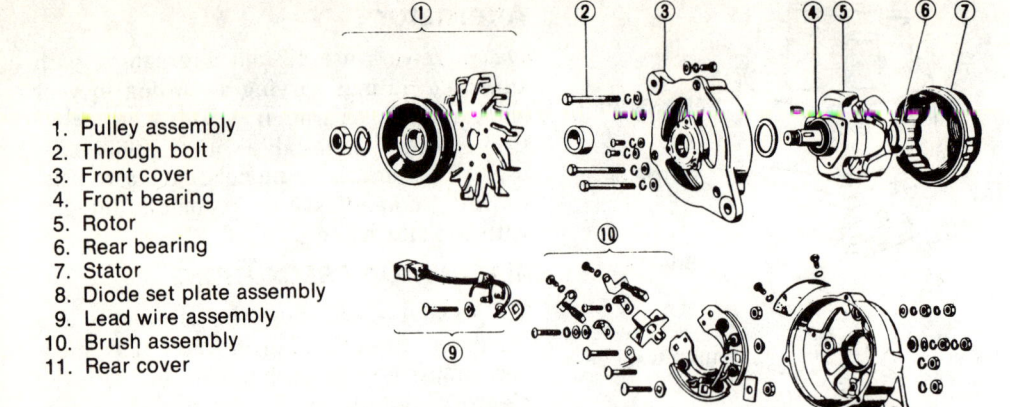

1970-71 alternator

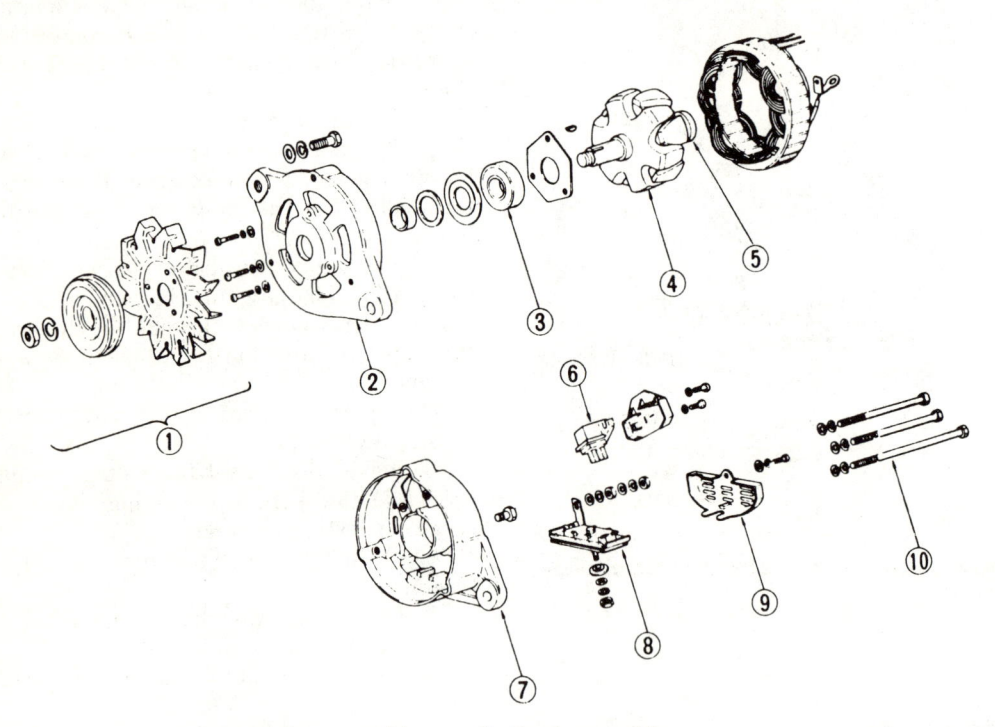

1. Pulley assembly
2. Front cover
3. Front bearing
4. Rotor
5. Rear bearing
6. Brush assembly
7. Rear cover
8. Diode (and plate) assembly
9. Diode cover
10. Through-bolts

1972-77 alternator

pulley and remove the belt from the alternator pulley.

4. Remove the nut at the rear end of the lower mounting bolt and then slide the bolt out the front while supporting the alternator.

5. Pull the alternator out of the engine compartment.

To install the alternator:

1. Put the alternator in position, lining up the two hinges with the bolt hole. Insert the bolt through the hinges and bolt hole from the front.

2. Install the nut at the rear of the mounting bolt.

3. Tilt the alternator until the adjusting bolt can be installed and install it.

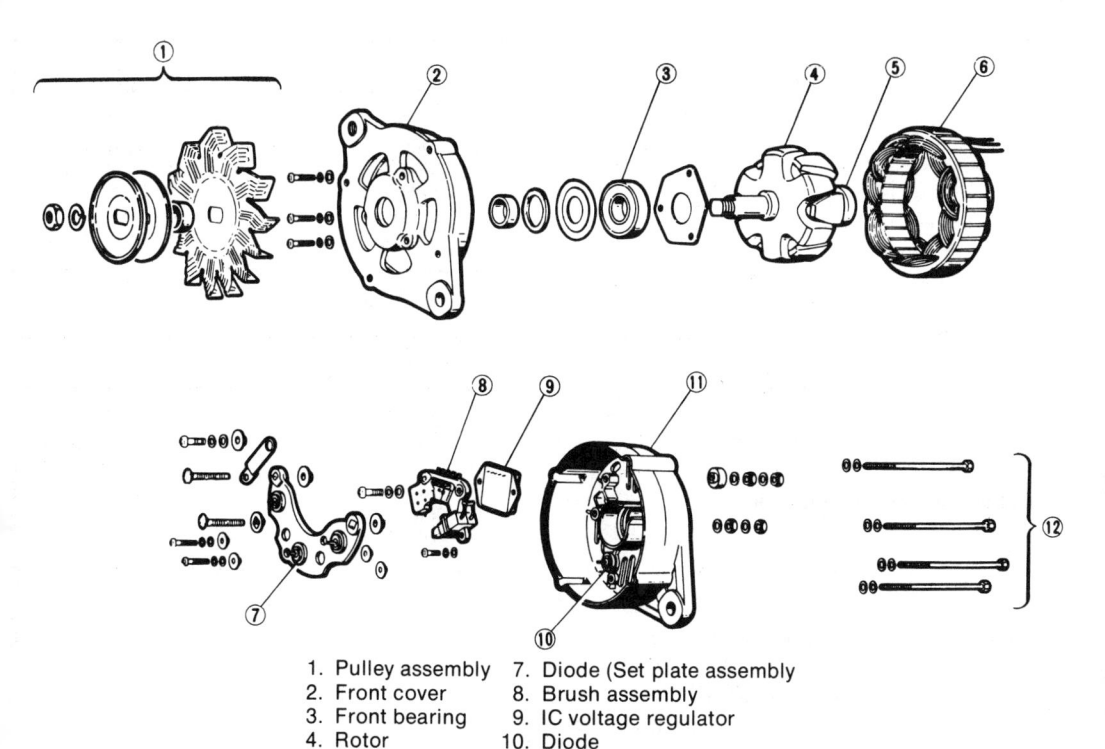

ENGINE AND ENGINE REBUILDING 65

1. Pulley assembly
2. Front cover
3. Front bearing
4. Rotor
5. Rear bearing
6. Stator
7. Diode (Set plate assembly
8. Brush assembly
9. IC voltage regulator
10. Diode
11. Rear cover
12. Through bolt

1978 and later alternator shown, 1981 and later similar

4. Install and tension the V-belt as described in Chapter 1.
5. Connect the plug connecting the alternator to the wiring harness and the two lead wires.
6. Connect the negative battery cable.

Regulator

REMOVAL AND INSTALLATION

1970–77

Disconnect the battery negative (−) cable. Then, unplug the connection between the regulator and wiring harness. Finally, remove the two mounting bolts and remove the regulator. To replace the regulator, reverse the removal procedures, but make sure to leave the battery disconnected until the last step.

1978 and Later

The transistorized regulator is soldered to the brush assembly inside the alternator. It is non-adjustable, and must be replaced together with the brush assembly if faulty.

1. Remove the alternator.
2. Remove the through bolts and separate the front cover from the stator housing.
3. Unsolder the stator lead wires from the diode terminals. Remove the screws securing the brush assembly. Remove the stator from the rear cover.
4. Unsolder the wires at the diode terminal. Remove the brush assembly and regulator mounting screws. Remove the brush assembly and regulator.
5. Assembly is the reverse. Apply soldering heat sparingly, carrying out the operation as quickly as possible to avoid heat damage to the transistors and diodes. Before assembling the alternator halves, bend a piece of wire into an "L" and slip it through the rear cover next to the brushes. Use the wire to hold the brushes in a retracted position until the case halves are assembled. Remove the wire carefully to prevent damage to the slip rings.

VOLTAGE ADJUSTMENT

1970–77

1. Using an ammeter rated at 10 amps, a 30-volt voltmeter, and a resistor rated at .25 ohms, connect up a test circuit as shown in the illustrations. On 1972 and earlier models, the regulator must be disconnected and held with the connector plug downward.

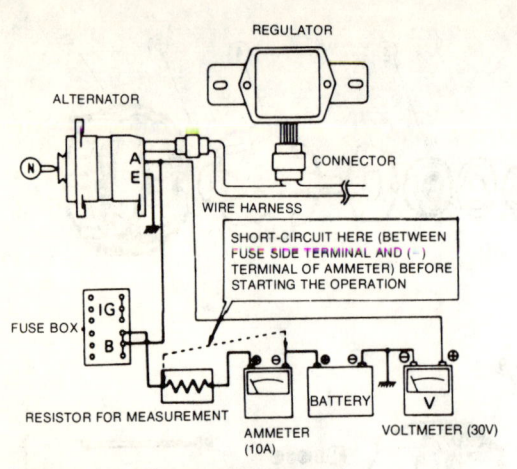

ENGINE AND ENGINE REBUILDING

Hookup for voltage measurement

Temperature °C(°F)	Voltage V
−10(14)	14.75 to 15.25
0(32)	14.60 to 15.10
10(50)	14.45 to 14.95
20(68)	14.30 to 14.80
30(86)	14.15 to 14.65
40(104)	14.00 to 14.50

Temperature/Voltage chart for 1970–74 models

Temperature °C(°F)	Voltage V
−10(14)	14.75 to 15.75
0(32)	14.60 to 15.60
10(50)	14.45 to 15.45
20(68)	14.30 to 15.30
30(86)	14.15 to 15.15
40(104)	14.00 to 15.00

Temperature/Voltage chart for 1975–77 models

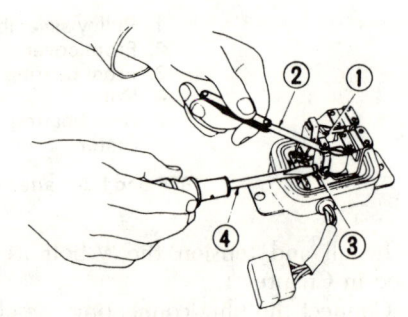

2. MAKE SURE TO SHORT CIRCUIT BETWEEN THE FUSE BOX SIDE OF THE RESISTOR AND THE NEGATIVE TERMINAL OF THE AMMETER EVERY TIME THE ENGINE IS STARTED. Then, disconnect the short circuit wire during testing.

3. Turn off all accessories. Operate the engine at 2,500 rpm for several minutes.

4. Make sure that the ammeter reading is below 5 amps. If not, the battery must be charged or another battery substituted so that the test may be made with the amperage within this range. Stop the engine.

5. Wait several minutes, then start the engine and slowly increase rpm to 2,500 rpm.

6. Compare the reading with the chart, allowing for the temperature around the regulator.

7. If the voltage is not within the specified range, adjust it as follows:

1. Adjust the voltage regulator core gap by loosening the screw which is used to secure the contact set on the yoke, and move the contact up or down as necessary. Retighten the screw. The gap should be 0.024–0.039 in.

2. Adjust the point gap of the voltage regulator coil by loosening the screw used to secure the upper contact and move the upper contact up or down. The gap should be 0.012–0.016 in. through 1975, 0.014–0.018 1976–77.

3. The core gap and point gap on the charge relay coil is or are adjusted in the same manner as previously outlined for the voltage regulator coil. The core gap is to be set at 0.032–0.039 in. and the point gap adjusted to 0.016–0.024 in.

1. Contact set
2. Thickness gauge
3. 4 mm (0.1575 in.) dia. screw
4. Crosshead screwdriver

Voltage regulator core gap adjustment

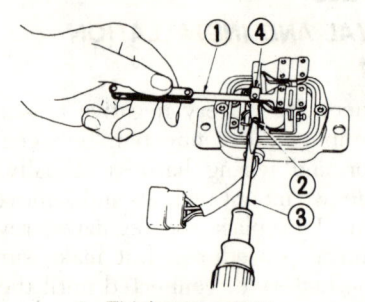

1. Thickness gauge
2. 3 mm (0.1181 in.) dia. screw
3. Crosshead screwdriver
4. Upper contact

Voltage regulator coil point gap adjustment

4. The regulated voltage is adjusted by loosening the locknut and turning the adjusting screw clockwise to increase, or counterclockwise to decrease the regulated volt-

ENGINE AND ENGINE REBUILDING   67

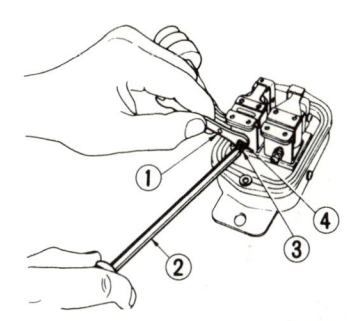

1. Wrench
2. Phillips screwdriver
3. Adjusting screw
4. Locknut

Regulated voltage adjustment

age. The voltage should be between 14.3–15.3 volts at 68° F.

Starter

A standard non-reduction gear starting motor is used on all models through 1977. This motor has its brushes located within the rear cover. Two versions are used: one for all manual transmission models through 1976, and one for automatic transmission models, 1973–77, and 1977 manual transmission models. Differences between these starters are minor. The 1970–76 manual transmission starter has no spring on the starter drive lever, and the armature simply locates in the rear cover bearing, while on the other starter the armature is retained by thrust washers and an E-clip.

A reduction gear starting motor is used on all 1978 and later models. The brushes are on a plate located just behind the starter drive housing; the rear cover serves only to locate the armature shaft.

REMOVAL AND INSTALLATION

1. Disconnect the negative battery cable.
2. Disconnect and label the wires from the terminals on the solenoid.
3. Remove the two bolts which secure the starter to the flywheel housing and pull the starter forward and out. To install, reverse the removal procedure.

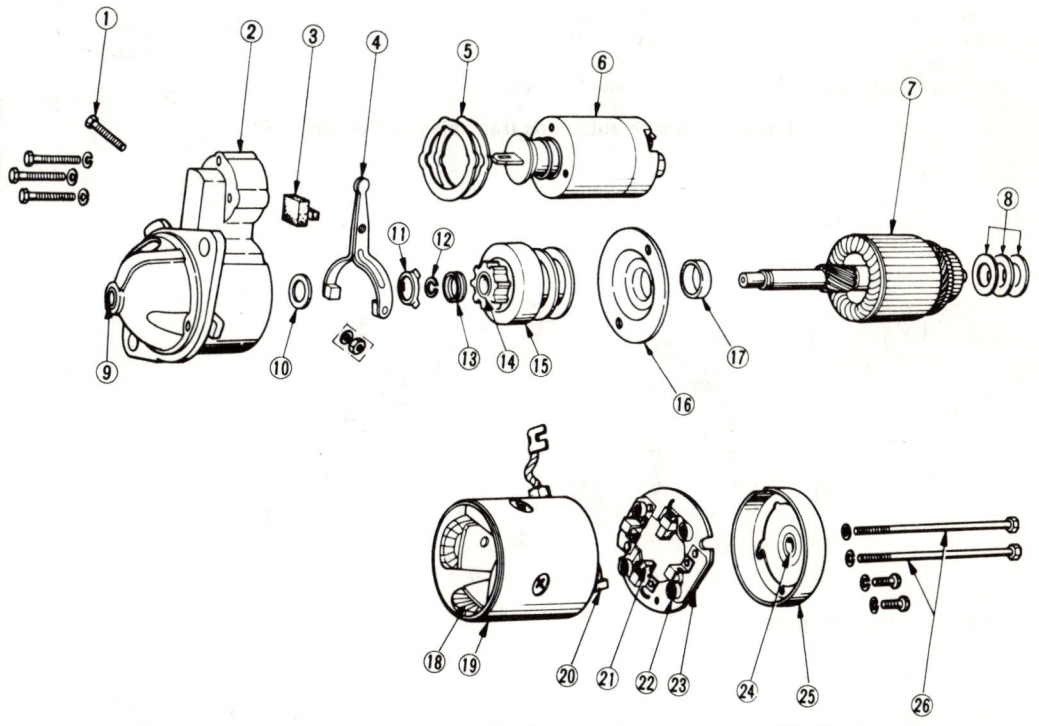

1. Shift lever pin
2. Gear case
3. Dust cover
4. Shift lever
5. Dust cover
6. Solenoid
7. Armature
8. Thrust washer
9. Bushing
10. Thrust washer
11. Stopper washer
12. Stopper clip
13. Pinion stopper
14. Pinion
15. Overrunning clutch
16. Center bracket
17. Center bearing
18. Field coil
19. Yoke
20. Brush (+)
21. Brush (−)
22. Brush spring
23. Brush holder assembly
24. Bushing
25. Rear cover
26. Through bolt

Starter used with manual transmission through 1976

68 ENGINE AND ENGINE REBUILDING

1. Solenoid
2. Dust cover (Adjusting washer)
3. Torsion spring
4. Shift lever
5. Dust cover
6. Thrust washer
7. E-ring
8. Rear cover bushing
9. Through bolt
10. Rear cover
11. Brush holder assembly
12. Brush (−)
13. Brush spring
14. Brush (+)
15. Yoke
16. Field coil assembly
17. Armature assembly
18. Center bearing
19. Center bracket
20. Pinion assembly
21. Dust cover
22. Pinion stopper
23. Stopper clip
24. Gear case
25. Gear case bushing

Starter used with automatic transmission through 1977

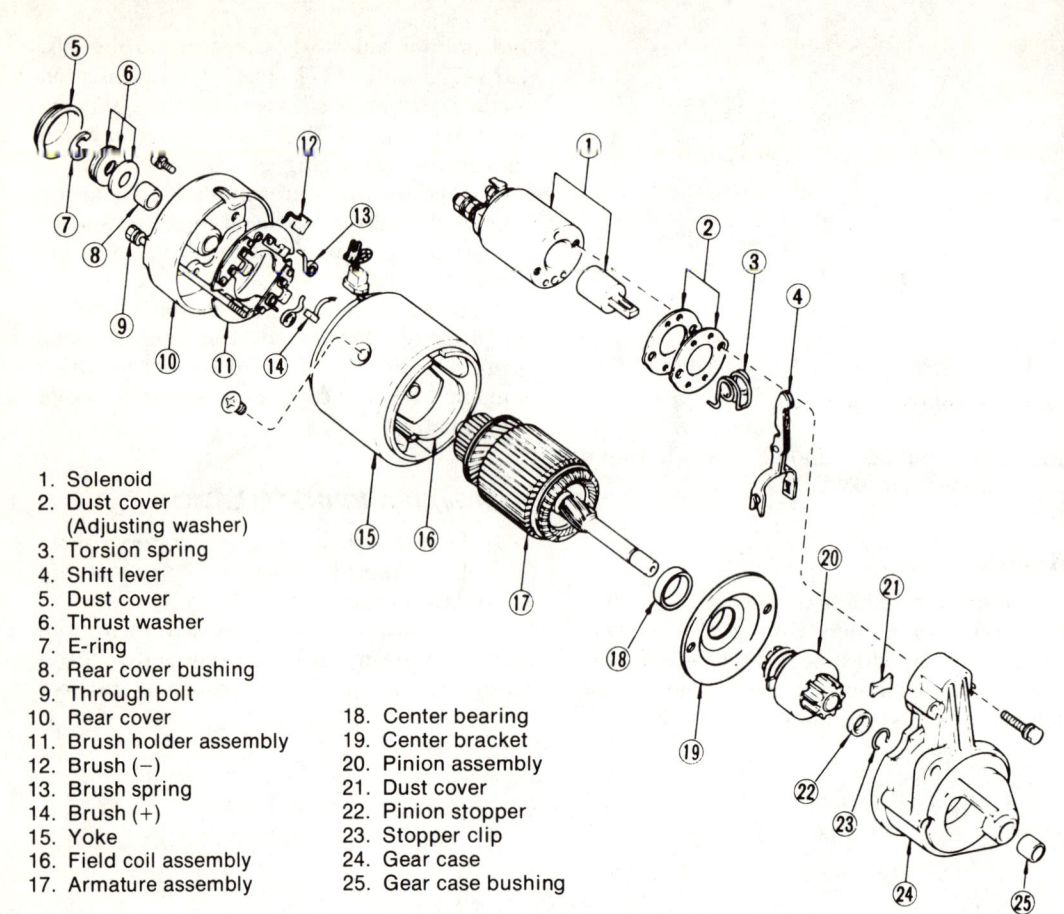

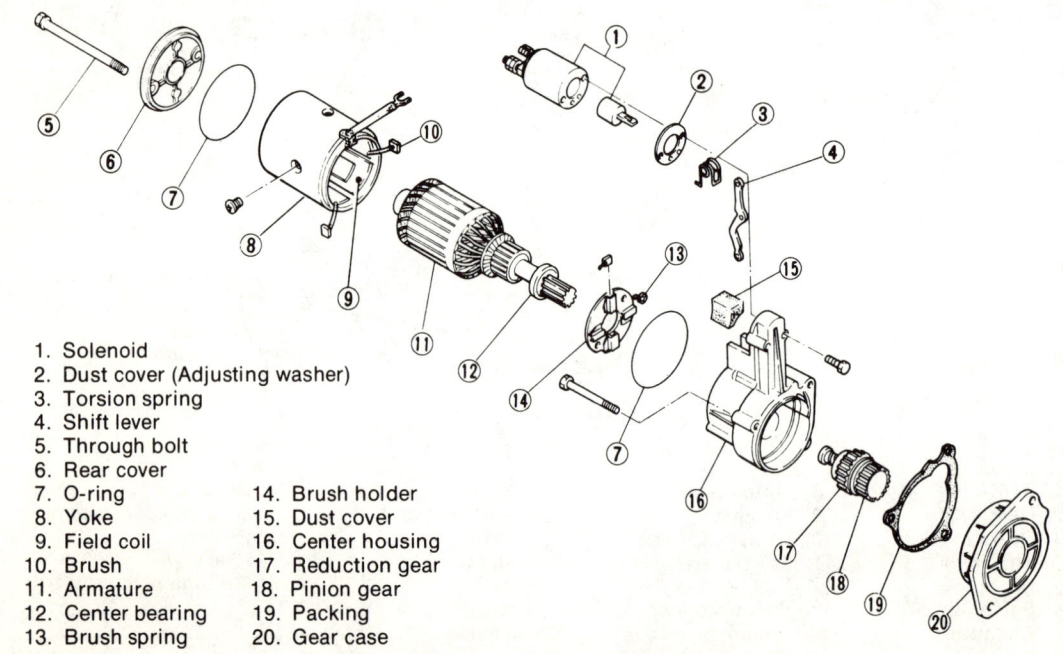

1. Solenoid
2. Dust cover (Adjusting washer)
3. Torsion spring
4. Shift lever
5. Through bolt
6. Rear cover
7. O-ring
8. Yoke
9. Field coil
10. Brush
11. Armature
12. Center bearing
13. Brush spring
14. Brush holder
15. Dust cover
16. Center housing
17. Reduction gear
18. Pinion gear
19. Packing
20. Gear case

Reduction gear starter, 1978 and later

ENGINE AND ENGINE REBUILDING 69

BRUSH REPLACEMENT
1970–77

1. Remove the starter. On automatic transmission models, 1973–76, and all 1977 models, remove the dust cover, the E-ring, and the two thrust washers from the rear cover. Remove the two brush holder set screws from the rear cover.
2. On all models, remove the two through bolts and remove the rear cover.
3. Remove the brushes from their holders by lifting the brush spring away from the brush; you can use a hook fabricated from wire to do this.
4. Unsolder the brush electrical connections.
5. Remove the brushes.

To install:

6. Insert the brushes into the holder. Solder the brush electrical connections. Raise the brushes far enough to permit installing the brush holder over the commutator.
7. Install the rear cover through bolts. On the models mentioned in Step 1, replace the brush holder set screws, and replace the thrust washers, E-ring, and the dust cover.

1978 and Later

1. Remove the starter. Remove the solenoid.
2. Remove the through bolts and the rear cover. The cover can be pried off with a screwdriver, but be careful not to damage the O-ring.
3. Remove the starter housing, armature, and brush holder from the center housing. They can be removed as an assembly.
4. Remove the positive side brush from its holder. The positive brush is insulated from the brush holder, and its lead wire is connected to the field coil.
5. Carefully lift the negative brush from the commutator and remove it from the holder.
6. Unsolder the brush electrical connections. Remove the brushes.
7. Install the new brushes and solder their wires to the connections. Install the brush holder, armature, and starter housing to the center housing. Install the rear cover and O-ring. Install the solenoid.

DRIVE REPLACEMENT
1970–77

1. Loosen the locknut and remove the connection going to the "M" terminal of the solenoid. Remove the securing screws and remove the solenoid.
2. On 1973–76 automatic transmission models and all 1977 models, first remove the dust cover, E-ring, thrust washers, and the two screws retaining the brush holder assembly. Remove the brush cover through-bolts and remove the cover assembly (all models).
3. Lift the brushes to free them from the commutator and remove the brush holder.
4. Tap the yoke assembly lightly with a wooden hammer and remove it from the field and case.
5. Remove the nut and bolt which serve as a pin for the shift lever, carefully retaining the associated washers.
6. Remove the armature assembly and shift lever.
7. Push the stop ring (located at the end of the armature shaft) toward the clutch and remove the snap-ring. Remove the stop ring.
8. Remove the clutch assembly from the armature shaft.

To install the drive:

1. Install the clutch assembly onto the armature shaft.
2. Put the stop ring on and hold it toward the clutch while installing the snap-ring.
3. Install the armature assembly and shift lever into the yoke.
4. Install the washers, nut and bolt which serve as a shift lever pivot pin.
5. Install the field back onto the yoke assembly.
6. Lift the brushes and install the brush holder. Install the brush cover and through-bolts.
7. On 1973–76 automatic transmission models, and all 1977 models, replace the brush holder set screws, the thrust washers, E-ring, and the dust cover.
8. Install the solenoid. Reconnect the wire to the "M" terminal of the solenoid.

1978 and Later

1. Remove the starter.
2. Remove the solenoid and the shift lever.
3. Remove the bolts securing the center housing to the front cover and separate the parts.
4. Remove the gears and the starter drive.
5. Installation is the reverse.

ENGINE AND ENGINE REBUILDING

Alternator and Regulator Specifications

	Alternator			Charge Relay		Regulator			
Year	Part No. or Manufacturer	Output (amps)	Part No. or Manufacturer	Core Gap in. (mm)	Point Gap in. (mm)	Volts to Close	Core Gap in. (mm)	Point Gap in. (mm)	Volts @ 68°F
1970–71	Hitachi LT145-35	45	TL1Z-37	.0315–.0394 (.8–1.0)	.0157–.0236 (.4–.6)	8–10①	.0236–.0394 (.6–1.0)	.0118–.0157 (.3–.4)	14.3–15.3
1972	Hitachi LT150-05	50	TL1Z-57	.0315–.0394 (.8–1.0)	.0157–.0236 (.4–.6)	4.2–5.2②	.0236–.0394 (.6–1.0)	.0118–.0157 (.3–.4)	14.3–15.3
1973	Hitachi LT150-10③	50③	TL1Z-57	.0315–.0394 (.8–1.0)	.0157–.0236 (.4–.6)	4.2–5.2②	.0236–.0394 (.6–1.0)	.0118–.0157 (.3–.4)	14.3–15.3
1974	Hitachi LT150-10③	50③	TL1Z-79	.0315–.0394 (.8–1.0)	.0157–.0236 (.4–.6)	4.2–5.2②	.024–.039 (.6–1.0)	.012–.016 (.3–.4)	14.3–15.3

Year							
1975	Hitachi LT160-23	60	TL1Z-85	.0315–.0394 (.8–1.0)	.0157–.0236 (.4–.6)	4.2–5.2 ②	.024–.039 (.6–1.0)	.012–.016 (.3–.4)	14.3–15.3
1976	Hitachi LT160-23	60	TL1Z-85B	.031–.039 (.8–1.0)	.016–.024 (.4–.6)	4.2–5.2 ②	.024–.039 (.6–1.0)	.014–.018 (.35–.45)	14.3–15.3
1977	Hitachi LT160-23C	60	TL1Z-85C	.031–.039 (.8–1.0)	.016–.024 (.4–.6)	4.2–5.2 ②	.024–.039 (.6–1.0)	.014–.018 (.35–.45)	14.3–15.3
1978	Hitachi LR160-42	60	Integral			Non-Adjustable			14.4–15.0
1979	Hitachi LR160-42B	60	Integral			Non-Adjustable			14.4–15.0
1980	Hitachi LR160-42B	60	Integral			Non-Adjustable			14.4–15.0
1981–82	Hitachi LR160-82	60	Integral			Non-Adjustable			14.4–15.0

① At terminal A
② At terminal N
③ Lt160-23, 60 amps—Canada

ENGINE AND ENGINE REBUILDING

SOLENOID REPLACEMENT
All Models

1. Loosen the locknut and remove the connection going to the "M" terminal of the solenoid.
2. Remove the three securing screws and remove the solenoid.

To install, reverse the removal procedures.

Battery

Refer to Chapter 1 for details on battery maintenance.

REMOVAL AND INSTALLATION

1. Disconnect the negative (ground) cable from the terminal, and then the positive cable. Special pullers are available to remove the cable clamps.

NOTE: *To avoid sparks, always disconnect the ground cable first, and connect it last.*

2. Remove the battery hold-down clamp.
3. Remove the battery, being careful not to spill the acid.

NOTE: *Spilled acid can be neutralized with a baking soda/water solution. If you somehow get acid into your eyes, flush it out with lots of water and get to a doctor.*

4. Clean the battery posts thoroughly before reinstalling, or when installing a new battery.
5. Clean the cable clamps, using a wire brush, both inside and out.
6. Install the battery and the hold-down clamp or strap. Connect the positive, and then the negative cable. Do not hammer them in place. The terminals should be coated lightly (externally) with grease to prevent corrosion. There are also felt washers impregnated with an anti-corrosion substance which are slipped over the battery posts before installing the cables; these are available in auto parts stores.

CAUTION: *Make absolutely sure that the battery is connected properly before you turn on the ignition switch. Reversed polarity can burn out your alternator and regulator within a matter of seconds.*

Battery and Starter Specifications

Year	Engine Displacement cu in. (cc)	BATTERY Ampere Hour Capacity	Volts	Terminal Grounded	STARTER Lock Test Amps	Volts	Torque ft lbs (kg)	No-Load Test Amps	Volts	RPM	Brush Spring Tension lbs (kg)
1970–72	146 (2393)	60	12	Neg	460	6	10.1 (1.4)	60	12	5000	1.76 ① (0.8)
1973–74	146 (2393), 156 (2565)	60	12	Neg	460 ①	6 ②	10.1 (1.4)	60	12	5000 ③	3.53 (1.6)
1975–77	168 (2753)	65	12	Neg	Not Recommended			60	12	5000 ③	3.53 (1.6)
1978	168 (2753)	65	12	Neg	Not Recommended			100	12	4300	3.96 (1.8)
1979	168 (2753)	60 ⑤	12	Neg	Not Recommended			100	12	4300	3.96 (1.8)
1980	168 (2753)	60 ⑤	12	Neg	Not Recommended			100	11	3900	3.96 (1.8)

① 3.52 (1.6)—1972
② Automatic—500 amps
③ Automatic—5 volts
④ Automatic—6000 rpm
⑤ 70 amps—Canada; optional, U.S.A.

ENGINE AND ENGINE REBUILDING

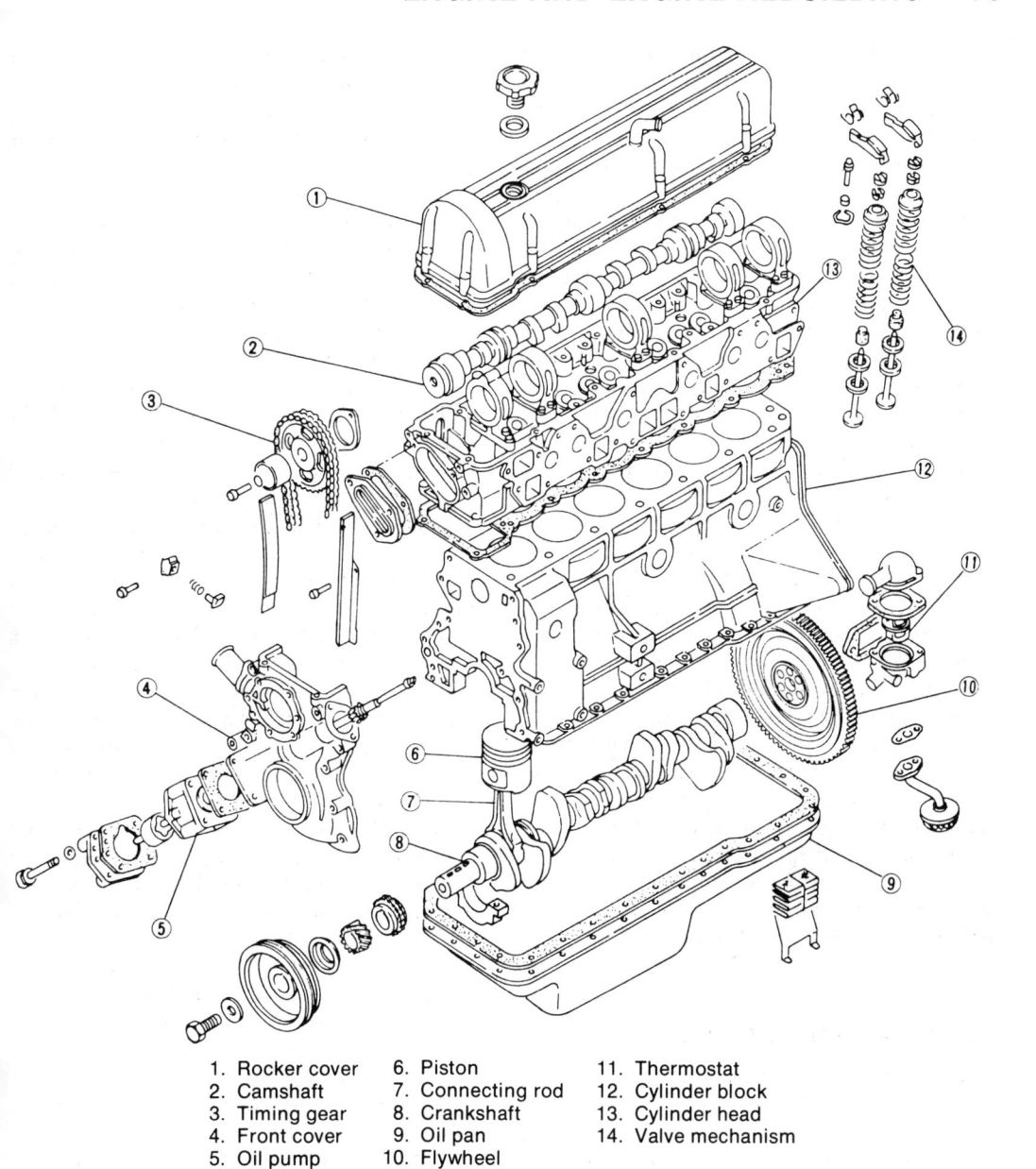

1. Rocker cover
2. Camshaft
3. Timing gear
4. Front cover
5. Oil pump
6. Piston
7. Connecting rod
8. Crankshaft
9. Oil pan
10. Flywheel
11. Thermostat
12. Cylinder block
13. Cylinder head
14. Valve mechanism

Exploded view of the engine

ENGINE MECHANICAL

Design

The L24, L26, and L28 engines are all single overhead camshaft, in-line six cylinder powerplants. The main difference between the three are varying bores and strokes to achieve the different displacements. The engine has a great deal of similarity to the four cylinder engines used in the 510, 610, and 710 series with obvious difference of an extra pair of cylinders.

The block is a single casting, providing seven main bearing supports for quiet and durable operation. The block is especially rigid due to the existence of a deep skirt around the crankshaft. Minimal weight is assured through the use of an overhead cam which eliminates the need for a tappet chamber. The main oil gallery runs parallel to the cylinder bores and an oil hole connects each main bearing with the gallery.

The crankshaft, made of forged steel, is precision balanced and fully counterweighted.

ENGINE AND ENGINE REBUILDING

The pistons are of cast aluminum and are of the slipper skirt type with struts. The piston pin is a hollow steel fabrication, and is press fitted into the connecting rod.

The connecting rods are of forged steel and are pressure lubricated via oil passages drilled between the connecting rod and main bearing journals.

The cylinder head is of an aluminum alloy which is chosen partially for its excellent heat transfer. Replaceable valve seats are used. While intake seats are aluminum and exhaust seats are iron in the L24 engine, the L26 and L28 engines employ brass and steel seats, respectively. The seats are hot press fitted. The heads also include five alloy brackets for support of the camshaft bearings.

The camshaft is of cast iron alloy and features five bearings. It is lubricated via holes through the support brackets which intersect with the main oil gallery for the head. The camshaft is driven via a double row roller chain. The chain tensioner is controlled through both spring and oil pressure.

The valve actuating mechanism consists of inner and outer springs and pivot type rocker arms which are driven directly off the camshaft. The elimination of pushrods substantially reduces valve train mass for stress-free operation at high rpm and long service life.

The intake manifold is cast aluminum while the exhaust manifold is of cast iron and is ram-tuned for minimum backpressure.

Removal and Installation

The instructions below provide for removal of the engine and transmission as a unit, as this makes the operation easier and faster, and transmission removal is easier after the engine is out.

All operations involving hoisting the engine-transmission unit should be done with extreme care and should be carefully planned beforehand. Read the procedure through before beginning. It is best to use fender covers so that the fenders will not be damaged during removal or installation.

1. On fuel injected models, the fuel system should be discharged before the battery is disconnected. See the procedure for changing the fuel filter, given in Chapter 1. Disconnect the battery cables, negative cable first.
2. Mark the location of each hood hinge on the hood to facilitate reinstallation.
3. Carefully support the hood so that its weight will not be resting on the hinge bolts. Then, remove the bolts.
4. Remove the hood with the help of an assistant.
5. Remove the air cleaner.
6. Drain the radiator and crankcase.
7. On automatic transmission models, remove the splash shield. Disconnect and plug the two fluid cooler lines at the radiator. Disconnect the vacuum modulator hose at the intake manifold.
8. Disconnect the radiator hoses at the radiator. Remove the radiator mounting bolts and remove the radiator and shroud.
9. On models with air conditioning, loosen the compressor mounting bolts and remove the drive belt. Unbolt the compressor and move it aside, but do not disconnect any of the refrigerant lines. If there is not enough slack in the lines (this may be the case on some earlier models), the system will have to be discharged and the lines disconnected. Unless you are thoroughly familiar with air conditioning systems, this job should be referred to a specialist with proper training. The escaping refrigerant is extremely dangerous.
10. On models with power steering, loosen the pump mounting bolts and remove the drive belt. Remove the mounting bolts and move the pump away from the engine. Do not disconnect the power steering hoses.
11. Disconnect the accelerator linkage on carbureted models (see the illustration).
12. Disconnect and label the:
    a. battery ground cable at the engine;
    b. starter wiring;
    c. coil-to-distributor high-tension cable;
    d. primary wire to the distributor at the connection;
    e. wire to the temperature senders;

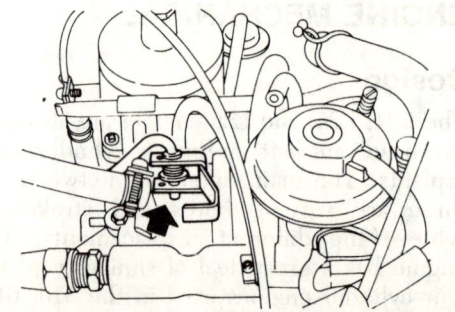

Disconnecting the accelerator linkage (through 1974)

ENGINE AND ENGINE REBUILDING   75

General Engine Specifications

Year	Engine Displacement cu in. (cc)	Carburetor Type	Horsepower @ rpm (Gross)	Torque @ rpm (ft lbs)	Bore x Stroke in. (mm)	Compression Ratio	Oil Pressure (psi)
1970–73	146 (2393)	Twin SU	151 @ 5600	146 @ 4400	3.27 (83) x 2.90 (74)	8.8:1	50–57
1974	156 (2565)	Twin SU	162 @ 5600	154 @ 4400	3.26 (83) x 3.11 (79)	8.8:1	50–57
1975–78	168 (2753)	Fuel Injection	170 @ 5600	177 @ 4400	3.39 (86) x 3.11 (79)	8.3:1	50–57
1979	168 (2753)	Fuel Injection	135 @ 5200 ①	144 @ 4400	3.39 (86) x 3.11 (79)	8.3:1	50–57
1980	168 (2753)	Fuel Injection	132 @ 5200 ①	144 @ 4000	3.39 (86) x 3.11 (79)	8.3:1	50–57
1981–82	168 (2753)	Fuel Injection	145 @ 5200	156 @ 4000	3.39 (86) x 3.11 (79)	8.8:1	50–57
1981–82 (Turbo)	168 (2753)	Fuel Injection	180 @ 5600	202 @ 2800	3.39 (86) x 3.11 (79)	7.4:1	—

① Net horsepower

Valve Specifications

Year	Engine Displacement cu in. (cc)	Seat Angle (deg)	Spring Test Pressure lbs @ in. (kg @ mm)	Spring Installed Height in. (mm)	Stem To Guide ① Clearance in. (mm) Intake	Stem To Guide ① Clearance in. (mm) Exhaust	Stem Diameter in. (mm) Intake	Stem Diameter in. (mm) Exhaust
All	All	45 ④	108 @ 1.16 ② (49 @ 29.5)	1.575 ③ (40.0)	.0008–.0021 (.020–.053)	.0016–.0029 (.040–.073)	.3136–.3142 (7.965–7.980)	.3128–.3134 (7.945–7.960)

① Guides are replaceable
② Inner spring—56.2 @ 0.965 (25.5 @ 24.5)
③ Inner spring—1.378 (35.0)
④ 1979 and later—45°30'

f. wire to the water temperature switch at the connector;
g. alternator wires;
h. choke heat wires (1974) or linkage;
i. throttle solenoid wire (manual transmission) and throttle linkage;
j. EGR solenoid wire at the connector, if equipped;
k. wire to the vacuum solenoid (manual transmission);
l. fuel line(s) (two for 1974 models); on fuel injected models be sure to relieve fuel line pressure as outlined in fuel filter replacement in Chapter 1 and to disconnect

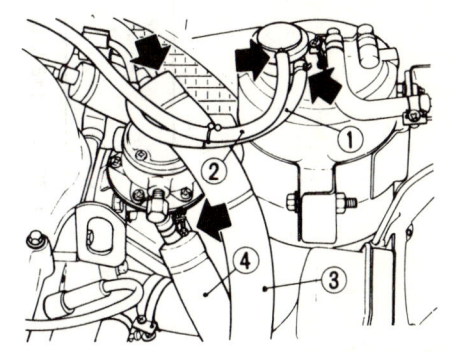

Remove: canister purge hose (1), vacuum signal hose (2), fuel return hose (3), and fuel charge hose (4); 1974 shown, later models similar

ENGINE AND ENGINE REBUILDING

Crankshaft and Connecting Rod Specifications
All measurements are given in inches (mm)

Year	Engine Displacement cu in. (cc)	Crankshaft Main Brg Journal Dia	Crankshaft Main Brg Oil Clearance	Crankshaft Shaft End-Play	Thrust on No.	Connecting Rod Journal Diameter	Connecting Rod Oil Clearance	Connecting Rod Side Clearance
1970–72	146 (2393)	2.1631–2.1636 (54.942–54.955)	.0008–.0028 (.020–.072)	.0020–.0071 (.05–.18)	center	1.9670–1.9675 (49.961–49.974)	.0006–.0022 (.014–.066)	.0079–.0118 (.20–.30)
1973–78	146 (2393), 156 (2565), 168 (2753)	2.1631–2.1636 (54.942–54.955)	.0008–.0028 (.020–.072)	.0020–.0071 (.05–.18)	center	1.9670–1.9675 (49.961–49.974)	.0010–.0022 (.025–.055)	.0079–.0118 (.20–.30)
1979–82	168 (2753)	2.1631–2.1636 (54.942–54.955)	.0008–.0026 (.020–.066)	.0020–.0071 (.05–.18)	center	1.9670–1.9675 (49.961–49.974)	.0009–.0026 (.024–.066)	.0079–.0118 (.20–.30)

Piston and Ring Specifications
All measurements in inches (mm)

Year	Engine Displacement cu in. (cc)	Piston Clearance	Ring Gap Top Compression	Ring Gap Bottom Compression	Ring Gap Oil Control	Ring Side Clearance Top Compression	Ring Side Clearance Bottom Compression	Ring Side Clearance Oil Control
1970–72	146 (2393)	.0010–.0018 (.025–.045)	.0091–.0150 (.23–.38)	.0059–.0118 (.15–.30)	.0059–.0118 (.15–.30)	.0018–.0031 (.45–.080)	.0012–.0025 (.030–.063)	.0010–.0025 (.025–.063)
1973–76	146 (2393), 156 (2565), 168 (2753)	.0010–.0018 (.025–.045)	.0091–.0150 (.23–.38)	.0059–.0118 (.15–.30)	.0059–.0118 (.15–.30)	.0018–.0031 (.045–.080)	.0012–.0028 (.030–.070)	0
1977–78	168 (2753)	.0010–.0018 (.025–.045)	.0098–.0157 (.25–.40)	.0118–.0197 (.30–.50)	.0118–.0354 (.30–.90)	.0016–.0029 (.040–.073)	.0012–.0028 (.030–.070)	0
1979–80	168 (2753)	.0010–.0018 (.025–.045)	.0098–.0157 (.25–.40)	.0118–.0197 (.30–.50)	.0118–.0354 (.30–.90)	.0016–.0029 (.040–.073)	.0012–.0025 (.030–.063)	0
1981–82	168 (2753)	.0010–.0018 (.025–.045)	.0098–.0157 (.25–.40)	.0059–.0118 (.15–.30)	.012–.035 (.3–.9)	.0016–.0029 (.040–.073)	.012–.025 (.030–.063)	—
1981–82 (Turbo)	168 (2753)	.0010–.0018 (.025–.045)	.0075–.0130 (.19–.33)	.0059–.0118 (.15–.30)	.012–.035 (.3–.9)	.0016–.0029 (.040–.073)	.012–.025 (.030–.063)	.0009–.0028 (.023–.070)

ENGINE AND ENGINE REBUILDING

Torque Specifications
All readings in ft lbs (kg-m)

Year	Engine Displacement cu in. (cc)	Cylinder Head Bolts	Rod Bearing Bolts	Main Bearing Bolts	Crankshaft Pulley Bolt	Flywheel To Crankshaft Bolts	Manifolds	Camshaft Sprocket Bolt
1970–72	146 (2393)	47 ①② (6.5)	19.5–23.9 (2.7–3.3)	33–40 (4.5–5.5)	115–130 (16–18)	101 (14)	5.8–8.7 (0.8–1.2)	36–43 (5–6)
1973	146 (2393)	47–61 ③ (6.5–8.5)	33–40 (4.5–5.5)	33–40 (4.5–5.5)	87–116 (12–16)	101–116 (14–16)	5.8–8.7 (0.8–1.2)	86–116 (12–16)
1974	156 (2565)	54–61 ③ (7.5–8.5)	27–31 (3.7–4.3)	33–40 (4.5–5.5)	94–108 (13–15)	94–108 (13–15)	5.8–8.7 (0.8–1.2)	94–108 (13–15)
1975–82	168 (2753)	54–61 ③ (7.5–8.5)	33–40 (4.5–5.5)	33–40 (4.5–5.5)	94–108 ④ (13–15)	94–108 (13–15)	⑤	94–108 (13–15)

① Tighten in two steps: 1st, 33(4.5); 2nd, 47(6.5)
② 1972: tighten in two steps: 1st, 47(6.5); 2nd, 55(7.5)
③ Tighten in three steps: 1st, 30(4.0); 2nd, 44(6.0); 3rd, 54–61(7.5–8.5)
④ 1977–78: 87–116(12–16); 1979–82; 101–116(14–16)
⑤ Small bolts (8M): 1975–78 10–13(1.4–1.8); 1979–82 11–18(1.5–2.5) large bolts (10M): 1975–78 25–36(3.5–5.0) 1979–82 25–33(3.5–4.5)

all electrical wiring to the fuel injection;
  m. heater hoses;
  n. vacuum line to the brake cylinder at the manifold;

  o. wires for the back-up lights, neutral safety switch, and top detecting switch;
  p. inhibitor switch and kick-down solenoid wires (automatic only).

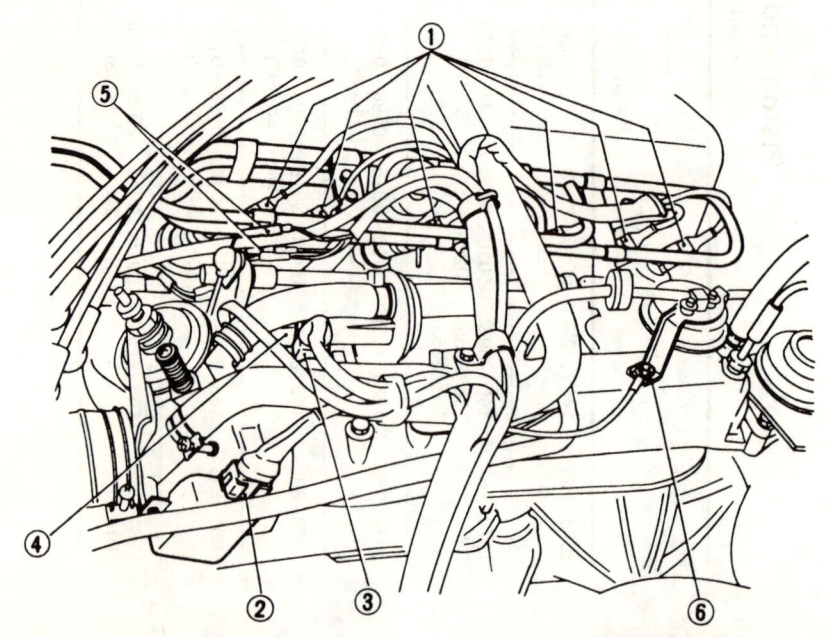

1. Injector connector
2. Throttle valve switch connector
3. Cold start valve connector
4. Air regulator connector
5. E.F.I. sub-harness connector
6. Engine ground

Removing the EFI harness

ENGINE AND ENGINE REBUILDING

13. Remove the clutch master cylinder (manual transmission only).

14. Disconnect the speedometer cable where it enters the rear extension housing of the transmission.

15. Disconnect the transmission control linkage.

16. Remove the shift lever (manual transmission) or disconnect the range selector (automatic transmission).

17. Disconnect the exhaust tube at the manifold.

18. Mark the companion flange and driveshaft for installation in the same place and disconnect the shaft at the rear by removing the four bolts. Remove the shaft from the rear of the transmission and seal the opening.

19. Support the transmission carefully to remove all weight from the rear mounts. Remove the bolts which secure the rear mounts to the body.

20. Connect an adequate cable or chain between the two lifting hooks on the engine. Hook the cable or chain to a hoist and apply just enough lift to take all weight off the front mounts.

21. Remove the bolts which attach the engine support to the front mounting insulators.

22. Working carefully to avoid damaging engine or body parts, tilt the engine, lowering the transmission jack as necessary, until it can be pulled up and out of the engine compartment, front first. The engine should be mounted on a secure stand as soon as possible.

When reinstalling the engine, first carefully inspect the engine mounts. If any part of the mount is damaged or if the bonded surface is deteriorated or separated, replace the mount.

The front mounts are identical, but are installed in different positions on the right and left. The rear mount must also be installed in the proper direction.

In all other respects engine installation is accomplished in the reverse of removal. Make sure that all engine mounts are properly assembled and tight before removing support.

Cylinder Head

REMOVAL AND INSTALLATION

1. Crank the engine until the No. 1 piston is at TDC of the compression stroke. Disconnect the negative battery cable, drain the coolant, and remove the air cleaner and attending hoses.

2. To provide clearance, remove the upper radiator hose, thermostat housing (coolant outlet elbow), and the thermostat. The housing, thermotime switch (fuel injected models), temperature switch(es), and vacuum switching valve can be removed as an assembly. Label the electrical connectors.

3. If equipped with power steering, unbolt the pump and move it aside. Do not disconnect the lines. It may be desirable to remove the alternator, on some models, to provide working room.

4. Label and disconnect the spark plug wires. Remove the spark plugs.

5. Disconnect the fuel lines. On fuel injected models, be sure to relieve fuel line pressure as outlined in fuel filter replacement in Chapter 1; disconnect all electrical wiring to the fuel injection.

Remove the fuel pump on models through 1974.

6. On models through 1974, disconnect the water, air, vacuum, and fuel hoses or lines from the carburetors.

7. On fuel injected models, the fuel injection assembly will be removed intact with the intake manifold. Disconnect the hose from the rocker cover which runs to the throttle chamber. Remove the coolant pipe/fuel pipe retaining bolt from the cylinder head.

8. Disconnect and remove the EGR control tube, then remove the EGR valve on 1973 and later models so equipped.

9. Disconnect the coolant piping and the exhaust gas inlet tube from the intake manifold.

10. Most 1979 and later models have an auxiliary cooling fan on the right side of the engine, with ducting which runs over the rocker cover to the intake manifold. Remove this ducting, if equipped.

11. Remove the rocker cover.

12. Remove the air conditioner fast idle mechanism and bracket, if equipped.

13. Remove the coolant tube from the balance tube of the manifold, then remove the balance tube, if equipped.

14. Remove the exhaust heat shield plate. Disconnect the exhaust pipe from the exhaust manifold or from the turbocharger exhaust outlet if so equipped. Disconnect the EGR tube from the exhaust manifold. On models with air injection, remove the air

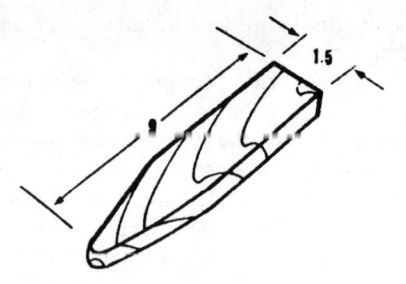

Dimensions for fabricating the wooden wedge used to support the timing chain

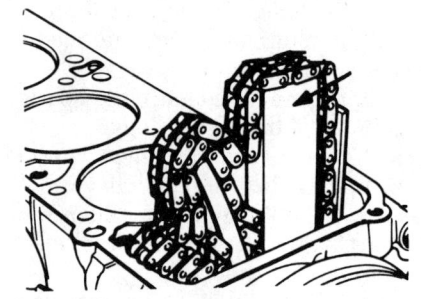

Support the timing chain with a wedge

pump hose from the air injection gallery pipe. Remove the exhaust manifold.

15. Remove the intake manifold.
16. Disconnect the cylinder head temperature sender.
17. Mark the relationship of the camshaft sprocket to the timing chain with paint or chalk. If this is done, it will not be necessary to locate the factory timing marks. Before removing the camshaft sprocket, it will be necessary to wedge the chain in place so that it will not fall down into the front cover. The factory procedure is to wedge the timing chain in place with the wooden wedge shown here. The problem with this is that it may allow the chain tensioner to move out far enough to cock itself against the chain. If this

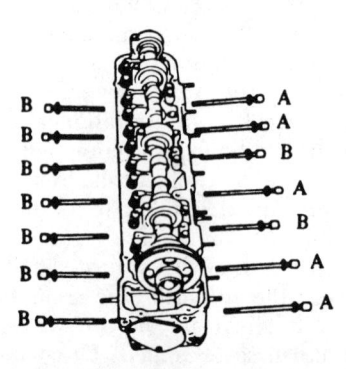

Note the use and position of different length bolts, labeled A or B

happens, you'll find that the chain won't go back over the sprocket after you've put the sprocket back on. In this case, it will be necessary to remove the front cover and push the tensioner back.

After installing the wedge, unbolt and remove the camshaft sprocket.

18. Remove the valve train oil gallery pipe on early models so equipped.
19. Loosen and remove the cylinder head bolts in the reverse order of the tightening sequence to prevent head warpage. You will need a 10 mm Allen wrench to remove the head bolts. Keep the bolts in order, because they are of different lengths. Lift the cylinder head from the engine; this may require the assistance of a strong friend.
20. Thoroughly clean the cylinder block and head mating surfaces. Check the block and head for flatness before installing the head. See the "Engine Rebuilding" section at the end of this chapter for details on how to do this. Install a new cylinder head gasket on the block. Do not use sealer on the gasket.
21. With the crankshaft turned so that the No. 1 piston is at TDC of the compression stroke (if not already done so as mentioned in Step 1), make sure that the camshaft sprocket timing mark and the oblong groove in the camshaft retaining plate are aligned.
22. Place the cylinder head in position on the block, being careful not to allow any of the valves to contact any of the pistons. Do not rotate the crankshaft or camshaft separately because of possible damage which might occur to the valves.
23. Temporarily install and tighten the two center right and left cylinder head bolts to 14.5 ft. lbs.
24. Install the camshaft sprocket together with the timing chain to the camshaft. Make sure that the marks you made earlier line up. If the chain will not stretch over the sprocket, the problem lies in the tensioner. See "Timing Chain Removal and Installation" for timing procedure, if necessary.
25. Install the cylinder head bolts. Note that two lengths are used. Tighten the bolts

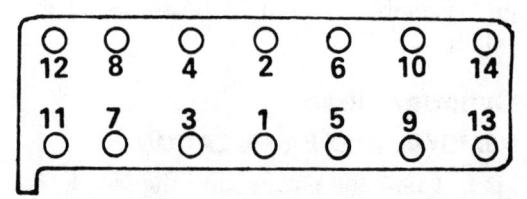

Head bolt tightening sequence—reverse the order for removal

ENGINE AND ENGINE REBUILDING

in two stages, on models through 1971: first to 33 ft lbs, second to 47 ft lbs.

Tighten the bolts in two stages, on 1972 models: first to 47 ft lbs, second to 55 ft lbs.

On 1973 and later models, tighten the bolts in three stages: first to 30 ft lbs, second to 44 ft lbs, third to 54–61 ft lbs.

On all models, be sure to tighten the bolts in the proper sequence, according to the accompanying diagram.

26. Install and assemble the remaining components in the reverse order of removal.

27. Adjust the valves to a preliminary cold clearance of 0.008 in., intake, 0.010 in., exhaust. Operate the engine until it is at normal operating temperature, retorque the head bolts (loosen them slightly and retighten to the final torque figure), and adjust the valves to the hot clearance specification.

VALVE GUIDE REMOVAL AND INSTALLATION

1. Measure the clearance between each valve guide and the valve stem with a micrometer and telescope hole gauge. Measure the valve stem diameter at top, center, and bottom; determine the highest reading. Then, with the hole gauge, measure the bore of the valve guide at the center. Subtract the highest stem diameter from the guide bore, and check to see if the stem-to-guide clearance is within specifications. If this procedure cannot be performed, install the valve in its normal closed position in the head and move it back-and-forth parallel with the position of the rocker arm. If the tip deflects 0.0079 in. (.19 mm) or more, stem-to-guide clearance is excessive.

2. Remove guides that are excessively worn with a press and drift pin. This requires about two tons pressure. This procedure is easier to perform if the cylinder head is heated before attempting it. Press toward the camshaft cover.

3. Allow the head to cool to room temperature, as necessary, and ream the guide hole to 0.4794–0.4802 in. (12.185–12.196 mm).

4. Heat the cylinder head to 302–392° F (150–200° C). Press 0.008 in. (0.2 mm) oversize guides into the head. Interference fit of the guide should be 0.0011–0.0019 in. (0.027–0.049 mm).

5. Ream the bore of the new guides to 0.3150–0.3157 in. (8.000–8.018 mm).

6. Correct the valve seat surface as described under "Valve Seat Removal and Installation" if a new seat is not required.

VALVE SEAT REMOVAL AND INSTALLATION

1. Check the valve seat inserts for pitting where the valve contacts them and recut the seat, or replace it as necessary.

2. Bore the old seat until it collapses, setting the machine depth stop so boring cannot affect the bottom of the insert recess.

Valve Seat Interference Fit—in. (mm)

Year	Intake	Exhaust
1970–73	0.0031–0.0043 (0.08–0.11)	0.0024–0.0039 (0.06–0.10)
1974–82	0.0032–0.0044 (0.081–0.113)	0.0025–0.0038 (0.064–0.096)

3. Select a standard or 0.020 in. (0.5 mm) oversize seat as determined by measuring the cylinder head recess. Machine the recess to the proper size concentric with the valve guide center, according to a measurement of the outside diameter of the seat, and the following charts. Do this at room temperature.

4. Heat the cylinder head to 302–392° F (150–200° C).

5. Press the insert in and make sure that it seats properly in the recess.

6. Cut the seat to the dimensions shown in the correct illustration.

7. Put a small amount of fine grinding compound onto the valve seat face, put the valve into the guide, and lap until the proper seal is obtained. Remove the valve and clean the valve and seat.

OVERHAUL

Inspect the cylinder head for cracks and other flaws. Measure the head on the cylinder block mating surface to check for warpage, employing a straightedge and feeler gauge. If warpage exceeds 0.0039 in. (0.1 mm) or there is other damage, repair or replace the head as required. See the "Engine Rebuilding" section for additional information.

Valve Rockers

REMOVAL AND INSTALLATION

1. Remove the rocker spring.
2. Loosen the rocker pivot locknut, lower

ENGINE AND ENGINE REBUILDING

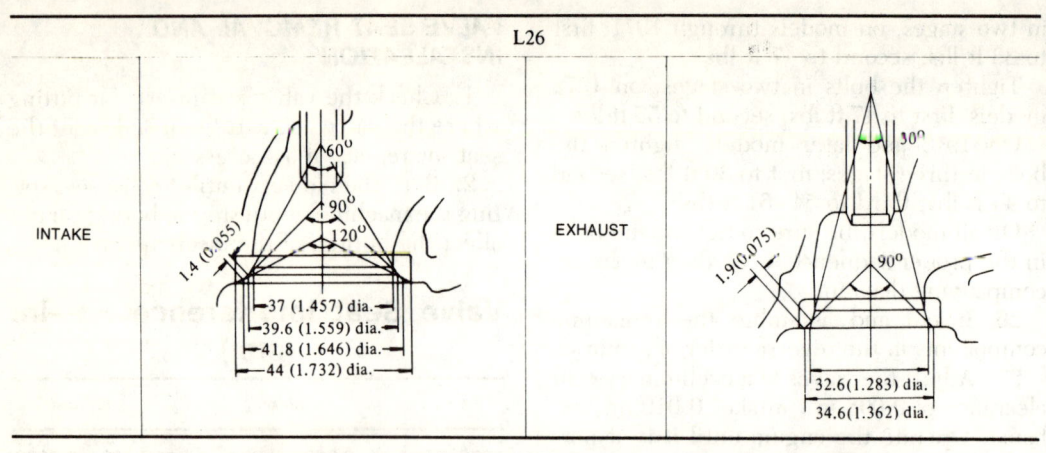

L26

INTAKE — 60°, 90°, 120°, 1.4 (0.055)
- 37 (1.457) dia.
- 39.6 (1.559) dia.
- 41.8 (1.646) dia.
- 44 (1.732) dia.

EXHAUST — 30°, 90°, 1.9 (0.075)
- 32.6 (1.283) dia.
- 34.6 (1.362) dia.

Valve seat dimensions in mm for the 2600 cc engine (inches in parentheses)

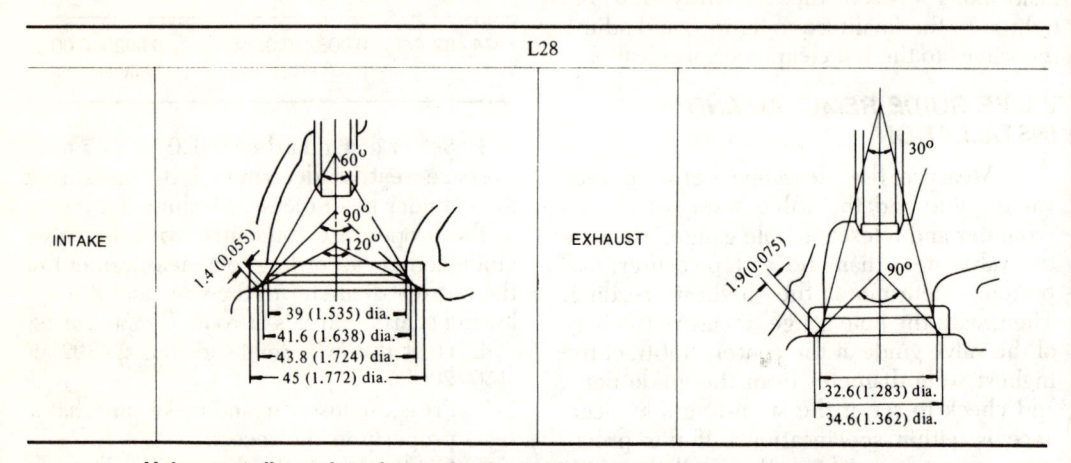

L28

INTAKE — 60°, 90°, 120°, 1.4 (0.055)
- 39 (1.535) dia.
- 41.6 (1.638) dia.
- 43.8 (1.724) dia.
- 45 (1.772) dia.

EXHAUST — 30°, 90°, 1.9 (0.075)
- 32.6 (1.283) dia.
- 34.6 (1.362) dia.

Valve seat dimensions in mm for the 2800 cc engine (inches in parentheses)

Cylinder Head Recess Diameter—in. (mm)

Year-Type	Intake	Exhaust
1970–72	1.791–1.7918 (45.5–45.52)	1.476–1.4768 (37.5–37.52)
1973		
Standard	1.732–1.734 (43.987–44.003)	1.456–1.458 (36.980–37.036)
Service	1.749–1.751 (44.433–44.487)	1.476–1.478 (37.480–37.536)
1974–82		
Standard	1.7323–1.7329 ① (44.0–44.016)	1.4567–1.4573 (37.0–37.016)
Service	1.7520–1.7526 ② (44.5–44.516)	1.4764–1.4770 (37.5–37.516)

① For 1975–80 1.7717–1.7723 (45.000–45.016)
② For 1977–80 1.7913–1.7920 (45.50–45.516)

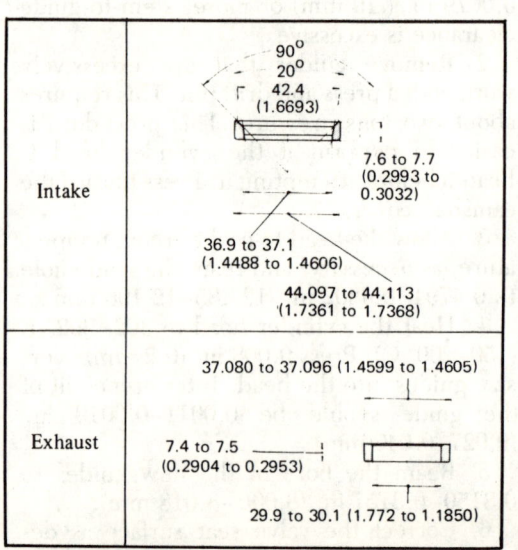

Intake — 90°, 20°, 42.4 (1.6693)
- 7.6 to 7.7 (0.2993 to 0.3032)
- 36.9 to 37.1 (1.4488 to 1.4606)
- 44.097 to 44.113 (1.7361 to 1.7368)

Exhaust
- 37.080 to 37.096 (1.4599 to 1.4605)
- 7.4 to 7.5 (0.2904 to 0.2953)
- 29.9 to 30.1 (1.772 to 1.1850)

Valve seat dimensions in mm for 1973 engines (inches in parentheses)

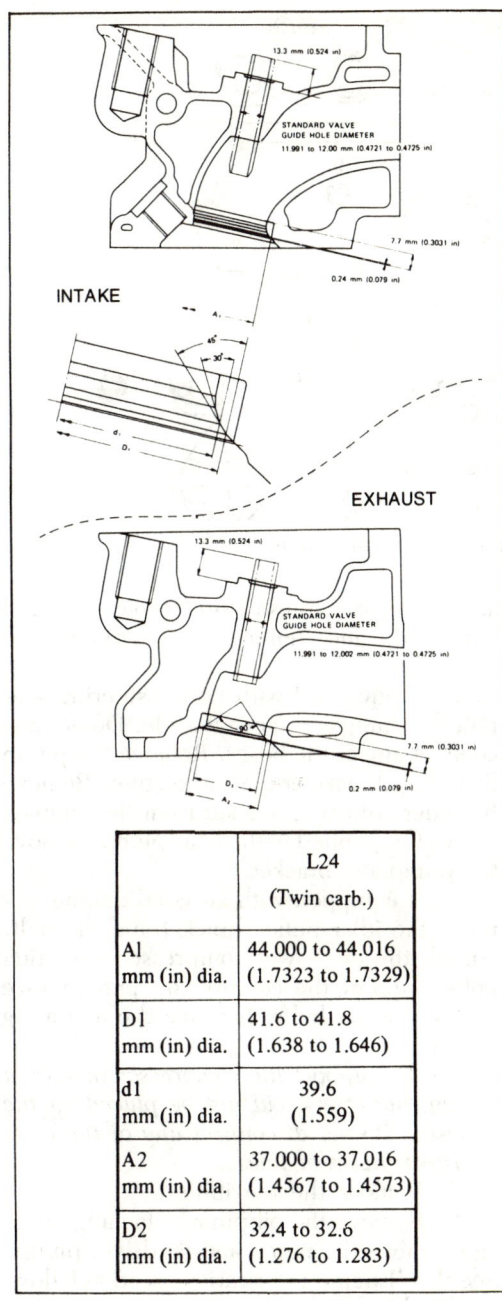

ENGINE AND ENGINE REBUILDING

Valve seat dimensions for 1972 and earlier engines

	L24 (Twin carb.)
A1 mm (in) dia.	44.000 to 44.016 (1.7323 to 1.7329)
D1 mm (in) dia.	41.6 to 41.8 (1.638 to 1.646)
d1 mm (in) dia.	39.6 (1.559)
A2 mm (in) dia.	37.000 to 37.016 (1.4567 to 1.4573)
D2 mm (in) dia.	32.4 to 32.6 (1.276 to 1.283)

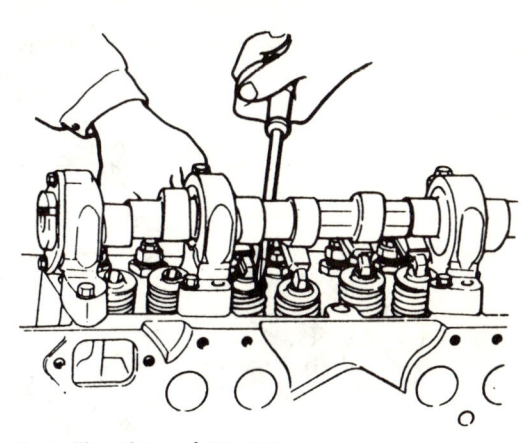

Installing the rocker arms

INSPECTION

Inspect the pivot head, cam and pivot contact surfaces for damage or excessive wear. If wear is excessive, the faulty parts should be replaced. Whenever the pivot is defective, replace the rocker arm also.

Intake and Exhaust Manifolds

REMOVAL AND INSTALLATION

NOTE: *It is important to replace the gasket whenever either manifold is removed. Because the manifolds share a common gasket, it is necessary to remove both manifolds for access to the gasket. Be sure to get the correct replacement gasket for your car. 1979–82 models have square exhaust ports, instead of the round ports used on 1970–78 models. The gaskets are not interchangeable.*

1. Disconnect the air and vacuum hoses from the air cleaner. Disconnect the hose linking the balance tube and the temperature sensor at the balance tube end, on carbureted models.
2. Remove the air cleaner.
3. On carbureted models: disconnect the coolant, air, vacuum, and fuel hoses from the intake manifold and carburetors (drain enough coolant from the bottom of the radiator to perform this without losing coolant). Remove the carburetors from the manifold. Disconnect the rear coolant inlet pipe and the exhaust gas inlet tube at the manifold. Remove the air conditioner fast idle mechanism and bracket from the manifold, if equipped. Remove the securing nut and disconnect the coolant tube from the balance tube.
4. On fuel injected models: relieve fuel

the pivot by screwing it down into the cylinder head, and remove the rocker arm by pressing down on the valve spring.

3. To remove the rocker pivots, loosen the locknut, then unscrew the pivot from the cylinder head.
4. Install the pivots and rockers in the reverse order of removal.

ENGINE AND ENGINE REBUILDING

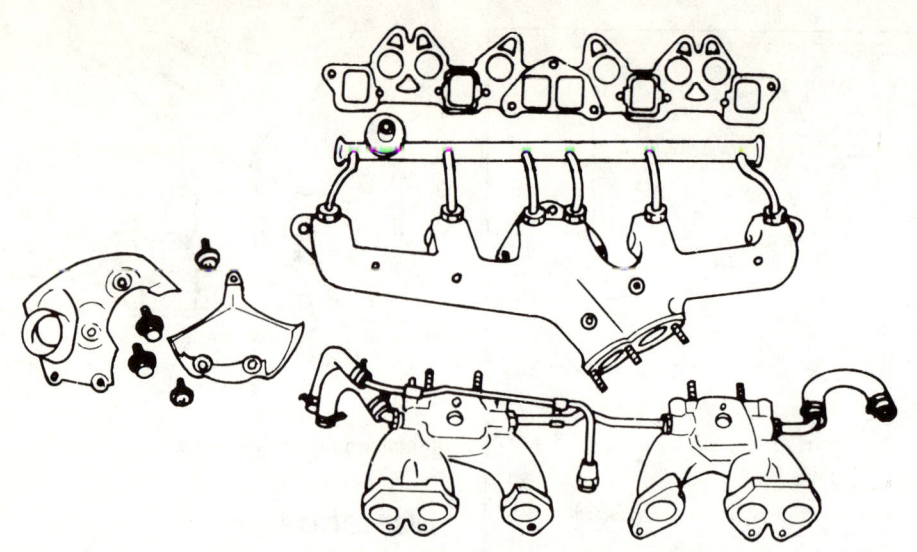

Intake and exhaust manifolds—carbureted models

line pressure as outlined in the fuel filter replacement procedure in Chapter 1. Disconnect the fuel injection wiring harness. Disconnect the hose from the rocker cover to the throttle chamber at the rocker cover. Drain the coolant into a clean container. Disconnect the coolant hose which runs from the heater to the coolant inlet at the inlet. Remove the bolt securing the coolant pipe/fuel pipe to the cylinder head. Remove the tube connecting the heater to the thermostat housing. Disconnect the fuel lines.

5. Disconnect the vacuum hose to the EGR valve, and the EGR tube from the exhaust manifold.

6. On models with an air pump, disconnect the air injection hose from the air injection gallery on the exhaust manifold at the check valve.

7. Disconnect the exhaust pipe from the exhaust manifold or from the exhaust outlet of the turbocharger if so equipped. Remove the exhaust manifold heat shield.

8. Remove the intake and exhaust manifolds.

9. Install the manifolds in the reverse order of removal. Always use a new gasket; air leaks will cause burnt valves and misfiring. Tighten the manifold bolts from the center outwards, in two progressive steps, to the proper torque.

Timing Cover

REMOVAL AND INSTALLATION

1. Disconnect the negative battery cable. Drain the coolant, remove the radiator hoses and automatic transmission cooler lines, if equipped, and remove the radiator and shroud.

2. If equipped with power steering, unbolt the pump and move it aside. Do not disconnect any of the hoses. Remove the pump mounting bracket from the engine. Remove the idler adjusting bracket from the engine.

3. If equipped with an air pump, remove the pump and bracket.

4. If equipped with air conditioning, remove the idler pulley bracket and the belt. Unbolt the two lower compressor mounting bolts, support the compressor, and remove the two upper bolts. Remove the mounting bracket.

NOTE: *Support the compressor in such a way that stress will not be placed on the hoses. Do not disconnect any of the compressor hoses or lines.*

5. Remove the distributor.

6. Remove the oil pump attaching bolts, and remove the pump and its drive spindle. See the "Engine Lubrication" section following for details.

7. Remove the engine cooling fan and pulley, together with the drive belt.

8. Remove the water pump.

9. Remove the crankshaft pulley bolt and remove the pulley. You will have to lock up the engine to do this. The best way is to remove the flywheel inspection cover between the engine and transmission and lock the flywheel with a tool made for the purpose. These are available in auto parts stores.

10. Remove the bolts holding the front cover to the front of the cylinder block, the

ENGINE AND ENGINE REBUILDING

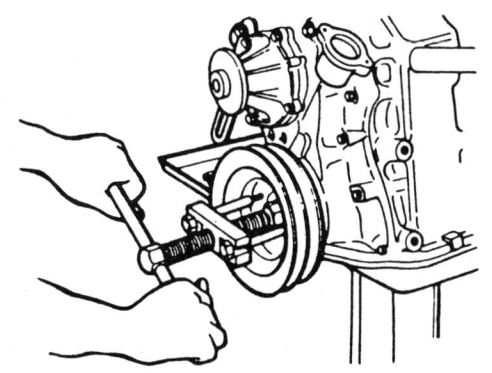

Remove the crankshaft pulley with a puller

four bolts which retain the front of the oil pan to the bottom of the front cover, and the two bolts which are screwed down through the front of the cylinder head into the top of the front cover.

11. Carefully pry the front cover off the engine.

12. Cut the exposed front section of the oil pan gasket away from the oil pan. Do the same to the gasket at the top of the front cover. Remove the two side gaskets and clean all the mating surfaces thoroughly.

13. Cut the portions needed from a new oil pan gasket and top front cover gasket.

14. Apply sealer to all of the gaskets and position them on the engine in their proper places.

15. Apply a light coating of oil to the crankshaft oil seal and carefully mount the front cover to the engine. Install all of the mounting bolts.

Tighten the 8 mm bolts to 7–12 ft lbs, and the 6 mm bolts to 3–6 ft lbs. Tighten the oil pan attaching bolts to 4–7 ft lbs.

16. Before installing the oil pump, place the gasket over the shaft and make sure that the mark on the drive spindle faces (is aligned with) the oil pump hole. Install the

APPLY SEALANT AT THESE POINTS

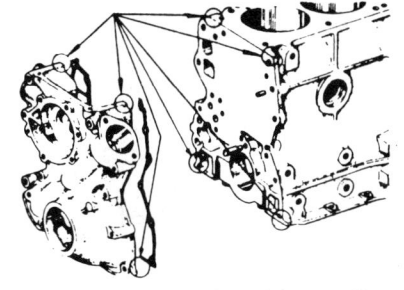

Apply sealant to the timing cover at the points shown

oil pump so that the projection on the top of the shaft is located in the exact position as when it was removed, or is in the 11:25 o'clock position with the piston in the No. 1 cylinder placed at TDC on the compression stroke, if the engine was disturbed since disassembly. This will ensure proper distributor timing.

Tighten the oil pump attaching bolts to 8–10 ft lbs. See "Oil Pump Removal and Installation."

17. The rest of installation is the reverse of removal.

Oil Seal

1. Remove the front cover.

2. Pry the old seal from the cover with a pointed piece of plastic or wood. A plastic knitting needle makes a perfect removal tool. Do not use a screwdriver, or other metal tool, which will damage the sealing lip.

3. Oil the lip of the new seal. Do not use grease. Press the seal into place, making sure the flat side faces forward and the lip faces the front of the engine. Use a seal driver made for the purpose, if possible, or a socket of the proper diameter.

4. Oil the crankshaft and the newly installed seal, and install the front cover.

Timing Chain and Tensioner

REMOVAL AND INSTALLATION

1. Before beginning any disassembly procedures, position the No. 1 piston at TDC on the compression stroke.

2. Remove the front cover. Remove the camshaft cover.

3. With the No. 1 piston at TDC, the timing marks on the camshaft sprocket and the timing chain should be visible. Mark both of them with paint. Also mark the relationship of the camshaft sprocket to the camshaft. At this point you will see that there are three sets of timing marks and locating holes in the sprocket. They are for making adjustments to compensate for timing chain stretch. See the "Timing Chain Adjustment" section following for details.

4. With the timing marks on the cam sprocket clearly marked, locate and mark the timing marks on the crankshaft sprocket. Also mark the chain timing mark. Of course, if the chain is not to be reused, marking it is useless.

5. Unbolt the camshaft sprocket and remove the sprocket along with the chain. As

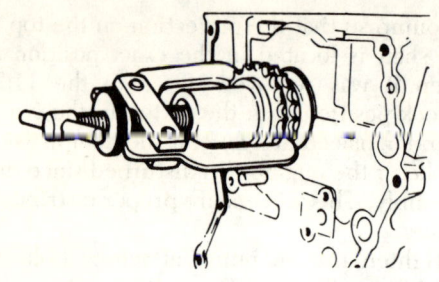

86 ENGINE AND ENGINE REBUILDING

The crankshaft sprocket can be removed with a puller if necessary

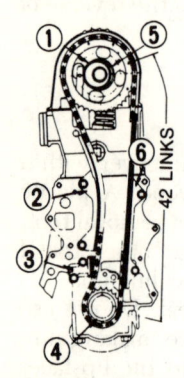

1. Fuel pump drive cam
2. Chain guide
3. Chain tensioner
4. Crank sprocket
5. Cam sprocket
6. Chain guide

Installing the timing chain. The number of "links" refers to the pins

you remove the chain, hold it where the chain tensioner contacts it. When the chain is removed, the tensioner is going to come apart. Hold on to it and you won't lose any of the parts.

The crankshaft sprocket can be removed with a puller, if necessary. There is no need to remove the chain guide unless it is being replaced.

6. Install the timing chain and the camshaft sprocket together after first positioning the chain over the crankshaft sprocket. Position the sprocket so that the marks made earlier line up. This is assuming that the engine has not been disturbed. The camshaft and the crankshaft keys should both be pointing upward. If a new chain and/or gear is being installed, position the sprocket so that the timing marks on the chain align with the marks on the sprocket (with both keys pointing up). The marks are on the right-hand side of the sprockets as you face the engine. When the chain is installed correctly, there will be 42 pins between the mating marks of the chain and sprockets on models through 1978. 1979 and later engines have two marked links which align with the marks on the sprockets, as an aid to proper timing. The factory refers to the pins as links, but in American terminology this is incorrect. Count the pins. There are two pins per chain link. This is an important step. If you do not get the exact number of pins between the timing marks, valve timing will be incorrect, and the engine will either not run at all or run very badly.

7. Install the chain tensioner. Adjust the protrusion of the chain tensioner spindle to zero clearance.

8. With a new seal installed in the front cover and a light coat of oil applied to the seal, assemble the remaining components of the engine in the reverse order of disassembly.

TIMING CHAIN ADJUSTMENT

When the timing chain stretches excessively, valve timing will be incorrect. There are three sets of holes and timing marks on the camshaft sprocket which are provided to correct the valve timing.

If the stretch of the chain roller links is excessive, adjust the camshaft sprocket location by transferring the camshaft set position of the camshaft sprocket from the factory position of No. 1 to No. 2 or 3 as follows:

1. Turn the crankshaft until the No. 1 piston is at TDC of the compression stroke. Check to see if the camshaft sprocket location notch is to the left of the oblong groove on the camshaft retaining plate. If the notch is to the left of the groove in the retaining plate, then the chain is stretched and needs to be adjusted.

2. Remove the camshaft sprocket together with the chain and install the sprocket and chain with the locating dowel on the camshaft inserted into either of the other two holes in the sprocket. Use No. 2 or No. 3 hole, depending on how badly the chain is stretched. If, for example, the chain stretch could be corrected by moving the sprocket to the No. 2 position, then the locating dowel on the camshaft would be inserted into the No. 2

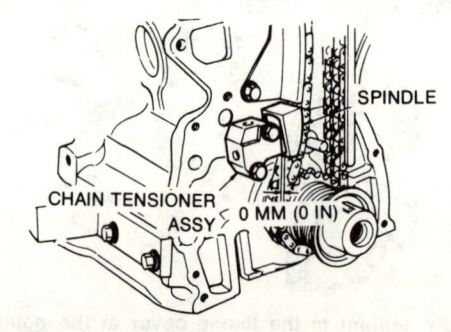

Installing the timing chain tensioner

ENGINE AND ENGINE REBUILDING 87

hole of the sprocket and the timing mark on the chain would be aligned with the No. 2 mark on the sprocket. The amount of modification for each location is 4° of crankshaft rotation.

3. Recheck the valve timing as outlined in Step 1 of this procedure. The notch in the sprocket should be to the right of the groove in the camshaft retaining plate.

4. If or when the notch cannot be brought to the right of the groove with the sprocket installed in the No. 3 hole, the timing chain must be replaced to gain the proper valve timing.

Camshaft

REMOVAL AND INSTALLATION

1. Remove the cylinder head.
2. For each valve rocker:
   a. Remove the valve rocker spring;
   b. Loosen the rocker pivot locknut, loosen the adjustment as far as possible, depress the valve spring, and remove the rocker.
3. Remove the camshaft locating plate.
4. Pull the camshaft slowly out toward the front of the head, being especially careful to avoid damaging the lobes and bearings.

To install the camshaft:
1. Coat the camshaft bearings and the cam lobes with clean motor oil. Carefully slide the camshaft in place in the camshaft carrier.
2. Install the camshaft locating plate with the groove in the upward position.
3. Install the cylinder head.

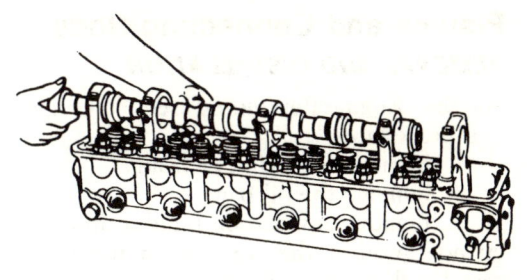

Installing the camshaft

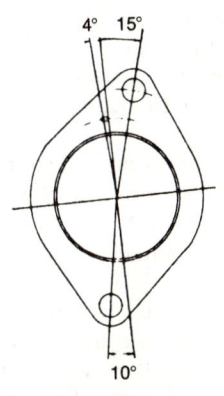

The camshaft locating plate

4. Install the camshaft drive sprocket in the same position.
5. Install the valve rockers.

NOTE: *The camshaft may be removed with the head in place, if you wish. First, remove the radiator and the hood. Then follow all instructions, including preliminary cylinder head removal procedures. Be especially careful not to disturb the timing.*

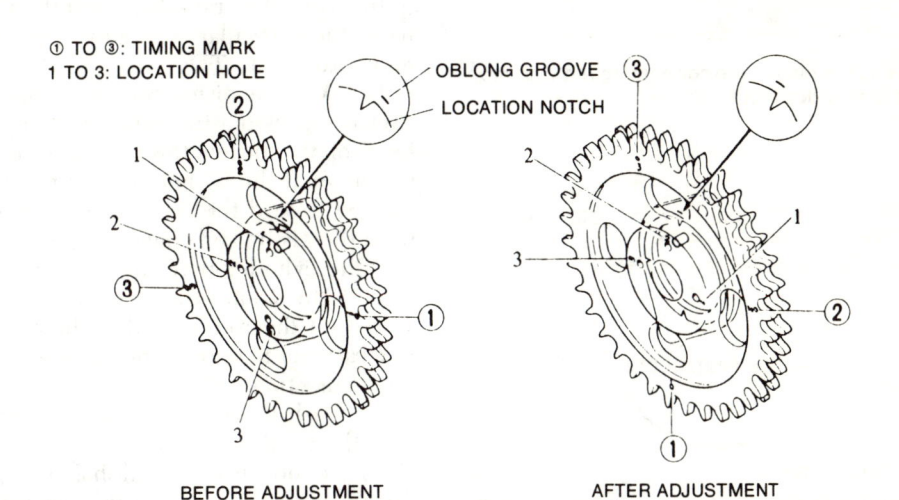

① TO ③: TIMING MARK
1 TO 3: LOCATION HOLE

OBLONG GROOVE
LOCATION NOTCH

BEFORE ADJUSTMENT   AFTER ADJUSTMENT

Adjusting the camshaft sprocket location

ENGINE AND ENGINE REBUILDING

Pistons and Connecting Rods

REMOVAL AND INSTALLATION

See the "Engine Rebuilding" section for general procedures.

1. Remove the cylinder head.
2. Remove the oil pan.
3. Remove any carbon buildup from the cylinder wall at the top end of the piston travel with a ridge reamer tool.
4. Position the piston to be removed at the bottom of its stroke so that the connecting rod bearing cap can be reached easily from under the engine.
5. Unscrew the connecting rod bearing cap and remove the cap and lower half of the bearing.
6. Push the piston and connecting rod up and out of the cylinder block with a length of wood. Use care not to scratch the cylinder wall with the connecting rod or the wooden tool.
7. Keep all of the components from each cylinder together and install them in the cylinder from which they were removed.
8. Coat the bearing face of the connecting rod and the outer face of the pistons with engine oil.
9. On engines through 1978, turn the top compression ring to bring its gap to about the 1:30 o'clock position. Set the remaining rings so that their gaps are positioned 180° apart around the piston. The oil ring gap will be directly under the top compression ring gap.

On 1979 and later engines, set the top ring gap at the 1:00 o'clock position. Position the second ring gap 180° opposite the top ring gap. The top oil ring rail gap should then be placed under the top ring gap, the expander ring should be at the 3:00 o'clock position, and the bottom oil ring rail gap should be under the second ring gap. See the illustration for details.

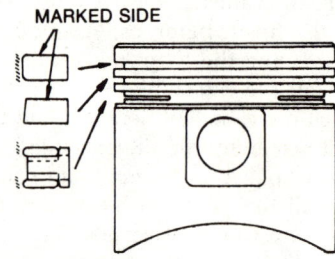

Arrangement of the piston ring gaps around the piston, 1979 and later

Removing the piston and connecting rod assembly from the cylinder block

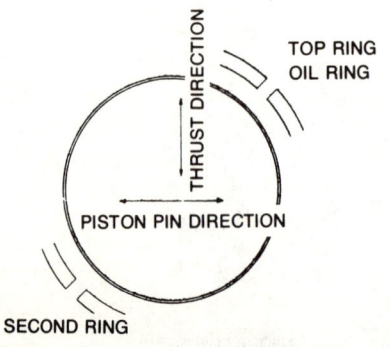

Piston ring installation

Arrangement of the piston ring gaps around the piston through 1978

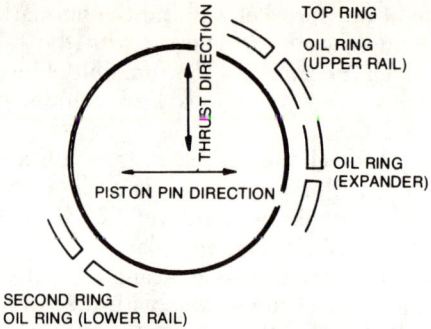

10. Turn the crankshaft until the rod journal of the particular cylinder you are working on is brought to TDC.
11. With the piston and rings clamped in a ring compressor, the notched mark on the head of the piston toward the front of the engine, and the oil hole side of the connecting rod toward the right side of the engine, push the piston and connecting rod assembly into the cylinder bore until the big bearing end of the connecting rod contacts and is seated on the rod journal of the crankshaft. Use care not to scratch the cylinder wall with the connecting rod.
12. Push down farther on the piston and turn the crankshaft while the connecting rod rides around on the crankshaft rod journal. Turn the crankshaft until the crankshaft rod journal is at BDC (bottom dead center).

ENGINE AND ENGINE REBUILDING

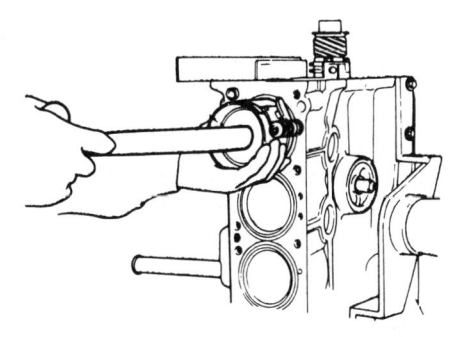

Installing the piston and connecting rod

13. Align the mark on the connecting rod bearing cap with that on the connecting rod and tighten the bearing cap bolts to the specified torque.

14. Install all of the piston/connecting rod assemblies in the manner outlined above and assemble the oil pan and cylinder head to the engine in the reverse order of removal.

IDENTIFICATION AND POSITIONING

The pistons are marked with a notch in the piston head. When installed in the engine, the notch markings are to be facing toward the front of the engine.

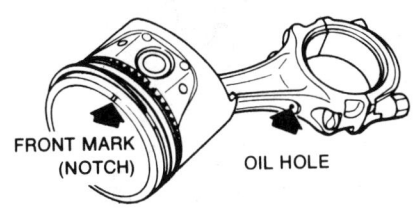

Piston and connecting rod identification and positioning

The connecting rods are installed in the engine with the oil hole facing toward the right side of the engine.

NOTE: *It is advisable to number the pistons, connecting rods, and bearing caps in some manner so that they can be reinstalled in the same cylinder, facing the same direction, from which they are removed.*

ENGINE LUBRICATION

Oil Pan

REMOVAL AND INSTALLATION

1. If the engine is in the vehicle, attach a lift, support the engine, and remove the engine mounting bolts as described in "Engine Removal and Installation".

2. Raise the engine just slightly, watching to make sure that no hoses or wires are damaged.

3. Drain the engine oil.

4. Remove the oil pan bolts and slide the pan out to the rear.

To install the pan:

1. Use a new gasket, coated on both sides with sealer.

2. Apply a thin bead of silicone seal to the engine block at the junction of the block and front cover, and the junction of the block and main bearing cap. Then apply a thin coat of silicone seal to the new oil pan gasket, install the gasket to the block and install the pan.

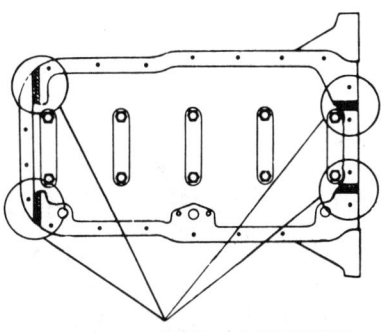

Apply a thin bead of silicone seal to these areas before installing the oil pan gasket on the block

3. Tighten the pan bolts in a circular pattern from the center to the ends, to 4–7 ft lbs. Overtightening will distort the pan lip, causing leakage.

4. Reinstall engine mounting bolts as described under "Engine Removal and Installation," using the specified torque and maintaining support until all mounts are secure.

5. Refill the oil pan to the specified level.

Rear Main Oil Seal

REPLACEMENT

In order to replace the rear main oil seal, the rear main bearing cap must be removed. Removal of the rear main bearing cap requires the use of a special rear main bearing cap puller. Also, the oil seal is installed with a special crankshaft rear oil seal drift. Unless these or similar tools are available to you, it is recommended that the oil seal be replaced by a Datsun service center.

1. Remove the engine and transmission from the car.

ENGINE AND ENGINE REBUILDING

2. Separate the transmission from the engine.
3. Remove the clutch from the flywheel (manual transmissions only).
4. Remove the flywheel from the crankshaft.

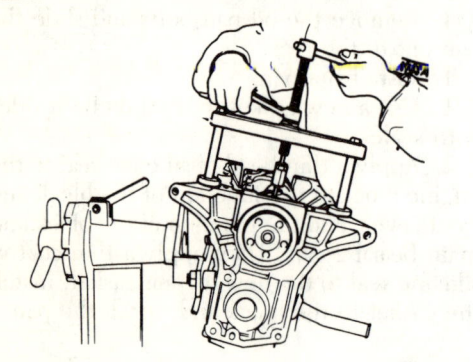

Removing the rear main bearing cap with a puller

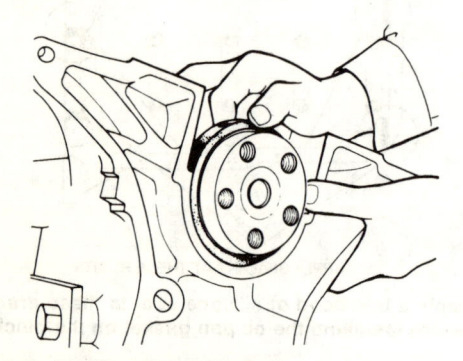

Removing the rear main seal

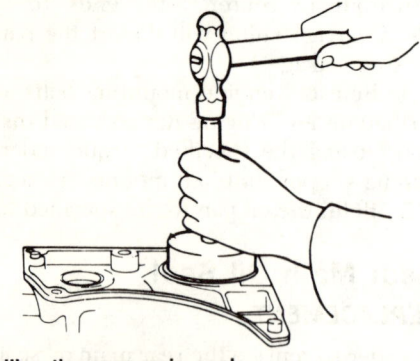

Installing the rear main seal

5. Remove the rear main bearing cap using a special tool made for the purpose. Remove the bearing cap side seals.
6. Remove the rear main oil seal from around the crankshaft.
7. Apply oil to the sealing lip of the oil seal and install the seal around the crankshaft.

8. Apply sealer to the rear main bearing cap as indicated in the illustration. Install the cap and tighten the bolts evenly in three stages to 33–40 ft lbs.
9. Apply sealant to the rear main bearing cap side seals and install the side seals, driving the seals into place with a drift.
10. Assemble the engine and install in the car.

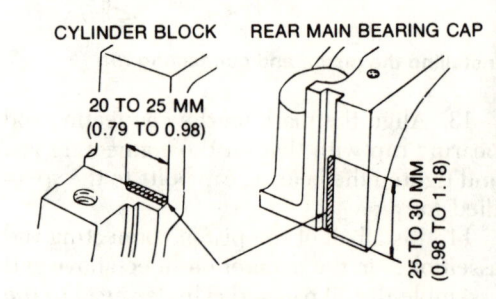

Application of sealer to the rear main bearing cap

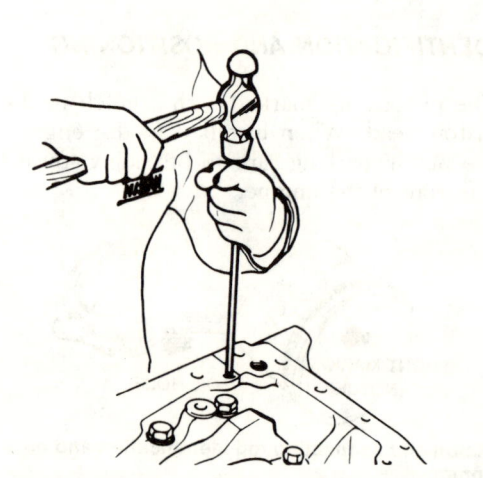

Installing the rear main bearing cap side seals

Oil Pump

REMOVAL AND INSTALLATION

1970–79

1. Turn the engine over until the No. 1 cylinder is at TDC on the compression stroke.
2. Drain the oil pan. Remove the splash shield if so equipped.
3. Remove high-tension wires, and unbolt and remove the distributor.
4. Remove the four pump bolts, and pull the oil pump out.

To install:
1. Replace the oil pump gasket. Fill the pump housing with clean engine oil.
2. Align the drive pump hole and spindle

ENGINE AND ENGINE REBUILDING

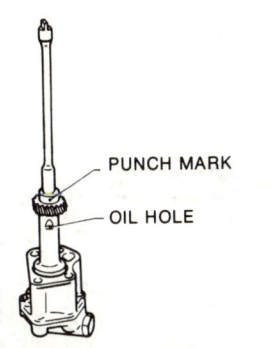

Lining up the marks on the oil pump and the distributor drive spindle

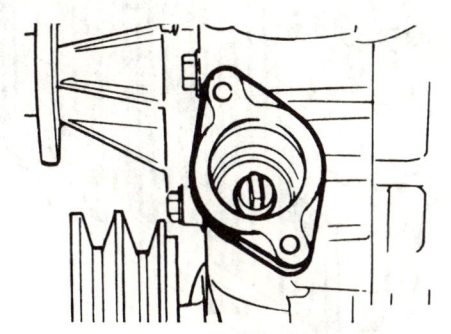

Proper alignment of the distributor drive spindle

mark by turning the spindle. Then, turn the spindle one gear tooth to the right.

3. Install the pump with the mounting bolts, torquing them to 8.0–10.8 ft lbs (1.1–1.5 kg-m).
4. The projection on top of the spindle should now be at the 11:25 o'clock position, with the smaller half of the spindle facing forward.
5. Reinstall the splash shield.
6. Refill the oil pan to the specified level.
7. Reinstall the distributor, carefully rotating the rotor back-and-forth until the bottom of the distributor shaft engages the projection on top of the oil pump spindle. Install mounting bolts.

1980 and Later

1. Drain the oil from the oil pan.
2. Turn the crankshaft so that the No. 1 piston is at top dead center on its compression stroke.
3. Remove the distributor cap and mark the position of the distributor rotor in relation to the distributor base with a piece of chalk.
4. Remove the front stabilizer bar, if so equipped.
5. Remove the splash shield.
6. Remove the oil pump body with the drive spindle assembly.
7. To install, fill the pump housing with engine oil, align the punch mark on the spindle with the hole in the oil pump. The No. 1 piston should be at top dead center (TDC) on its compression stroke.
8. With a new gasket placed over the drive spindle, install the oil pump and drive spindle assembly, making sure the tip of the drive spindle fits into the distributor shaft notch securely. The distributor rotor should be pointing to the match mark you made earlier.
NOTE: *Great care must be taken not to disturb the distributor rotor while installing the oil pump, or the ignition timing may be wrong.*
9. Assemble the remaining components in the reverse order of removal.

ENGINE COOLING

Radiator

REMOVAL AND INSTALLATION

1. Drain the radiator coolant by opening the drain cock at the bottom. Removal of the pressure cap will speed the process.
2. Disconnect the upper and lower hoses at the radiator.
3. On air conditioned models, unbolt the lower radiator shroud and remove it from underneath.
4. On automatic transmission equipped cars, disconnect both transmission cooler lines and cap them.
5. Remove the radiator mounting bolts and remove it (and shroud) by pulling it upward and out of the compartment.

To install the radiator, reverse these procedures. Refill both radiator and transmission to the specified levels. Operate the engine and continue filling radiator to the proper level until all air bubbles are expelled.

Water Pump

REMOVAL AND INSTALLATION

1. Drain the radiator coolant through the lower drain cock.
2. Remove the fan shroud mounting bolts and remove the shroud.
3. Loosen and then remove the fan belt.
4. Remove the fan and pulley from the water pump hub.

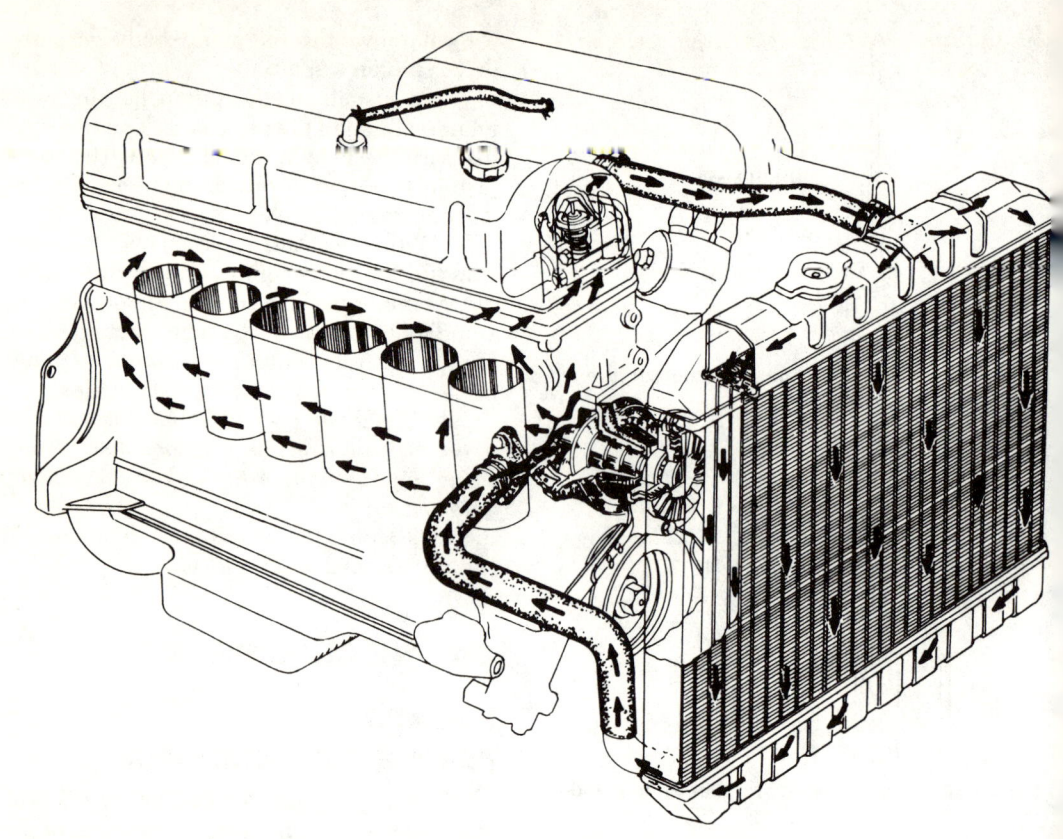

ENGINE AND ENGINE REBUILDING

Cooling system flow diagram—260-Z; others similar

5. Remove the pump and gasket.

To install, first clean all traces of old gasket material from both surfaces and install a new gasket coated with sealer.

Then, reverse the removal procedure. Finally, refill the radiator with the engine idling to remove all air bubbles.

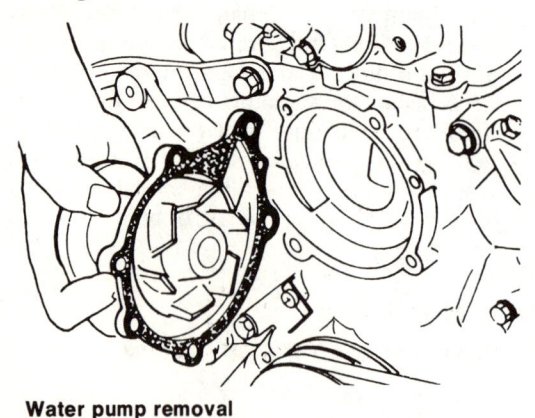

Water pump removal

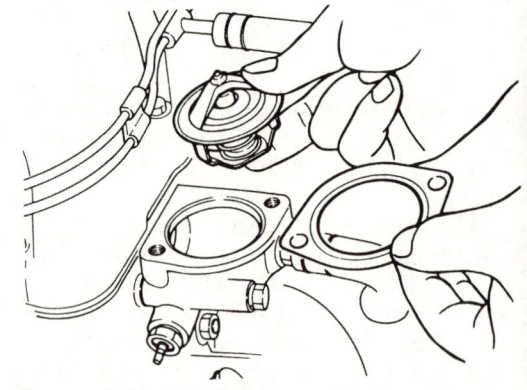

Thermostat installation; the spring faces down

Thermostat

The factory-installed thermostat opening temperature is 180° F (82° C) for cars sold in the U.S., 190° F (88° C) for cars sold in Canada.

REMOVAL AND INSTALLATION

1. Drain the radiator coolant through the lower drain cock.
2. Disconnect the upper radiator hose at the water outlet.
3. Loosen the mounting bolts and remove the water outlet, gasket, and thermostat.

To install the thermostat, reverse the above procedures. Install the thermostat with the wax pellet downward and use a new water outlet gasket coated with scaler. 1979 and later models use a thermostat with an air bleed hole in the flange. The thermostat should be installed with the hole facing the left side of the engine. If it is necessary to replace the thermostat, be sure the new one has a bleed hole.

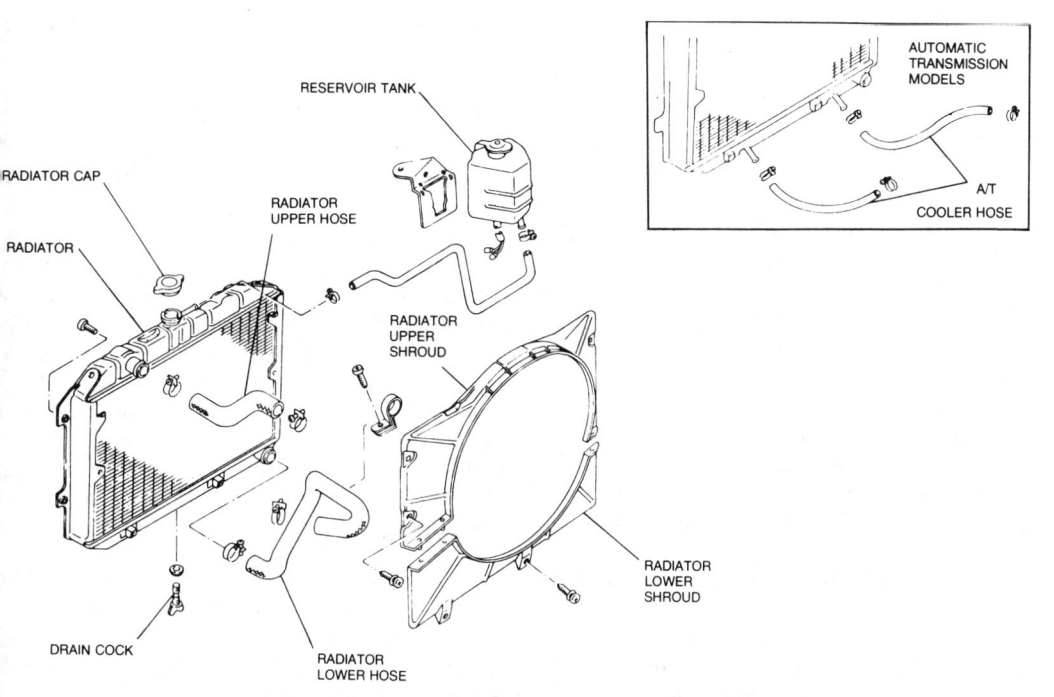

Radiator installation details, ZX models; Z series similar

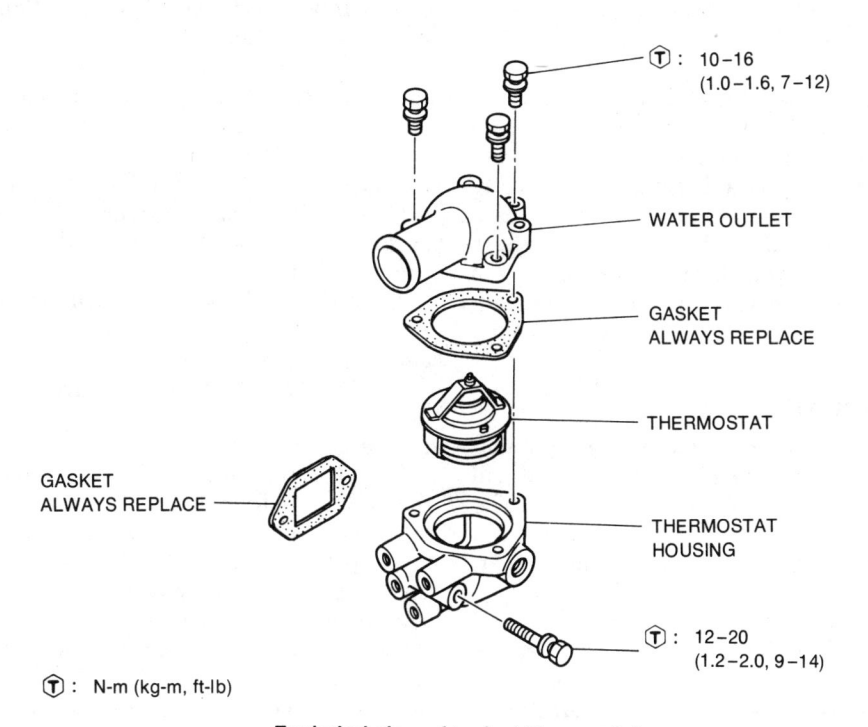

⊤ : N-m (kg-m, ft-lb)

Exploded view of typical Thermostat

ENGINE REBUILDING

Most procedures involved in rebuilding an engine are fairly standard, regardless of the type of engine involved. This section is a guide to accepted rebuilding procedures. Examples of standard rebuilding practices are illustrated and should be used along with specific details concerning your particular engine, found earlier in this chapter.

The procedures given here are those used by any competent rebuilder. Obviously some of the procedures cannot be performed by the do-it-yourself mechanic, but are provided so that you will be familiar with the services that should be offered by rebuilding or machine shops. As an example, in most instances, it is more profitable for the home mechanic to remove the cylinder heads, buy the necessary parts (new valves, seals, keepers, keys, etc.) and deliver these to a machine shop for the necessary work. In this way you will save the money to remove and install the cylinder head and the mark-up on parts.

On the other hand, most of the work involved in rebuilding the lower end is well within the scope of the do-it-yourself mechanic. Only work such as hot-tanking, actually boring the block or Magnafluxing (invisible crack detection) need be sent to a machine shop.

Tools

The tools required for basic engine rebuilding should, with a few exceptions, be those included in a mechanic's tool kit. An accurate torque wrench, and a dial indicator (reading in thousandths) mounted on a universal base should be available. Special tools, where required, are available from the major tool suppliers. The services of a competent automotive machine shop must also be readily available.

Precautions

Aluminum has become increasingly popular for use in engines, due to its low weight and excellent heat transfer characteristics. The following precautions must be observed when handling aluminum (or any other) engine parts:
—Never hot-tank aluminum parts.
—Remove all aluminum parts (identification tags, etc.) from engine parts before hot-tanking (otherwise they will be removed during the process).
—Always coat threads lightly with engine oil or anti-seize compounds before installation to prevent seizure.
—Never over-torque bolts or spark plugs in aluminum threads. Should stripping occur, threads can be restored using any of a number of thread repair kits available (see next section).

Inspection Techniques

Magnaflux and Zyglo are inspection techniques used to locate material flaws, such as stress cracks. Magnaflux is a magnetic process, applicable only to ferrous materials. The Zyglo process coats the material with a fluorescent dye penetrant, and any material may be tested using Zyglo. Specific checks of suspected surface cracks may be made at lower cost and more readily using spot check dye. The dye is sprayed onto the suspected area, wiped off, and the area is then sprayed with a developer. Cracks then will show up brightly.

Overhaul

The section is divided into two parts. The first, Cylinder Head Reconditioning, assumes that the cylinder head is removed from the engine, all manifolds are removed, and the cylinder head is on a workbench. The camshaft should be removed from overhead cam cylinder heads. The second section, Cylinder Block Reconditioning, covers the block, pistons, connecting rods and crankshaft. It is assumed that the engine is mounted on a work stand, and the cylinder head and all accessories are removed.

Procedures are identified as follows:
Unmarked—Basic procedures that must be performed in order to successfully complete the rebuilding process.
Starred (*)—Procedures that should be performed to ensure maximum performance and engine life.
Double starred (**)—Procedures that may be performed to increase engine performance and reliability.

When assembling the engine, any parts that will be in frictional contact must be pre-lubricated, to provide protection on initial start-up. Any product specifically formulated for this purpose may be used. NOTE: *Do not use engine oil*. Where semi-permanent (locked but removable) installation of bolts or nuts is desired, threads should be cleaned and located with Loctite® or a similar product (non-hardening).

Repairing Damaged Threads

Several methods of repairing damaged threads are available. Heli-Coil® (shown here), Keenserts® and Microdot® are among the most widely used. All involve basically the same principle—drilling out stripped threads, tapping the hole and installing a pre-wound insert—making welding, plugging and oversize fasteners unnecessary.

Two types of thread repair inserts are usually supplied—a standard type for most Inch Coarse, Inch Fine, Metric Coarse and Metric Fine thread sizes and a spark plug type to fit most spark plug port sizes. Consult the individual manufacturer's catalog to determine exact applications. Typical thread repair kits will contain a selection of pre-wound threaded inserts, a tap (corresponding to the outside diameter threads of the insert) and an installation tool. Spark plug inserts usually differ because they require a tap equipped with pilot threads and a combined reamer/tap section. Most manufacturers also supply blister-packed thread repair inserts separately in addition to a master kit containing a variety of taps and inserts plus installation tools.

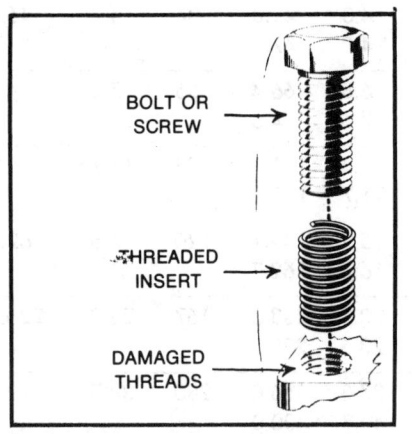

Before effecting a repair to a threaded hole, remove any snapped, broken or damaged bolts or studs. Penetrating oil can be used to free frozen threads; the offending item can be removed with locking pliers or with a screw or stud extractor. After the hole is clear, the thread can be repaired, as follows:

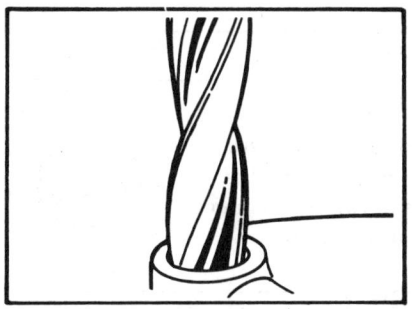

Drill out the damaged threads with specified drill. Drill completely through the hole or to the bottom of a blind hole

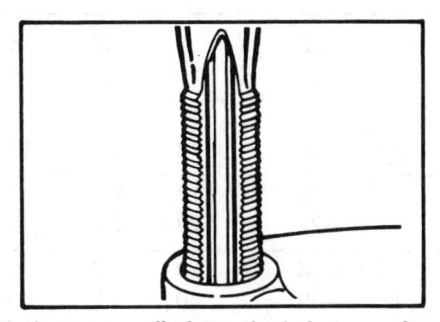

With the tap supplied, tap the hole to receive the thread insert. Keep the tap well oiled and back it out frequently to avoid clogging the threads

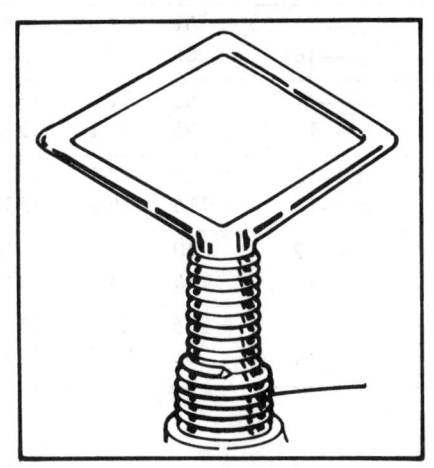

Damaged bolt holes can be repaired with thread repair inserts

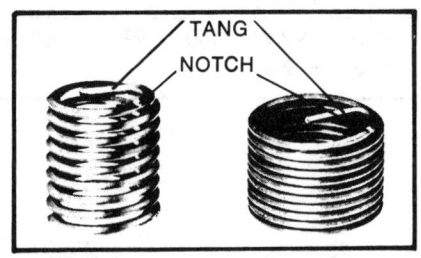

Standard thread repair insert (left) and spark plug thread insert (right)

Screw the threaded insert onto the installation tool until the tang engages the slot. Screw the insert into the tapped hole until it is ¼–½ turn below the top surface. After installation break off the tang with a hammer and punch

Standard Torque Specifications and Fastener Markings

The Newton-metre has been designated the world standard for measuring torque and will gradually replace the foot-pound and kilogram-meter. In the absence of specific torques, the following chart can be used as a guide to the maximum safe torque of a particular size/grade of fastener.

- There is no torque difference for fine or coarse threads.
- Torque values are based on clean, dry threads. Reduce the value by 10% if threads are oiled prior to assembly.
- The torque required for aluminum components or fasteners is considerably less.

U. S. BOLTS

SAE Grade Number	1 or 2			5			6 or 7		
Bolt Markings Manufacturer's marks may vary—number of lines always 2 less than the grade number.									
Usage	Frequent			Frequent			Infrequent		
Bolt Size (inches)—(Thread)	Maximum Torque			Maximum Torque			Maximum Torque		
	Ft-Lb	kgm	Nm	Ft-Lb	kgm	Nm	Ft-Lb	kgm	Nm
¼—20	5	0.7	6.8	8	1.1	10.8	10	1.4	13.5
—28	6	0.8	8.1	10	1.4	13.6			
5/16—18	11	1.5	14.9	17	2.3	23.0	19	2.6	25.8
—24	13	1.8	17.6	19	2.6	25.7			
3/8—16	18	2.5	24.4	31	4.3	42.0	34	4.7	46.0
—24	20	2.75	27.1	35	4.8	47.5			
7/16—14	28	3.8	37.0	49	6.8	66.4	55	7.6	74.5
—20	30	4.2	40.7	55	7.6	74.5			
½—13	39	5.4	52.8	75	10.4	101.7	85	11.75	115.2
—20	41	5.7	55.6	85	11.7	115.2			
9/16—12	51	7.0	69.2	110	15.2	149.1	120	16.6	162.7
—18	55	7.6	74.5	120	16.6	162.7			
5/8—11	83	11.5	112.5	150	20.7	203.3	167	23.0	226.5
—18	95	13.1	128.8	170	23.5	230.5			
¾—10	105	14.5	142.3	270	37.3	366.0	280	38.7	379.6
—16	115	15.9	155.9	295	40.8	400.0			
7/8— 9	160	22.1	216.9	395	54.6	535.5	440	60.9	596.5
—14	175	24.2	237.2	435	60.1	589.7			
1— 8	236	32.5	318.6	590	81.6	799.9	660	91.3	894.8
—14	250	34.6	338.9	660	91.3	849.8			

ENGINE AND ENGINE REBUILDING

METRIC BOLTS

NOTE: *Metric bolts are marked with a number indicating the relative strength of the bolt. These numbers have nothing to do with size.*

Description	Torque ft-lbs (Nm)	
Thread size x pitch (mm)	Head mark—4	Head mark—7
6 x 1.0	2.2–2.9 (3.0–3.9)	3.6–5.8 (4.9–7.8)
8 x 1.25	5.8–8.7 (7.9–12)	9.4–14 (13–19)
10 x 1.25	12–17 (16–23)	20–29 (27–39)
12 x 1.25	21–32 (29–43)	35–53 (47–72)
14 x 1.5	35–52 (48–70)	57–85 (77–110)
16 x 1.5	51–77 (67–100)	90–120 (130–160)
18 x 1.5	74–110 (100–150)	130–170 (180–230)
20 x 1.5	110–140 (150–190)	190–240 (160–320)
22 x 1.5	150–190 (200–260)	250–320 (340–430)
24 x 1.5	190–240 (260–320)	310–410 (420–550)

NOTE: *This engine rebuilding section is a guide to accepted rebuilding procedures. Typical examples of standard rebuilding procedures are illustrated. Use these procedures along with the detailed instructions earlier in this chapter, concerning your particular engine.*

Cylinder Head Reconditioning

Procedure	Method
Remove the cylinder head:	See the engine service procedures earlier in this chapter for details concerning specific engines.
Identify the valves:	Invert the cylinder head, and number the valve faces front to rear, using a permanent felt-tip marker.
Remove the camshaft:	See the engine service procedures earlier in this chapter for details concerning specific engines.
Remove the valves and springs:	Using an appropriate valve spring compressor (depending on the configuration of the cylinder head), compress the valve springs. Lift out the keepers with needlenose pliers, release the compressor, and remove the valve, spring, and spring retainer. See the engine service procedures earlier in this chapter for details concerning specific engines.
Check the valve stem-to-guide clearance:	Clean the valve stem with lacquer thinner or a similar solvent to remove all gum and varnish. Clean the valve guides using solvent and an expanding wire-type valve guide cleaner. Mount a dial indicator so that the stem is at 90° to the valve stem, as close to the valve guide as possible. Move the valve off its seat, and measure the valve guide-to-stem clearance by rocking the stem back and forth to actuate the dial indicator. Measure the valve stems using a micrometer, and compare to specifications, to determine whether stem or guide wear is responsible for excessive clearance. NOTE: *Consult the Specifications tables earlier in this chapter.*

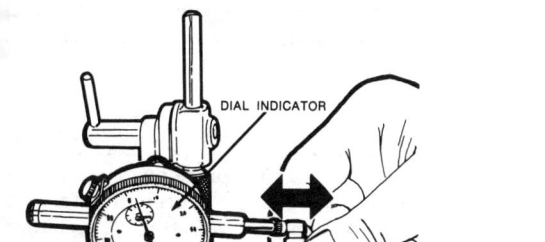

Check the valve stem-to-guide clearance

ENGINE AND ENGINE REBUILDING

Cylinder Head Reconditioning

Procedure	Method
De-carbon the cylinder head and valves: 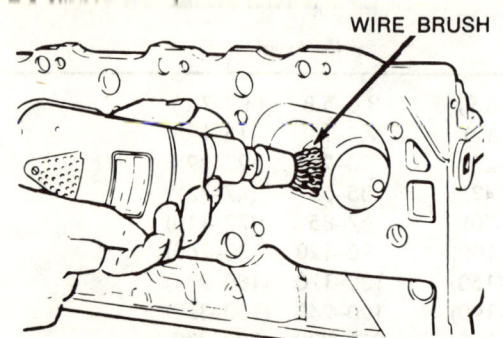 Remove the carbon from the cylinder head with a wire brush and electric drill	Chip carbon away from the valve heads, combustion chambers, and ports, using a chisel made of hardwood. Remove the remaining deposits with a stiff wire brush. *NOTE: Be sure that the deposits are actually removed, rather than burnished.*
Hot-tank the cylinder head (cast iron heads only): CAUTION: *Do not hot-tank aluminum parts.*	Have the cylinder head hot-tanked to remove grease, corrosion, and scale from the water passages. *NOTE: In the case of overhead cam cylinder heads, consult the operator to determine whether the camshaft bearings will be damaged by the caustic solution.*
Degrease the remaining cylinder head parts:	Clean the remaining cylinder head parts in an engine cleaning solvent. Do not remove the protective coating from the springs.
Check the cylinder head for warpage: 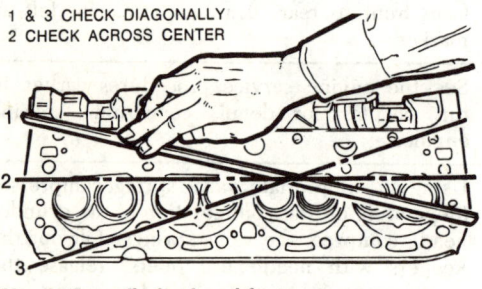 1 & 3 CHECK DIAGONALLY 2 CHECK ACROSS CENTER Check the cylinder head for warpage	Place a straight-edge across the gasket surface of the cylinder head. Using feeler gauges, determine the clearance at the center of the straight-edge. If warpage exceeds .003″ in a 6″ span, or .006″ over the total length, the cylinder head must be resurfaced. *NOTE: If warpage exceeds the manufacturer's maximum tolerance for material removal, the cylinder head must be replaced.* When milling the cylinder heads of V-type engines, the intake manifold mounting position is altered, and must be corrected by milling the manifold flange a proportionate amount.
*****Knurl the valve guides:** 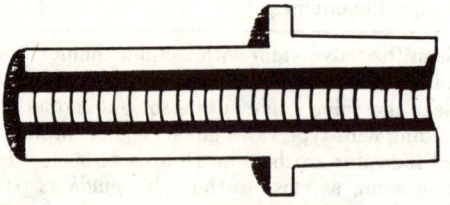 Cut-away view of a knurled valve guide	*****Valve guides which are not excessively worn or distorted may, in some cases, be knurled rather than replaced. Knurling is a process in which metal is displaced and raised, thereby reducing clearance. Knurling also provides excellent oil control. The possibility of knurling rather than replacing valve guides should be discussed with a machinist.
Replace the valve guides: NOTE: *Valve guides should only be replaced if damaged or if an oversize valve stem is not available.*	See the engine service procedures earlier in this chapter for details concerning specific engines. Depending on the type of cylinder head, valve guides may be pressed, hammered, or shrunk in. In cases where the guides are shrunk into the head, replacement should be left to an equipped machine shop. In other

ENGINE AND ENGINE REBUILDING

Cylinder Head Reconditioning

Procedure	Method
	cases, the guides are replaced using a stepped drift (see illustration). Determine the height above the boss that the guide must extend, and obtain a stack of washers, their I.D. similar to the guide's O.D., of that height. Place the stack of washers on the guide, and insert the guide into the boss. NOTE: *Valve guides are often tapered or beveled for installation.* Using the stepped installation tool (see illustration), press or tap the guides into position. Ream the guides according to the size of the valve stem.

A—VALVE GUIDE I.D. B—LARGER THAN THE VALVE GUIDE O.D.

WASHERS

A—VALVE GUIDE I.D. B—LARGER THAN THE VALVE GUIDE O.D.

Valve guide installation tool using washers for installation

Replace valve seat inserts:	Replacement of valve seat inserts which are worn beyond resurfacing or broken, if feasible, must be done by a machine shop.
Resurface (grind) the valve face:	Using a valve grinder, resurface the valves according to specifications given earlier in this chapter. CAUTION: *Valve face angle is not always identical to valve seat angle.* A minimum margin of 1/32″ should remain after grinding the valve. The valve stem top should also be squared and resurfaced, by placing the stem in the V-block of the grinder, and turning it while pressing lightly against the grinding wheel. NOTE: *Do not grind sodium filled exhaust valves on a machine. These should be hand lapped.*

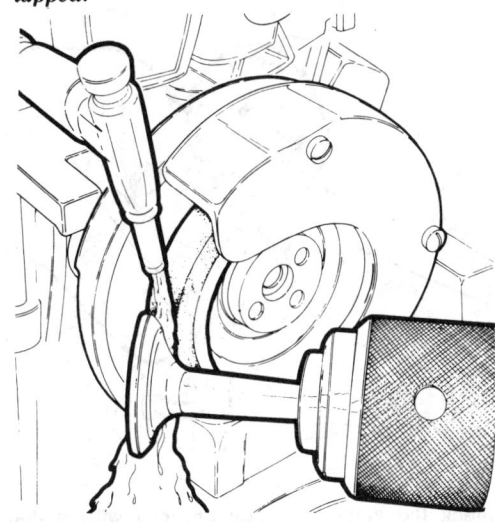

FOR DIMENSIONS, REFER TO SPECIFICATIONS

CHECK FOR BENT STEM

DIAMETER

VALVE FACE ANGLE

1/32″ MINIMUM

THIS LINE PARALLEL WITH VALVE HEAD

Critical valve dimensions

Valve grinding by machine

ENGINE AND ENGINE REBUILDING

Cylinder Head Reconditioning

Procedure	Method
Resurface the valve seats using reamers or grinder: *Valve seat width and centering* *Reaming the valve seat with a hand reamer*	Select a reamer of the correct seat angle, slightly larger than the diameter of the valve seat, and assemble it with a pilot of the correct size. Install the pilot into the valve guide, and using steady pressure, turn the reamer clockwise. **CAUTION:** *Do not turn the reamer counterclockwise.* Remove only as much material as necessary to clean the seat. Check the concentricity of the seat (following). If the dye method is not used, coat the valve face with Prussian blue dye, install and rotate it on the valve seat. Using the dye marked area as a centering guide, center and narrow the valve seat to specifications with correction cutters. **NOTE:** *When no specifications are available, minimum seat width for exhaust valves should be $5/64''$, intake valves $1/16''$.* After making correction cuts, check the position of the valve seat on the valve face using Prussian blue dye. To resurface the seat with a power grinder, select a pilot of the correct size and coarse stone of the proper angle. Lubricate the pilot and move the stone on and off the valve seat at 2 cycles per second, until all flaws are gone. Finish the seat with a fine stone. If necessary the seat can be corrected or narrowed using correction stones.
Check the valve seat concentricity: *Check the valve seat concentricity with a dial gauge*	Coat the valve face with Prussian blue dye, install the valve, and rotate it on the valve seat. If the entire seat becomes coated, and the valve is known to be concentric, the seat is concentric. *Install the dial gauge pilot into the guide, and rest of the arm on the valve seat. Zero the gauge, and rotate the arm around the seat. Run-out should not exceed .002″.

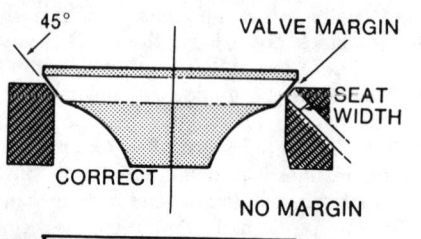

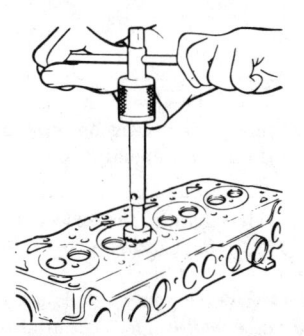

ENGINE AND ENGINE REBUILDING

Cylinder Head Reconditioning

Procedure	Method
*Lap the valves: NOTE: *Valve lapping is done to ensure efficient sealing of resurfaced valves and seats.*	Invert the cyclinder head, lightly lubricate the valve stems, and install the valves in the head as numbered. Coat valve seats with fine grinding compound, and attach the lapping tool suction cup to a valve head. NOTE: *Moisten the suction cup.* Rotate the tool between the palms, changing position and lifting the tool often to prevent grooving. Lap the valve until a smooth, polished seat is evident. Remove the valve and tool, and rinse away all traces of grinding compound.
	**Fasten a suction cup to a piece of drill rod, and mount the rod in a hand drill. Proceed as above, using the hand drill as a lapping tool. CAUTION: *Due to the higher speeds involved when using the hand drill, care must be exercised to avoid grooving the seat.* Lift the tool and change direction of rotation often.

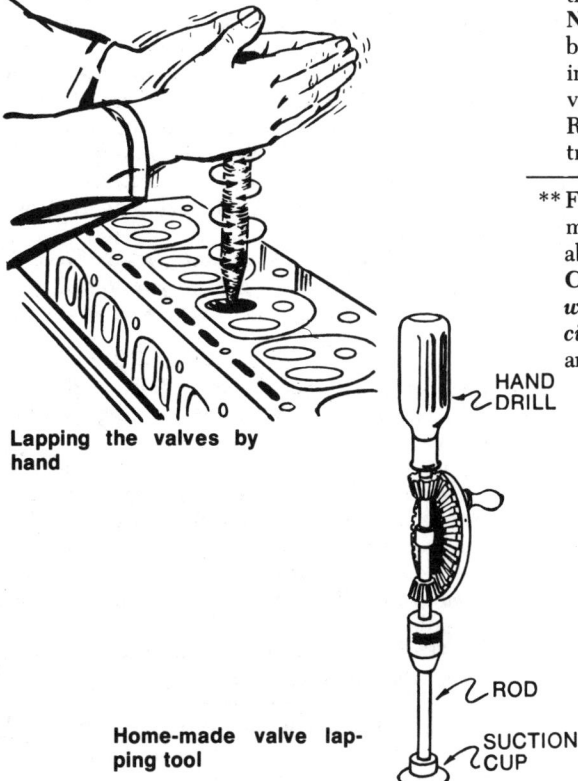

Lapping the valves by hand

Home-made valve lapping tool

Check the valve springs:	Place the spring on a flat surface next to a square. Measure the height of the spring, and rotate it against the edge of the square to measure distortion. If spring height varies (by comparison) by more than $1/16''$ or if distortion exceeds $1/16''$, replace the spring.
	**In addition to evaluating the spring as above, test the spring pressure at the installed and compressed (installed height minus valve lift) height using a valve spring tester. Springs used on small displacement engines (up to 3 liters) should be ∓ 1 lb of all other springs in either position. A tolerance of ∓ 5 lbs is permissible on larger engines.

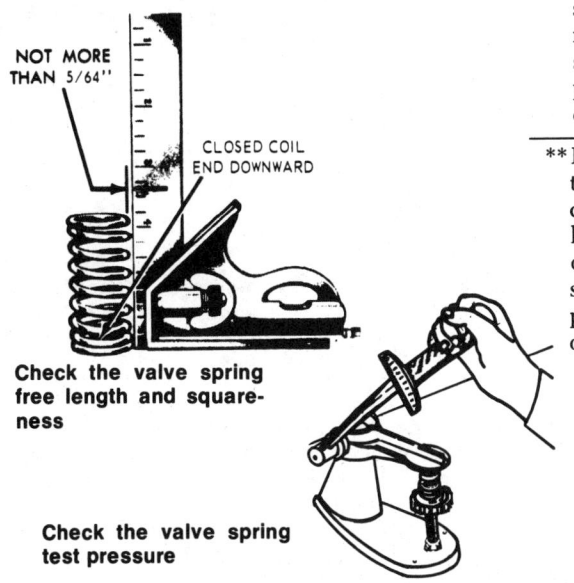

Check the valve spring free length and squareness

Check the valve spring test pressure

ENGINE AND ENGINE REBUILDING

Cylinder Head Reconditioning

Procedure	Method
*Install valve stem seals: *Install valve stem seals*	*Due to the pressure differential that exists at the ends of the intake valve guides (atmospheric pressure above, manifold vacuum below), oil is drawn through the valve guides into the intake port. This has been alleviated somewhat since the addition of positive crankcase ventilation, which lowers the pressure above the guides. Several types of valve stem seals are available to reduce blow-by. Certain seals simply slip over the stem and guide boss, while others require that the boss be machined. Recently, Teflon guide seals have become popular. Consult a parts supplier or machinist concerning availability and suggested usages. NOTE: *When installing seals, ensure that a small amount of oil is able to pass the seal to lubricate the valve guides; otherwise, excessive wear may result.*
Install the valves:	See the engine service procedures earlier in this chapter for details concerning specific engines. Lubricate the valve stems, and install the valves in the cylinder head as numbered. Lubricate and position the seals (if used) and the valve springs. Install the spring retainers, compress the springs, and insert the keys using needlenose pliers or a tool designed for this purpose. NOTE: *Retain the keys with wheel bearing grease during installation.*
Check valve spring installed height: *Valve spring installed height (A)*	Measure the distance between the spring pad the lower edge of the spring retainer, and compare to specifications. If the installed height is incorrect, add shim washers between the spring pad and the spring. CAUTION: *Use only washers designed for this purpose.* *Measure the valve spring installed height (A) with a modified steel rule*
Clean and inspect the camshaft:	Degrease the camshaft, using solvent, and clean out all oil holes. Visually inspect cam lobes and bearing journals for excessive wear. If a lobe is questionable, check all lobes as indicated below. If a journal or lobe is worn, the camshaft must be reground or replaced.

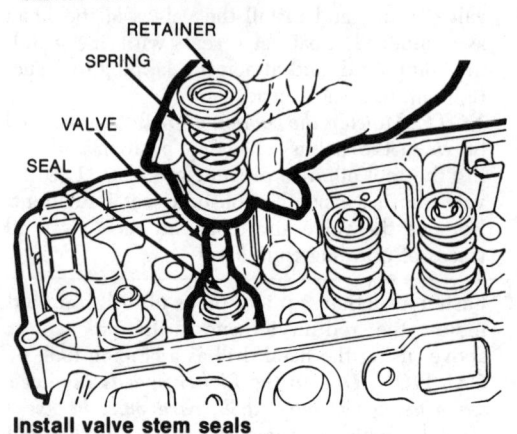

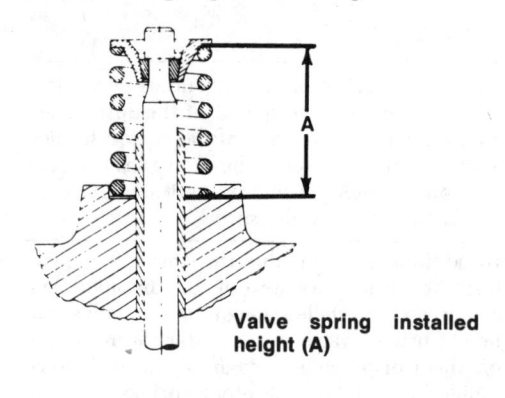

ENGINE AND ENGINE REBUILDING

Cylinder Head Reconditioning

Procedure	Method
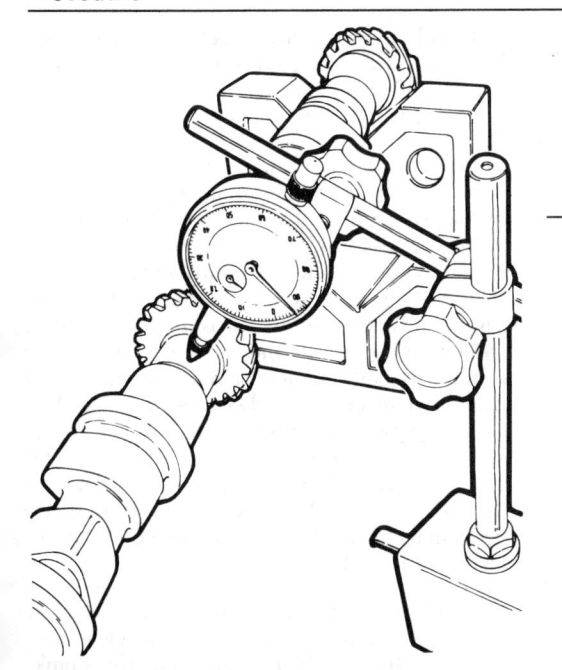	NOTE: *If a journal is worn, there is a good chance that the bushings are worn.* If lobes and journals appear intact, place the front and rear journals in V-blocks, and rest a dial indicator on the center journal. Rotate the camshaft to check straightness. If deviation exceeds .001″, replace the camshaft.
	*Check the camshaft lobes with a micrometer, by measuring the lobes from the nose to base and again at 90° (see illustration). The lift is determined by subtracting the second measurement from the first. If all exhaust lobes and all intake lobes are not identical, the camshaft must be reground or replaced.
Check the camshaft for straightness	Camshaft lobe measurement
Install the camshaft:	See the engine service procedures earlier in this chapter for details concerning specific engines.
Install the rocker arms:	See the engine service procedures earlier in this chapter for details concerning specific engines.

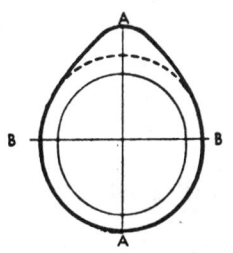

Cylinder Block Reconditioning

Procedure	Method
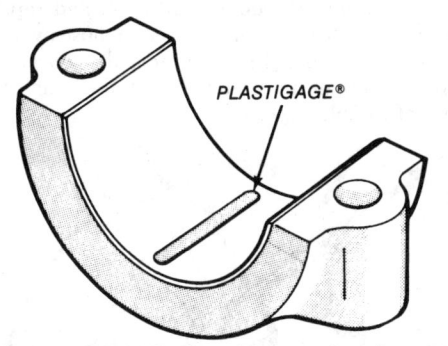 Checking the main bearing clearance:	Invert engine, and remove cap from the bearing to be checked. Using a clean, dry rag, thoroughly clean all oil from crankshaft journal and bearing insert. NOTE: *Plastigage® is soluble in oil; therefore, oil on the journal or bearing could result in erroneous readings.* Place a piece of Plastigage along the full length of journal, reinstall cap, and torque to specifications. NOTE: *Specifications are given in the engine specifications earlier in this chapter.* Remove bearing cap, and determine bearing clearance by comparing width of Plastigage to the scale on Plastigage envelope. Journal taper is determined by comparing width of the Plastigage strip near its ends. Rotate crankshaft 90° and retest, to determine journal eccentricity. NOTE: *Do not rotate crankshaft with Plastigage installed.* If bearing insert and journal appear in-
Plastigage® installed on the lower bearing shell	

ENGINE AND ENGINE REBUILDING

Cylinder Block Reconditioning

Procedure	Method
Measure Plastigage® to determine main bearing clearance	tact, and are within tolerances, no further main bearing service is required. If bearing or journal appear defective, cause of failure should be determined before replacement. * Remove crankshaft from block (see below). Measure the main bearing journals at each end twice (90° apart) using a micrometer, to determine diameter, journal taper and eccentricity. If journals are within tolerances, reinstall bearing caps at their specified torque. Using a telescope gauge and micrometer, measure bearing I.D. parallel to piston axis and at 30° on each side of piston axis. Subtract journal O.D. from bearing I.D. to determine oil clearance. If crankshaft journals appear defective, or do not meet tolerances, there is no need to measure bearings; for the crankshaft will require grinding and/or undersize bearings will be required. If bearing appears defective, cause for failure should be determined prior to replacement.
Check the connecting rod bearing clearance:	Connecting rod bearing clearance is checked in the same manner as main bearing clearance, using Plastigage. Before removing the crankshaft, connecting rod side clearance also should be measured and recorded. * Checking connecting rod bearing clearance, using a micrometer, is identical to checking main bearing clearance. If no other service is required, the piston and rod assemblies need not be removed.
Remove the crankshaft: **Match the connecting rod to the cylinder with a number stamp**	Using a punch, mark the corresponding main bearing caps and saddles according to position (i.e., one punch on the front main cap and saddle, two on the second, three on the third, etc.). Using number stamps, identify the corresponding connecting rods and caps, according to cylinder (if no numbers are present). Remove the main and connecting rod caps, and replace sleeves of plastic tubing or vacuum hose over the connecting rod bolts, to protect the journals as the crankshaft is removed. Lift the crankshaft out of the block. **Match the connecting rod and cap with scribe marks**

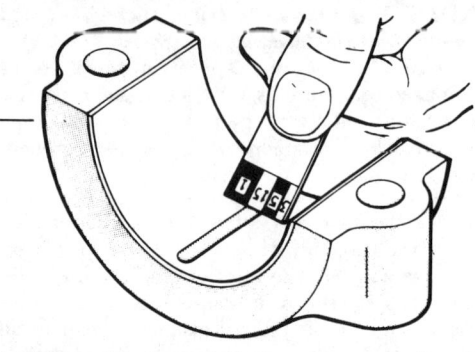

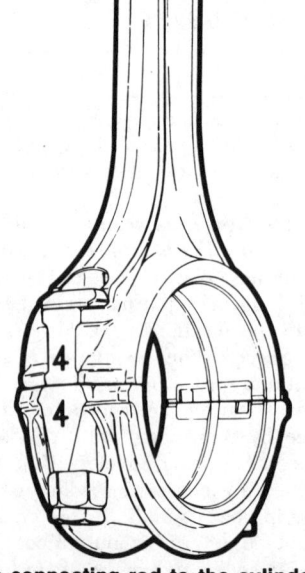

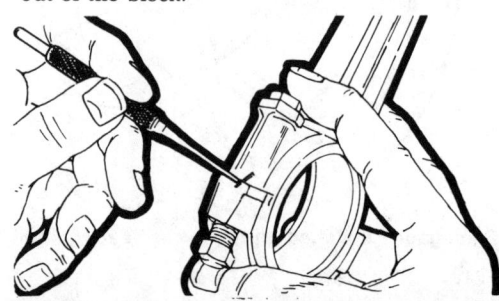

ENGINE AND ENGINE REBUILDING

Cylinder Block Reconditioning

Procedure	Method
Remove the ridge from the top of the cylinder: 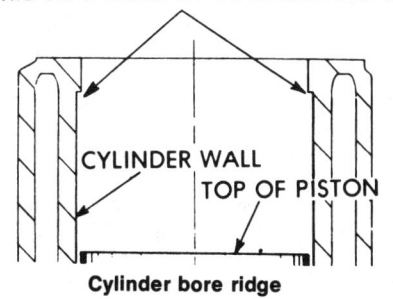 *[Illustration: Cylinder bore ridge — RIDGE CAUSED BY CYLINDER WEAR, CYLINDER WALL, TOP OF PISTON]*	In order to facilitate removal of the piston and connecting rod, the ridge at the top of the cylinder (unworn area; see illustration) must be removed. Place the piston at the bottom of the bore, and cover it with a rag. Cut the ridge away using a ridge reamer, exercising extreme care to avoid cutting too deeply. Remove the rag, and remove cuttings that remain on the piston. **CAUTION:** *If the ridge is not removed, and new rings are installed, damage to rings will result.*
Remove the piston and connecting rod: 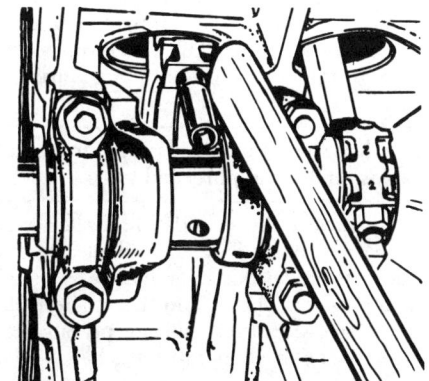 *[Illustration: Push the piston out with a hammer handle]*	Invert the engine, and push the pistons and connecting rods out of the cylinders. If necessary, tap the connecting rod boss with a wooden hammer handle, to force the piston out. **CAUTION:** *Do not attempt to force the piston past the cylinder ridge* (see above).
Service the crankshaft:	Ensure that all oil holes and passages in the crankshaft are open and free of sludge. If necessary, have the crankshaft ground to the largest possible undersize.
	**Have the crankshaft Magnafluxed, to locate stress cracks. Consult a machinist concerning additional service procedures, such as surface hardening (e.g., nitriding, Tuftriding) to improve wear characteristics, cross drilling and chamfering the oil holes to improve lubrication, and balancing.
Removing freeze plugs:	Drill a small hole in the middle of the freeze plugs. Thread a large sheet metal screw into the hole and remove the plug with a slide hammer.
Remove the oil gallery plugs:	Threaded plugs should be removed using an appropriate (usually square) wrench. To remove soft, pressed in plugs, drill a hole in the plug, and thread in a sheet metal screw. Pull the plug out by the screw using pliers.
Hot-tank the block: **NOTE:** *Do not hot-tank aluminum parts.*	Have the block hot-tanked to remove grease, corrosion, and scale from the water jackets. **NOTE:** *Consult the operator to determine whether the camshaft bearings will be damaged during the hot-tank process.*

ENGINE AND ENGINE REBUILDING

Cylinder Block Reconditioning

Procedure	Method

Check the block for cracks:	Visually inspect the block for cracks or chips. The most common locations are as follows:
	    Adjacent to freeze plugs.
	    Between the cylinders and water jackets.
	    Adjacent to the main bearing saddles.
	    At the extreme bottom of the cylinders.
	Check only suspected cracks using spot check dye (see introduction). If a crack is located, consult a machinist concerning possible repairs.

	** Magnaflux the block to locate hidden cracks. If cracks are located, consult a machinist about feasibility of repair.
Install the oil gallery plugs and freeze plugs:	Coat freeze plugs with sealer and tap into position using a piece of pipe, slightly smaller than the plug, as a driver. To ensure retention, stake the edges of the plugs. Coat threaded oil gallery plugs with sealer and install. Drive replacement soft plugs into block using a large drift as a driver.
	* Rather than reinstalling lead plugs, drill and tap the holes, and install threaded plugs.
Check the bore diameter and surface:	Visually inspect the cylinder bores for roughness, scoring, or scuffing. If evident, the cylinder bore must be bored or honed oversize to eliminate imperfections, and the smallest possible oversize piston used. The new pistons should be given to the machinist with the block, so that the cylinders can be bored or honed exactly to the piston size (plus clearance). If no flaws are evident, measure the bore diameter using a telescope gauge and micrometer, or dial gauge, parallel and perpendicular to the engine centerline, at the top (below the ridge) and bottom of the bore. Subtract the bottom measurements from the top to determine taper, and the parallel to the centerline measurements from the perpendicular measurements to determine eccentricity. If the measurements are not within specifications, the cylinder must be bored or honed, and an oversize piston installed. If the measurements are within specifications the cylinder may

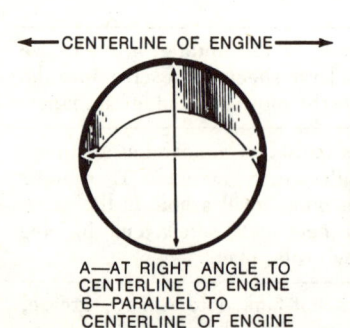

Measure the cylinder bore with a dial gauge

Cylinder bore measuring points
A—AT RIGHT ANGLE TO CENTERLINE OF ENGINE
B—PARALLEL TO CENTERLINE OF ENGINE

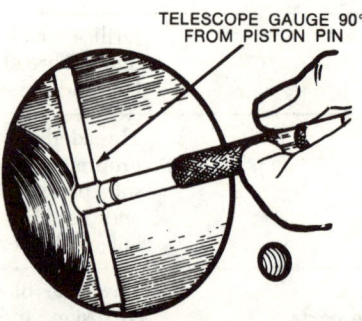

Measure the cylinder bore with a telescope gauge

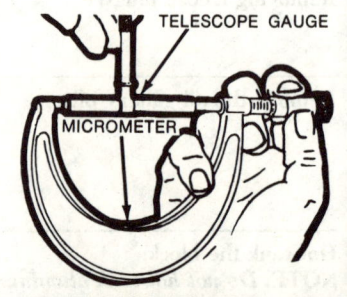

Measure the telescope gauge with a micrometer to determine the cylinder bore

ENGINE AND ENGINE REBUILDING

Cylinder Block Reconditioning

Procedure	Method
	be used as is, with only finish honing (see below). **NOTE:** *Prior to submitting the block for boring, perform the following operation(s).*
Check the cylinder block bearing alignment: **Check the main bearing saddle alignment**	Remove the upper bearing inserts. Place a straightedge in the bearing saddles along the centerline of the crankshaft. If clearance exists between the straightedge and the center saddle, the block must be alignbored.
*Check the deck height:	The deck height is the distance from the crankshaft centerline to the block deck. To measure, invert the engine, and install the crankshaft, retaining it with the center maincap. Measure the distance from the crankshaft journal to the block deck, parallel to the cylinder centerline. Measure the diameter of the end (front and rear) main journals, parallel to the centerline of the cylinders, divide the diameter in half, and subtract it from the previous measurement. The results of the front and rear measurements should be identical. If the difference exceeds .005", the deck height should be corrected. **NOTE:** *Block deck height and warpage should be corrected at the same time.*
Check the block deck for warpage:	Using a straightedge and feeler gauges, check the block deck for warpage in the same manner that the cylinder head is checked (see Cylinder Head Reconditioning). If warpage exceeds specifications, have the deck resurfaced. **NOTE:** *In certain cases a specification for total material removal (cylinder head and block deck) is provided. This specification must not be exceeded.*
Clean and inspect the pistons and connecting rods: RING EXPANDER **Remove the piston rings**	Using a ring expander, remove the rings from the piston. Remove the retaining rings (if so equipped) and remove piston pin. **NOTE:** *If the piston pin must be pressed out, determine the proper method and use the proper tools; otherwise the piston will distort.* Clean the ring grooves using an appropriate tool, exercising care to avoid cutting too deeply. Thoroughly clean all carbon and varnish from the piston with solvent. **CAUTION:** *Do not use a wire brush or caustic solvent on pistons.* Inspect the pistons for scuffing, scoring, cracks, pitting, or excessive ringsgroove wear. If wear is evident, the piston must be replaced. Check the connecting rod length by measuring

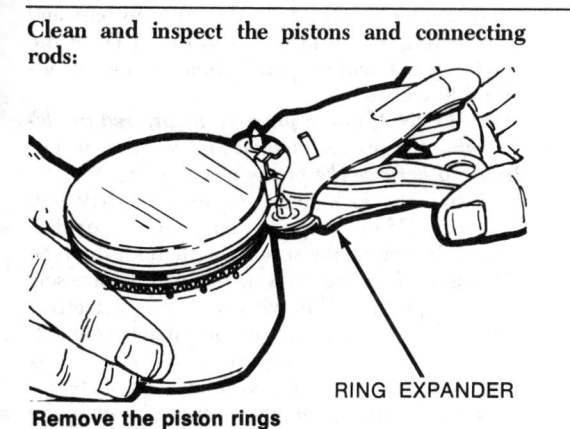

ENGINE AND ENGINE REBUILDING

Cylinder Block Reconditioning

Procedure	Method
Clean the piston ring grooves (RING GROOVE CLEANER)	the rod from the inside of the large end to the inside of the small end using calipers (see illustration). All connecting rods should be equal length. Replace any rod that differs from the others in the engine. * Have the connecting rod alignment checked in an alignment fixture by a machinist. Replace any twisted or bent rods. * Magnaflux the connecting rods to locate stress cracks. If cracks are found, replace the connecting rod.
Check the connecting rod length (arrow)	
Fit the pistons to the cylinders: Measure the piston prior to fitting	Using a telescope gauge and micrometer, or a dial gauge, measure the cylinder bore diameter perpendicular to the piston pin, 2½" below the deck. Measure the piston perpendicular to its pin on the skirt. The difference between the two measurements is the piston clearance. If the clearance is within specifications or slightly below (after boring or honing), finish honing is all that is required. If the clearance is excessive, try to obtain a slightly larger piston to bring clearance within specifications. Where this is not possible, obtain the first oversize piston, and hone (of if necessary, bore) the cylinder to size.
Assemble the pistons and connecting rods: Install the piston pin lock-rings (if used)	Inspect piston pin, connecting rod small end bushing, and piston bore for galling, scoring, or excessive wear. If evident, replace defective part(s). Measure the I.D. of the piston boss and connecting rod small end, and the O.D. of the piston pin. If within specifications, assemble piston pin and rod. **CAUTION:** *If piston pin must be pressed in, determine the proper method and use the proper tools; otherwise the piston will distort.* Install the lock rings; ensure that they seat properly. If the parts are not within specifications, determine the service method for the type of engine. In some cases, piston and pin are serviced as an assembly when either is defective. Others specify reaming the piston and connecting rods for an oversize pin. If the connecting rod bushing is worn, it may in many cases be replaced. Reaming the piston and replacing the rod bushing are machine shop operations.

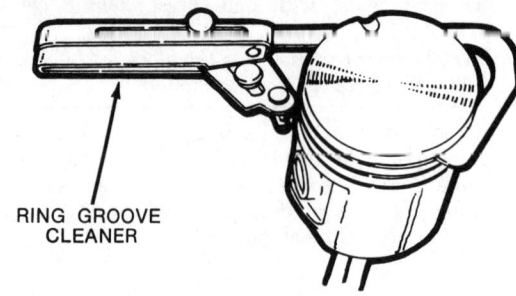

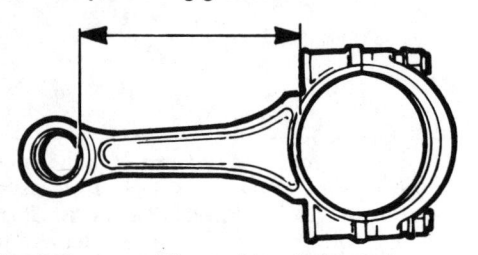

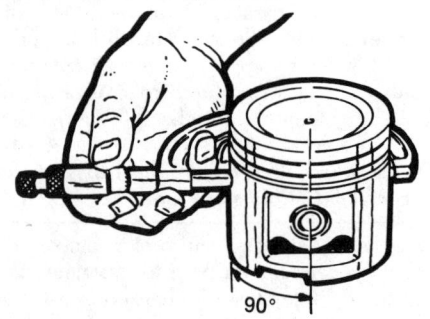

ENGINE AND ENGINE REBUILDING

Cylinder Block Reconditioning

Procedure	Method
Finish hone the cylinders:	Chuck a flexible drive hone into a power drill, and insert it into the cylinder. Start the hone, and move it up and down in the cylinder at a rate which will produce approximately a 60° cross-hatch pattern. **NOTE:** *Do not extend the hone below the cylinder bore.* After developing the pattern, remove the hone and recheck piston fit. Wash the cylinders with a detergent and water solution to remove abrasive dust, dry, and wipe several times with a rag soaked in engine oil.

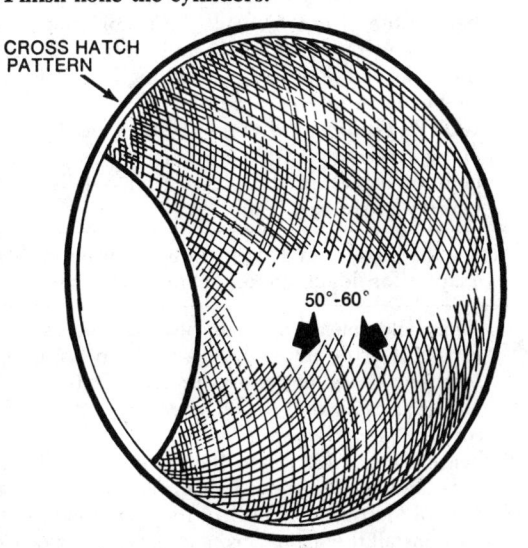

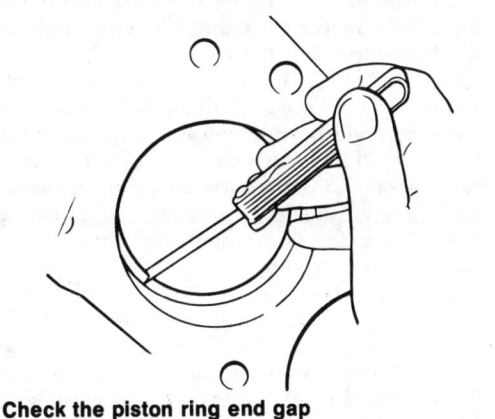

Check the piston ring end gap

Check piston ring end-gap:	Compress the piston rings to be used in a cylinder, one at a time, into that cylinder, and press them approximately 1″ below the deck with an inverted piston. Using feeler gauges, measure the ring end-gap, and compare to specifications. Pull the ring out of the cylinder and file the ends with a fine file to obtain proper clearance. **CAUTION:** *If inadequate ring end-gap is utilized, ring breakage will result.*

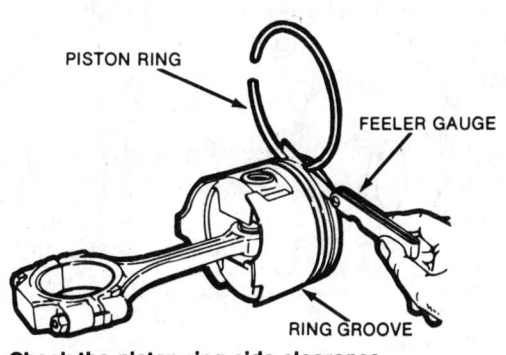

Check the piston ring side clearance

Install the piston rings:	Inspect the ring grooves in the piston for excessive wear or taper. If necessary, recut the groove(s) for use with an overwidth ring or a standard ring and spacer. If the groove is worn uniformly, overwidth rings, or standard rings and spaces may be installed without recutting. Roll the outside of the ring around the groove to check for burrs or deposits. If any are found, remove with a fine file. Hold the ring in the groove, and measure side clearance. If necessary, correct as indicated above. **NOTE:** *Always install any additional spacers above the piston ring.* The ring groove must be deep enough to allow the ring to seat below the lands (see illustration). In many cases, a "go-no-go" depth gauge will be provided with the piston rings. Shallow grooves may be corrected by recutting, while deep

ENGINE AND ENGINE REBUILDING

Cylinder Block Reconditioning

Procedure	Method
	grooves require some type of filler or expander behind the piston. Consult the piston ring supplier concerning the suggested method. Install the rings on the piston, lowest ring first, using a ring expander. NOTE: *Position the rings as specified by the manufacturer.* Consult the engine service procedures earlier in this chapter for details concerning specific engines.
Install the rear main seal:	See the engine service procedures earlier in this chapter for details concerning specific engines.
Install the crankshaft: **Remove or install the upper bearing insert using a roll-out pin** **Home-made bearing roll-out pin** **Aligning the thrust bearing**	Thoroughly clean the main bearing saddles and caps. Place the upper halves of the bearing inserts on the saddles and press into position. NOTE: *Ensure that the oil holes align.* Press the corresponding bearing inserts into the main bearing caps. Lubricate the upper main bearings, and lay the crankshaft in position. Place a strip of Plastigage on each of the crankshaft journals, install the main caps, and torque to specifications. Remove the main caps, and compare the Plastigage to the scale on the Plastigage envelope. If clearances are within tolerances, remove the Plastigage, turn the crankshaft 90°, wipe off all oil and retest. If all clearances are correct, remove all Plastigage, thoroughly lubricate the main caps and bearing journals, and install the main caps. If clearances are not within tolerance, the upper bearing inserts may be removed, without removing the crankshaft, using a bearing roll out pin (see illustration). Roll in a bearing that will provide proper clearance, and retest. Torque all main caps, excluding the thrust bearing cap, to specifications. Tighten the thrust bearing cap finger tight. To properly align the thrust bearing, pry the crankshaft the extent of its axial travel several times, the last movement held toward the front of the engine, and torque the thrust bearing cap to specifications. Determine the crankshaft end-play (see below), and bring within tolerance with thrust washers.
Measure crankshaft end-play:	Mount a dial indicator stand on the front of the block, with the dial indicator stem resting on the

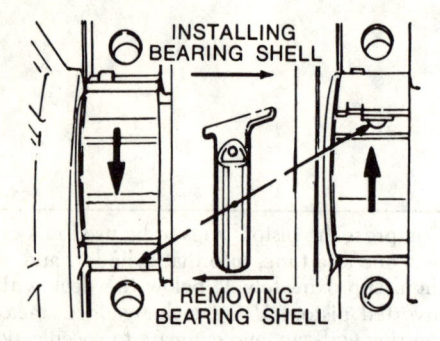

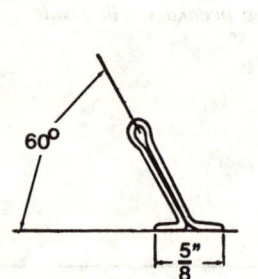

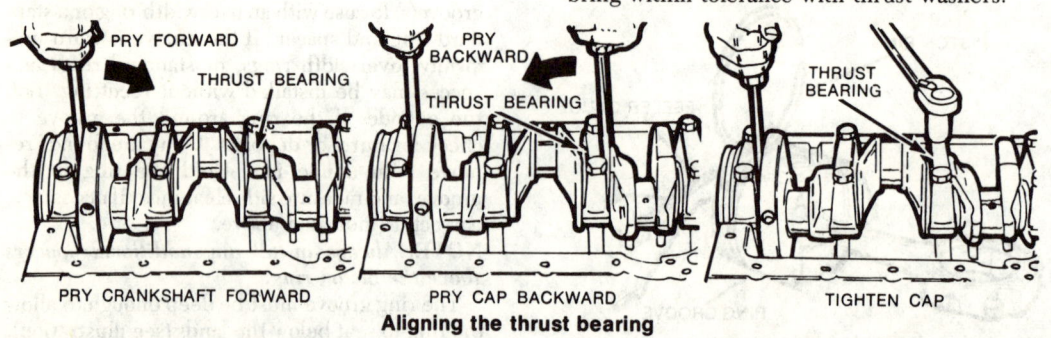

Cylinder Block Reconditioning

Procedure	Method

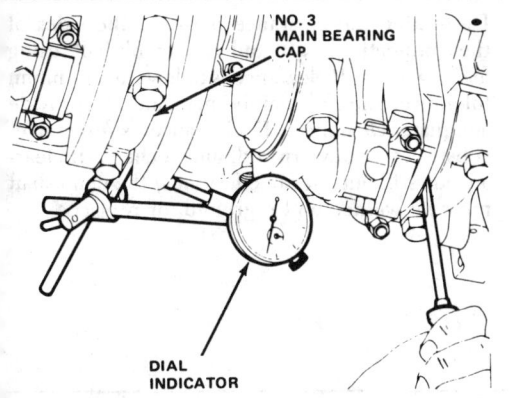

Check the crankshaft end-play with a dial indicator

Check the crankshaft end-play with a feeler gauge

Install the pistons:

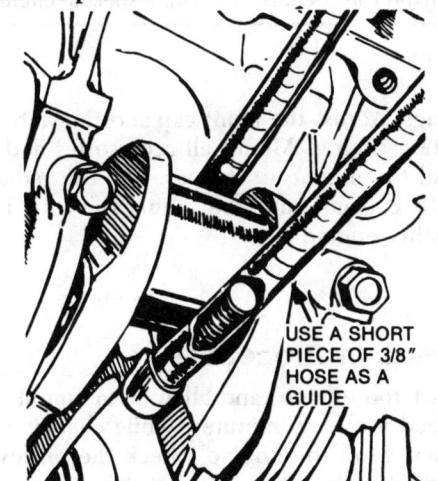

Use lengths of vacuum hose or rubber tubing to protect the crankshaft journals and cylinder walls during piston installation

RING COMPRESSOR

nose of the crankshaft, parallel to the crankshaft axis. Pry the crankshaft the extent of its travel rearward, and zero the indicator. Pry the crankshaft forward and record crankshaft end-play.
NOTE: *Crankshaft end-play also may be measured at the thrust bearing, using feeler gauges (see illustration).*

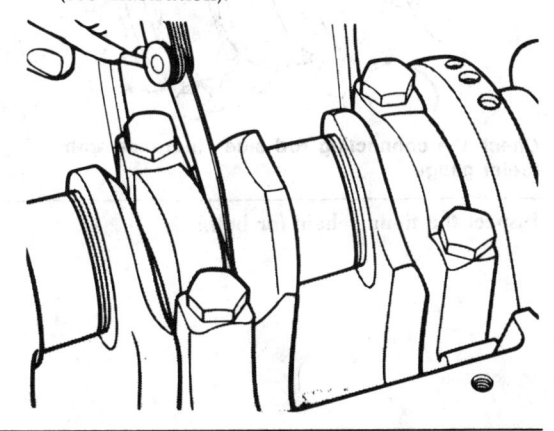

Press the upper connecting rod bearing halves into the connecting rods, and the lower halves into the connecting rod caps. Position the piston ring gaps according to specifications (see car section), and lubricate the pistons. Install a ring compresser on a piston, and press two long (8″) pieces of plastic tubing over the rod bolts. Using the tubes as a guide, press the pistons into the bores and onto the crankshaft with a wooden hammer handle. After seating the rod on the crankshaft journal, remove the tubes and install the cap finger tight. Install the remaining pistons in the same manner. Invert the engine and check the bearing clearance at two points (90° apart) on each journal with Plastigage.
NOTE: *Do not turn the crankshaft with Plastigage installed.*

If clearance is within tolerances, remove *all* Plastigage, thoroughly lubricate the journals, and torque the rod caps to specifications. If clearance is not within specifications, install different thickness bearing inserts and recheck.
CAUTION: *Never shim or file the connecting rods or caps.*

Always install plastic tube sleeves over the rod bolts when the caps are not installed, to protect the crankshaft journals.

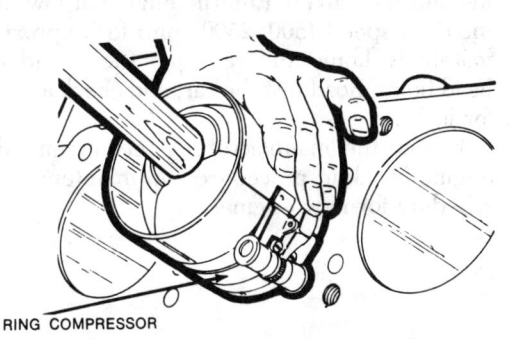

Install the piston using a ring compressor

ENGINE AND ENGINE REBUILDING

Cylinder Block Reconditioning

Procedure	Method
Check connecting rod side clearance: *Check the connecting rod side clearance with a feeler gauge*	Determine the clearance between the sides of the connecting rods and the crankshaft using feeler gauges. If clearance is below the minimum tolerance, the rod may be machined to provide adequate clearance. If clearance is excessive, substitute an unworn rod, and recheck. If clearance is still outside specifications, the crankshaft must be welded and reground, or replaced.
Inspect the timing chain (or belt):	Visually inspect the timing chain for broken or loose links, and replace the chain if any are found. If the chain will flex sideways, it must be replaced. Install the timing chain as specified. Be sure the timing belt is not stretched, frayed or broken. NOTE: *If the original timing chain is to be reused, install it in its original position.* See the engine service procedures earlier in this chapter for details concerning specific engines.

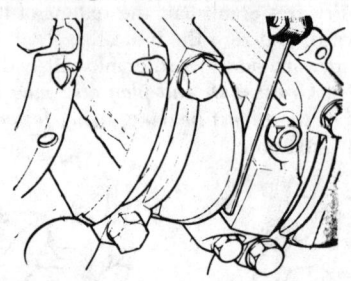

Completing the Rebuilding Process

Following the above procedures, complete the rebuilding process as follows:

Fill the oil pump with oil, to prevent cavitating (sucking air) on initial engine start up. Install the oil pump and the pickup tube on the engine. Coat the oil pan gasket as necessary, and install the gasket and the oil pan. Mount the flywheel and the crankshaft vibration damper or pulley on the crankshaft.

NOTE: *Always use new bolts when installing the flywheel.* Inspect the clutch shaft pilot bushing in the crankshaft. If the bushing is excessively worn, remove it with an expanding puller and a slide hammer, and tap a new bushing into place.

Position the engine, cylinder head side up. Install the cylinder head, and torque it as specified. Install the rocker arms and adjust the valves.

Install the intake and exhaust manifolds, the carburetor(s), the distributor and spark plugs. Adjust the point gap and the static ignition timing. Mount all accessories and install the engine in the car. Fill the radiator with coolant, and the crankcase with high quality engine oil.

Break-in Procedure

Start the engine, and allow it to run at low speed for a few minutes, while checking for leaks. Stop the engine, check the oil level, and fill as necessary. Restart the engine, and fill the cooling system to capacity. Check the point dwell angle and adjust the ignition timing and the valves. Run the engine at low to medium speed (800–2500 rpm) for approximately ½ hour, and retorque the cylinder head bolts. Road test the car, and check again for leaks.

Follow the manufacturer's recommended engine break-in procedure and maintenance schedule for new engines.

Emission Controls and Fuel System

EMISSION CONTROLS

There are three sources of automotive pollutants: crankcase fumes, exhaust gases, and gasoline evaporation. The pollutants formed from these substances fall into three categories: unburnt hydrocarbons (HC), carbon monoxide (CO), and oxides of nitrogen (NOx). The equipment used to limit these pollutants is called emission control equipment.

Due to varying state, federal, and provincial regulations, specific emission control equipment have been devised for each. The U.S. emission equipment is divided into two categories: California and 49 State. In this section, the term "California" applies only to cars originally built to be sold in California. California emissions equipment is generally not shared with equipment installed on cars built to be sold in the other 49 States. Models built to be sold in Canada also have specific emissions equipment, although in most years 49 State and Canadian equipment is the same.

Crankcase Ventilation System

A closed, positive crankcase ventilation system is employed on all Datsun 240-Z, 260-Z, 280-Z, and 280-ZX vehicles. This system cycles incompletely burned fuel which works its way past the piston rings back into the intake manifold for reburning with the fuel/air mixture. The oil filler cap is sealed and air is drawn from the top of the crankcase into the intake manifold through a valve with a variable orifice.

This valve (commonly known as the PCV valve) employs spring pressure and a sliding plunger to regulate the flow of air into the manifold according to the amount of manifold vacuum. When the carburetor throttles are open fairly wide, this valve opens to maximize the flow. However, at idle speed, when manifold vacuum is at maximum, the PCV valve throttles the flow in order not to unnecessarily affect the small volume of mixture passing to the engine.

A ventilating line connects the valve cover with the air cleaner. During most driving conditions, manifold vacuum is high and all of the vapor from the crankcase, plus a small amount of excess air, is drawn into the manifold via the PCV. However, at full-throttle, the increase in the volume of blow-by and the decrease in manifold vacuum make the flow via the PCV inadequate. Under these conditions excess vapors are drawn into the air cleaner and pass through the carburetors and into the engine.

114 EMISSION CONTROLS AND FUEL SYSTEM

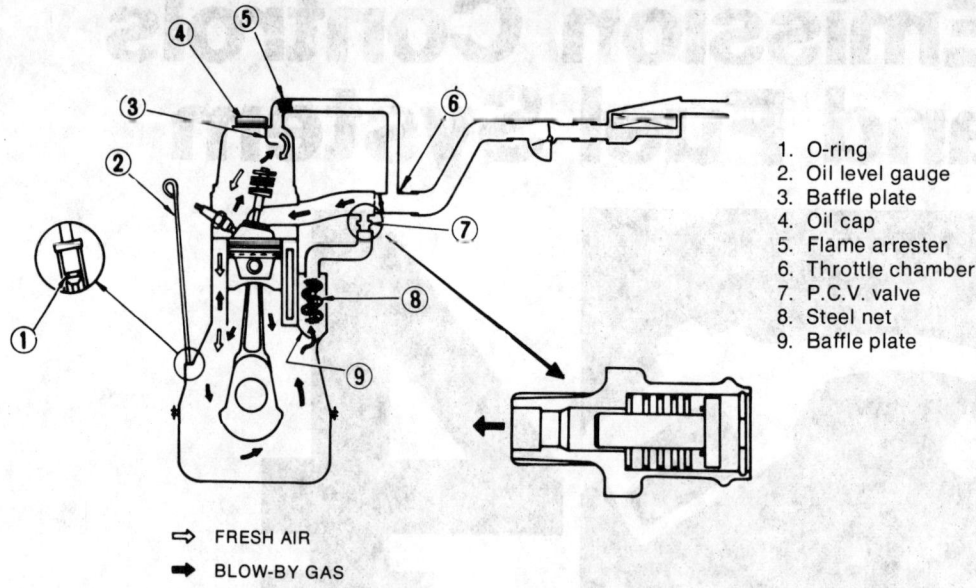

1. O-ring
2. Oil level gauge
3. Baffle plate
4. Oil cap
5. Flame arrester
6. Throttle chamber
7. P.C.V. valve
8. Steel net
9. Baffle plate

⇨ FRESH AIR
➡ BLOW-BY GAS

Crankcase emission control system, except turbocharged engines

SERVICE CHECKS

After every 12,000 miles or every year, perform the following services:

1. Check the condition of the hoses and the connectors to ensure that there is no leakage. Replace parts if necessary.
2. Disconnect the hoses and blow them clean with compressed air. Where extreme clogging is encountered, replace the hose.
3. Check the PCV valve as follows:

 a. Start the engine and allow it to idle. Then, disconnect the ventilating hose from the PCV valve, allowing air to be drawn into the manifold through the valve. The flow of air should produce an audible

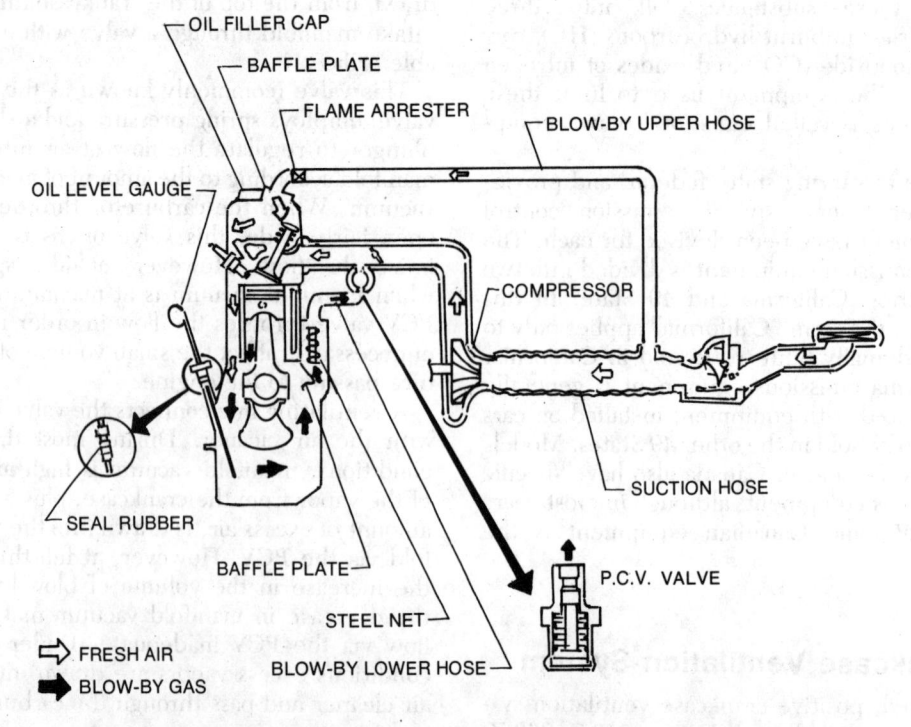

⇨ FRESH AIR
➡ BLOW-BY GAS

Crankcase emission control system, turbocharged engines

EMISSION CONTROLS AND FUEL SYSTEM

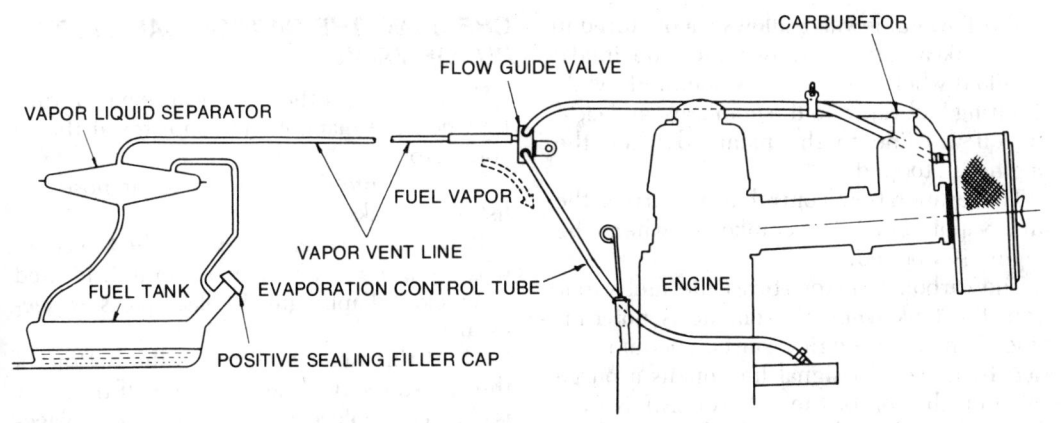

Evaporative emission control system (1970–73)

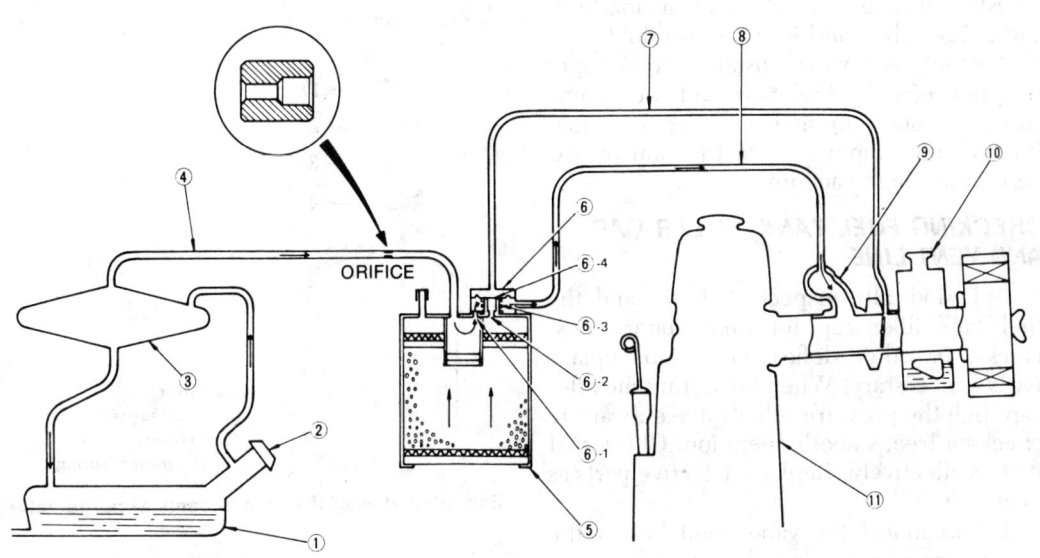

1. Fuel tank
2. Positive sealing filler cap
3. Vapor liquid separator
4. Vapor vent line
5. Carbon canister
6. Purge control valve
6-1. Small orifice
6-2. Large orifice
6-3. Diaphragm spring
6-4. Diaphragm
7. Vacuum signal line
8. Canister purge line
9. Balance tube
10. Carburetor
11. Engine

Evaporative emission control system (1974–75—later similar)

"hiss" and it should be possible to feel a strong vacuum when placing a finger over the valve inlet. If the valve is clogged, replace it as it is not serviceable. Replace the valve every two years.

Evaporative Emission Control System

The Evaporative Emission Control System employs:
1. A sealed filler cap.
2. A vapor-liquid separator and vent line.
3. A flow guide valve (240-Z).
4. An evaporation control tube (240-Z).
5. A carbon storage canister (260-Z, 280-Z, and 280-ZX).
6. A fuel check valve (1976 and later models).

The sealed filler cap allows vacuum (created as the fuel pump empties the tank) to draw air into the tank to replace the used fuel. This avoids damaging the tank or starving the fuel system. It will not, however, allow fuel vapor to escape.

The vapor-liquid separator allows a vent line to collect the vapor formed in the gas tank and store it in the crankcase or in a carbon canister, but prohibits liquid fuel from passing into the vent line.

116 EMISSION CONTROLS AND FUEL SYSTEM

The flow guide valve allows vapor stored in the crankcase to be drawn into the intake manifold when the engine is operated, while shunting fuel vapor to the crankcase and closing off the line to the manifold when the engine is stopped.

The evaporation control tube carries the fuel vapor into the crankcase when the engine is stopped.

The carbon canister stores the fuel vapor from the tank when the engine is not running. When the engine starts, vacuum carried by a vacuum signal line opens a purge valve on the top of the canister. Air is then drawn through a filter on the bottom of the canister, through the charcoal, a nozzle in the purge valve, and into the manifold.

The fuel check valve, installed in the vapor line between the fuel tank and the carbon canister, allows air flow into the fuel tank, but prevents vapor flow to the canister except under high vacuum.

CHECKING FUEL TANK, FILLER CAP, AND VENT LINE

1. Periodically inspect all hoses and the fuel tank filler cap for poor connections, cracks, or other deficiencies, and replace parts as necessary. When inspecting the filler cap, pull the pressure relief valve outward to check for free, smooth operation. Check that it seals effectively. Replace defective parts as necessary.

2. Disconnect the vapor vent line at the canister or flow guide valve. Install a "T," connecting a source of air pressure and a pressure gauge which reads in inches of water.

3. Slowly apply pressure until the pressure gauge reads 14.5 inches. Close off the air supply, and wait 2½ minutes.

4. Check the reading on the gauge. It should not have dropped below 13.5 inches.

5. Remove the filler cap. The pressure should drop to zero in a few seconds. If not, the vent line is clogged.

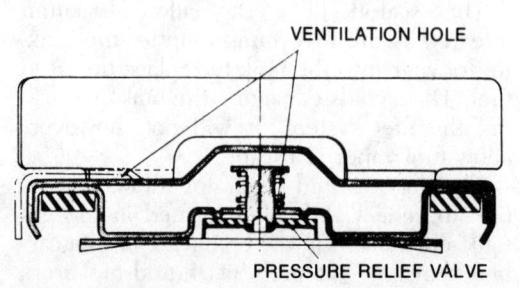

Fuel filler cap

CHECKING THE CARBON CANISTER PURGE VALVE

1. Disconnect the rubber hose which runs between the manifold and canister at the T connector.

2. Blow into the open end of the hose and listen for leaks.

3. If there are leaks, remove the top cover of the purge valve and check for a dislocated or cracked diaphragm. Replace parts as necessary.

4. At this time the filter on the bottom of the canister should be inspected. If the filter is clogged, replace it. Inspection and replacement can be accomplished without removing the canister.

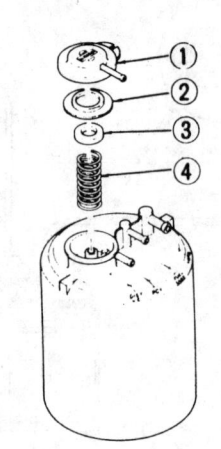

1. Cover
2. Diaphragm
3. Retainer
4. Diaphragm spring

Exploded view of the carbon canister purge valve

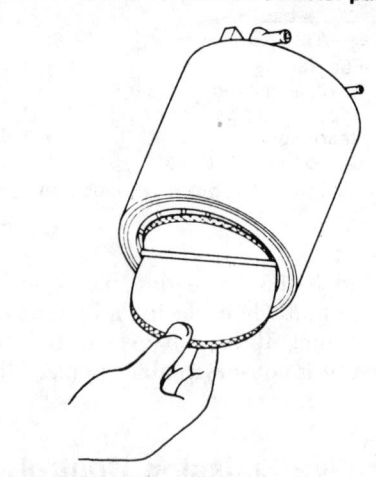

Replacing the canister filter

CHECKING THE FLOW GUIDE VALVE

1. Disconnect all hoses to the valve.
2. Force low pressure air into the fuel tank vent connection. Air should emerge from the crankcase side.

EMISSION CONTROLS AND FUEL SYSTEM

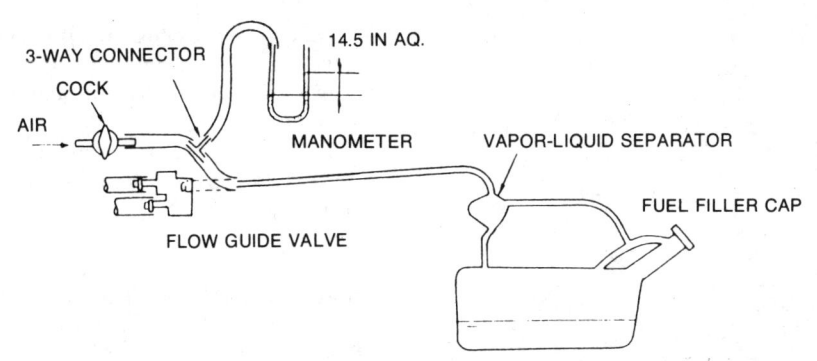

Gauge hook-up for checking the evaporative emission control system

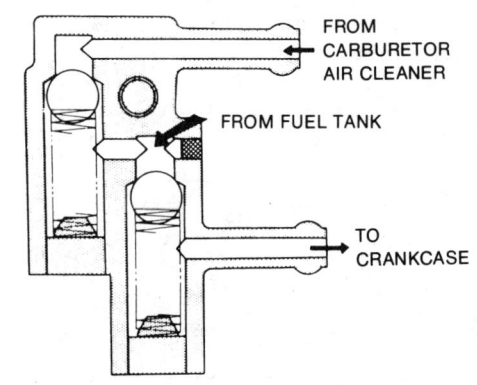

The flow guide valve (1970–73 models only)

3. Force air into the air cleaner connection. Air should emerge from the fuel tank and/or crankcase vent connection.
4. Force air into the crankcase vent line connection. There should be no leakage.
5. If the valve fails any of these tests, replace it.

CHECKING THE FUEL CHECK VALVE

1976–78

1. Remove the valve from the vapor line.
2. Blow through the fuel tank side connector. Resistance should be felt, and only a small flow of air should be felt at the engine side of the valve.
3. Blow through the engine side connector. Air should flow smoothly through the valve, emerging at the fuel tank side.

If the valve does not function correctly, replace it.

1979 and Later

1. Remove the valve from the vapor line.
2. Suck air through the carbon canister connector. Air should flow only under high vacuum.
3. Suck air through the fuel tank side of the valve. Air should flow only under high vacuum.
4. Repeat Step 3 while closing off the carbon canister connector with your finger. Air should flow only under extremely high vacuum.

If the valve does not function correctly, replace it.

Air Injection Reactor

Some 240 and 260-Z models are equipped with a positive displacement air pump to inject fresh air into the exhaust ports to accelerate combustion in the manifold. The system includes:
1. An antibackfire valve. When the throttle is suddenly closed, this valve diverts the air pump discharge into the intake manifold in order to promote combustion in the combustion chambers and minimize combustion in the exhaust manifold.
2. A check valve. This device prevents exhaust gases from traveling back into the air pump when exhaust pressure exceeds air pump discharge pressure.
3. An air pump relief valve. This valve controls the air pump discharge pressure in order to protect the pump from excessive pressure.

TESTING THE AIR PUMP AND VALVES

1. Operate the engine until it reaches operating temperature.
2. Inspect all hoses and connections, replace any damaged hoses or clamps, and retighten connections as necessary.
3. Check the air pump belt tension and adjust as necessary.
4. Disconnect the air supply hose at the check valve.
5. Insert the open end of a special Air Pump Test Gauge Adapter into the air supply

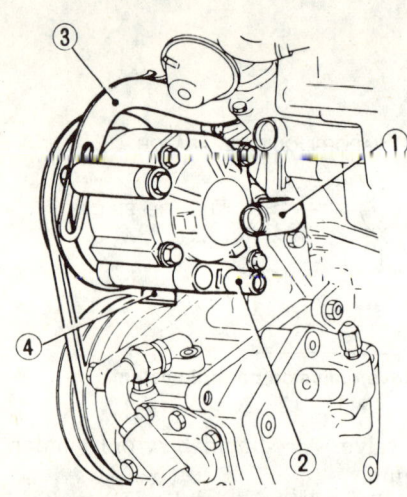

118 EMISSION CONTROLS AND FUEL SYSTEM

Rear view of the air pump 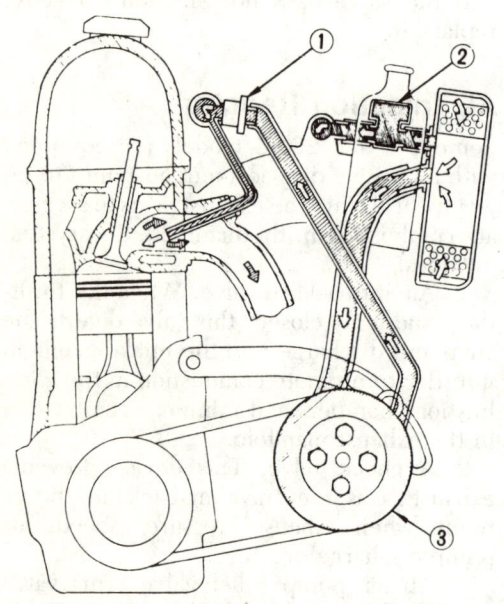
1. Inlet port
2. Outlet port
3. Belt adjusting bar
4. Relief valve

The air injection system
1. Check valve 2. Antibackfire valve 3. Air pump

The antibackfire valve air inlet hole

9. Stop the engine. Inspect the check valve plate position. The plate should be lightly in contact with the seat away from the air manifold.

10. Insert a small screwdriver into the valve connection, depress the valve plate, and release it. It should return to the seat freely.

11. Start the engine and slowly bring its speed to 1,500 rpm. There should be no leakage of exhaust gas from the check valve although a slight fluttering at idle is normal.

12. If the check valve fails any of the tests, replace it.

13. Reconnect the air supply hose and remove the air cleaner cover.

14. Lightly position a finger over the inlet hole for the antibackfire valve (see the illustration). Do not shut the hole off entirely.

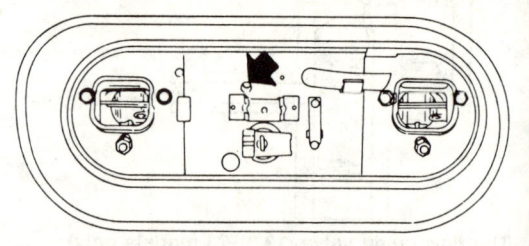

15. Raise the engine rpm to between 3,000 and 3,500, and then suddenly release the linkage. There should be a sudden flow of air during deceleration. If there is no airflow or if airflow exists under other than deceleration conditions, replace the valve.

AIR PUMP REMOVAL AND INSTALLATION

1. Disconnect all hoses from the housing.
2. Remove the bolt used to position the pump on the belt adjusting bar. Remove the bolt which secures the pump to the mounting bracket.
3. Remove the belt, and remove the pump.

To install the pump:
1. Put the pump and belt into position. Install the pump mounting bolt.
2. Install the bolt which positions the pump loosely on the adjusting bar. Adjust the belt tension to specifications and tighten the nut.
3. Reinstall all hoses.

ANTIBACKFIRE VALVE REPLACEMENT

No special instructions are required except that the valve *must* be replaced with its dia-

hose and clamp it securely. This adapter is required because it provides a relief port of critical size.

6. Operate the engine at 1,500 rpm and read the test gauge. The pressure should be 0.63 in. Hg. (16 mm) or more.

7. With the engine still at 1,500 rpm, close the relief port in the gauge adapter and listen for leaks. If there is any leakage from the relief valve, it is faulty.

8. If the system fails the pressure test, the pump must be replaced unless the problem is in the relief valve.

EMISSION CONTROLS AND FUEL SYSTEM

phragm chamber upward. Never attempt to disassemble and repair the valve.

CHECK VALVE REMOVAL AND INSTALLATION

1. Disconnect the air supply hose.
2. While removing the valve, put opposing pressure on the flange of the air manifold with a wrench.

To install the valve:
1. Reverse the removal procedure, again putting pressure in opposition to installation torque on the air manifold flange. Never attempt to disassemble and repair the valve.

Air Induction System

1980 49 State models have an Air Induction System to supply fresh air to the exhaust manifold. The system is not used on models sold in California or Canada.

Components include an air pipe connecting the air cleaner to the exhaust manifold. An air induction valve is installed in the pipe. The valve is simply a four petal reed valve, which allows air to pass into the exhaust manifold during periods of negative exhaust pressure, and closes during periods of positive exhaust pressure. In this way, fresh air is siphoned into the exhaust manifold without the need for an air pump. The fresh air promotes burning of hot HC and CO gases which otherwise would escape the combustion process.

SERVICE

The only periodic maintenance required is replacement of the air induction filter at 24,000 mile or 30 month intervals. This procedure is covered in Chapter 1.

Throttle Opener

All 1970–73 models and 1974 models equipped with a manual transmission have a throttle opener to reduce emissions during deceleration.

ADJUSTMENT

1. Bring the engine to operating temperature.
2. Disconnect the vacuum hose at point "A." Connect a vacuum gauge which gives quick response where the hose was removed.
3. On 1973 and later models, disconnect the throttle opener solenoid harness.
4. Rev the engine to approximately 3,000 rpm and release the throttle. Note the reading on the pressure gauge between the time that the throttle actuator begins to work and the time that the throttle reaches normal idle position. The reading should be constant between these two points.

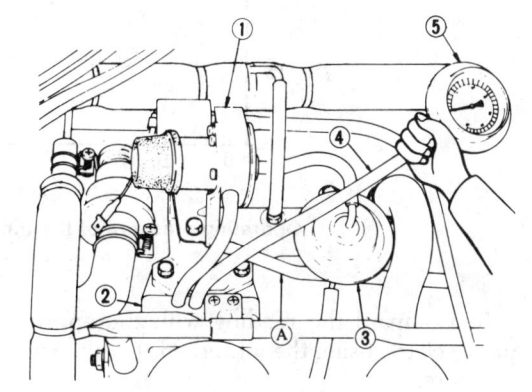

1. Throttle opener control valve
2. Intake manifold
3. Servo diaphragm
4. Vacuum gauge hose
5. Vacuum gauge

Connecting the vacuum gauge to the manifold

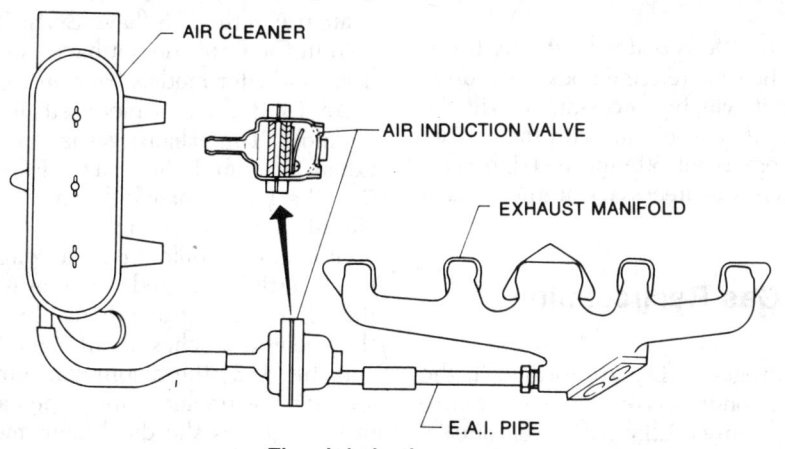

The air induction system

120 EMISSION CONTROLS AND FUEL SYSTEM

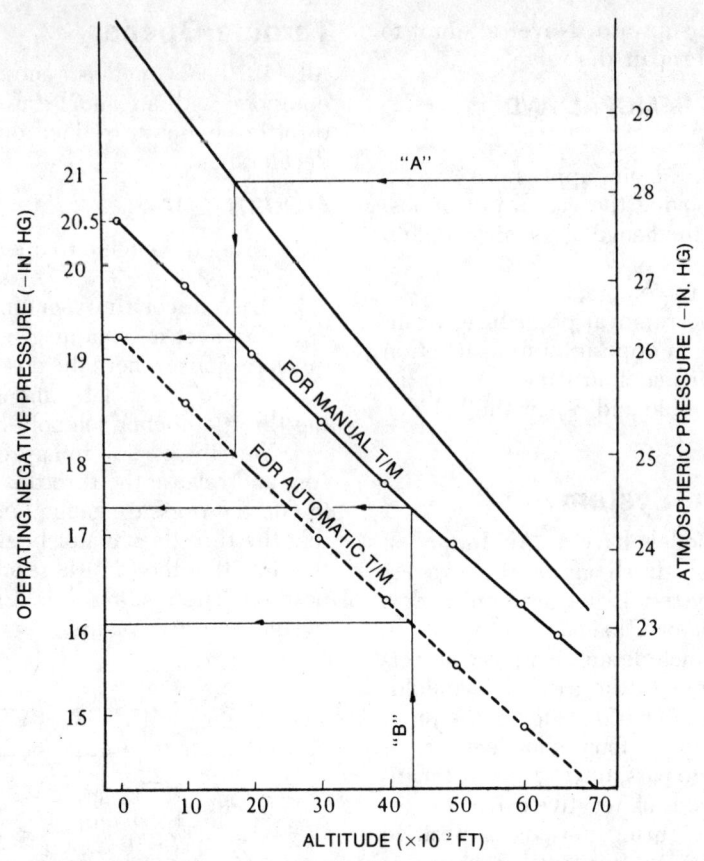

Operating pressure of the throttle opener—1972 and earlier

5. Compare the reading with the appropriate chart, using the altitude or barometric pressure.

6. Loosen the vacuum adjusting screw locknut and adjust the pressure as necessary. If the pressure is too low, adjust the screw clockwise. If it is too high, turn the screw counterclockwise.

7. Tighten the locknut and recheck the adjustment.

8. If the throttle actuator holds the throttle open all the time (engine does not drop to idle speed), it will be necessary to rig the gauge so that it can be read with the car decelerating from about 50 mph in High gear. Adjust the screw as necessary on the basis of this test.

Exhaust Gas Recirculation System

Oxides of nitrogen (NOx) are formed in the engine under conditions of high temperature and high pressure. Elimination of one of these two conditions reduces the formation of NOx. Exhaust gas recirculation is used to reduce combustion temperatures in the engine.

All Except Turbocharged Engines

All 1973 and 1974 models have EGR. Only models sold in California have EGR in 1975 and 1976. All 1977–79 models have EGR, and all 1980 models sold in Canada and for 49 State use in the U.S. have EGR; 1980 models sold in California do not have the system. All 1981 and later models have an EGR system.

An EGR valve is mounted on the intake manifold. The exhaust gas is drawn from the exhaust manifold, through the EGR valve, and into the intake manifold. The EGR valve is closed when the engine is idling; exhaust gas recirculation would cause a rough idle. As the throttle is opened, vacuum is applied to the EGR valve vacuum diaphragm. When the vacuum reaches about 2 inches of mercury (in. Hg.) the diaphragm moves against spring pressure and is fully open at 8 in. Hg. of vacuum. As the diaphragm moves up, it pulls the EGR valve pintle from its seat,

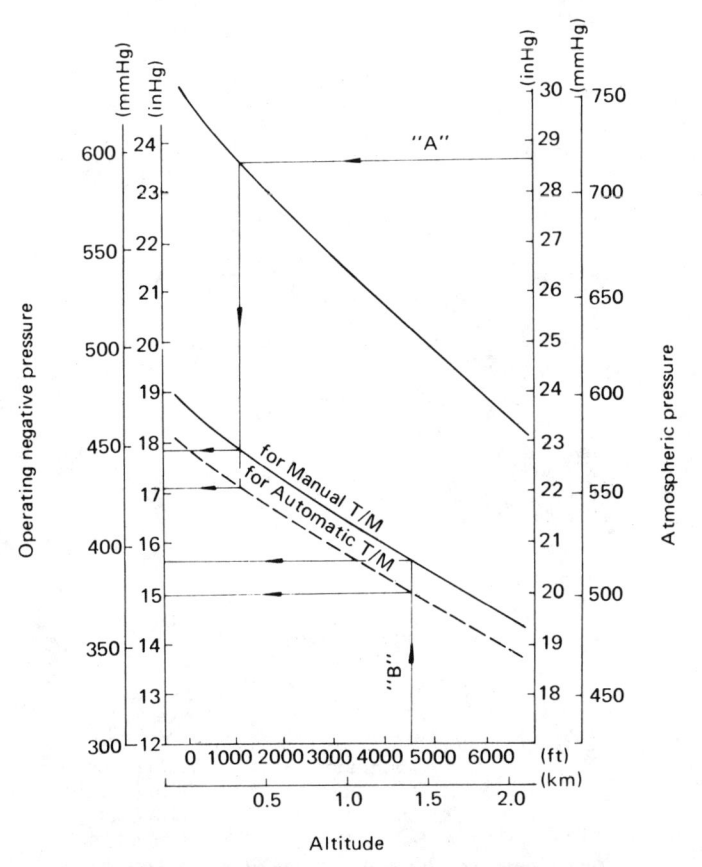

Operating pressure of the throttle opener—1973 and later

allowing exhaust gas to be pulled into the intake manifold by intake vacuum. The valve closes at full throttle, when EGR is not needed, as a means of improving fuel economy.

1973-76 models have an electrically operated solenoid valve mounted on the EGR valve. The vacuum signal to the EGR valve must travel through the solenoid valve. The solenoid valve prevents EGR when the engine is cold. Temperature signals to the solenoid valve are sent by a passenger compartment temperature sensor in 1973; as long as the temperature inside the car is below freezing, the solenoid valve blocks vacuum to the EGR valve, preventing exhaust recirculation. 1974-76 models use a temperature switch installed in the engine coolant outlet housing; as long as engine coolant temperatures remain below approximately 106° F (41° C) in 1974, or below approximately 122° F (50° C), 1975-76, the solenoid valve blocks vacuum to the EGR valve. When the temperature of the engine coolant, or the passenger compartment, reaches normal operating temperature, the solenoid is de-activated and intake manifold vacuum is allowed to act upon the EGR valve diaphragm and exhaust gas recirculation takes place.

On 1977 and later models, a thermal vacuum valve (TVV) controls the application of vacuum to the EGR valve. When the engine coolant reaches a predetermined temperature, the TVV opens and allows vacuum to be routed to the EGR valve. Below the predetermined temperature, the TVV closes and blocks vacuum to the EGR valve.

All 1977-78 models, all 1979 U.S. models, and all 1980 49 State U.S. models have a back pressure transducer (BPT) valve installed between the EGR valve and the thermal vacuum valve. The BPT valve has a diaphragm raised or lowered by exhaust back pressure. The diaphragm opens or closes an air bleed, which is connected into the EGR vacuum line. High pressure results in higher levels of EGR, because the BPT diaphragm is raised, closing off the air bleed, which allows more vacuum to reach and open the EGR valve.

122 EMISSION CONTROLS AND FUEL SYSTEM

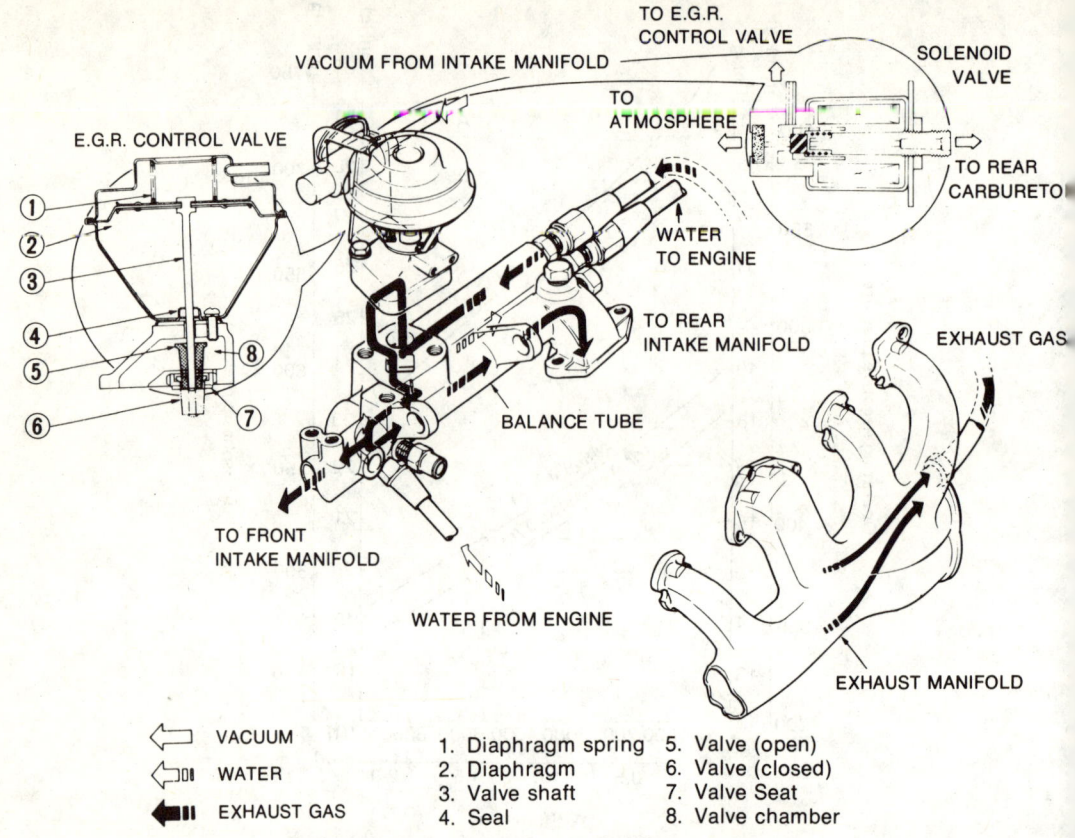

1. Diaphragm spring
2. Diaphragm
3. Valve shaft
4. Seal
5. Valve (open)
6. Valve (closed)
7. Valve Seat
8. Valve chamber

The 1973–74 exhaust gas recirculation system

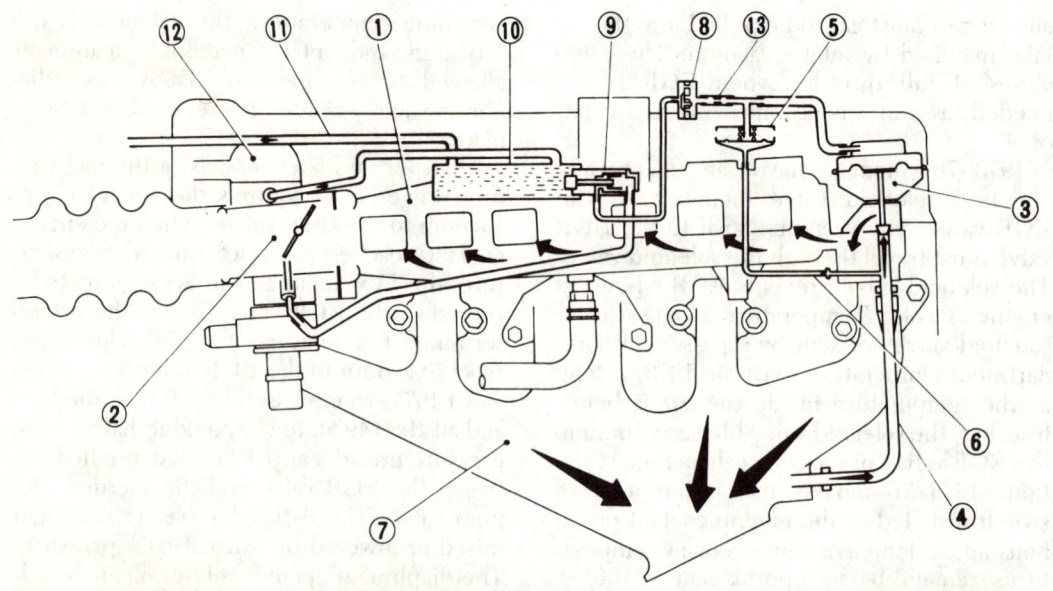

1. Intake manifold
2. Throttle chamber
3. E.G.R. control valve
4. E.G.R. tube
5. B.P.T. valve
6. B.P.T. valve control tube
7. Exhaust manifold
8. Vacuum delay valve (Models equipped with catalytic converter)
9. Thermal vacuum valve
10. Heater housing
11. Water return tube
12. Thermostat housing
13. Vacuum orifice

EGR system schematic, typical of all 1975 and later models (1979 shown)

EMISSION CONTROLS AND FUEL SYSTEM

Thus, the amount of recirculated exhaust gas varies with exhaust pressure.

1977–78 models sold in California, 1979 models with a catalytic converter, and 1980 49 State models have a vacuum delay valve (VDV) installed in the line between the thermal vacuum valve and the EGR valve. The valve delays rapid drops in vacuum in the EGR signal line, thus effecting a longer EGR time.

Turbocharged Engines

E.G.R. is controlled by the central electronic control unit adjusting to the engine operating conditions.

Cylinder head temperature, engine rpm, engine load, air temperature and barometric pressure are used for the determination of the E.G.R. amount.

These signals are transmitted to the control unit where optimum E.G.R. quantities are recorded. To obtain the optimum E.G.R. quantity that corresponds to the engine operating conditions at the time, an electric signal is sent to the vacuum control modulator (V.C.M.). The vacuum control modulator transforms the electric signal to a vacuum signal, which in turn controls the E.G.R. valve.

A one-way valve is utilized for the purpose of preventing the V.C.M. from applying positive pressure in high speed conditions.

This valve is installed in the vacuum line leading to V.C.M.

INSPECTION

1973–76

1. Visually inspect the entire EGR control system. Clean the mechanism of any oil or dirt. Replace any rubber hoses found to be cracked or broken. On 1973 models, check the vacuum tube which runs from the solenoid to the carburetor; if deformed, replace it. Tightening torque for this tube is 3.0 ft lbs (0.4 kg-m).
2. Check the solenoid electrical connections for corrosion, breaks in the insulation, etc., and correct as necessary.
3. Start the engine and allow it to reach normal operating temperature. On 1973 models, the temperature in the passenger compartment must be over 60° F. Increase the engine speed to 3,000–3,500 rpm. The plate of the EGR control diaphragm and the valve shaft should move upward. This can be more easily seen with a mirror placed under the EGR valve.
4. Disconnect the EGR solenoid electrical leads and connect them directly to the car battery with a pair of jumper wires. Race the engine again with the solenoid connected to the battery. The EGR valve diaphragm should remain stationary.
5. With the engine running at idle, reach up under the EGR valve and raise the diaphragm by pushing it upwards with your fingers. Wear a heavy glove to protect your hand from the hot engine. When the diaphragm is raised, the idle should become rough, indicating that exhaust gases are recirculating. If the roughness does not occur, the EGR passages are blocked.

Inspect the individual components as follows:

1. Remove the EGR valve from the intake manifold.
2. Apply 6.0 in. Hg of vacuum to the EGR valve vacuum connection. The valve should open. Pinch off the connection with the vacuum still applied. The valve should remain in the raised position for at least 30 seconds.
3. Inspect the EGR valve for any signs of warpage or damage, and replace as necessary.
4. Clean the EGR valve seat with a brush and compressed air.
5. Connect the solenoid to a 12 volt DC power source. The solenoid should click when power is applied. If the valve clicks, it is considered to be working properly.
6. Check the 1974–76 temperature switch by removing it from the engine (drain the engine coolant first) and placing it in a container of water together with a thermometer. Connect a self-powered test light to the temperature switch electrical leads. Heat the water. The switch should conduct current when the water temperature is below 77° F (25° C) on 1974 models, or below 122° F (50° C) on 1975–76 models. The switch should stop conduction somewhere between 88–106° F (31–41° C) on 1974 models, or between 134–145° F (57–63° C) on 1975–76 models. Replace the switch if it behaves otherwise.

1977 and Later

1. Remove the EGR valve. Apply enough vacuum to the EGR valve vacuum connection to raise the diaphragm and open the valve. Pinch off the vacuum connection. The valve should remain open for at least thirty seconds. If not, the diaphragm is leaking and the valve must be replaced.

124 EMISSION CONTROLS AND FUEL SYSTEM

EGR valve (left) and BPT valve (right)

2. Check the valve for damage (warpage, cracks, etc) and replace as necessary.

3. Clean the valve seat with a wire brush and compressed air.

4. Install the EGR valve on the engine. Start the engine and allow it to idle. With the engine idling, reach up under the EGR valve and raise the diaphragm by pushing it upwards with your fingers. Wear a glove to protect your hand if the engine is hot. When the diaphragm is raised, the engine idle should become rough, indicating that exhaust gases are recirculating. If the roughness does not occur, the EGR passages are blocked.

5. To check the operation of the thermal vacuum valve, drain the engine coolant and remove the valve. Connect two lengths of vacuum hose to the two TVV vacuum connections. Place the valve in a container of water together with a thermostat, with the vacuum hoses above the level of the water. Do not allow water to get into the valve. When the water temperature is below 177° F (47° C), the vacuum passage should be closed. You can check this by sucking on one of the vacuum hoses.

6. Heat the water. On 1977 models, the valve should open (conduct vacuum) when the water temperature reaches 117–127° F (47–53° C). On 1978–80 models, the valve should open at about 122° F (50° C), and remain open until the water temperature reaches about 203° F (95°C). On 1978 and later models only, the valve should close again when water temperature reaches about 208° F (98° C). Replace the valve if it behaves otherwise.

7. To test the BPT valve installed on some 1977 and later models, disconnect the two vacuum hoses on the valve. Plug one of the ports. While applying pressure to the bottom of the valve, apply vacuum to the unplugged port and check for leakage. If any exists, replace the valve.

8. To check the delay valve installed on some 1977 and later models, remove the valve and blow into the side which connects to the EGR or BPT valve. Air should flow. When air is applied to the other side, air flow resistance should be greater. If not, replace the valve.

EGR VALVE AND BALANCE TUBE REMOVAL AND INSTALLATION

1. Disconnect the vacuum line from the EGR valve.

2. Remove the two valve mounting bolts and remove the valve.

3. To remove the balance tube on 1973–74 models, disconnect:
   a. The fuel hose to the rear carburetor;
   b. The hose between the air cleaner and rocker cover;
   c. The hose between the anti-backfire valve and balance tube;
   d. The vacuum lines between the balance tube and air cleaner, intake manifold and throttle opener valve, and throttle opener valve and air cleaner.

EMISSION CONTROLS AND FUEL SYSTEM

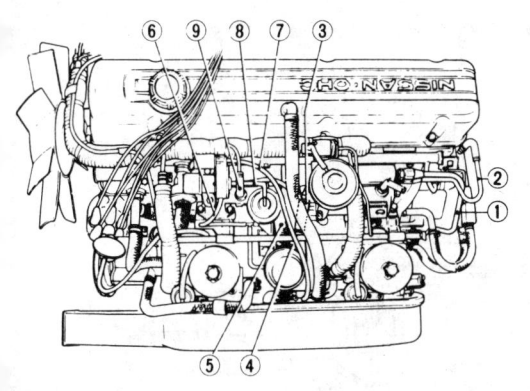

1. Exhaust gas return tube
2. Water outlet tube
3. ISS hose
4. Crankcase ventilation hose
5. Antibackfire valve hose
6. Throttle opener vacuum signal hose
7. Throttle opener hose (throttle opener to air cleaner)
8. Throttle opener hose (throttle opener to servo diaphragm)
9. Canister purge hose

EGR connections through 1974

4. Remove the throttle opener valve and servo.
5. Disconnect the water tube between the thermostat housing and balance tube.
6. Remove the exhaust gas return tube and water outlet hose.
7. Disconnect the throttle linkage at the joint.
8. Remove the four mounting bolts and pull the balance tube off the engine. Disconnect the hose which runs between the idle screw block and air/fuel by-pass tube.

To install, reverse the removal procedures exactly.

Automatic Temperature Control Air Cleaner (1970–74)

This system is designed to stabilize the temperature of air going to the carburetors in order to permit smooth operation with leaner fuel/air mixtures. It incorporates a temperature sensor which feeds a vacuum motor varying amounts of vacuum according to the temperature of the air in the air cleaner. The vacuum motor controls an air door which in turn controls the amount of air to pass over the exhaust manifold on its way to the air cleaner.

A.T.C. SYSTEM TEST

1. Allow the engine to cool until the engine compartment is below 86° F (30° C). Make sure that the air door is open.
2. Start the engine and operate it at idle. If the air door closes right away, it and the vacuum motor are in good condition.
3. Watch the air door to ensure that it opens gradually. In hot weather, it will eventually open all the way while in cold weather, it will open only slightly.
4. If there is doubt about the operation of the system, tape a small thermometer to the inside of the air cleaner cover, as close as possible to the sensor. Then operate the engine

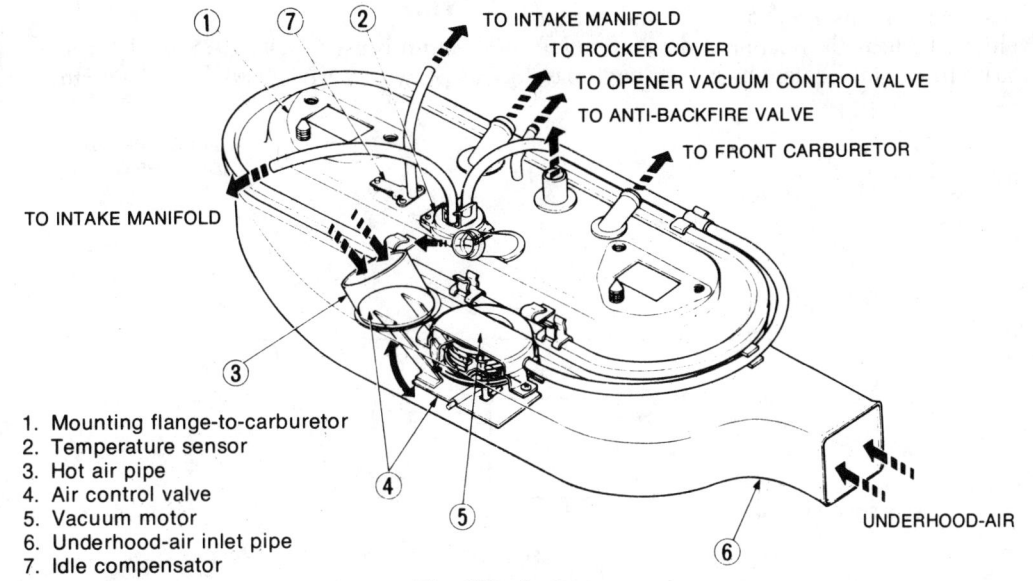

1. Mounting flange-to-carburetor
2. Temperature sensor
3. Hot air pipe
4. Air control valve
5. Vacuum motor
6. Underhood-air inlet pipe
7. Idle compensator

The ATC air cleaner

EMISSION CONTROLS AND FUEL SYSTEM

FLOW OF COOLANT

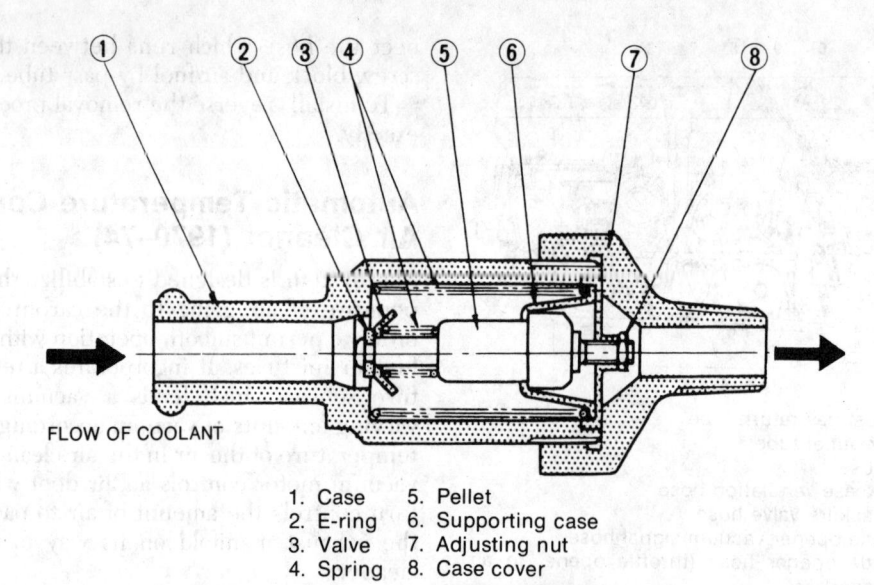

1. Case
2. E-ring
3. Valve
4. Spring
5. Pellet
6. Supporting case
7. Adjusting nut
8. Case cover

The manifold heat control thermostat

until the thermometer has had a chance to reach a stable reading. Finally, open the air cleaner and read the thermometer. It should read between 100–130° F (38–55° C).

5. If the system is faulty, the vacuum motor may be tested by removing its vacuum supply hose from the temperature sensor and connecting it directly to the manifold. If the valve closes with the engine operating at idle speed, the problem must be in the temperature sensor or the hoses.

Manifold Heat Control Thermostat

This device is installed on 1972 and earlier vehicles to heat the manifold during engine warmup. Engine coolant passes through passages in the manifold until a temperature of about 150° F exists. At this point, the thermostat closes off the flow of coolant through the manifold.

To test the thermostat, remove it and attach a length of rubber hose to the inlet end. Then immerse the thermostat in water heated to 175° F. After the thermostat has had a minute or so to reach the temperature of the water, force air at low pressure into the hose. If bubbles come out the other end of the thermostat, replace it.

Boost Controlled Deceleration Device

This unit is used on all 1975 and later models except with turbocharged engines, to per-

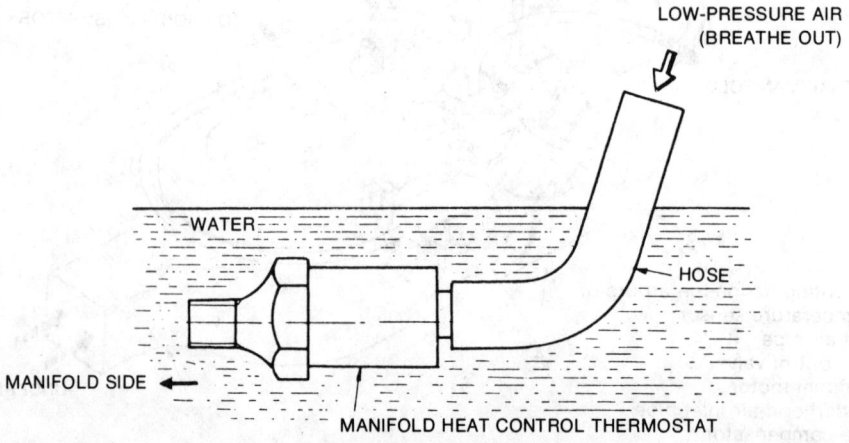

LOW-PRESSURE AIR (BREATHE OUT)

WATER

HOSE

MANIFOLD SIDE

MANIFOLD HEAT CONTROL THERMOSTAT

Checking the manifold heat control thermostat

form the same function as the throttle opener used on earlier models, to reduce emissions of HC during deceleration. The device is a part of the throttle chamber and is located at the bottom. If the throttle hangs open for long periods during deceleration, it's a sign that the BCDD requires adjustment. This should be referred to your Datsun dealer.

Catalytic Converter

All 1975 and later models sold in California, some 1979 models sold in the other 49 States of the U.S., and all 1980 and later models sold in the U.S. and Canada have a catalytic converter, which is a muffler-shaped device installed into the exhaust system. The converter is filled with a monolithic substrate coated with small amounts of platinum and palladium. Through catalytic action, a chemical change converts carbon monoxide and hydrocarbons into carbon dioxide and water. 1980 models sold in California and all 1981 and later models have a three-way catalytic converter. Platinum, palladium, and rhodium are used in an oxidation-reduction process which acts on all three major constituents of exhaust pollution; HC and CO are oxidized in the usual manner into H_2O and CO_2, and oxides of nitrogen are reduced to free oxygen and nitrogen (O_2 and N_2 respectively).

1975-78 models (all California models) have a floor temperature warning system, consisting of a temperature sensor installed onto the floor of the car above the converter; a relay, located under the passenger seat; and a light, installed on the instrument panel. The lamp illuminates when floor temperatures become abnormally high, due to converter or engine malfunction. The light also comes on when the ignition switch is turned to Start, to check its operation. 1979 and later models do not have the warning system.

1980 California models and all 1981 and later models have an oxygen sensor warning light on the dashboard, which illuminates at the first 30,000 mile interval, signaling the need for oxygen sensor replacement. The oxygen sensor is part of the Mixture Ratio Feedback System, described later in this section. The Feedback System uses the three-way converter as one of its major components.

No regular maintenance is required for the catalytic converter system, except for periodic replacement of the Air Induction System filter on 1980 49 State models sold in the U.S. The Air Induction System is described earlier in this chapter; filter replacement procedures are in Chapter 1. The Air Induction System is used to supply the catalytic converter with fresh air; oxygen present in the air is used in the oxidation process.

Mixture Ratio Feedback System

The need for better fuel economy coupled to increasingly strict emission control regulations dictate a more exact control of the engine air/fuel mixture. Datsun has developed a Mixture Ratio Feedback System in response to these needs. The system is installed on all 1980 models sold in California and all 1981 and later models.

The principle of the system is to control the air/fuel mixture exactly, so that more complete combustion can occur in the engine, and more thorough oxidation and reduction of the exhaust gases can occur in the catalytic converter. The object is to maintain a stoichiometric air/fuel mixture, which is chemically correct for theoretically complete combustion. The stoichiometric ratio is 14.7:1 (air to fuel). At that point, the converter's efficiency is greatest in oxidizing and reducing HC, CO, and NOx into CO_2, H_2O, O_2, and N_2.

Components used in the system include an oxygen sensor, installed in the exhaust manifold upstream of the converter; a three-way oxidation-reduction catalytic converter; an electronic control unit, which is part of the electronic fuel injection control unit; and the fuel injection system itself.

The oxygen sensor reads the oxygen content of the exhaust gases. It generates an electrical signal which is sent to the control unit. The control unit then decides how to adjust the mixture to keep it at the correct air/fuel ratio. For example, if the mixture is too lean, the control unit increases the fuel metering to the injectors. The monitoring process is a continual one, so that fine mixture adjustments are going on at all times.

The system has two modes of operation: open loop and closed loop. Open loop operation takes place when the engine is still cold. In this mode, the control unit ignores signals from the oxygen sensor and provides a fixed signal to the fuel injection unit. Closed loop operation takes place when the engine and catalytic converter have warmed to normal operating temperature. In closed loop operation, the control unit uses the oxygen sensor

128　EMISSION CONTROLS AND FUEL SYSTEM

signals to adjust the mixture; the burned mixture's oxygen content is read by the oxygen sensor, which continues to signal the control unit, and so on. Thus, the closed loop mode is an interdependent system of information feedback.

Mixture is, of course, not readily adjustable in this system. All system adjustments require the use of a CO meter; thus, they should be entrusted to a qualified dealer with access to the equipment and special training in the system's repair. The only regularly scheduled maintenance is replacement of the oxygen sensor at 30,000 mile intervals. This procedure is covered in the following section.

It should be noted that proper operation of the system is entirely dependent on the oxygen sensor. Thus, if the sensor is not replaced at the correct interval, or if the sensor fails during normal operation, the engine fuel mixture will be incorrect, resulting in poor fuel economy, starting problems, or stumbling and stalling of the engine when warm.

OXYGEN SENSOR INSPECTION AND REPLACEMENT

An exhaust gas sensor warning light will illuminate on the instrument panel when the car has reached 30,000 miles. This is a signal that the oxygen sensor must be replaced.

Note that the warning light is not part of a repeating system; that is, after the first 30,000 mile service, the warning light will not illuminate again. However, it is important to replace the oxygen sensor every 30,000 miles, to ensure proper monitoring and control of the engine air/fuel mixture.

The oxygen sensor can be inspected using the following procedure:

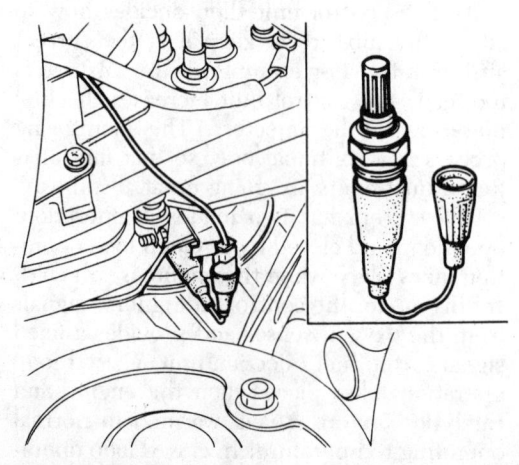

1. Start the engine and allow it to reach normal operating temperature.
2. Run the engine at approximately 2,000 rpm under no load. Block the front wheels and set the parking brake.
3. An inspection lamp has been provided on the bottom of the control unit, which is located in the passenger compartment on the driver's side kick panel, next to the clutch or brake pedal. If the oxygen sensor is operating correctly, the inspection lamp will go on and off more than 5 times in 10 seconds. The inspection lamp can be more easily seen with the aid of a mirror.
4. If the lamp does not go on and off as specified, the system is not operating correctly. Check the battery, ignition system, engine oil and coolant levels, all fuses, the fuel injection wiring harness connectors, all vacuum hoses, the oil filler cap and dipstick for proper seating, and the valve clearance and engine compression. If all of these parts are in good order, and the inspection lamp still does not go on and off at least 5 times in 10 seconds, the oxygen sensor is probably faulty. However, the possibility exists that the malfunction could be in the fuel injection control unit. The system should be tested by a qualified dealer with specific training in the Mixture Ratio Feedback System.

To replace the oxygen sensor:

1. Disconnect the negative cable from the battery.
2. Disconnect the sensor electrical lead. Unscrew the sensor from the exhaust manifold.
3. Coat the threads of the replacement sensor with a nickel base anti-seize compound. Do not use other types of compounds, since they may electrically insulate the sensor. Install the sensor into the mani-

Oxygen sensor

UNDER THE RIGHT SIDE OF INSTRUMENT PANEL

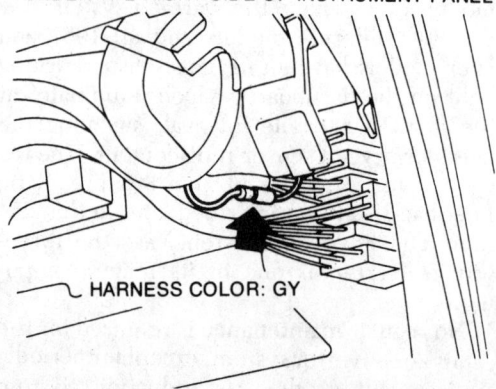

HARNESS COLOR: GY

Oxygen sensor warning lamp harness connector

EMISSION CONTROLS AND FUEL SYSTEM

fold. Installation torque for the sensor is 29-36 ft lbs (4.0-5.0 kg-m). Connect the electrical lead. Be careful handling the electrical lead; it is easily damaged.

4. Connect the negative battery cable.

After the first 30,000 mile replacement, the warning lamp harness connector should be unplugged to extinguish the lamp. The connector is located under the right side of the instrument panel; the harness wire color is green with a yellow stripe.

Spark Timing Control System—1970-76

Retardation of the ignition timing can be used to control the emission of oxides of nitrogen and hydrocarbons. 1970-73 automatic transmission models have a dual point distributor to provide advanced and retarded distributor characteristics. 1974 automatic transmission models, and all 1975-76 49 States and Canada models use a distributor with dual pick-ups for the same purpose.

The distributor has two sets of breaker points or two electronic ignition pick-ups which operate independently of each other and are positioned with a relative phase angle of 10° (1970-73), 7° (1974), or 6° (1975-76) apart. This makes one set the advanced set and the other the retarded set.

The two sets are connected in parallel to the primary side of the ignition circuit. One set of points or pick-ups controls the firing of the spark plugs, and hence the ignition timing, depending on whether or not the retarded set is energized.

When both sets are electrically energized, the first set to open has no control over breaking the ignition coil primary circuit because the retarded set is still closed and maintaining a complete circuit to ground. When the retarded set opens, the advanced set is still open, and the primary circuit is broken causing the electromagnetic field in the ignition coil to collapse and the ignition spark to be produced.

When the retarded set is removed from the primary ignition circuit through the operation of a distributor relay inserted into the retarded circuit, the advanced set controls the primary circuit.

PHASE DIFFERENCE ADJUSTMENT

1. On 1970-73 models, disconnect the distributor wiring harness from the engine harness. Connect the black wire of the engine harness to the black wire of the distributor harness using a jumper wire. This connects the advanced set of points.

On 1974 models, disconnect the engine harness from the coolant temperature switch. This activates the advanced pick-up.

On 1975-76 models, disconnect the red engine harness wire from the coolant temperature switch. Ground the engine harness wire to the engine block (use a jumper wire if necessary).

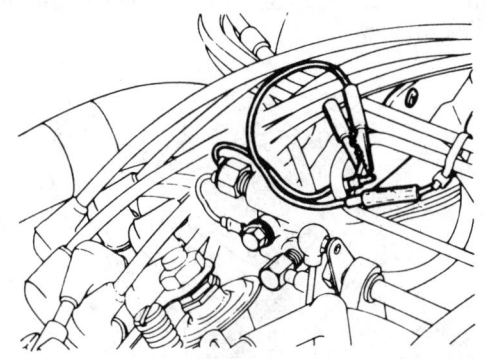

Ground the engine harness wire (1975-76)

2. With the engine at normal operating temperature and idling at the specified idling speed (see the "Tune-Up Specifications" chart in Chapter 2), adjust the engine timing to the advanced specification.

3. On 1970-73 models, disconnect the jumper wire from the black wire of the distributor harness and connect it to the yellow wire of the distributor harness. This connects the retarded set of points.

To connect the retarded pick-ups on 1974 models, use a jumper wire to short circuit the engine harness wire disconnected from the temperature switch in Step 1. This will short circuit the advance control relay.

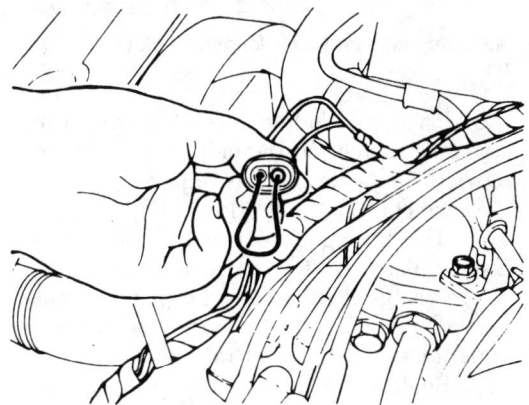

Jumper wire connection to the engine harness (1974)

130 EMISSION CONTROLS AND FUEL SYSTEM

On 1975–76 models, remove the ground from the engine harness red wire, leaving the wire disconnected.

4. With the engine idling, check the ignition timing. It should be retarded from the advanced setting as follows:
10°—1970–73
7°—1974
6°—1975–76

5. To adjust the phase angle of the ignition timing, loosen the adjuster plate set screws on the same side as the retarded point or pick-up set.

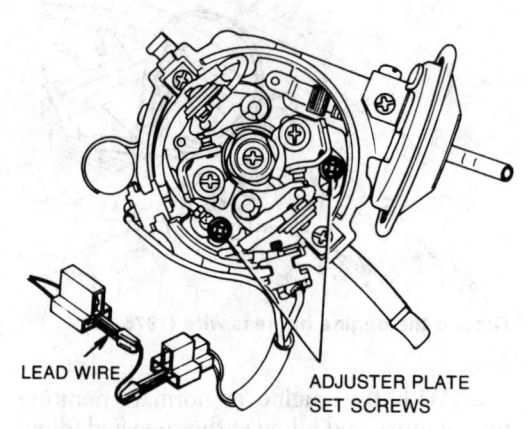

Adjuster plate set screw location—1970–73

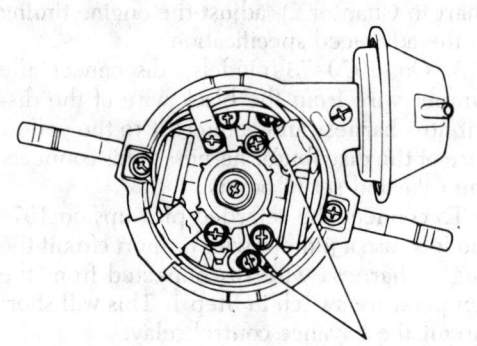

Adjuster plate set screw location—electronic ignition

6. Place the blade of a screwdriver in the adjusting notch of the adjuster plate and move the adjuster plate as required to obtain the correct retarded ignition timing specification. The timing is retarded when the adjuster plate is turned counterclockwise. There are graduations on the plate to make the adjustment easier: one graduation is equal to 4° of crankshaft rotation.

7. Replace the distributor cap, start the engine, and check the ignition timing with the retarded side activated (as in Step 3).

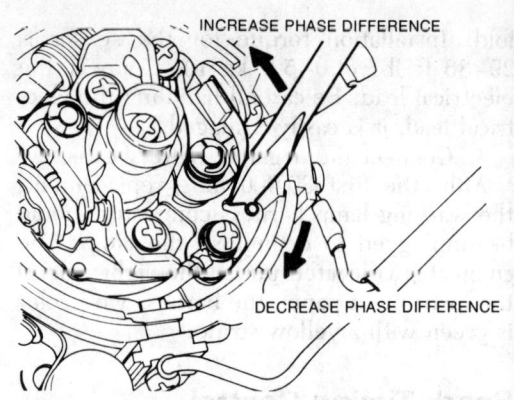

Move the adjuster plate to change the phase difference—point type models

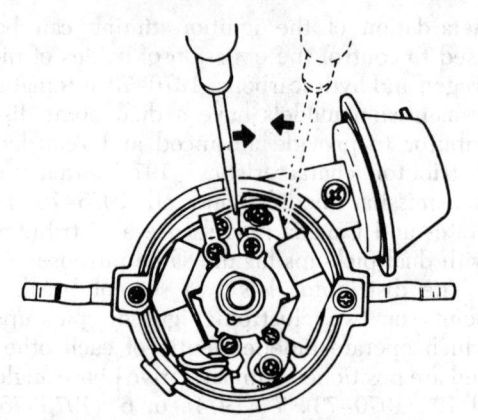

Phase difference adjustment on electronic ignition models

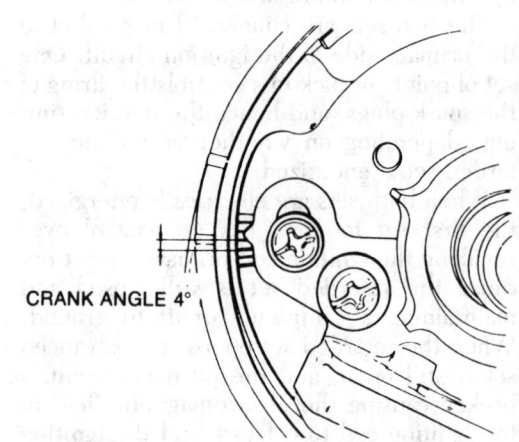

The graduations on the adjuster plate equal 4° of crankshaft rotation

8. Repeat Steps 6 and 7 as necessary to properly set the retarded ignition timing.

Transmission Controlled Spark Advance—1975–76

This system is used on all 1975–76 manual transmission equipped models, except those

EMISSION CONTROLS AND FUEL SYSTEM

delivered in California. The system consists of a transmission mounted electrical switch and a vacuum switching valve. The switch functions to limit vacuum advance to operation in fourth gear only. The vacuum switching valve is energized in all gears except fourth and vents vacuum from the throttle chamber into the atmosphere. When the transmission is shifted into fourth gear, the switch breaks the circuit and the vacuum valve is deenergized and vacuum reaches the advance unit on the distributor.

Spark Timing Control System—1979 and Later

Two different systems are used in 1979 and 1980, but both are given the name of Spark Timing Control System. Basically, both systems are designed to control distributor vacuum advance.

1979

All U.S. models with a catalytic converter and all models sold in Canada have this system. It is designed to control distributor vacuum advance during acceleration to limit emissions of HC and NOx.

The system simply consists of a vacuum delay valve spliced into the distributor vacuum advance hose. During acceleration, the valve restricts the amount of air flow in the vacuum hose. Inside the valve are a metering disc and a one-way umbrella valve. Air flows freely past the umbrella valve, from the throttle to the distributor. The metering valve restricts air flow in the opposite direction, from the distributor to the throttle.

Inspection

1. Remove the valve from the distributor vacuum hose.
2. Blow through the valve from the throttle side. This is the black side of the valve. Air should flow through freely.
3. Blow through the distributor side of the valve. This is the brown side. There should be resistance to the air flow.
4. If the valve does not perform correctly, replace it. When installing the valve, be sure the brown side is connected to the distributor hose and the black side is connected to the throttle hose.

1980 AND LATER

This system is slightly more complicated than the 1979 system. Spark timing is controlled by a single Thermal Vacuum Valve (TVV) on models sold in California and Canada. 1980 California models and all 1981 and later models sold in U.S.A. have a TVV installed in the engine thermostat housing. The valve has two vacuum connections: one for fresh air from the vacuum connector, the other to the distributor vacuum advance. 1980 and later Canadian models have a TVV installed in the intake manifold heater housing. The valve has three vacuum connections: one for fresh air, one to the EGR valve, and one to the distributor vacuum advance.

U.S.A. State models have two TVVs and a one-way valve. One TVV is installed in the intake manifold in the same manner as the Canadian TVV; it has the same connections as the Canadian TVV. The other TVV is installed in the thermostat housing, and also has three vacuum connections: one to the one-way valve, one to the distributor vacuum advance unit, and one to a vacuum source on the throttle chamber. The one-way valve is installed in the line between the vacuum connector and the TVV installed in the thermostat housing.

Inspection

This inspection procedure applies to the entire system, regardless of the specific components used.

1. Check all vacuum hoses for leaks, kinks, breaks, improper connections, etc., and correct as necessary.
2. Check that the distributor vacuum advance unit is working properly.
3. Connect a timing light to the engine.
4. Check the TVV as follows:
    a. Start the engine. It must be cold. Check and record the ignition timing.
    b. As the engine warms up, check and record the ignition timing. The timing should be retarded from its cold setting.
    c. Allow the engine to warm up to normal operating temperature. The timing should advance to its normal setting.
5. If the timing does not change as specified, replace the TVV (both TVVs on U.S.A. State models).

The one-way valve installed on U.S.A State models can be inspected as follows:

1. Remove the one-way valve.
2. Blow air through the vacuum connector side of the valve (black side). Air should flow through freely.
3. Blow air through the TVV side of the

132 EMISSION CONTROLS AND FUEL SYSTEM

valve (white side). There should be resistance to the air flow.

4. If the valve does not perform correctly, replace it. When installing the valve, be sure that the black side is connected to the vacuum connector hose and the white side is connected to the TVV hose.

Deceleration Control System
VACUUM CONTROL VALVE

This system is used on 1981 and later models with a turbocharged engine and is designed to control the intake manifold vacuum under decelerating driving conditions so as to reduce oil consumption. Air is directed from a 3-way connector through an air hose and vacuum control valve. To keep oil consumption low, as the air enters, the intake manifold vacuum will be maintained at less than the specified level. To check the operation of the vacuum control valve proceed as follows:

1. Disconnect one end (Air regulator side) of the air hose connecting the 3 way connector to the control valve.
2. Make sure that the vacuum control valve operates when engine speed is decreased from 3,500–4,000 to idle.
3. Place fingers on the hose end to check for valve operation. If the intake vacuum is not present at the end of the air hose, replace the vacuum control valve.

NOTE: *The above procedure is not accurate at altitudes above 2,300 to 4,000 ft range.*

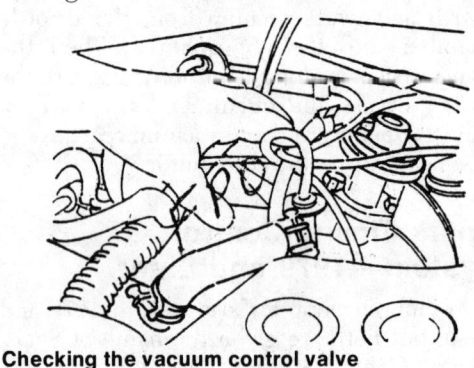

Checking the vacuum control valve

FUEL SYSTEM

Mechanical Fuel Pump (1970–74)
REMOVAL AND INSTALLATION

1. Disconnect the inlet and outlet lines from the pump.

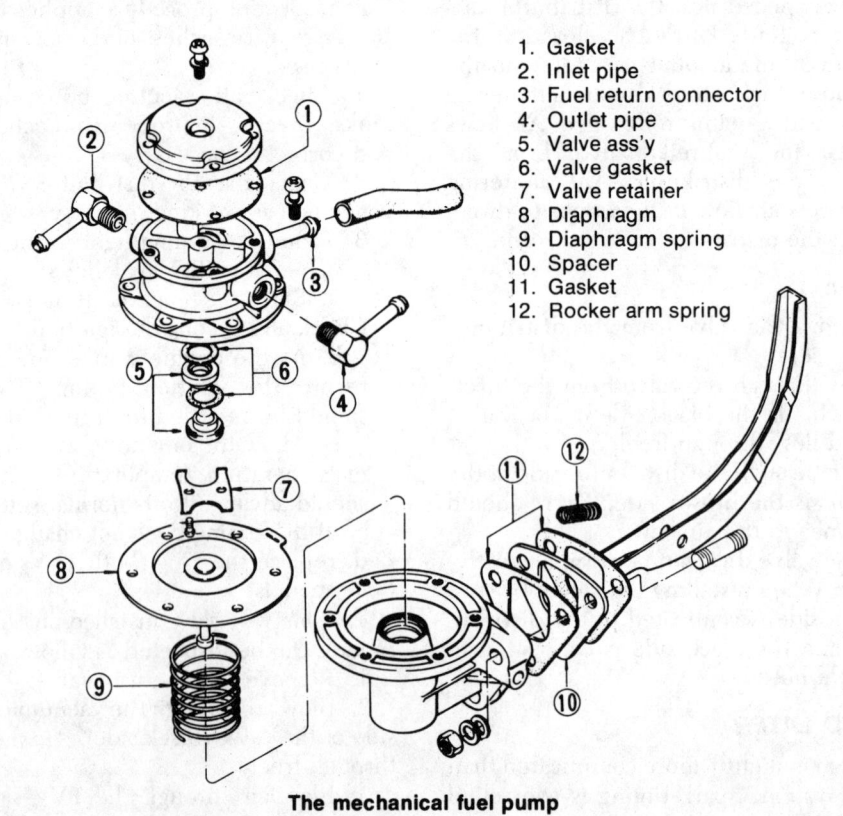

1. Gasket
2. Inlet pipe
3. Fuel return connector
4. Outlet pipe
5. Valve ass'y
6. Valve gasket
7. Valve retainer
8. Diaphragm
9. Diaphragm spring
10. Spacer
11. Gasket
12. Rocker arm spring

The mechanical fuel pump

EMISSION CONTROLS AND FUEL SYSTEM

2. Remove the mounting bolts.
3. Remove the pump and discard the gasket.
4. Lubricate the rocker arm, rocker arm pin, and lever pin of the pump.
5. Put a new gasket in position and bolt the pump in place.
6. Connect the fuel lines.

FUEL PUMP TEST

1. Disconnect the line from the fuel pump to the carburetor at the pump.
2. Tee in a pressure gauge going as close to the carburetor as possible.
3. Start the engine and operate it at various speeds. The fuel pump pressure should be 3.4–4.25 psi (0.24–0.30 kg/cm²).

Pressure below these specifications indicates excessive wear, while high pressure indicate a faulty spring or diaphragm. In either case, the pump requires removal and disassembly for replacement of faulty parts. If the pump passes the pressure test, but if there is still a question that its performance may not be adequate, proceed with the capacity test below.

1. Disconnect the pressure gauge from the tee, and position a large container under the open end.
2. Start the engine and operate it at 1,000 rpm for 15 seconds. The pump should deliver at least 0.42 qts (400 cc) of fuel in this time.

Failure of this test indicates a faulty pump or clogged suction line.

Electric Fuel Pump (1974–82)
LOCATION AND TYPE

The electric pump used on 260-Z models is a transistorized plunger type which force feeds the conventional mechanical fuel pump in order to minimize the chances of vapor lock or other fuel deficiency problems. The pump is located in the corner where the differential mounting member intersects the side member. The 1975–82 Z and ZX models are equipped with one electric fuel pump mounted near the fuel tank and the right rear wheel.

REMOVAL AND INSTALLATION
1974

1. Disconnect the negative battery cable.
2. Remove the inlet hose at the fuel strainer. Remove the outlet hose at the pump and drain the remaining fuel into a suitable container.
3. Disconnect both electrical connections at the pump.

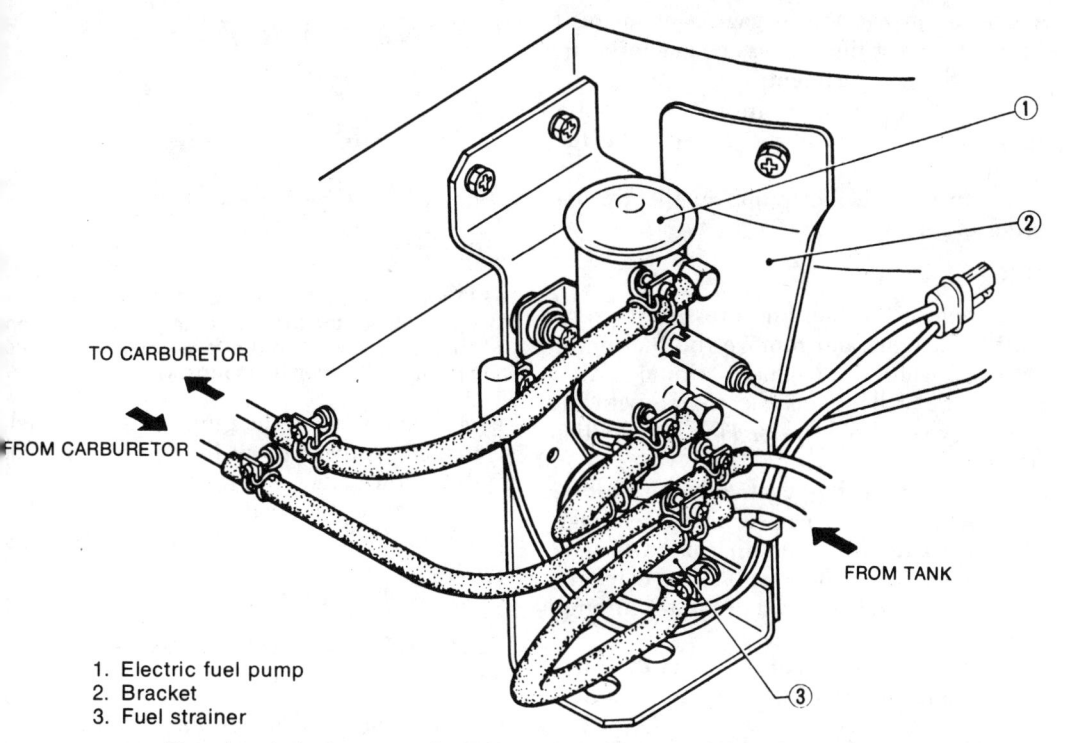

1. Electric fuel pump
2. Bracket
3. Fuel strainer

The electric fuel pump and strainer; 1974 shown, later models similar

134 EMISSION CONTROLS AND FUEL SYSTEM

4. Remove the mounting bolts, and remove the pump from the bracket.

To install, reverse the removal procedures.

1975–79

1. Disconnect the battery ground cable.
2. Disconnect the wiring harness to the cold start valve.
3. Using two jumper wires from the battery, energize the cold start valve for two or three seconds to relieve pressure in the fuel system.

CAUTION: *Be careful not to short the two jumpers together.*

4. Jack up the rear of the car and safely support it on stands. Have a can and a rag handy to catch any spilled fuel.
5. Clamp the hose between the fuel tank and the fuel pump.
6. Loosen the hose clamps on the fuel lines at both ends of the pump and remove the lines from the pump.
7. Remove the two retaining screws and remove the fuel pump bracket.
8. Disconnect the fuel pump harness connector. On 280-Z models, roll back the carpet behind the passenger seat to reach the connector. On 280-Z 2+2 models, remove the rear seat and remove the harness cover. Disconnect the wiring. On ZX models, remove the mat in the luggage compartment, and disconnect the harness connector at the rear of the compartment.
9. Pull the harness through the rubber grommet in the floor and remove the fuel pump.
10. Install the fuel pump in the reverse order of removal.

1980

1. Reduce the fuel line pressure to zero: start the engine and remove the fuel pump relay #2 while the engine is running. After the engine stalls, crank the engine with the starter two or three times. Turn the ignition off.
2. Disconnect the negative battery cable.
3. Remove the luggage compartment mat. Disconnect the fuel pump harness wiring at the connector at the rear of the compartment. Push the wires and grommet through the floor.
4. Raise and support the rear of the car.
5. Clamp the hose between the fuel tank and the pump.
6. Loosen the fuel line clamps and disconnect the hoses from the pump. Have a metal container ready to catch the fuel which will spill from the lines.
7. Remove the bolts which secure the pump bracket to the body and remove the pump.
8. Installation is the reverse.

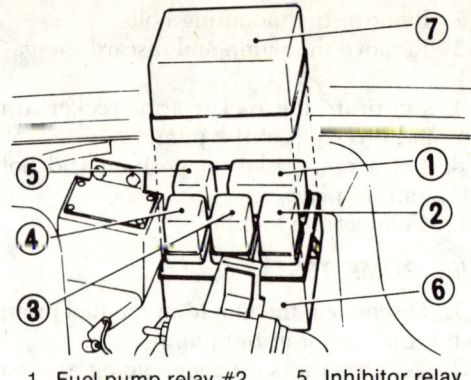

1. Fuel pump relay #2
2. Lighting relay
3. Bulb check relay
4. Air conditioner relay
5. Inhibitor relay
6. Relay bracket
7. Relay cover

Fuel pump relay # 2—1980 and later

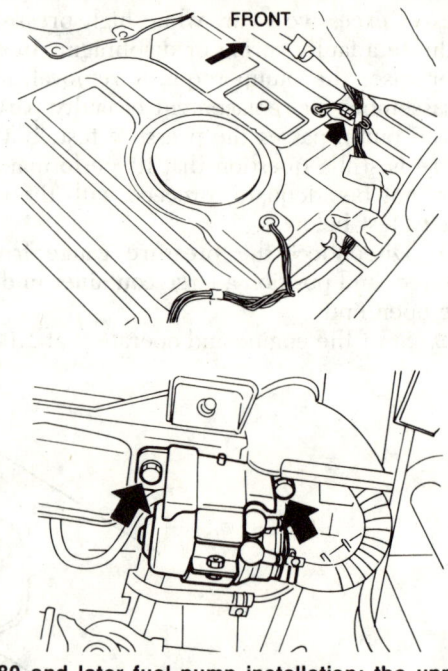

1980 and later fuel pump installation; the upper diagram shows the location of the harness wiring connector (arrow), and the lower diagram shows the pump installation bolts (arrow)

ELECTRIC FUEL PUMP TEST
1974

1. Disconnect the fuel pump outlet hose.
2. Connect a hose with an inside diameter

EMISSION CONTROLS AND FUEL SYSTEM

of 6 mm (0.236 in.) to the pump outlet. Do not use a hose of a smaller diameter. Raise the end of the hose above the level of the pump.

3. Start the engine and allow it to run for a minute. Capacity should be 1,400 cc (85.5 cu. in.) in one minute or less. There is normally enough fuel in the carburetor float bowls to perform this test.

4. If capacity is sufficient but there is still some doubt about the pump's performance, connect a pressure gauge to the pump outlet with a hose of the same diameter as used in Step 2. Pressure should be 4.6 psi (0.32 kg/cm^2).

1975-78
FUNCTIONAL TEST

1. Disconnect the cable from the "S" terminal of the starter motor solenoid.
2. Unplug the cold start valve wiring harness connector.
3. Turn the ignition key to Start. You should be able to hear the fuel pump running. If not, check the wiring circuits and fuses. If the circuits and fuses are in order, replace the pump.

PRESSURE TEST

1. Reduce the fuel line pressure to zero, following Steps 1–3 of the pump removal and installation procedure.
2. Connect a pressure gauge into the fuel line in the engine compartment between the fuel tube and the fuel filter outlet hose.
3. Disconnect the wire from the "S" terminal of the starter motor solenoid.
4. Connect the negative battery cable.
5. Turn the ignition key to Start.
6. Pressure should be approximately 36.3 psi (2.55 kg/cm^2).
7. If not, replace the pressure regulator (see the replacement procedure following) and repeat the tests. If the pressure is still not correct, check all fuel lines for kinks or blockage, and replace the pump as necessary.

1979-82
FUNCTIONAL TEST

1. Disconnect either the wire to the alternator "L" terminal, or the oil pressure switch connector.
2. Turn the ignition key to Start. You should be able to hear the fuel pump running. If not, check the wiring circuits and fuses; if they are in order, replace the fuel pump.

PRESSURE TEST

1. Reduce the fuel pressure to zero. For 1979 models, follow Steps 1–3 of the 1975–79 fuel pump replacement procedure. For 1980–82 models, follow Step 1 of the 1980 fuel pump replacement procedure.
2. On 1979 models, connect the negative battery cable.
3. Connect a fuel pressure gauge into the fuel line in the engine compartment between the fuel pipe and the fuel filter outlet hose.
4. Start the engine and read the fuel pressure. It should be approximately 30 psi (2.1 kg/cm^2) at idle, and approximately 37 psi (2.6 kg/cm^2) at any speed above idle.
5. If the pressure is incorrect, replace the pressure regulator, following the replacement procedure given later in this chapter. After replacement of the regulator, repeat the pressure test. If still incorrect, check the fuel lines for kinks or blockage, and replace the pump as necessary.

Fuel Pressure Regulator
REMOVAL AND INSTALLATION
1975-82

1. Reduce the fuel line pressure to zero, using the appropriate procedure given under the fuel pump replacement instructions.
2. Disconnect the vacuum hose from the pressure regulator.
3. Remove the regulator attaching screws.
4. Place a rag under the regulator to catch the fuel which will spill when the fuel lines

Fuel pressure regulator

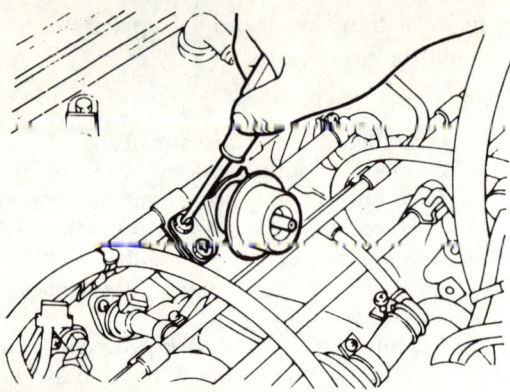

136 EMISSION CONTROLS AND FUEL SYSTEM

Fuel pressure regulator removal

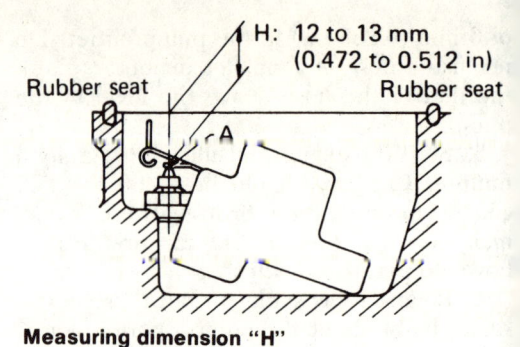

Measuring dimension "H"

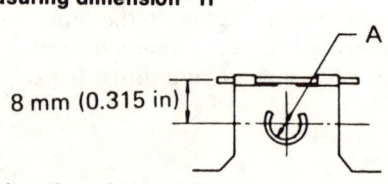

The location of point "A"

are disconnected. Loosen the hose clamps and remove the fuel lines from the regulator.

5. Installation is the reverse.

Carburetors

REMOVAL AND INSTALLATION

1. Remove the three thumbscrews and detach the air cleaner cover.
2. Disconnect all hoses between air cleaner and other components.
3. Remove the six screws retaining the air cleaner flange to the carburetors and remove it.
4. Remove the fuel and ISS hoses from both carburetors. Remove the by-pass hose from the front carburetor.
5. Remove the distributor and canister vacuum hose from the front carburetor.
6. Remove the EGR vacuum hose from the rear carburetor (on 1973 and later models).
7. Remove the coolant inlet hose from the front carburetor and the outlet hose from the rear carburetor.
8. Disconnect the throttle linkage and, on earlier models, the choke linkage.
9. Remove the attaching nuts and remove the carburetors.
10. To separate the two carburetors, disconnect and remove the air by-pass and coolant hoses.
11. Reverse the removal procedures to install.

FLOAT LEVEL ADJUSTMENT

1974

1. Remove the carburetor from the intake manifold. Remove the seven attaching screws and remove the float chamber cover.
2. Turn the carburetor upside down to check the position of the float lever. Both floats should touch the inner wall of the carburetor.
3. Measure dimension "H" between the end face of the float chamber and the float lever tongue which contacts the needle valve (point "A"). It should be 0.472–0.512 in. (12–13 mm).
4. If necessary, bend the float lever near the float to bring the dimension to within specifications.
5. Turn the carburetor right side up. Measure the gap ("G") between the power valve nozzle and float. It should be 0.020–0.079 in. (0.5–2.0 mm).

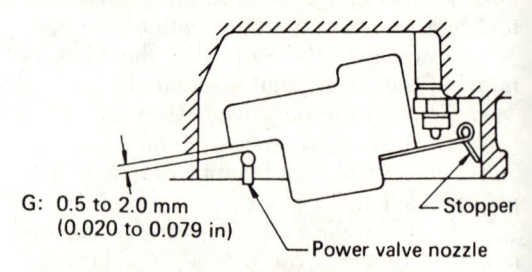

The location of dimension "G"

6. Adjust the gap, as necessary, by bending the stop as required. Then, recheck dimension "H."
7. Install the float chamber cover and install the carburetor on the engine.
8. When the engine is operating, the fuel level should be even with the center line of the float level window.

1973

1. Remove the carburetor from the engine. Remove the float chamber cover.

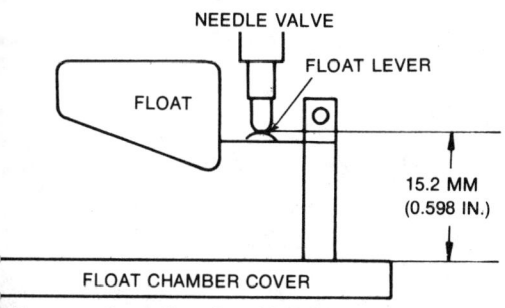

EMISSION CONTROLS AND FUEL SYSTEM

Where to check float level height—1973 models

2. Measure the distance between the portion of the float lever which contacts the needle valve and the float chamber cover. It should be 0.598 in. (15.2 mm).
3. If necessary, bend the float lever to adjust the dimension. Recheck to make sure that the dimension is to specification.
4. Install the float chamber cover and reinstall the carburetor on the engine.
5. Check float level by operating the engine and checking that the fuel level is in the center of the float level window.

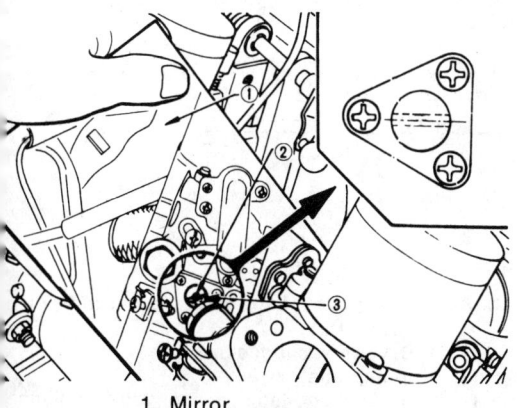

1970–72

1. Remove the four float chamber cover screws and remove the cover.
2. Place the cover on a flat surface with the float upward.
3. Lift the float up until the needle valve is open and then lower it just until the needle valve contacts the seat.
4. See the illustration and measure the distance between fuel level and the top of the float chamber. It should be 0.5512–0.5906 in. (14–15 mm).
5. If necessary, correct the dimension by bending the float lever.
6. Replace the float chamber cover.

FAST IDLE ADJUSTMENT

1973–74

1. Place the fast idle screw on the first step of the fast idle cam.
2. Adjust the screw so that the clearance between the throttle valve and the lower throttle bore is 0.023–0.025 in. (0.59–0.64 mm).

1970–72

1. Measure the clearance between the throttle valve and bore when the choke lever

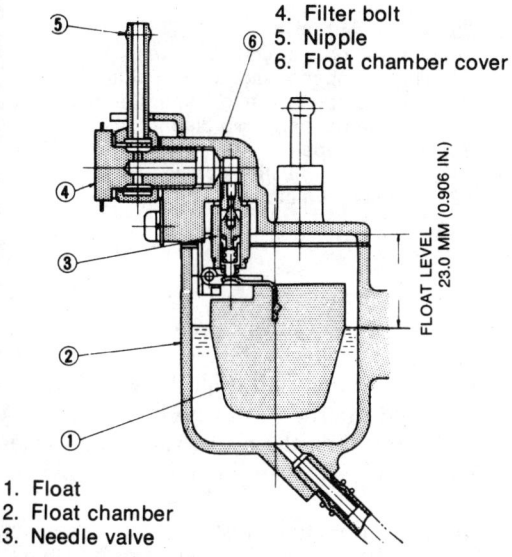

1. Mirror
2. Float level point
3. Float level window

Checking the float level with a mirror

4. Filter bolt
5. Nipple
6. Float chamber cover

1. Float
2. Float chamber
3. Needle valve

Adjustment of the float level —1972 and earlier

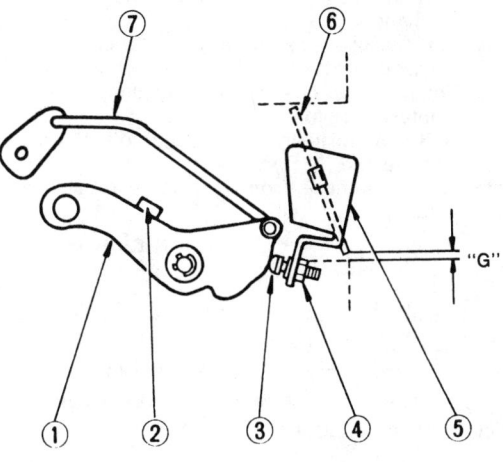

1. Choke lever
2. Choke lever stopper
3. Fast idle screw
4. Locknut
5. Fast idle lever
6. Throttle valve
7. Connecting rod

Adjusting the fast idle opening—260-Z

138 EMISSION CONTROLS AND FUEL SYSTEM

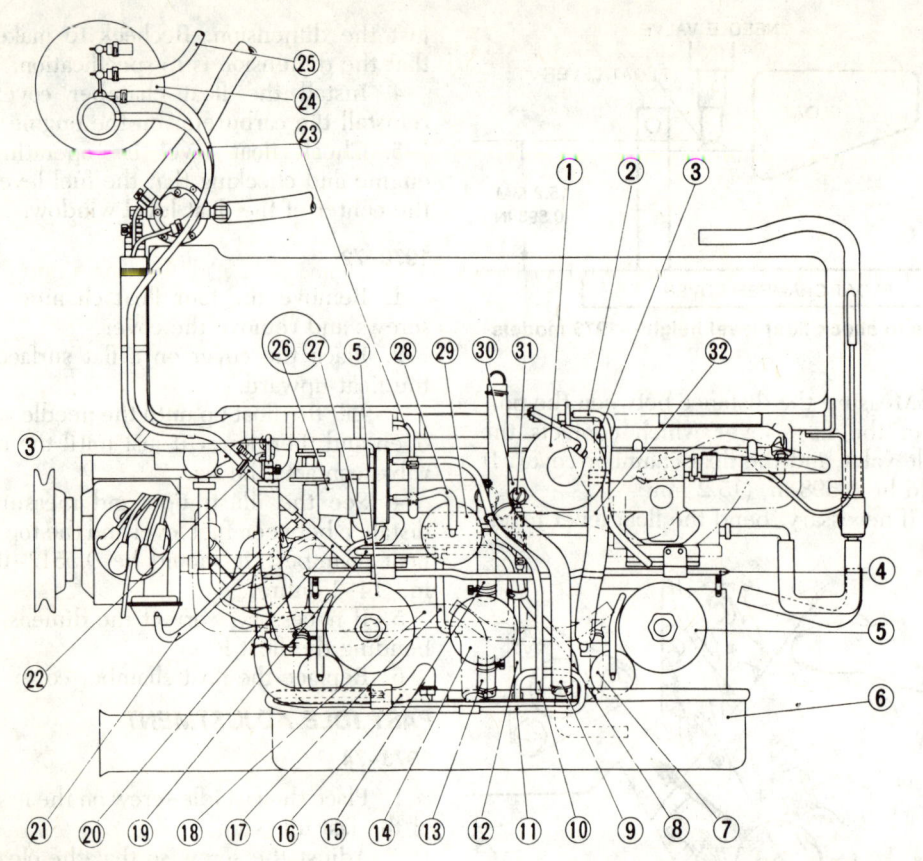

1. E.G.R. control valve
2. E.G.R. vacuum signal hose
3. Fuel inlet hose
4. I.S.S. tube
5. Carburetor
6. Air cleaner
7. Air by-pass hose
8. Idle compensator hose
9. Crankcase ventilation hose
10. Throttle opener hose (from throttle opener solenoid to air cleaner)
11. Temp. sensor hose (from temp. sensor to vacuum motor)
12. Temp. sensor hose (from temp. sensor to intake manifold)
13. A. B. valve hose (from air cleaner to A. B. valve)
14. Antibackfire (A. B.) valve
15. A. B. valve hose (from A. B. valve to balance tube)
16. Air by-pass hose (from air cleaner to front carburetor)
17. A. B. valve vacuum signal hose
18. Air pump inlet hose
19. A. B. valve and temp. sensor vacuum signal hose
20. Distributor and canister vacuum signal hose
21. Distributor vacuum signal hose
22. Canister vacuum signal hose
23. Canister purge hose
24. Carbon canister
25. Vapor vent hose
26. Throttle opener control valve
27. Throttle opener vacuum signal hose
28. Throttle opener servo diaphragm hose
29. Throttle opener servo diaphragm
30. Balance tube
31. Idle speed adjusting screw
32. Heat shield material

Carburetor and air cleaner piping

is out all the way. The clearance should be 0.232–0.271 in. (0.59–0.69 mm).

2. Correct the clearance by bending the connecting rod. Making the rod longer increases the clearance.

CHOKE PISTON ADJUSTMENT
1974

1. Close the choke valve all the way.
2. Hold the valve shut by stretching a rubber band between the lever connected to the choke wire and the carburetor.
3. Using a pair of pliers, gently grip the diaphragm rod and pull it all the way out.
4. Hold the rod in this position and check the gap between the choke valve and carburetor body. The gap should be 0.0925 in. (2.35 mm).
5. Bend the choke piston rod as necessary to secure the proper adjustment.

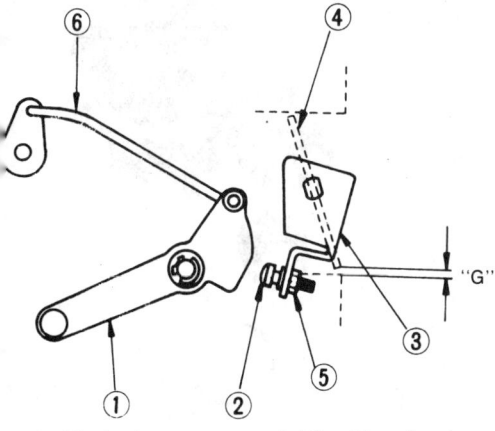

EMISSION CONTROLS AND FUEL SYSTEM 139

1. Choke lever
2. Fast idle screw
3. Fast idle lever
4. Throttle valve
5. Locknut
6. Connecting rod

Adjusting the fast idle opening—1973 models

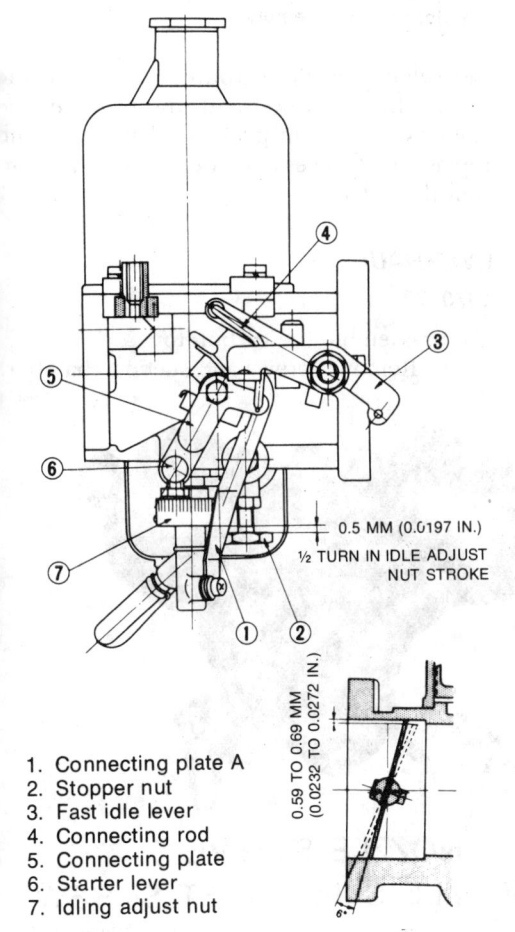

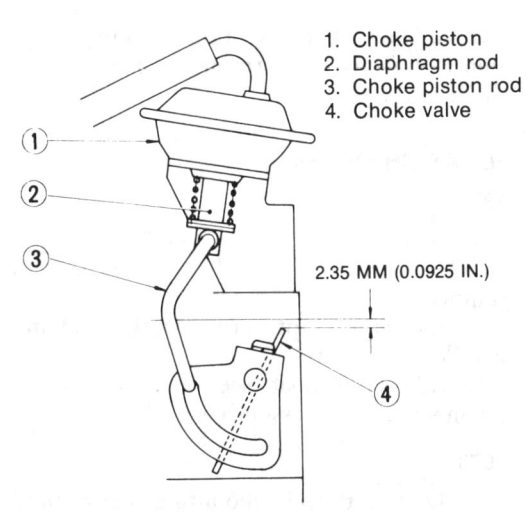

1. Choke piston
2. Diaphragm rod
3. Choke piston rod
4. Choke valve

2.35 MM (0.0925 IN.)

Adjusting the 260-Z choke piston

Location of the suction piston lifter

1. Connecting plate A
2. Stopper nut
3. Fast idle lever
4. Connecting rod
5. Connecting plate
6. Starter lever
7. Idling adjust nut

0.5 MM (0.0197 IN.)
½ TURN IN IDLE ADJUST NUT STROKE

0.59 TO 0.69 MM (0.0232 TO 0.0272 IN.)

Adjusting the fast idle opening—1970–72

SUCTION PISTON AND CHAMBER INSPECTION

1. Remove the air cleaner and the oil cap nut.

2. Gradually raise the suction piston with a suitable probe on 1973 and later models. On 1972 and earlier carburetors, the piston should be raised so that the lifter is well beyond the point where the lifter head contacts the suction piston.

3. Release the piston. The piston should drop smoothly and a sucking sound should be audible.

4. Install the oil cap nut. Raise the suction with your finger, going in through the throttle bore, and then let it drop. The piston should resist rising due to damper operation and it should return to the bottom of its travel smoothly. Otherwise, the piston and chamber require cleaning.

OVERHAUL
1973–74

On 1973 and later models the factory does not recommend overhaul, except as de-

140 EMISSION CONTROLS AND FUEL SYSTEM

scribed below, because of the extreme precision with which carburetors are calibrated at the factory.

FLOAT CHAMBER
1974

1. Remove the seven mounting screws which secure the float chamber cover and remove it.
2. Do not attempt to remove the float and needle valve parts.
3. Adjust the float (see "Float Level Adjustment"), and reassemble.

1973

1. Loosen the six mounting screws and remove the float chamber cover.
2. Remove the clip and remove the needle valve parts. Do not touch the needle jet setting nut or bend the float stopper.
3. Reassemble parts of the needle valve. Adjust the float level as described above.
4. Install the float chamber cover.

POWER VALVE
1973–74

If the carbon monoxide (CO) emissions in the exhaust are abnormally high and there is no obvious reason, check the power valve. Remove the three mounting screws and remove

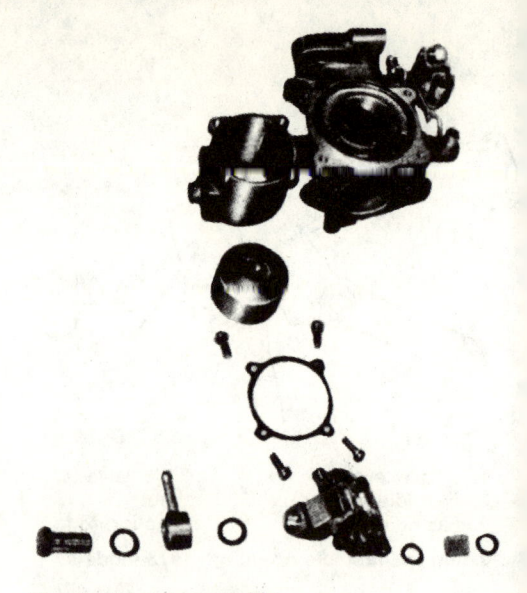

The float bowl assembly

the valve from the carburetor. Remove the other three screws and disassemble the valve. Carefully inspect the diaphragm and replace it if necessary. Reassemble and install the valve.

OVERHAUL
1970–72

To disassemble the carburetors:
1. Remove screws and suction chamber.

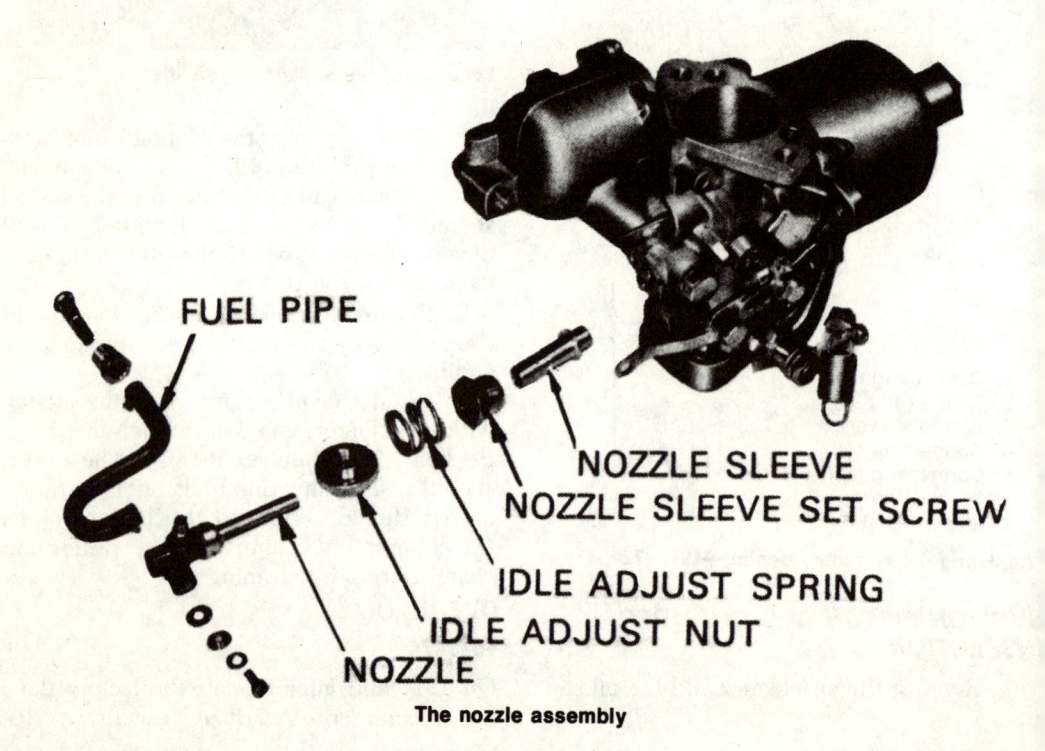

The nozzle assembly

CHILTON'S
FUEL ECONOMY & TUNE-UP TIPS

Tune-Up • Spark Plug Diagnosis • Emission Controls
Fuel System • Cooling System • Tires and Wheels
General Maintenance

55 WAYS TO IMPROVE FUEL ECONOMY

CHILTON'S FUEL ECONOMY & TUNE-UP TIPS

Fuel economy is important to everyone, no matter what kind of vehicle you drive. The maintenance-minded motorist can save both money and fuel using these tips and the periodic maintenance and tune-up procedures in this Repair and Tune-Up Guide.

There are more than 130,000,000 cars and trucks registered for private use in the United States. Each travels an average of 10-12,000 miles per year, and, in total they consume close to 70 billion gallons of fuel each year. This represents nearly 2/3 of the oil imported by the United States each year. The Federal government's goal is to reduce consumption 10% by 1985. A variety of methods are either already in use or under serious consideration, and they all affect your driving and the cars you will drive. In addition to "down-sizing", the auto industry is using or investigating the use of electronic fuel delivery, electronic engine controls and alternative engines for use in smaller and lighter vehicles, among other alternatives to meet the federally mandated Corporate Average Fuel Economy (CAFE) of 27.5 mpg by 1985. The government, for its part, is considering rationing, mandatory driving curtailments and tax increases on motor vehicle fuel in an effort to reduce consumption. The government's goal of a 10% reduction could be realized — and further government regulation avoided — if every private vehicle could use just 1 less gallon of fuel per week.

How Much Can You Save?

Tests have proven that almost anyone can make at least a 10% reduction in fuel consumption through regular maintenance and tune-ups. When a major manufacturer of spark plugs sur-

TUNE-UP

1. Check the cylinder compression to be sure the engine will really benefit from a tune-up and that it is capable of producing good fuel economy. A tune-up will be wasted on an engine in poor mechanical condition.

2. Replace spark plugs regularly. New spark plugs alone can increase fuel economy 3%.

3. Be sure the spark plugs are the correct type (heat range) for your vehicle. See the Tune-Up Specifications.

Heat range refers to the spark plug's ability to conduct heat away from the firing end. It must conduct the heat away in an even pattern to avoid becoming a source of pre-ignition, yet it must also operate hot enough to burn off conductive deposits that could cause misfiring.

The heat range is usually indicated by a number on the spark plug, part of the manufacturer's designation for each individual spark plug. The numbers in bold-face indicate the heat range in each manufacturer's identification system.

Manufacturer	Typical Designation
AC	R **45** TS
Bosch (old)	WA **145** T30
Bosch (new)	HR **8** Y
Champion	RBL **15** Y
Fram/Autolite	**415**
Mopar	P-**62** PR
Motorcraft	BRF-**42**
NGK	BP **5** ES-15
Nippondenso	W **16** EP
Prestolite	14GR **5** 2A

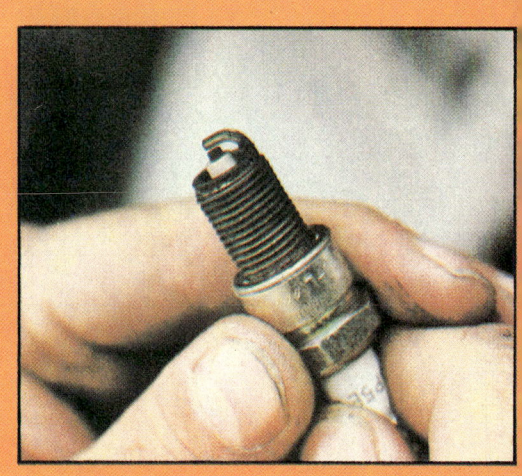

Periodically, check the spark plugs to be sure they are firing efficiently. They are excellent indicators of the internal condition of your engine.

On AC, Bosch (new), Champion, Fram/Autolite, Mopar, Motorcraft and Prestolite, a higher number indicates a hotter plug. On Bosch (old), NGK and Nippondenso, a higher number indicates a colder plug.

4. Make sure the spark plugs are properly gapped. See the Tune-Up Specifications in this book.

5. Be sure the spark plugs are firing efficiently. The illustrations on the next 2 pages show you how to "read" the firing end of the spark plug.

6. Check the ignition timing and set it to specifications. Tests show that almost all cars

veyed over 6,000 cars nationwide, they found that a tune-up, on cars that needed one, increased fuel economy over 11%. Replacing worn plugs alone, accounted for a 3% increase. The same test also revealed that 8 out of every 10 vehicles will have some maintenance deficiency that will directly affect fuel economy, emissions or performance. Most of this mileage-robbing neglect could be prevented with regular maintenance.

Modern engines require that all of the functioning systems operate properly for maximum efficiency. A malfunction anywhere wastes fuel. You can keep your vehicle running as efficiently and economically as possible, by being aware of your vehicles operating and performance characteristics. If your vehicle suddenly develops performance or fuel economy problems it could be due to one or more of the following:

PROBLEM	POSSIBLE CAUSE
Engine Idles Rough	Ignition timing, idle mixture, vacuum leak or something amiss in the emission control system.
Hesitates on Acceleration	Dirty carburetor or fuel filter, improper accelerator pump setting, ignition timing or fouled spark plugs.
Starts Hard or Fails to Start	Worn spark plugs, improperly set automatic choke, ice (or water) in fuel system.
Stalls Frequently	Automatic choke improperly adjusted and possible dirty air filter or fuel filter.
Performs Sluggishly	Worn spark plugs, dirty fuel or air filter, ignition timing or automatic choke out of adjustment.

Check spark plug wires on conventional point type ignition for cracks by bending them in a loop around your finger.

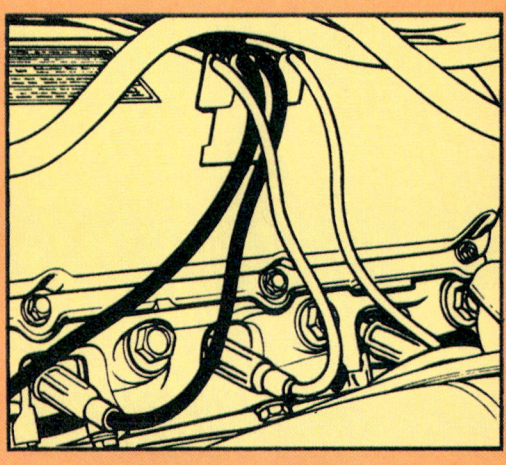

Be sure that spark plug wires leading to adjacent cylinders do not run too close together. (Photo courtesy Champion Spark Plug Co.)

have incorrect ignition timing by more than 2°.

7. If your vehicle does not have electronic ignition, check the points, rotor and cap as specified.

8. Check the spark plug wires (used with conventional point-type ignitions) for cracks and burned or broken insulation by bending them in a loop around your finger. Cracked wires decrease fuel efficiency by failing to deliver full voltage to the spark plugs. One misfiring spark plug can cost you as much as 2 mpg.

9. Check the routing of the plug wires. Misfiring can be the result of spark plug leads to adjacent cylinders running parallel to each other and too close together. One wire tends to pick up voltage from the other causing it to fire "out of time".

10. Check all electrical and ignition circuits for voltage drop and resistance.

11. Check the distributor mechanical and/or vacuum advance mechanisms for proper functioning. The vacuum advance can be checked by twisting the distributor plate in the opposite direction of rotation. It should spring back when released.

12. Check and adjust the valve clearance on engines with mechanical lifters. The clearance should be slightly loose rather than too tight.

SPARK PLUG DIAGNOSIS

Normal

APPEARANCE: This plug is typical of one operating normally. The insulator nose varies from a light tan to grayish color with slight electrode wear. The presence of slight deposits is normal on used plugs and will have no adverse effect on engine performance. The spark plug heat range is correct for the engine and the engine is running normally.

CAUSE: Properly running engine.

RECOMMENDATION: Before reinstalling this plug, the electrodes should be cleaned and filed square. Set the gap to specifications. If the plug has been in service for more than 10-12,000 miles, the entire set should probably be replaced with a fresh set of the same heat range.

Oil Deposits

APPEARANCE: The firing end of the plug is covered with a wet, oily coating.

CAUSE: The problem is poor oil control. On high mileage engines, oil is leaking past the rings or valve guides into the combustion chamber. A common cause is also a plugged PCV valve, and a ruptured fuel pump diaphragm can also cause this condition. Oil fouled plugs such as these are often found in new or recently overhauled engines, before normal oil control is achieved, and can be cleaned and reinstalled.

RECOMMENDATION: A hotter spark plug may temporarily relieve the problem, but the engine is probably in need of work.

Incorrect Heat Range

APPEARANCE: The effects of high temperature on a spark plug are indicated by clean white, often blistered insulator. This can also be accompanied by excessive wear of the electrode, and the absence of deposits.

CAUSE: Check for the correct spark plug heat range. A plug which is too hot for the engine can result in overheating. A car operated mostly at high speeds can require a colder plug. Also check ignition timing, cooling system level, fuel mixture and leaking intake manifold.

RECOMMENDATION: If all ignition and engine adjustments are known to be correct, and no other malfunction exists, install spark plugs one heat range colder.

Photos Courtesy Champion Spark Plug Co.

Carbon Deposits

APPEARANCE: Carbon fouling is easily identified by the presence of dry, soft, black, sooty deposits.

CAUSE: Changing the heat range can often lead to carbon fouling, as can prolonged slow, stop-and-start driving. If the heat range is correct, carbon fouling can be attributed to a rich fuel mixture, sticking choke, clogged air cleaner, worn breaker points, retarded timing or low compression. If only one or two plugs are carbon fouled, check for corroded or cracked wires on the affected plugs. Also look for cracks in the distributor cap between the towers of affected cylinders.

RECOMMENDATION: After the problem is corrected, these plugs can be cleaned and reinstalled if not worn severely.

MMT Fouled

APPEARANCE: Spark plugs fouled by MMT (Methycyclopentadienyl Maganese Tricarbonyl) have reddish, rusty appearance on the insulator and side electrode.

CAUSE: MMT is an anti-knock additive in gasoline used to replace lead. During the combustion process, the MMT leaves a reddish deposit on the insulator and side electrode.

RECOMMENDATION: No engine malfunction is indicated and the deposits will not affect plug performance any more than lead deposits (see Ash Deposits). MMT fouled plugs can be cleaned, regapped and reinstalled.

High Speed Glazing

APPEARANCE: Glazing appears as shiny coating on the plug, either yellow or tan in color.

CAUSE: During hard, fast acceleration, plug temperatures rise suddenly. Deposits from normal combustion have no chance to fluff-off; instead, they melt on the insulator forming an electrically conductive coating which causes misfiring.

RECOMMENDATION: Glazed plugs are not easily cleaned. They should be replaced with a fresh set of plugs of the correct heat range. If the condition recurs, using plugs with a heat range one step colder may cure the problem.

Ash (Lead) Deposits

APPEARANCE: Ash deposits are characterized by light brown or white colored deposits crusted on the side or center electrodes. In some cases it may give the plug a rusty appearance.

CAUSE: Ash deposits are normally derived from oil or fuel additives burned during normal combustion. Normally they are harmless, though excessive amounts can cause misfiring. If deposits are excessive in short mileage, the valve guides may be worn.

RECOMMENDATION: Ash-fouled plugs can be cleaned, gapped and reinstalled.

Detonation

APPEARANCE: Detonation is usually characterized by a broken plug insulator.

CAUSE: A portion of the fuel charge will begin to burn spontaneously, from the increased heat following ignition. The explosion that results applies extreme pressure to engine components, frequently damaging spark plugs and pistons.

Detonation can result by over-advanced ignition timing, inferior gasoline (low octane) lean air/fuel mixture, poor carburetion, engine lugging or an increase in compression ratio due to combustion chamber deposits or engine modification.

RECOMMENDATION: Replace the plugs after correcting the problem.

Photos Courtesy Fram Corporation

EMISSION CONTROLS

13. Be aware of the general condition of the emission control system. It contributes to reduced pollution and should be serviced regularly to maintain efficient engine operation.

14. Check all vacuum lines for dried, cracked or brittle conditions. Something as simple as a leaking vacuum hose can cause poor performance and loss of economy.

15. Avoid tampering with the emission control system. Attempting to improve fuel econ-

FUEL SYSTEM

Check the air filter with a light behind it. If you can see light through the filter it can be reused.

Extremely clogged filters should be discarded and replaced with a new one.

18. Replace the air filter regularly. A dirty air filter richens the air/fuel mixture and can increase fuel consumption as much as 10%. Tests show that ⅓ of all vehicles have air filters in need of replacement.

19. Replace the fuel filter at least as often as recommended.

20. Set the idle speed and carburetor mixture to specifications.

21. Check the automatic choke. A sticking or malfunctioning choke wastes gas.

22. During the summer months, adjust the automatic choke for a leaner mixture which will produce faster engine warm-ups.

COOLING SYSTEM

29. Be sure all accessory drive belts are in good condition. Check for cracks or wear.

30. Adjust all accessory drive belts to proper tension.

31. Check all hoses for swollen areas, worn spots, or loose clamps.

32. Check coolant level in the radiator or expansion tank.

33. Be sure the thermostat is operating properly. A stuck thermostat delays engine warm-up and a cold engine uses nearly twice as much fuel as a warm engine.

34. Drain and replace the engine coolant at least as often as recommended. Rust and scale

TIRES & WHEELS

38. Check the tire pressure often with a pencil type gauge. Tests by a major tire manufacturer show that 90% of all vehicles have at least 1 tire improperly inflated. Better mileage can be achieved by over-inflating tires, but never exceed the maximum inflation pressure on the side of the tire.

39. If possible, install radial tires. Radial tires deliver as much as ½ mpg more than bias belted tires.

40. Avoid installing super-wide tires. They only create extra rolling resistance and decrease fuel mileage. Stick to the manufacturer's recommendations.

41. Have the wheels properly balanced.

omy by tampering with emission controls is more likely to worsen fuel economy than improve it. Emission control changes on modern engines are not readily reversible.

16. Clean (or replace) the EGR valve and lines as recommended.

17. Be sure that all vacuum lines and hoses are reconnected properly after working under the hood. An unconnected or misrouted vacuum line can wreak havoc with engine performance.

---

23. Check for fuel leaks at the carburetor, fuel pump, fuel lines and fuel tank. Be sure all lines and connections are tight.

24. Periodically check the tightness of the carburetor and intake manifold attaching nuts and bolts. These are a common place for vacuum leaks to occur.

25. Clean the carburetor periodically and lubricate the linkage.

26. The condition of the tailpipe can be an excellent indicator of proper engine combustion. After a long drive at highway speeds, the inside of the tailpipe should be a light grey in color. Black or soot on the insides indicates an overly rich mixture.

27. Check the fuel pump pressure. The fuel pump may be supplying more fuel than the engine needs.

28. Use the proper grade of gasoline for your engine. Don't try to compensate for knocking or "pinging" by advancing the ignition timing. This practice will only increase plug temperature and the chances of detonation or pre-ignition with relatively little performance gain.

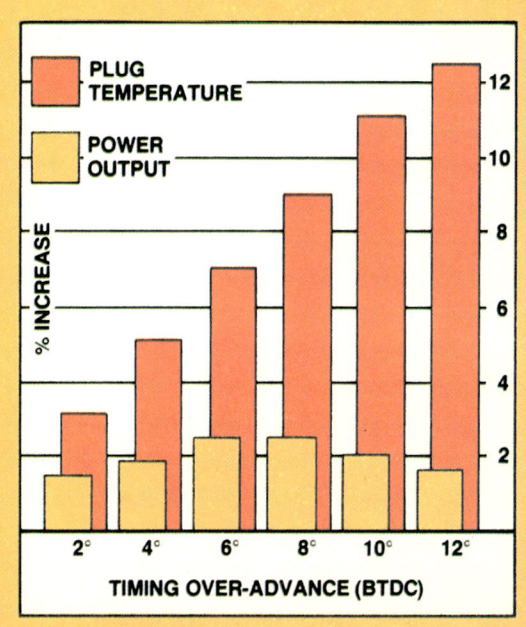

Increasing ignition timing past the specified setting results in a drastic increase in spark plug temperature with increased chance of detonation or preignition. Performance increase is considerably less. (Photo courtesy Champion Spark Plug Co.)

---

that form in the engine should be flushed out to allow the engine to operate at peak efficiency.

35. Clean the radiator of debris that can decrease cooling efficiency.

36. Install a flex-type or electric cooling fan, if you don't have a clutch type fan. Flex fans use curved plastic blades to push more air at low speeds when more cooling is needed; at high speeds the blades flatten out for less resistance. Electric fans only run when the engine temperature reaches a predetermined level.

37. Check the radiator cap for a worn or cracked gasket. If the cap does not seal properly, the cooling system will not function properly.

---

42. Be sure the front end is correctly aligned. A misaligned front end actually has wheels going in different directions. The increased drag can reduce fuel economy by .3 mpg.

43. Correctly adjust the wheel bearings. Wheel bearings that are adjusted too tight increase rolling resistance.

Check tire pressures regularly with a reliable pocket type gauge. Be sure to check the pressure on a cold tire.

GENERAL MAINTENANCE

Check the fluid levels (particularly engine oil) on a regular basis. Be sure to check the oil for grit, water or other contamination.

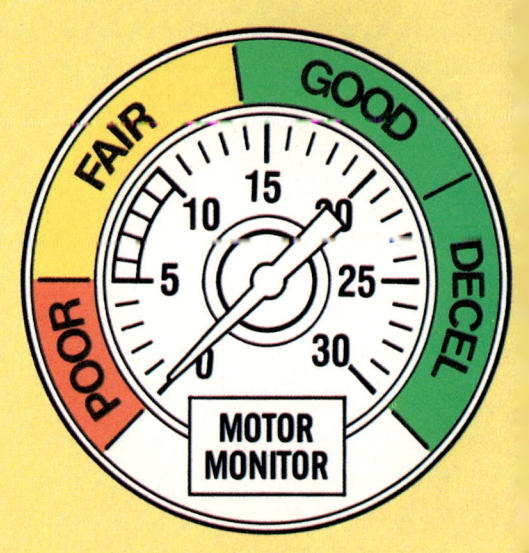

A vacuum gauge is another excellent indicator of internal engine condition and can also be installed in the dash as a mileage indicator.

44. Periodically check the fluid levels in the engine, power steering pump, master cylinder, automatic transmission and drive axle.

45. Change the oil at the recommended interval and change the filter at every oil change. Dirty oil is thick and causes extra friction between moving parts, cutting efficiency and increasing wear. A worn engine requires more frequent tune-ups and gets progressively worse fuel economy. In general, use the lightest viscosity oil for the driving conditions you will encounter.

46. Use the recommended viscosity fluids in the transmission and axle.

47. Be sure the battery is fully charged for fast starts. A slow starting engine wastes fuel.

48. Be sure battery terminals are clean and tight.

49. Check the battery electrolyte level and add distilled water if necessary.

50. Check the exhaust system for crushed pipes, blockages and leaks.

51. Adjust the brakes. Dragging brakes or brakes that are not releasing create increased drag on the engine.

52. Install a vacuum gauge or miles-per-gallon gauge. These gauges visually indicate engine vacuum in the intake manifold. High vacuum = good mileage and low vacuum = poorer mileage. The gauge can also be an excellent indicator of internal engine conditions.

53. Be sure the clutch is properly adjusted. A slipping clutch wastes fuel.

54. Check and periodically lubricate the heat control valve in the exhaust manifold. A sticking or inoperative valve prevents engine warm-up and wastes gas.

55. Keep accurate records to check fuel economy over a period of time. A sudden drop in fuel economy may signal a need for tune-up or other maintenance.

© 1980 Chilton Book Company, Radnor, PA 19089

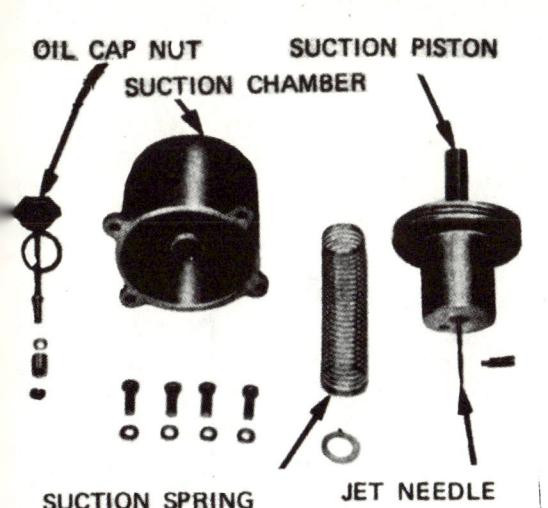

EMISSION CONTROLS AND FUEL SYSTEM

The suction chamber assembly

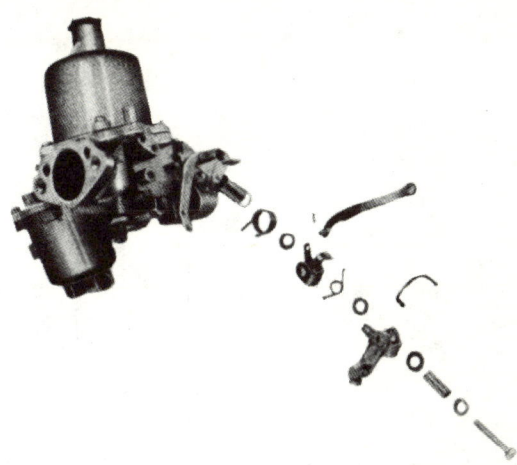

Choke linkage—exploded view

2. Remove suction spring, nylon packing, and suction piston from chamber. Be extremely careful not to bend the jet needle.

3. Do not remove the jet needle from the suction piston unless it must be replaced. To remove, loosen jet needle setscrew. Hold the needle with pliers at a point no more than 0.10 in. from the piston. Remove needle by pulling and turning slowly. Replace the needle with the shoulder portion flush with the piston surface. Check this with a straightedge. Tighten the setscrew.

4. Clean all parts of suction chamber assembly with a safe solvent. Reassemble, using all new parts supplied in overhaul kit. Do not lubricate piston.

5. To dismantle nozzle assembly, remove 4 mm screw and remove connecting plate from nozzle head by pulling lightly on starter (choke) lever. Remove fuel line and nozzle. Be careful not to bend jet needle if suction chamber assembly is mounted on carburetor.

Remove idle (mixture) adjusting nut and spring. Do not remove nozzle sleeve unless absolutely necessary. Special care is required to replace this part. Remove nozzle sleeve setscrew and nozzle sleeve.

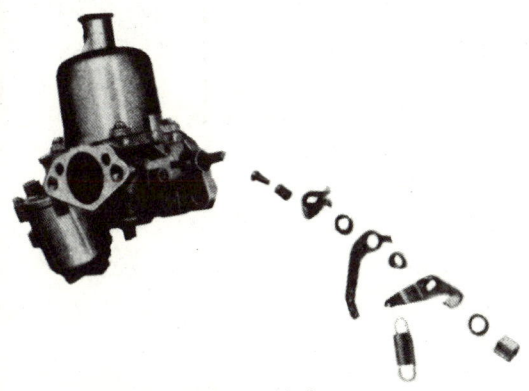

6. Clean all parts of nozzle assembly with a safe solvent. Be very careful of nozzle. Do not pass anything through nozzle for cleaning purposes.

7. The jet needle must now be carefully centered in the nozzle, unless the nozzle sleeve and setscrew were not disturbed. Even so, it is a good idea to check this. To center the jet needle, insert nozzle sleeve into carburetor body with setscrew loose. Carefully install the suction piston assembly without the plunger rod. Insert the nozzle without spring and mixture adjusting nut until the nozzle contacts the nozzle sleeve. Position the nozzle sleeve so that the jet needle is centered inside the sleeve and does not contact the sleeve. Test centering by raising and releasing suction piston. It should drop smoothly, making a metallic sound when it hits the stop. Tighten the nozzle sleeve setscrew when the needle is centered.

8. Reassemble nozzle assembly. Replace fuel line. Replace damper plunger rod.

9. Pull starter lever slightly, replace connecting plate and 4 mm screw.

10. Carburetor synchronization and mixture adjustments must be performed after reinstalling carburetors.

Fuel Injection

The 1975 and later 280-Zs and ZXs are equipped with electronic fuel injection built under Bosch patents. The Bosch L-Jetronic

Throttle linkage—exploded view

EMISSION CONTROLS AND FUEL SYSTEM

Carburetor Specifications
in. (mm)

Engine and Year	Make and Type	Bore Dia	Venturi Dia	Fuel Pressure psi (kg/cm²)	Needle Valve Dia	Nozzle No.	Power Jet No.	Jet Needle No.	Suction Spring No.	Suction Hole Dia	Fast Idle Throttle Opening	Damper Plunger Dia
L24 1970–72	Hitachi HJG46W-3A	1.811 (46)	1.339 (34)	3.4 (.24)	.0787 (2.0)	A	—	N-27	23	—	—	—
L24 1973	Hitachi HMB46W-1	1.811 (46)	1.654 (42)	3.4 (.24)	—	—	40	N-62	50	.295 (7.5)	.0232–.0252 (.59–.64)	.3–.9 (8.36)
L26 1974	Hitachi HMB46W-4	1.811 (46)	1.654 (42)	4.6 (.32)	—	—	40	—	50	.295 (7.5)	.0232–.0252 (.59–.64)	.3–.9 (8.36)

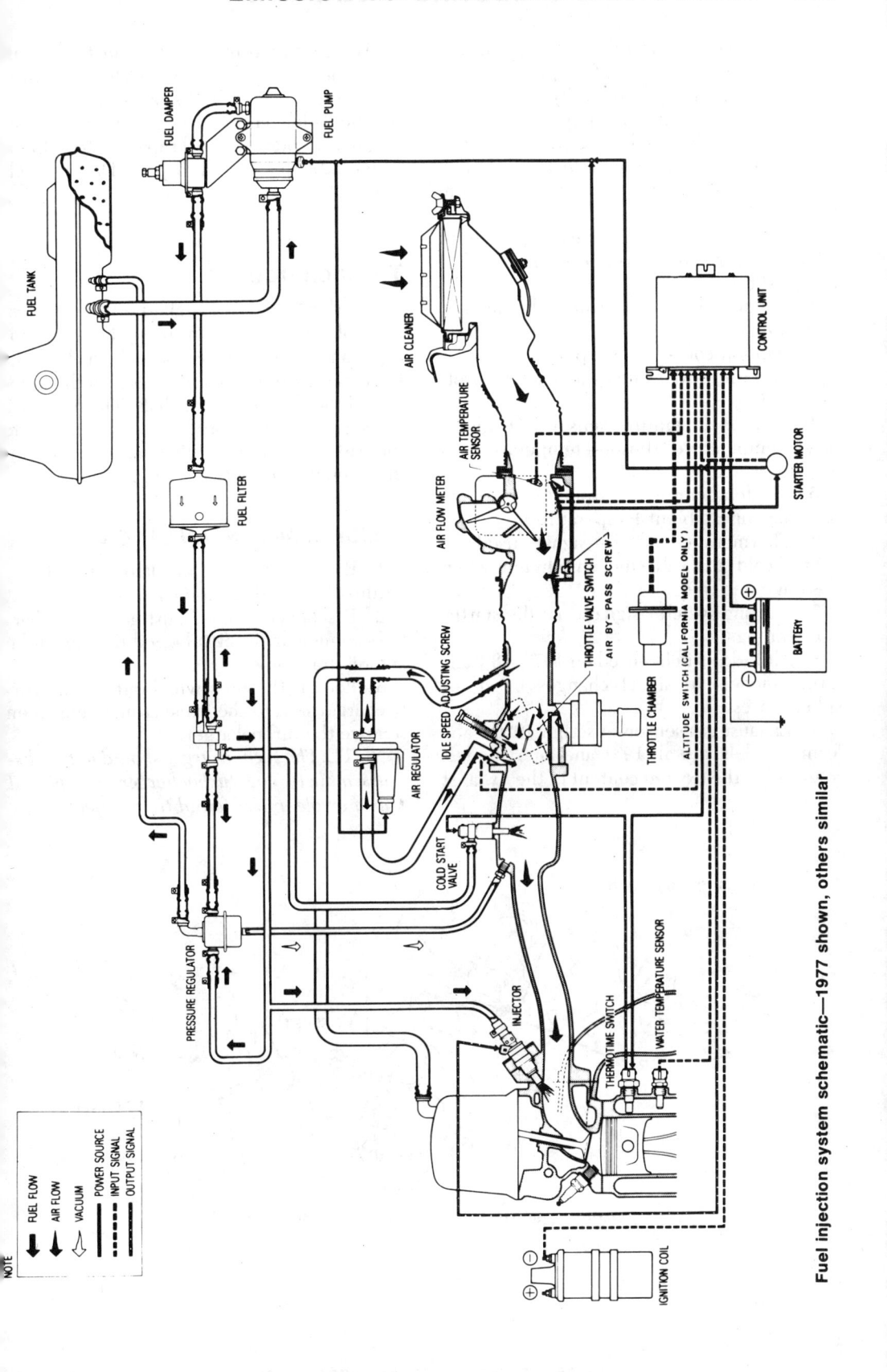

EMISSION CONTROLS AND FUEL SYSTEM 143

Fuel injection system schematic—1977 shown, others similar

EMISSION CONTROLS AND FUEL SYSTEM

system precisely controls fuel injection to match engine requirements, reducing emissions and increasing driveability.

The electric fuel pump pumps fuel through a damper and filter to the pressure regulator. The six fuel injectors are electric solenoid valves which open and close by signals from the control unit.

The control unit receives input from various sensors to determine engine operating condition.

1. Air flow meter—measures the amount of intake air.
2. Ignition coil—engine rpm.
3. Throttle valve switch—amount of throttle opening.
4. Water temperature sensor or cylinder head temperature sensor—temperature of coolant or engine.
5. Air temperature sensor—temperature of intake air (ambient temperature).
6. Thermotime switch—signal used to control cold start valve fuel enrichment when the engine is cold.
7. Starting switch—signals that the starter is operating.
8. Altitude switch—used on 1977-78 California models to signal changes in atmospheric pressure.
9. Exhaust gas sensor—used in 1980 California models and all 1981 and later models to measure the oxygen content of the exhaust gas.

The sensors provide the input to the control unit, which determines the amount of fuel to be injected by its preset program.

The L-Jetronic fuel injection system is highly complex unit. All repair or adjustment should be left to an expert Datsun technician.

Turbocharger

The turbocharger is installed on the exhaust manifold. This system utilizes exhaust gas energy to rotate the turbine wheel which drives the compressor turbine installed on the other end of the turbine wheel shaft. The compressor supplies compressed air to the engine to increase the charging efficiency so as to improve engine output and torque.

REMOVAL AND INSTALLATION

1. Remove the heat insulator, inlet tube, air duct hose and suction air pipe.
2. Disconnect the exhaust gas sensor harness connector, front tube, oil delivery tube and oil drain pipe.
3. Loosen the nuts which attach the turbocharger unit to the exhaust manifold, then remove the turbocharger.

NOTE: *The turbocharger should not be disassembled. The turbocharger is replaced as a whole unit if found to be defective.*

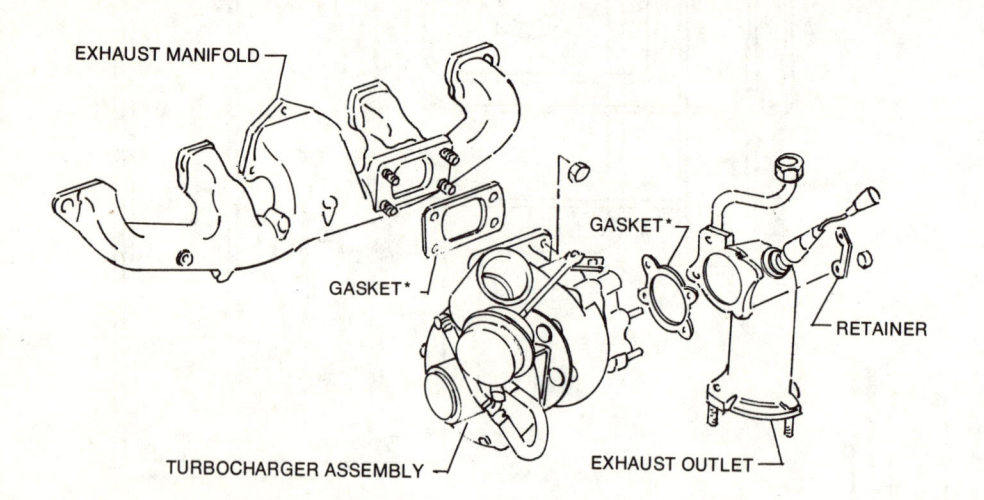

*: Replace if necessary.

Turbocharger assembly, removal and installation

EMISSION CONTROLS AND FUEL SYSTEM

Fuel Tank

REMOVAL AND INSTALLATION

1970-78

1. Disconnect the negative battery cable.
2. Remove the drain plug and drain all fuel from the tank.
3. Disconnect the gauge unit electrical wiring. Disconnect the outlet or outlet and return hose(s) at the tank. Label the wires.
4. Remove the nuts from the two tank securing bands and lower the tank slightly.
5. Disconnect and label the three ventilation hoses used on models with evaporative emission control. Disconnect the fuel tank filler pipe. Remove the tank.
6. The tank should be checked carefully for dents or cracks which might cause leaks. Replace the tank as necessary.
7. Installation is the reverse of removal. Be sure to connect the filler hose after the tank was been mounted, to prevent leakage at the connection. Be careful not to kink hoses or overtighten fittings when reconnecting.

1979 and Later

1. Reduce the fuel line pressure to zero. Follow the appropriate steps under the fuel pump removal procedure.
2. The tank has no drain plug. Fuel must be drained as follows:
   a. Disconnect the fuel outlet hose from the fuel pipe.
   b. Place the hose into a metal container and seal the opening with a rag.
   c. Disconnect the alternator "L" terminal or the oil pressure switch electrical lead.
   d. Connect the negative battery cable.
   e. Turn the ignition switch to On.
   f. Allow the fuel pump to empty the tank into the container.
   CAUTION: *Stop the fuel pump before the tank is completely empty to prevent damage to the pump. Disconnect the negative battery cable after emptying the tank.*
3. Remove the fuel filler pipe protector inside the right rear wheel opening. Disconnect the filler hose and the evaporative emission control hose. Plug the hose openings.
4. Remove the luggage compartment mat. Remove the cover over the tank sending unit and hose connections. Disconnect the gauge electrical harness and the ventilation, fuel feed and fuel return hoses.
5. Remove the nuts and the fuel tank retaining straps. Remove the tank.
6. Installation is the reverse. Be careful not to twist or kink any of the hoses.

Chassis Electrical

5

HEATER

Blower (without Air Conditioning)

REMOVAL AND INSTALLATION

1970–78

1. Disconnect the negative battery cable.
2. Remove the clamp at the air intake duct so as to disconnect the air intake box control cable.
3. Disconnect blower and resistor wires at the connectors.

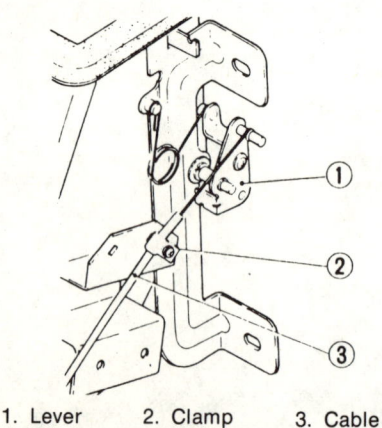

1. Lever 2. Clamp 3. Cable

Disconnecting the intake door control cable (1970–78)

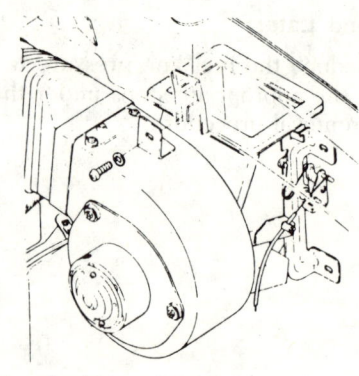

Removing the blower housing through 1978

4. Remove the retaining screws and remove the blower unit.
5. The motor and fan may be separated from the blower unit by removing the three mounting screws. Be careful to retain the washers and spacers.
6. Reassembly is accomplished in reverse order. When reassembling the control cable for the air intake door, set the AIR lever in the OFF position and position the wire in the clamp so that the door will just be closed.

1979 and Later

1. Disconnect the negative battery cable.
2. Remove the lower instrument panel cover and the glove box.

CHASSIS ELECTRICAL 147

3. Remove the floor nozzle, defroster duct, and the side defroster duct on the right side.
4. Remove the heater duct.
5. Disconnect the blower motor wiring harness.
6. Disconnect the control cable at the blower assembly by removing the clip.
7. Remove the bolts securing the blower assembly to the firewall and remove the blower assembly.
8. The motor and fan can be removed by removing the three motor retaining screws. The fan simply bolts onto the motor shaft.
9. Installation is the reverse.

The motor and fan can also be removed without removing the entire blower housing assembly:
1. Disconnect the negative battery cable.
2. Remove the lower instrument panel cover and the floor nozzle on the right side.
3. Disconnect the blower motor wiring harness.
4. Remove the three motor attaching screws and remove the motor and fan as a unit from the blower housing.

Blower (with Air Conditioning)
REMOVAL AND INSTALLATION
1970-78

1. Disconnect the battery negative cable. Disconnect the vacuum hose at the intake door actuator.
2. Remove the defroster duct which is located near the passenger seat.
3. Disconnect the connectors at the blower motor and at the resistor.
4. Remove the three housing mounting bolts and remove the housing.

5. The motor may be removed by removing the three bolts and pulling it out. Be careful to retain the three washers and three spacers.
6. Installation is the reverse of removal.

1979 and Later

1. Disconnect the negative battery cable.
2. Remove the instrument panel lower cover on the right side. Remove the glove box.
3. Remove the floor nozzle, the defroster

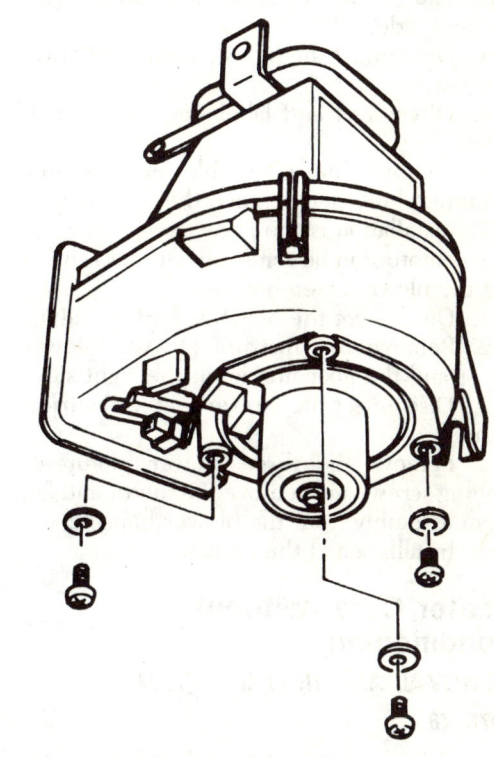

ZX blower motor and fan removal

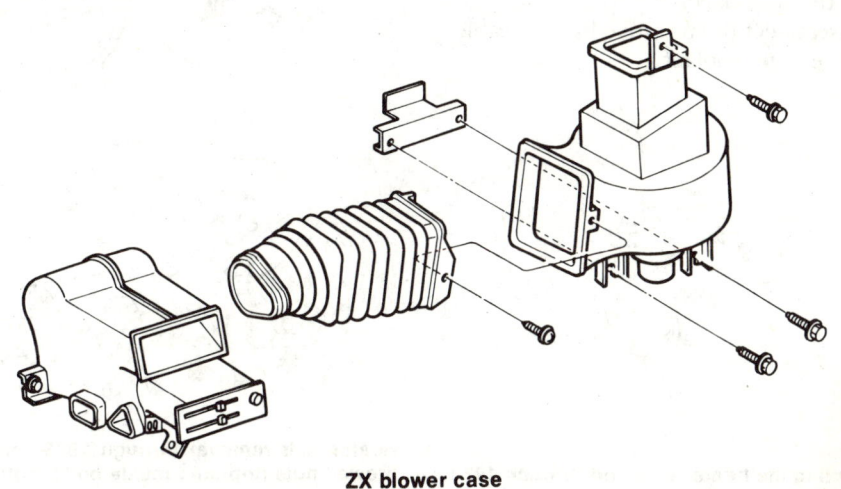

ZX blower case

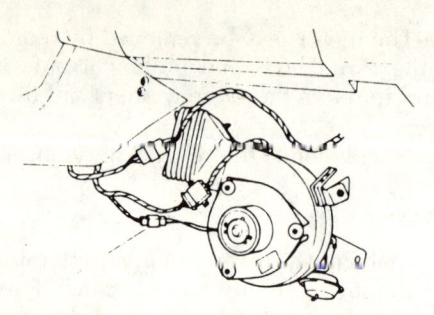

148 CHASSIS ELECTRICAL

Removing the blower housing with air conditioning through 1978

duct, and the side defroster duct on the passenger's side.

4. Disconnect the blower motor electrical harness.
5. Disconnect and label the two vacuum hoses.
6. Remove the three blower assembly mounting bolts and remove the assembly.
7. Installation is the reverse.

The motor can be removed without removing the blower assembly:

1. Disconnect the negative battery cable.
2. Remove the instrument panel lower cover and the floor nozzle on the right side.
3. Disconnect the blower motor electrical harness.
4. Remove the three blower motor attaching screws and remove the motor and fan as an assembly from the blower housing.
5. Installation is the reverse.

Heater Core (Without Air Conditioning)

REMOVAL AND INSTALLATION

1970-78

The entire heater unit must be removed for access to the heater core.

1. Disconnect the negative battery cable. Drain the engine coolant.

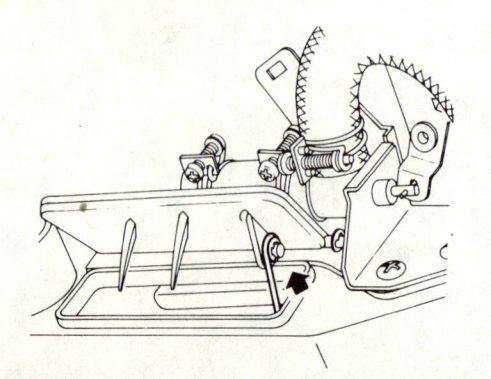

2. Remove the floor console.
3. Remove the four screws retaining the finish panel around the heater control and pull the panel out slightly. Disconnect the wires and remove the panel.
4. Remove the two screws retaining the duct to the instrument panel bracket and the four screws retaining the brackets. Remove the brackets. Disconnect the ventilator duct hose from the ventilator outlet and remove the outlet from the center panel.
5. Remove the heater control:

   a. Remove the control cables at the air intake duct, the heat control valve, and the floor heater door and disconnect the door control rod.

   b. Disconnect the wires from the heater control to the heater harness at the connectors.

   c. Remove the two screws retaining the control assembly to the instrument panel.

   d. Remove the screws holding the heater control panel reinforcement to the instrument panel and remove the reinforcement.

   e. Remove the two screws retaining the heater control to the heater unit.

6. Disconnect the defroster ducts from the heater unit. Remove the clamps for the heater inlet and outlet hoses and remove the hoses from the tubes.

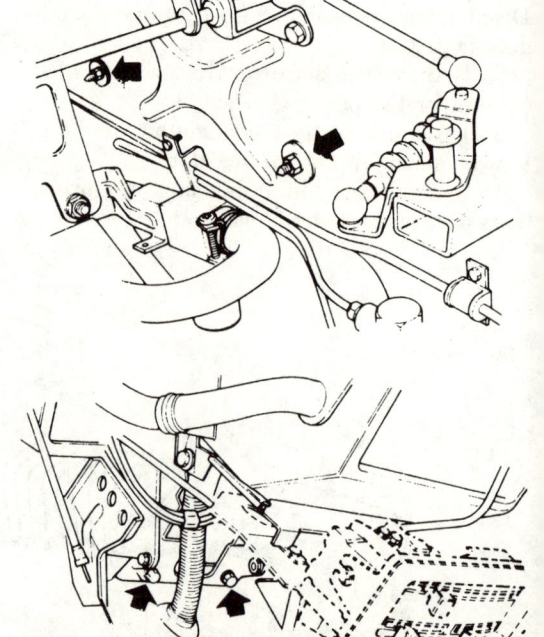

Disconnecting the heater door rod through 1978

Heater unit removal through 1978—engine side firewall nuts (top) and inside bolts (bottom)

CHASSIS ELECTRICAL 149

7. Remove the two screws retaining the duct adapter to the heater unit.

8. Remove the two nuts and two screws retaining the heater unit to the firewall. The two nuts are on the engine side of the firewall; the screws are under the heater control unit.

9. Pull the heater out slightly and turn it 90° to the left. Remove the heater unit from the instrument panel.

10. Loosen the hose clamps on the heat control valve and disconnect the hoses.

11. Remove the two screws retaining the valve to its bracket.

12. Remove the four heater bracket screws from the unit and remove the bracket.

13. Remove the two screws retaining the capillary tube bracket to the unit and remove the capillary tube from the unit. Remove the valve at the same time.

CAUTION: *Be careful not to bend or twist the tube too much. If the tube must be bent slightly, be sure the valve is open to prevent any change in the operating characteristics of the capillary tube.*

14. Remove the screws retaining the heat control valve bracket to the unit and the hose connector to the unit.

15. Loosen the hose clamps from the heater core tubes and disconnect the hoses from the core tubes. Remove the heat control valve bracket and hose connector.

16. Disconnect the floor door operating rod from the door.

17. Remove the side cover from the unit.

18. Open the floor door to prevent scratching the heater core, and remove the core from the unit.

19. Assembly and installation is the reverse. Adjust the air intake door, the mode door, the floor door, and the heat control valve cables so that:

　a. When the AIR lever is OFF, the air intake door is closed.

　b. When the AIR lever is on HEAT, the mode door lever is moved toward the firewall.

　c. When the AIR lever is on DEF, the floor door lever is pushed forward toward the firewall to the defrost position.

　d. When the TEMP lever is on HOT, the heat control valve is open (pulled towards you).

1979 and Later

The heater unit must be removed for access to the heater core.

1. Disconnect the negative battery cable.

2. Set the TEMP lever to HOT. Drain the coolant.

3. Remove the instrument panel lower covers, the floor nozzles, the defroster ducts, the instrument console, and the center ventilator.

4. Remove the glove box.

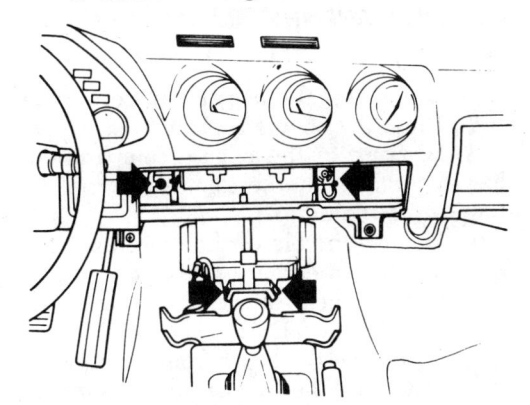

ZX heater unit removal

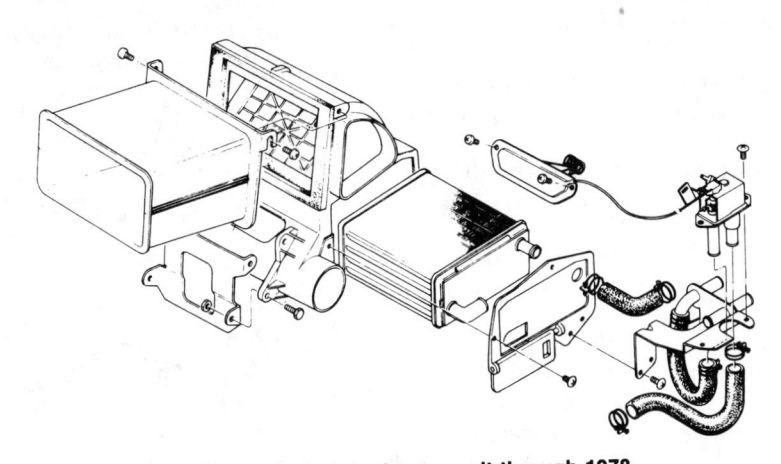

Exploded view of the heater unit through 1978

CHASSIS ELECTRICAL

5. Remove the heater duct.
6. Remove the control cables and rod from the heater unit. Remove the heater control assembly attaching screws and remove the control assembly.
7. Disconnect the heater inlet and outlet hoses inside the passenger compartment.
8. Remove the blower assembly. Refer to the procedure earlier in this chapter.
9. Remove the bolts retaining the heater unit to the firewall and remove the unit. All the bolts are on the passenger compartment side of the firewall, and are accessible through the center of the instrument panel opening.
10. Remove the heat control valve.
11. Remove the clips from the heater case seam and separate the case. Remove the core.
12. Assembly and installation is the reverse.

Heater Core (With Air Conditioning)

REMOVAL AND INSTALLATION

1970–78

1. Disconnect the negative battery cable.
2. Drain the engine coolant.
3. Working in the engine compartment, loosen the heater hose clamps and pull the hoses from the tubes.
4. Remove the blower housing, using the procedure given earlier in this chapter.
5. Remove the heater control valve:
   a. Move the TEMP lever to HOT.
   b. Remove the hoses from the valve.
   c. Remove the two screws retaining the valve to its bracket. Be careful not to twist or bend the capillary tube excessively.
   d. Remove the hose which runs from the vacuum valve to the heater core outlet.
   e. Remove the two screws from the vacuum valve and the two screws from the heater valve bracket.
   f. Remove the vacuum hose. Remove the vacuum valve and heater valve bracket as an assembly.
6. Disengage the control cable from the heater door and remove the rod from the door.
7. Remove the two cover screws and remove the heater core cover. Pull the core from the housing. Keep the heater door open when doing this to prevent damage to the core.

8. Assembly and installation is the reverse.

1979 and Later

CAUTION: *This procedure requires evacuation of the air conditioning refrigerant. Do not attempt to discharge the system unless you are thoroughly familiar with air conditioning systems. Escaping refrigerant will freeze any surface it contacts. If you do not have proper training, have the system discharged and recharged by a professional.*

1. Disconnect the negative battery cable. Set the TEMP lever to HOT and drain the coolant.
2. Remove the blower unit using the procedure given earlier in this chapter.
3. Remove the cooling unit:
   a. Discharge the cooling system.
   b. Loosen the flare nuts at each of the inlet and outlet pipe connections at the evaporator. Plug all openings immediately to prevent the entry of moisture or dirt.
   c. Remove the passenger side defroster duct.
   d. Remove the mounting bolts and remove the cooling unit from beneath the instrument panel.
4. Remove the heater controls:
   a. Remove the lower instrument panel trim covers.
   b. Remove the console.
   c. Remove the ventilator and duct from the center of the instrument panel.
   d. Disconnect the cable from the heat control valve.
   e. Disconnect the wiring connector. Disconnect and label the vacuum hoses, or disconnect and label the connections of the vacuum selector.
   f. Remove the attaching screws and remove the control assembly.

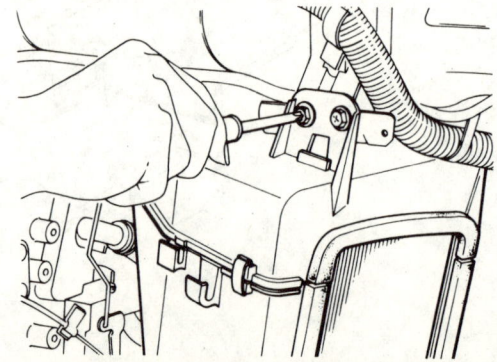

ZX cooling unit removal

CHASSIS ELECTRICAL 151

5. Remove the instrument panel lower cover and the floor nozzle on the driver's side.
6. Disconnect the heater inlet and outlet hoses.
7. Remove the bolts which attach the heater unit to the firewall and remove the unit.
8. Remove the heat control valve.
9. Remove the clips from the heater case seam and separate the two halves of the case.
10. Remove the heater core.
11. Assembly and installation is the reverse. Be sure to adjust the heat control cables after installation.

RADIO

REMOVAL AND INSTALLATION
240-Z

1. Disconnect the negative battery cable.
2. Remove the four mounting screws for the instrument console finish panel, and remove the panel.
3. Pull off the two radio knobs and remove the retaining nuts behind them. Disconnect the power and speaker wiring and the antenna cable at the connectors.
4. Remove the radio.
5. Installation is the reverse.

260-Z and 280-Z

1. Disconnect the negative battery cable. Remove the five screws holding the floor console in place. Remove the choke control wire from the console. Disconnect the wiring harness and remove the console.

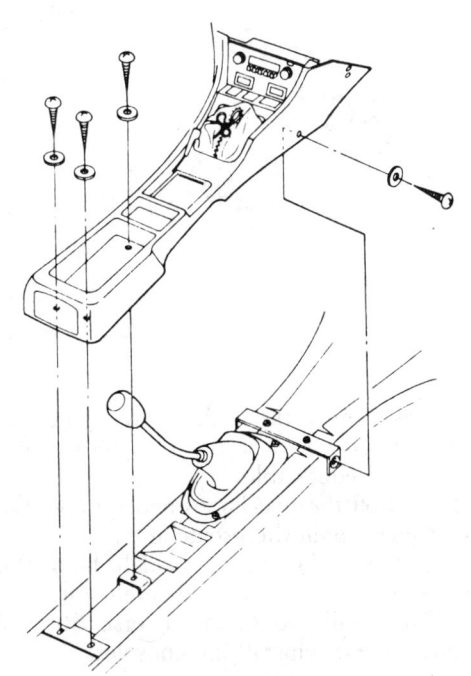

Console removal through 1978

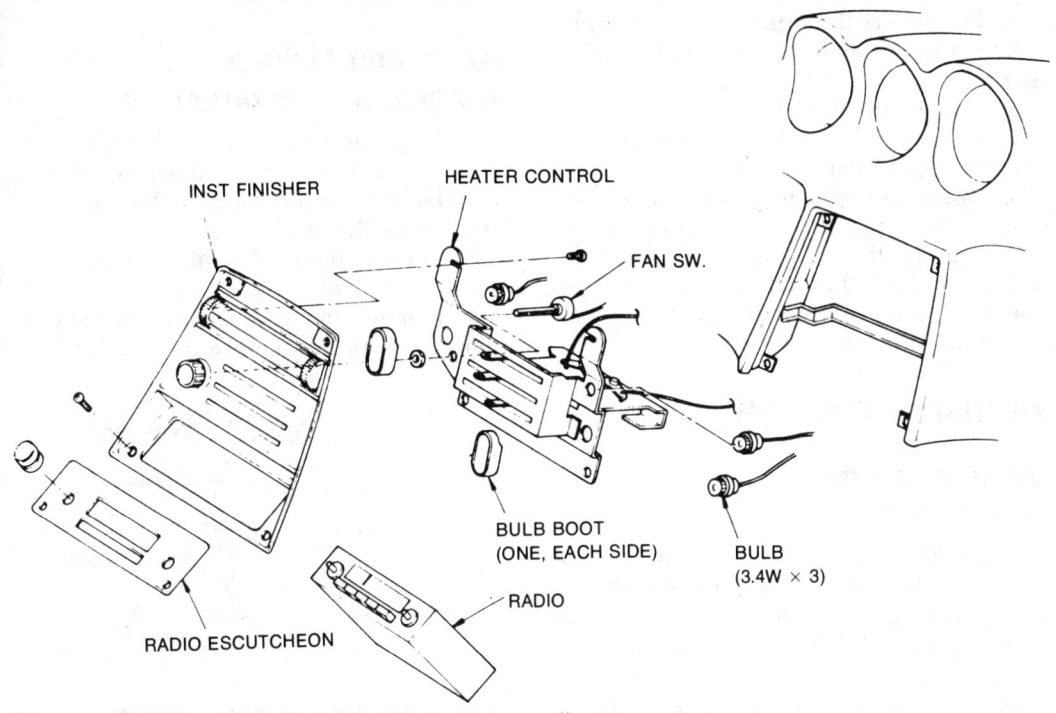

Removing the radio through 1978

152 CHASSIS ELECTRICAL

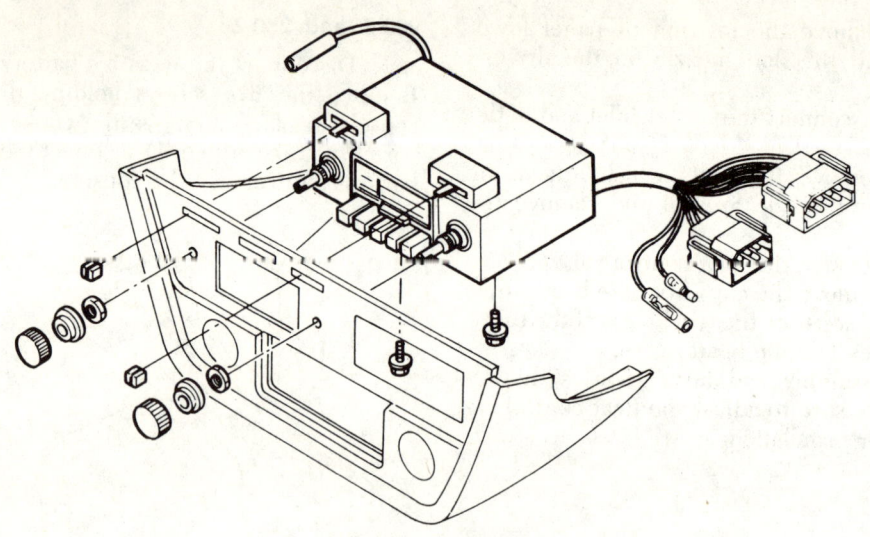

ZX radio removal

2. Disconnect the radio power and antenna switch wires at the connectors. Remove the feeder cable.
3. Pull off the two knobs and remove the nuts which retain the escutcheon.
4. Remove the screws which hold the radio to the console box and remove it.
5. To install the radio, reverse Steps 2 through 4 and reinstall the console.

280-ZX

1. Disconnect the negative battery cable.
2. Remove the lower instrument panel cover.
3. Remove the console.
4. Pull the radio knobs off the shafts. Remove the nuts from the shafts.
5. Disconnect the power, speaker, and antenna wiring from the rear of the radio.
6. Remove the retaining bolts from the bottom of the radio and remove the radio from behind the instrument panel.
7. Installation is the reverse.

WINDSHIELD WIPERS

Blade and Arm
REPLACEMENT

1. On 240, 260, and 280-Z models, raise the wiper blade off the glass, unscrew the retaining nut on the shaft, and pull the arm from the shaft. On ZX models, pry the cover upwards to expose the retaining nut, unscrew the nut, and pull the arm from the shaft.

2. Before installing the arm, be sure the motor is in its park position. Turn the ignition switch on, and cycle the motor a few times. Then turn off the wiper motor with the wiper switch, not the ignition switch. Turn the ignition off and press the arm onto the shaft. Proper arm installation figures for the Z models is given in the illustration. For ZX models, the blade should be parked approximately 8 mm (0.315 in.) from the bottom windshield molding.

Motor and Linkage
REMOVAL AND INSTALLATION

1. Disconnect the negative battery cable. Remove the wiper arms as described above.
2. Disconnect the wiper motor connector from under the hood.
3. Remove the cowl retaining screws and remove the cowl.
4. Remove the wiper motor bracket retaining screws and remove the bracket.

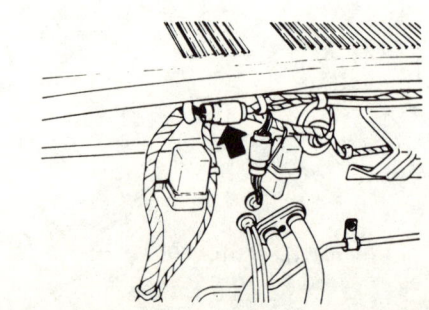

Arrow shows the wiper motor connector through 1978

CHASSIS ELECTRICAL 153

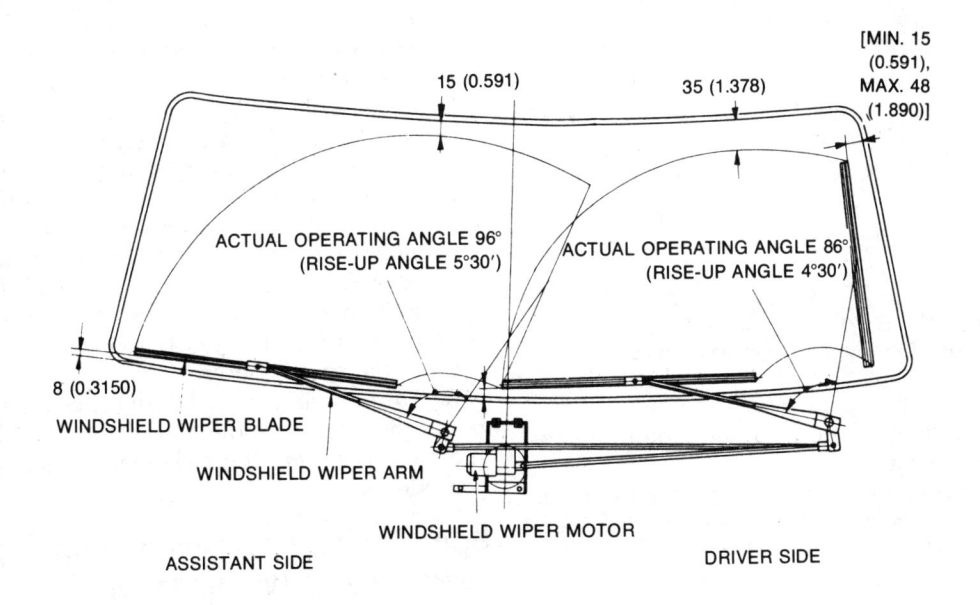

15 (0.591)   35 (1.378)   [MIN. 15 (0.591), MAX. 48 (1.890)]

ACTUAL OPERATING ANGLE 96° (RISE-UP ANGLE 5°30′)

ACTUAL OPERATING ANGLE 86° (RISE-UP ANGLE 4°30′)

8 (0.3150)

WINDSHIELD WIPER BLADE
WINDSHIELD WIPER ARM
WINDSHIELD WIPER MOTOR

ASSISTANT SIDE   DRIVER SIDE

UNIT: MM (IN.)

Wiper motor and linkage through 1978

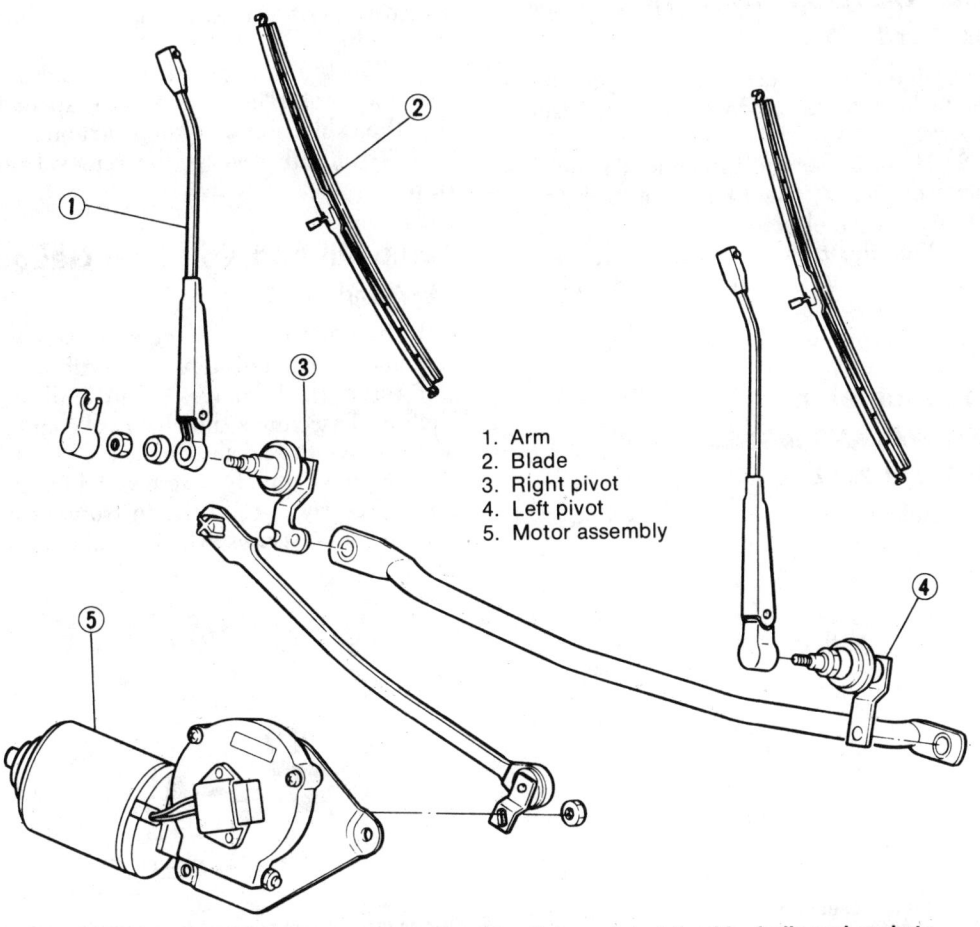

1. Arm
2. Blade
3. Right pivot
4. Left pivot
5. Motor assembly

ZX wiper motor and linkage components. The linkage is retained by balls and sockets

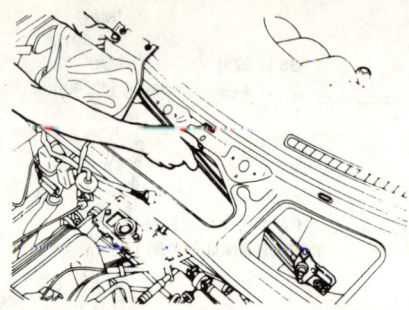

154 CHASSIS ELECTRICAL

Removing the wiper linkage on Z models

5. If only the motor is to be removed, disconnect the linkage from the motor and remove the motor.
6. If the motor and linkage are to be removed, remove the screws which retain each pivot and remove the linkage.
7. Install in the reverse order.

GAUGES

Tachometer

REMOVAL AND INSTALLATION

260-Z and 280-Z

1. Remove the screw, located just above the tachometer face, which retains the tach at the top.
2. From under the instrument panel, remove the screw which holds the tach to the instrument panel bracket.
3. Pull the tach out, disconnect the instrument harness connector, and fully remove the tach.
4. Reverse the procedure to install.

Speedometer

REMOVAL AND INSTALLATION

260-Z and 280-Z

1. Remove the tachometer, as described above.

2. Disconnect the speedometer cable at the junction screw on speedometer back.
3. Disconnect the trip meter reset cable going in through the tachometer opening.
4. Disconnect the two retaining screws for the speedometer in the same way as the two tachometer retaining screws were removed. Disconnect the resistor lead wire from the connector while under the instrument panel.
5. Pull speedometer out slightly, disconnect the instrument harness connector and remove the speedometer.
6. To reinstall, first install the speedometer in the reverse of the above, then install the tach, reversing the tachometer removal procedures.

Speedometer or Tachometer

REMOVAL AND INSTALLATION

240-Z

1. Remove the heater air duct which passes behind the instruments.
2. Remove the wing nuts and washers which retain the instrument to be removed from behind.
3. Pull the instrument down slightly, remove wires and, in the case of the speedometer, the cable. Remove the instrument.
4. To install, reverse the removal procedure.

Temp-Oil and Volt-Fuel Gauges

260-Z and 280-Z

1. Remove the four retaining screws for the instrument finish panel (located under the three small gauges), and pull it out slightly. Disconnect the electrical connectors and remove the finish panel.
2. Remove the two screws which retain the three-way duct to the instrument panel and the four screws which retain it to the bracket.

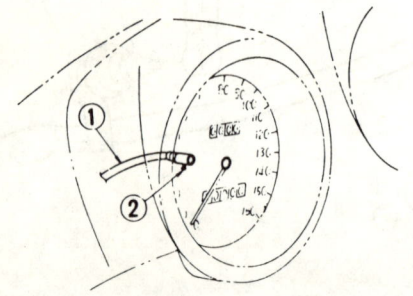

1. Trip meter reset cable   2. Retaining screw

Removing the reset cable on Z models

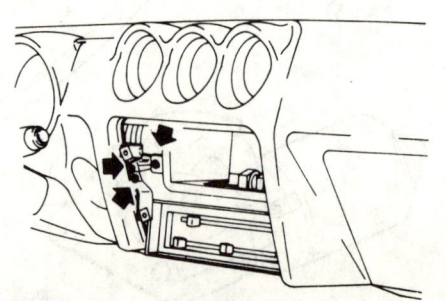

Removing the three-way duct retaining screws on Z models

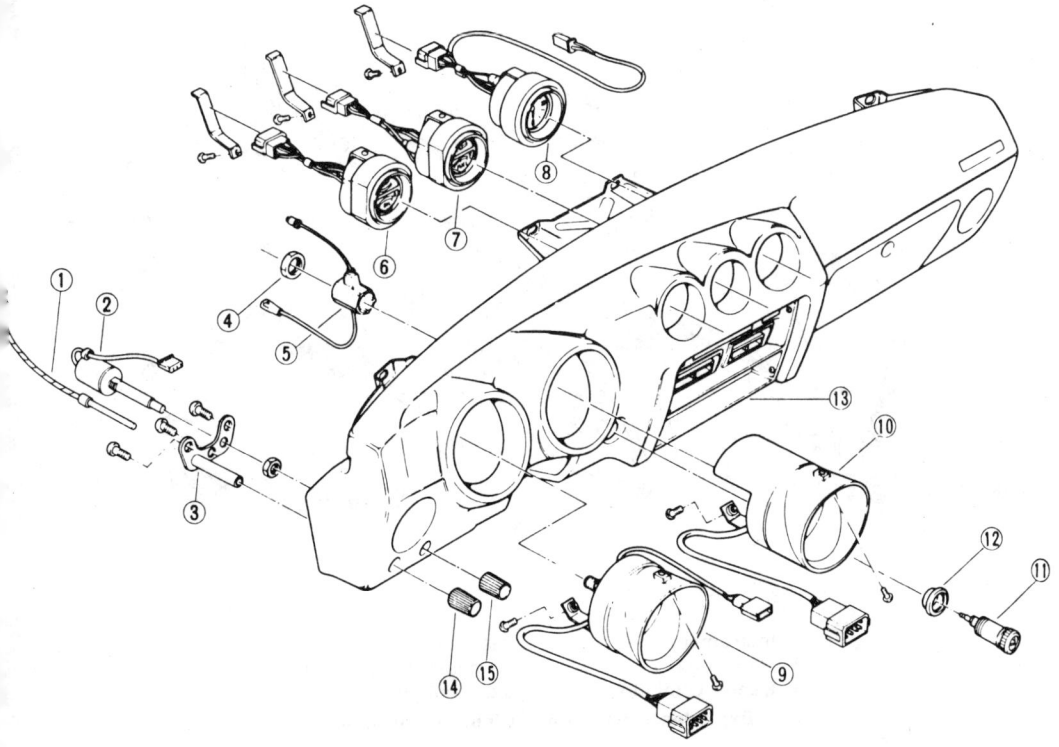

CHASSIS ELECTRICAL 155

1. Trip meter reset knob
2. Resistor (illumination control)
3. Bracket
4. Cigarette lighter retaining nut
5. Cigarette lighter housing
6. Oil-temp gauge
7. Amp-fuel gauge
8. Clock
9. Speedometer
10. Tachometer
11. Cigarette lighter
12. Escutcheon
13. Instrument finish panel
14. Knob (trip meter reset)
15. Knob (resistor)

Exploded view of the Z model instrument panel

3. Disconnect the duct hoses and remove the duct.
4. Remove the screw(s) retaining the gauge or gauges to be removed from the instrument panel.
5. Pull the gauge to the rear, disconnect the connector(s), and remove the gauge.
6. Install reversing the above procedures.

240-Z

1. Remove the instrument panel finish panel.

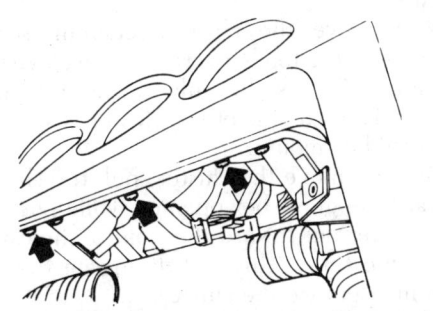

2. Go in where the panel was with a pair of pliers and carefully loosen the hex-head screws on the back of the instrument to be removed.
3. Pull the gauge to the rear, disconnect the connector(s), and remove it.
4. Reverse the procedure to install.

Removing the gauge retaining screws on Z models

Removing the mounting screws for the temperature/oil pressure gauge on Z models

156 CHASSIS ELECTRICAL

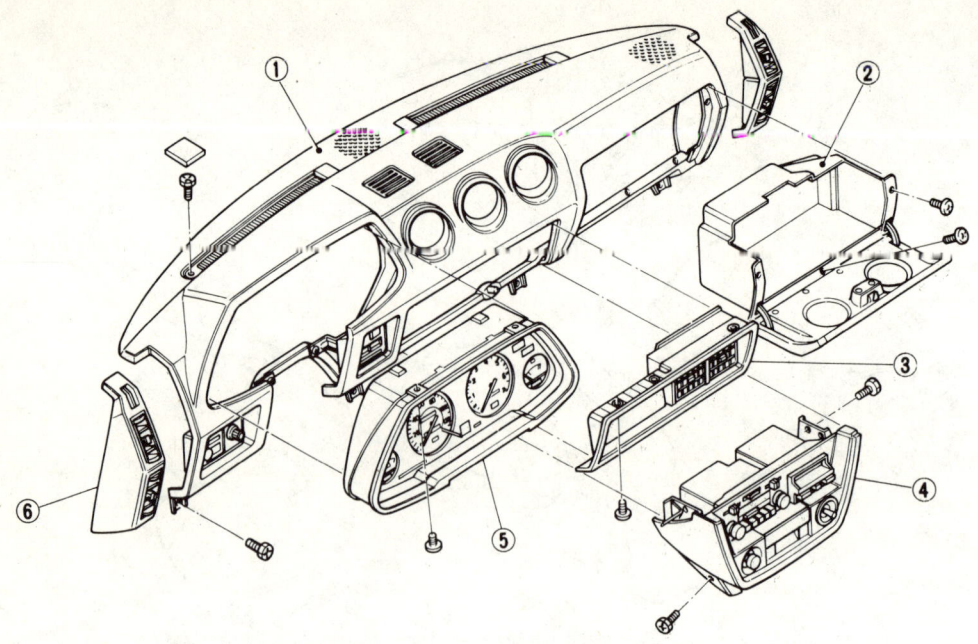

1. Instrument pad
2. Glove box
3. Center ventilator
4. Instrument console
5. Main instrument cluster
6. Side ventilator

Exploded view of the ZX instrument panel

MAIN INSTRUMENT CLUSTER
REMOVAL AND INSTALLATION
280-ZX

1. Disconnect the negative battery cable.
2. Remove the steering wheel. See Chapter 8 for the correct procedure.
3. Remove the steering column trim covers (shell).
4. Remove the lower instrument panel trim cover on the left side.
5. Disconnect the speedometer cable at the connector inside the passenger compartment.
6. Remove the combination switch:
   a. Disconnect the combination switch wiring harness at the connector.
   b. Remove the retaining screw holding the combination switch to the steering column and remove the switch.
7. Remove the four instrument cluster retaining screws. There are two at the top and two which secure brackets next to the steering column.
8. Pull the cluster out slightly and disconnect the wiring harness. Pull the cluster from the instrument panel.
9. Installation is the reverse.

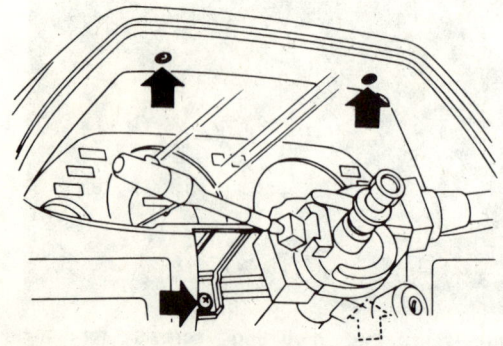

ZX main instrument cluster removal

Oil, Volt, and Clock Cluster
REMOVAL AND INSTALLATION
280-ZX

1. Disconnect the negative battery cable.
2. Remove the glove box.
3. Disconnect the wiring harness to the cluster.
4. Remove the cluster retaining screw which is at the top left corner of the glove box opening. This is the only cluster retaining screw. The left side of the cluster is secured by a rubber mount.
5. To remove the cluster, pull the cluster toward the glove box opening while pushing the cluster out toward the front of the car at the same time. This will disengage the left mount. Remove the cluster.
6. Installation is the reverse.

CHASSIS ELECTRICAL 157

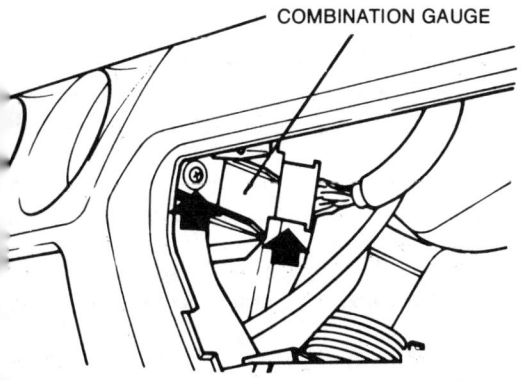

ZX oil, volt, and clock cluster removal: retaining screw (left arrow) and harness connection (right arrow) accessible through the glove box opening

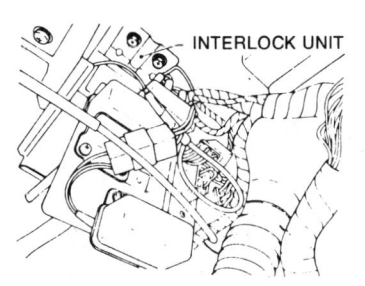

Location of the seatbelt interlock unit

Speedometer Cable Replacement

All Models

1. Reach up under the instrument panel and disconnect the cable housing from the back of the speedometer. It is attached by a knurled knob which simply unscrews.
2. On 240, 260, and 280-Z models, remove the screw under the instrument panel which retains the speedometer cable to a bracket.
3. Pull the cable from the housing. ZX models have an intermediate connection in the passenger compartment. Unscrew the intermediate connection and pull the two cables from the housings.
4. If the cable is broken, the other half of the cable will have to be removed from the transmission end. Unscrew the retaining knob and remove the cable from the transmission.
5. Lubricate the cable with graphite powder or speedometer cable lubricant and feed the cable into the housing. It is best to start at the speedometer end and feed the cable down towards the transmission. It is also usually necessary to unscrew the transmission connection and install the cable end to the gear, then reconnect the housing to the transmission. Slip the cable end into the speedometer and reconnect the cable housing to the speedometer. Install the bracket on Z models.

260-Z SEATBELT INTERLOCK SYSTEM

This system is designed to prevent the engine from starting unless all persons in the car have seat belts on. If either seat is unoccupied, a sensor in the seat by-passes the belt switch for that seat. If system failure prevents the car from starting, it can be started by turning the ignition switch, depressing the button in the engine compartment, and then turning the key to the start position. In addition, whenever a seat is occupied and the belt is not connected, a warning light and buzzer will be activated.

The system should be checked out using a special factory Interlock Checker. However, once the cause of trouble has been located, an individual component can be replaced using the following procedures.

Interlock Unit

REMOVAL AND INSTALLATION

The interlock unit is located behind the relay bracket, under the dash.

1. Disconnect the interlock relay lead wires at the connectors.
2. Remove the three relay bracket retaining screws and remove the relay bracket and relays.
3. Remove the two screws which hold the interlock unit to the dash side panel and remove the unit.
4. To install, reverse these procedures.

Seat Belt Switch and Fastener

REMOVAL AND INSTALLATION

1. Slide the seat all the way forward.
2. Remove the belt fastener securing bolt.
3. Disconnect the belt switch lead wire at the connector. Remove the fastener.
4. Install in reverse sequence.

Seat Switch

REMOVAL AND INSTALLATION

1. Remove the four seat mounting bolts.
2. Lift the seat and disconnect the seat switch wires at the connector.

158 CHASSIS ELECTRICAL

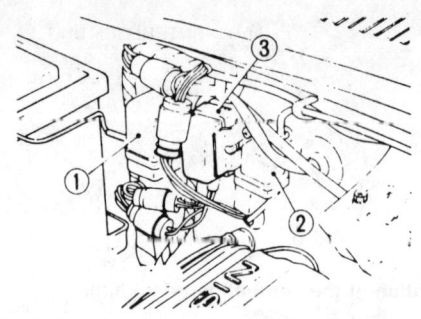

1. Fusible link box 2. Seat belt warning relay
3. Interlock relay

Location of the seat belt warning relay and interlock relay

3. Remove the seat from the car.
4. Install a new seat in reverse order, as the seat switch is integral with the seat assembly.

Interlock Relay

REMOVAL AND INSTALLATION

1. Open the hood. Disconnect the relay lead wires at the connector.
2. Remove the two screws which attach the relay to the front of the dash panel and remove the relay.
3. Install in reverse order.

Seat Belt Warning Relay (Automatic Transmission only)

See the procedures for removal of the Interlock Relay. This relay is retained by the same screws which retain the interlock relay, although wiring is separate.

Emergency Switch

This switch is located on the right-side of the engine compartment, except when the car is equipped with air conditioning. In this case it is located on the vacuum tank retainer. Simply disconnect the wires and remove the retaining screws to remove it. Reverse the procedure to install.

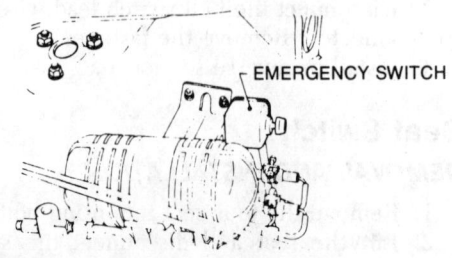

Location of the emergency switch

Warning Buzzer

REMOVAL AND INSTALLATION

1. Disconnect the negative battery cable. Remove the speedometer as described above.
2. Going in through the speedometer hole, disconnect the lead wires for the buzzer at the connector.
3. Remove the retaining screw and remove the buzzer, gaining access the same way.
4. Install by reversing the above procedures.

Warning Lamp Bulb

REMOVAL AND INSTALLATION

1. Remove the heater control knobs and the four screws retaining the finish panel to the instrument panel.
2. Pull the finish panel out slightly and disconnect the map lamp and seat belt lamp connector. Remove the finish panel.
3. Twist the socket mounted at the rear of the seat belt warning lamp and remove it. The bulb may now be removed and replaced.
4. Install the socket and then replace the finish panel in reverse of the above.

LIGHTING

Headlamp

REMOVAL AND INSTALLATION
1970–78

1. Disconnect the headlamp connector behind the front fender panel.
2. Go in through the wheel opening and remove the four headlamp housing retaining screws.
3. Pull the headlamp assembly out.
4. Loosen the retaining ring screws, rotate the ring, and remove it.
5. Disconnect the connector and remove the sealed beam unit.

To install:

1. Connect the wiring connector to the new sealed beam unit, and position it so that the three location tabs fit the hollows in the mounting ring. The letters on the sealed beam must be in an upright position.
2. Install the retaining ring and new lamp by positioning the ring and rotating it in the reverse of removal. Tighten the ring retaining screws.

CHASSIS ELECTRICAL 159

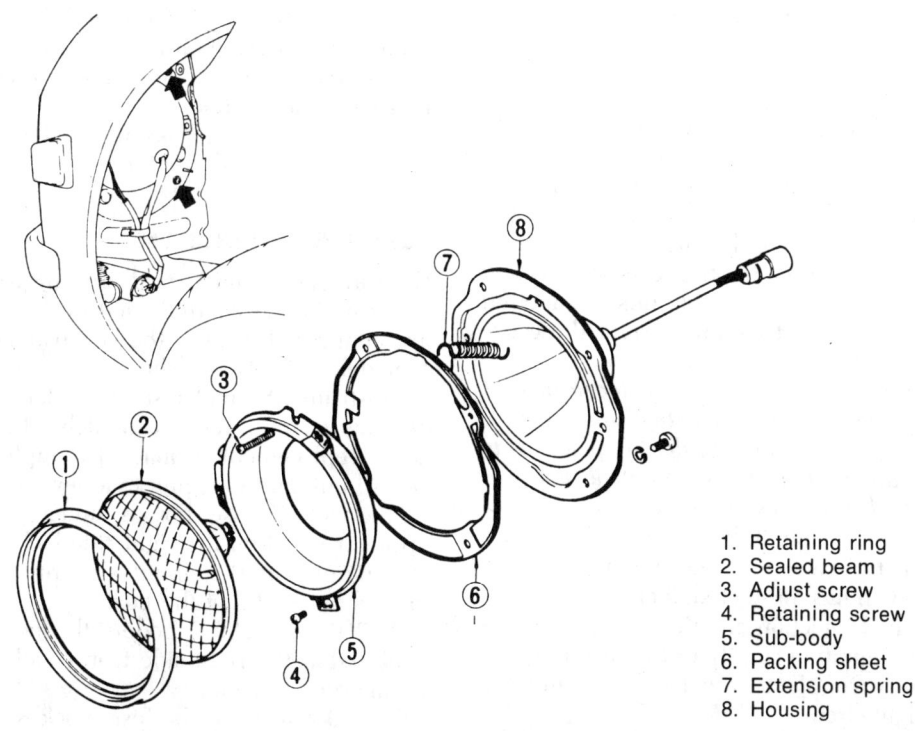

Exploded view of the headlamp parts—Z models

1. Retaining ring
2. Sealed beam
3. Adjust screw
4. Retaining screw
5. Sub-body
6. Packing sheet
7. Extension spring
8. Housing

3. Install the housing to the fender panel with the four screws and connect the wiring connector.
4. Aim the new headlamp, if necessary.

1979 and Later

1. The headlights are accessible through the engine compartment. For access to the left headlight, remove the headlight cleaner reservoir tank, if so equipped. For access to the right headlight, remove the coolant reservoir tank and the charcoal canister.
2. Disconnect the headlamp wiring from the rear of the bulb.
3. Remove the three bolts retaining the headlight bracket.
4. Pull the bracket back and remove the three screws holding the headlight retaining ring. Remove the ring and remove the headlight. Be careful not to touch the headlight aiming screws, located at the top and the outside of the ring.
5. Installation is the reverse.

HEADLIGHT ADJUSTMENT

The headlight aiming screws are accessible by going through the cutting hole of the headlight case. The vertical screw is located on top, while the horizontal screw is to the side.

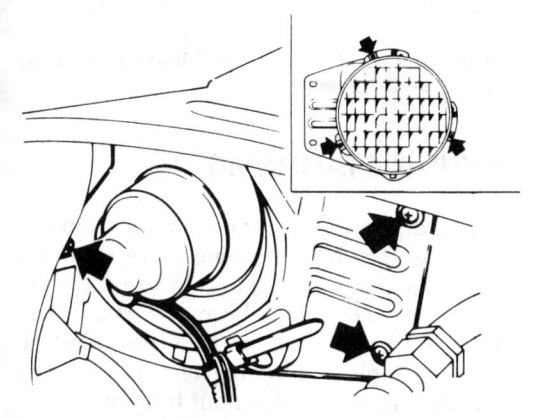

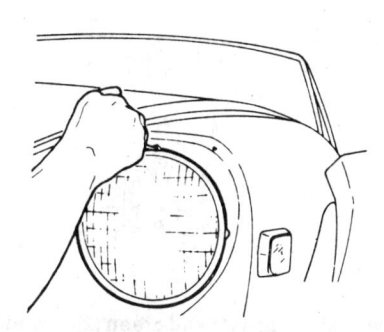

ZX headlamp removal

Headlamp aiming adjustment

CHASSIS ELECTRICAL

CIRCUIT PROTECTION

Fusible Links

Fusible links are protective devices used in the electrical circuits. When current increases beyond the amperage the link is designed to withstand, the fusible metal of the link melts, breaking the circuit and preventing further damage to other components and wiring. Whenever a fusible link has melted because of a short circuit, correct the cause before installing a new link.

> CAUTION: *Always use replacements of the same electrical capacity as the original, available from your dealer. Replacements of a different electrical value will not provide adequate system protection.*

All 280-ZX fusible links are located in a case next to the battery in the engine compartment. Circuits protected include the electronic fuel injection circuit, the ignition circuit, the ignition supply to the fuse box, the accessory supply to the fuse box, and the headlight circuit.

The 280-Z fusible links are located on the relay bracket on the inner right fender in front of the battery. The fuel injection fusible link is connected between the battery positive cable and the fuel injection harness.

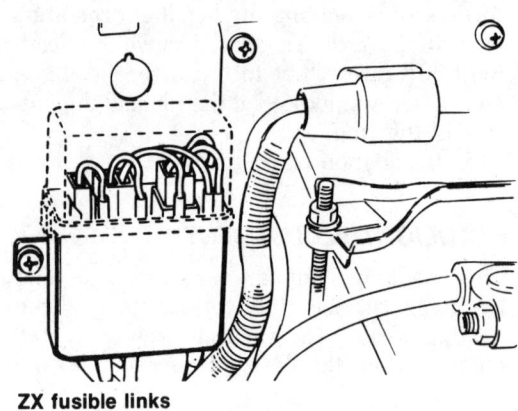

On the 260-Z, the fusible link box is located on the firewall on the right-side of the engine compartment. These links protect the alternator and starter.

On the 240-Z, the links are located at the starter motor and alternator.

Fuses And Flashers

The turn signal and hazard warning flashers are located underneath the left side of the instrument panel, next to the kick panel on all Z models. The two flasher units are under the instrument panel just to the left of the steering column on ZX models. In both cases, replacement is made by unplugging the old unit and plugging in a new one.

The 280-ZX fuse box is under the instrument panel on the right side kick panel. Fuse ratings and the circuits they protect are marked on the lid of the box.

On 260-Z and 280-Z models, the fuse block is located at the right-side trim panel under the instrument panel.

On 240-Z models, the fuse block is in the console under the ash tray.

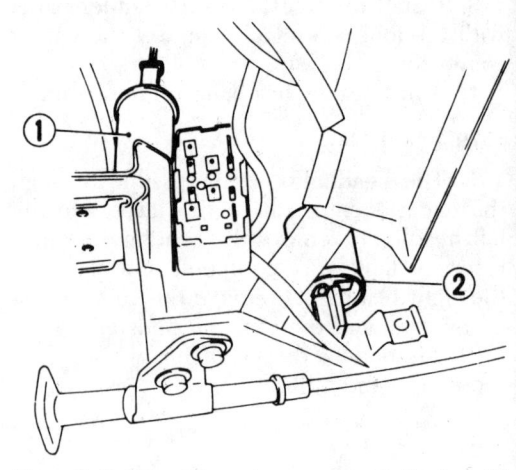

ZX fusible links

Hazard flasher (1) and turn signal flasher (2) locations—Z models

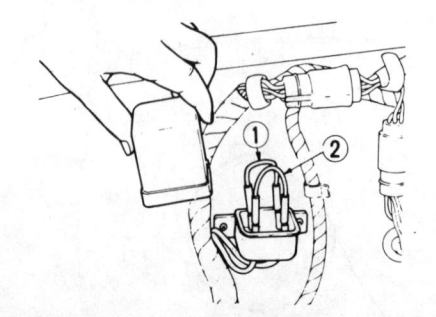

Fusible links—black (1) and green (2)—used in the 260-Z

WIRING DIAGRAMS

Wiring diagrams have been omitted from this book. As cars have become more complex, wiring diagrams have grown in size and complexity as well. It has become virtually impossible to provide a readable reproduction in a reasonable number of pages. Information on obtaining wiring diagrams from the manufacturer is available at your Datsun dealer.

CHASSIS ELECTRICAL

Light Bulb Specifications

Model/Year	Wattage or Candle Power	SAE Trade Number
240-Z, 1970–71		
Headlamp	50/40	612
Front Park/Turn Signal	23/7 cp	—
Side Marker	7.5	—
Rear Combination		
Tail	7	—
Stop	23	—
Turn	23	—
Back-up	23	—
240-Z, 1972–73		
Headlamp	50/40	612
Front Park/Turn Signal	32/3 cp	1034
Side Marker	4 cp	67
Rear Combination		
Stop/Tail	32/3 cp	1034
Turn	32	1073
Back-up	32	1073
260-Z and 280-Z, 1974–78		
Headlamp	50/40	6012
Front Combination		
Park/Turn Signal	23/8	1034
Side Marker	8	67
Rear Combination		
Stop/Tail	23/8	1034
Tail	8	67
Turn	23	1073
Back-up	23	1073
280-ZX, 1979–82		
Headlamp	50/40 [1]	6012
Front Combination		
Park/Turn	27/8	1157
Side Marker	3.4	158
Rear Combination		
Stop/Tail	27/8	1157
Turn	27	1156
Back-up	27	1156

[1] 1981–82—60/50 (Halogen)

Clutch and Transmission

MANUAL TRANSMISSION

The Datsun 240-Z uses a model F4W71A four speed transmission in 1970 and 1971. 1972–76 models use the F4W71B four speed transmission. 1977 and later models use either the F4W71B four speed or the FS5W71B five speed transmission. All models use a single top rail shifter with internal linkage. No shift linkage adjustments are necessary or possible.

NEUTRAL SAFETY SWITCH REMOVAL AND INSTALLATION

1. Disconnect the lead wires (green with black stripe and green with white stripe) at the connectors.
2. Unscrew the neutral safety switch from the transmission rear extension housing and remove it.
3. Install in reverse order.

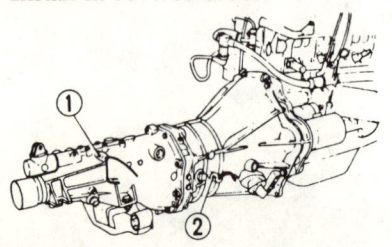

Neutral safety switch (1) and back-up lamp switch (2)

TRANSMISSION REMOVAL AND INSTALLATION

1. Disconnect the battery negative cable and the accelerator linkage to the carburetor. Drain the transmission oil.
2. Remove the screws holding the console in place. Remove the choke control wire from the console. Disconnect the wiring harness and remove the console. Remove the shift lever boot.
3. Put the transmission in Neutral and remove the E-ring from the gearshift lever pin. Then, remove the pin and remove the gearshift lever.
4. Support the vehicle on safety stands or a lift.
5. Disconnect the exhaust pipe at the front. Remove the exhaust pipe bracket from the extension housing. Support the pipe with a length of wire.

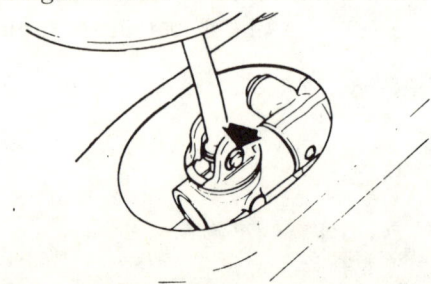

Disconnecting the gearshift lever C-clip

CLUTCH AND TRANSMISSION 163

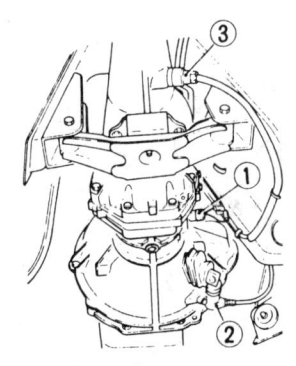

1. Neutral safety switch
2. Clutch slave cylinder
3. Speedometer

The underside of the transmission

6. Disconnect the back-up light and neutral safety switch wires.
7. Remove the clutch operating cylinder.
8. Disconnect the speedometer cable at the rear extension housing.
9. Remove the resonator and muffler hanger bolts.
10. Scribe matchmarks on the rear of the driveshaft and on the companion flange.
11. Remove rear driveshaft bolts, pull the rear down, and then draw the driveshaft sleeve yoke out of the transmission. Draw the shaft out carefully so as not to damage the spline, yoke, or transmission oil seal. Plug the opening in the transmission with a clean rag.
12. Support the engine under the oil pan with a jack. Place a wood block between the jack and pan.
13. Place a jack under the transmission. Do not place the jack under the drain plug.
14. Remove the nut attaching the transmission to the rear crossmember. Remove the crossmember attaching bolts and remove it.
15. Disconnect the wiring and remove the starter motor.
16. Remove the bolts holding the transmission to the engine.
17. Slide the transmission slightly to the rear, then slowly downward, and remove it.

On installation:
1. Clean the mating surfaces of the engine and transmission case.
2. Lightly grease the clutch disc and mainshaft splines.
3. Reverse the above removal procedures. Installation torque for the engine-to-transmission bolts is 32–43 ft lbs (4.4–5.9 kg-m) for the top four bolts, and 6.5–8.7 ft lbs (0.9–1.2 kg-m) for the bottom two bolts.
4. Refill the transmission to the level of the filler plug with the recommended oil.

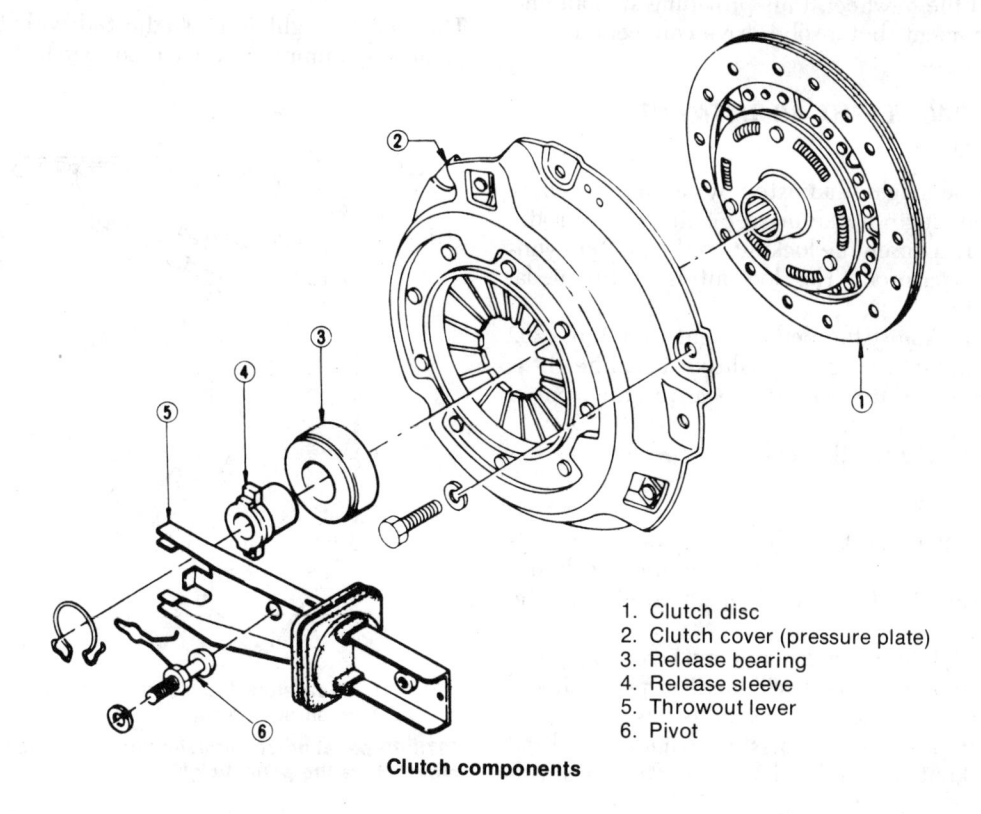

1. Clutch disc
2. Clutch cover (pressure plate)
3. Release bearing
4. Release sleeve
5. Throwout lever
6. Pivot

Clutch components

164 CLUTCH AND TRANSMISSION

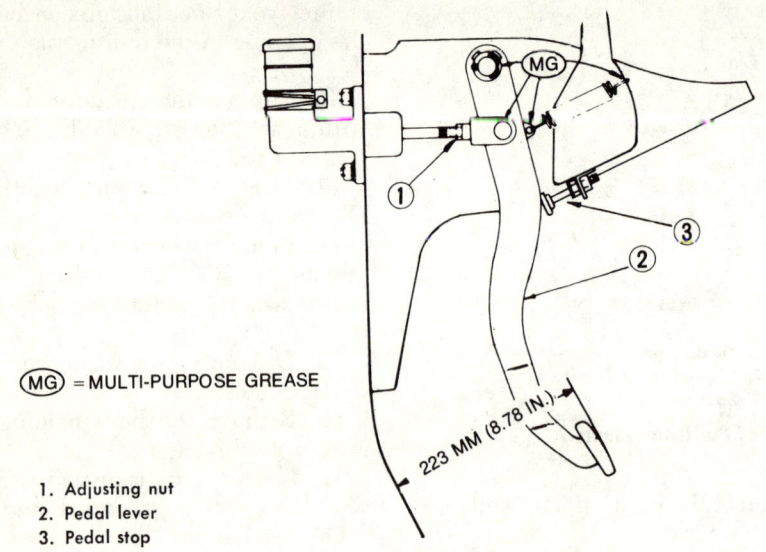

(MG) = MULTI-PURPOSE GREASE

1. Adjusting nut
2. Pedal lever
3. Pedal stop

Adjusting the clutch pedal free-play, 1972–75

CLUTCH

The clutch consists of a driven disc splined to the transmission mainshaft and a pressure plate which is bolted to the engine flywheel. When the clutch pedal is released, the pressure plate moves toward the flywheel and sandwiches the driven disc between itself and the flywheel, thus providing smooth engagement, but a solid drive connection.

PEDAL HEIGHT ADJUSTMENT

1970–71

Pedal height is adjusted by varying the effective length of the master cylinder pushrod.

1. Loosen the locknut on the master cylinder pushrod. The locknut is at the pedal clevis.
2. Adjust the pedal height to 8.0 in. (202 mm) by turning the pushrod. Pedal height is measured from the floorboard to the front of the pedal pad.
3. Tighten the locknut.

1972–75

The height is first adjusted by varying the effective length of the master cylinder pushrod. Height is then adjusted with the pedal stop bumper.

1. Loosen the locknut and screw the pedal stop in as far as it will go. The pedal should be free to move out as far as possible.
2. Loosen the master cylinder pushrod locknut. It is located at the pedal clevis. Adjust the rod so that the pedal height is 8.9 in. (226 mm). Pedal height is measured from the floorboard to the front of the pedal pad. Tighten the locknut.
3. Screw the pedal stop back out until the pedal height is 8.78 in. (223 mm). Tighten the locknut.

1976–79

The pedal height is first adjusted with the pedal stop bumper or the clutch switch. Free

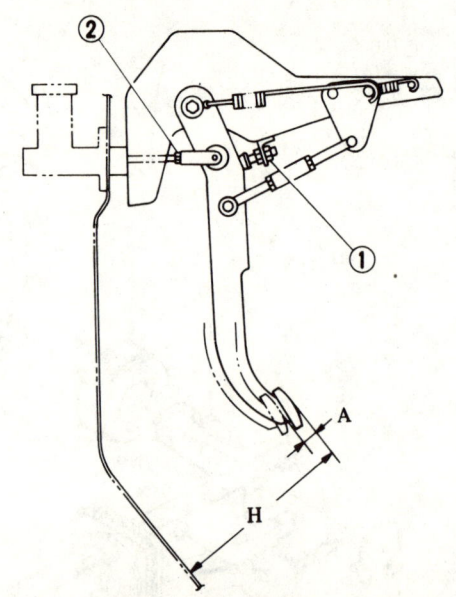

1. Pedal stop/clutch switch locknut
2. Pushrod locknut

1976–79 pedal height adjustment: "A" is the free-play; "H" is the pedal height

CLUTCH AND TRANSMISSION 165

play is then adjusted by varying the effective length of the master cylinder pushrod.

1. Loosen the locknut on the pedal stop bumper or clutch switch. Turn the bumper or switch in or out until the pedal height is 8.8 in. (223 mm), 1976–78, or 7.87–8.11 in. (200–206 mm), 1979. Pedal height is measured from the floorboard to the front of the pedal pad. Tighten the locknut.

2. Loosen the master cylinder pushrod locknut. The locknut is at the pedal clevis.

3. Adjust the pedal free play by turning the pushrod. Free play should be 0.04–0.12 in. (1.0–3.0 mm) in 1976 and 1977. Free play should be 0.04–0.20 in. (1.0–5.0 mm) in 1978 and 1979. Tighten the locknut.

1980 and Later

Three adjustments are to be made. The first is to the adjusting rod, which connects the pedal arm to the return spring pivot. The second is made by varying the effective length of the master cylinder pushrod. The third is made by adjusting the clutch switch or pedal stop bumper.

1. Check the length of the adjusting rod. The distance between the center of each end should be 6.10 in. (155 mm). If not, loosen the locknuts and turn the adjuster until the length is correct. Tighten the locknuts.

2. Loosen the clutch switch or the pedal stop bumper locknut. Turn the switch or bumper all the way in so that the pedal arm does not make contact.

3. Loosen the master cylinder pushrod locknut (located at the pedal clevis). Adjust the pedal height by turning the master cylinder pushrod. Pedal height is measured from the floorboard to the front of the pedal pad. The height should be 8.11 in. (206 mm). Tighten the locknut.

4. Turn the clutch switch or the pedal stop until the pedal height measures 7.99 in. (203 mm). Tighten the locknut on the switch or stop.

5. Check the pedal free play. It should be 0.04–0.20 in. (1.0–5.0 mm). If incorrect, adjust with the master cylinder pushrod.

REMOVAL AND INSTALLATION

1. Remove the transmission as described above.

2. Insert a clutch aligning bar or similar tool all the way into the clutch disc hub. This must be done so as to support the weight of the clutch disc during removal. Mark the

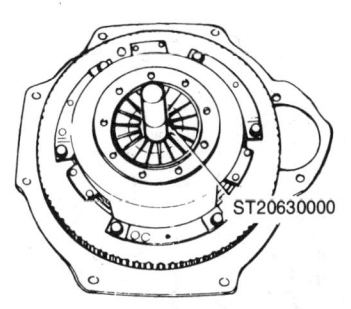

Support the clutch assembly with a clutch alignment tool

clutch assembly-to-flywheel relationship with paint or a center punch so that the clutch assembly can be assembled in the same position from which it is removed.

3. Loosen the pressure plate-to-flywheel bolts evenly, one turn at a time, until all spring pressure is released.

4. Remove the bolts and pull the pressure plate and disc off the flywheel.

5. Inspect the flywheel for scoring, roughness, or signs of overheating. Light scoring may be cleaned up with emery cloth, but any deep grooves or scoring warrant replacement or refacing (if possible) of the flywheel. If the clutch facings or flywheel are oily, inspect the transmission front cover oil seal, the pilot bushing, and the engine rear seals for leakage, and correct before replacing the clutch. If the pilot bushing in the crankshaft is worn, replace it. Install it using a soft hammer. The installation depth should be 0.18–0.20 in. (4.5–5.0 mm), 1970–77; 0.374 in. (9.5 mm), 1978; or 0.157 in. (4.0 mm), 1979–80. Installation depth is measured from the end of the crankshaft flange to the transmission end of the pilot bushing. The factory-supplied part does not have to be oiled, but check the procedure if you are using an aftermarket part. Inspect the clutch cover for wear or scoring, and replace as necessary. The pressure plate and spring cannot be disassembled; you must replace the clutch cover as an assembly.

6. Inspect the clutch release bearing. If it is rough or noisy, it should be replaced. The bearing can be removed from the sleeve with a puller; this requires a press to install the new bearing. After installation, coat the groove in the sleeve, the contact surfaces of the release lever, pivot pin and sleeve, and the release bearing contact surfaces on the transmission front cover with a light coat of grease. Be careful not to use too much grease, which will run at high temperatures

CLUTCH AND TRANSMISSION

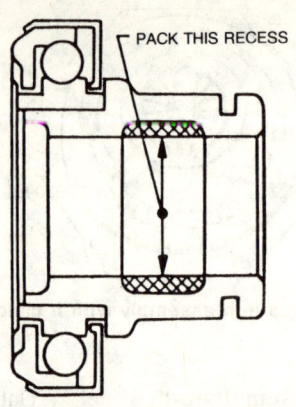

Coat the area indicated in the bearing sleeve with grease

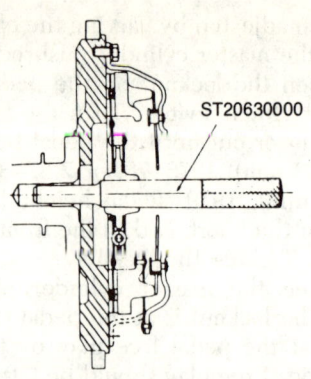

Center the clutch cover with an alignment tool

and get onto the clutch facings. Reinstall the release bearing on the lever.

7. Apply a thin coat of grease to the pressure plate wire ring, diaphragm spring, clutch cover grooves and the drive bosses on the pressure plate.

8. Apply a thin coat of Lubriplate® to the splines in the driven plate. Slide the clutch disc into the splines, and move it back and forth several times. Remove the disc and wipe off the excess lubricant. Be very careful not to get any grease on the clutch facings.

9. Assemble the clutch cover and the clutch plate on the clutch alignment tool.

10. Align the marks made on the clutch cover and the flywheel (if the old cover is being used) and install the six clutch cover-to-flywheel bolts. Three dowels are used to locate the clutch cover on the flywheel. Tighten the bolts in a criss-cross pattern, one turn at a time, to 12–15 ft lbs (1.6–2.1 kg-m). Remove the clutch alignment tool.

11. Install the transmission.

Clutch Master Cylinder
REMOVAL AND INSTALLATION

1. Remove the pushrod clevis pin. Disconnect the tube going to the slave cylinder and drain the fluid.

2. Remove the windshield washer tank and dropping resistor out of the way on vehicles with fuel injection.

3. Remove the mounting bolts and remove the cylinder from the car.

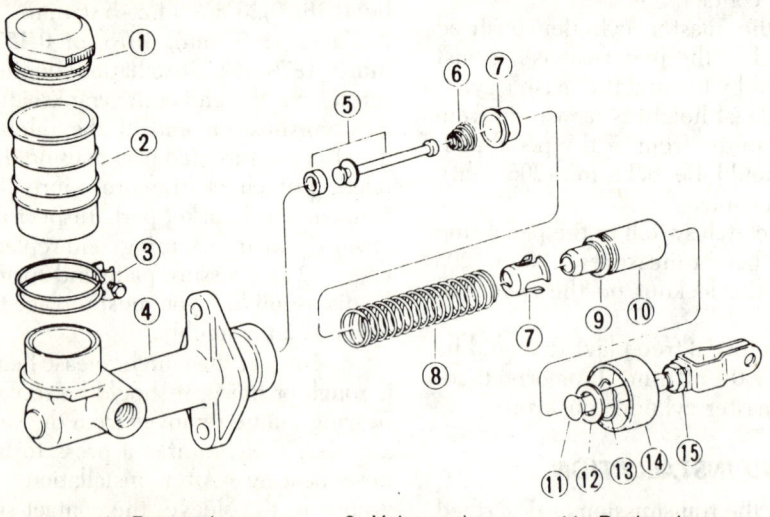

1. Reservoir cap
2. Reservoir
3. Reservoir band
4. Cylinder body
5. Valve assembly
6. Valve spring
7. Spring seat
8. Return spring
9. Piston cup
10. Piston
11. Pushrod
12. Stopper
13. Stopper ring
14. Dust cover
15. Nut

Exploded view of the clutch master cylinder—typical of all models

CLUTCH AND TRANSMISSION

4. On installation, reverse the above procedures.
5. Bleed the system as described below.

SYSTEM BLEEDING

1. Fill the master cylinder with the recommended fluid to the proper level.
2. Clean any dirt from the bleeder screw on the slave cylinder and install at bleeder hose. Submerge the free end of the hose in a container of brake fluid.
3. Have someone depress the clutch pedal slowly. Loosen the bleeder screw as the pedal starts moving down and retighten it before the pedal stops moving downward.
4. Have your assistant release the clutch pedal, then repeat Step 3 until the fluid in the bleed hose is bubble-free. Keep your eye on the fluid level and refill the reservoir with fresh fluid as necessary.
5. When all air is bled, refill the master cylinder, tighten the bleeder screw snugly, and remove the bleeder hose.

OVERHAUL

1. Remove the dust cover. Remove the stopper ring.
2. Remove the pushrod and piston assembly.
3. Remove the spring seat. Remove the piston cup and discard it. Wash all parts in brake fluid.
4. Check the cylinder for uneven wear/or damage and measure the clearance between the piston and cylinder. The clearance should not be more than 0.0059 in. (0.15 mm). If defects are found, replace master cylinder.
5. Install a new piston cup.
6. Inspect the dust cover, oil reservoir, cap, and replace parts as necessary.
7. Inspect the return valve springs and replace if broken or weak.
8. Inspect the hose and tube. Replace parts as necessary.
9. Reassemble the master cylinder, reversing Steps 1–3. Dip the piston cup in brake fluid and coat the piston and cylinder with fluid before installing. Make sure that the piston is facing the right way!

Clutch Slave Cylinder

REMOVAL AND INSTALLATION

1. Remove the return spring. Detach the line going to the master cylinder and drain the fluid.

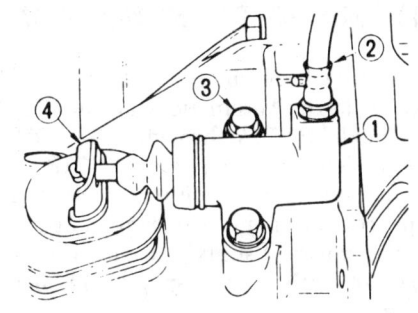

1. Clutch slave cylinder   3. Mounting bolts
2. Clutch hose   4. Withdrawal lever

Slave cylinder mounting

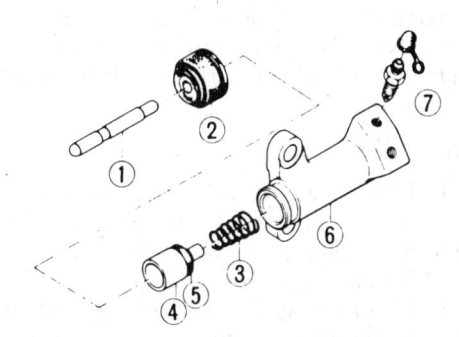

1. Pushrod   5. Piston cup
2. Dust cover   6. Operating cylinder
3. Piston spring   7. Bleeder screw
4. Piston

Exploded view of the clutch slave cylinder

2. Remove the mounting bolts and remove the cylinder.
3. To install, reverse the above procedure and then bleed the system as previously described in "System Bleeding."

OVERHAUL

1. Remove the pushrod and dust cover.
2. Remove the piston and piston spring.
3. Remove the bleeder screw.
4. Clean all parts in brake fluid and inspect for damage. Check the piston and cylinder for excessive wear or scoring. The cylinder must not be worn beyond 0.7500 in. (19.05 mm).
5. Install a new piston cup. Dip it in brake fluid first, and be sure that it is installed in the right direction.
6. Check the dust cover for damage and check the return spring for a break or weakened condition.
7. Assemble the cylinder in the reverse order of Steps 1–3, dipping the piston in brake fluid and also coating the cylinder with it.

CLUTCH AND TRANSMISSION

AUTOMATIC TRANSMISSION

The optional automatic transmission is a JATCO (Japan Automatic Transmission Co., Ltd.) model 3N71A through 1972; 1973 and later models use the JATCO 3N71B. It is a fully automatic unit with a three element torque converter and two planetary gear sets. The transmission shifts gears in response to signals of both engine speed and manifold vacuum.

While it is unlikely that you will ever disassemble the transmission yourself, there are a few adjustments you can perform which will prolong the transmission's life if performed accurately. The most important thing is to change the fluid regularly, which is covered in Chapter 1.

PAN REMOVAL

1. Remove all pan mounting bolts.
2. Remove the pan slowly, keeping it level to avoid spilling fluid. Drain the fluid.

To install:
1. Clean the gasket surfaces of both the pan and the transmission.
2. Use a new gasket.
3. When tightening mounting bolts, go back-and-forth in a criss-cross fashion, tightening the bolts evenly to 3.6–5.1 ft lbs (0.5–0.7 kg-m).
4. Refill with Dexron® fluid and check the level as described in Chapter 1.

BRAKE BAND ADJUSTMENT

1. Remove the oil pan as previously described.
2. Loosen the locknut on the piston stem. Tighten the piston stem to *exactly* 9–11 ft lbs (1.2–1.5 kg-m).
3. Loosen the piston stem *exactly* two turns. Hold the stem and tighten the locknut to 11–29 ft lbs (1.5–4.0 kg-m). If the stem turns when the locknut is tightened, loosen the locknut and repeat the adjustment.
4. Replace the oil pan and refill the transmission as described above.

NEUTRAL SAFETY SWITCH ADJUSTMENT

1. Apply the brakes and check to see that the starter works only in the "P" and "N" transmission ranges. If the starter works with the transmission in gear, adjust the switch as described below.
2. Remove the fastening nut of the range selector lever and the bolts which hold the switch body in place. Remove the machine screw under the switch body.
3. Put the manual shaft in the "N" position by moving the selector lever so that the slot in the shaft is vertical and the detent mechanism clicks.
4. Align the screw hole with the internal rotor pin hole and insert a 0.059 in. (1.5 mm) pin to ensure and retain alignment.

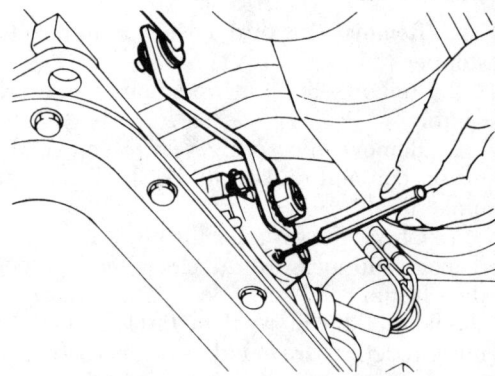

Insert the alignment pin into the hole for neutral safety switch alignment

5. Install the switch bolts, pull out the pin, and put the machine screw back into the hole. Install the range selector lever nut.
6. Test again as in step 1. If the switch does not work, replace it.

SHIFT LINKAGE ADJUSTMENT

1970–72

1. Loosen the trunnion locknuts at the lower end of the control lever. Remove the selector lever knob and console.
2. Put the transmission selector in "N" and put the transmission shift lever in the Neutral position by pushing it all the way back, then moving it forward two stops.
3. Check the vertical clearance between

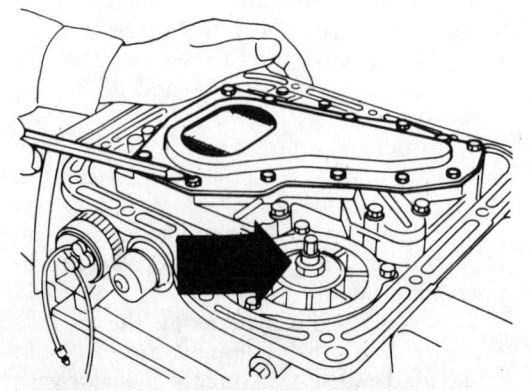

Brake band piston stem and locknut (arrow)

CLUTCH AND TRANSMISSION 169

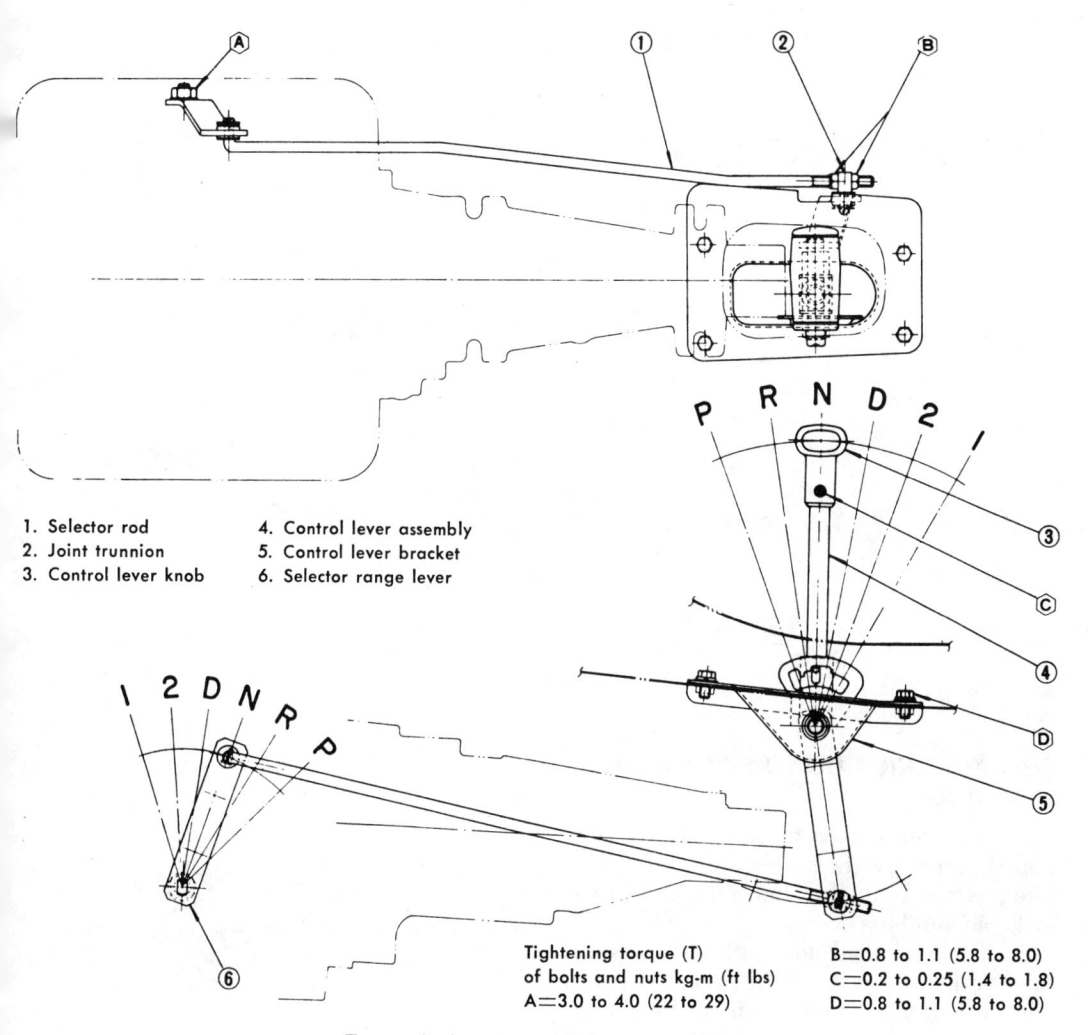

1. Selector rod
2. Joint trunnion
3. Control lever knob
4. Control lever assembly
5. Control lever bracket
6. Selector range lever

Tightening torque (T) of bolts and nuts kg-m (ft lbs)
A=3.0 to 4.0 (22 to 29)
B=0.8 to 1.1 (5.8 to 8.0)
C=0.2 to 0.25 (1.4 to 1.8)
D=0.8 to 1.1 (5.8 to 8.0)

Transmission control linkage—1973-78

the top of the shift lever pin and transmission control bracket ("A" in the illustration). It should be 0.020-0.059 in. (0.5-1.5 mm). Adjust the nut at the lower end of the selector lever compression rod, as necessary.

4. Check the horizontal clearance ("B") between the shift lever pin and transmission control bracket. It should be 0.020 in. (0.5 mm). Adjust the trunion locknuts as necessary to get this clearance.

5. Replace the console with the shift pointer correctly aligned. Install the shift knob.

1973-78

1. Loosen the adjusting nuts ("B").
2. Set both transmission control lever and range selector lever in the "N" position.
3. Tighten the adjusting nuts so that they both just touch the trunnion ("2").
4. Tighten the nuts. Test the shifter for proper operation.

1979 and Later

Adjustment is made at the locknuts at the base of the shifter, which control the length of the shift control rod.

1. Place the shift lever in "D".
2. Loosen the locknuts and move the shift lever until it is firmly in the "D" range, the pointer is aligned, and the transmission is in "D" range.
3. Tighten the locknuts.
4. Check the adjustment. Start the car and apply the parking brake. Shift through all the ranges, starting in "P". As the lever is moved from "P" to "1", you should be able to feel the detents in each range. If proper adjustment is not possible, the grommets are probably worn and should be replaced.

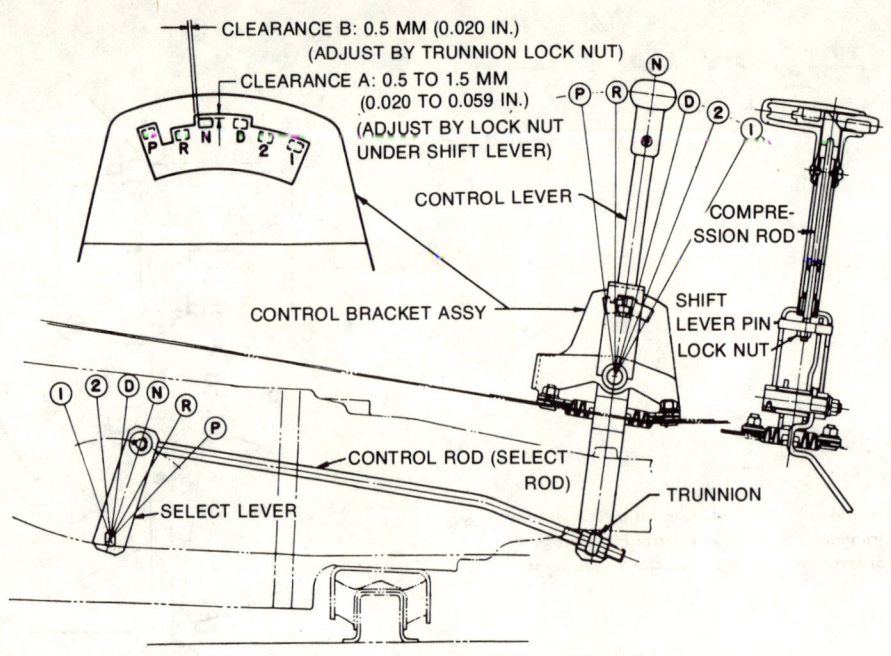

CLUTCH AND TRANSMISSION

Transmission control linkage—1970–72

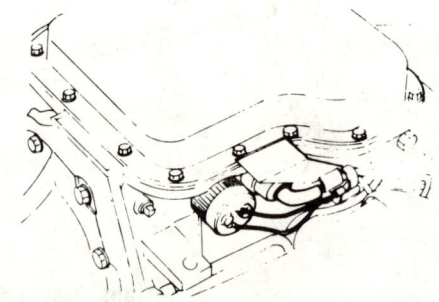

Location of the downshift solenoid

CHECKING KICK-DOWN SWITCH AND SOLENOID

1. Turn the key to the normal ON position, and depress the accelerator all the way. The solenoid in the transmission should make an audible click.
2. If the solenoid does not work, inspect the wiring, and test it electrically to determine whether the problem is in the wiring, the kick-down switch, or the solenoid.
3. If the solenoid requires replacement, drain a little over 2 pts (1 liter) of fluid from the transmission before removing it.

Drive Train

7

DRIVELINE

Driveshaft and U-Joints

REMOVAL AND INSTALLATION

1. Raise the car. It may be necessary to move the exhaust pipe and insulator out of the way on some models.
2. Scribe matchmarks on the rear of the driveshaft and the companion flange.
3. Remove the bolts and nuts from the companion flange.
4. Pull the rear of the driveshaft downward and pull the splined portion at the front out of the transmission. Plug the hole in the transmission extension housing.
5. To install, reverse these procedures, oiling the splines before assembly. Make sure that the marks made in Step 3 align.

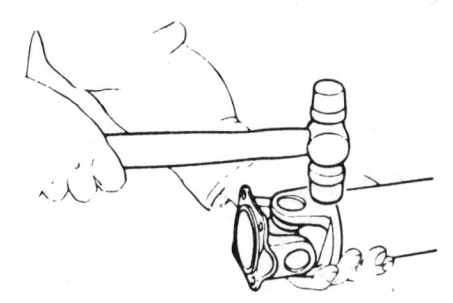

Removing the U-joint bearings

Torque the flange bolts to 18–23 ft lbs (2.5–3.2 kg-m) on 1970–74 models, 25–33 ft lbs (3.5–4.5 kg-m) on 1975–82 models.

U-JOINT OVERHAUL

NOTE: *The universal joints used on 1975 and later models cannot be disassembled. If defective, the entire driveshaft must be replaced as a unit.*

1. Clean all parts in a safe solvent.
2. Mark the driveshaft and joint so that they can be reassembled in exactly the same position.
3. Remove the snap-rings with a screwdriver.
4. Lightly tap the base of the yoke with a soft hammer and remove each bearing race.
5. Check the spider bearing journals for dents or brinell marks. Make sure that the yoke holes are not worn.
6. Check the snap-rings, bearings, and seal rings. Replace parts as necessary.
7. Check the shaft tube for dents or cracks, and replace if necessary.
8. Assemble in reverse order. The needle rollers may be held in the races with grease. Reusable bearings should be carefully packed with grease.
9. Install snap-rings that are equal in thickness opposite each other. Choose

DRIVE TRAIN

thickness so that play will not exceed 0.0008 in. (0.02 mm). See the following chart.

Snap-Rings

Thickness in. (mm)	Color
.0787 (2.0)	White
.0795 (2.02)	Yellow
.0803 (2.04)	Red
.0811 (2.06)	Green
.0819 (2.08)	Blue
.0827 (2.10)	Brown
.0835 (2.12)	Unpainted
.0843 (2.43)	Pink

10. Check that the frictional resistance of the joint does not exceed 9 in. lbs (10 kg-cm) on 240-Z models, or 13 in. lbs (15 kg-cm) on 260-Z models.

Axle Shaft

Two methods are used to join the axle shaft to the differential. All 1970–73 models, all 1975 and 1976 models, and all 1977 and later manual transmission models have a four bolt flange at the differential end. All 1974 models, and all 1977 and later automatic transmission models have axle shafts retained to the differential by a single center bolt. All axle shafts have a four bolt flange at the outside end, which mates to the stub axle flange (companion flange). The stub axle flange is retained by a bolt to the stub axle, which is also splined to the flange. The stub axle is carried in two wheel bearings. The bearings are carried in a housing attached to the rear suspension lower arm.

REMOVAL AND INSTALLATION

1. Raise and support the car.
2. Remove the U-joint yoke flange bolts at the outside. Remove the U-joint flange bolts or the center bolt at the differential.
3. Remove the axle shaft.
4. Installation is the reverse. Torque the outside flange bolts to 36–43 ft lbs (5.0–6.0 kg-m). Tighten the four differential side flange bolts to 36–43 ft lbs (5.0–6.0 kg-m). On axle shafts retained to the differential

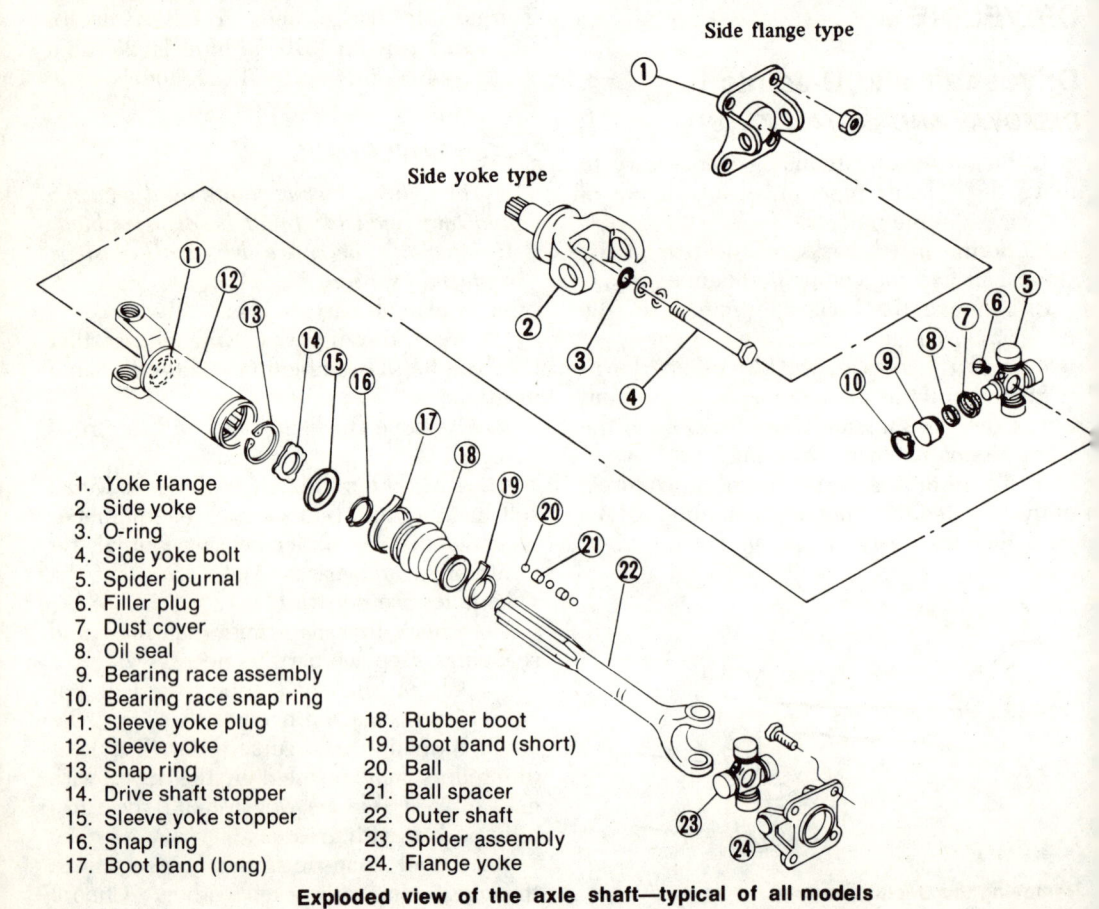

1. Yoke flange
2. Side yoke
3. O-ring
4. Side yoke bolt
5. Spider journal
6. Filler plug
7. Dust cover
8. Oil seal
9. Bearing race assembly
10. Bearing race snap ring
11. Sleeve yoke plug
12. Sleeve yoke
13. Snap ring
14. Drive shaft stopper
15. Sleeve yoke stopper
16. Snap ring
17. Boot band (long)
18. Rubber boot
19. Boot band (short)
20. Ball
21. Ball spacer
22. Outer shaft
23. Spider assembly
24. Flange yoke

Exploded view of the axle shaft—typical of all models

DRIVE TRAIN

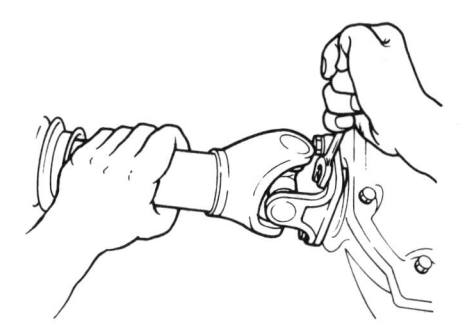

Removing the yoke flange bolts at the differential

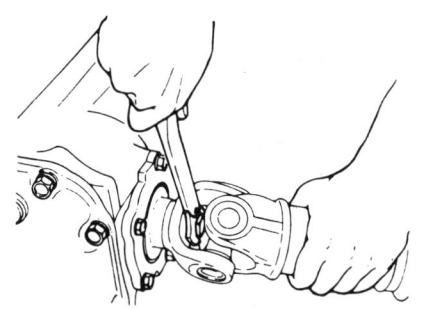

Removing the yoke flange center bolt at the differential

with a single center bolt, tighten the bolt to 17–23 ft lbs (2.4–3.2 kg-m), 1974 and 1977, or 23–31 ft lbs (3.2–4.3 kg-m), 1978 and later.

INSPECTION

Before disassembling the axle shaft, inspect it as follows:

1. Check the parts for wear or damage. Replace the shaft as an assembly if defects are found.
2. Extend and compress the axle shaft (full stroke). Check the action for smoothness.
3. Check the play in the axle shaft. Fully compress the shaft and check the play with a dial indicator. If play exceeds 0.004 in (0.1 mm) through 1978, or 0.008 (0.2 mm), 1979–80, the shaft must be replaced. The sleeve yoke, balls, spacers and outer shaft are *not* available as service parts.

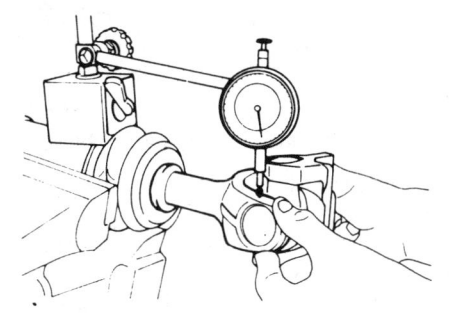

Measuring the play in the axle shaft

4. Check the U-joints for smoothness. If movement is notchy or loose, overhaul the U-joints.
5. Check the U-joint axial play. If it exceeds 0.0008 in. (0.02 mm), overhaul the U-joints.

OVERHAUL

You will need a pair of snap ring pliers for this job.

1. Matchmark the parts across the U-joint journals, and across the sliding yoke (outer shaft to sleeve yoke). The axle shaft was balanced as a unit and must be rebuilt as originally assembled.
2. Remove the snap rings from the U-joints and disassemble them as outlined in the "U-joint Overhaul" procedure in this chapter.
3. Cut the boot band and remove the boot from the sleeve yoke.
4. Remove the snap ring from the sleeve yoke at the boot end.
5. Remove the outer shaft carefully; do not lose any of the balls or spacers.
6. It is not necessary to remove the snap ring and sleeve yoke plug at the differential end of the sleeve yoke, because the parts are not available for service. If any damage is present, the entire axle shaft must be replaced.
7. Clean the spacers, balls, and sleeve yoke and outer shaft grooves in solvent. Check the parts for wear, brinelling, distortion, cracks, straightness, etc. If there is any question as to the integrity of the part, replace the axle shaft.
8. Check the snap ring, grease seal, and dust seal for wear or damage. These parts are available for service and should be replaced as necessary.
9. Apply a fairly generous amount of grease to the yoke and shaft grooves. Install the balls and spacers onto the shaft. The grease will retain them. Be sure they are in the correct sequence.
10. Before assembling the shaft and sleeve yoke, apply a large glob of grease to the inner end of the sleeve yoke. You can put a blob of grease on the end of the shaft, too.
11. Align the parts according to the matchmarks made in Step 1. Slide the shaft into the sleeve yoke, making sure none of the balls or spacers is displaced.
12. Compress the shaft and check the play again. Refer to the inspection procedure. Replace the shaft if necessary.

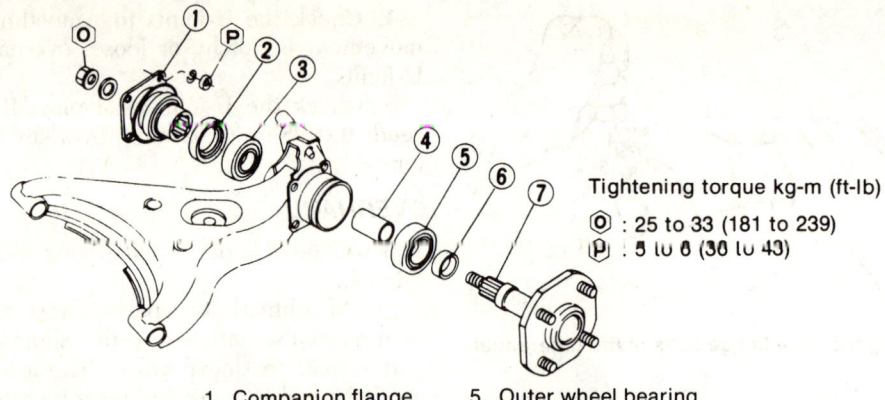

DRIVE TRAIN

1. Companion flange
2. Grease seal
3. Inner wheel bearing
4. Spacer
5. Outer wheel bearing
6. Bearing spacer
7. Stub axle

Tightening torque kg-m (ft-lb)
◎ : 25 to 33 (181 to 239)
ⓟ : 5 to 6 (36 to 43)

Stub axle and rear wheel bearings, 1979–80 shown, other models similar

13. Install the boot onto the sleeve yoke and retain with a new boot band.

14. Clean, repack, and assemble the U-joints. Select snap rings which will yield 0.0008 in. (0.02 mm) of axial play. Be certain to use the same thickness snap ring on opposite sides of the journals to retain driveline balance, and to keep the stresses evenly distributed.

15. Install the axle shaft.

Stub Axle and Rear Wheel Bearings

REMOVAL AND INSTALLATION

1. Block the front wheels. Loosen the wheel nuts, raise and support the car, and remove the wheel.

2. Remove the axle shaft.

3. On cars with rear disc brakes, unbolt the caliper and move it aside. See Chapter 9. Do not disconnect the hose from the caliper. Do not allow the caliper to hang by the hose; support the caliper with a length of wire or rest it on a suspension member.

4. Remove the brake disc on models with rear disc brakes. Remove the brake drum on cars with drum brakes. See Chapter 9.

5. Remove the stub axle nut. You will have to hold the stub axle at the outside while removing the nut from the axle shaft side. The nut will require a good deal of force to remove, so be sure to hold the stub axle firmly.

6. Remove the stub axle with a slide hammer and an adapter. The outer wheel bearing will come off with the stub axle.

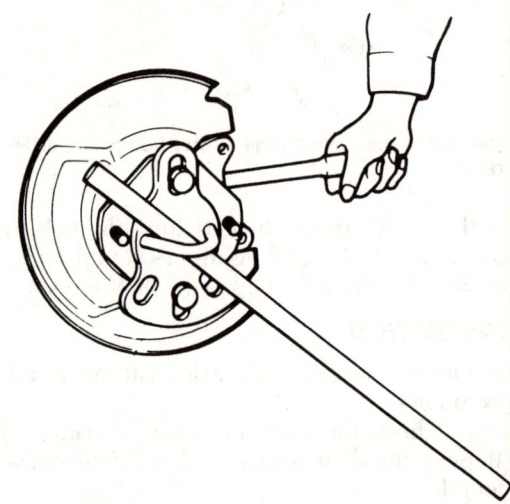

Hold the stub axle while removing the nut from the axle shaft side

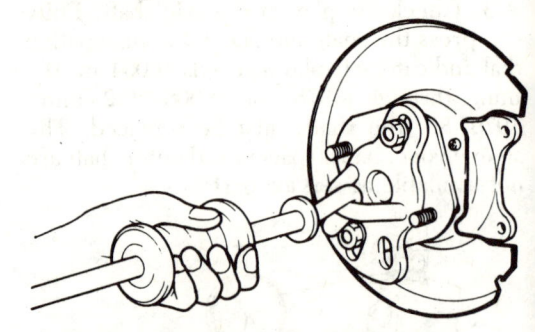

Remove the stub axle with a slide hammer

7. Remove the companion flange from the lower arm.

8. Remove and discard the grease seal and inner bearing from the lower arm using a drift made for the purpose or a length of pipe of the proper diameter.

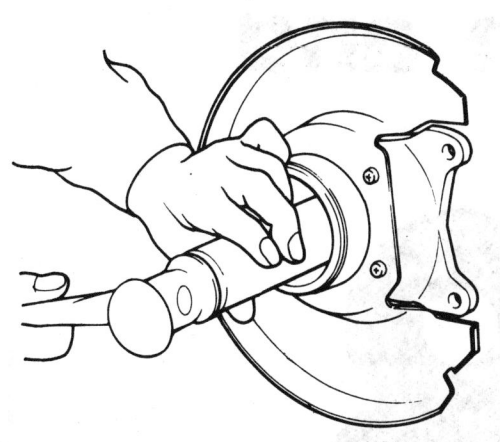

Remove the grease seal and inner bearing with a drift or driver

The outer bearing can be removed from the stub axle with a puller. If the grease seal or the bearings are removed, new parts must be used on assembly.

9. Clean all the parts to be reused in solvent.
10. Sealed-type bearings are used. When the new bearings are installed, the sealed side must face out. Install the sealed side of the outer bearing facing the wheel, and the sealed side of the inner bearing facing the differential.
11. Press the outer bearing onto the stub axle.
12. The bearing housing is stamped with an "A", "B", or "C", through 1978. 1979 and later models have an "N", "M", or "P". Select a spacer with the same marking. Install the spacer on the stub axle.
13. Install the stub axle into the lower arm.
14. Install the new inner bearing into the lower arm with the stub axle in place. Install a new grease seal.
15. Install the companion flange onto the stub axle.
16. Install the stub axle nut. Tighten to 181–239 ft lbs (25–33 kg-m).
17. Install the brake disc or drum, and the caliper if removed.
18. Install the axle shaft. Install the wheel and lower the car.

Suspension and Steering

8

FRONT SUSPENSION

The front suspension system is of the MacPherson strut type. The struts used on either side are a combination spring and shock absorber with the outer casing of the shock actually supporting the spring at the bottom and forming a major structural component of the suspension. The wheel spindle is welded to the bottom of the strut. A strut mounting thrust bearing at the top and a ball joint at the bottom allow the entire strut to rotate in cornering maneuvers.

A rubber-bushed transverse link (lower arm) connects the lower portion of the strut to the main front crossmember via the ball joint; the link thus allows for vertical movement. Compression rods, through 1978, connect the outer ends of the transverse links to the chassis at points in back of the outer ends, thus preventing excessive fore-and-aft movement. In 1979, the compression rods were replaced by tension rods, which mount to brackets at the front of the car and run back to the transverse links, controlling fore-and-aft movement.

Springs and Shock Absorbers
TESTING SHOCK ABSORBER ACTION

Shock absorbers require replacement if the vehicle fails to recover quickly after a large bump is encountered, if there is a tendency for the vehicle to sway or nose dive excessively, or, sometimes, if the suspension is overly susceptible to vibration.

A good way to test the shocks is to intermittently apply downward pressure to one corner of the vehicle until it is moving up and down for almost the full suspension travel, then release it and watch the recovery. If the vehicle bounces slightly about one more time and then comes to rest, the shock absorbers are serviceable. If the vehicle goes on bouncing, the shocks require replacement.

Strut
REMOVAL AND INSTALLATION

The struts are precision parts and retain the springs under tremendous pressure even when removed from the car. For these reasons, several expensive special tools and substantial specialized knowledge are required to safely and effectively work on these parts. We recommend that if spring or shock absorber repair work is required, you remove the strut or struts involved and take them to a repair facility which is fully equipped and familiar with the car.

1. Jack up the car and support the chassis with stands as shown in Chapter 1.
2. Remove the hub nuts and remove the wheel.

SUSPENSION AND STEERING 177

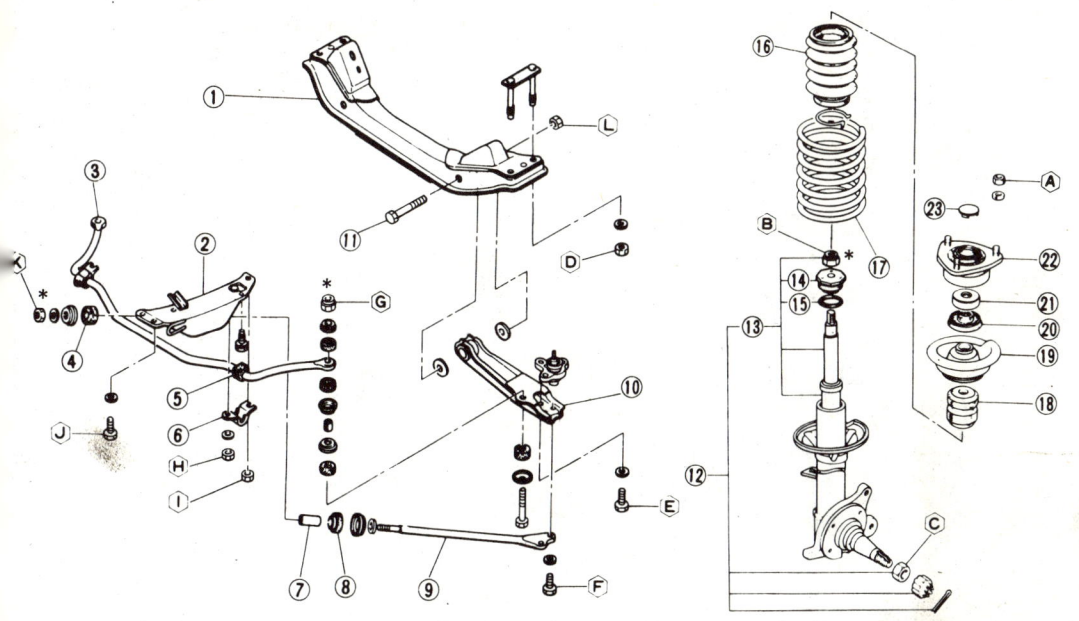

1. Suspension crossmember
2. Tension rod bracket
3. Stabilizer bar
4. Tension rod mounting bushing
5. Stabilizer bushing
6. Stabilizer bracket
7. Tension rod collar
8. Tension rod mounting bushing
9. Tension rod
10. Transverse link
11. Transverse link mounting bolt
12. Strut assembly
13. Shock absorber
14. Gland packing
15. O-ring
16. Dust cover
17. Front spring
18. Bound bumper
19. Front spring upper seat
20. Dust seal
21. Strut mounting bearing
22. Strut mounting insulator
23. Cap

*: Replace self-locking nut whenever strut is disassembled.

Tightening torque in ft. lbs. (kg-m)

A. 22–29 (3.0–4.0)
B. 43–54 (6.0–7.5)
C. 18–22 (2.5–3.0)
D. 51–65 (7.0–9.0)
E. 33–40 (4.5–5.5)
F. 33–40 (4.5–5.5)
G. 12–16 (1.6–2.2)
H. 20–27 (2.7–3.7)
I. 20–27 (2.7–3.7)
J. 23–31 (3.2–4.3)
K. 33–40 (4.5–5.5)
L. 58–72 (8.0–10.0)

ZX front suspension

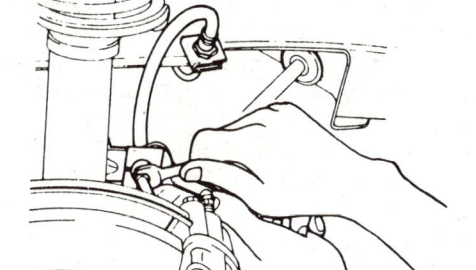

Brake hose disconnection—Z model shown

3. Remove the splash board, if necessary.
4. Loosen the brake hose connection. Remove the hose locking spring, pull the plate off, and remove the hose from the strut assembly bracket. Cap the hose so that dust cannot enter.
5. Remove the brake caliper retaining bolts and remove the caliper assembly. See Chapter 9 for details.
6. Remove the bolts connecting the strut to the knuckle arm.
7. Separate the knuckle arm from the strut

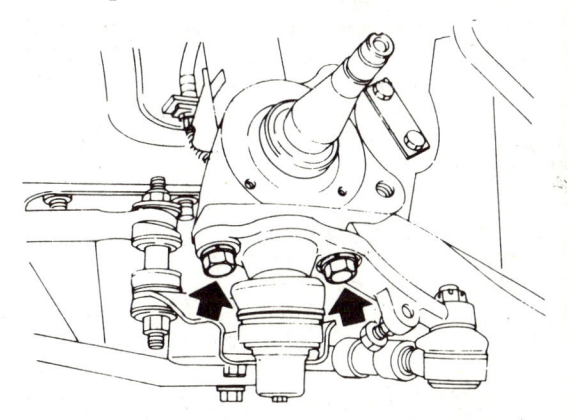

Knuckle arm-to-strut bolts—ZX shown

178 SUSPENSION AND STEERING

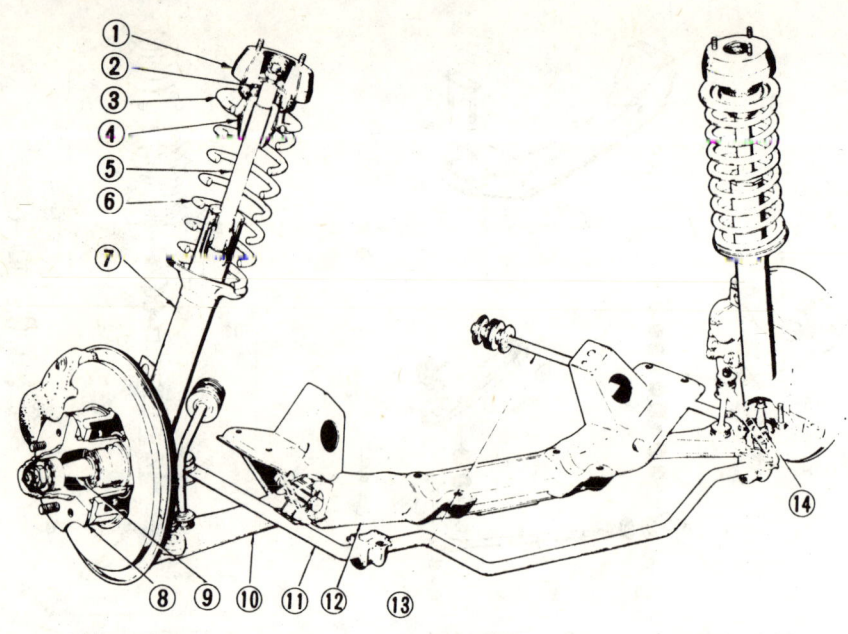

1. Strut mounting insulator
2. Strut mounting bearing
3. Upper spring seat
4. Bumper rubber
5. Piston rod
6. Front spring
7. Strut assembly
8. Hub assembly
9. Spindle
10. Transverse link
11. Stabilizer
12. Suspension member
13. Compression rod
14. Ball joint

Z model front suspension

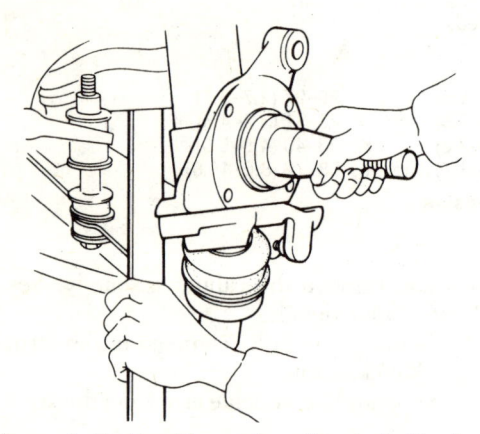

Separate the knuckle arm from the strut with a bar

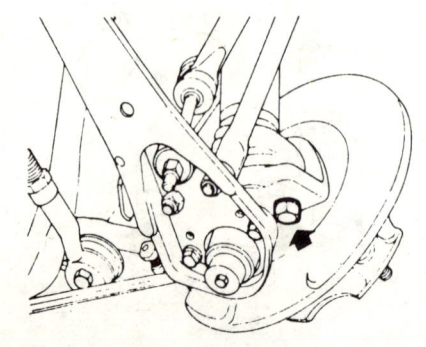

Knuckle arm bolts—Z models

by forcing the transverse link (lower arm) down with a long bar.

8. Support the strut assembly. Remove the three nuts inside the engine compartment which retain the strut at the top. Remove the strut assembly.

To install:

1. Inspect all bushings and replace as necessary.
2. Reverse the removal procedures, using the following torque figures:

   a. Strut securing nuts (to body):
   - 1970–78: 18–25 ft lbs (2.5–3.5 kg-m);
   - 1979–82; 22–29 ft lbs (3.0–4.0 kg-m).

   b. Knuckle arm bolts: 53–72 ft lbs (7.3–9.9 kg-m), all models.

Coil Spring

REMOVAL AND INSTALLATION

This procedure requires the use of a spring compressor. It cannot be performed without one. If you do not have access to the special tool, do not disassemble the strut.

WARNING: *The coil springs are retained under considerable pressure. They can exert enough force to cause serious injury. Exercise extreme caution when disassembling the strut for coil spring removal.*

SUSPENSION AND STEERING

1. Remove the strut assembly.
2. Bolt the bottom of the strut to a plate and secure the plate in a vise.
3. Install a spring compressor on the coil spring. Be sure to engage the tool evenly on a minimum of three coils, paying particular attention not to contact or stress the strut piston rod.
4. Compress the spring just enough to allow the upper mount to be turned by hand.
5. Hold the upper mount with a rod and unscrew the self-locking nut from the piston rod. Discard this nut and use a new one on assembly.
6. Remove the mounting insulator, strut bearing, dust seal, spring seat, and dust cover.
7. Slowly and cautiously unscrew the spring compressor until all spring tension is relieved. Remove the spring and the rubber bumper.
8. Do not disassemble the shock absorber.

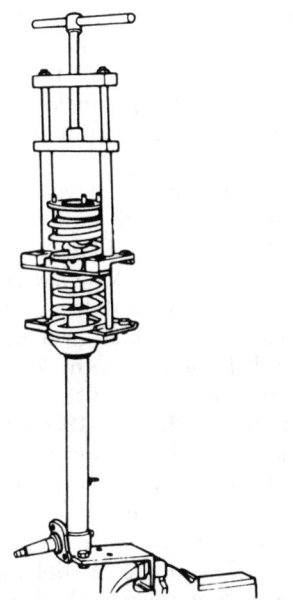

To install:
1. Pull the piston rod to the top of its stroke. Install the rubber bumper to hold the rod in place.
2. Install the spring compressor on the coil spring. Leave the upper 2½ to 3 coils free to prevent interference with the upper spring seat. Compress the spring and install on the strut.
3. Lubricate the dust seal with multi-purpose grease. Lubrication points are shown in the illustration.
4. Install the dust cover, upper spring seat, dust seal, bearing, and insulator.

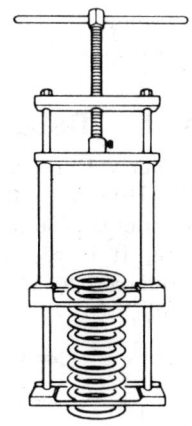

Spring compressor installed on the coil spring for removal

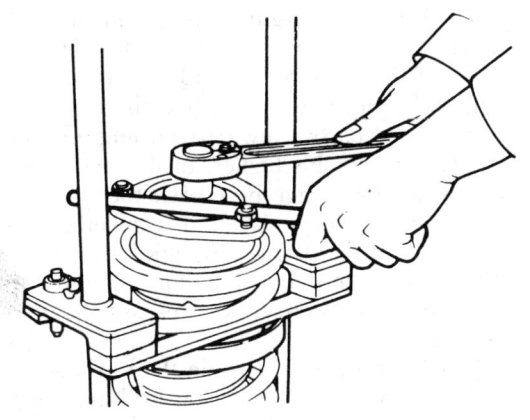

Spring compressor installed on the coil spring for installation—leave the upper coils free

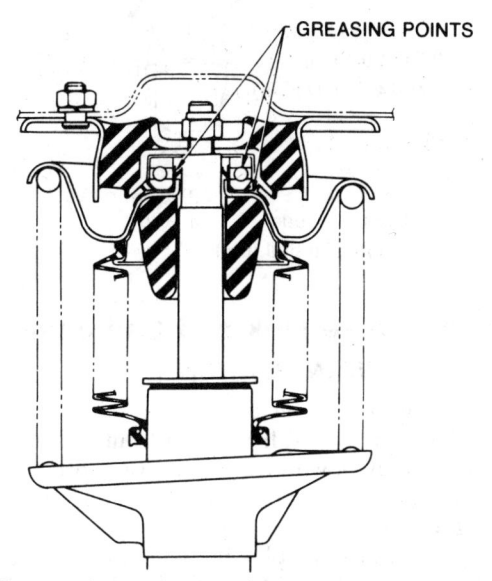

Hold the upper mount with a rod to unscrew the piston rod nut

Dust seal greasing locations

NOTE: *Do not allow the piston rod to retract into the shock absorber. If it falls, screw a nut onto the rod and pull the rod out. Do not use pliers or the like to grip the rod, because they will damage its surface, resulting in leaks, uneven operation, and seal damage. Be extremely careful in all operations not to stress or contact the rod.*

5. Install a new self-locking nut on the piston rod. Tighten the nut temporarily to about 35 ft lbs (5.5 kg-m).

6. Place the spring in position between the upper and lower spring seats. Slowly and carefully unscrew the compressor until all spring tension is relieved. Remove the compressor.

7. Move the rubber bumper to the upper spring seat.

8. Install the strut. After installation, tighten the piston rod nut to 54–69 ft lbs (7.5–9.5 kg-m) through 1978, or 43–54 ft lbs (6.0–7.5 kg-m), 1979 and later.

Shock Absorber Rebuilding

The shock absorber within the strut housing can be rebuilt. However, this procedure requires a number of special tools and a good deal of expertise. It is recommended that rebuilding be referred to your dealer or a qualified mechanic.

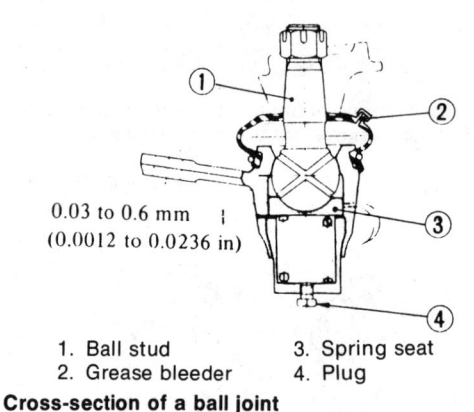

0.03 to 0.6 mm
(0.0012 to 0.0236 in)

1. Ball stud
2. Grease bleeder
3. Spring seat
4. Plug

Cross-section of a ball joint

Transverse Link and Ball Joint

BALL JOINT INSPECTION

1. Put the vehicle on a lift so that all weight is removed from both front wheels.

2. Apply downward and upward pressure to the outer end of the transverse link, avoiding any compression of the spring.

3. Measure the play between the link and the bottom of the strut which effectively is the axial play in the ball joint. If play exceeds 0.0236 in. (0.6 mm), replace the ball joint as later described.

REMOVAL AND INSTALLATION

1. Loosen the wheel nuts. Raise and support the car. Remove the wheel.

2. Remove the splash shield.

3. Remove the cotter pin from the steering linkage ball joint at the steering knuckle. Separate the steering linkage from the knuckle with a ball joint removal tool.

4. Remove the bolts retaining the knuckle to the MacPherson strut. Separate the knuckle from the strut. See Step 7 of the strut removal procedure.

5. Remove the compression rod (through 1978) or tension rod (1979 and later) and the stabilizer bar.

6. Remove the transverse link (lower arm) mounting bolt and remove the link from the car, complete with the knuckle and ball joint.

To remove the ball joint from the transverse link:

7. Place the link in a vise. Remove the bolt retaining the ball joint to the link; remove the ball joint and knuckle arm.

8. To remove the knuckle arm, remove the cotter pin and nut from the ball joint stud. Place the knuckle arm in a vise and press the ball joint from the knuckle.

To inspect the ball joint:

1. On models through 1974, check the ball joint axial play. Hook a spring scale onto the ball joint stud and measure the amount of force necessary to move it. It should be 0.28–1.25 in. oz (20–90 gr-cm).

2. On 1975 and later models, measure the ball joint turning torque. Hook a spring scale into the cotter pin hole and measure the amount of force necessary to turn the ball joint. The torque figures are: 35 in. lbs (40 kg-cm), 1975; more than 43 in. lbs (50 kg-cm), 1976–78; more than 13 in. lbs (15 kg-cm), 1979 and later. Note that these figures are for used parts. New part turning torques will be considerably higher. In all cases, these are the minimum figures; replace the ball joint if the turning torque is less than specified.

To inspect the transverse link bushing:

1. Check the bushing for melted or cracked areas where it adheres to the inner or outer tubes.

2. Check for cracks inside the bushing.

3. If damage is found, the bushing must be pressed from the link. This will require a driver or a length of pipe of the same outer

SUSPENSION AND STEERING

Transverse link mounting bolt

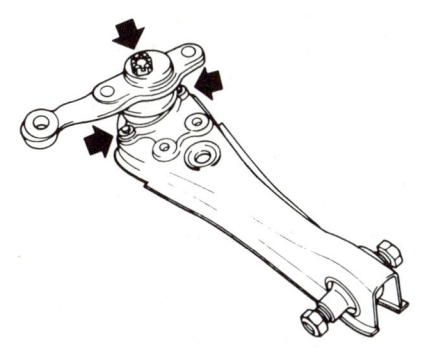

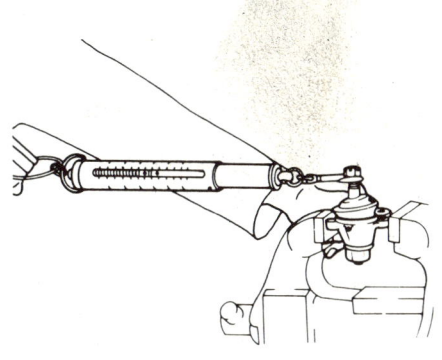

Measuring the ball joint axial play

Two lower arrows show ball joint retaining bolts; upper arrow is the ball joint stud nut which secures the knuckle arm (Z model shown)

diameter as the bushing, and a spacer to be placed under the link, through which the bushing can pass as it is pressed from the link. The new bushing must be pressed into the link, using the driver used for removal.

To install the parts:

1. Remove the bolt from the bottom of the ball joint and install a grease nipple. Pump multi-purpose grease (NLGI #2 lithium soap base) into the ball joint until all old grease is expelled and the joint is full. Do not allow new grease to be forced past the clamped portion of the joint. Remove the grease nipple and install the plug.

2. Install the parts in the reverse order of removal. The ball joint stud nut (castle nut) torques are: 40–54 ft lbs (5.5–7.5 kg-m), 1970–78; 71–88 ft lbs (9.8–12.2 kg-m), 1979 and later. Install a new cotter pin after installation.

The ball joint installation bolt torque figures are: 35–45 ft lbs (4.9–6.3 kg-m), 1970–73; 44–51 ft lbs (6.1–7.1 kg-m), 1974; 14–18 ft lbs (1.9–2.5 kg-m), 1975–78; 33–40 ft lbs (4.5–5.5 kg-m), 1979 and later.

3. When installing the transverse link, install the pivot bolt and tighten it enough to hold it in place. When assembly is complete, lower the car and torque the transverse link bolt to its final figure with the weight of the car on its wheels. The torque specifications are: 80–94 ft lbs (11.0–13.0 kg-m), 1970–73; 80–100 ft lbs (11.1–14.0 kg-m), 1974–78; 58–80 ft lbs (8.0–11.0 kg-m), 1979 and later.

Front End Alignment

Alignment should be performed after it has been verified that all parts of the steering and suspension systems are in good condition. Tire pressures must be correct with tires cold.

Camber and caster angles are determined by the basic geometry of the suspension, and cannot be adjusted except through repair of faulty or bent components. Ride height also is nonadjustable and if the car is not level, a replacement spring of appropriate length must be substituted for a weak one.

TOE

Toe is the amount, measured in a fraction of an inch, that the front wheels are closer together at one end than the other. Toe-in means that the front wheels are closer together at the front of the tire than at the rear of the tire; toe-out means that the rear of the tires are closer together than the front. The Z and ZX are designed to have a slight amount of toe-in. Toe-in compensates for the tendency of the front wheels to be forced outwards when the car is moving forward.

Toe-in is adjusted by turning the tie-rods, which have right-hand threads on one side and left-hand threads on the other. You can make this adjustment yourself if you make very careful measurements, although it is recommended that the adjustment be made by your dealer or a qualified shop. The wheels must be dead straight ahead. The car must have a full tank of gas, all fluids must be at their proper levels, the wheel bearings must be properly adjusted, and the tires

182 SUSPENSION AND STEERING

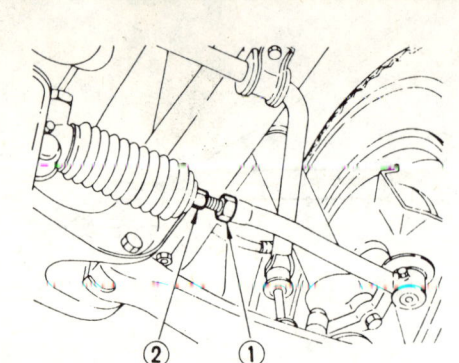

Location of locknut (1) and adjusting nut (2) for toe-in

must be properly inflated to their cold specification.

1. Toe-in can be determined by measuring the distance between the centers of the tire treads, at the front of the tire and at the rear. If the tread pattern on your car's tires makes this impossible, you can measure between the edges of the wheel rims, but be sure to move the car forward and measure in a couple of places to avoid errors caused by bent rims or wheel runout.

2. If the measurement is not within specification, loosen the locknuts at both tie-rods. On 1979 and later models with power steering, loosen the clamp nuts.

3. Turn the tie-rods, or the adjusting sleeve on power steering models, equally in opposite directions until toe-in is correct. Tighten the locknuts or clamp nuts and recheck the adjustment.

NOTE: *After the adjustment is made, be sure that the tie-rod threads are engaged into the steering rack ends to a depth of at least 1.38 in. (38 mm) with manual steering. On power steering models, the adjusting sleeve must engage at least 0.08–0.16 in. (2–4 mm) of the tie-rod threads, and the clamp bolts should be towards the rear of the car.*

REAR SUSPENSION

The independent rear suspension is a MacPherson strut type. Two different designs are used. Models through 1978 have unequal length A-arms (transverse links) which pivot in rubber bushings at the differential carrier. The struts are mounted to the body at the upper end. The lower end of the struts carry the wheel bearing housings, which are welded to the strut. 1979 and later models use a semi-trailing arm design. The lower arms (transverse links) pivot in rubber bushings in the suspension carrier, which is bolted to the body. The arms carry the wheel bearings in this design, and the struts bolt to the arms directly above the wheel bearing housings. The upper ends of the struts bolt to the body. In both designs, a stabilizer bar is used which bolts to the centers of the lower arms.

The axle shafts, which are two piece designs joined by splines to accommodate length changes, have U-joints at either end and thus do not support the car in any way. The differential housing is bolted to a crossmember at the front; rear retention is through a leaf spring, through 1978, or a body-mounted bracket, 1979 and later.

Springs and Shock Absorbers
TESTING SHOCK ABSORBER ACTION

Shocks require replacement if the vehicle fails to recover quickly after hitting a large bump or if the vehicle sways excessively with a change in steering wheel position.

A good way to test the shocks is to intermittently apply downward pressure to one corner of the vehicle until it is moving up and down for almost the full suspension travel, then release it and watch the recovery. If the vehicle bounces slightly about one more time and then comes to rest, the shocks are serviceable. If the vehicle goes on bouncing, replace the shocks.

MacPherson Strut

The struts are precision parts and retain the springs under tremendous pressure even when removed from the car. For these reasons, several expensive special tools and substantial specialized knowledge are required to safely and effectively work on these parts. We recommend that if a spring or shock absorber repair is required, you remove the strut(s) involved and take them to a repair facility which is fully equipped and familiar with the car.

REMOVAL AND INSTALLATION
1970–78

This procedure can be used to remove the strut, wheel bearing housing, bearings, stub axle, and rear brake assembly as a unit. If you wish to remove the stub axle first, refer to Chapter 7. In any case, it is easiest to remove

Wheel Alignment

Year	Model	Caster Range (deg)	Camber Range (deg)	Toe-in ① Inches (mm)	Steering Axis Inclination (deg)	Wheel Pivot Ratio (deg) Inner Wheel	Wheel Pivot Ratio (deg) Outer Wheel
1970–73	240-Z	2°55' ±30'	50' ±30'	0–0.12 (0–3) ②	12°10' ±30'	33° ±30'	31.7° ±30'
1974	260-Z	2°54' ±45'	46' ±45'	0–0.12 (0–3) ②	12°10' ±30'	33° ±30'	31.7° ±30'
1975–78	280-Z	2°3'–3°33'	18'–1°48'	0–0.12 (0–3)	11°14'–12°44'	33°54'–34°54'	32°6'–34°6'
	280-Z 2+2	2°3'–3°33'	21'–1°51'	0–0.12 (0–3)	11°14'–12°44'	36°18'–37°18'	34°24'–36°24'
1979–81	280-ZX	4°10'–5°40'	–35'–+55'	0.04–0.12 (1–3)	8°35'–10°5'	33°30'–37°30' ③	29°–33° ④

① Car fully laden—see text
② Car laden plus two 150 pound passengers
③ 32°–36° with power steering
④ 24°30'–28°30' with power steering

184 SUSPENSION AND STEERING

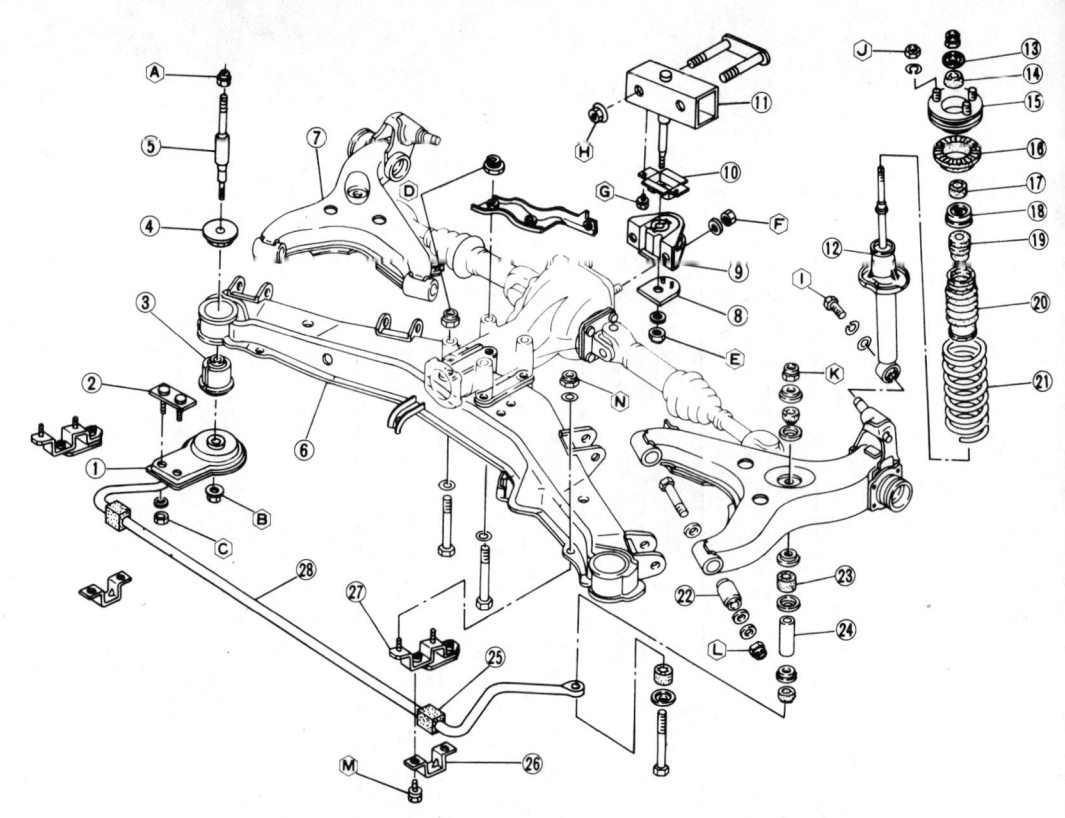

1. Suspension member mounting stay
2. Suspension member mounting bolt
3. Member mounting insulator
4. Member mounting upper stopper
5. Suspension mounting bolt
6. Suspension member assembly
7. Suspension arm assembly
8. Differential mounting plate
9. Differential mounting insulator
10. Differential mounting adapter plate
11. Differential mounting bracket
12. Shock absorber assembly
13. Special washer
14. Shock absorber mounting bushing A
15. Shock absorber mounting insulator
16. Spring seat rubber
17. Shock absorber mounting bushing B
18. Bound bumper cover
19. Bound bumper
20. Dust cover
21. Coil spring
22. Suspension arm bushing
23. Stabilizer bushing
24. Stabilizer collar
25. Stabilizer mounting bushing
26. Stabilizer mounting clip
27. Stabilizer mounting bracket
28. Rear stabilizer

Tightening torque in ft. lbs. (kg-m)
A. 87–116 (12–16)
B. 58–72 (8–10)
C. 14–19 (2.0–2.6)
D. 43–58 (6.0–8.0)
E. 87–108 (12–15)
F. 65–87 (9–12)—R200 differential
   43–58 (6–8)—R180 differential
G. 23–31 (3.2–4.3)
H. 43–58 (6–8)
I. 43–58 (6–8)
J. 22–29 (3–4)
K. 12–15 (1.6–2.1)
L. 58–72 (8–10)
M. 12–15 (1.6–2.1)
N. 12–15 (1.6–2.1)

Exploded view of the ZX rear suspension

the brake with the strut, and disassemble the parts after removal from the car.

1. Loosen the wheel nuts, jack the car up, and support it on stands as shown in Chapter 1.
2. Remove the wheel nuts and wheels. Disconnect the brake hose at (1) and the linkage at (2).
3. Disconnect the stabilizer bar at the crossmember and transverse link.
4. Remove the transverse link outer spindle self-locking nuts (2), and the spindle bolt (1). Pull the spindle out and separate the transverse link and strut.
5. Disconnect the driveshaft at the outer end.

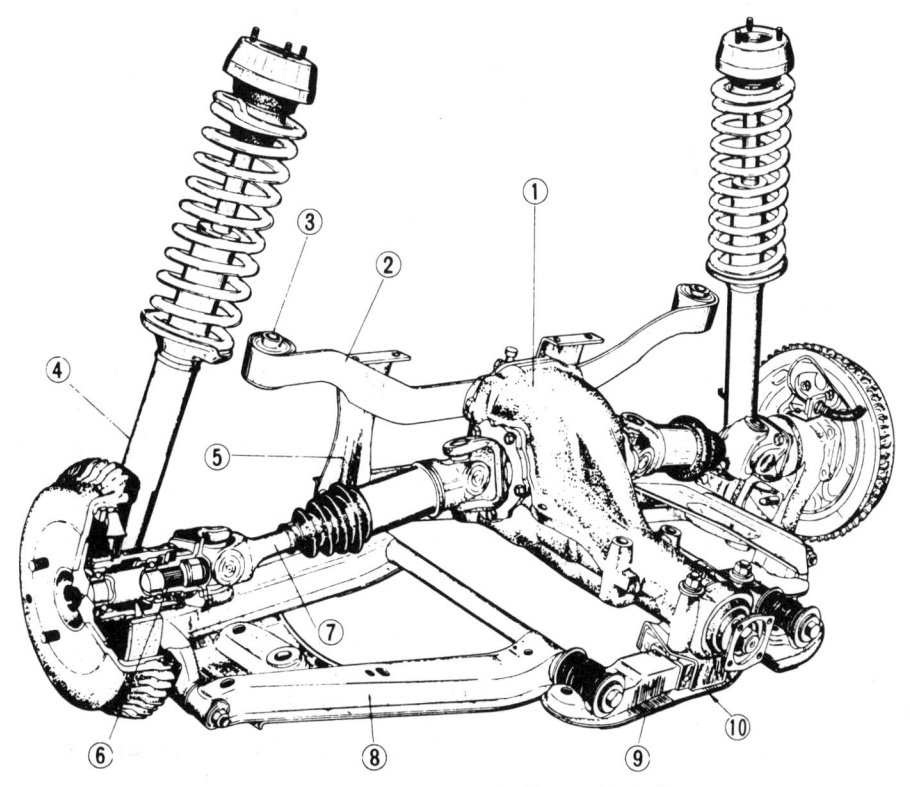

SUSPENSION AND STEERING 185

1. Gear carrier
2. Differential case mounting rear member
3. Differential case mounting rear insulator
4. Strut assembly
5. Link mounting brace
6. Rear axle shaft
7. Driveshaft
8. Transverse link
9. Differential case mounting front member
10. Differential case mounting front insulator

Z model rear suspension

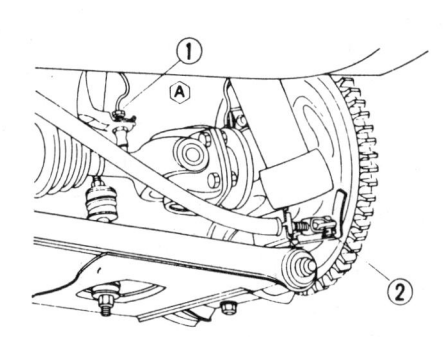

TIGHTENING TORQUE:
Ⓐ: 1.5 TO 1.8 KG-M (11 TO 13 FT-LB)

Disconnect the brake line at (1) and the side linkage at (2)—Z models

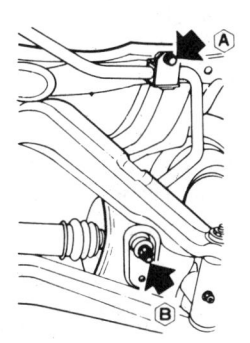

TIGHTENING TORQUE:
Ⓐ: 1.0 TO 1.2 KG-M (7.2 TO 8.7 FT-LB)
Ⓑ: 1.2 TO 1.7 KG-M (8.7 TO 12.3 FT-LB))

Arrows show stabilizer bar retaining bolts—Z models

6. Place a jack under the lower end of the strut. Remove the strut installation nuts from inside the passenger compartment. Lower the strut carefully with the jack.

To install:

1. Inspect all bushings and replace as necessary.
2. Reverse the removal procedures, installing the spindle so that the shorter length, when measured from the locking bolt notch, is toward the front.
3. Use the following torque figures:

Axle shaft flange bolts at differential side: 36–43 ft lbs (5.0–6.0 kg-m); except: 23–31 ft lbs (3.2–4.3), 1973–74 and 1978; 17–23 ft lbs (2.4–3.2 kg-m), 1977

SUSPENSION AND STEERING

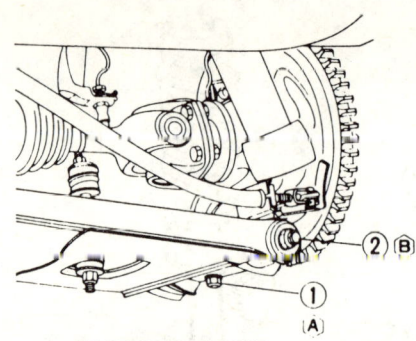

TIGHTENING TORQUE:
(A) : 1.0 TO 1.2 KG-M (7.2 TO 8.7 FT-LB)
(B) : 7.5 TO 9.5 KG-M (54 TO 69 FT-LB)

Transverse link lockbolt (1) and nuts (2)—Z models

Axle shaft flange bolts at wheel side: 36–43 ft lbs (5.0–6.0 kg-m)
Strut installation nuts: 12–15 ft lbs (1.6–2.1 kg-m), 1970–72; 18–25 ft lbs (2.5–3.5 kg-m), 1973–78
Link spindle locknuts: 54–69 ft lbs (7.5–9.5 kg-m)
Link spindle lock bolt: 7.2–8.7 ft lbs (1.0–1.2 kg-m)
Stabilizer bar at link: 8.7–12.3 ft lbs (1.2–1.7 kg-m)
Stabilizer bar at crossmember: 7.2–8.7 ft lbs (1.0–1.2 kg-m)
Brake line connector: 11–13 ft lbs (1.5–1.8 kg-m)

4. Fill and bleed brake system.

1979 and Later

1. Block the front wheels.
2. Raise and support the rear of the car. The car should be far enough off the ground that the rear spring does not support any weight.
3. Working inside the luggage compartment, turn and remove the caps above the strut mounts. Remove the three strut mounting nuts.
4. Remove the mounting bolt for the strut at the lower arm (transverse link) and remove the strut.

Installation is the reverse. Install the top end first and secure with the nuts snugged down but not tightened to the final torque figure. Attach the lower end of the strut to the lower arm, then tighten the top mounting nuts to 22–29 ft lbs (3–4 kg-m). Tighten the strut bolt at the lower arm to 43–58 ft lbs (6–8 kg-m).

Coil Spring

REMOVAL AND INSTALLATION

A spring compressor is required to remove the coil spring from the MacPherson strut. It is recommended that this job be referred to your dealer. However, if you have access to the proper equipment, the coil spring can be removed in the same manner as the front coil springs. The procedure is given earlier in this chapter.

Rear Suspension Adjustments

The rear suspension is not adjustable for wheel alignment. However, alignment should be checked periodically and repairs made to defective or bent parts, as necessary.

STEERING

Steering Wheel

REMOVAL AND INSTALLATION

1. Disconnect the battery negative terminal.
2. On models through 1978, depress the horn pad, turn it counterclockwise, and remove it. On 1979 and later ZX models, pull the horn pad off.
3. Remove the steering wheel nut.
4. Install a puller, threading the anchor screws into the holes provided for this purpose in the wheel.
5. Turn the center bolt of the puller counterclockwise until the wheel comes off.

CAUTION: *Do not hammer on the end of the steering shaft. Striking the shaft will damage the bearing or impair the collapsibility of the column.*

To install:
1. Apply grease to all portions which will slide together during installation.
2. Put the punch mark on the top of the column shaft and install the wheel in a straight-ahead position.
3. Torque the steering wheel nut to 36–51 ft lbs (5–7 kg-m) on 1970–76 models; 29–36 ft lbs (4–5 kg-m) on 1977 and later models.
4. Turn the wheel through the whole range of the steering system and make sure that it does not grab.
5. Install the horn pad, reconnect the battery, and test the horn.

SUSPENSION AND STEERING 187

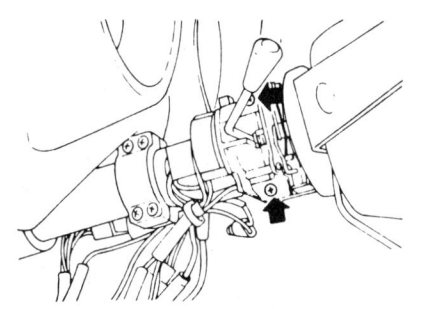

Combination switch retaining screws (arrows)—Z models

Combination Switch

REMOVAL AND INSTALLATION

The combination switch operates the lights, wipers, windshield washer, turn signals, and the dimmer switch through 1978. The 1979 and later combination switch operates the headlights, high beam flasher, and turn signals.

1970–78

1. Disconnect the negative terminal from the battery.
2. Remove the screws which hold the shell cover halves together and remove them from the column jacket.
3. Disconnect all six (five on 1977 and later models) electrical connectors.
4. Remove the two screws which hold the switch to the column jacket.
5. Separate the switch halves (without disconnecting the connector which connects the two halves electrically) and remove the switch.

To install:

1. Reverse the above procedures, ensuring that the location tab inside the turn signal switch lines up with the hole in the jacket of the steering column.

1979 and Later

1. Disconnect the negative cable from the battery.
2. Remove the horn pad.
3. Remove the steering wheel.
4. Remove the steering column cover.
5. Unplug the combination switch wires at the electrical connector.
6. Remove the retaining screw and remove the combination switch assembly.
7. Installation is the reverse.

Ignition Switch

REMOVAL AND INSTALLATION

1. Disconnect the negative battery cable. Remove the screws holding the shell cover halves together, separate, and remove the cover halves.
2. Disconnect the lead wires at the connector located at the bottom of the steering lock.
3. Remove the screw which holds the switch to the steering lock, and remove the switch.
4. Install in reverse order of the above procedure.

Tie-rod and Steering Ball Joint

REMOVAL AND INSTALLATION

Manual Steering

1. Raise the car, put it on stands, and remove the front wheel(s).
2. Remove the splash board.
3. Remove the cotter pins and nuts which hold the ball studs in the knuckle arms (arrowed).
4. Use a ball joint removal tool (steering linkage puller) to separate the ball joint from the steering knuckle arm.
5. Loosen the tie-rod locknut and unscrew the rod from the steering system.

To install:

1. Reverse the removal procedure, tightening the ball joint stud nut (castle nut) to 40–55 ft lbs (5.5–7.6 kg-m) through 1978, or 40–72 ft lbs (5.5–10.0 kg-m), 1979 and later. Install a new cotter pin. You can tighten the castle nut to align the cotter pin holes, but do not loosen it.
2. Check and adjust the toe-in.

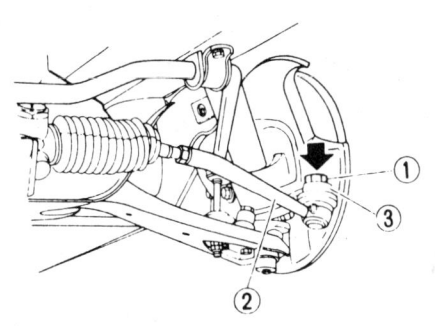

Arrow shows the location of the outer ball stud nut (1). (2) indicates the tie-rod, and (3) the knuckle arm—Z model shown

188 SUSPENSION AND STEERING

Separate the ball joint from the knuckle with a puller (power steering model shown)

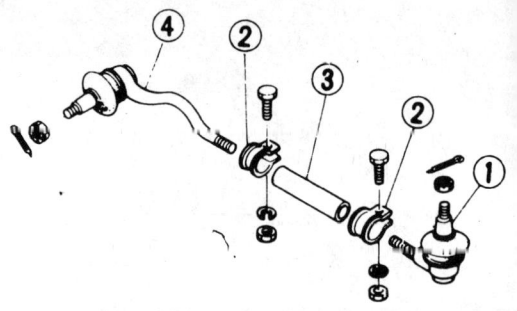

1. Tie-rod end
2. Clamp
3. Adjusting sleeve
4. Inner tie-rod

Exploded view of the power steering tie-rod

Power Steering

1. Raise and support the front of the car. Block the rear wheels.
2. Remove and discard the cotter pin from the ball joint stud at the steering knuckle arm. Remove the castle nut from the ball joint stud.
3. Separate the ball joint from the knuckle with a ball joint removal tool (steering linkage puller).
4. Loosen the adjusting sleeve clamp nut on the tie-rod side and unscrew the tie-rod.
5. Installation is the reverse. Tighten the ball joint castle nut to 40 ft lbs (5.5 kg-m), then continue to tighten until the cotter pin holes align. Torque limit is 72 ft lbs (10 kg-m). Install a new cotter pin.
6. Check and adjust the toe-in as necessary.

Brakes

9

Datsun 240, 260, and 280-Z automobiles are equipped with a vacuum-assisted, proportioned braking system employing discs on the front and finned aluminum drums on the rear. The vacuum-assist cylinder is 6.0 in. in diameter on 1970–72 vehicles, and 7.5 in. in diameter on 1973 and later models (except 2+2 models which use a 9 in.). The S-16 Girling-Sumitomo disc brake calipers are the two-piston type, and the rear brakes are self-adjusting, leading-trailing type. The handbrake is mechanical, employing cables for actuation of the rear drum brakes.

The master cylinder is a dual cylinder de-

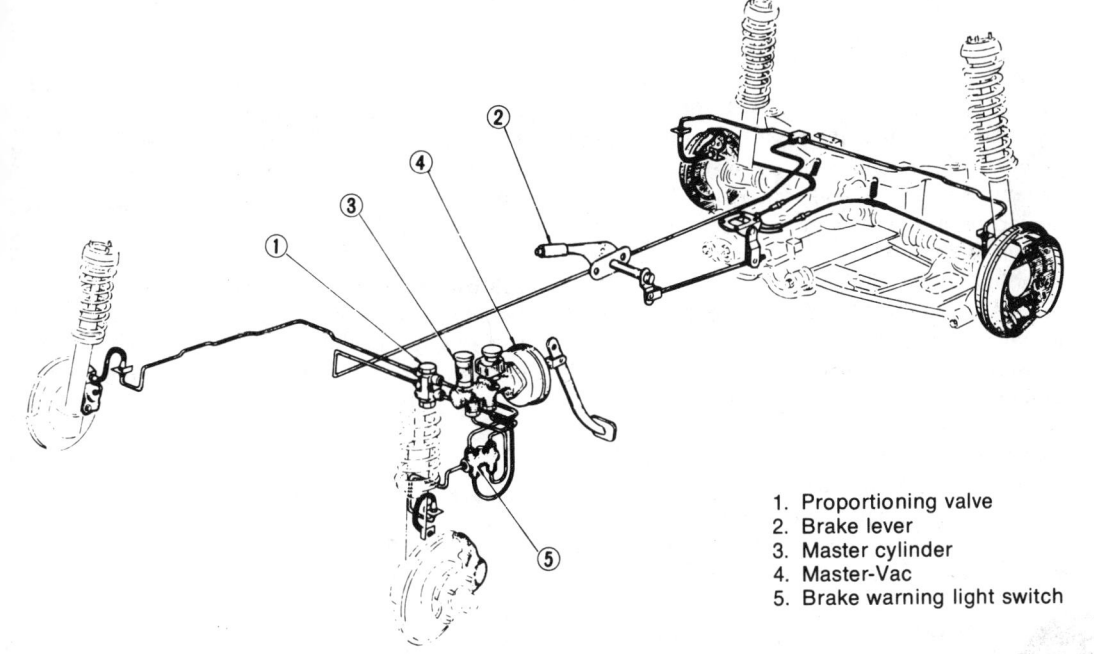

1. Proportioning valve
2. Brake lever
3. Master cylinder
4. Master-Vac
5. Brake warning light switch

The brake system, 1973–74; later models similar

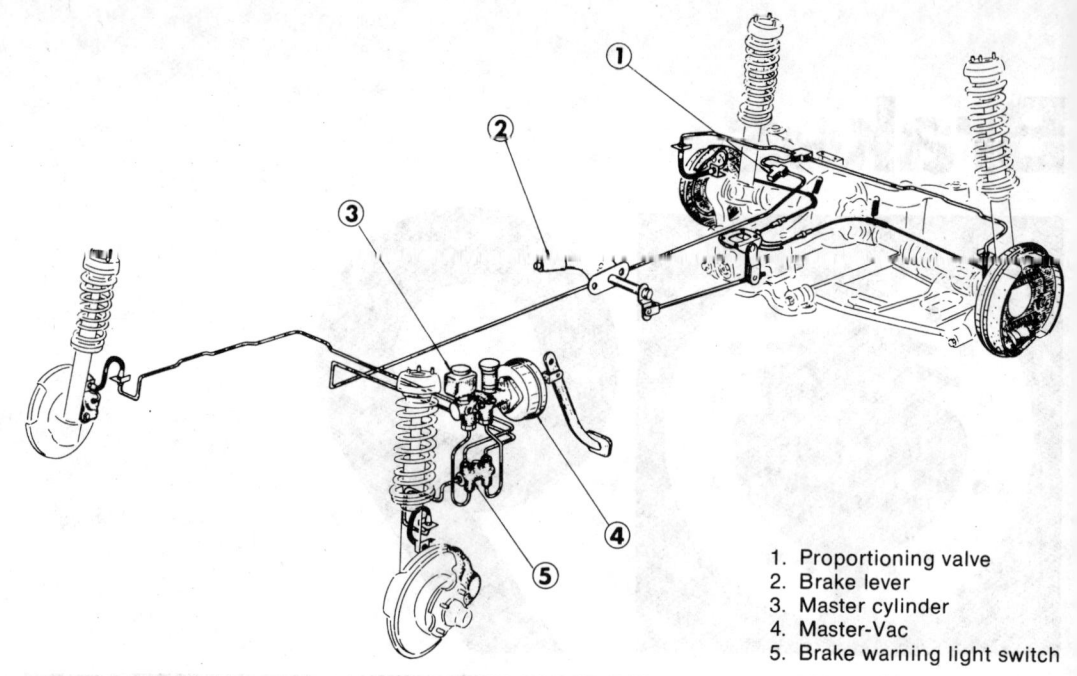

BRAKES

1. Proportioning valve
2. Brake lever
3. Master cylinder
4. Master-Vac
5. Brake warning light switch

The 1970–72 brake system

sign so that failure of either the front or rear brakes causes the brake system at the opposite end of the vehicle to be sealed off at the master cylinder and continue to operate normally.

The "Master-Vac" assist system employs manifold vacuum against a diaphragm to assist in application of the brakes. The vacuum is regulated to be proportional to the pressure placed on the pedal.

The system also incorporates a warning light which is operated by a hydraulic electric switch which connects the front and rear hydraulic systems. If pressure in one system is not counter-balanced by pressure in the other, as when a leak has caused it to be sealed off at the master cylinder, the switch piston is forced to one side and closes the warning light switch.

Ordinarily in a hydraulic brake system, application of pressure at the master cylinder causes equal pressure to be built up at all wheel cylinders or caliper pistons at the wheels. While this is appropriate during normal braking, weight transfer from the back wheels to the front under very hard braking lessens rear brake pressure requirements. Stable braking cannot be achieved if the rear wheels cease to turn as tire tread will track only if it is rolling along the road. As a result, a proportioning valve is used. The valve permits equal pressure in all parts of the system until system pressure reached a certain point. Then, through the motion of sprung pistons in the valve, rear brake pressure is throttled and maintained at a reduced percentage of front brake pressure.

In 1970–72 models, the proportioning valve is located in the rear of the main brake line going to the back of the car, while in later vehicles, it is located in the engine compartment and links the front and rear systems.

ZX models are equipped with vacuum-assisted disc brakes at all four wheels. The front discs are CL28V single piston sliding caliper models with ventilated rotors. Rear brakes are Annette AN14H single piston sliding caliper models. The inner piston is equipped with a toggle and strut actuated parking brake mechanism which locks the inner pad against the solid rotor. A 9 inch "Master-Vac" booster is used on all models, and is similar to the one installed on the 1973–78 2 + 2 Z, but is not interchangeable. The warning light and proportioning valve systems are the same as those used on the Z series.

BRAKE SYSTEM

Adjustment

PEDAL HEIGHT

1970–78

1. Loosen the locknut and turn the pushrod clevis to get a pedal height of 8.11

BRAKES

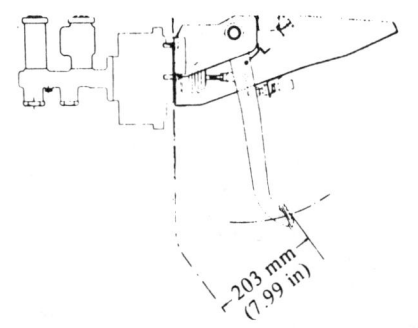

Pedal height adjustment; the figures are for models through 1978

in. (206 mm). If necessary, loosen the locknut and adjust the pedal stop back and out of the way so that it has no effect on pedal height. Tighten the pushrod locknut.

2. Adjust the stop back until height becomes 7.99 in. (203 mm). Tighten the stop locknut.

3. Check the stop lamp switch to ensure that the end surface of the installation screw is flush with the bracket. The lamp should go on when the pedal is depressed 0.59 in. (15 mm) and should go off when the pedal is released.

1979 and Later

Pedal height is adjusted with the brake light switch and the pushrod.

1. Measure the pedal height from the floorboard (beneath the mat) to the front of the brake pedal. The distance should be 7.13–7.36 in. for manual transmission models, or 7.48–7.72 in. for automatic transmission models.

2. If the pedal height is incorrect, loosen the brake light switch locknut and turn the body of the switch to screw it in or out. When the pedal height is correct, tighten the locknut.

3. In some cases, the switch adjustment will not have enough range. In this case, loosen the pushrod locknut and adjust the pedal height by turning the pushrod. Tighten the locknut after adjustment.

4. Check the operation of the brake lights after all adjustments are complete.

DISC BRAKES

All disc brakes are inherently self-adjusting. No periodic adjustment is either necessary or possible.

DRUM BRAKES

The rear drum brakes used on 1970–78 models are equipped with automatic adjusters actuated by the parking brake mechanism. No periodic adjustment of the drum brakes is necessary if this mechanism is working properly. If the brake shoe to drum clearance is incorrect, and applying and releasing the parking brake a few times does not adjust it properly, the parts will have to be disassembled for repair.

HYDRAULIC SYSTEM

Master Cylinder

REMOVAL AND INSTALLATION

1. On ZX models, remove the heat shield plate.

2. Disconnect the wiring to the brake fluid level gauge at the electrical connector. Early models do not have the gauge.

3. Place some cloths under the master cylinder to catch spilled fluid.

4. Unbolt the brake tubes from the master cylinder. Use a flare nut wrench, if possible, to avoid damage to the lines.

NOTE: *Brake fluid will damage paint; wipe up any spilled fluid immediately, then flush the area with clear water.*

5. Cap the brake tubes.

6. Remove the nuts securing the master cylinder to the vacuum booster and remove the master cylinder from the car.

7. To install, position the master cylinder on the vacuum booster studs and install the nuts. Tighten to 5.0–8.0 ft lbs (0.8–1.1 kg-m).

8. Install the brake lines. Tighten to 11–13 ft lbs (1.5–1.8 kg-m).

9. Bleed the brake system as described later in this chapter. Check the system for leaks.

10. Adjust the brake pedal height, if necessary.

OVERHAUL

This is a tedious, time-consuming job. You can save yourself a lot of trouble by buying a rebuilt master cylinder from your dealer or a parts supply house. The small difference in cost between a rebuilding kit and a rebuilt part usually makes it more economical, in terms of time and work, to buy the rebuilt part.

NOTE: *Datsun has two suppliers for brake parts: Nabco and Tokico. These parts are not interchangeable. Be certain to get the*

192 BRAKES

1. Reservoir cap
2. Disc brake reservoir
3. Drum brake reservoir
4. Master cylinder
5. Piston assembly (A)
6. Piston cup
7. Cylinder spring
8. Primary piston cup
9. Piston assembly (B)
10. Secondary piston cup
11. Stop
12. Snap-ring
13. Valve spring
14. Check valve assembly
15. Check valve assembly
16. Packing
17. Valve cap screw
19. Stop bolt
20. Bleeder

1970–72 master cylinder

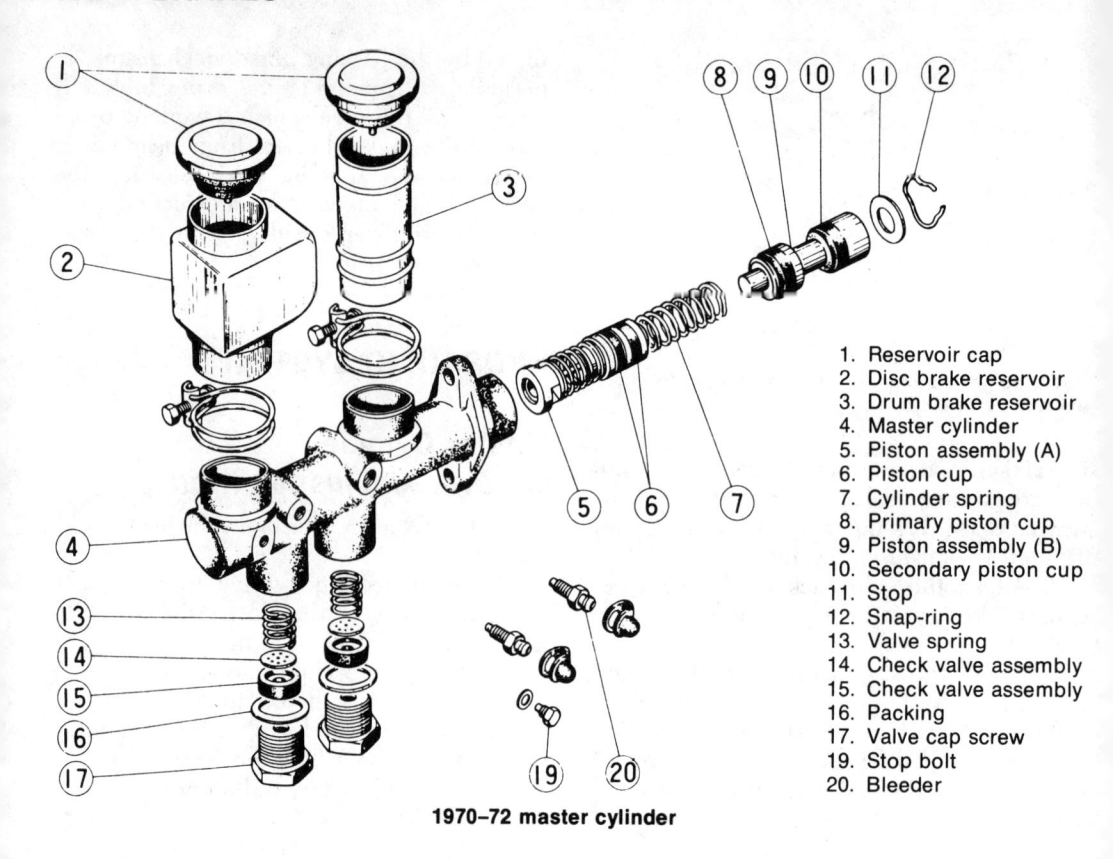

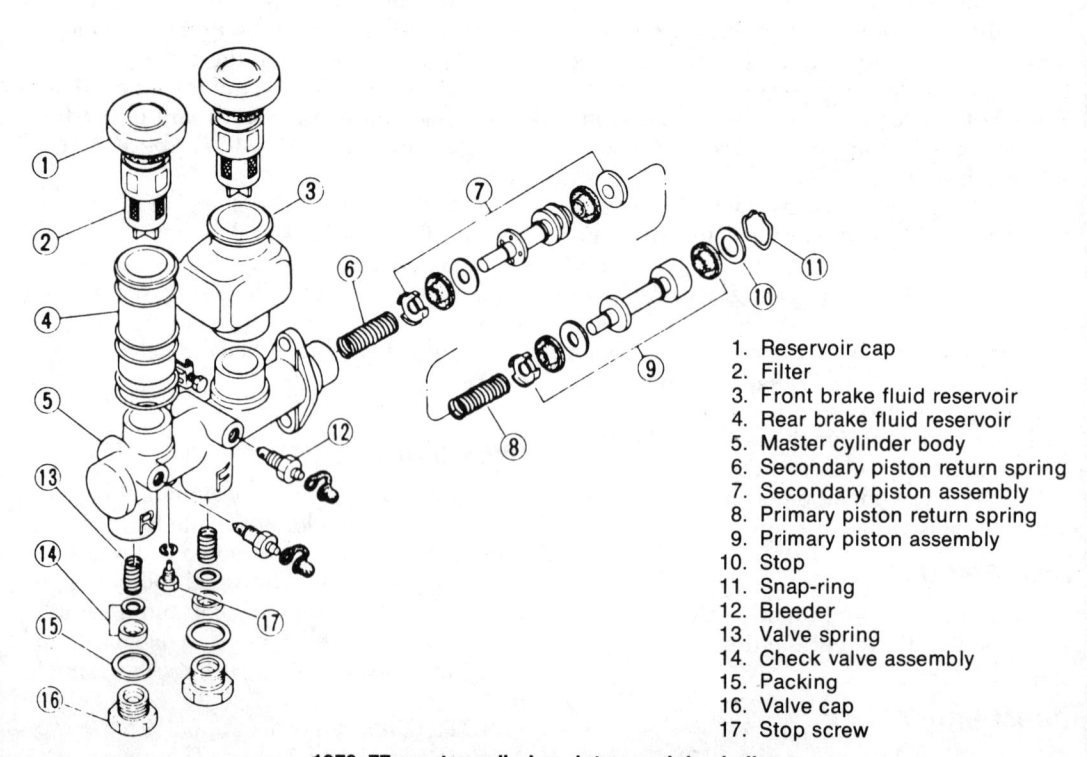

1. Reservoir cap
2. Filter
3. Front brake fluid reservoir
4. Rear brake fluid reservoir
5. Master cylinder body
6. Secondary piston return spring
7. Secondary piston assembly
8. Primary piston return spring
9. Primary piston assembly
10. Stop
11. Snap-ring
12. Bleeder
13. Valve spring
14. Check valve assembly
15. Packing
16. Valve cap
17. Stop screw

1973–77 master cylinder—later models similar

correct rebuilding parts for your car's master cylinder. The manufacturer's name is clearly stamped on the part.

1. Remove the master cylinder from the car.
2. Remove the reservoir caps and filters and drain the brake fluid. Discard this fluid.
3. Pry the piston stopper snap-ring from the open end of the master cylinder with a screwdriver.
4. Remove the stopper screw and washer from the bottom of the master cylinder and then remove the primary and secondary piston assemblies from the master cylinder bore.
5. Remove the caps on the underside of the master cylinder to gain access to the check valves for cleaning.

NOTE: *Do not disassemble the brake fluid level gauge, if equipped.*

6. Discard all used rubber parts and gaskets. These parts should be replaced with the new components included in the rebuilding kit.

NOTE: *Do not remove the master cylinder reservoir tanks unless they are leaking. If they are removed for any reason, they must be replaced with new ones.*

7. Clean all the parts in clean brake fluid. Do *not* use mineral oil or alcohol for cleaning.
8. Check the cylinder bore and piston for wear, scoring, corrosion, or any other damage. The piston and cylinder bore can be dressed with crocus cloth soaked in brake fluid. Move the crocus cloth around the cylinder bore, not in and out. Do the same to the piston, if necessary. Wash both the cylinder bore and the piston with clean brake fluid.
9. Check the piston-to-cylinder bore clearance; it should measure less than 0.0059 in. (0.15 mm) for all models. If greater clearance exists, replace the piston, the cylinder, or both. The cylinder bore diameter should be 7/8 in. (22.23 mm) through 1978, or 15/16 in. (23.81 mm), 1979 and later.
10. Assemble the master cylinder in the reverse order of disassembly. Soak all of the components in clean brake fluid before assembling them.
11. Clamp the master cylinder in a vise by one of its flanges. Fill the reservoirs with fresh fluid, and pump the piston with a screwdriver until fluid squirts from the outlet ports. Install the master cylinder and bleed the system.

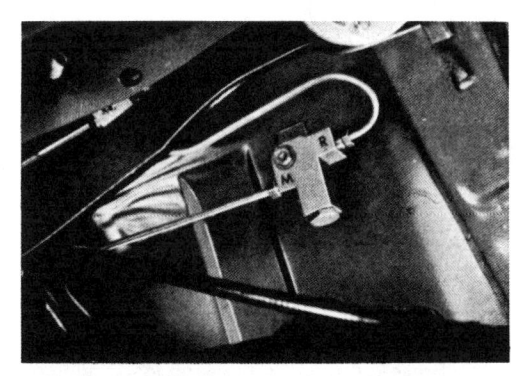

1970–72 proportioning valve

Note: Identification for inlet and outlet is facilitated by an arrow mark.

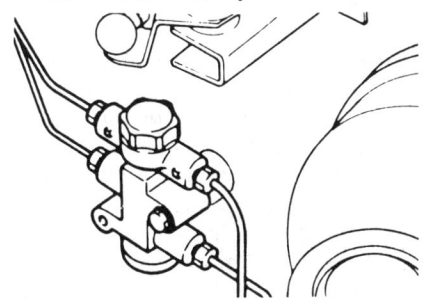

1973 and later proportioning valve

Proportioning Valve
REMOVAL AND INSTALLATION

1. Disconnect the brake lines at the valve.
2. Remove the mounting bolt and remove the valve.

NOTE: *Do not disassemble the valve.*

To install:

1. On 1970–72 models, the "M" faces toward the master cylinder and the "R" toward the rear brakes. On 1973–82 models, the "F" faces the front brakes, and the arrow faces the rear brake side.
2. Install the mounting bolt, connect the lines, and bleed the system.

Brake Warning Light Switch
1970–77

This assembly is unrepairable, and must be replaced as a unit if problems occur. Replacement is made by disconnecting the brake lines (use a flare nut wrench, if possible, to avoid damage to the lines) and removing the part. Install the lines onto the new switch and bleed the system.

194 BRAKES

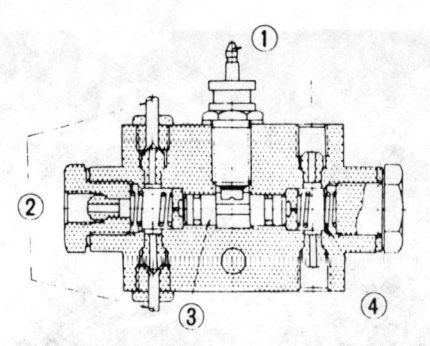

1. Wire terminal
2. Brake tubes
3. Valve assembly
4. Piston load spring

Cross-section of the brake warning light switch through 1977

1978 and Later

The warning light switches are installed in the master cylinder reservoir caps in these models. The switches can be tested by removing each cap in turn and holding it above the reservoir, allowing the switch float to drop to the bottom of its travel. With the ignition on and the parking brake released, the warning light should glow. If the switches do not operate properly, they must be replaced. They are available only as complete units.

Bleeding

The purpose of bleeding the brakes is to expel air trapped in the hydraulic system. The system must be bled whenever the pedal feels spongy, indicating that compressible air has entered the system. It must also be bled whenever the system has been opened or repaired. You will need a helper for this job.

CAUTION: *Never reuse brake fluid which has been bled from the system.*

The sequence for bleeding is as follows:

1970–78: Right rear, left rear, right front, left front.

1979–80: Master cylinder front, master cylinder rear, right rear, left rear, right front, left front.

1. Clean all dirt from around the master cylinder reservoir caps. Remove the caps and fill the master cylinder to the proper level with clean, fresh brake fluid meeting DOT 3 specifications.

NOTE: *Brake fluid picks up moisture from the air, which reduces its effectiveness and causes brake line corrosion. Don't leave the master cylinder or the fluid container open any longer than necessary. Be careful not to spill brake fluid on painted surfaces;* wipe up any spilled fluid immediately and rinse the area with clear water.

2. Clean all the bleeder screws. You may want to give each one a shot of penetrating solvent to loosen it up; seizure is a common problem with bleeder screws, which then break off, sometimes requiring replacement of the part to which they are attached.

3. Attach a length of clear vinyl tubing to the bleeder screw on the wheel cylinder (or master cylinder). Insert the other end of the tube into a clear, clean jar half filled with brake fluid.

4. Have your helper slowly depress the brake pedal. As this done, open the bleeder screw 1/3—1/2 of a turn, and allow the fluid to run through the tube. Close the bleeder screw before the pedal reaches the end of its travel. Have your assistant slowly release the pedal. Repeat this process until no air bubbles appear in the expelled fluid.

5. Repeat the procedure on the other three brakes, checking the fluid level in the master cylinder reservoirs often. Do not allow the reservoirs to run dry, or the bleeding process will have to be repeated.

FRONT DISC BRAKES

Disc Brake Pads

INSPECTION

1970–78

The pads must be removed from the caliper for inspection. Refer to the removal procedure.

1. Clean the pad with a safe solvent.
2. Check the pad for:
   a. Heavy saturation with fluid or grease.

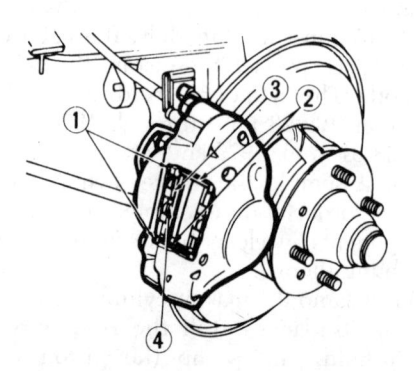

1. Clip
2. Retaining pin
3. Anti-squeal spring
4. Pad

Parts of the front disc brake through 1978

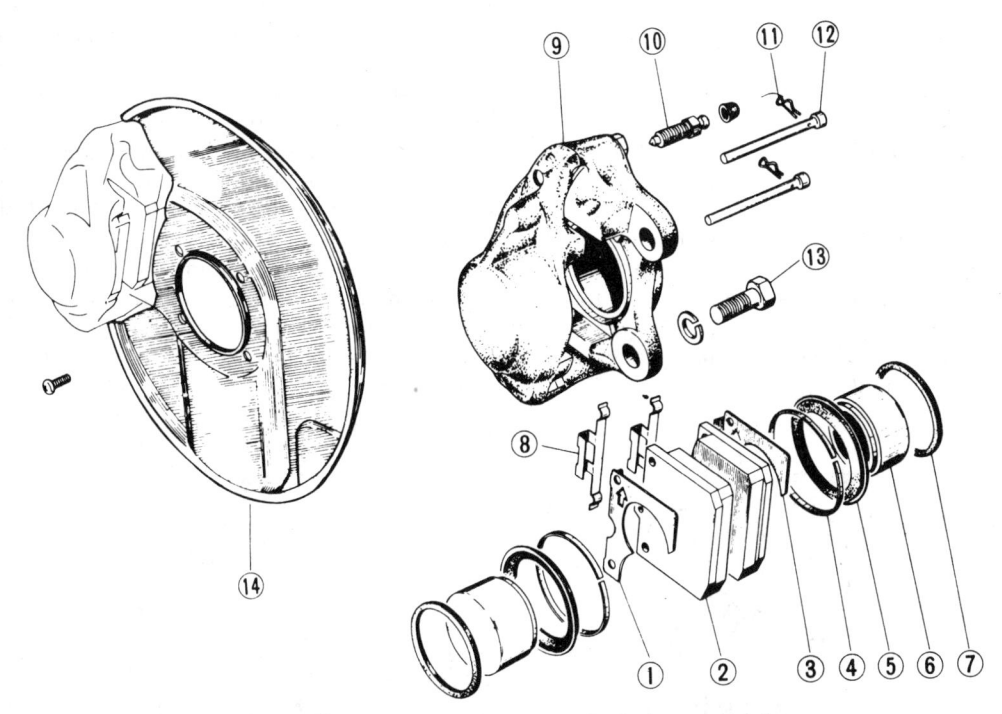

BRAKES 195

1. Anti-squeal shim (right-side)
2. Pad
3. Anti-squeal shim (left-side)
4. Retaining ring
5. Dust cover
6. Piston
7. Piston seal
8. Anti-squeal spring
9. Caliper assembly
10. Bleeder
11. Clip
12. Retaining pin
13. Caliper mounting bolt
14. Baffle plate

Exploded view of the S-16 Girling-Sumitomo front disc brake (1970–78)

b. Friction material thickness of less than 0.079 in. (2 mm) or overall thickness of less than 0.295 in. (7.5 mm).

If either "a" or "b" apply, replace *both* pads with a new *set*.

NOTE: *This minimum thickness measurement may disagree with your state inspection laws.*

1979 and Later

An inspection slot is provided in the top of the caliper for checking the pad thickness. However, if the thickness seems marginal, the pads should be removed from the caliper and checked. Minimum thickness for the pads is 0.08 in. (2 mm). This measurement may disagree with your state inspection laws.

NOTE: *Always replace all pads on both front wheels at the same time. When inspecting or replacing the pads, check the surface of the rotors for scoring or wear. The rotors should be removed for resurfacing if badly scored.*

REMOVAL AND INSTALLATION

1970–78

1. Raise the front of the car and support it securely. Remove the wheel.
2. Remove the clips, retaining pins, and anti-squeal spring.
3. Remove the pad and anti-squeal shim.

To install:
1. Clean all caliper and pad locating parts.
2. Loosen the master cylinder "F" reservoir cap. Force the piston back into the cylinder to accommodate the greater thickness of a new pad.
3. Apply a light coat of grease to the sliding surfaces of the caliper and both sides of the shim. The shim should only be greased along the round cut-out which fits around the piston.
4. Install the pad and anti-squeal shim. The shim arrow must point in the direction of forward rotation. Install the anti-squeal spring and retaining pin, and secure them with the clip.

196 BRAKES

5. Depress and release the brake pedal several times.

1979 and Later

1. Raise and support the front of the car. Remove the wheels.
2. Remove the lower pin bolt which retains the caliper to the torque member.
3. Rotate the caliper upward out of the way, exposing the pads. Do not try to move the caliper sideways.
4. Remove the pad retainers, inner and outer shims, and pads.

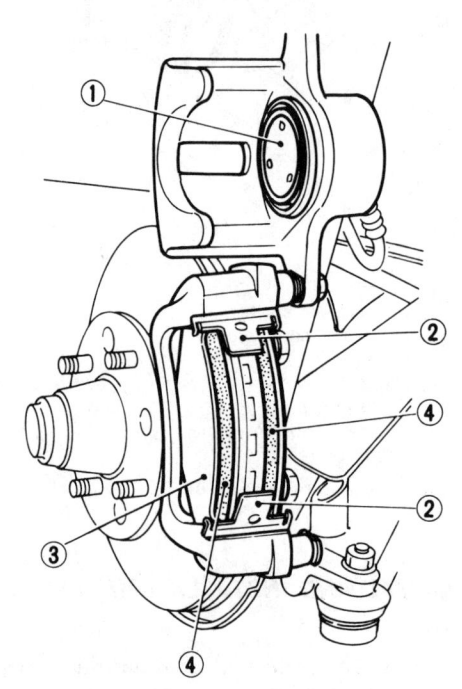

5. To install, clean the piston end and pin bolts.
6. Install a new inner pad. Rotate the caliper back down into place, slightly open the bleeder screw, then, with a long bar, lever the caliper to the outside to press the piston into place. Rotate the caliper back up out of the way.
7. Lightly coat the sliding surfaces of the torque member with grease. Install a new outer pad and inner and outer shims. Install the pad retainers; be careful not to install upside down.

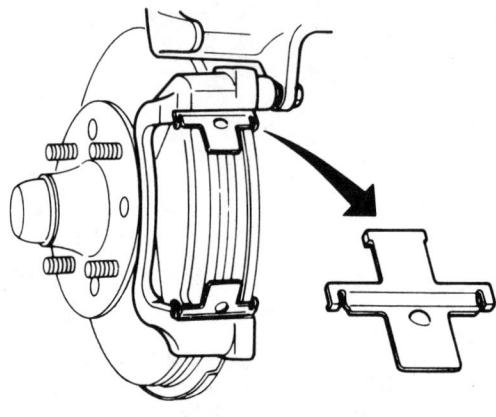

Pad retainer installation, 1979 and later

8. Rotate the caliper down and install the pin bolt. Tighten to 16–23 ft lbs (2.2–3.2 kg-m).
9. Apply the brakes a few times to seat the pads. Check the master cylinder level, and add fluid if necessary. Bleed the brakes if necessary.

Disc Brake Calipers

REMOVAL AND INSTALLATION
1970–78

1. Remove the pads, as previously described.

1. Inner shim   3. Outer shim
2. Pad retainer 4. Pads

Brake pad removal, 1979 and later

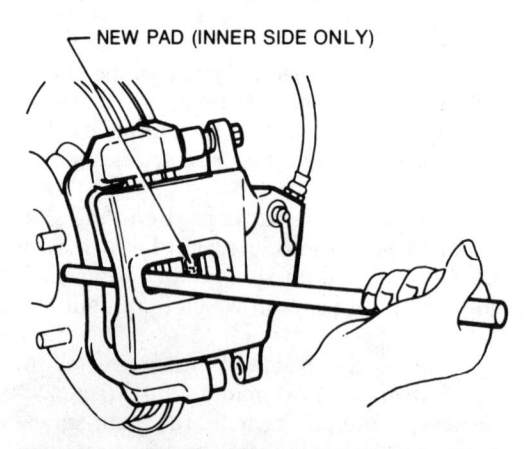

Lever the caliper to the outside to press the piston back, 1979 and later

Brake line (1) and caliper installation bolts (2), 1970–78

BRAKES

2. Disconnect the brake line, remove the caliper installation bolt, and remove the caliper assembly.

To install:

1. Put the caliper in position and install the installation bolt. Tighten to 53–72 ft lbs (7.3–9.9 kg-m).
2. Reconnect the brake line. Bleed the system, as previously described (bleeding of only the disconnected line should be necessary).

1979 and Later

1. Raise and support the front of the car. Remove the wheel.
2. Disconnect and plug the brake hose. Use a flare nut wrench if possible.
3. The caliper is retained to the knuckle spindle by two bolts. Remove the bolts and remove the caliper assembly.
4. To install, place the caliper in position on the spindle without the pads or pad retainer. Install the upper caliper bolt loosely. Install the pads and pad retainer.
5. Swing the caliper down and install the lower bolt. Tighten both bolts to 53–72 ft lbs (7.3–9.9 kg-m).
6. Install the brake hose. Tightening torque is 11–13 ft lbs (1.5–1.8 kg-m). Bleed the brakes.

OVERHAUL
1970–78

The caliper halves must not be separated. If brake fluid leaks from the bridge seal, replace the caliper assembly.

1. Clean the caliper assembly of all accumulated mud and dust.
2. Remove the retaining rings. Remove the dust covers.
3. Hold one piston with a finger so that it will not come out and gradually apply air pressure to the brake line fitting. This should cause the other piston to come out, but if the piston you are holding begins moving before the other, switch your finger over and remove the more movable one first.
4. Carefully push the other piston out.
5. With a finger, carefully remove both piston seals.
6. Thoroughly clean all parts in brake fluid.
7. Inspect, as follows:
   a. Check cylinder walls for damage or excessive wear. Light rust, etc. should be removed with fine emery paper. If the wall is heavily rusted, replace the caliper assembly.
   b. Inspect the pad, as previously described.
   c. Inspect the piston for uneven wear, damage or any rust. Replace the piston if there is any rust, as it is chrome plated and cannot be cleaned.
   d. Replace piston seals and dust covers.
8. Coat the piston seal with brake fluid and carefully install the piston seal.
9. Install the dust seal onto the piston. Coat the piston with brake fluid. Install the piston and seal assembly and install the retaining ring.
10. Repeat Steps 8 and 9 for the other piston.

1979 and Later

1. Raise and support the front of the car. Remove the wheels. Remove the brake hose. Plug the caliper and hose to prevent leakage.
2. Remove the two mounting bolts and remove the caliper from the spindle.
3. Remove the two pin bolts.
4. Separate the caliper from the torque member.
5. Remove the pad retainers and pads.
6. Gradually apply compressed air to the fluid inlet and remove the pistons and dust seals. Remove the piston seals.
7. Check the caliper bore for scoring, wear, corrosion, etc. Minor damage can be cleaned up with crocus cloth, but deep pits or wear warrant caliper replacement. The piston is plated and must not be polished.
8. Install the piston seals.
9. Lubricate the piston, dust seals, and caliper bore with clean brake fluid. Install the dust seal to the piston, then install the other lip of the seal into the caliper bore groove. Install the piston.
10. Apply a thin coat of grease to the

RETAINING RING

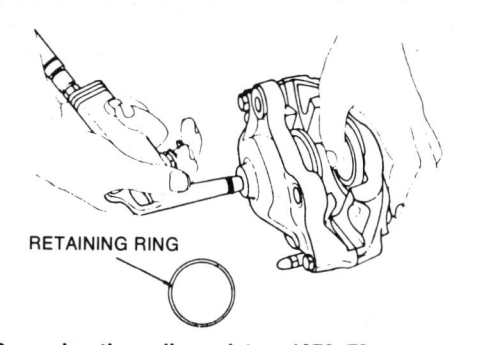

Removing the caliper piston, 1970–78

198 BRAKES

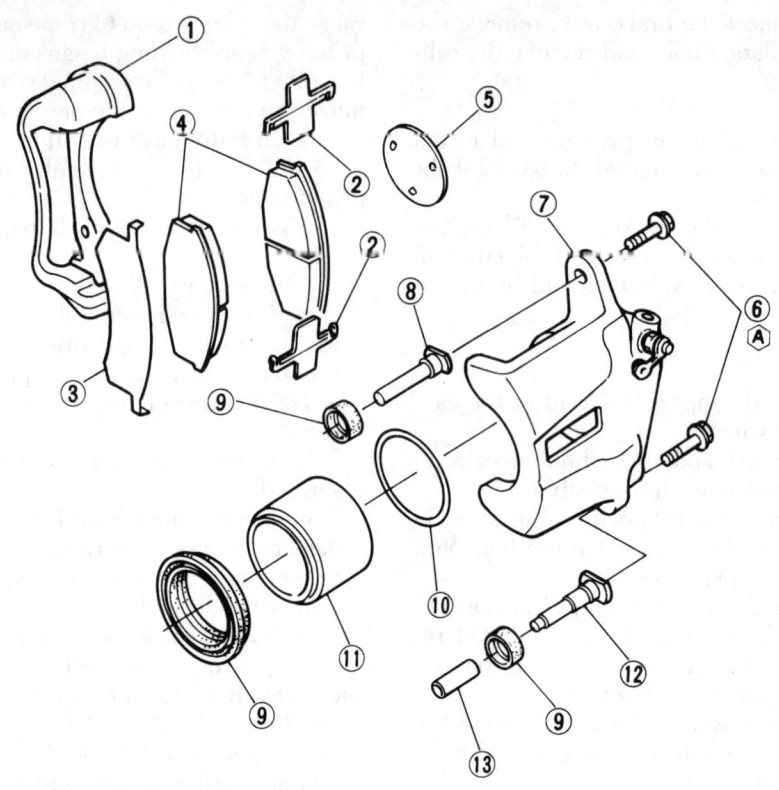

1. Torque member
2. Pad retainer
3. Outer shim
4. Pad
5. Inner shim
6. Pin bolt
7. Cylinder body
8. Main pin
9. Dust seal
10. Piston seal
11. Piston
12. Sub pin
13. Rubber seal

Tightening torque kg-m (ft-lb)
A : 2.2 to 3.2 (16 to 23)

Exploded view of the CL28V front disc brake, 1979 and later

torque member (where it contacts the pads) and the pin bushings and pins.

11. Install the pin bolts, tightening to 16–23 ft lbs (2.2–3.2 kg-m).

12. Install the caliper.

Brake Disc

REMOVAL AND INSTALLATION

All Models

1. Raise the vehicle and support it securely. Remove the front wheel. Remove the caliper as previously described.

2. Pry off the hub cap with two flat bladed screwdrivers.

3. Remove the cotter pin. Remove the wheel bearing locknut.

4. Remove the hub and rotor and wheel bearing and seal as an assembly from the spindle. Remove the seal and bearings from the hub.

5. Remove the bolts holding the rotor to the hub and remove the rotor.

To inspect the wheel bearings:

1. Remove all old grease with solvent.

2. Put the bearings back in position in the hub, and slowly rotate to check for smooth rotation. Check for roughness, burrs, discoloration, or other defects. If any defects are noted, supply new parts and remove and replace the outer races, as later described. Otherwise, go on to the installation procedure.

3. Utilizing the two grooves inside the wheel hub, tap each outer bearing race to remove it from the hub.

4. Install the new outer races with a drift, as shown.

To install:

1. Install the rotor onto the hub, install the mounting bolts, and torque to 28–38 ft lbs (3.9–5.3 kg-m) 1979 and 40–54 ft lbs (5.5–7.5 kg-m) 1980 and later.

BRAKES 199

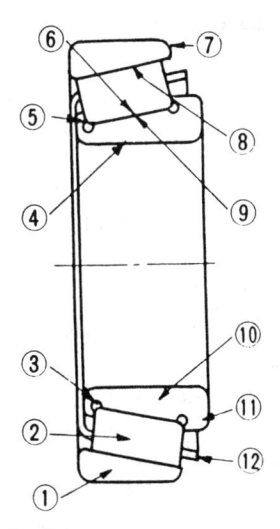

1. Outer race
2. Roller
3. Small collar
4. Collar surface
5. Inner race fitted surface
6. Inner race surface
7. Outer race fitted surface
8. Outer race surface
9. Roller rolling surface
10. Inner race
11. Large roller
12. Supporter

Wheel bearing

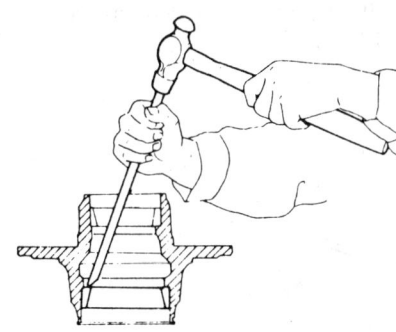

Removing the outer race

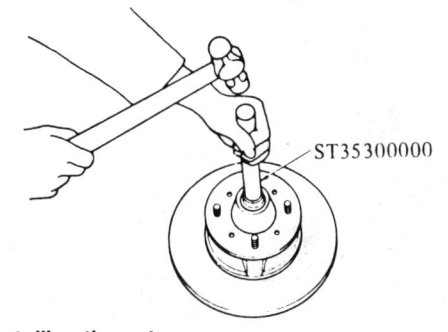

Installing the outer race

2. Carefully reassemble the bearings and seal in the hub, employing a new seal if leakage was noted during disassembly.

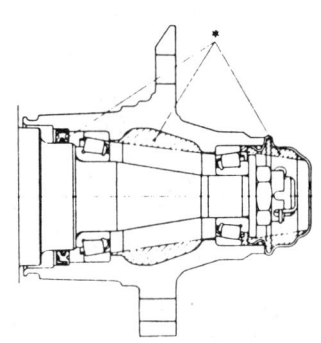

Greasing the points in the hub

3. Fill the spaces between the rollers and the pocket in the seal lip with wheel bearing grease. Fill the hub and hub cap with grease as indicated in the illustration.
4. Coat the spindle shaft and threads, the seal, and the locknut with bearing grease.
5. Install the inner bearing and seal onto the spindle.
6. Install the hub and outer bearing onto the spindle.
7. Install and tighten the locknut to 18–22 ft lbs (2.5–3.0 kg-m). Turn the hub back and forth several turns to seat the bearing, and retorque the locknut to the same figure.
8. Turn the locknut back out at least 60° and up to 75° until the nut is aligned properly for the cotter pin.

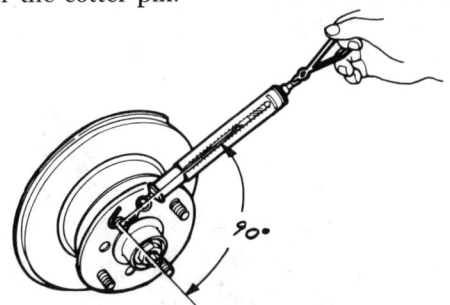

Checking wheel bearing rotation torque

9. Rotate the hub back and forth several times, then measure the starting torque at the wheel hub bolt with a spring scale. It should be 3.5–7.4 in. lbs (4.0–8.5 kg-cm) with new parts or 0.9–3.9 in. lbs (1.0–4.5 kg-cm) with used parts.
10. If the torque is correct, install the cotter pin and hub cap.
11. Replace the caliper, and bleed the hydraulic system. Replace the wheel.

INSPECTION

1. Remove the wheel. Remove the caliper as previously described.

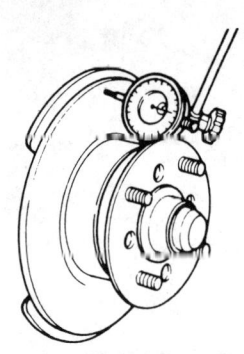

200 BRAKES

Measuring rotor deflection

2. Mount a dial indicator so that deflection at the center of pad contact surface can be measured. Maximum deflection is 0.0079 in. (0.2 mm), 1970-78, or 0.0039 in. (0.1 mm), 1979-80. If necessary, adjust the wheel bearing.

3. Measure the thickness of the rotor all the way around with a micrometer. Maximum variation should be 0.0012 in. (0.03 mm) or less with a used rotor, or 0.0028 in. (0.07 mm) when new.

4. If the rotor is machined, the minimum thickness is 0.413 in. (10.5 mm), 1970-78, or 0.709 in. (18.0 mm), 1979 and later. Replace the disc if the minimum thickness will be less after machining.

Wheel Bearings
ADJUSTMENT

1. Support the vehicle securely. Remove the wheel. Remove the hub cap.
2. Remove the cotter pin, and loosen the hub locknut fully.
3. Follow Steps 7-10 of the "Brake Disc Installation" procedure.
4. Install the wheel and lower the vehicle.

REMOVAL, INSTALLATION, AND PACKING

Follow all steps of the "Brake Disc Removal and Installation" procedure except Step 5 of the removal procedure and Step 1 of the installation procedure, which involve removing the disc from the hub.

REAR DRUM BRAKES

Brake Drums
REMOVAL AND INSTALLATION

1. Raise the vehicle and support it securely.
2. Remove the wheel. The brake drum may now be removed. If the drum will not pull off readily, proceed as follows on 1970-76 models:

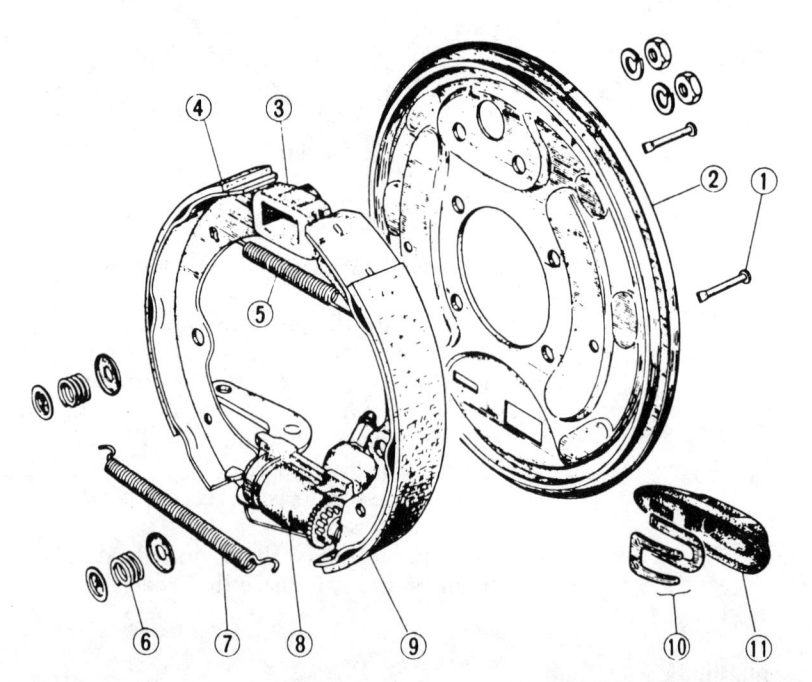

1. Anti-rattle pin
2. Brake plate
3. Anchor block
4. Rear shoe assembly
5. Return spring
6. Anti-rattle spring
7. Return spring
8. Wheel cylinder
9. Front shoe
10. Retaining shim
11. Dust cover

Disassembled view of the 1970-76 rear drum brake

BRAKES 201

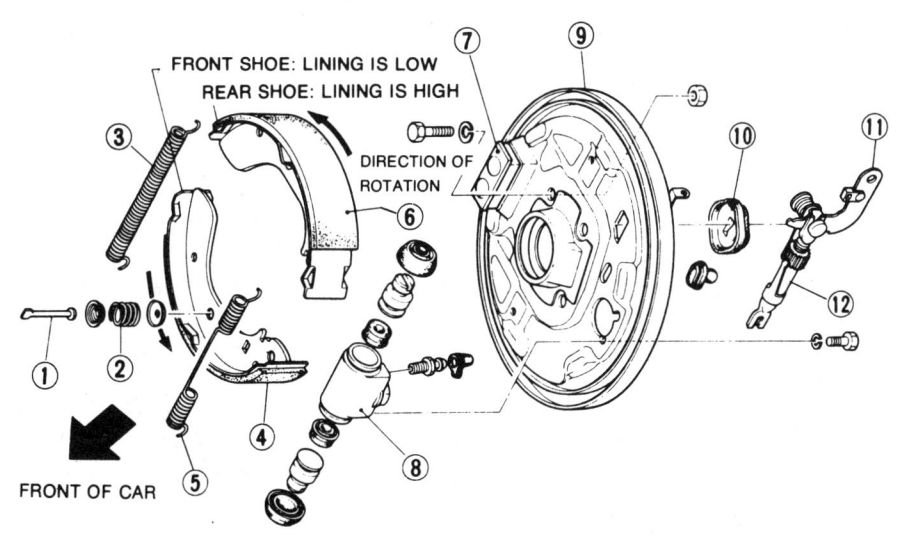

1. Anti-rattle pin
2. Anti-rattle spring
3. Return spring
4. Leading shoe assembly
5. Return spring
6. Trailing shoe assembly
7. Anchor block
8. Wheel cylinder
9. Backing plate
10. Dust cover
11. Parking brake toggle lever
12. Adjuster

Exploded view of the 1977–78 rear drum brake

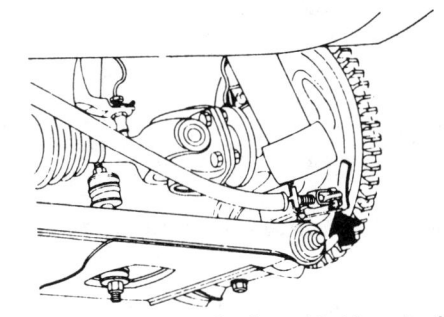

Disconnecting the handbrake cable (drum brakes)

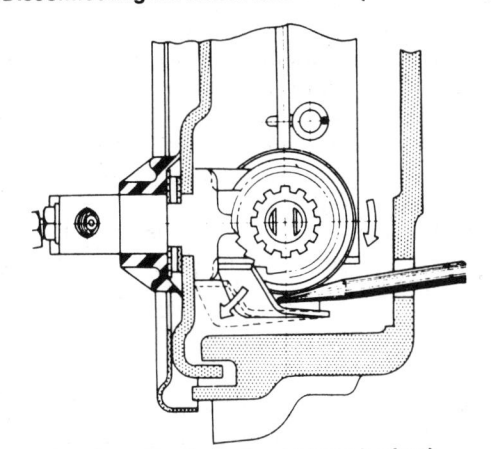

Turning the adjusting wheel (drum brakes)

a. Remove the handbrake clevis pin from the wheel cylinder lever and disconnect the handbrake cable;
b. Remove the plug from the adjusting hole in the drum, and, using a screwdriver, remove the adjusting lever from the adjusting wheel;
c. Turn the adjusting wheel in a downward direction, using a screwdriver until the drum is movable. Remove the drum.

To remove a stubborn 1977–78 model drum:
a. Fully apply the hand brake;
b. Push or tap the cotter pin out and remove the stop from the parking brake lever on the rear of the drum;
c. Release the parking brake. Remove the drum.

To install:
1. Install the drum onto the wheel studs.
2. Using a screwdriver and going in through the adjusting hole, turn the adjusting wheel in an upward direction until the brake shoes lightly touch the drum.

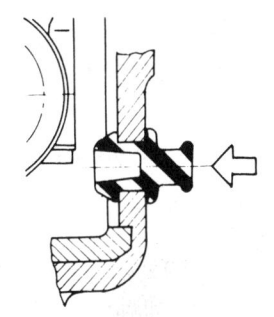

The adjusting hole plug (drum brakes)

202 BRAKES

3. Reconnect the handbrake cable with the clevis pin. Operate the handbrake until the adjusting mechanism no longer clicks.
4. Install the adjusting hole plug making sure that it is installed so that the inner lip is on the inside of the drum all the way around.
5. Install the wheel and lower the vehicle.

INSPECTION

1. Remove the brake drum. Wipe out the accumulated dust with a damp cloth.
   WARNING: *Do not blow the brake dust out of the drums with compressed air or lungpower. Brake linings contain asbestos, a known cancer causing substance. Dispose of the cloth after use.*
2. Inspect the drum for uneven wear, wear in steps, or scoring.
3. The drum may be machined until it reaches the wear limit shown in the "Brake Specifications" chart. The drum requires machining if the inner diameter is more than 0.0020 in. (0.05 mm) out-of-round.

Brake Shoes

REMOVAL AND INSTALLATION

1. Remove the brake drum as previously described.
2. Remove the anti-rattle springs.
3. Remove both brake shoes together.

To install:
1. Apply grease to the adjusting wheel and to the threaded and sliding portions of the adjust screw.
2. Apply multipurpose grease to the backing plate, anchor block, and sliding portions of the wheel cylinder, carefully avoiding getting any grease onto the lining surfaces.
3. Install the shoes. Install the anti-rattle springs and return spring.
4. Install the drum, and adjust the adjuster mechanism, as previously described, under "Brake Drum Removal and Installation."

Wheel Cylinders

REMOVAL AND INSTALLATION

1970–76

1. Remove the brake drums and shoes, as previously described.
2. Disconnect the brake line (1), and remove the dust cover (2).
3. Drive out the locking shim (3) toward the front and remove the other shim by pulling it to the rear.
4. Remove the cylinder.

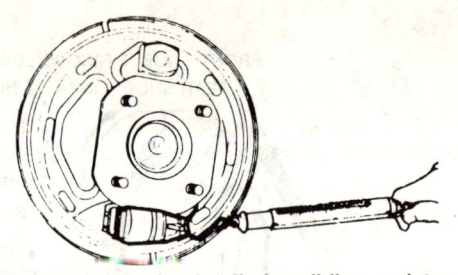

Measuring the wheel cylinder sliding resistance through 1976

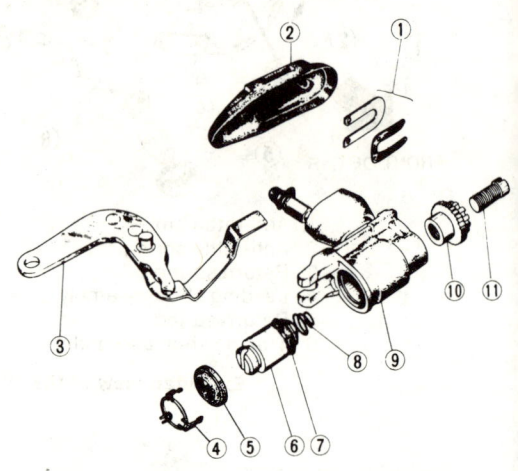

1. Retaining shim
2. Dust cover
3. Wheel cylinder lever
4. Retainer
5. Dust cover
6. Piston
7. Piston cup
8. Spring
9. Wheel cylinder
10. Adjust wheel
11. Adjust screw

Wheel cylinder components through 1976

To install:
1. Apply grease to the cylinder, backing plate, and shims. Also apply grease to the wheel cylinder lever fulcrum.
2. Put the cylinder in position and install shims in reverse of the removal procedure. Install the dust cover.
3. Measure the sliding resistance of the cylinder with a spring scale. It should be 4.41–15.43 lbs (2–7 kg).
4. Reconnect the brake line, install the brake shoes, install the drum, bleed the hydraulic system, and adjust the adjuster as previously described.

1977–78

1. Raise and support the rear of the car.
2. Remove the wheel, brake drum, and brake shoes.
3. Remove and plug the brake line. Use a flare nut wrench, if possible.
4. Remove the wheel cylinder retaining bolts and remove the wheel cylinder.
5. Installation is the reverse.

BRAKES

OVERHAUL

This is one of those jobs where it is usually easier to just replace the part rather than rebuild it. Rebuilding kits contain all the parts of a wheel cylinder except the body and piston.

NOTE: *Datsun has two suppliers for wheel cylinder parts: Nabco and Tokico. The parts are not interchangeable. Be sure to get the correct rebuilding kit for the parts on your car. The name of the manufacturer is stamped on the wheel cylinder.*

1. Remove the wheel cylinder from the backing plate.
2. Remove the dust boots and remove the piston. Discard the piston cup. The dust boots can be reused if necessary, but it is better to replace them.
3. Wash all of the components in clean brake fluid.
4. Inspect the piston and piston bore. Replace them if corroded, scored, or worn. The piston and bore can be polished lightly with crocus cloth. Move the crocus cloth around the piston bore, not in and out.
5. Wash the wheel cylinder and piston thoroughly in clean brake fluid, allowing them to remain wet for assembly. Lubricate the piston cups and dust seals with brake fluid.
6. Apply rubber grease sparingly to the inside of the dust boot lip.
7. Assemble the wheel cylinder and install it in the reverse order of removal. Assemble the remaining components and bleed the brakes.

REAR DISC BRAKES

Disc Brake Pads

INSPECTION

1. Raise and support the rear of the car. Remove the wheel.
2. The pads can be inspected through the top of the yoke. However, it is better to remove the pads to measure their thickness.
3. Minimum pad thickness is 0.08 in. (2 mm). This minimum thickness may disagree with your state inspection laws.

NOTE: *If the pads are worn, always replace all pads on both wheels at the same time.*

4. Check the condition of the rotor while you are about the task of inspecting the pads. If it is scored, cracked, or worn beyond the minimum thickness (0.339 in./8.6 mm), replace it.

REMOVAL AND INSTALLATION

1. Raise and support the rear of the car. Remove the wheels.
2. Remove the clip at the outside of the pad pins.

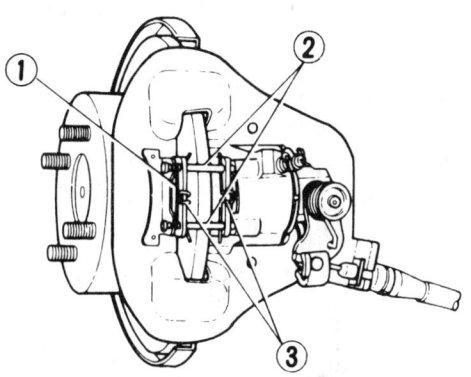

1. Clip 2. Pad pins 3. Anti-squeal springs

Rear disc brake pad removal, 1979 and later

3. Remove the pad pins. Hold the anti-squeal springs in place with your finger.
4. Remove the pads.
5. To install, first clean the end of the piston with clean brake fluid.
6. Lightly coat the caliper-to-pad, the yoke-to-pad, retaining pin-to-pad, and retaining pin-to-bracket surfaces with grease. Do not allow grease to get on the rotor or pad surfaces.
7. Push the piston into place with a screwdriver by pushing in on the piston while at

Push and turn the piston into the bore (rear disc brakes)

204 BRAKES

the same time turning it clockwise into the bore. Then, with a lever between the rotor and yoke, push the yoke over until the clearance to install the pads is equal.

8. Install the shims and pads, anti-squeal springs and pins. Install the clip. Note that the inner pad has a tab which must fit into the piston notch. Therefore, be sure that the piston notch is centered to allow proper pad installation.

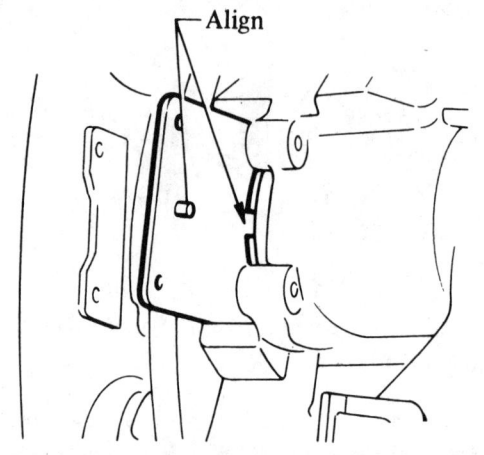

Align the tab with the piston notch (rear disc brakes)

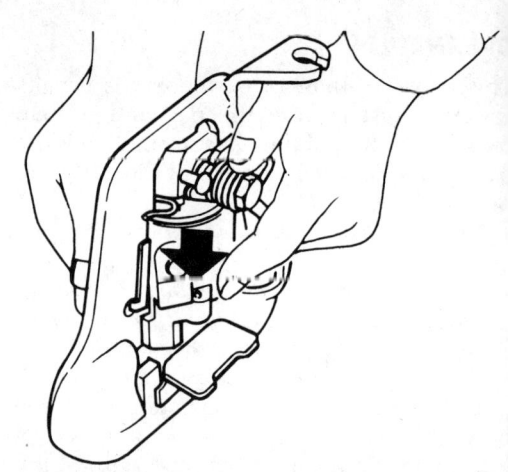

Push on the caliper to remove it from the yoke (rear disc brakes)

9. Apply the brakes a few times to center the pads. Check the master cylinder fluid level and add if necessary.

Caliper

REMOVAL AND INSTALLATION

1. Disconnect and plug the brake line from the caliper. Use a flare nut wrench to disconnect the line, to prevent damage to the line or the fitting.
2. Disconnect the hand brake cable at the lever.
3. Remove the caliper mounting bolts and remove the caliper.
4. To install, place the caliper into position and install the mounting bolts. Tighten to 28–38 ft lbs (3.9–5.3 kg-m).
5. Connect the hand brake cable.
6. Unplug and connect the brake line. Tighten to 11–13 ft lbs (1.5–1.8 kg-m). Bleed the brakes.

OVERHAUL

1. Remove the caliper from the car.
2. Remove the pads.
3. Stand the caliper assembly on end, large end down, and push on the caliper to separate it from the yoke.
4. Remove the retaining rings and dust seals from both pistons. Discard the dust seals.
5. Push in on the outer piston to force out the piston assembly. Remove and discard the piston seals.
6. Remove the yoke spring from the yoke.
7. Disengage the piston assembly by turning the outer piston counterclockwise.
8. Disassemble the outer piston by removing the snap ring.
9. Disassemble the inner piston by removing the snap ring. This will allow the spring cover, spring, and spring seat to come out. Remove the inner snap ring to remove the key plate, push rod, and strut.
10. To install, assemble the pistons in the reverse order of disassembly. Apply a thin coat of grease to the groove in the push rod, its O-ring, the strut ends, oil seal, piston seal, and the inside of the dust seal. The piston seals, dust seals, oil seal, and push rod O-ring should be replaced with new ones whenever the caliper is disassembled. New parts are included in the rebulding kit.
11. Install the piston seals. Apply a thin coat of grease to the groove in the sliding surfaces of the piston and caliper bore. Install the pistons into the caliper. Install the retainers onto the dust seals.
12. Install the yoke springs on the yoke.
13. Lightly coat the yoke and caliper body contact surfaces, and the pad pin hole, with silicone grease. Assemble the yoke to the caliper.

BRAKES

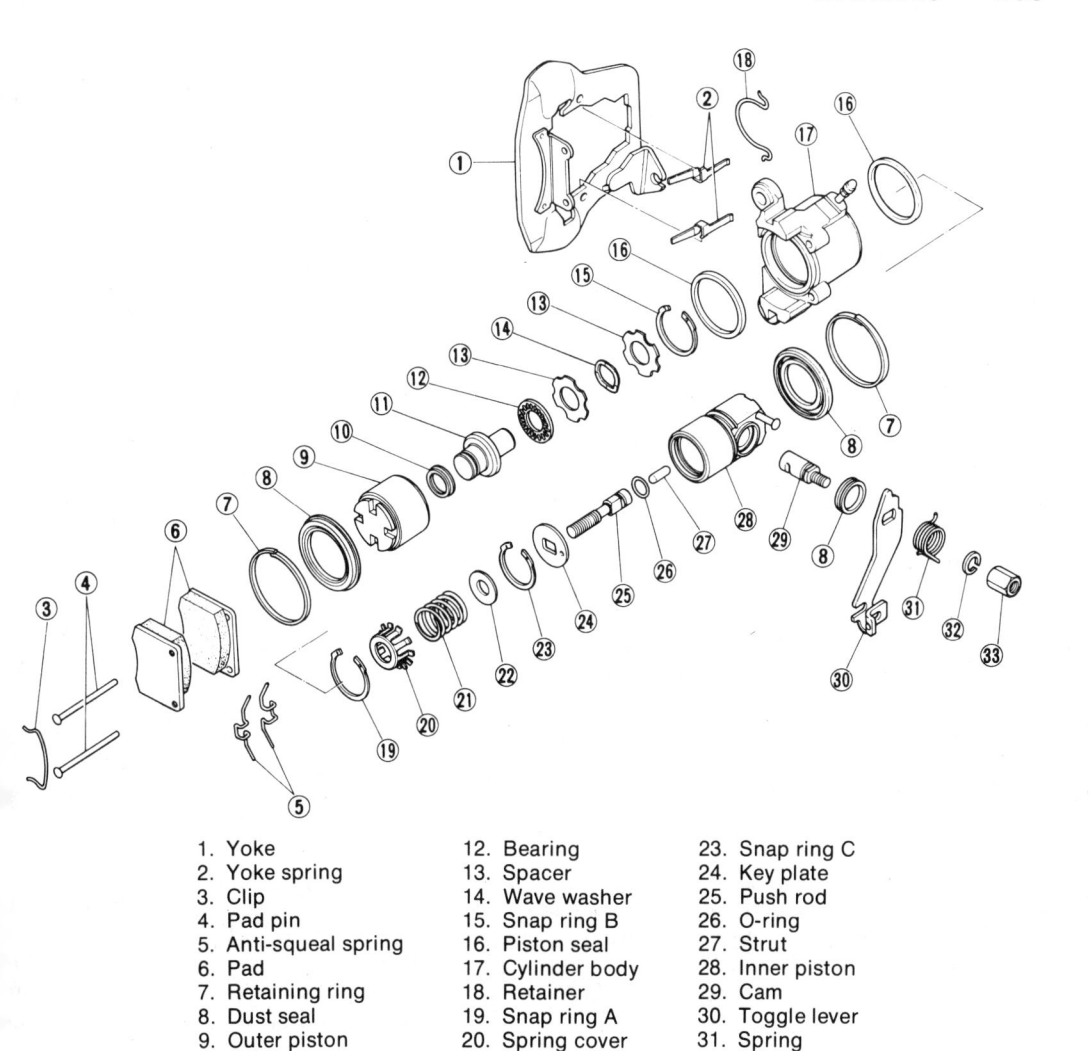

1. Yoke
2. Yoke spring
3. Clip
4. Pad pin
5. Anti-squeal spring
6. Pad
7. Retaining ring
8. Dust seal
9. Outer piston
10. Oil seal
11. Adjusting nut
12. Bearing
13. Spacer
14. Wave washer
15. Snap ring B
16. Piston seal
17. Cylinder body
18. Retainer
19. Snap ring A
20. Spring cover
21. Spring
22. Spring seat
23. Snap ring C
24. Key plate
25. Push rod
26. O-ring
27. Strut
28. Inner piston
29. Cam
30. Toggle lever
31. Spring
32. Washer
33. Nut

Annette AN14H rear disc brake

14. Install the pads.
15. Install the caliper.

Disc (Rotor)

REMOVAL AND INSTALLATION

1. Remove the caliper.
2. Remove the rotor.
3. Installation is the reverse.

INSPECTION

1. Check the surface for wear or scoring. Deep scoring, grooves, or rust pitting can be removed by refacing. Minimum thickness is 0.339 in. (8.6 mm). If the rotor will be thinner than this after refinishing, it must be replaced.
2. Check disc parallelism; it must be less than 0.0012 in. (0.03 mm). If over this specification, the disc must be replaced.
3. Install the disc and the wheel nuts. Check the runout with a dial indicator. If runout exceeds 0.0059 in. (0.15 mm), the disc needs to be refinished or replaced.

Rear Wheel Bearings

Rear wheel bearing service is covered in Chapter 7.

PARKING BRAKE

Cable

NOTE: *The driveshaft must be removed, as described in Chapter 7, to adjust or*

BRAKES

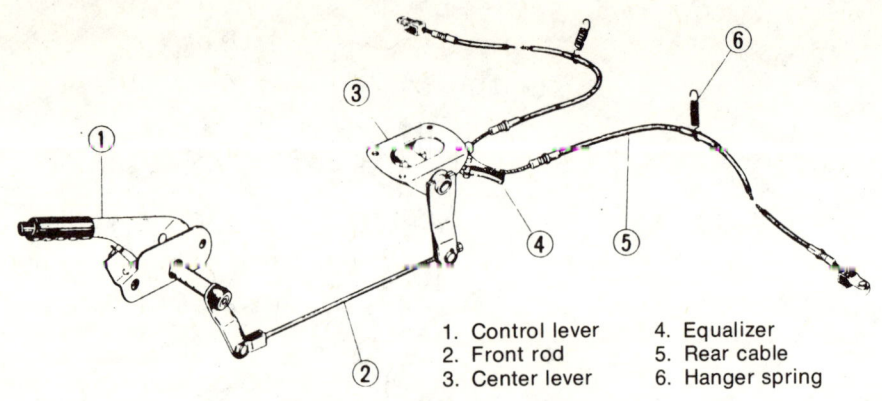

1. Control lever
2. Front rod
3. Center lever
4. Equalizer
5. Rear cable
6. Hanger spring

Handbrake linkage through 1978

replace the handbrake cable on models through 1978.

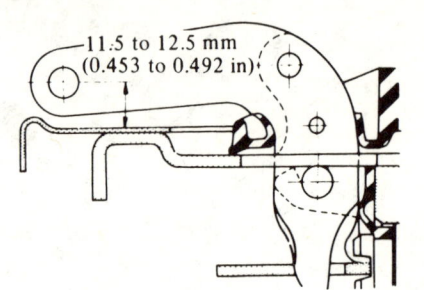

Handbrake adjustment dimensions through 1978

ADJUSTMENT

1970-78

1. Release the handbrake fully and block the vehicle wheels.
2. Loosen the locknut at the rear of the front rod.
3. Measure the dimension between the wheel cylinder lever pin hole centers and their respective buffer plates.
4. Rotate the front rod to bring the dimension to 0.453–0.492 in. (11.5–12.5 mm) on both sides.
5. Tighten the locknut at the rear of the front rod.

1979-82

1. Pull up the handbrake lever, counting the number of ratchet clicks for full engagement. Full engagement should be reached in 4–6 notches.
2. Release the parking brake.
3. Adjust the lever stroke at the cable equalizer under the car: loosen the locknut and tighten the adjusting nut to reduce the number of ratchet clicks necessary for engagement. Tighten the locknut.
4. Check the adjustment and repeat as necessary.

Brake Specifications
All measurements are given in in. (mm)

Year	Model	Master Cylinder Bore	Wheel Cylinder or Caliper Inner Diameter Front	Wheel Cylinder or Caliper Inner Diameter Rear	Brake Disc or Drum Diameter Front	Brake Disc or Drum Diameter Rear
1970–71	240-Z	.8748 (22.22)	2.1252 (53.98)	.8748 (22.22)	10.67 (271)	9.04 (229.6)
1972–78	240-Z, 260-Z, 280-Z	.8748 (22.22)	2.1252 (53.98)	.8748 (22.22)	10.67 (271)	9.00 (228.6)①
1979–82	280-ZX	15/16 (23.81)	2.386 (60.6)	1.685 (42.8)	9.92 (252)	10.59 (2.69)

① Wear limit: 9.055(230.0)

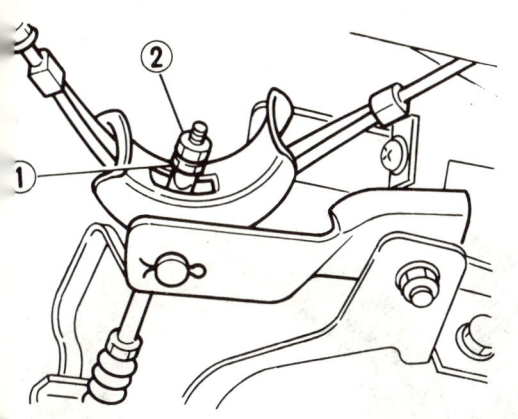

BRAKES 207

Parking brake equalizer; (1) is the adjusting nut and (2) is the locknut

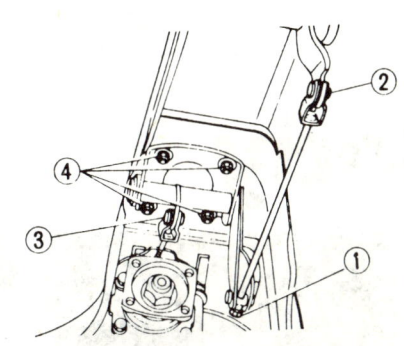

Handbrake locknut and adjusting nut (1), clevis pins (2 and 3), and brake handle mounting bracket bolts (4)—1970–78 models

5. After adjustment, check to see that the rear brake levers (at the calipers) return to their full off positions when the lever is released, and that the rear cables are not slack when the lever is released.
6. To adjust the warning lamp, bend the warning lamp switch plate down so that the light comes on when the lever is engaged one notch.

REMOVAL AND INSTALLATION

1970–78

1. Remove the hanger spring and clevis pin located at (3).
2. Remove the clevis pins at both wheel cylinder levers.
3. Remove the cable retainers at the wheels and disconnect the cable from both hanger springs.
4. Remove the retainers at the forward (equalizer end) and remove the cable.

To install:
1. Reverse the above procedures.
2. Adjust the cable, as previously described.

1979 and Later

FRONT CABLE

1. Remove the passenger seat.
2. Disconnect the warning switch electrical connector.
3. Remove the two bolts securing the lever to the floor.
4. Under the car, remove the locknut, adjusting nut and equalizer.
5. Pull the cable out through the passenger compartment and remove from the car. Installation is the reverse.

REAR CABLE

1. Disconnect the cable at the equalizer.
2. Remove the cable lock plate from the rear suspension member and the rear discs.
3. Remove the clevis pin and clevis at the rear disc levers.
4. Disconnect the cable from the suspension arm. Remove the cable.
5. Installation is the reverse.

Body 10

You can repair most minor auto body damage yourself. Minor damage usually falls into one of several categories: (1) small scratches and dings in the paint that can be repaired without the use of body filler, (2) deep scratches and dents that require body filler, but do not require pulling, or hammering metal back into shape and (3) rust-out repairs. The repair sequences illustrated in this chapter are typical of these types of repairs. If you want to get involved in more complicated repairs including pulling or hammering sheet metal back into shape, you will probably need more detailed instructions. Chilton's *Minor Auto Body Repair, 2nd Edition* is a comprehensive guide to repairing auto body damage yourself.

TOOLS AND SUPPLIES

The list of tools and equipment you may need to fix minor body damage ranges from very basic hand tools to a wide assortment of specialized body tools. Most minor scratches, dings and rust holes can be fixed using an electric drill, wire wheel or grinder attachment, half-round plastic file, sanding block, various grades of sandpaper (#36, which is coarse through #600, which is fine) in both wet and dry types, auto body plastic, primer, touch-up paint, spreaders, newspaper and masking tape.

Most manufacturers of auto body repair products began supplying materials to professionals. Their knowledge of the best most-used products has been translated into body repair kits for the do-it-yourselfer. Kits are available from a number of manufacturers and contain the necessary materials in the required amounts for the repair identified on the package.

Kits are available for a wide variety of uses including:
- Rusted out metal
- All purpose kit for dents and holes
- Dents and deep scratches
- Fiberglass repair kit
- Epoxy kit for restyling.

Kits offer the advantage of buying what you need for the job. There is little waste and little chance of materials going bad from not being used. The same manufacturers also merchandise all of the individual products used—spreaders, dent pullers, fiberglass cloth, polyester resin, cream hardener, body filler, body files, sandpaper, sanding discs and holders, primer, spray paint, etc.

CAUTION: *Most of the products you will be using contain harmful chemicals, so be extremely careful. Always read the complete label before opening the containers. When*

BODY 209

you put them away for future use, be sure they are out of children's reach!

Most auto body repair kits contain all the materials you need to do the job right in the kit. So, if you have a small rust spot or dent you want to fix, check the contents of the kit before you run out and buy any additional tools.

ALIGNING BODY PANELS

Doors

There are several methods of adjusting doors. Your vehicle will probably use one of those illustrated.

Whenever a door is removed and is to be reinstalled, you should matchmark the position of the hinges on the door pillars. The holes of the hinges and/or the hinge attaching points are usually oversize to permit alignment of doors. The striker plate is also moveable, through oversize holes, permitting up-and-down, in-and-out and fore-and-aft movement. Fore-and-aft movement is made by adding or subtracting shims from behind the striker and pillar post. The striker should be adjusted so that the door closes fully and remains closed, yet enters the lock freely.

DOOR HINGES

Don't try to cover up poor door adjustment with a striker plate adjustment. The gap on each side of the door should be equal and uniform and there should be no metal-to-metal contact as the door is opened or closed.

1. Determine which hinge bolts must be loosened to move the door in the desired direction.
2. Loosen the hinge bolt(s) just enough to allow the door to be moved with a padded pry bar.
3. Move the door a small amount and check the fit, after tightening the bolts. Be sure that there is no bind or interference with adjacent panels.
4. Repeat this until the door is properly positioned, and tighten all the bolts securely.

Hood, Trunk or Tailgate

As with doors, the outline of hinges should be scribed before removal. The hood and trunk can be aligned by loosening the hinge bolts in their slotted mounting holes and moving the hood or trunk lid as necessary.

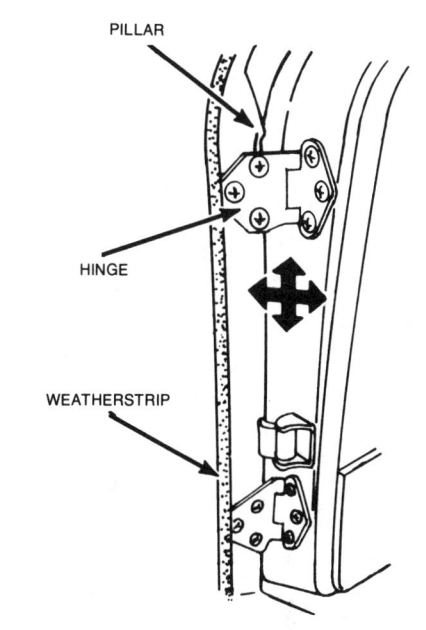

Door hinge adjustment

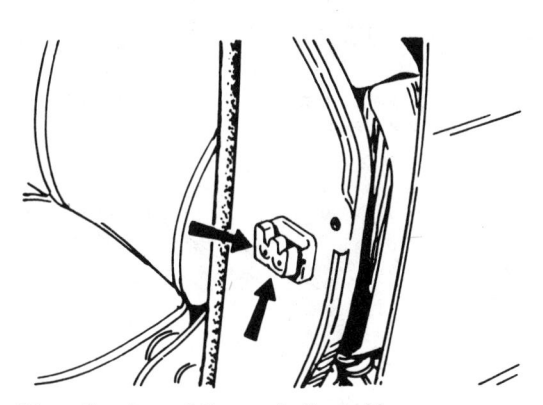

Move the door striker as indicated by arrows

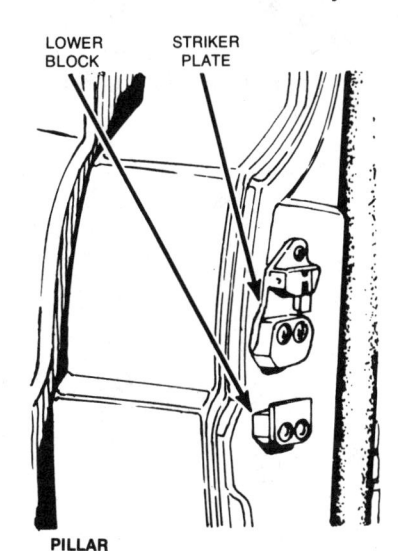

Striker plate and lower block

BODY

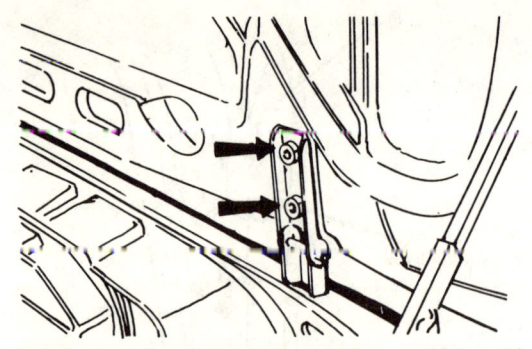

Loosen the hinge boots to permit fore-and-aft and horizontal adjustment

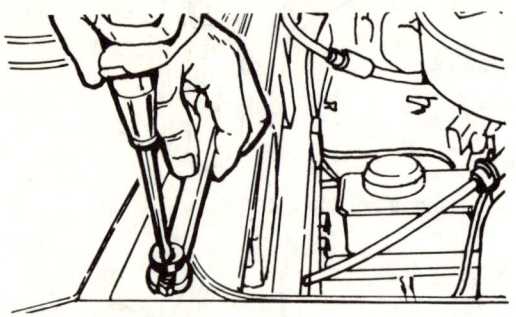

The hood is adjusted vertically by stop-screws at the front and/or rear

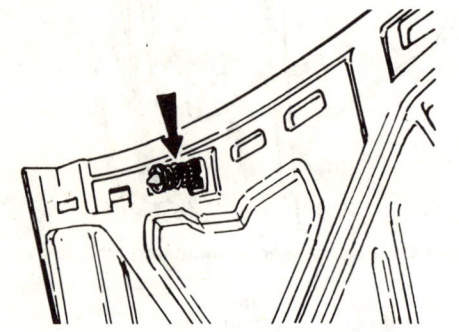

The hood pin can be adjusted for proper lock engagement

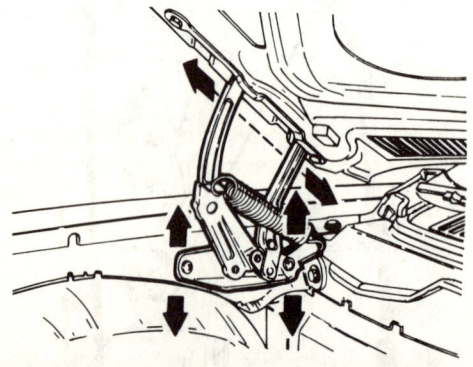

The height of the hood at the rear is adjusted by loosening the bolts that attach the hinge to the body and moving the hood up or down

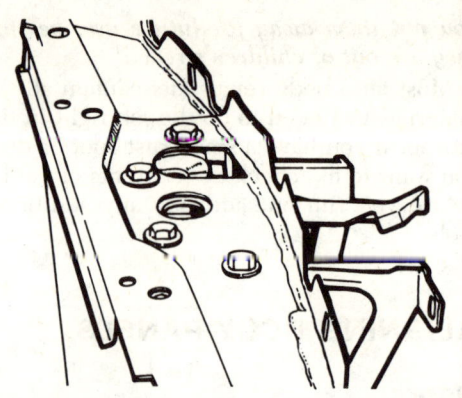

The base of the hood lock can also be repositioned slightly to give more positive lock engagement

The hood and trunk have adjustable catch locations to regulate lock engagement. Bumpers at the front and/or rear of the hood provide a vertical adjustment and the hood lockpin can be adjusted for proper engagement.

The tailgate on the station wagon can be adjusted by loosening the hinge bolts in their slotted mounting holes and moving the tailgate on its hinges. The latchplate and latch striker at the bottom of the tailgate opening can be adjusted to stop rattle. An adjustable bumper is located on each side.

RUST, UNDERCOATING, AND RUSTPROOFING

Rust

Rust is an electrochemical process. It works on ferrous metals (iron and steel) from the inside out due to exposure of unprotected surfaces to air and moisture. The possibility of rust exists practically nationwide—anywhere humidity, industrial pollution or chemical salts are present, rust can form. In coastal areas, the problem is high humidity and salt air; in snowy areas, the problem is chemical salt (de-icer) used to keep the roads clear, and in industrial areas, sulphur dioxide is present in the air from industrial pollution and is changed to sulphuric acid when it rains. The rusting process is accelerated by high temperatures, especially in snowy areas, when vehicles are driven over slushy roads and then left overnight in a heated garage.

Automotive styling also can be a contributor to rust formation. Spot welding of panels creates small pockets that trap moisture and form an environment for rust formation. Fortunately, auto manufacturers have been working hard to increase the corrosion protection of their products. Galvanized sheet metal enjoys much wider use, along with the increased use of plastic and various rust retardant coatings. Manufacturers are also designing out areas in the body where rust-forming moisture can collect.

To prevent rust, you must stop it before it gets started. On new vehicles, there are two ways to accomplish this.

First, the car or truck should be treated with a commercial rustproofing compound. There are many different brands of franchised rustproofers, but most processes involve spraying a waxy "self-healing" compound under the chassis, inside rocker panels, inside doors and fender liners and similar places where rust is likely to form. Prices for a quality rustproofing job range from $100-$250, depending on the area, the brand name and the size of the vehicle.

Ideally, the vehicle should be rustproofed as soon as possible following the purchase. The surfaces of the car or truck have begun to oxidize and deteriorate during shipping. In addition, the car may have sat on a dealer's lot or on a lot at the factory, and once the rust has progressed past the stage of light, powdery surface oxidation rustproofing is not likely to be worthwhile. Professional rustproofers feel that once rust has formed, rustproofing will simply seal in moisture already present. Most franchised rustproofing operations offer a 3-5 year warranty against rust-through, but will not support that warranty if the rustproofing is not applied within three months of the date of manufacture.

Undercoating should not be mistaken for rustproofing. Undercoating is a black, tar-like substance that is applied to the underside of a vehicle. Its basic function is to deaden noises that are transmitted from under the car. It simply cannot get into the crevices and seams where moisture tends to collect. In fact, it may clog up drainage holes and ventilation passages. Some undercoatings also tend to crack or peel with age and only create more moisture and corrosion attracting pockets.

The second thing you should do immediately after purchasing the car is apply a paint sealant. A sealant is a petroleum based product marketed under a wide variety of brand names. It has the same protective properties as a good wax, but bonds to the paint with a chemically inert layer that seals it from the air. If air can't get at the surface, oxidation cannot start.

The paint sealant kit consists of a base coat and a conditioning coat that should be applied every 6-8 months, depending on the manufacturer. The base coat must be applied before waxing, or the wax must first be removed.

Third, keep a garden hose handy for your car in winter. Use it a few times on nice days during the winter for underneath areas, and it will pay big dividends when spring arrives. Spraying under the fenders and other areas which even car washes don't reach will help remove road salt, dirt and other build-ups which help breed rust. Adjust the nozzle to a high-force spray. An old brush will help break up residue, permitting it to be washed away more easily.

It's a somewhat messy job, but worth it in the long run because rust often starts in those hidden areas.

At the same time, wash grime off the door sills and, more importantly, the under portions of the doors, plus the tailgate if you have a station wagon or truck. Applying a coat of wax to those areas at least once before and once during winter will help fend off rust.

When applying the wax to the under parts of the doors, you will note small drain holes. These holes often are plugged with undercoating or dirt. Make sure they are cleaned out to prevent water build-up inside the doors. A small punch or penknife will do the job.

Water from the high-pressure sprays in car washes sometimes can get into the housings for parking and taillights, so take a close look. If they contain water merely loosen the retaining screws and the water should run out.

212 BODY

Repairing Scratches and Small Dents

Step 1. This dent (arrow) is typical of a deep scratch or minor dent. If deep enough, the dent or scratch can be pulled out or hammered out from behind. In this case no straightening is necessary

Step 2. Using an 80-grit grinding disc on an electric drill grind the paint from the surrounding area down to bare metal. This will provide a rough surface for the body filler to grab

Step 3. The area should look like this when you're finished grinding

BODY 213

Step 4. Mix the body filler and cream hardener according to the directions

Step 5. Spread the body filler evenly over the entire area. Be sure to cover the area completely

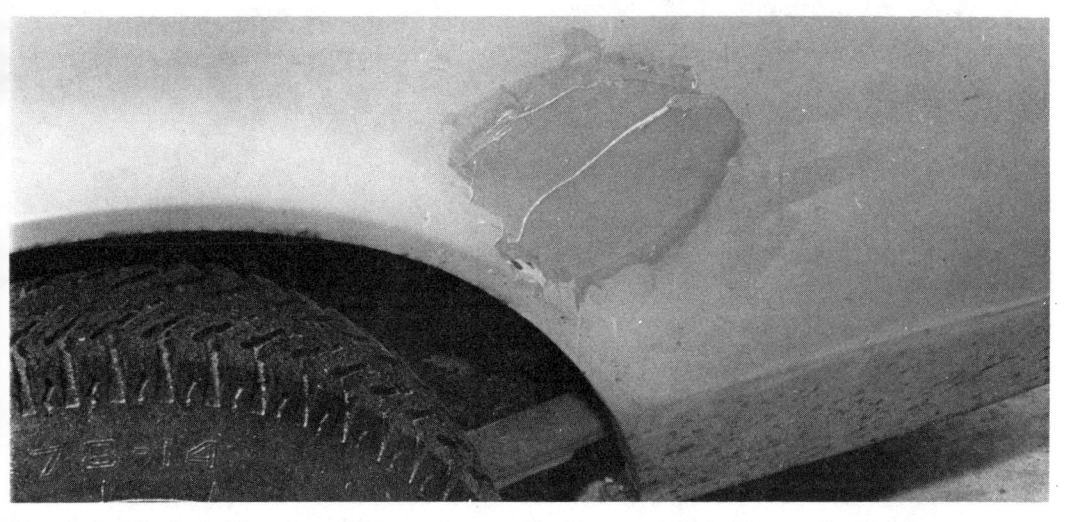

Step 6. Let the body filler dry until the surface can just be scratched with your fingernail

214   BODY

Step 7. Knock the high spots from the body filler with a body file

Step 8. Check frequently with the palm of your hand for high and low spots. If you wind up with low spots, you may have to apply another layer of filler

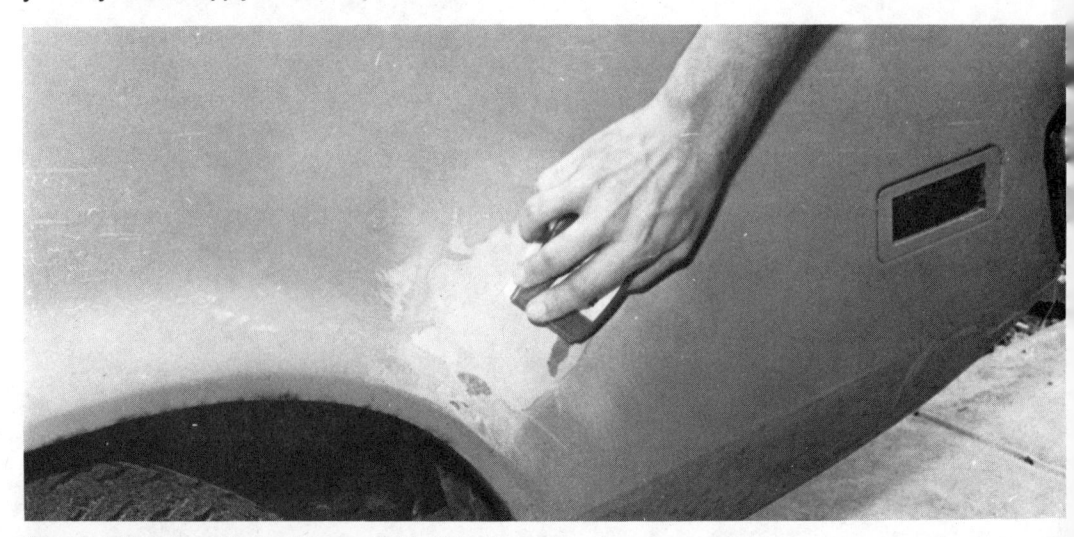

Step 9. Block sand the entire area with 320 grit paper

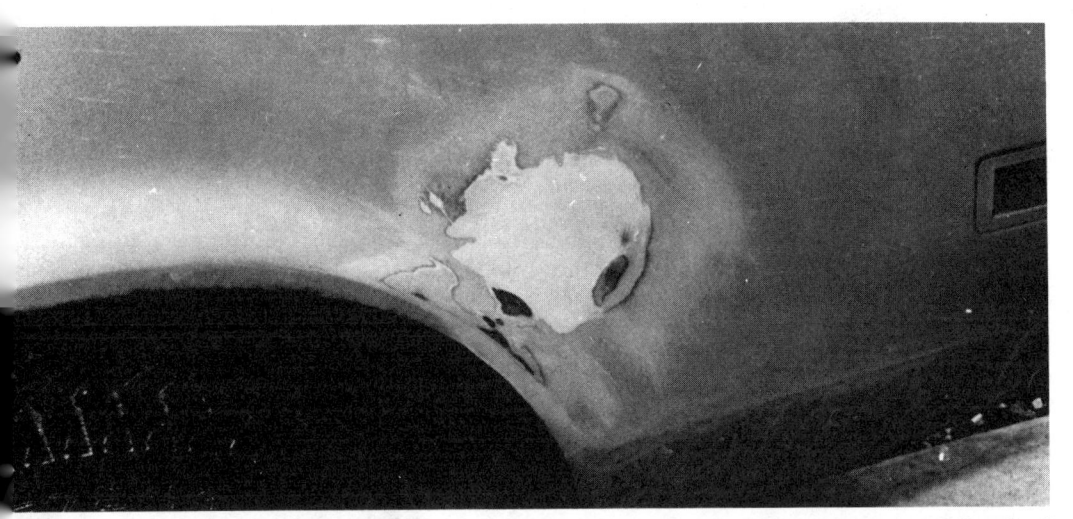

BODY 215

Step 10. When you're finished, the repair should look like this. Note the sand marks extending 2—3 inches out from the repaired area

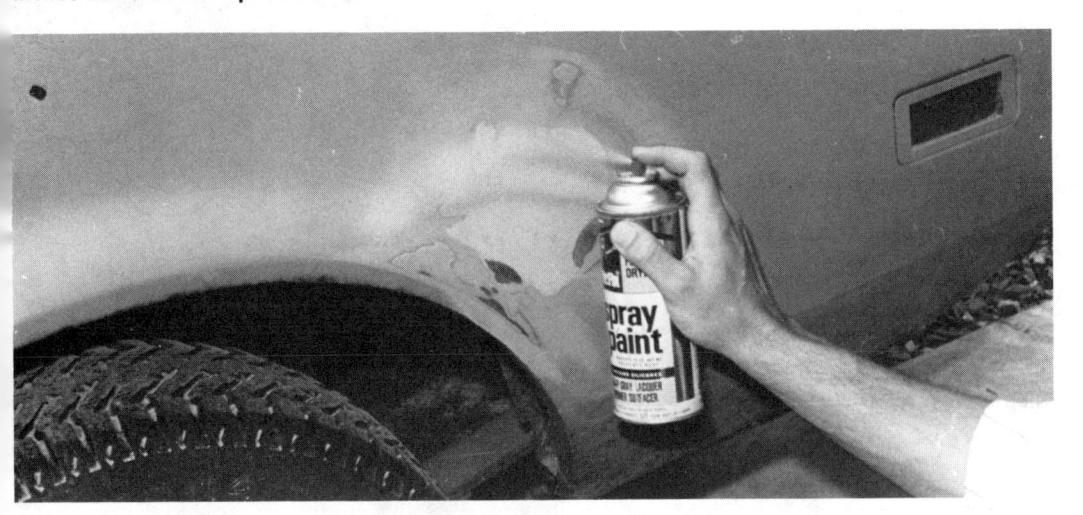

Step 11. Prime the entire area with automotive primer

Step 12. The finished repair ready for the final paint coat. Note that the primer has covered the sanding marks (see Step 10). A repair of this size should be able to be spotpainted with good results

216 BODY

REPAIRING RUST HOLES

One thing you have to remember about rust: even if you grind away all the rusted metal in a panel, and repair the area with any of the kits available, *eventually* the rust will return. There are two reasons for this. One, rust is a chemical reaction that causes pressure under the repair from the inside out. That's how the blisters form. Two, the back side of the panel (and the repair) is wide open to moisture, and unpainted body filler acts like a sponge. That's why the best solution to rust problems is to remove the rusted panel and install a new one or have the rusted area cut out and a new piece of sheet metal welded in its place. The trouble with welding is the expense; sometimes it will cost more than the car or truck is worth.

One of the better solutions to do-it-yourself rust repair is the process using a fiberglass cloth repair kit (shown here). This will give a strong repair that resists cracking and moisture and is relatively easy to use. It can be used on large or small holes and also can be applied over contoured surfaces.

Step 1. Rust areas such as this are common and are easily fixed

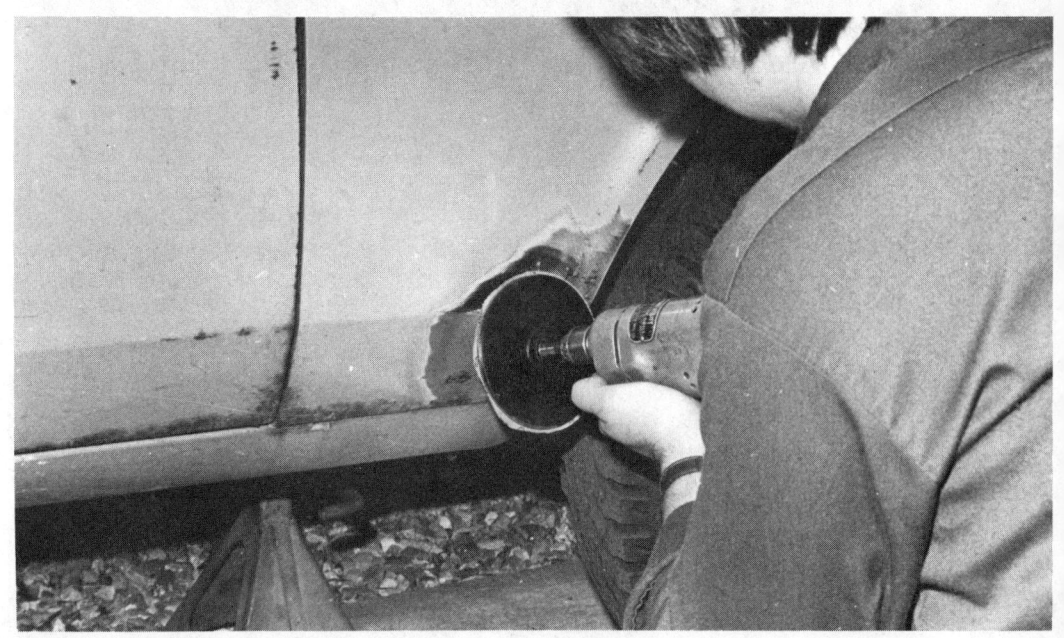

Step 2. Grind away all traces of rust with a 24-grit grinding disc. Be sure to grind back 3—4 inches from the edge of the hole down to bare metal and be sure all traces of rust are removed

BODY 217

Step 3. Be sure all rust is removed from the edges of the metal. The edges must be ground back to un-rusted metal

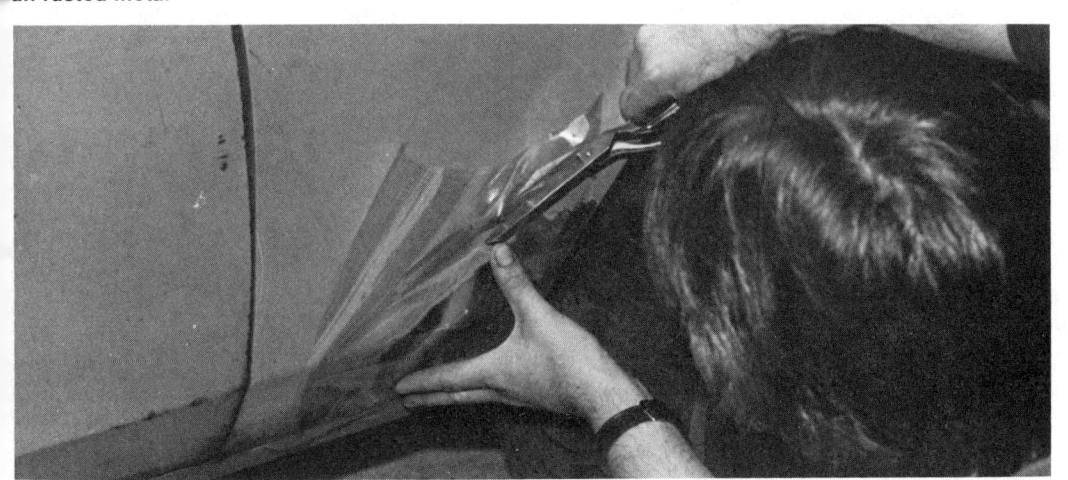

Step 4. If you are going to use release film, cut a piece about 2" larger than the area you have sanded. Place the film over the repair and mark the sanded area on the film. Avoid any unnecessary wrinkling of the film

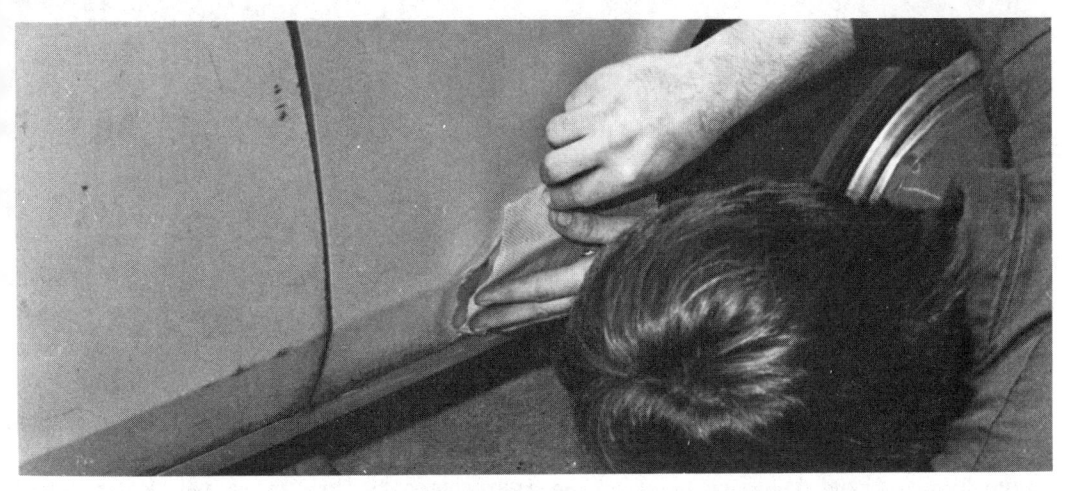

Step 5. Cut 2 pieces of fiberglass matte. One piece should be about 1" smaller than the sanded area and the second piece should be 1" smaller than the first. Use sharp scissors to avoid loose ends

218 BODY

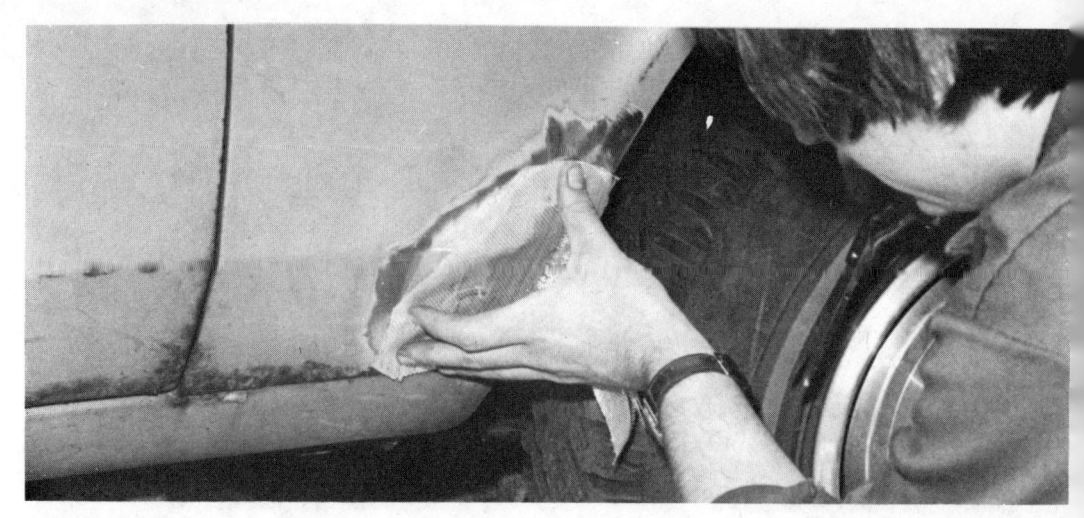

Step 6. Check the dimensions of the release film and cloth by holding them up to the repair area

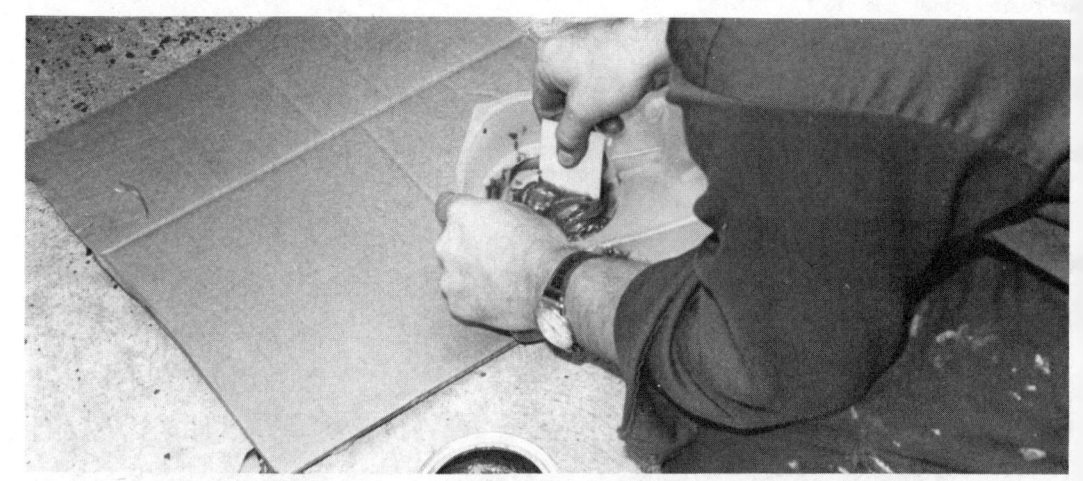

Step 7. Mix enough repair jelly and cream hardener in the mixing tray to saturate the fiberglass material or fill the repair area. Follow the directions on the container

Step 8. Lay the release sheet on a flat surface and spread an even layer of filler, large enough to cover the repair. Lay the smaller piece of fiberglass cloth in the center of the sheet and spread another layer of repair jelly over the fiberglass cloth. Repeat the operation for the larger piece of cloth. If the fiberglass cloth is not used, spread the repair jelly on the release film, concentrated in the middle of the repair

BODY 219

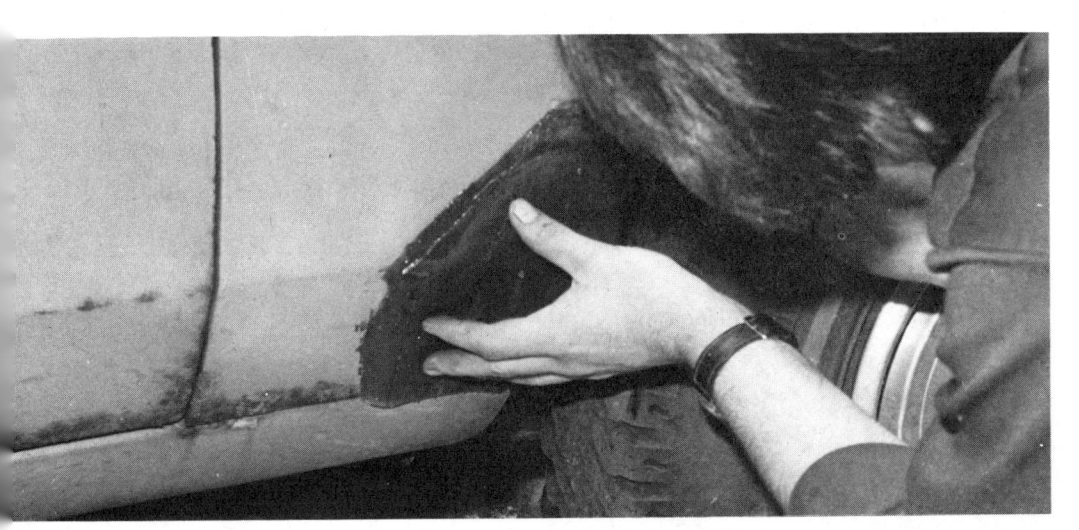

Step 9. Place the repair material over the repair area, with the release film facing outward

Step 10. Use a spreader and work from the center outward to smooth the material, following the body contours. Be sure to remove all air bubbles

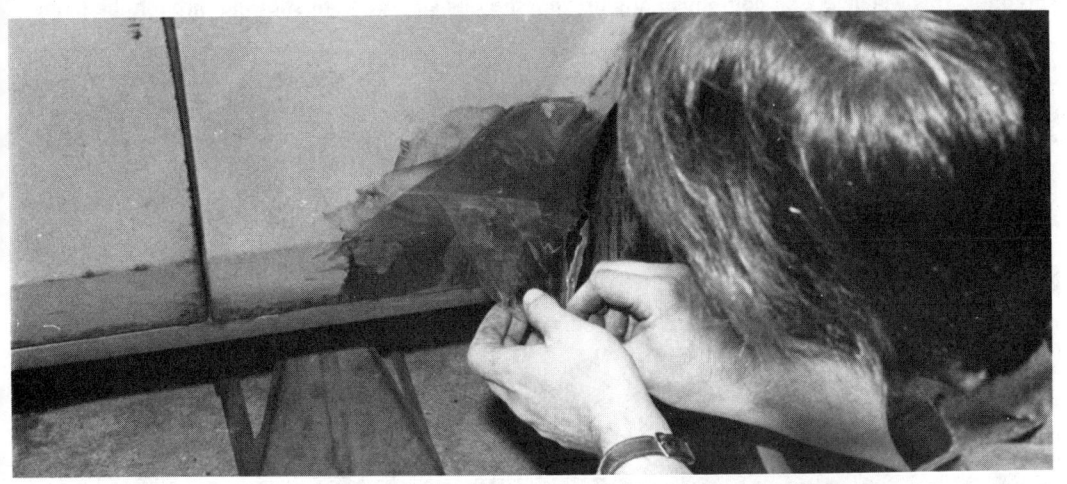

Step 11. Wait until the repair has dried tack-free and peel off the release sheet. The ideal working temperature is 65—90° F. Cooler or warmer temperatures or high humidity may require additional curing time

220   BODY

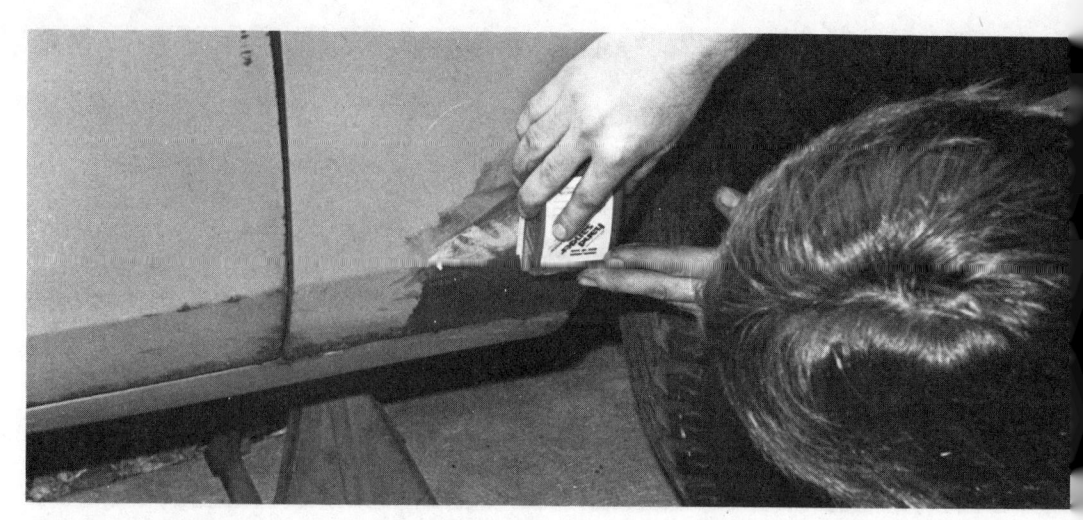

Step 12. Sand and feather-edge the entire area. The initial sanding can be done with a sanding disc on an electric drill if care is used. Finish the sanding with a block sander

Step 13. When the area is sanded smooth, mix some topcoat and hardener and apply it directly with a spreader. This will give a smooth finish and prevent the glass matte from showing through the paint

Step 14. Block sand the topcoat with finishing sandpaper

BODY 221

Step 15. To finish this repair, grind out the surface rust along the top edge of the rocker panel

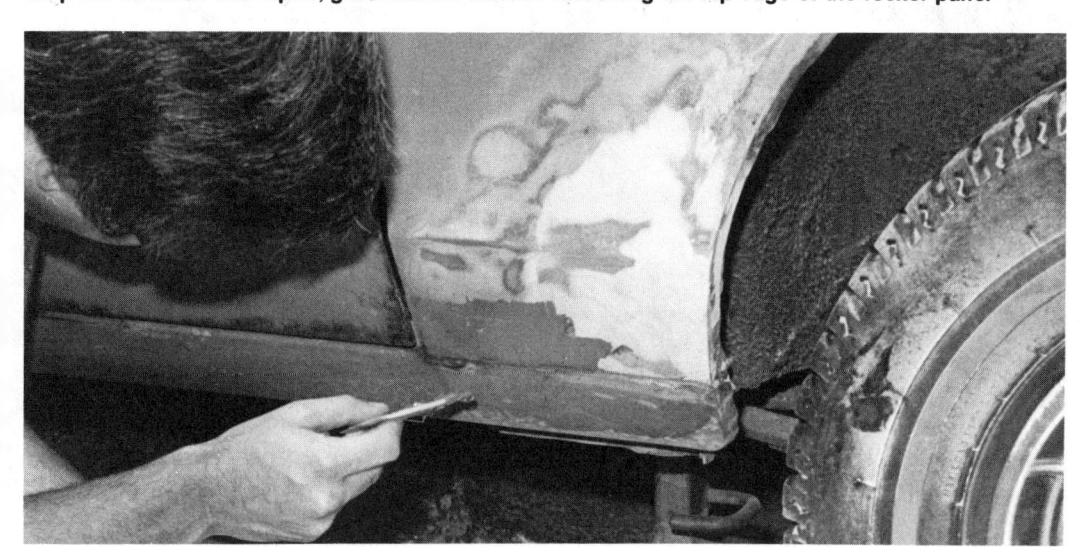

Step 16. Mix some more repair jelly and cream hardener and apply it directly over the surface

Step 17. When it dries tack-free, block sand the surface smooth

Step 18. If necessary, mask off adjacent panels and spray the entire repair with primer. You are now ready for a color coat

AUTO BODY CARE

There are hundreds—maybe thousands—of products on the market, all designed to protect or aid your car's finish in some manner. There are as many different products as there are ways to use them, but they all have one thing in common—the surface must be clean.

Washing

The primary ingredient for washing your car is water, preferably "soft" water. In many areas of the country, the local water supply is "hard" containing many minerals. The little rings or film that is left on your car's surface after it has dried is the result of "hard" water.

Since you usually can't change the local water supply, the next best thing is to dry the surface before it has a chance to dry itself.

Into the water you usually add soap. Don't use detergents or common, coarse soaps. Your car's paint never truly dries out, but is always evaporating residual oils into the air. Harsh detergents will remove these oils, causing the paint to dry faster than normal. Instead use warm water and a non-detergent soap made especially for waxed surfaces or a liquid soap made for waxed surfaces or a liquid soap made for washing dishes by hand.

Other products that can be used on painted surfaces include baking soda or plain soda water for stubborn dirt.

Wash the car completely, starting at the top, and rinse it completely clean. Abrasive grit should be loaded off under water pressure; scrubbing grit off will scratch the finish. The best washing tool is a sponge, cleaning mitt or soft towel. Whichever you choose, replace it often as each tends to absorb grease and dirt.

Other ways to get a better wash include:

• Don't wash your car in the sun or when the finish is hot.
• Use water pressure to remove caked-on dirt.
• Remove tree-sap and bird effluence immediately. Such substances will eat through wax, polish and paint.

One of the best implements to dry your car is a turkish towel or an old, soft bath towel. Anything with a deep nap will hold any dirt in suspension and not grind it into the paint.

Harder cloths will only grind the grit into the paint making more scratches. Always start drying at the top, followed by the hood and trunk and sides. You'll find there's always more dirt near the rocker panels and wheelwells which will wind up on the rest of the car if you dry these areas first.

Cleaners, Waxes and Polishes

Before going any farther you should know the function of various products.

Cleaners—remove the top layer of dead pigment or paint.

Rubbing or polishing compounds—used to remove stubborn dirt, get rid of minor scratches, smooth away imperfections and partially restore badly weathered paint.

Polishes—contain no abrasives or waxes; they shine the paint by adding oils to the paint.

Waxes—are a protective coating for the polish.

CLEANERS AND COMPOUNDS

Before you apply any wax, you'll have to remove oxidation, road film and other types of pollutants that washing alone will not remove.

The paint on your car never dries completely. There are always residual oils evaporating from the paint into the air. When enough oils are present in the paint, it has a healthy shine (gloss). When too many oils evaporate the paint takes on a whitish cast known as oxidation. The idea of polishing and waxing is to keep enough oil present in the painted surface to prevent oxidation; but when it occurs, the only recourse is to remove the top layer of "dead" paint, exposing the healthy paint underneath.

Products to remove oxidation and road film are sold under a variety of generic names—polishes, cleaner, rubbing compound, cleaner/polish, polish/cleaner, self-polishing wax, pre-wax cleaner, finish restorer and many more. Regardless of name there are two types of cleaners—abrasive cleaners (sometimes called polishing or rubbing compounds) that remove oxidation by grinding away the top layer of "dead" paint, or chemical cleaners that dissolve the "dead" pigment, allowing it to be wiped away.

Abrasive cleaners, by their nature, leave thousands of minute scratches in the finish, which must be polished out later. These should only be used in extreme cases, but are usually the only thing to use on badly oxidized paint finishes. Chemical cleaners are much milder but are not strong enough for severe cases of oxidation or weathered paint.

The most popular cleaners are liquid or paste abrasive polishing and rubbing compounds. Polishing compounds have a finer abrasive grit for medium duty work. Rubbing compounds are a coarser abrasive and for heavy duty work. Unless you are familiar with how to use compounds, be very careful. Excessive rubbing with any type of compound or cleaner can grind right through the paint to primer or bare metal. Follow the directions on the container—depending on type, the cleaner may or may not be OK for your paint. For example, some cleaners are not formulated for acrylic lacquer finishes.

When a small area needs compounding or heavy polishing, it's best to do the job by hand. Some people prefer a powered buffer for large areas. Avoid cutting through the paint along styling edges on the body. Small, hand operations where the compound is applied and rubbed using cloth folded into a thick ball allow you to work in straight lines along such edges.

To avoid cutting through on the edges when using a power buffer, try masking tape. Just cover the edge with tape while using power. Then finish the job by hand with the tape removed. Even then work carefully. The paint tends to be a lot thinner along the sharp ridges stamped into the panels.

Whether compounding by machine or by hand, only work on a small area and apply the compound sparingly. If the materials are spread too thin, or allowed to sit too long, they dry out. Once dry they lose the ability to deliver a smooth, clean finish. Also, dried out polish tends to cause the buffer to stick in one spot. This in turn can burn or cut through the finish.

WAXES AND POLISHES

Your car's finish can be protected in a number of ways. A cleaner/wax or polish/cleaner followed by wax or variations of each all provide good results. The two-step approach (polish followed by wax) is probably slightly better but consumes more time and effort. Properly fed with oils, your paint should never need cleaning, but despite the best polishing job, it won't last unless it's protected with wax. Without wax, polish must be renewed at least once a month to prevent oxidation. Years ago (some still swear by it today), the best wax was made from the Brazilian palm, the Carnuba, favored for its vegetable base and high melting point. However, modern synthetic waxes are harder, which means they protect against moisture better, and chemically inert silicone is used for a long lasting protection. The only problem with silicone wax is that it penetrates all layers of paint. To repaint or touch up a panel or car protected by silicone wax, you have to completely strip the finish to avoid "fisheyes."

Under normal conditions, silicone waxes will last 4–6 months, but you have to be careful of wax build-up from too much waxing. Too thick a coat of wax is just as bad as no wax at all; it stops the paint from breathing.

Combination cleaners/waxes have become popular lately because they remove the old layer of wax plus light oxidation, while putting on a fresh coat of wax at the same time. Some cleaners/waxes contain abrasive cleaners which require caution, although many cleaner/waxes use a chemical cleaner.

Applying Wax or Polish

You may view polishing and waxing your car as a pleasant way to spend an afternoon, or as a boring chore, but it has to be done to keep the paint on your car. Caring for the paint doesn't require special tools, but you should follow a few rules.

1. Use a good quality wax.
2. Before applying any wax or polish, be sure the surface is completely clean. Just because the car looks clean, doesn't mean it's ready for polish or wax.
3. If the finish on your car is weathered, dull, or oxidized, it will probably have to be compounded to remove the old or oxidized paint. If the paint is simply dulled from lack of care, one of the non-abrasive cleaners known as polishing compounds will do the trick. If the paint is severely scratched or really dull, you'll probably have to use a rubbing compound to prepare the finish for waxing. If you're not sure which one to use, use the polishing compound, since you can easily ruin the finish by using too strong a compound.
4. Don't apply wax, polish or compound in direct sunlight, even if the directions on the can say you can. Most waxes will not cure properly in bright sunlight and you'll probably end up with a blotchy looking finish.
5. Don't rub the wax off too soon. The result will be a wet, dull looking finish. Let the wax dry thoroughly before buffing it off.
6. A constant debate among car enthusiasts is how wax should be applied. Some maintain pastes or liquids should be applied in a circular motion, but body shop experts have long thought that this approach results in barely detectable circular abrasions, especially on cars that are waxed frequently. They advise rubbing in straight lines, especially if any kind of cleaner is involved.
7. If an applicator is not supplied with the wax, use a piece of soft cheesecloth or very soft lint-free material. The same applies to buffing the surface.

SPECIAL SURFACES

One-step combination cleaner and wax formulas shouldn't be used on many of the special surfaces which abound on cars. The one-step materials contain abrasives to achieve a clean surface under the wax top coat. The abrasives are so mild that you could clean a car every week for a couple of years without fear of rubbing through the paint. But this same level of abrasiveness might, through repeated use, damage decals used for special trim effects. This includes wide stripes, wood-grain trim and other appliques.

Painted plastics must be cleaned with care. If a cleaner is too aggressive it will cut through the paint and expose the primer. If bright trim such as polished aluminum or chrome is painted, cleaning must be performed with even greater care. If rubbing compound is being used, it will cut faster than polish.

Abrasive cleaners will dull an acrylic finish. The best way to clean these newer finishes is with a non-abrasive liquid polish. Only dirt and oxidation, not paint, will be removed.

Taking a few minutes to read the instructions on the can of polish or wax will help prevent making serious mistakes. Not all preparations will work on all surfaces. And some are intended for power application while others will only work when applied by hand.

Don't get the idea that just pouring on some polish and then hitting it with a buffer will suffice. Power equipment speeds the operation. But it also adds a measure of risk. It's very easy to damage the finish if you use the wrong methods or materials.

Caring for Chrome

Read the label on the container. Many products are formulated specifically for chrome, but others contain abrasives that will scratch the chrome finish. If it isn't recommended for chrome, don't use it.

Never use steel wool or kitchen soap pads to clean chrome. Be careful not to get chrome cleaner on paint or interior vinyl surfaces. If you do, get it off immediately.

Troubleshooting 11

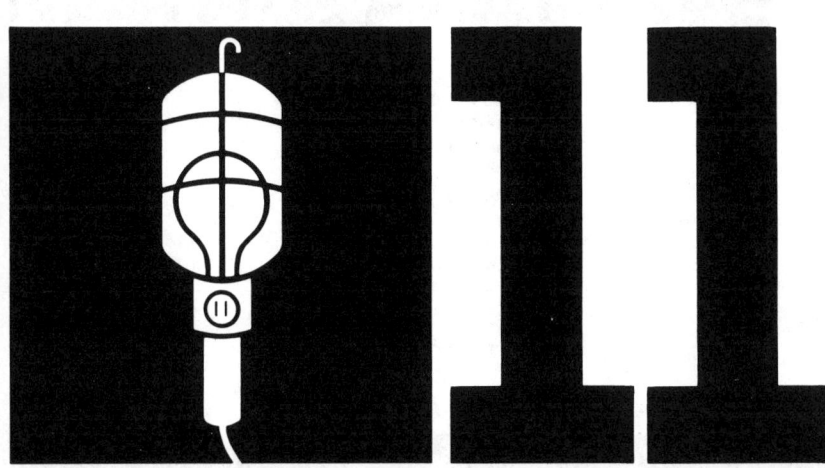

This section is designed to aid in the quick, accurate diagnosis of automotive problems. While automotive repairs can be made by many people, accurate troubleshooting is a rare skill for the amateur and professional alike.

In its simplest state, troubleshooting is an exercise in logic. It is essential to realize that an automobile is really composed of a series of systems. Some of these systems are interrelated; others are not. Automobiles operate within a framework of logical rules and physical laws, and the key to troubleshooting is a good understanding of all the automotive systems.

This section breaks the car or truck down into its component systems, allowing the problem to be isolated. The charts and diagnostic road maps list the most common problems and the most probable causes of trouble. Obviously it would be impossible to list every possible problem that could happen along with every possible cause, but it will locate MOST problems and eliminate a lot of unnecessary guesswork. The systematic format will locate problems within a given system, but, because many automotive systems are interrelated, the solution to your particular problem may be found in a number of systems on the car or truck.

USING THE TROUBLESHOOTING CHARTS

This book contains all of the specific information that the average do-it-yourself mechanic needs to repair and maintain his or her car or truck. The troubleshooting charts are designed to be used in conjunction with the specific procedures and information in the text. For instance, troubleshooting a point-type ignition system is fairly standard for all models, but you may be directed to the text to find procedures for troubleshooting an individual type of electronic ignition. You will also have to refer to the specification charts throughout the book for specifications applicable to your car or truck.

TOOLS AND EQUIPMENT

The tools illustrated in Chapter 1 (plus two more diagnostic pieces) will be adequate to troubleshoot most problems. The two other tools needed are a voltmeter and an ohmmeter. These can be purchased separately or in combination, known as a VOM meter.

In the event that other tools are required, they will be noted in the procedures.

TROUBLESHOOTING

Troubleshooting Engine Problems
See Chapters 2, 3, 4 for more information and service procedures.

Index to Systems

System	To Test	Group
Battery	Engine need not be running	1
Starting system	Engine need not be running	2
Primary electrical system	Engine need not be running	3
Secondary electrical system	Engine need not be running	4
Fuel system	Engine need not be running	5
Engine compression	Engine need not be running	6
Engine vacuum	Engine must be running	7
Secondary electrical system	Engine must be running	8
Valve train	Engine must be running	9
Exhaust system	Engine must be running	10
Cooling system	Engine must be running	11
Engine lubrication	Engine must be running	12

Index to Problems

Problem: Symptom	Begin at Specific Diagnosis, Number
Engine Won't Start:	
Starter doesn't turn	1.1, 2.1
Starter turns, engine doesn't	2.1
Starter turns engine very slowly	1.1, 2.4
Starter turns engine normally	3.1, 4.1
Starter turns engine very quickly	6.1
Engine fires intermittently	4.1
Engine fires consistently	5.1, 6.1
Engine Runs Poorly:	
Hard starting	3.1, 4.1, 5.1, 8.1
Rough idle	4.1, 5.1, 8.1
Stalling	3.1, 4.1, 5.1, 8.1
Engine dies at high speeds	4.1, 5.1
Hesitation (on acceleration from standing stop)	5.1, 8.1
Poor pickup	4.1, 5.1, 8.1
Lack of power	3.1, 4.1, 5.1, 8.1
Backfire through the carburetor	4.1, 8.1, 9.1
Backfire through the exhaust	4.1, 8.1, 9.1
Blue exhaust gases	6.1, 7.1
Black exhaust gases	5.1
Running on (after the ignition is shut off)	3.1, 8.1
Susceptible to moisture	4.1
Engine misfires under load	4.1, 7.1, 8.4, 9.1
Engine misfires at speed	4.1, 8.4
Engine misfires at idle	3.1, 4.1, 5.1, 7.1, 8.4

Sample Section

Test and Procedure	Results and Indications	Proceed to
4.1—Check for spark: Hold each spark plug wire approximately ¼" from ground with gloves or a heavy, dry rag. Crank the engine and observe the spark.	If no spark is evident:	4.2
	If spark is good in some cases:	4.3
	If spark is good in all cases:	4.6

TROUBLESHOOTING

Specific Diagnosis

This section is arranged so that following each test, instructions are given to proceed to another, until a problem is diagnosed.

Section 1—Battery

Test and Procedure	Results and Indications	Proceed to
1.1—Inspect the battery visually for case condition (corrosion, cracks) and water level.	If case is cracked, replace battery:	1.4
	If the case is intact, remove corrosion with a solution of baking soda and water (**CAUTION**: *do not get the solution into the battery*), and fill with water:	1.2
Inspect the battery case		
1.2—Check the battery cable connections: Insert a screwdriver between the battery post and the cable clamp. Turn the headlights on high beam, and observe them as the screwdriver is gently twisted to ensure good metal to metal contact.	If the lights brighten, remove and clean the clamp and post; coat the post with petroleum jelly, install and tighten the clamp:	1.4
	If no improvement is noted:	1.3
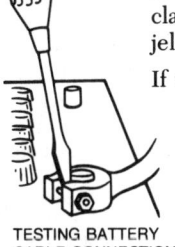 *TESTING BATTERY CABLE CONNECTIONS USING A SCREWDRIVER*		
1.3—Test the state of charge of the battery using an individual cell tester or hydrometer.	If indicated, charge the battery. **NOTE:** *If no obvious reason exists for the low state of charge (i.e., battery age, prolonged storage), proceed to:*	1.4

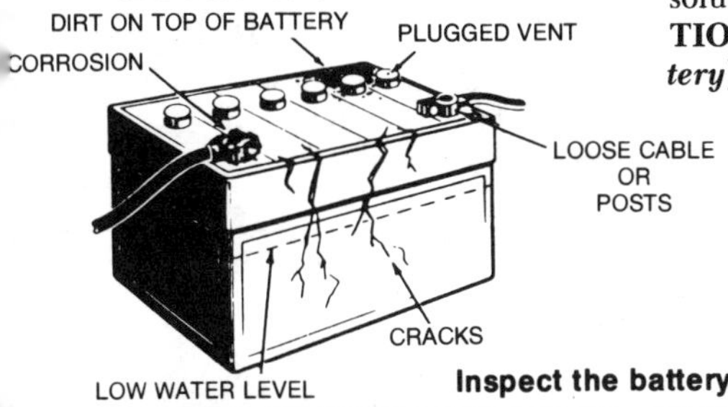

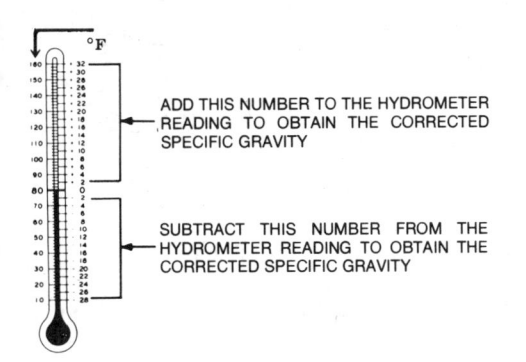

Specific Gravity (@ 80° F.)

Minimum	Battery Charge
1.260	100% Charged
1.230	75% Charged
1.200	50% Charged
1.170	25% Charged
1.140	Very Little Power Left
1.110	Completely Discharged

ADD THIS NUMBER TO THE HYDROMETER READING TO OBTAIN THE CORRECTED SPECIFIC GRAVITY

SUBTRACT THIS NUMBER FROM THE HYDROMETER READING TO OBTAIN THE CORRECTED SPECIFIC GRAVITY

The effects of temperature on battery specific gravity (left) and amount of battery charge in relation to specific gravity (right)

1.4—Visually inspect battery cables for cracking, bad connection to ground, or bad connection to starter.	If necessary, tighten connections or replace the cables:	2.1

Section 2—Starting System
See Chapter 3 for service procedures

Test and Procedure	Results and Indications	Proceed to
Note: Tests in Group 2 are performed with coil high tension lead disconnected to prevent accidental starting.		
2.1—Test the starter motor and solenoid: Connect a jumper from the battery post of the solenoid (or relay) to the starter post of the solenoid (or relay).	If starter turns the engine normally:	2.2
	If the starter buzzes, or turns the engine very slowly:	2.4
	If no response, replace the solenoid (or relay).	3.1
	If the starter turns, but the engine doesn't, ensure that the flywheel ring gear is intact. If the gear is undamaged, replace the starter drive.	3.1
2.2—Determine whether ignition override switches are functioning properly (clutch start switch, neutral safety switch), by connecting a jumper across the switch(es), and turning the ignition switch to "start".	If starter operates, adjust or replace switch:	3.1
	If the starter doesn't operate:	2.3
2.3—Check the ignition switch "start" position: Connect a 12V test lamp or voltmeter between the starter post of the solenoid (or relay) and ground. Turn the ignition switch to the "start" position, and jiggle the key.	If the lamp doesn't light or the meter needle doesn't move when the switch is turned, check the ignition switch for loose connections, cracked insulation, or broken wires. Repair or replace as necessary:	3.1
	If the lamp flickers or needle moves when the key is jiggled, replace the ignition switch.	3.3

Checking the ignition switch "start" position

STARTER RELAY (IF EQUIPPED)

2.4—Remove and bench test the starter, according to specifications in the engine electrical section.	If the starter does not meet specifications, repair or replace as needed:	3.1
	If the starter is operating properly:	2.5
2.5—Determine whether the engine can turn freely: Remove the spark plugs, and check for water in the cylinders. Check for water on the dipstick, or oil in the radiator. Attempt to turn the engine using an 18" flex drive and socket on the crankshaft pulley nut or bolt.	If the engine will turn freely only with the spark plugs out, and hydrostatic lock (water in the cylinders) is ruled out, check valve timing:	9.2
	If engine will not turn freely, and it is known that the clutch and transmission are free, the engine must be disassembled for further evaluation:	Chapter 3

TROUBLESHOOTING

Section 3—Primary Electrical System

Test and Procedure	Results and Indications	Proceed to
3.1—Check the ignition switch "on" position: Connect a jumper wire between the distributor side of the coil and ground, and a 12V test lamp between the switch side of the coil and ground. Remove the high tension lead from the coil. Turn the ignition switch on and jiggle the key.	If the lamp lights:	3.2
	If the lamp flickers when the key is jiggled, replace the ignition switch:	3.3
	If the lamp doesn't light, check for loose or open connections. If none are found, remove the ignition switch and check for continuity. If the switch is faulty, replace it:	3.3

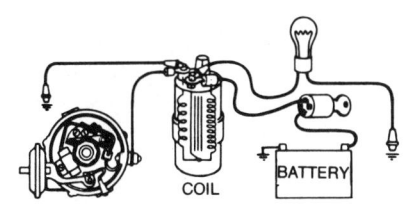

Checking the ignition switch "on" position

3.2—Check the ballast resistor or resistance wire for an open circuit, using an ohmmeter. See Chapter 3 for specific tests.	Replace the resistor or resistance wire if the resistance is zero. **NOTE:** *Some ignition systems have no ballast resistor.*	3.3

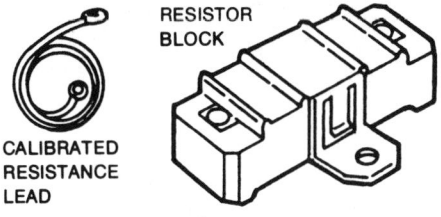

Two types of resistors

3.3—On point-type ignition systems, visually inspect the breaker points for burning, pitting or excessive wear. Gray coloring of the point contact surfaces is normal. Rotate the crankshaft until the contact heel rests on a high point of the distributor cam and adjust the point gap to specifications. On electronic ignition models, remove the distributor cap and visually inspect the armature. Ensure that the armature pin is in place, and that the armature is on tight and rotates when the engine is cranked. Make sure there are no cracks, chips or rounded edges on the armature.	If the breaker points are intact, clean the contact surfaces with fine emery cloth, and adjust the point gap to specifications. If the points are worn, replace them. On electronic systems, replace any parts which appear defective. If condition persists:	3.4

230 TROUBLESHOOTING

Test and Procedure	Results and Indications	Proceed to
3.4—On point-type ignition systems, connect a dwell-meter between the distributor primary lead and ground. Crank the engine and observe the point dwell angle. On electronic ignition systems, conduct a stator (magnetic pickup assembly) test. See Chapter 3.	On point-type systems, adjust the dwell angle if necessary. **NOTE:** *Increasing the point gap decreases the dwell angle and vice-versa.* If the dwell meter shows little or no reading; On electronic ignition systems, if the stator is bad, replace the stator. If the stator is good, proceed to the other tests in Chapter 3.	3.6 3.5

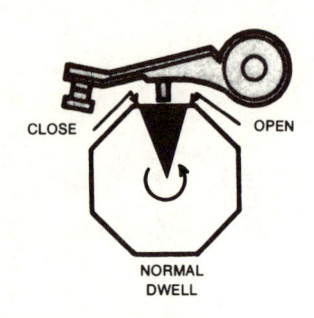

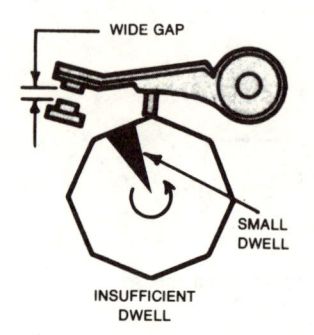

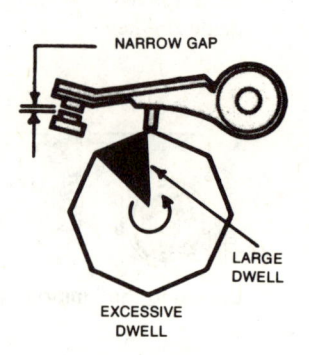

Dwell is a function of point gap

3.5—On the point-type ignition systems, check the condenser for short: connect an ohmeter across the condenser body and the pigtail lead.	If any reading other than infinite is noted, replace the condenser	3.6

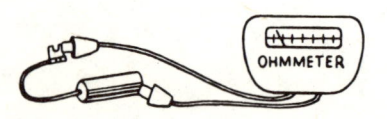

Checking the condenser for short

3.6—Test the coil primary resistance: On point-type ignition systems, connect an ohmmeter across the coil primary terminals, and read the resistance on the low scale. Note whether an external ballast resistor or resistance wire is used. On electronic ignition systems, test the coil primary resistance as in Chapter 3.	Point-type ignition coils utilizing ballast resistors or resistance wires should have approximately 1.0 ohms resistance. Coils with internal resistors should have approximately 4.0 ohms resistance. If values far from the above are noted, replace the coil.	4.1

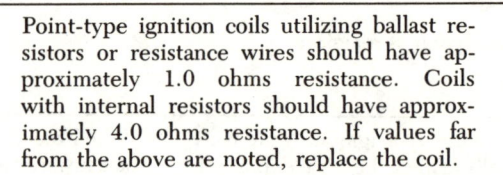

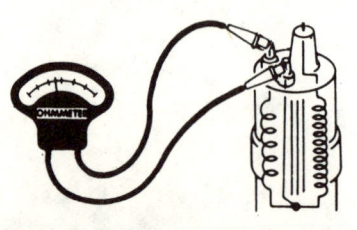

Check the coil primary resistance

TROUBLESHOOTING 231

Section 4—Secondary Electrical System
See Chapters 2–3 for service procedures

Test and Procedure	Results and Indications	Proceed to
4.1—Check for spark: Hold each spark plug wire approximately ¼" from ground with gloves or a heavy, dry rag. Crank the engine, and observe the spark.	If no spark is evident:	4.2
	If spark is good in some cylinders:	4.3
	If spark is good in all cylinders:	4.6

Check for spark at the plugs

4.2—Check for spark at the coil high tension lead: Remove the coil high tension lead from the distributor and position it approximately ¼" from ground. Crank the engine and observe spark. **CAUTION**: *This test should not be performed on engines equipped with electronic ignition.*	If the spark is good and consistent:	4.3
	If the spark is good but intermittent, test the primary electrical system starting at 3.3:	3.3
	If the spark is weak or non-existent, replace the coil high tension lead, clean and tighten all connections and retest. If no improvement is noted:	4.4
4.3—Visually inspect the distributor cap and rotor for burned or corroded contacts, cracks, carbon tracks, or moisture. Also check the fit of the rotor on the distributor shaft (where applicable).	If moisture is present, dry thoroughly, and retest per 4.1:	4.1
	If burned or excessively corroded contacts, cracks, or carbon tracks are noted, replace the defective part(s) and retest per 4.1:	4.1
	If the rotor and cap appear intact, or are only slightly corroded, clean the contacts thoroughly (including the cap towers and spark plug wire ends) and retest per 4.1:	
	If the spark is good in all cases:	4.6
	If the spark is poor in all cases:	4.5

Inspect the distributor cap and rotor

232 TROUBLESHOOTING

Test and Procedure	Results and Indications	Proceed to
4.4—Check the coil secondary resistance: On point-type systems connect an ohmmeter across the distributor side of the coil and the coil tower. Read the resistance on the high scale of the ohmmeter. On electronic ignition systems, see Chapter 3 for specific tests.	The resistance of a satisfactory coil should be between 4,000 and 10,000 ohms. If resistance is considerably higher (i.e., 40,000 ohms) replace the coil and retest per 4.1. **NOTE:** *This does not apply to high performance coils.*	

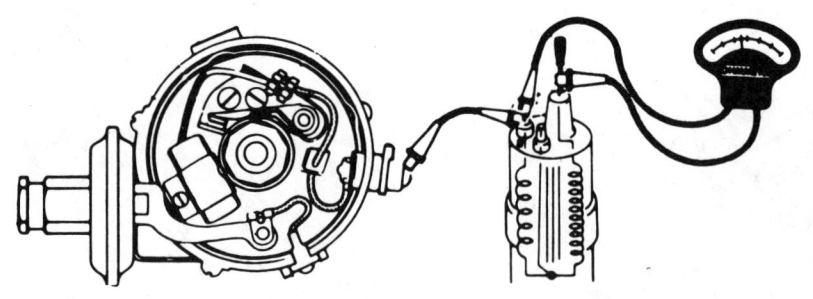

Testing the coil secondary resistance

4.5—Visually inspect the spark plug wires for cracking or brittleness. Ensure that no two wires are positioned so as to cause induction firing (adjacent and parallel). Remove each wire, one by one, and check resistance with an ohmmeter.	Replace any cracked or brittle wires. If any of the wires are defective, replace the entire set. Replace any wires with excessive resistance (over 8000 Ω per foot for suppression wire), and separate any wires that might cause induction firing.	4.6

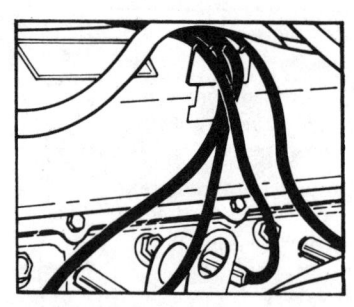

Misfiring can be the result of spark plug leads to adjacent, consecutively firing cylinders running parallel and too close together

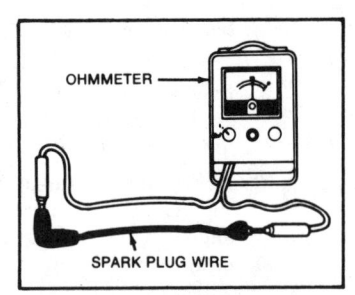

On point-type ignition systems, check the spark plug wires as shown. On electronic ignitions, do not remove the wire from the distributor cap terminal; instead, test through the cap

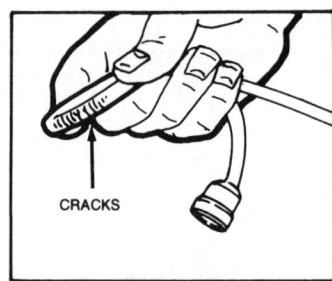

Spark plug wires can be checked visually by bending them in a loop over your finger. This will reveal any cracks, burned or broken insulation. Any wire with cracked insulation should be replaced

4.6—Remove the spark plugs, noting the cylinders from which they were removed, and evaluate according to the color photos in the middle of this book.	See following.	See following.

TROUBLESHOOTING 233

Test and Procedure	Results and Indications	Proceed to
4.7—Examine the location of all the plugs.	The following diagrams illustrate some of the conditions that the location of plugs will reveal.	4.8

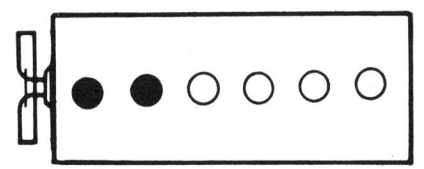

Two adjacent plugs are fouled in a 6-cylinder engine, 4-cylinder engine or either bank of a V-8. This is probably due to a blown head gasket between the two cylinders

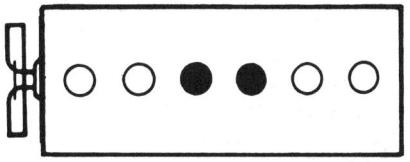

The two center plugs in a 6-cylinder engine are fouled. Raw fuel may be "boiled" out of the carburetor into the intake manifold after the engine is shut-off. Stop-start driving can also foul the center plugs, due to overly rich mixture. Proper float level, a new float needle and seat or use of an insulating spacer may help this problem

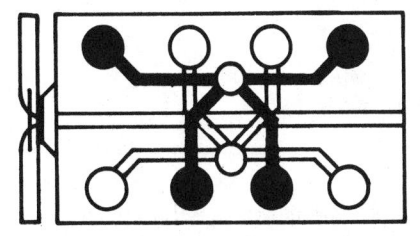

An unbalanced carburetor is indicated. Following the fuel flow on this particular design shows that the cylinders fed by the right-hand barrel are fouled from overly rich mixture, while the cylinders fed by the left-hand barrel are normal

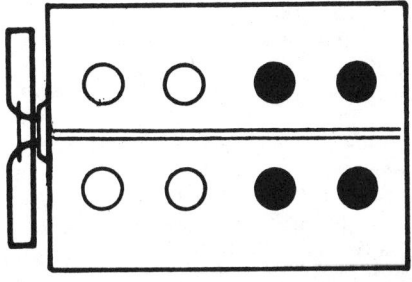

If the four rear plugs are overheated, a cooling system problem is suggested. A thorough cleaning of the cooling system may restore coolant circulation and cure the problem

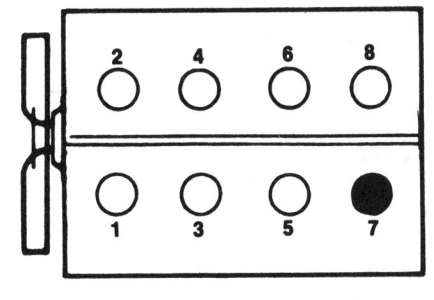

Finding one plug overheated may indicate an intake manifold leak near the affected cylinder. If the overheated plug is the second of two adjacent, consecutively firing plugs, it could be the result of ignition cross-firing. Separating the leads to these two plugs will eliminate cross-fire

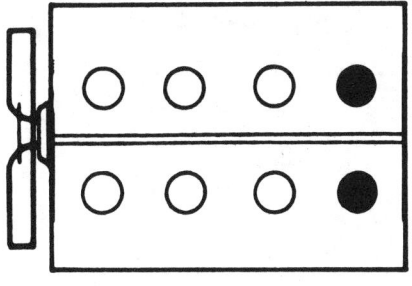

Occasionally, the two rear plugs in large, lightly used V-8's will become oil fouled. High oil consumption and smoky exhaust may also be noticed. It is probably due to plugged oil drain holes in the rear of the cylinder head, causing oil to be sucked in around the valve stems. This usually occurs in the rear cylinders first, because the engine slants that way

TROUBLESHOOTING

Test and Procedure	Results and Indications	Proceed to
4.8—Determine the static ignition timing. Using the crankshaft pulley timing marks as a guide, locate top dead center on the compression stroke of the number one cylinder.	The rotor should be pointing toward the No. 1 tower in the distributor cap, and, on electronic ignitions, the armature spoke for that cylinder should be lined up with the stator.	4.8
4.9—Check coil polarity. Connect a voltmeter negative lead to the coil high tension lead, and the positive lead to ground (**NOTE:** *Reverse the hook-up for positive ground systems*). Crank the engine momentarily.	If the voltmeter reads up-scale, the polarity is correct:	5.1
	If the voltmeter reads down-scale, reverse the coil polarity (switch the primary leads):	5.1

Checking coil polarity

Section 5—Fuel System
See Chapter 4 for service procedures

Test and Procedure	Results and Indications	Proceed to
5.1—Determine that the air filter is functioning efficiently: Hold paper elements up to a strong light, and attempt to see light through the filter.	Clean permanent air filters in solvent (or manufacturer's recommendation), and allow to dry. Replace paper elements through which light cannot be seen:	5.2
5.2—Determine whether a flooding condition exists: Flooding is identified by a strong gasoline odor, and excessive gasoline present in the throttle bore(s) of the carburetor.	If flooding is not evident:	5.3
	If flooding is evident, permit the gasoline to dry for a few moments and restart. If flooding doesn't recur:	5.7
	If flooding is persistent:	5.5

If the engine floods repeatedly, check the choke butterfly flap

5.3—Check that fuel is reaching the carburetor: Detach the fuel line at the carburetor inlet. Hold the end of the line in a cup (not styrofoam), and crank the engine.	If fuel flows smoothly:	5.7
	If fuel doesn't flow (**NOTE:** *Make sure that there is fuel in the tank*), or flows erratically:	5.4

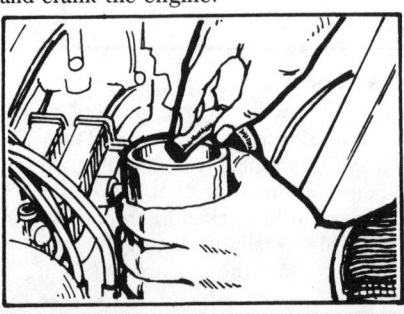

Check the fuel pump by disconnecting the output line (fuel pump-to-carburetor) at the carburetor and operating the starter briefly

TROUBLESHOOTING

Test and Procedure	Results and Indications	Proceed to
5.4—Test the fuel pump: Disconnect all fuel lines from the fuel pump. Hold a finger over the input fitting, crank the engine (with electric pump, turn the ignition or pump on); and feel for suction.	If suction is evident, blow out the fuel line to the tank with low pressure compressed air until bubbling is heard from the fuel filler neck. Also blow out the carburetor fuel line (both ends disconnected):	5.7
	If no suction is evident, replace or repair the fuel pump: NOTE: *Repeated oil fouling of the spark plugs, or a no-start condition, could be the result of a ruptured vacuum booster pump diaphragm, through which oil or gasoline is being drawn into the intake manifold (where applicable).*	5.7
5.5—Occasionally, small specks of dirt will clog the small jets and orifices in the carburetor. With the engine cold, hold a flat piece of wood or similar material over the carburetor, where possible, and crank the engine.	If the engine starts, but runs roughly the engine is probably not run enough. If the engine won't start:	5.9
5.6—Check the needle and seat: Tap the carburetor in the area of the needle and seat.	If flooding stops, a gasoline additive (e.g., Gumout) will often cure the problem:	5.7
	If flooding continues, check the fuel pump for excessive pressure at the carburetor (according to specifications). If the pressure is normal, the needle and seat must be removed and checked, and/or the float level adjusted:	5.7
5.7—Test the accelerator pump by looking into the throttle bores while operating the throttle.	If the accelerator pump appears to be operating normally:	5.8
	If the accelerator pump is not operating, the pump must be reconditioned. Where possible, service the pump with the carburetor(s) installed on the engine. If necessary, remove the carburetor. Prior to removal:	5.8

Check for gas at the carburetor by looking down the carburetor throat while someone moves the accelerator

5.8—Determine whether the carburetor main fuel system is functioning: Spray a commercial starting fluid into the carburetor while attempting to start the engine.	If the engine starts, runs for a few seconds, and dies:	5.9
	If the engine doesn't start:	6.1

TROUBLESHOOTING

Test and Procedure	Results and Indications	Proceed to
5.9—Uncommon fuel system malfunctions: See below:	If the problem is solved:	6.1
	If the problem remains, remove and recondition the carburetor.	

Condition	Indication	Test	Prevailing Weather Conditions	Remedy
Vapor lock	Engine will not restart shortly after running.	Cool the components of the fuel system until the engine starts. Vapor lock can be cured faster by draping a wet cloth over a mechanical fuel pump.	Hot to very hot	Ensure that the exhaust manifold heat control valve is operating. Check with the vehicle manufacturer for the recommended solution to vapor lock on the model in question.
Carburetor icing	Engine will not idle, stalls at low speeds.	Visually inspect the throttle plate area of the throttle bores for frost.	High humidity, 32–40° F.	Ensure that the exhaust manifold heat control valve is operating, and that the intake manifold heat riser is not blocked.
Water in the fuel	Engine sputters and stalls; may not start.	Pump a small amount of fuel into a glass jar. Allow to stand, and inspect for droplets or a layer of water.	High humidity, extreme temperature changes.	For droplets, use one or two cans of commercial gas line anti-freeze. For a layer of water, the tank must be drained, and the fuel lines blown out with compressed air.

Section 6—Engine Compression
See Chapter 3 for service procedures

6.1—Test engine compression: Remove all spark plugs. Block the throttle wide open. Insert a compression gauge into a spark plug port, crank the engine to obtain the maximum reading, and record.	If compression is within limits on all cylinders:	7.1
	If gauge reading is extremely low on all cylinders:	6.2
	If gauge reading is low on one or two cylinders: (If gauge readings are identical and low on two or more adjacent cylinders, the head gasket must be replaced.)	6.2

Checking compression

6.2—Test engine compression (wet): Squirt approximately 30 cc. of engine oil into each cylinder, and retest per 6.1.	If the readings improve, worn or cracked rings or broken pistons are indicated:	See Chapter 3
	If the readings do not improve, burned or excessively carboned valves or a jumped timing chain are indicated: NOTE: *A jumped timing chain is often indicated by difficult cranking.*	7.1

TROUBLESHOOTING 237

Section 7—Engine Vacuum
See Chapter 3 for service procedures

Test and Procedure	Results and Indications	Proceed to
7.1—Attach a vacuum gauge to the intake manifold beyond the throttle plate. Start the engine, and observe the action of the needle over the range of engine speeds.	See below.	See below

INDICATION: normal engine in good condition

Proceed to: 8.1

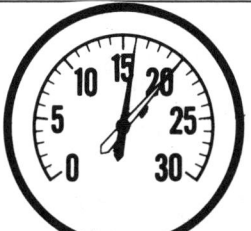

Normal engine
Gauge reading: steady, from 17–22 in./Hg.

INDICATION: sticking valves or ignition miss

Proceed to: 9.1, 8.3

Sticking valves
Gauge reading: intermittent fluctuation at idle

INDICATION: late ignition or valve timing, low compression, stuck throttle valve, leaking carburetor or manifold gasket

Proceed to: 6.1

Incorrect valve timing
Gauge reading: low (10–15 in./Hg) but steady

INDICATION: improper carburetor adjustment or minor intake leak.

Proceed to: 7.2

Carburetor requires adjustment
Gauge reading: drifting needle

INDICATION: ignition miss, blown cylinder head gasket, leaking valve or weak valve spring

Proceed to: 8.3, 6.1

Blown head gasket
Gauge reading: needle fluctuates as engine speed increases

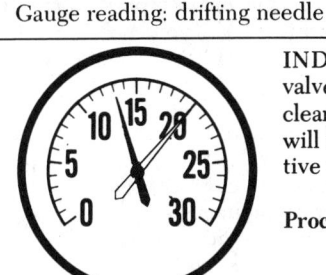

INDICATION: burnt valve or faulty valve clearance. Needle will fall when defective valve operates

Proceed to: 9.1

Burnt or leaking valves
Gauge reading: steady needle, but drops regularly

INDICATION: choked muffler, excessive back pressure in system

Proceed to: 10.1

Clogged exhaust system
Gauge reading: gradual drop in reading at idle

INDICATION: worn valve guides

Proceed to: 9.1

Worn valve guides
Gauge reading: needle vibrates excessively at idle, but steadies as engine speed increases

White pointer = steady gauge hand

Black pointer = fluctuating gauge hand

238 TROUBLESHOOTING

Test and Procedure	Results and Indications	Proceed to
7.2—Attach a vacuum gauge per 7.1, and test for an intake manifold leak. Squirt a small amount of oil around the intake manifold gaskets, carburetor gaskets, plugs and fittings. Observe the action of the vacuum gauge.	If the reading improves, replace the indicated gasket, or seal the indicated fitting or plug. If the reading remains low:	8.1 7.3
7.3—Test all vacuum hoses and accessories for leaks as described in 7.2. Also check the carburetor body (dashpots, automatic choke mechanism, throttle shafts) for leaks in the same manner.	If the reading improves, service or replace the offending part(s): If the reading remains low:	8.1 6.1

Section 8—Secondary Electrical System
See Chapter 2 for service procedures

Test and Procedure	Results and Indications	Proceed to
8.1—Remove the distributor cap and check to make sure that the rotor turns when the engine is cranked. Visually inspect the distributor components.	Clean, tighten or replace any components which appear defective.	8.2
8.2—Connect a timing light (per manufacturer's recommendation) and check the dynamic ignition timing. Disconnect and plug the vacuum hose(s) to the distributor if specified, start the engine, and observe the timing marks at the specified engine speed.	If the timing is not correct, adjust to specifications by rotating the distributor in the engine: (Advance timing by rotating distributor opposite normal direction of rotor rotation, retard timing by rotating distributor in same direction as rotor rotation.)	8.3
8.3—Check the operation of the distributor advance mechanism(s): To test the mechanical advance, disconnect the vacuum lines from the distributor advance unit and observe the timing marks with a timing light as the engine speed is increased from idle. If the mark moves smoothly, without hesitation, it may be assumed that the mechanical advance is functioning properly. To test vacuum advance and/or retard systems, alternately crimp and release the vacuum line, and observe the timing mark for movement. If movement is noted, the system is operating.	If the systems are functioning: If the systems are not functioning, remove the distributor, and test on a distributor tester:	8.4 8.4
8.4—Locate an ignition miss: With the engine running, remove each spark plug wire, one at a time, until one is found that doesn't cause the engine to roughen and slow down.	When the missing cylinder is identified:	4.1

Section 9—Valve Train
See Chapter 3 for service procedures

Test and Procedure	Results and Indications	Proceed to
9.1—Evaluate the valve train: Remove the valve cover, and ensure that the valves are adjusted to specifications. A mechanic's stethoscope may be used to aid in the diagnosis of the valve train. By pushing the probe on or near push rods or rockers, valve noise often can be isolated. A timing light also may be used to diagnose valve problems. Connect the light according to manufacturer's recommendations, and start the engine. Vary the firing moment of the light by increasing the engine speed (and therefore the ignition advance), and moving the trigger from cylinder to cylinder. Observe the movement of each valve.	Sticking valves or erratic valve train motion can be observed with the timing light. The cylinder head must be disassembled for repairs.	See Chapter 3
9.2—Check the valve timing: Locate top dead center of the No. 1 piston, and install a degree wheel or tape on the crankshaft pulley or damper with zero corresponding to an index mark on the engine. Rotate the crankshaft in its direction of rotation, and observe the opening of the No. 1 cylinder intake valve. The opening should correspond with the correct mark on the degree wheel according to specifications.	If the timing is not correct, the timing cover must be removed for further investigation.	See Chapter 3

Section 10—Exhaust System

Test and Procedure	Results and Indications	Proceed to
10.1—Determine whether the exhaust manifold heat control valve is operating: Operate the valve by hand to determine whether it is free to move. If the valve is free, run the engine to operating temperature and observe the action of the valve, to ensure that it is opening.	If the valve sticks, spray it with a suitable solvent, open and close the valve to free it, and retest.	
	If the valve functions properly:	10.2
	If the valve does not free, or does not operate, replace the valve:	10.2
10.2—Ensure that there are no exhaust restrictions: Visually inspect the exhaust system for kinks, dents, or crushing. Also note that gases are flowing freely from the tailpipe at all engine speeds, indicating no restriction in the muffler or resonator.	Replace any damaged portion of the system:	11.1

TROUBLESHOOTING

Section 11—Cooling System
See Chapter 3 for service procedures

Test and Procedure	Results and Indications	Proceed to
11.1—Visually inspect the fan belt for glazing, cracks, and fraying, and replace if necessary. Tighten the belt so that the longest span has approximately ½" play at its midpoint under thumb pressure (see Chapter 1).	Replace or tighten the fan belt as necessary: *Checking belt tension*	11.2
11.2—Check the fluid level of the cooling system.	If full or slightly low, fill as necessary:	11.5
	If extremely low:	11.3
11.3—Visually inspect the external portions of the cooling system (radiator, radiator hoses, thermostat elbow, water pump seals, heater hoses, etc.) for leaks. If none are found, pressurize the cooling system to 14–15 psi.	If cooling system holds the pressure:	11.5
	If cooling system loses pressure rapidly, reinspect external parts of the system for leaks under pressure. If none are found, check dipstick for coolant in crankcase. If no coolant is present, but pressure loss continues:	11.4
	If coolant is evident in crankcase, remove cylinder head(s), and check gasket(s). If gaskets are intact, block and cylinder head(s) should be checked for cracks or holes.	
	If the gasket(s) is blown, replace, and purge the crankcase of coolant:	12.6
	NOTE: *Occasionally, due to atmospheric and driving conditions, condensation of water can occur in the crankcase. This causes the oil to appear milky white. To remedy, run the engine until hot, and change the oil and oil filter.*	
11.4—Check for combustion leaks into the cooling system: Pressurize the cooling system as above. Start the engine, and observe the pressure gauge. If the needle fluctuates, remove each spark plug wire, one at a time, noting which cylinder(s) reduce or eliminate the fluctuation.	Cylinders which reduce or eliminate the fluctuation, when the spark plug wire is removed, are leaking into the cooling system. Replace the head gasket on the affected cylinder bank(s). *Pressurizing the cooling system*	

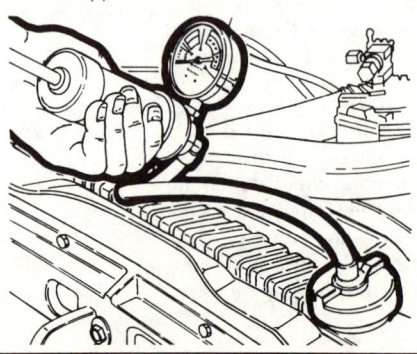

TROUBLESHOOTING 241

est and Procedure	Results and Indications	Proceed to
1.5—Check the radiator pressure cap: Attach a radiator pressure tester to the radiator cap (wet the seal prior to installation). Quickly pump up the pressure, noting the point at which the cap releases.	If the cap releases within ± 1 psi of the specified rating, it is operating properly:	**11.6**
	If the cap releases at more than ± 1 psi of the specified rating, it should be replaced:	**11.6**

Checking radiator pressure cap

11.6—Test the thermostat: Start the engine cold, remove the radiator cap, and insert a thermometer into the radiator. Allow the engine to idle. After a short while, there will be a sudden, rapid increase in coolant temperature. The temperature at which this sharp rise stops is the thermostat opening temperature.	If the thermostat opens at or about the specified temperature:	**11.7**
	If the temperature doesn't increase: (If the temperature increases slowly and gradually, replace the thermostat.)	**11.7**
11.7—Check the water pump: Remove the thermostat elbow and the thermostat, disconnect the coil high tension lead (to prevent starting), and crank the engine momentarily.	If coolant flows, replace the thermostat and retest per 11.6:	**11.6**
	If coolant doesn't flow, reverse flush the cooling system to alleviate any blockage that might exist. If system is not blocked, and coolant will not flow, replace the water pump.	

Section 12—Lubrication
See Chapter 3 for service procedures

Test and Procedure	Results and Indications	Proceed to
12.1—Check the oil pressure gauge or warning light: If the gauge shows low pressure, or the light is on for no obvious reason, remove the oil pressure sender. Install an accurate oil pressure gauge and run the engine momentarily.	If oil pressure builds normally, run engine for a few moments to determine that it is functioning normally, and replace the sender.	—
	If the pressure remains low:	**12.2**
	If the pressure surges:	**12.3**
	If the oil pressure is zero:	**12.3**
12.2—Visually inspect the oil: If the oil is watery or very thin, milky or foamy, replace the oil and oil filter.	If the oil is normal:	**12.3**
	If after replacing oil the pressure remains low:	**12.3**
	If after replacing oil the pressure becomes normal:	—

242 TROUBLESHOOTING

Test and Procedure	Results and Indications	Proceed to
12.3—Inspect the oil pressure relief valve and spring, to ensure that it is not sticking or stuck. Remove and thoroughly clean the valve, spring, and the valve body.	If the oil pressure improves: If no improvement is noted:	— 12.4
12.4—Check to ensure that the oil pump is not cavitating (sucking air instead of oil): See that the crankcase is neither over nor underfull, and that the pickup in the sump is in the proper position and free from sludge.	Fill or drain the crankcase to the proper capacity, and clean the pickup screen in solvent if necessary. If no improvement is noted:	12.5
12.5—Inspect the oil pump drive and the oil pump:	If the pump drive or the oil pump appear to be defective, service as necessary and retest per 12.1:	12.1
	If the pump drive and pump appear to be operating normally, the engine should be disassembled to determine where blockage exists:	See Chapter 3
12.6—Purge the engine of ethylene glycol coolant: Completely drain the crankcase and the oil filter. Obtain a commercial butyl cellosolve base solvent, designated for this purpose, and follow the instructions precisely. Following this, install a new oil filter and refill the crankcase with the proper weight oil. The next oil and filter change should follow shortly thereafter (1000 miles).		

TROUBLESHOOTING EMISSION CONTROL SYSTEMS

See Chapter 4 for procedures applicable to individual emission control systems used on specific combinations of engine/transmission/model.

TROUBLESHOOTING THE CARBURETOR
See Chapter 4 for service procedures

Carburetor problems cannot be effectively isolated unless all other engine systems (particularly ignition and emission) are functioning properly and the engine is properly tuned.

TROUBLESHOOTING

Condition	Possible Cause
Engine cranks, but does not start	1. Improper starting procedure 2. No fuel in tank 3. Clogged fuel line or filter 4. Defective fuel pump 5. Choke valve not closing properly 6. Engine flooded 7. Choke valve not unloading 8. Throttle linkage not making full travel 9. Stuck needle or float 10. Leaking float needle or seat 11. Improper float adjustment
Engine stalls	1. Improperly adjusted idle speed or mixture **Engine hot** 2. Improperly adjusted dashpot 3. Defective or improperly adjusted solenoid 4. Incorrect fuel level in fuel bowl 5. Fuel pump pressure too high 6. Leaking float needle seat 7. Secondary throttle valve stuck open 8. Air or fuel leaks 9. Idle air bleeds plugged or missing 10. Idle passages plugged **Engine Cold** 11. Incorrectly adjusted choke 12. Improperly adjusted fast idle speed 13. Air leaks 14. Plugged idle or idle air passages 15. Stuck choke valve or binding linkage 16. Stuck secondary throttle valves 17. Engine flooding—high fuel level 18. Leaking or misaligned float
Engine hesitates on acceleration	1. Clogged fuel filter 2. Leaking fuel pump diaphragm 3. Low fuel pump pressure 4. Secondary throttle valves stuck, bent or misadjusted 5. Sticking or binding air valve 6. Defective accelerator pump 7. Vacuum leaks 8. Clogged air filter 9. Incorrect choke adjustment (engine cold)
Engine feels sluggish or flat on acceleration	1. Improperly adjusted idle speed or mixture 2. Clogged fuel filter 3. Defective accelerator pump 4. Dirty, plugged or incorrect main metering jets 5. Bent or sticking main metering rods 6. Sticking throttle valves 7. Stuck heat riser 8. Binding or stuck air valve 9. Dirty, plugged or incorrect secondary jets 10. Bent or sticking secondary metering rods. 11. Throttle body or manifold heat passages plugged 12. Improperly adjusted choke or choke vacuum break.
Carburetor floods	1. Defective fuel pump. Pressure too high. 2. Stuck choke valve 3. Dirty, worn or damaged float or needle valve/seat 4. Incorrect float/fuel level 5. Leaking float bowl

TROUBLESHOOTING

Condition	Possible Cause
Engine idles roughly and stalls	1. Incorrect idle speed 2. Clogged fuel filter 3. Dirt in fuel system or carburetor 4. Loose carburetor screws or attaching bolts 5. Broken carburetor gaskets 6. Air leaks 7. Dirty carburetor 8. Worn idle mixture needles 9. Throttle valves stuck open 10. Incorrectly adjusted float or fuel level 11. Clogged air filter
Engine runs unevenly or surges	1. Defective fuel pump 2. Dirty or clogged fuel filter 3. Plugged, loose or incorrect main metering jets or rods 4. Air leaks 5. Bent or sticking main metering rods 6. Stuck power piston 7. Incorrect float adjustment 8. Incorrect idle speed or mixture 9. Dirty or plugged idle system passages 10. Hard, brittle or broken gaskets 11. Loose attaching or mounting screws 12. Stuck or misaligned secondary throttle valves
Poor fuel economy	1. Poor driving habits 2. Stuck choke valve 3. Binding choke linkage 4. Stuck heat riser 5. Incorrect idle mixture 6. Defective accelerator pump 7. Air leaks 8. Plugged, loose or incorrect main metering jets 9. Improperly adjusted float or fuel level 10. Bent, misaligned or fuel-clogged float 11. Leaking float needle seat 12. Fuel leak 13. Accelerator pump discharge ball not seating properly 14. Incorrect main jets
Engine lacks high speed performance or power	1. Incorrect throttle linkage adjustment 2. Stuck or binding power piston 3. Defective accelerator pump 4. Air leaks 5. Incorrect float setting or fuel level 6. Dirty, plugged, worn or incorrect main metering jets or rods 7. Binding or sticking air valve 8. Brittle or cracked gaskets 9. Bent, incorrect or improperly adjusted secondary metering rods 10. Clogged fuel filter 11. Clogged air filter 12. Defective fuel pump

TROUBLESHOOTING FUEL INJECTION PROBLEMS

Each fuel injection system has its own unique components and test procedures, for which it is impossible to generalize. Refer to Chapter 4 of this Repair & Tune-Up Guide for specific test and repair procedures, if the vehicle is equipped with fuel injection.

TROUBLESHOOTING ELECTRICAL PROBLEMS

See Chapter 5 for service procedures

For any electrical system to operate, it must make a complete circuit. This simply means that the power flow from the battery must make a complete circle. When an electrical component is operating, power flows from the battery to the component, passes through the component causing it to perform its function (lighting a light bulb), and then returns to the battery through the ground of the circuit. This ground is usually (but not always) the metal part of the car or truck on which the electrical component is mounted.

Perhaps the easiest way to visualize this is to think of connecting a light bulb with two wires attached to it to the battery. If one of the two wires attached to the light bulb were attached to the negative post of the battery and the other were attached to the positive post of the battery, you would have a complete circuit. Current from the battery would flow to the light bulb, causing it to light, and return to the negative post of the battery.

The normal automotive circuit differs from this simple example in two ways. First, instead of having a return wire from the bulb to the battery, the light bulb returns the current to the battery through the chassis of the vehicle. Since the negative battery cable is attached to the chassis and the chassis is made of electrically conductive metal, the chassis of the vehicle can serve as a ground wire to complete the circuit. Secondly, most automotive circuits contain switches to turn components on and off as required.

Every complete circuit from a power source must include a component which is using the power from the power source. If you were to disconnect the light bulb from the wires and touch the two wires together (don't do this) the power supply wire to the component would be grounded before the normal ground connection for the circuit.

Because grounding a wire from a power source makes a complete circuit—less the required component to use the power—this phenomenon is called a short circuit. Common causes are: broken insulation (exposing the metal wire to a metal part of the car or truck), or a shorted switch.

Some electrical components which require a large amount of current to operate also have a relay in their circuit. Since these circuits carry a large amount of current, the thickness of the wire in the circuit (gauge size) is also greater. If this large wire were connected from the component to the control switch on the instrument panel, and then back to the component, a voltage drop would occur in the circuit. To prevent this potential drop in voltage, an electromagnetic switch (relay) is used. The large wires in the circuit are connected from the battery to one side of the relay, and from the opposite side of the relay to the component. The relay is normally open, preventing current from passing through the circuit. An additional, smaller, wire is connected from the relay to the control switch for the circuit. When the control switch is turned on, it grounds the smaller wire from the relay and completes the circuit. This closes the relay and allows current to flow from the battery to the component. The horn, headlight, and starter circuits are three which use relays.

It is possible for larger surges of current to pass through the electrical system of your car or truck. If this surge of current were to reach an electrical component, it could burn it out. To prevent this, fuses, circuit breakers or fusible links are connected into the current supply wires of most of the major electrical systems. When an electrical current of excessive power passes through the component's fuse, the fuse blows out and breaks the circuit, saving the component from destruction.

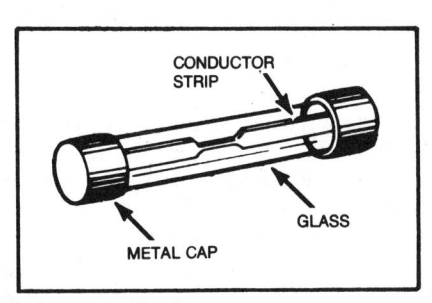

Typical automotive fuse

A circuit breaker is basically a self-repairing fuse. The circuit breaker opens the circuit the same way a fuse does. However, when either the short is removed from the circuit or the surge subsides, the circuit breaker resets itself and does not have to be replaced as a fuse does.

A fuse link is a wire that acts as a fuse. It is normally connected between the starter relay and the main wiring harness. This connection is usually under the hood. The fuse link (if installed) protects all the

TROUBLESHOOTING

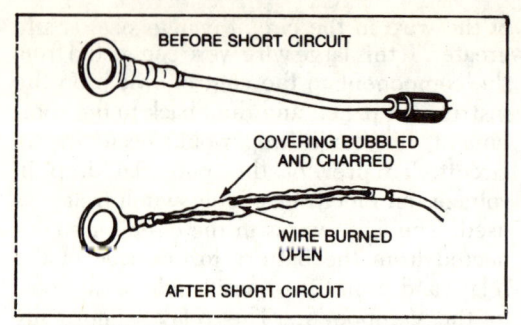

Most fusible links show a charred, melted insulation when they burn out

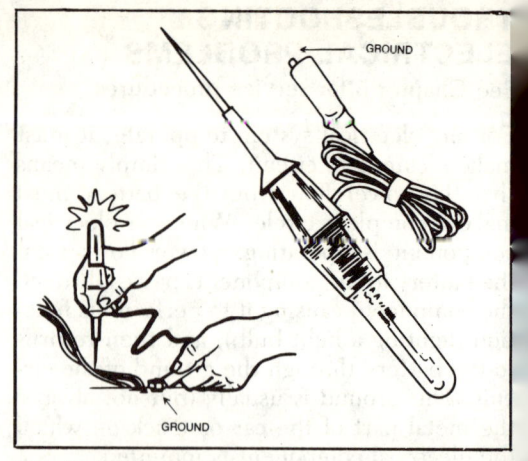

The test light will show the presence of current when touched to a hot wire and grounded at the other end

chassis electrical components, and is the probable cause of trouble when none of the electrical components function, unless the battery is disconnected or dead.

Electrical problems generally fall into one of three areas:

1. The component that is not functioning is not receiving current.
2. The component itself is not functioning.
3. The component is not properly grounded.

The electrical system can be checked with a test light and a jumper wire. A test light is a device that looks like a pointed screwdriver with a wire attached to it and has a light bulb in its handle. A jumper wire is a piece of insulated wire with an alligator clip attached to each end.

If a component is not working, you must follow a systematic plan to determine which of the three causes is the villain.

1. Turn on the switch that controls the inoperable component.
2. Disconnect the power supply wire from the component.
3. Attach the ground wire on the test light to a good metal ground.
4. Touch the probe end of the test light to the end of the power supply wire that was disconnected from the component. If the component is receiving current, the test light will go on.

NOTE: *Some components work only when the ignition switch is turned on.*

If the test light does not go on, then the problem is in the circuit between the battery and the component. This includes all the switches, fuses, and relays in the system. Follow the wire that runs back to the battery. The problem is an open circuit between the battery and the component. If the fuse is blown and, when replaced, immediately blows again, there is a short circuit in the system which must be located and repaired. If there is a switch in the system, bypass it with a jumper wire. This is done by connecting one end of the jumper wire to the power supply wire into the switch and the other end of the jumper wire to the wire coming out of the switch. If the test light lights with the jumper wire installed, the switch or whatever was bypassed is defective.

NOTE: *Never substitute the jumper wire for the component, since it is required to use the power from the power source.*

5. If the bulb in the test light goes on, then the current is getting to the component that is not working. This eliminates the first of the three possible causes. Connect the power supply wire and connect a jumper wire from the component to a good metal ground. Do this with the switch which controls the component turned on, and also the ignition switch turned on if it is required for the component to work. If the component works with the jumper wire installed, then it has a bad ground. This is usually caused by the metal area on which the component mounts to the chassis being coated with some type of foreign matter.

6. If neither test located the source of the trouble, then the component itself is defective. Remember that for any electrical system to work, all connections must be clean and tight.

TROUBLESHOOTING

Troubleshooting Basic Turn Signal and Flasher Problems

See Chapter 5 for service procedures

Most problems in the turn signals or flasher system can be reduced to defective flashers or bulbs, which are easily replaced. Occasionally, the turn signal switch will prove defective.

F = Front   R = Rear   ● = Lights off   ○ = Lights on

Condition	Possible Cause
Turn signals light, but do not flash	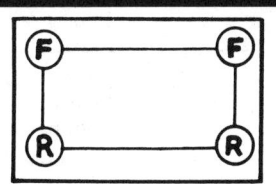 Defective flasher
No turn signals light on either side	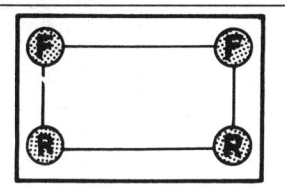 Blown fuse. Replace if defective. Defective flasher. Check by substitution. Open circuit, short circuit or poor ground.
Both turn signals on one side don't work	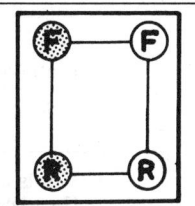 Bad bulbs. Bad ground in both (or either) housings.
One turn signal light on one side doesn't work	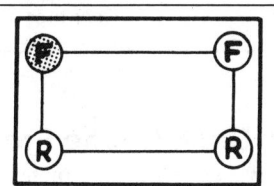 Defective bulb. Corrosion in socket. Clean contacts. Poor ground at socket.
Turn signal flashes too fast or too slowly	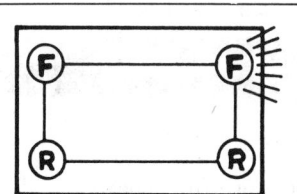 Check any bulb on the side flashing too fast. A heavy-duty bulb is probably installed in place of a regular bulb. Check the bulb flashing too slowly. A standard bulb was probably installed in place of a heavy-duty bulb. Loose connections or corrosion at the bulb socket.
Indicator lights don't work in either direction	 Check if the turn signals are working. Check the dash indicator lights. Check the flasher by substitution.
One indicator light doesn't light	 On systems with one dash indicator: See if the lights work on the same side. Often the filaments have been reversed in systems combining stoplights with taillights and turn signals. Check the flasher by substitution. On systems with two indicators: Check the bulbs on the same side. Check the indicator light bulb. Check the flasher by substitution.

TROUBLESHOOTING

Troubleshooting Lighting Problems
See Chapter 5 for service procedures

Condition	Possible Cause
One or more lights don't work, but others do	1. Defective bulb(s) 2. Blown fuse(s) 3. Dirty fuse clips or light sockets 4. Poor ground circuit
Lights burn out quickly	1. Incorrect voltage regulator setting or defective regulator 2. Poor battery/alternator connections
Lights go dim	1. Low/discharged battery 2. Alternator not charging 3. Corroded sockets or connections 4. Low voltage output
Lights flicker	1. Loose connection 2. Poor ground. (Run ground wire from light housing to frame) 3. Circuit breaker operating (short circuit)
Lights "flare"—Some flare is normal on acceleration—If excessive, see "Lights Burn Out Quickly"	High voltage setting
Lights glare—approaching drivers are blinded	1. Lights adjusted too high 2. Rear springs or shocks sagging 3. Rear tires soft

Troubleshooting Dash Gauge Problems

Most problems can be traced to a defective sending unit or faulty wiring. Occasionally, the gauge itself is at fault. See Chapter 5 for service procedures.

Condition	Possible Cause

COOLANT TEMPERATURE GAUGE

Gauge reads erratically or not at all	1. Loose or dirty connections 2. Defective sending unit. 3. Defective gauge. To test a bi-metal gauge, remove the wire from the sending unit. Ground the wire for an instant. If the gauge registers, replace the sending unit. To test a magnetic gauge, disconnect the wire at the sending unit. With ignition ON gauge should register COLD. Ground the wire; gauge should register HOT.

AMMETER GAUGE—TURN HEADLIGHTS ON (DO NOT START ENGINE). NOTE REACTION

Ammeter shows charge Ammeter shows discharge Ammeter does not move	1. Connections reversed on gauge 2. Ammeter is OK 3. Loose connections or faulty wiring 4. Defective gauge

TROUBLESHOOTING 249

Condition	Possible Cause

OIL PRESSURE GAUGE

Gauge does not register or is inaccurate	1. On mechanical gauge, Bourdon tube may be bent or kinked. 2. Low oil pressure. Remove sending unit. Idle the engine briefly. If no oil flows from sending unit hole, problem is in engine. 3. Defective gauge. Remove the wire from the sending unit and ground it for an instant with the ignition ON. A good gauge will go to the top of the scale. 4. Defective wiring. Check the wiring to the gauge. If it's OK and the gauge doesn't register when grounded, replace the gauge. 5. Defective sending unit.

ALL GAUGES

All gauges do not operate All gauges read low or erratically All gauges pegged	1. Blown fuse 2. Defective instrument regulator 3. Defective or dirty instrument voltage regulator 4. Loss of ground between instrument voltage regulator and frame 5. Defective instrument regulator

WARNING LIGHTS

Light(s) do not come on when ignition is ON, but engine is not started	1. Defective bulb 2. Defective wire 3. Defective sending unit. Disconnect the wire from the sending unit and ground it. Replace the sending unit if the light comes on with the ignition ON.
Light comes on with engine running	4. Problem in individual system 5. Defective sending unit

Troubleshooting Clutch Problems

It is false economy to replace individual clutch components. The pressure plate, clutch plate and throwout bearing should be replaced as a set, and the flywheel face inspected, whenever the clutch is overhauled. See Chapter 6 for service procedures.

Condition	Possible Cause
Clutch chatter	1. Grease on driven plate (disc) facing 2. Binding clutch linkage or cable 3. Loose, damaged facings on driven plate (disc) 4. Engine mounts loose 5. Incorrect height adjustment of pressure plate release levers 6. Clutch housing or housing to transmission adapter misalignment 7. Loose driven plate hub
Clutch grabbing	1. Oil, grease on driven plate (disc) facing 2. Broken pressure plate 3. Warped or binding driven plate. Driven plate binding on clutch shaft
Clutch slips	1. Lack of lubrication in clutch linkage or cable (linkage or cable binds, causes incomplete engagement) 2. Incorrect pedal, or linkage adjustment 3. Broken pressure plate springs 4. Weak pressure plate springs 5. Grease on driven plate facings (disc)

TROUBLESHOOTING

Troubleshooting Clutch Problems (cont.)

Condition	Possible Cause
Incomplete clutch release	1. Incorrect pedal or linkage adjustment or linkage or cable binding 2. Incorrect height adjustment on pressure plate release levers 3. Loose, broken facings on driven plate (disc) 4. Bent, dished, warped driven plate caused by overheating
Grinding, whirring grating noise when pedal is depressed	1. Worn or defective throwout bearing 2. Starter drive teeth contacting flywheel ring gear teeth. Look for milled or polished teeth on ring gear.
Squeal, howl, trumpeting noise when pedal is being released (occurs during first inch to inch and one-half of pedal travel)	Pilot bushing worn or lack of lubricant. If bushing appears OK, polish bushing with emery cloth, soak lube wick in oil, lube bushing with oil, apply film of chassis grease to clutch shaft pilot hub, reassemble. NOTE: Bushing wear may be due to misalignment of clutch housing or housing to transmission adapter
Vibration or clutch pedal pulsation with clutch disengaged (pedal fully depressed)	1. Worn or defective engine transmission mounts 2. Flywheel run out. (Flywheel run out at face not to exceed 0.005") 3. Damaged or defective clutch components

Troubleshooting Manual Transmission Problems
See Chapter 6 for service procedures

Condition	Possible Cause
Transmission jumps out of gear	1. Misalignment of transmission case or clutch housing. 2. Worn pilot bearing in crankshaft. 3. Bent transmission shaft. 4. Worn high speed sliding gear. 5. Worn teeth or end-play in clutch shaft. 6. Insufficient spring tension on shifter rail plunger. 7. Bent or loose shifter fork. 8. Gears not engaging completely. 9. Loose or worn bearings on clutch shaft or mainshaft. 10. Worn gear teeth. 11. Worn or damaged detent balls.
Transmission sticks in gear	1. Clutch not releasing fully. 2. Burred or battered teeth on clutch shaft, or sliding sleeve. 3. Burred or battered transmission mainshaft. 4. Frozen synchronizing clutch. 5. Stuck shifter rail plunger. 6. Gearshift lever twisting and binding shifter rail. 7. Battered teeth on high speed sliding gear or on sleeve. 8. Improper lubrication, or lack of lubrication. 9. Corroded transmission parts. 10. Defective mainshaft pilot bearing. 11. Locked gear bearings will give same effect as stuck in gear.
Transmission gears will not synchronize	1. Binding pilot bearing on mainshaft, will synchronize in high gear only. 2. Clutch not releasing fully. 3. Detent spring weak or broken. 4. Weak or broken springs under balls in sliding gear sleeve. 5. Binding bearing on clutch shaft, or binding countershaft. 6. Binding pilot bearing in crankshaft. 7. Badly worn gear teeth. 8. Improper lubrication. 9. Constant mesh gear not turning freely on transmission mainshaft. Will synchronize in that gear only.

TROUBLESHOOTING 251

Condition	Possible Cause
Gears spinning when shifting into gear from neutral	1. Clutch not releasing fully. 2. In some cases an extremely light lubricant in transmission will cause gears to continue to spin for a short time after clutch is released. 3. Binding pilot bearing in crankshaft.
Transmission noisy in all gears	1. Insufficient lubricant, or improper lubricant. 2. Worn countergear bearings. 3. Worn or damaged main drive gear or countergear. 4. Damaged main drive gear or mainshaft bearings. 5. Worn or damaged countergear anti-lash plate.
Transmission noisy in neutral only	1. Damaged main drive gear bearing. 2. Damaged or loose mainshaft pilot bearing. 3. Worn or damaged countergear anti-lash plate. 4. Worn countergear bearings.
Transmission noisy in one gear only	1. Damaged or worn constant mesh gears. 2. Worn or damaged countergear bearings. 3. Damaged or worn synchronizer.
Transmission noisy in reverse only	1. Worn or damaged reverse idler gear or idler bushing. 2. Worn or damaged mainshaft reverse gear. 3. Worn or damaged reverse countergear. 4. Damaged shift mechanism.

TROUBLESHOOTING AUTOMATIC TRANSMISSION PROBLEMS

Keeping alert to changes in the operating characteristics of the transmission (changing shift points, noises, etc.) can prevent small problems from becoming large ones. If the problem cannot be traced to loose bolts, fluid level, misadjusted linkage, clogged filters or similar problems, you should probably seek professional service.

Transmission Fluid Indications

The appearance and odor of the transmission fluid can give valuable clues to the overall condition of the transmission. Always note the appearance of the fluid when you check the fluid level or change the fluid. Rub a small amount of fluid between your fingers to feel for grit and smell the fluid on the dipstick.

If the fluid appears:	It indicates:
Clear and red colored	Normal operation
Discolored (extremely dark red or brownish) or smells burned	Band or clutch pack failure, usually caused by an overheated transmission. Hauling very heavy loads with insufficient power or failure to change the fluid often result in overheating. Do not confuse this appearance with newer fluids that have a darker red color and a strong odor (though not a burned odor).
Foamy or aerated (light in color and full of bubbles)	1. The level is too high (gear train is churning oil) 2. An internal air leak (air is mixing with the fluid). Have the transmission checked professionally.
Solid residue in the fluid	Defective bands, clutch pack or bearings. Bits of band material or metal abrasives are clinging to the dipstick. Have the transmission checked professionally.
Varnish coating on the dipstick	The transmission fluid is overheating

TROUBLESHOOTING

TROUBLESHOOTING DRIVE AXLE PROBLEMS

First, determine when the noise is most noticeable.

Drive Noise: Produced under vehicle acceleration.

Coast Noise: Produced while coasting with a closed throttle.

Float Noise: Occurs while maintaining constant speed (just enough to keep speed constant) on a level road.

External Noise Elimination

It is advisable to make a thorough road test to determine whether the noise originates in the rear axle or whether it originates from the tires, engine, transmission, wheel bearings or road surface. Noise originating from other places cannot be corrected by servicing the rear axle.

ROAD NOISE

Brick or rough surfaced concrete roads produce noises that seem to come from the rear axle. Road noise is usually identical in Drive or Coast and driving on a different type of road will tell whether the road is the problem.

TIRE NOISE

Tire noise can be mistaken as rear axle noise, even though the tires on the front are at fault. Snow tread and mud tread tires or tires worn unevenly will frequently cause vibrations which seem to originate elsewhere; *temporarily, and for test purposes only,* inflate the tires to 40–50 lbs. This will significantly alter the noise produced by the tires, but will not alter noise from the rear axle. Noises from the rear axle will normally cease at speeds below 30 mph on coast, while tire noise will continue at lower tone as speed is decreased. The rear axle noise will usually change from drive conditions to coast conditions, while tire noise will not. Do not forget to lower the tire pressure to normal after the test is complete.

ENGINE/TRANSMISSION NOISE

Determine at what speed the noise is most pronounced, then stop in a quiet place. With the transmission in Neutral, run the engine through speeds corresponding to road speeds where the noise was noticed. Noises produced with the vehicle standing still are coming from the engine or transmission.

FRONT WHEEL BEARINGS

Front wheel bearing noises, sometimes confused with rear axle noises, will not change when comparing drive and coast conditions. While holding the speed steady, lightly apply the footbrake. This will often cause wheel bearing noise to lessen, as some of the weight is taken off the bearing. Front wheel bearings are easily checked by jacking up the wheels and spinning the wheels. Shaking the wheels will also determine if the wheel bearings are excessively loose.

REAR AXLE NOISES

Eliminating other possible sources can narrow the cause to the rear axle, which normally produces noise from worn gears or bearings. Gear noises tend to peak in a narrow speed range, while bearing noises will usually vary in pitch with engine speeds.

Noise Diagnosis

The Noise Is:	Most Probably Produced By:
1. Identical under Drive or Coast	Road surface, tires or front wheel bearings
2. Different depending on road surface	Road surface or tires
3. Lower as speed is lowered	Tires
4. Similar when standing or moving	Engine or transmission
5. A vibration	Unbalanced tires, rear wheel bearing, unbalanced driveshaft or worn U-joint
6. A knock or click about every two tire revolutions	Rear wheel bearing
7. Most pronounced on turns	Damaged differential gears
8. A steady low-pitched whirring or scraping, starting at low speeds	Damaged or worn pinion bearing
9. A chattering vibration on turns	Wrong differential lubricant or worn clutch plates (limited slip rear axle)
10. Noticed only in Drive, Coast or Float conditions	Worn ring gear and/or pinion gear

TROUBLESHOOTING

Troubleshooting Steering & Suspension Problems

Condition	Possible Cause
Hard steering (wheel is hard to turn)	1. Improper tire pressure 2. Loose or glazed pump drive belt 3. Low or incorrect fluid 4. Loose, bent or poorly lubricated front end parts 5. Improper front end alignment (excessive caster) 6. Bind in steering column or linkage 7. Kinked hydraulic hose 8. Air in hydraulic system 9. Low pump output or leaks in system 10. Obstruction in lines 11. Pump valves sticking or out of adjustment 12. Incorrect wheel alignment
Loose steering (too much play in steering wheel)	1. Loose wheel bearings 2. Faulty shocks 3. Worn linkage or suspension components 4. Loose steering gear mounting or linkage points 5. Steering mechanism worn or improperly adjusted 6. Valve spool improperly adjusted 7. Worn ball joints, tie-rod ends, etc.
Veers or wanders (pulls to one side with hands off steering wheel)	1. Improper tire pressure 2. Improper front end alignment 3. Dragging or improperly adjusted brakes 4. Bent frame 5. Improper rear end alignment 6. Faulty shocks or springs 7. Loose or bent front end components 8. Play in Pitman arm 9. Steering gear mountings loose 10. Loose wheel bearings 11. Binding Pitman arm 12. Spool valve sticking or improperly adjusted 13. Worn ball joints
Wheel oscillation or vibration transmitted through steering wheel	1. Low or uneven tire pressure 2. Loose wheel bearings 3. Improper front end alignment 4. Bent spindle 5. Worn, bent or broken front end components 6. Tires out of round or out of balance 7. Excessive lateral runout in disc brake rotor 8. Loose or bent shock absorber or strut
Noises (see also "Troubleshooting Drive Axle Problems")	1. Loose belts 2. Low fluid, air in system 3. Foreign matter in system 4. Improper lubrication 5. Interference or chafing in linkage 6. Steering gear mountings loose 7. Incorrect adjustment or wear in gear box 8. Faulty valves or wear in pump 9. Kinked hydraulic lines 10. Worn wheel bearings
Poor return of steering	1. Over-inflated tires 2. Improperly aligned front end (excessive caster) 3. Binding in steering column 4. No lubrication in front end 5. Steering gear adjusted too tight
Uneven tire wear (see "How To Read Tire Wear")	1. Incorrect tire pressure 2. Improperly aligned front end 3. Tires out-of-balance 4. Bent or worn suspension parts

HOW TO READ TIRE WEAR

The way your tires wear is a good indicator of other parts of the suspension. Abnormal wear patterns are often caused by the need for simple tire maintenance, or for front end alignment.

Excessive wear at the center of the tread indicates that the air pressure in the tire is consistently too high. The tire is riding on the center of the tread and wearing it prematurely. Occasionally, this wear pattern can result from outrageously wide tires on narrow rims. The cure for this is to replace either the tires or the wheels.

Over-inflation

This type of wear usually results from consistent under-inflation. When a tire is under-inflated, there is too much contact with the road by the outer treads, which wear prematurely. When this type of wear occurs, and the tire pressure is known to be consistently correct, a bent or worn steering component or the need for wheel alignment could be indicated.

Under-inflation

Feathering is a condition when the edge of each tread rib develops a slightly rounded edge on one side and a sharp edge on the other. By running your hand over the tire, you can usually feel the sharper edges before you'll be able to see them. The most common causes of feathering are incorrect toe-in setting or deteriorated bushings in the front suspension.

Feathering

When an inner or outer rib wears faster than the rest of the tire, the need for wheel alignment is indicated. There is excessive camber in the front suspension, causing the wheel to lean too much putting excessive load on one side of the tire. Misalignment could also be due to sagging springs, worn ball joints, or worn control arm bushings. Be sure the vehicle is loaded the way it's normally driven when you have the wheels aligned.

One side wear

Cups or scalloped dips appearing around the edge of the tread almost always indicate worn (sometimes bent) suspension parts. Adjustment of wheel alignment alone will seldom cure the problem. Any worn component that connects the wheel to the suspension can cause this type of wear. Occasionally, wheels that are out of balance will wear like this, but wheel imbalance usually shows up as bald spots between the outside edges and center of the tread.

Cupping

Second-rib wear is usually found only in radial tires, and appears where the steel belts end in relation to the tread. It can be kept to a minimum by paying careful attention to tire pressure and frequently rotating the tires. This is often considered normal wear but excessive amounts indicate that the tires are too wide for the wheels.

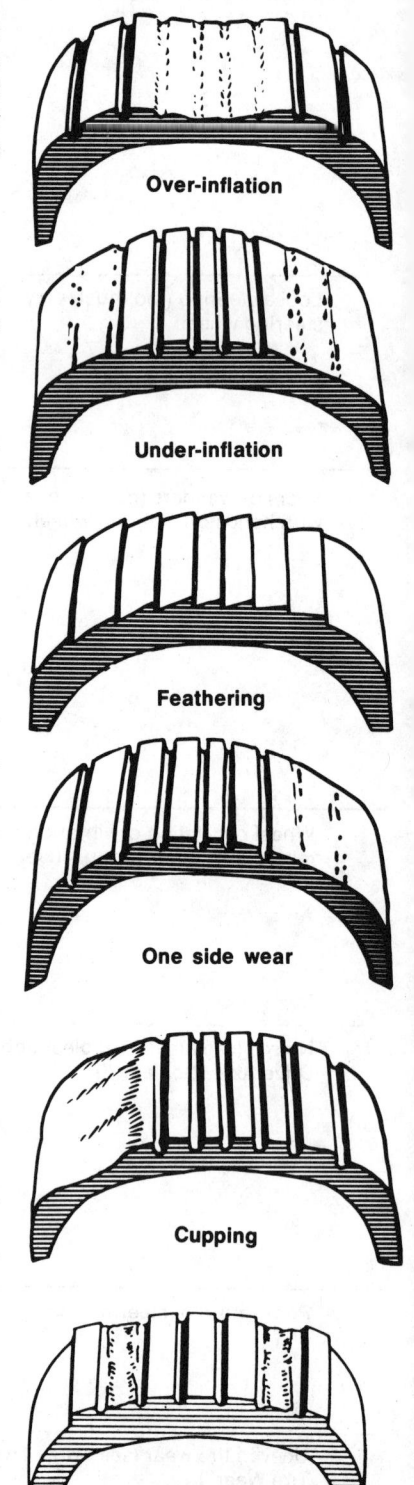

Second-rib wear

TROUBLESHOOTING

Troubleshooting Disc Brake Problems

Condition	Possible Cause
Noise—groan—brake noise emanating when slowly releasing brakes (creep-groan)	Not detrimental to function of disc brakes—no corrective action required. (This noise may be eliminated by slightly increasing or decreasing brake pedal efforts.)
Rattle—brake noise or rattle emanating at low speeds on rough roads, (front wheels only).	1. Shoe anti-rattle spring missing or not properly positioned. 2. Excessive clearance between shoe and caliper. 3. Soft or broken caliper seals. 4. Deformed or misaligned disc. 5. Loose caliper.
Scraping	1. Mounting bolts too long. 2. Loose wheel bearings. 3. Bent, loose, or misaligned splash shield.
Front brakes heat up during driving and fail to release	1. Operator riding brake pedal. 2. Stop light switch improperly adjusted. 3. Sticking pedal linkage. 4. Frozen or seized piston. 5. Residual pressure valve in master cylinder. 6. Power brake malfunction. 7. Proportioning valve malfunction.
Leaky brake caliper	1. Damaged or worn caliper piston seal. 2. Scores or corrosion on surface of cylinder bore.
Grabbing or uneven brake action—Brakes pull to one side	1. Causes listed under "Brakes Pull". 2. Power brake malfunction. 3. Low fluid level in master cylinder. 4. Air in hydraulic system. 5. Brake fluid, oil or grease on linings. 6. Unmatched linings. 7. Distorted brake pads. 8. Frozen or seized pistons. 9. Incorrect tire pressure. 10. Front end out of alignment. 11. Broken rear spring. 12. Brake caliper pistons sticking. 13. Restricted hose or line. 14. Caliper not in proper alignment to braking disc. 15. Stuck or malfunctioning metering valve. 16. Soft or broken caliper seals. 17. Loose caliper.
Brake pedal can be depressed without braking effect	1. Air in hydraulic system or improper bleeding procedure. 2. Leak past primary cup in master cylinder. 3. Leak in system. 4. Rear brakes out of adjustment. 5. Bleeder screw open.
Excessive pedal travel	1. Air, leak, or insufficient fluid in system or caliper. 2. Warped or excessively tapered shoe and lining assembly. 3. Excessive disc runout. 4. Rear brake adjustment required. 5. Loose wheel bearing adjustment. 6. Damaged caliper piston seal. 7. Improper brake fluid (boil). 8. Power brake malfunction. 9. Weak or soft hoses.

Troubleshooting Disc Brake Problems (cont.)

Condition	Possible Cause
Brake roughness or chatter (pedal pumping)	1. Excessive thickness variation of braking disc. 2. Excessive lateral runout of braking disc. 3. Rear brake drums out-of-round. 4. Excessive front bearing clearance.
Excessive pedal effort	1. Brake fluid, oil or grease on linings. 2. Incorrect lining. 3. Frozen or seized pistons. 4. Power brake malfunction. 5. Kinked or collapsed hose or line. 6. Stuck metering valve. 7. Scored caliper or master cylinder bore. 8. Seized caliper pistons.
Brake pedal fades (pedal travel increases with foot on brake)	1. Rough master cylinder or caliper bore. 2. Loose or broken hydraulic lines/connections. 3. Air in hydraulic system. 4. Fluid level low. 5. Weak or soft hoses. 6. Inferior quality brake shoes or fluid. 7. Worn master cylinder piston cups or seals.

Troubleshooting Drum Brakes

Condition	Possible Cause
Pedal goes to floor	1. Fluid low in reservoir. 2. Air in hydraulic system. 3. Improperly adjusted brake. 4. Leaking wheel cylinders. 5. Loose or broken brake lines. 6. Leaking or worn master cylinder. 7. Excessively worn brake lining.
Spongy brake pedal	1. Air in hydraulic system. 2. Improper brake fluid (low boiling point). 3. Excessively worn or cracked brake drums. 4. Broken pedal pivot bushing.
Brakes pulling	1. Contaminated lining. 2. Front end out of alignment. 3. Incorrect brake adjustment. 4. Unmatched brake lining. 5. Brake drums out of round. 6. Brake shoes distorted. 7. Restricted brake hose or line. 8. Broken rear spring. 9. Worn brake linings. 10. Uneven lining wear. 11. Glazed brake lining. 12. Excessive brake lining dust. 13. Heat spotted brake drums. 14. Weak brake return springs. 15. Faulty automatic adjusters. 16. Low or incorrect tire pressure.

TROUBLESHOOTING

Condition	Possible Cause
Squealing brakes	1. Glazed brake lining. 2. Saturated brake lining. 3. Weak or broken brake shoe retaining spring. 4. Broken or weak brake shoe return spring. 5. Incorrect brake lining. 6. Distorted brake shoes. 7. Bent support plate. 8. Dust in brakes or scored brake drums. 9. Linings worn below limit. 10. Uneven brake lining wear. 11. Heat spotted brake drums.
Chirping brakes	1. Out of round drum or eccentric axle flange pilot.
Dragging brakes	1. Incorrect wheel or parking brake adjustment. 2. Parking brakes engaged or improperly adjusted. 3. Weak or broken brake shoe return spring. 4. Brake pedal binding. 5. Master cylinder cup sticking. 6. Obstructed master cylinder relief port. 7. Saturated brake lining. 8. Bent or out of round brake drum. 9. Contaminated or improper brake fluid. 10. Sticking wheel cylinder pistons. 11. Driver riding brake pedal. 12. Defective proportioning valve. 13. Insufficient brake shoe lubricant.
Hard pedal	1. Brake booster inoperative. 2. Incorrect brake lining. 3. Restricted brake line or hose. 4. Frozen brake pedal linkage. 5. Stuck wheel cylinder. 6. Binding pedal linkage. 7. Faulty proportioning valve.
Wheel locks	1. Contaminated brake lining. 2. Loose or torn brake lining. 3. Wheel cylinder cups sticking. 4. Incorrect wheel bearing adjustment. 5. Faulty proportioning valve.
Brakes fade (high speed)	1. Incorrect lining. 2. Overheated brake drums. 3. Incorrect brake fluid (low boiling temperature). 4. Saturated brake lining. 5. Leak in hydraulic system. 6. Faulty automatic adjusters.
Pedal pulsates	1. Bent or out of round brake drum.
Brake chatter and shoe knock	1. Out of round brake drum. 2. Loose support plate. 3. Bent support plate. 4. Distorted brake shoes. 5. Machine grooves in contact face of brake drum (Shoe Knock). 6. Contaminated brake lining. 7. Missing or loose components. 8. Incorrect lining material. 9. Out-of-round brake drums. 10. Heat spotted or scored brake drums. 11. Out-of-balance wheels.

Troubleshooting Drum Brakes (cont.)

Condition	Possible Cause
Brakes do not self adjust	1. Adjuster screw frozen in thread. 2. Adjuster screw corroded at thrust washer. 3. Adjuster lever does not engage star wheel. 4. Adjuster installed on wrong wheel.
Brake light glows	1. Leak in the hydraulic system. 2. Air in the system. 3. Improperly adjusted master cylinder pushrod. 4. Uneven lining wear. 5. Failure to center combination valve or proportioning valve.

Appendix

General Conversion Table

Multiply by	To convert	To	
2.54	Inches	Centimeters	.3937
30.48	Feet	Centimeters	.0328
.914	Yards	Meters	1.094
1.609	Miles	Kilometers	.621
6.45	Square inches	Square cm.	.155
.836	Square yards	Square meters	1.196
16.39	Cubic inches	Cubic cm.	.061
28.3	Cubic feet	Liters	.0353
.4536	Pounds	Kilograms	2.2045
3.785	Gallons	Liters	.264
.068	Lbs./sq. in. (psi)	Atmospheres	14.7
.138	Foot pounds	Kg. m.	7.23
1.014	H.P. (DIN)	H.P. (SAE)	.9861
—	To obtain	From	Multiply by

Note: 1 cm. equals 10 mm.; 1 mm. equals .0394".

Conversion—Common Fractions to Decimals and Millimeters

Common Fractions	Decimal Fractions	Millimeters (approx.)	Common Fractions	Decimal Fractions	Millimeters (approx.)	Common Fractions	Decimal Fractions	Millimeters (approx.)
1/128	.008	0.20	11/32	.344	8.73	43/64	.672	17.07
1/64	.016	0.40	23/64	.359	9.13	11/16	.688	17.46
1/32	.031	0.79	3/8	.375	9.53	45/64	.703	17.86
3/64	.047	1.19	25/64	.391	9.92	23/32	.719	18.26
1/16	.063	1.59	13/32	.406	10.32	47/64	.734	18.65
5/64	.078	1.98	27/64	.422	10.72	3/4	.750	19.05
3/32	.094	2.38	7/16	.438	11.11	49/64	.766	19.45
7/64	.109	2.78	29/64	.453	11.51	25/32	.781	19.84
1/8	.125	3.18	15/32	.469	11.91	51/64	.797	20.24
9/64	.141	3.57	31/64	.484	12.30	13/16	.813	20.64
5/32	.156	3.97	1/2	.500	12.70	53/64	.828	21.03
11/64	.172	4.37	33/64	.516	13.10	27/32	.844	21.43
3/16	.188	4.76	17/32	.531	13.49	55/64	.859	21.83
13/64	.203	5.16	35/64	.547	13.89	7/8	.875	22.23
7/32	.219	5.56	9/16	.563	14.29	57/64	.891	22.62
15/64	.234	5.95	37/64	.578	14.68	29/32	.906	23.02
1/4	.250	6.35	19/32	.594	15.08	59/64	.922	23.42
17/64	.266	6.75	39/64	.609	15.48	15/16	.938	23.81
9/32	.281	7.14	5/8	.625	15.88	61/64	.953	24.21
19/64	.297	7.54	41/64	.641	16.27	31/32	.969	24.61
5/16	.313	7.94	21/32	.656	16.67	63/64	.984	25.00
21/64	.328	8.33						

Conversion—Millimeters to Decimal Inches

mm	inches	mm	inches	mm	inches	mm	inches	mm	inches
1	.039 370	31	1.220 470	61	2.401 570	91	3.582 670	210	8.267 700
2	.078 740	32	1.259 840	62	2.440 940	92	3.622 040	220	8.661 400
3	.118 110	33	1.299 210	63	2.480 310	93	3.661 410	230	9.055 100
4	.157 480	34	1.338 580	64	2.519 680	94	3.700 780	240	9.448 800
5	.196 850	35	1.377 949	65	2.559 050	95	3.740 150	250	9.842 500
6	.236 220	36	1.417 319	66	2.598 420	96	3.779 520	260	10.236 200
7	.275 590	37	1.456 689	67	2.637 790	97	3.818 890	270	10.629 900
8	.314 960	38	1.496 050	68	2.677 160	98	3.858 260	280	11.032 600
9	.354 330	39	1.535 430	69	2.716 530	99	3.897 630	290	11.417 300
10	.393 700	40	1.574 800	70	2.755 900	100	3.937 000	300	11.811 000
11	.433 070	41	1.614 170	71	2.795 270	105	4.133 848	310	12.204 700
12	.472 440	42	1.653 540	72	2.834 640	110	4.330 700	320	12.598 400
13	.511 810	43	1.692 910	73	2.874 010	115	4.527 550	330	12.992 100
14	.551 180	44	1.732 280	74	2.913 380	120	4.724 400	340	13.385 800
15	.590 550	45	1.771 650	75	2.952 750	125	4.921 250	350	13.779 500
16	.629 920	46	1.811 020	76	2.992 120	130	5.118 100	360	14.173 200
17	.669 290	47	1.850 390	77	3.031 490	135	5.314 950	370	14.566 900
18	.708 660	48	1.889 760	78	3.070 860	140	5.511 800	380	14.960 600
19	.748 030	49	1.929 130	79	3.110 230	145	5.708 650	390	15.354 300
20	.787 400	50	1.968 500	80	3.149 600	150	5.905 500	400	15.748 000
21	.826 770	51	2.007 870	81	3.188 970	155	6.102 350	500	19.685 000
22	.866 140	52	2.047 240	82	3.228 340	160	6.299 200	600	23.622 000
23	.905 510	53	2.086 610	83	3.267 710	165	6.496 050	700	27.559 000
24	.944 880	54	2.125 980	84	3.307 080	170	6.692 900	800	31.496 000
25	.984 250	55	2.165 350	85	3.346 450	175	6.889 750	900	35.433 000
26	1.023 620	56	2.204 720	86	3.385 820	180	7.086 600	1000	39.370 000
27	1.062 990	57	2.244 090	87	3.425 190	185	7.283 450	2000	78.740 000
28	1.102 360	58	2.283 460	88	3.464 560	190	7.480 300	3000	118.110 000
29	1.141 730	59	2.322 830	89	3.503 903	195	7.677 150	4000	157.480 000
30	1.181 100	60	2.362 200	90	3.543 300	200	7.874 000	5000	196.850 000

To change decimal millimeters to decimal inches, position the decimal point where desired on either side of the millimeter measurement shown and reset the inches decimal by the same number of digits in the same direction. For example, to convert 0.001 mm to decimal inches, reset the decimal behind the 1 mm (shown on the chart) to 0.001; change the decimal inch equivalent (0.039" shown) to 0.000039".

Tap Drill Sizes

National Fine or S.A.E.

Screw & Tap Size	Threads Per Inch	Use Drill Number
No. 5	44	37
No. 6	40	33
No. 8	36	29
No. 10	32	21
No. 12	28	15
¼	28	3
5/16	24	1
3/8	24	Q
7/16	20	W
½	20	29/64
9/16	18	33/64
5/8	18	37/64
¾	16	11/16
7/8	14	13/16
1⅛	12	1 3/64
1¼	12	1 11/64
1½	12	1 27/64

Tap Drill Sizes

National Coarse or U.S.S.

Screw & Tap Size	Threads Per Inch	Use Drill Number
No. 5	40	39
No. 6	32	36
No. 8	32	29
No. 10	24	25
No. 12	24	17
¼	20	8
5/16	18	F
3/8	16	5/16
7/16	14	U
½	13	27/64
9/16	12	31/64
5/8	11	17/32
¾	10	21/32
7/8	9	49/64
1	8	7/8
1⅛	7	63/64
1¼	7	1 7/64
1½	6	1 11/32

Decimal Equivalent Size of the Number Drills

Drill No.	Decimal Equivalent	Drill No.	Decimal Equivalent	Drill No.	Decimal Equivalent
80	.0135	53	.0595	26	.1470
79	.0145	52	.0635	25	.1495
78	.0160	51	.0670	24	.1520
77	.0180	50	.0700	23	.1540
76	.0200	49	.0730	22	.1570
75	.0210	48	.0760	21	.1590
74	.0225	47	.0785	20	.1610
73	.0240	46	.0810	19	.1660
72	.0250	45	.0820	18	.1695
71	.0260	44	.0860	17	.1730
70	.0280	43	.0890	16	.1770
69	.0292	42	.0935	15	.1800
68	.0310	41	.0960	14	.1820
67	.0320	40	.0980	13	.1850
66	.0330	39	.0995	12	.1890
65	.0350	38	.1015	11	.1910
64	.0360	37	.1040	10	.1935
63	.0370	36	.1065	9	.1960
62	.0380	35	.1100	8	.1990
61	.0390	34	.1110	7	.2010
60	.0400	33	.1130	6	.2040
59	.0410	32	.1160	5	.2055
58	.0420	31	.1200	4	.2090
57	.0430	30	.1285	3	.2130
56	.0465	29	.1360	2	.2210
55	.0520	28	.1405	1	.2280
54	.0550	27	.1440		

Decimal Equivalent Size of the Letter Drills

Letter Drill	Decimal Equivalent	Letter Drill	Decimal Equivalent	Letter Drill	Decimal Equivalent
A	.234	J	.277	S	.348
B	.238	K	.281	T	.358
C	.242	L	.290	U	.368
D	.246	M	.295	V	.377
E	.250	N	.302	W	.386
F	.257	O	.316	X	.397
G	.261	P	.323	Y	.404
H	.266	Q	.332	Z	.413
I	.272	R	.339		

APPENDIX

Anti-Freeze Chart

Temperatures Shown in Degrees Fahrenheit +32 is Freezing

Cooling System Capacity Quarts	1	2	3	4	5	6	7	8	9	10	11	12	13	14
10	+24°	+16°	+4°	−12°	−34°	−62°								
11	+25	+18	+8	−6	−23	−47								
12	+26	+19	+10	0	−15	−34	−57°							
13	+27	+21	+13	+3	−9	−25	−45							
14			+15	+6	−5	−18	−34							
15			+16	+8	0	−12	−26							
16			+17	+10	+2	−8	−19	−34	−52°					
17			+18	+12	+5	−4	−14	−27	−42					
18			+19	+14	+7	0	−10	−21	−34	−50°				
19			+20	+15	+9	+2	−7	−16	−28	−42				
20				+16	+10	+4	−3	−12	−22	−34	−48°			
21				+17	+12	+6	0	−9	−17	−28	−41			
22				+18	+13	+8	+2	−6	−14	−23	−34	−47°		
23				+19	+14	+9	+4	−3	−10	−19	−29	−40		
24				+19	+15	+10	+5	0	−8	−15	−23	−34	−46°	
25				+20	+16	+12	+7	+1	−5	−12	−20	−29	−40	−50°
26					+17	+13	+8	+3	−3	−9	−16	−25	−34	−44
27					+18	+14	+9	+5	−1	−7	−13	−21	−29	−39
28					+18	+15	+10	+6	+1	−5	−11	−18	−25	−34
29					+19	+16	+12	+7	+2	−3	−8	−15	−22	−29
30					+20	+17	+13	+8	+4	−1	−6	−12	−18	−25

For capacities over 30 quarts divide true capacity by 3. Find quarts Anti-Freeze for the ⅓ and multiply by 3 for quarts to add.

Quarts of ETHYLENE GLYCOL Needed for Protection to Temperatures Shown Below

For capacities under 10 quarts multiply true capacity by 3. Find quarts Anti-Freeze for the tripled volume and divide by 3 for quarts to add.

To Increase the Freezing Protection of Anti-Freeze Solutions Already Installed

Number of Quarts of ETHYLENE GLYCOL Anti-Freeze Required to Increase Protection

Cooling System Capacity Quarts	From +20° F. to					From +10° F. to					From 0° F. to			
	0°	−10°	−20°	−30°	−40°	0°	−10°	−20°	−30°	−40°	−10°	−20°	−30°	−40°
10	1¾	2¼	3	3½	3¾	¾	1½	2¼	2¾	3¼	¾	1½	2	2½
12	2	2¾	3½	4	4½	1	1¾	2½	3¼	3¾	1	1¾	2½	3¼
14	2¼	3¼	4	4¾	5½	1¼	2	3	3¾	4½	1	2	3	3½
16	2½	3½	4½	5¼	6	1¼	2½	3½	4¼	5¼	1¼	2¼	3¼	4
18	3	4	5	6	7	1½	2¾	4	5	5¾	1½	2½	3¾	4¾
20	3¼	4½	5¾	6¾	7½	1¾	3	4¼	5½	6½	1½	2¾	4¼	5¼
22	3½	5	6¼	7¼	8¼	1¾	3¼	4¾	6	7¼	1¾	3¼	4½	5½
24	4	5½	7	8	9	2	3½	5	6½	7½	1¾	3½	5	6
26	4¼	6	7½	8¾	10	2	4	5½	7	8¼	2	3¾	5½	6¾
28	4½	6¼	8	9½	10½	2¼	4¼	6	7½	9	2	4	5¾	7¼
30	5	6¾	8½	10	11½	2½	4½	6½	8	9½	2¼	4¼	6¼	7¾

Test radiator solution with proper hydrometer. Determine from the table the number of quarts of solution to be drawn off from a full cooling system and replace with undiluted anti-freeze, to give the desired increased protection. For example, to increase protection of a 22-quart cooling system containing Ethylene Glycol (permanent type) anti-freeze, from +20° F. to −20° F. will require the replacement of 6¼ quarts of solution with undiluted anti-freeze.

Index

A
Air cleaner, 8
Air conditioning
    Sight glass inspection, 14
Alternator, 63
Antifreeze, 17
Automatic transmission
    Adjustment, 168
    Filter change, 33
    Pan removal, 33, 168
Axle
    Fluid recommendations, 34
    Lubricant level, 23
Axle shaft
    Bearings and seals, 174

B
Ball joints, 180
Battery
    Jump starting, 35
    Maintenance, 15
    Removal and installation, 72
Belt tension adjustment, 11
Body, 208
Body work, 208
Brakes
    Adjustment, 190
    Bleeding, 194
    Caliper, 196, 204
    Fluid level, 22
    Fluid recommendations, 30
    Front brakes, 194
    Master cylinder, 22, 191
    Parking brake, 205
    Rear brakes, 200, 203
Bulbs, 161

C
Camber, 181
Camshaft and bearings, 87
Capacities, 27
Carburetor
    Adjustment, 136
    Overhaul, 139
    Replacement, 136
Caster, 181
Charging system, 63
Chassis lubrication, 34
Clutch
    Adjustment, 164
    Replacement, 165
Condenser, 43
Connecting rod and bearings, 88
Cooling system, 17, 91
Crankcase ventilation (PCV), 9, 113
Cylinder head
    Removal and installation, 79
    Torque sequence, 80

D
Dents and scratches, 213
Differential
    Fluid change, 34
Distributor
    Removal and installation, 60
    Breaker points, 43
Door panels, 209
Drive axle, 172
Driveshaft, 171
Dwell angle, 46
Dwell meter, 3, 46

E
Electrical
    Chassis, 146
    Engine, 60
Electronic ignition, 47, 52
Emission controls, 113
Engine
    Camshaft, 87
    Cylinder head torque sequence, 80
    Exhaust manifold, 83
    Front cover, 84
    Identification, 7
    Intake manifold, 83
    Oil recommendations, 30
    Pistons and rings, 88
    Rebuilding, 94
    Removal and installation, 74
    Rocker arm (or shaft), 81
    Specifications, 75
    Timing chain (or gears), 85
    Tune-up, 38
Evaporative canister, 116
Exhaust manifold, 83

F
Fan belt adjustment, 11
Firing order, 63
Fluid level checks
    Battery, 14
    Coolant, 22
    Engine oil, 20
    Master cylinder, 22
    Power steering pump, 24
    Rear axle, 23
    Steering gear, 23
    Transmission, 22
Fluid recommendations, 30
Front suspension
    Ball joints, 180
    Strut, 176
    Wheel alignment, 181
Front wheel bearing, 200
Fuel injection, 58, 141
Fuel filter, 27
Fuel pump, 132

INDEX

Fuel system, 132
Fuel tank, 145
Fuses and flashers, 160
Fusible links, 160

G

Gearshift linkage adjustment
    Automatic, 168
Generator (see Alternator)

H

Hand brake, 205
Headlights, 158
Heater, 146

I

Identification
    Vehicle, 6
    Engine, 7
    Transmission, 8
Idle speed and mixture, 56, 58
Ignition switch, 187
Instrument cluster, 154
Intake manifold, 83

J

Jacking points, 36
Jump starting, 35

L

Light bulb specifications, 161
Lubrication
    Chassis, 34
    Differential, 34
    Engine, 30, 89
    Transmission, 33

M

Maintenance intervals, 29
Manifolds
    Intake, 83
    Exhaust, 83
Manual transmission, 33, 162
Master cylinder, 22, 191
Model identification, 6

N

Neutral safety switch, 162, 168

O

Oil and fuel recommendations, 30
Oil change, 32
Oil filter (engine), 32
Oil pan, 89

Oil pump, 90
Oil level (engine), 20

P

Parking brake, 205
Pistons and rings
    Installation, 88
    Positioning, 88
PCV valve, 9, 113
Points, 43

R

Radiator, 91
Radio, 151
Rear axle, 172
Rear suspension, 182
Regulator, 65
Rear main oil seal, 89
Rings, 88
Rocker arm (or shaft), 81
Routine maintenance, 8
Rust spots, 211

S

Safety notice, ii
Scratches and dents, 213
Serial number location, 6
Shock absorbers
    Front, 176, 180
    Rear, 182
Spark plugs, 38
Specifications
    Alternator and regulator, 70
    Battery and starter, 72
    Brakes, 206
    Capacities, 27
    Carburetor, 142
    Crankshaft and connecting rod, 76
    General engine, 75
    Light bulb, 161
    Piston and ring, 77
    Torque, 78
    Tune-up, 40
    Valve, 75
    Wheel alignment, 183
Speedometer cable, 157
Springs
    Front, 176, 178
    Rear, 182, 186
Starter, 67
Steering
    Linkage, 187
    Wheel, 186
Stripped threads, 95
Strut, 176, 182

T

Thermostat, 92
Tie-rod, 187

INDEX

Timing (ignition), 52
Tires, 24
Tools, 2
Towing, 35
Transmission
    Automatic, 33
    Manual, 33, 162
    Fluid change, 33
Tranverse link, 180
Troubleshooting, 225
Tune-up
    Procedures, 38
    Specifications, 40
Turbocharger, 144
Turn signal switch, 187

U

U-joints, 171

V

Valves
    Adjustment, 54
    Service, 81
    Specifications, 75
Vehicle identification, 6

W

Water pump, 91
Wheel alignment, 181
Wheel bearings, 174, 198, 200
Wheel cylinders, 202
Windshield wipers
    Arm, 152
    Blade, 20, 152
    Linkage, 152
    Motor, 152

Chilton's Repair & Tune-Up Guides

The complete line covers domestic cars, imports, trucks, vans, RV's and 4-wheel drive vehicles.

CODE	TITLE	CODE	TITLE
#7199	AMC 75-82; all models	#6935	GM Sub-compact 71-81 inc. Vega, Monza, Astre, Sunbird, Starfire & Skyhawk
#7165	Alliance 1983		
#7323	Aries 81-82	#6937	Granada 75-80
#7032	Arrow Pick-Up 79-81	#5905	GTO 68-73
#7193	Aspen 76-80	#5821	GTX 68-73
#5902	Audi 70-73	#7204	Honda 73-82
#7028	Audi 4000/5000 77-81	#7191	Horizon 78-82
#6337	Audi Fox 73-75	#5912	International Scout 67-73
#5807	Barracuda 65-72	#7136	Jeep CJ 1945-81
#7203	Blazer 69-82	#6739	Jeep Wagoneer, Commando, Cherokee 66-79
#5576	BMW 59-70	#6962	Jetta 1980
#6844	BMW 70-79	#7203	Jimmy 69-82
#7027	Bobcat	#7059	J-2000 1982
#7307	Buick Century/Regal 75-83	#7165	Le Car 76-83
#7045	Camaro 67-81	#7323	Le Baron 1982
#6695	Capri 70-77	#5905	Le Mans 68-73
#7195	Capri 79-82	#7055	Lynx 81-82 inc. EXP & LN-7
#7059	Cavalier 1982	#6634	Maverick 70-77
#5807	Challenger 65-72	#7198	Mazda 71-82
#7037	Challenger (Import) 71-81	#7031	Mazda RX-7 79-81
#7041	Champ 78-81	#6065	Mercedes-Benz 59-70
#6316	Charger/Coronet 71-75	#5907	Mercedes-Benz 68-73
#7162	Chevette 76-82 inc. diesel	#6809	Mercedes-Benz 74-79
#7313	Chevrolet 68-83 all full size models	#7128	Mercury 68-71 all full sized models
#7167	Chevrolet/GMC Pick-Ups 70-82	#7194	Mercury Mid-Size 71-82 inc. Continental, Cougar, XR-7 & Montego
#7169	Chevrolet/GMC Vans 67-82		
#7310	Chevrolet S-10/GMC S-15 Pick-Ups 82-83	#7173	MG 61-80
#7051	Chevy Luv 72-81 inc. 4wd	#6973	Monarch 75-80
#7056	Chevy Mid-Size 64-82 inc. El Camino, Chevelle, Laguna, Malibu & Monte Carlo	#6542	Mustang 65-73
		#6812	Mustang II 74-78
#6841	Chevy II 62-79	#7195	Mustang 79-82
#7059	Cimarron 1982	#6841	Nova 69-79
#7049	Citation 80-81	#7049	Omega 81-82
#7037	Colt 71-81	#7191	Omni 78-82
#6634	Comet 70-77	#6575	Opel 71-75
#7194	Continental 1982	#5982	Peugeot 70-74
#6691	Corvair 60-69 inc. Turbo	#7049	Phoenix 81-82
#6576	Corvette 53-62	#7027	Pinto 71-80
#7192	Corvette 63-82	#8552	Plymouth 68-76 full sized models
#7190	Cutlass 70-82	#7168	Plymouth Vans 67-82
#6324	Dart 68-76	#5822	Porsche 69-73
#6962	Dasher 74-80	#7048	Porsche 924 & 928 77-81 inc. Turbo
#5790	Datsun 61-72	#6962	Rabbit 75-80
#7196	Datsun F10, 310, Nissan Stanza 77-82	#7323	Reliant 81-82
#7170	Datsun 200SX, 510, 610, 710, 810 73-82	#7165	Renault 75-83
#7197	Datsun 1200, 210/Nissan Sentra 73-82	#5821	Roadrunner 68-73
#7172	Datsun Z & ZX 70-82	#5988	Saab 69-75
#7050	Datsun Pick-Ups 70-81 inc. 4wd	#7041	Sapporo 78-81
#6324	Demon 68-76	#5821	Satellite 68-73
#6554	Dodge 68-77 all full sized models	#6962	Scirocco 75-80
#7323	Dodge 400 1982	#7059	Skyhawk 1982
#6486	Dodge Charger 67-70	#7049	Skylark 80-81
#7168	Dodge Vans 67-82	#7208	Subaru 70-82
#6326	Duster 68-76	#5905	Tempest 68-73
#7055	Escort 81-82 inc. EXP & LN-7	#6320	Torino 62-75
#6320	Fairlane 62-75	#5795	Toyota 66-70
#7312	Fairmont 78-83	#7043	Toyota Celica & Supra 71-81
#7042	Fiat 69-81	#7036	Toyota Corolla, Carina, Tercel, Starlet 70-81
#6846	Fiesta 78-80	#7044	Toyota Corona, Cressida, Crown, Mark II 70-81
#7046	Firebird 67-81	#7035	Toyota Pick-Ups 70-81
#7059	Firenza 1982	#5910	Triumph 69-73
#7128	Ford 68-81 all full sized models	#7162	T-1000 1982
#7140	Ford Bronco 66-81	#6326	Valiant 68-76
#6983	Ford Courier 72-80	#5796	Volkswagen 49-71
#7194	Ford Mid-Size 71-82 inc. Torino, Gran Torino, Ranchero, Elite, LTD II & Thunderbird	#6837	Volkswagen 70-81
		#7193	Volaré 76-80
#7166	Ford Pick-Ups 65-82 inc. 4wd	#6529	Volvo 56-69
#7171	Ford Vans 61-82	#7040	Volvo 70-80
#7165	Fuego 82-83	#7312	Zephyr 78-83

Chilton's Repair & Tune-Up Guides are available at your local retailer or by mailing a check or money order for $10.95 plus $1.00 to cover postage and handling to:

Chilton Book Company
Dept. DM
Radnor, PA 19089

NOTE: When ordering be sure to include your name & address, book code & title.